# STERLING
## Test Prep

MW01168514

# Regents

# Living Environment

## Review

4<sup>th</sup> edition

**Customer Satisfaction Guarantee**

Your feedback is important because we strive to provide the highest quality prep materials. Email us comments or suggestions.

info@sterling–prep.com

We reply to emails – check your spam folder

4   3   2   1

ISBN-13: 979-8-8855708-3-1

Sterling Test Prep materials are available at quantity discounts.

Contact info@sterling–prep.com

Sterling Test Prep
6 Liberty Square #11
Boston, MA 02109

© 2023 Sterling Test Prep

Published by Sterling Test Prep

 Printed in the U.S.A.

# STERLING
## Test Prep

Thousands of students use our study materials to achieve high test scores.

This book provides a thorough review of biology topics tested on Regents Living Environment, covering the principles and concepts necessary to answer test questions. Understanding key concepts, extracting and analyzing information, and distinguishing between similar answer choices are more effective than mere memorization. This review prepares you to achieve a high score by confidently applying your knowledge when choosing correct answers.

This text is clearly presented and systematically organized to provide targeted Regents Living Environment preparation. Learn the scientific foundations and essential biology topics needed to master the material and answer exam questions. These review chapters teach important principles and relationships and how they apply to the questions.

Experienced life science instructors analyzed the exam content and developed the material that builds knowledge and skills crucial for success. Our test preparation experts structured the content to match the current exam requirements.

Using this book will significantly improve your performance on the test!

240403frd

*Regents Living Environment Practice Questions* provides high-yield practice questions covering topics tested on Regents. Develop the ability to apply your knowledge and quickly choose the correct answer to increase your test score.

This review book will increase your score.

**Visit our Amazon store**

**Regents study aids by Sterling Test Prep**

**Regents Physical Science**

Physics Review

Physics Practice Questions

Chemistry Review

Chemistry Practice Questions

Living Environment Content Review

Living Environment Practice Questions

**Regents Social Studies**

U.S. History and Government Review

Global History and Geography Transition Review

Global History and Geography II Review

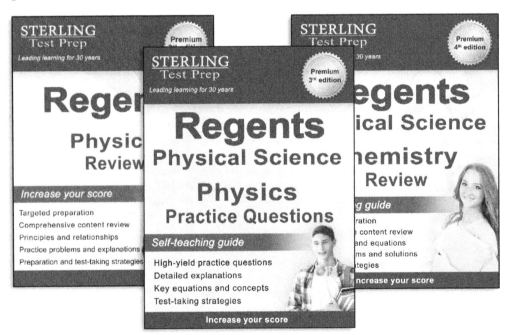

# Table of Contents

Table of Contents (continued)

# Table of Contents (*continued*)

**Table of Contents** (*continued*)

# Table of Contents (*continued*)

# Table of Contents (*continued*)

# Table of Contents (*continued*)

**Table of Contents** (*continued*)

# Table of Contents (*continued*)

**Table of Contents** (*continued*)

# Table of Contents (*continued*)

**Table of Contents** (*continued*)

**Table of Contents** (*continued*)

**Table of Contents** (*continued*)

**Table of Contents** (*continued*)

**Table of Contents** (*continued*)

**Table of Contents** (*continued*)

## Table of Contents (*continued*)

# Table of Contents (*continued*)

## Table of Contents (*continued*)

**Table of Contents** (*continued*)

## Table of Contents (*continued*)

**Table of Contents** (*continued*)

## Table of Contents (*continued*)

**Table of Contents** (*continued*)

## Table of Contents (*continued*)

---

**Customer Satisfaction Guarantee**

Your feedback is important because we strive to provide the highest quality prep materials. Email us comments or suggestions.

info@sterling–prep.com

We reply to emails – check your spam folder

---

**Highest quality guarantee**

Be the first to report a content error for a $10 reward or a grammatical mistake to receive a $5 reward.

**Thank you for choosing our book!**

---

## Regents Living Environment Preparation and Test-Taking Strategies

### Test preparation strategies

The best way to do well in Regents Living Environment is to be good at biology. There is no way around knowing the subject; proper preparation is key to success. Prepare to answer with confidence as many questions as possible.

#### *Study in advance*

Devote 3 to 6 months to studying. The information is manageable by studying regularly before the test.

Cramming is not a successful tactic. However, do not study too far in advance. Studying more than six months ahead is not advised and may result in fatigue and poor knowledge retention.

#### *Develop a realistic study and practice schedule*

Cramming eight hours a day is unfeasible and leads to burnout, which is detrimental to performance.

Commit to a realistic study and practice schedule.

#### *Remove distractions*

During this preparation period, temporarily eliminate distractions.

However, balance is critical, and it is crucial not to neglect physical well-being and social or family life. Prepare with full intensity but do not jeopardize your health or emotional well-being.

#### *Develop an understanding over memorization*

When studying, devote time to each topic.

After a study session, write a short concept outline to clarify relationships and increase knowledge retention.

#### *Make flashcards*

Avoid commercial flashcards because making cards help build and retain knowledge.

Consider using self-made flashcards to develop knowledge retention and quiz what you know.

#### *Find a study partner*

Occasionally studying with a friend to prepare for the test can motivate and provide accountability.

Explaining concepts to another improves and fine-tunes your understanding, integrates knowledge, bolsters competence, and identifies deficiencies in comprehension.

### Take practice tests

Do not take practice tests too early.

First, develop a comprehensive understanding of concepts. In the last weeks, use practice tests to fine-tune your final preparation. If you are not scoring well on practice tests, you want time to improve without undue stress.

Alternate studying and practicing to increase knowledge retention and identify areas for study. Taking practice tests accustoms you to the challenges of test-taking.

## Test day strategies

### Be well-rested and eat the right foods

Get a full night's sleep before the test for proper mental and physical capacity. If you are up late the night before, you will have difficulty concentrating and focusing on the test.

Avoid foods and drinks that lead to drowsiness (carbohydrates and protein). Avoid drinks high in sugar, causing glucose to spike and crash.

### Pack in advance

Check what you are allowed to bring to the test. Pay attention to the required check-in items (e.g., printed confirmation, identification).

Pack the day before to avoid the stress of not frantically looking for things on test day.

### Arrive at the testing center early

Starting right is an advantage. Allow time to check in and remain calm before the test begins.

Map and test the route to the center in advance and determine parking locations, if applicable. If you are not familiar with the test location, visit before the test day to practice and avoid travel errors. Plan your route correctly to arrive at the center without additional challenges and unnecessary stress.

### Maintain a positive attitude

Avoid falling into a mental spiral of negative emotions. Too much worry leads to underperformance.

If you become anxious, chances are higher for lower performance in preparation and during the test. Inner peace helps during preparation and the high-stakes test.

To do well on the test requires logical, systematic, and analytical thinking, so relax and remain calm.

### Focus on progress

Do not be concerned with other test-takers. Someone proceeding rapidly through the exam may be rushing or guessing on questions.

*Take breaks* and breathe deeply

Do not skip the available timed breaks. Refreshing breaks help you finish strong.

Eat a light snack to replenish your energy. Your mind and body will appreciate the available breaks.

The best approach to any test is *not* to keep your head down the whole session. While there is no time to waste, take a few seconds between questions to breathe deeply.

Momentarily clear your thoughts to relax your mind and muscles.

## Time management strategies

### *Timing*

Besides good preparation, time management is the critical strategy for the exam.

Timed practice is not the objective at this stage. While practicing, note how many questions you would have completed in the allotted time.

### *Average time per question*

In advance, determine the average time allotted for each question.

Use two different approaches depending on which preparation phase you are working on.

During the first preparation phase, acquire, fortify, and refine your knowledge.

During your final practice stage, use the time needed to develop analytical and thought processes related to specific questions.

### *Work systematically*

Note your comprehension compared to the correct answers to learn the material and identify conceptual weaknesses. Do not overlook explanations to questions as a source of content, analysis, and interdependent relationships.

During the second preparation phase, do not spend more than the average allotted time on each question when taking practice tests.

Pace your response time to develop a consistent pace and complete the test within the allotted time. If you are time-constrained during the final practice phase, work more efficiently, or your score will suffer.

### *Focus on the easy questions and skip the unfamiliar*

Easy or difficult questions are worth the same points. Score more points for three quickly answered questions than one hard-earned victory.

Answer the familiar and easy questions to maximize points if time runs out.

### *Identify strengths and weaknesses*

Skip unfamiliar questions in the first round as challenging questions require more than the average allotted time.

In the second review, questions that you cannot approach systematically or lack fundamental knowledge will likely not be answered through analysis.

Use the elimination and educated guessing strategy to select an answer and move on to another question.

### *Do not overinvest in any question*

Some questions consume more time than the average and make you think of investing more time. Stop thinking that investing more time in challenging questions is productive.

Do not get entangled with questions while losing track of time. The test is timed, so do not spend too much time on any questions.

### *Look at every question on the exam*

It is unfortunate not to earn points for a question you could have quickly answered because you did not see it.

If you are in the first half of the test and spending more than the average on a question, select the best option, note the question number, and move on. You do not want to rush through the remaining questions, causing you to miss more answers.

If time allows, return to marked questions and take a fresh look. However, do not change the original answer unless you have a reason to change it. University studies show that hastily changing answers often replace correct and incorrect answers.

### Multiple-choice questions

### *Answer all questions*

How many questions are correct, not how much work went into selecting the answers matters. An educated guess earns the same points as an answer known with confidence.

On the test, you need to think and analyze information quickly. The skill of analyzing information quickly cannot be gained from a college course, prep course, or textbook. Working efficiently and effectively is a skill developed through focused effort and applied practice.

### *Strategic approach*

Strategies, approaches, and perspectives for answering multiple-choice questions help maximize points.

Many strategies seem like common sense. However, these helpful approaches might be overlooked under the pressure of a timed test.

While no strategy replaces comprehensive preparation, apply probability for success on unfamiliar questions.

### *Understand the question*

Know what the question is asking before selecting an answer. It is surprising how many students do not read (and reread) carefully and rush to select the wrong answer.

The test-makers anticipate hasty mistakes, and many enticing answers include specious choices. A successful student reads the question and understands it precisely before looking at the answers.

### *Focus on the answer*

Separate the vital information from distracters and understand the design and thrust of the question.

Answer the question and not merely pick a factually accurate statement or answer a misconstrued question.

Rephrasing the question helps articulate what precisely the correct response requires. When rephrasing, do not change the meaning of the question; assume it is direct and to the point as written.

After selecting the answer, review the question and verify that the choice selected answers the question.

### *Answer the question before looking at choices*

This valuable strategy is applicable if the question asks for generalized factual details. Form a thought response first, then look for the choice that matches your preordained answer.

Select the predetermined statement as it is likely correct.

### *Factually correct, but wrong*

Questions often have incorrect choices that are factually correct but do not answer the question.

Predetermine the answer and do not choose merely a factually correct statement. Verify that the choice answers the question.

### *Do not fall for the familiar*

When in doubt, it is comforting to choose what is familiar. If you recognize a term or concept, you may be tempted to pick that choice impetuously.

However, do not go with familiar answers merely because they are familiar. Think through the answer and how it relates to the question before selecting it.

### *Experiments questions*

Determine the purpose, methods, variables, and controls of the experiment. Understanding the presented information helps answer the question.

With multiple experiments, understand variations of the same experiment by focusing on the differences.

For example, focus on the changes between the first and second experiments, second and third, and first and third. Direct comparison between experiments helps organize the information and apply it to the answer.

## Words of caution

The words *"all," "none,"* and *"except"* require attention. Be alert with questions containing these words, as the answer may not be apparent on the first read of the question.

## Double-check the question

After selecting an answer, return to the question to ensure the selected choice answers the question as asked.

## Fill the answers carefully

Many mistakes happen when filling in answers. Filling the answers correctly is simple but crucial. Be attentive to the question number and enter the answer accordingly. If you skip a question, skip it on the answer sheet.

## Elimination strategies

If the correct answer is not immediately apparent, use the process of elimination.

Use the strategy of educated guessing by eliminating one or two answers. Usually, at least one answer choice is easily identified as wrong. Eliminating one choice increases the odds of selecting the correct one.

## Process of elimination

Eliminate choices:

- Use proportionality for quantitative questions to eliminate choices too high or too low.

- Eliminate answers that are *almost right* or *half right*. Consider *half right* as *wrong* since distractor choices are purposely included.

- If two answers are direct opposites, the correct answer is likely one of them. However, note if they are direct opposites or another reason to consider them correct. Therefore, eliminate the other choices and narrow the search for the correct one.

- For numerical questions, eliminate the smallest and largest numbers (unless for a reason).

## Roman numeral questions

Roman numeral questions present several statements and ask which is/are correct. These questions are tricky for most test-takers because they have more than one potentially correct statement.

Roman numeral questions are often included in combinations with more than one answer. Eliminating a wrong Roman numeral statement eliminates all choices that include it.

## Educated guessing

## Correct ways to guess

Do not assume you must get every question right; this will add unnecessary stress during the exam. You will (likely) need to guess for some questions.

Answer as many questions correctly as possible without wasting time.

For challenging questions, random guessing does not help. Use educated guessing after elimination.

*Playing the odds*

Guessing is a form of "partial credit" because while you might not be sure of the correct answer, you have the relevant knowledge to identify some wrong choices.

There is a 25% chance of correctly guessing random responses since questions have four choices. Therefore, the odds are guessing 1 question correctly to 3 incorrectly.

*Guessing after elimination of answers*

After eliminating one answer as wrong, you have a 33% chance of a lucky guess. Therefore, your odds move from 1 question right to 2 questions wrong.

While this may not seem like a dramatic increase, it can make an appreciable difference in your score.

Confidently eliminating two wrong choices increases the chances of guessing correctly to 50%!

When using elimination:

- Do not rely on gut feelings alone to answer questions quickly.

  Understand and recognize the difference between *knowing* and *gut feeling* about the answer. Gut feelings should sparingly be used after the process of elimination.

- Do not fall for answers that sound "clever," and choose "bizarre" answers.

  Choose them only with a reason to believe they may be correct.

*Eliminating Roman numeral choices*

A workable strategy for Roman numeral questions is to guess the wrong statement.

For example:

> A. I only
>
> B. III only
>
> C. I and II only
>
> D. I and III only

Notice that statement II does not have an answer dedicated to it. This indicates that statement II is likely wrong and eliminates choice C, narrowing your search to three choices. However, if you are confident that statement II is the answer, do not apply this strategy.

## Constructed response questions

Free-response questions typically require processing information into existing conceptual frameworks.

There are some personal choices for writing the desired response.

### *Free-response question skills*

Be able to present and discuss relevant examples. Practice clarifying or evaluating principles.

Perform detailed analysis of relationships and respond to stimulus materials such as charts or graphs.

### *Understand the question*

As with the multiple-choice questions, understand what the question asks. Assume that the question, as written, is direct and to the point.

Mental rephrasing should not add or alter the meaning or essence of the question.

### *Answer the questions in order of competence*

You are not bound to answer the questions in their sequence. Survey all questions and decide which requires minimal effort or time.

Avoid getting entangled and frustrated to use time efficiently and maximize points.

### *Do not write more than needed*

Additional work beyond the question's stated directives does not earn a higher score or result in extra credit.

For time management and keeping responses relevant, answer the question but avoid superfluous responses.

### *Organize thoughts*

Before writing, brainstorm the questions' topics. Outline your thoughts on scratch paper during the composition process. Essential definitions, ideas, examples, or names are valid details when relevant.

Organized thoughts produce a coherent response. With practice, balance time between brainstorming and writing.

### *Follow the structure*

Structure responses to match the order specified in the question for a grader-friendly answer.

The reader/grader should not need to search for topics used in the grading criteria. A well-structured essay has complete sentences and paragraphs.

A formal introduction and conclusion are unnecessary; they go directly into answering the question.

### *Answer questions in their entirety*

It is essential to answer questions thoroughly, not just partially. For example, some questions ask to identify and explain. Performing only one step is inadequate and will be graded accordingly.

### Task verbs

Below are *task verbs* common for free-response questions – underline directives on practice questions and exams.

Refer to these tasks and verify when completed. Do not overlook them when writing a comprehensive response.

*Compare* – provide a description or explanation of similarities or differences.

*Define* – provide a specific meaning for a word or concept.

*Identify* – provide information about a specified topic without elaboration or explanation.

*Describe* – provide the relevant characteristics of a specified concept.

*Develop an argument* – articulate a claim and support it with evidence.

*Explain* – provide how (or why) relationships, processes, patterns, or outcomes occur, using evidence and reasoning.

*Conclude* – use available information to formulate an accurate statement demonstrating understanding based on evidence.

*How* questions typically require analyzing the relationship, process, pattern, or outcome.

*Why* questions typically require analyzing motivations or reasons for the relationship, process, or outcome.

### Write legibly

The reader must decipher your writing, so responses are scored appropriately. Practice writing under a time limit to produce a readable response. Ask a friend to read a sample response to understand the words expressed if this issue exists.

Consider printing key phrases or highlighting them cleanly (e.g., asterisk, underline) in your response.

### Use plain language

All claims should be directly stated. You do not want the graders to guess how something demonstrates a point.

Regardless of if they correctly guess your intentions, you will be graded critically for ambiguities. Present relevant information clearly and concisely to demonstrate the argument's primary points.

### Use facts to bolster arguments

Written responses should include specific facts and avoid unsubstantiated claims. Avoid contradictions, circular definitions, and question restatements. Do not use long, meandering responses filled with loosely-related facts regarding specific concepts.

### Review and correct answers

If questions are completed and time remains, review each response. Assess if anything is needed to be added or requires correction. Put a simple strikethrough through the error for a mistake, so the grader disregards that portion. If you add content, insert an asterisk (*) and refer the reader to the end of the essay. Thoughtful revisions earn crucial points.

*Notes for active learning*

# CHAPTER 1

# Ecosystems, Biosphere & Conservation Biology

- Ecosystems, Energy Flow and Nutrient Cycles
- Ecological Pyramids
- Biogeochemical cycles
- Biosphere
- Terrestrial Biomes
- Aquatic Biomes
- Conservation Biology
- Climate Change

## Ecosystems, Energy Flow and Nutrient Cycles

### Ecosystems

*Ecosystem* includes a biotic community and its abiotic environment. The biotic community is organized by which organisms fuel their metabolic activities.

*Autotrophs* are the basis of an ecosystem and feed *heterotrophs*. They synthesize their organic compounds using energy from the sun or inorganic compounds. They include photoautotrophs and chemoautotrophs.

*Photoautotrophs* (algae, cyanobacteria) use photosynthesis, converting solar energy into organic compounds.

*Chemoautotrophs* are bacteria that *oxidize* inorganic compounds (e.g., ammonia, nitrite, sulfide) to generate organic compounds. They are rare and typically found in caves, hydrothermal ocean vents, and environments lacking light.

*Heterotrophs* must obtain nutrients by consuming other organisms. Herbivores feed on autotrophs and are typically prey animals for carnivores and omnivores.

*Detritivores* degrade dead organic matter and recycle energy and nutrients within the ecosystem.

The smallest detritivores, such as fungi and bacteria, are *decomposers.*

Many decomposers are *saprotrophs,* digesting organic matter externally by secreting enzymes into the surrounding environment and absorbing degraded products.

### Energy flow

*Ecosystems* are characterized by nutrient production, movement, consumption, and recycling.

*Nutrients* are forms of *chemical energy* which flow throughout the system in predictable ways, governed by the laws of thermodynamics.

> *First law of thermodynamics* states that *energy can neither be created nor destroyed.*

> *Second law of thermodynamics* states that energy transformations *lose energy to the environment.*

*Energy flow* is assembled into the *food chain* of a community.

### Trophic levels

*Trophic levels* are the food chains that describe how an organism feeds. Arrows in the food chain show the direction of energy flow. The greater the number of energy pathways in a food web, the more stable the community.

At the base of every food chain are the autotrophs as *primary producers.*

*Primary producers* are responsible for *primary production*, creating organic compounds using energy from the sun or inorganic compounds.

*Chemical energy* created by primary production nourishes producers and other organisms in the food chain. It can be quantified by *biomass* or the amount of organic material in an area.

*Biomass* may be living or dead; the requirement is to contain *usable energy.*

*Herbivores* consuming primary producers are *primary consumers.* Those organisms which consume the primary consumers are *secondary consumers,* and so on.

Typically, food chains do not exceed the level of a tertiary consumer.

At the top of the food chain are *apex predators,* with no natural predators.

For example, a primary producer in a food chain may be a carrot plant. Its direct predator, the eastern cottontail rabbit, is a primary consumer. The red fox is a secondary consumer, and the golden eagle is the tertiary consumer and apex predator.

However, golden eagles often prey on rabbits in addition to foxes. An ecosystem involves many food chains interconnected into a food web. The basic linear food chain fails to capture the complex ecosystem interactions.

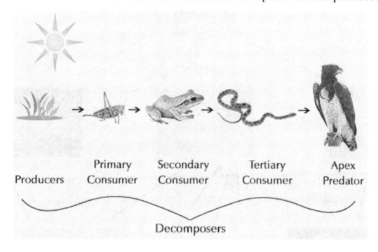

*Food chain from producers and consumers to apex predator*

*Detritivores* are challenging to place on a food web and are often conceptualized as separate.

*Grazing food webs* do not include detritivores; it places primary producers at the basal level.

*Detrital food webs* place detritivores at the bottom.

Food webs begin when producers receive energy from the sun through photosynthesis.

*Gross primary productivity* is the total amount of energy they generate via photosynthesis. However, much of this energy must be used by the producers themselves to fuel their metabolism.

*Net primary productivity* passed to heterotrophs is unused energy.

Due to the second law of thermodynamics, energy is lost at each trophic level because all organisms lose heat through cellular respiration.

*Organic matter* remains *undigested* at each trophic level and is lost as waste.

*Detritivores* help recycle undigested organic matter and release energy from these substances.

## Ecological Pyramids

### Ecological efficiency

*Ecological efficiency* is the proportion of energy at each trophic level transferred to the next. About 90% of an organism's energy is consumed for metabolism, and only 10% passes to the next trophic level. Therefore, 1,000 kilograms of plant biomass supports 100 kilograms of primary consumers, 10 kilograms of secondary consumers, and 1 kilogram of tertiary consumers.

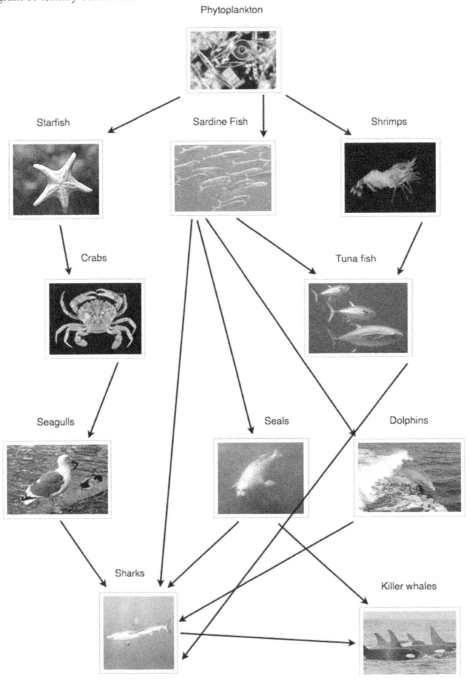

*Food web from phytoplankton producers through primary, secondary, and tertiary consumers*

Massive amounts of biomass are needed at the lower levels to support the apex predators at the top. This rapid energy loss is why food chains rarely have more than four links.

Ecological pyramids represent the trophic levels in a food web by their energy content, biomass, or the number of species. Energy and biomass are greatest at the primary producer level and lowest at the apex predator level. However, energy reclamation by decomposers dramatically improves the efficiency of the overall ecosystem.

*Apex predator* populations are the least stable and most heavily impacted by population fluctuations at lower trophic levels. The pyramid base is the producer trophic level, with increased consumer trophic levels.

*Ecological pyramid of numbers* is based on the number of organisms at each trophic level.

*Pyramid of energy* is based on how much energy each level generates.

*Pyramid of biomass* is based on the amount of living material (i.e., biomass) produced by a given area or volume on Earth's surface at each trophic level.

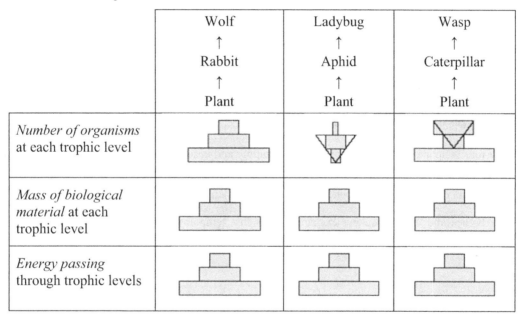

*Ecological pyramids; the ecological pyramid of numbers, the pyramid of energy, and the pyramid of biomass*

Most pyramids resemble a typical upright triangle. However, the pyramid may have inversion areas at points in time. For example, this occurs if an herbivore population feeds on a fast-growing producer, keeping its biomass low in comparison.

## Biogeochemical Cycles

### Nutrient cycles

Nutrients such as water, carbon, nitrogen, and phosphorous are limited in supply. They must be continually recycled through the biotic and abiotic components of an ecosystem via *biogeochemical cycles.* Reservoirs and exchange pools are abiotic portions of biogeochemical cycles.

*Reservoir* is an area that stores a particular nutrient for long periods, perhaps hundreds, thousands, or millions of years. Some nutrients in the reservoir are accessible to organisms by an *exchange pool,* which is temporary storage. Nutrients flow through living organisms (i.e., the biotic community).

### Water cycle

*Hydrologic cycle* is the movement of water throughout Earth's crust, atmosphere, water bodies, and organisms. At a basic level, the hydrologic cycle involves evaporating water from freshwater and saltwater bodies, which condenses and falls as precipitation.

Some water flows below Earth's surface and becomes *groundwater,* contained in *aquifers.*

*Water table* is the depth at which an aquifer is saturated with water. Some groundwater seeps back to the surface and forms freshwater bodies or runs off into the ocean.

*Freshwater* makes up about 3% of the world's water supply and is considered a renewable resource. Freshwater can, however, become locally unavailable when consumption exceeds supply or when it becomes polluted. Groundwater is an example of a biogeochemical reservoir, which makes up about 20% of the world's freshwater.

Freshwater bodies and the atmosphere exchange pools that temporarily store water and make it available to organisms. Ice in the polar regions and water in the deep oceans are reservoirs, like groundwater.

### Carbon cycle

*Carbon cycle* is the exchange of carbon between organisms and their environment. Terrestrial organisms and marine mammals exchange carbon dioxide ($CO_2$) directly with the atmosphere.

Aquatic organisms that do not breathe air do this exchange indirectly by inhaling or exhaling *dissolved carbon dioxide* as bicarbonate ($HCO_3^-$).

Terrestrial and aquatic autotrophs uptake carbon, convert it into organic compounds, and cycle through the food web. As heterotrophs respire, they return carbon dioxide to the air and water.

Photosynthesis and respiration occur at relatively equal rates, keeping the cycle balanced.

Organisms return carbon as organic compounds in the form of waste or ultimately from their decomposing bodies, which detritivores recycle. Some organic compounds are not decomposed but become preserved as coal, oil, and natural gas fossils. The global reservoirs of the carbon cycle are these fossil fuels, along with bicarbonate that remains deep in the oceans or becomes trapped as limestone.

**Greenhouse gases**

*Carbon dioxide* ($CO_2$) is one of three primary *greenhouse gases* that increase atmospheric temperature. Solar energy reaches the Earth and warms the planet, but a significant amount should be reflected, primarily as infrared radiation. The burning of fossil fuels and forests causes additional carbon dioxide to enter the atmosphere.

*Greenhouse gases* absorb reflected infrared radiation and trap it in the atmosphere, causing a rise in atmospheric temperatures. This additional $CO_2$ interferes with the typical exchange between photosynthesis and respiration and alters the carbon cycle. Oil spills are carbon pollution, releasing millions of gallons into oceans each year.

**Nitrogen cycle**

*Nitrogen gas* ($N_2$) makes up 78% of the atmosphere and is vital for plant and animal growth. Organisms use nitrogen compounds to assemble amino acids, nitrogenous bases, and nucleotides such as ATP and $NADP^+$. The cycle of nitrogen throughout its various forms is the nitrogen cycle.

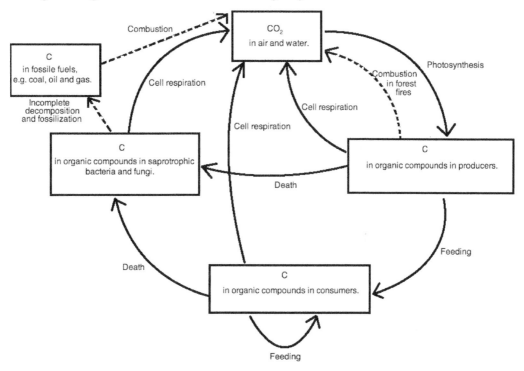

*Carbon cycle with the exchange of carbon among organisms and the atmosphere*

Plants rely on relationships with certain bacteria to convert nitrogen into forms that they can use, a process of *nitrogen fixation*. Nitrogen can be absorbed by plants as ammonium ($NH_4^+$) or nitrate ($NO_3^{-1}$). Nitrogen-fixing bacteria may live within plant roots or freely in the soil and water. They reduce nitrogen gas into ammonium which the plant can take up. Ammonium can be created from the urea in animal wastes.

Bacteria further convert ammonium into nitrate ($NO_3^{-1}$) by *nitrification*. This two-step process requires bacteria to convert ammonium to nitrite ($NO_2^-$), and other bacteria convert nitrite to nitrate. Nitrogen converts to nitrate when lightning or cosmic radiation provides energy for a reaction between atmospheric nitrogen and oxygen.

*Denitrification* refers to converting nitrate back to unusable nitrous oxide ($N_2O$) and nitrogen gas, thus completing the nitrogen cycle. Another class of bacteria performs this.

Human fertilizer production has significantly altered the nitrogen cycle, adding ammonium to the soil. Runoff from nitrogen-rich fields results in over-enrichment, or *eutrophication,* of lakes and oceans.

*Eutrophication* causes large algal blooms, overtaking the environment and killing off other organisms.

The burning of plants and fossil fuels adds nitrogen oxide to the atmosphere, contributing to air pollution. These emissions combine with atmospheric water vapor to form acids that precipitate and acidify soil, *acid deposition*.

Nitrogen oxides react with hydrocarbons in the atmosphere to form *photochemical smog,* which contains dangerous compounds that cause respiratory distress. These air pollutants can accumulate near the ground due to *thermal inversions*, in which warm air traps cold air just above the Earth's surface.

**Phosphorus cycle**

In the *phosphorus cycle,* plants take up phosphate ions ($PO_4^{3-}$ and $HPO_4^{2-}$) available in the soil, primarily from weathering of rocks. However, while most phosphorus is in sediments, phosphorus that runs off into water bodies is incorporated into organic compounds by algae.

Phosphate is the *limiting nutrient* in most ecosystems, and organisms rapidly take up phosphate. Animals eat these producers and incorporate phosphates into phospholipids, ATP, and nucleotides.

*Decay of organisms* and animal waste decomposition eventually make phosphate ions available again. However, phosphate incorporated into teeth, bones, and shells does not decay for long periods.

Like other biogeochemical cycles, humans have disrupted the phosphorus cycle. This is primarily due to the mining of phosphate ores and runoff from livestock wastes and fertilized fields.

Human and animal sewage contributes to phosphate in water bodies, polluting water and leading to *eutrophication*.

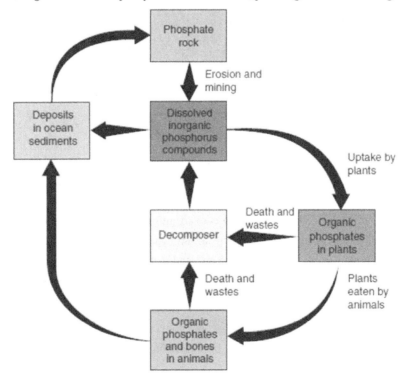

*Phosphorus cycle is when plants take up released phosphorous, primarily from soil*

## Biosphere

**Distinct environmental conditions**

Earth can be divided into layers, each with distinct environmental conditions.

*Geosphere* is the solid portion of Earth's surface, including the cryosphere and lithosphere.

*Cryosphere* contains all frozen water on Earth; most are found at the poles.

*Lithosphere* is the rocky surface of the Earth that extends down about 100 kilometers. It comprises the crust as well as the upper mantle.

*Hydrosphere* covers three-quarters of the *lithosphere*, the liquid water zone primarily contained in oceans. It supports a vast diversity of life and helps regulate global temperatures by absorbing and slowly releasing large amounts of heat.

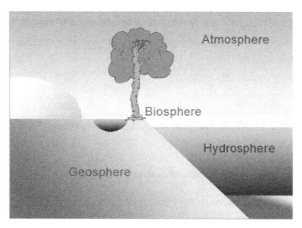

*The intersection of geosphere, hydrosphere, atmosphere, and biosphere*

**Atmosphere**

*Atmosphere* is the gaseous layer wrapped around the Earth, which helps regulate temperatures by insulating the Earth from the frigid temperatures of outer space. It is held in place by the planet's gravity and is concentrated near the Earth's surface. The major gases within the atmosphere are nitrogen and oxygen.

Nitrogen makes up more than 75% of the atmosphere and is essential for plants and animal growth. About 20% of the atmosphere is oxygen necessary for cellular respiration (ATP production) and makes up the protective ozone barrier that absorbs potentially damaging solar radiation. Other gases in the atmosphere include carbon dioxide, water vapor, and noble gases such as argon and neon.

Interacting with the geosphere, the atmosphere, and the hydrosphere is the *biosphere*, a thin layer that comprises all biomass on Earth. In a sense, the biosphere is the global ecosystem. It is further divided into large *biomes*, characterized by a certain climate that supports a unique community of plants and animals. Biomes change with latitude as well as elevation.

For example, the tundra yields coniferous forests and deciduous forests from the poles toward the equator. This same sequence can be seen as one moves from a mountain peak to ground elevation.

49

## Terrestrial Biomes

### Tundra

*Alpine tundra* is at the top of all high mountains, even the equator. *Tundra* is near the north and south poles, wherever there is no exposure to rock or ice-covered seas. It covers about 20% of the Earth's surface, including Greenland, Scandinavia, Siberia, northern Canada, Antarctica's coasts, and surrounding islands.

*Tundra* is characterized by a cold, dry climate that receives less than 20 cm of annual rainfall. If not for the water provided by melting snow, the tundra would be defined as a desert. Except for alpine tundra, most tundra has a perpetually frozen layer of *permafrost* soil. Tundra is a challenging environment for plants due to high winds, a short growing season, and hard permafrost. Trees cannot grow in the tundra, but short woody shrubs can survive as they flower and seed quickly during the short period of available sunlight.

In the summer, the ground of the tundra is covered with bogs, marshes, and streams, with abundant grasses and mosses. Tundra has low biodiversity, and few animals are adapted to live in the tundra year-round. The tundra supports insects and migratory birds and mammals during the summer, such as shorebirds, wolves, and reindeer.

### Coniferous forests

*Coniferous forests* have a milder climate than the tundra and higher annual precipitation. They are primarily made of conifers such as spruce, fir, hemlock, and pine trees. These evergreens are well adapted to a snowy, dry climate and have thick, protective leaves or needles.

Mountainous coniferous forests are *montane coniferous forests.*

Coniferous forests are divided into biomes, depending on convention.

*Coniferous forest biome* is a taiga or boreal forest just below the tundra. It extends across northern Europe, Asia, and North America and makes up nearly 30% of its forest cover. It is the largest land biome and is exceeded in coldness and dryness only by the tundra. The soil does not contain permafrost but is relatively thin and nutrient poor. It is acidic and covered by lichens, mosses, and fallen needles.

### Taiga

*Taiga* supports greater animal diversity than the tundra, with hundreds of bird species and many year-round large mammals such as bears, wolves, moose, elk, and bison. It supports many small mammals, including beavers, hares, and squirrels.

Unlike the tundra, cold-blooded reptiles and amphibians can survive in the taiga.

At the latitudes or elevations below the taiga are *temperate coniferous forests.* They have milder summers and winters than taiga and higher precipitation.

Temperate coniferous forests can be found throughout Europe, Asia, North America, and South America. They include the evergreens of the taiga and cedars, redwoods, juniper, and deciduous trees. The understory is larger and diverse, with various shrubs and herbaceous plants.

## Temperate deciduous forests

*Temperate deciduous forests* are at latitudes lower than the coniferous forests, primarily in eastern North America, eastern Asia, and much of Europe. They have four well-defined seasons, with a growing season between 140 and 300 days. The climate is moderate with mild winters and appreciable rainfall, about 75 to 150 cm per year.

*Deciduous trees* are characterized by their leaves, which they shed in the fall and regrow in spring.

*Deciduous forests* support a wide variety of life, including countless birds, mammals, amphibians, and reptiles. The forest is well-stratified, with large, mature trees shading saplings, shrubs, herbaceous plants, lichens, and mosses. This well-developed understory is possible because of the broad leaves of deciduous trees, which allow sunlight to penetrate the canopy. Major tree species in a typical deciduous forest are maples, oaks, and elms.

## Tropical forests

*Tropical forests* are at or near the equator and can be subdivided into several categories, depending on the biome classification system in use.

*Tropical rainforests* are within 30° north and south of the equator in South America, Central America, Africa, India, Southeast Asia, and Oceania. They have a warm climate and abundant rainfall, from 190 to 1,000 cm per year.

Tropical rainforests are warm and humid year-round, with little change between the seasons. This climate sustains the highest diversity of any land biome with a staggering amount of insect life. Colorful birds and amphibians are abundant, as are snakes and lizards.

Many primates and other mammals are in rainforests. The largest carnivores are big cats such as jaguars and leopards. The forest is highly stratified, with a tall canopy of evergreens and dense understory. The forest floor has rich soil but sustains few plants due to the heavy shade.

A type of tropical rainforest found on high mountains is a *montane rain forest* or *cloud forest* and has a frigid climate compared to lowland tropical rain forests.

Other tropical forests are drier and may exhibit a mix of deciduous and evergreen trees. They are found north and south of the equatorial rainforest belt in Africa, India, Southeast Asia, and South America. One of the largest of these biomes is the *tropical seasonal forest*, which is warm year-round but has long dry seasons. The tropical seasonal forest is less diverse than the tropical rainforest but has much fauna. This biome often gives way to grasslands.

## Shrublands

*Shrubland* (or *scrubland*) is dominated by short, woody shrubs with thick evergreen leaves. These shrubs are highly resistant to forest fires and drought since shrubland is characterized by hot, dry summers and mild winters. Seeds of many plants in the shrubland require heat from fires to induce germination. Shrublands found throughout California and along coasts in South America, Western Australia, and the Mediterranean are *chaparral*.

*Chaparral* is adapted to the climate, with extensive root systems and large leaves that retain water. The chaparral is composed of oaks, manzanitas, sages, and other short, thorny shrubs in California.

*Xeric shrubland* is drier shrubland mixed with interior desert regions. The American West and other desert regions in Asia, South America, and Africa have large expanses of xeric shrubland.

## Grasslands

*Grasslands* are relatively arid but receive greater than 25 cm of annual rainfall. Grasslands are in areas too wet for desert and too dry for forests and once covered 40% of Earth's surface. They are now significantly diminished since their rich soil is ideal for agriculture. Grasslands are adapted to droughts, flooding, fires, and grazing from the many herbivores in these regions.

The two types of grassland are *temperate grasslands* and *tropical grasslands*.

*Temperate grasslands* are characterized by a mild climate and relatively low and predictable diversity. They are located throughout North America, South America, Eurasia, and South Africa, including *prairies, pampas, steppes, and veldts*.

Many temperate grassland animals are large grazing mammals like bison and antelope. Other grassland prey animals are mostly birds and rodents. They are preyed on by coyotes, foxes, lynxes, wolves, snakes, and predatory birds.

*Temperate grasslands* divide into *tall-grass* and *short-grass* regions. Tall grasslands can support trees, are more humid and milder, and are found in the lowlands.

Short grasslands are drier, cannot support trees, and may be found in cold highlands (e.g., steppes of Russia and Ukraine). Many short grasslands mix with deserts and shrublands.

## Savannas

*Tropical grasslands* are *savannas*, containing some trees but are mostly open. They have a relatively cool, dry season followed by a hot, rainy one. The well-known savannas are in Africa, although they can be found in South America and Australia.

*Savannas* support higher biodiversity than temperate grasslands and have the largest variety of herbivores. Insect life in savannas is plentiful and varied. Antelopes, zebras, wildebeests, water buffalo, elephants, and giraffes make their homes in savannas and large carnivores like lions, cheetahs, hyenas, and leopards.

## Deserts

*Deserts* are found at about 30° north and south of the equator, where dry air descends from the Hadley cell. They have an annual rainfall of less than 25 cm and a lack of cloud cover. The absence of clouds makes the days hot and the nights cold. Due to their inhospitable conditions, deserts have some of the *lowest biodiversity*.

Most desert animals are small insects, reptiles, birds, and rodents since a large size is a problem for heat regulation.

However, large birds, camels, kangaroos, and coyotes are in various deserts. Their plants are highly adapted to heat and drought, but some deserts, such as the Sahara, are nearly devoid of vegetation.

Well-known deserts are in low, interior regions, but a desert may be near coasts or at high altitudes as *cold deserts*.

Some researchers classify the tundra as a *polar desert* since it supports little life and is dry.

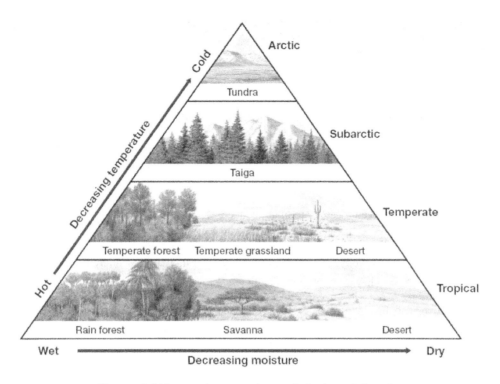

*Terrestrial biomes changes relate to latitude and elevation*

## Aquatic Biomes

### Freshwater and saltwater

*Aquatic biomes* make up most of Earth's biosphere, roughly classified as freshwater or saltwater (i.e., marine).

Marshes, swamps, and bogs are aquatic biomes called *wetlands* found on coastlands across the globe. Wetlands may be freshwater, marine, or a mix, known as *brackish*. They have incredible diversity, with countless amphibians, reptiles, and birds.

*Hydrophytes,* plants adapted to live in water, are in abundance.

*Estuaries* are where a freshwater river merges with the ocean. This may be a bay, lagoon, an inlet, sound, or another partially enclosed aquatic body. Estuaries are brackish, but they are considered marine biomes because of their importance to the seas. They are intertwined with *wetlands*.

Over half of marine fish are believed to have been born or raised in estuaries. Estuaries are provided with nutrients from rivers, ocean tides, and decayed vegetation, making them rich environments supporting much aquatic *flora* (i.e., plants) and *fauna* (i.e., animals). They are a unique biome that has been dramatically threatened by habitat destruction and pollution, leading to the collapse of many vital ecosystems.

### Oceans

*Oceans* comprise the other marine biome. The movement of water in oceans is influenced mainly by temperature, friction of surface winds, salinity, and the Coriolis effect. These factors combine to create ocean currents. Since ocean currents are bounded by land, they move in a circular path, *counterclockwise* in the Northern Hemisphere and *clockwise* in Southern Hemisphere. These currents are vital to regulating ocean temperatures and the global climate.

Currents induce *upwelling,* the circulation of cold, nutrient-rich waters to the surface. Ocean regions that experience upwelling are typically the most diverse and productive because they fuel the activities of *plankton,* a large group of free-swimming microorganisms.

### Plankton

*Plankton* is the basis of aquatic food chains because they are a food source for many organisms.

*Phytoplankton* is microscopic photosynthetic algae, while zooplankton is animals that feed on plankton. Phytoplankton creates most primary productivity in oceans, with macroalgae, cyanobacteria, and hydrophytes.

Plankton is in freshwater biomes, including lakes, ponds, rivers, and streams. Streams and rivers are connected to ecosystems and can exhibit remarkable spatial heterogeneity. They contain salt in less than 1% concentration.

*Headwaters* of the river are cool, clear, and well oxygenated. Nutrient content and species diversity increase as the river travels towards the sea or a lake.

Waters at the mouth of the river are murkiest due to sediment accumulation, which affects light penetrance. There may be lower diversity, lower oxygen, and lower productivity.

Plant life in rivers and streams must *anchor tightly* to the riverbed. In calmer waters, bottom-dwellers can be found that stay in place. In fast-moving waters, nearly all animals are fish that traverse great distances.

Many lakes and ponds have *limited diversity* due to their *isolation* from other regions. Ponds and lakes lack currents and have stable, permanent life forms. Aquatic plants, algae, insects, mollusks, crustaceans, amphibians, and fishes may be in lakes. Birds and reptiles such as turtles, snakes, or crocodiles may prey on these organisms.

**Lake zones**

Lakes are divided into four zones defined by their depth and distance from the shore.

*Littoral zone* includes the shallow areas closest to shore, where the warmest water is penetrated by light. Plants root themselves in the lakebed in this region and support animals such as mollusks, crustaceans, insects, amphibians, and small fishes. Many larval organisms are reared in nurseries of the littoral zone.

*Limnetic zone* is the sunlit area in the open waters of lakes and is home to many plankton and fish. Most photosynthesis occurs here.

*Profundal zone* is below the limnetic zone in deeper waters, home to larger fish, turtles, and snakes. Many birds dive to the profundal zone to capture prey. There is little photosynthesis because sunlight cannot sufficiently penetrate the deeper waters.

*Benthic zone* is at the bottom of a pond or lake and is made of soft sediment that receives little sunlight. It is inhabited by organisms that can tolerate low oxygen levels, including worms, mollusks, and crustaceans. These filter feeders thrive on the debris which falls from the higher zones.

**Lake stratifications**

In the temperate latitudes, deep lakes are stratified depending on the season. The surface waters are warm in summer due to the sun's heat, while the depths are cold. These layers are separated by the *thermocline,* a layer of abrupt temperature change.

In winter, this is reversed, with the depths remaining temperate due to insulation by surface ice and the surface being cold since it is closest to the frigid outside temperatures. In fall and spring, changing temperatures cause mixing that returns the lake to a uniform temperature without a significant thermocline. Lake animals are adapted to these seasonal changes and may migrate to different depths for favorable conditions

Lakes can be classified from *oligotrophic* (nutrient-poor) to *eutrophic* (nutrient-rich).

*Oligotrophic lakes* cannot sustain much plant life and have low levels of primary productivity; consequently, they are dominated by fish. They have clear waters and are often in cold, alpine regions.

*Eutrophic lakes* have high productivity and can support an abundance of plants that outcompete fish. Excessive eutrophication produces massive algal blooms, which deplete oxygen as they decompose. This creates hypoxic conditions that kill off animals.

An influx of nutrients can change an oligotrophic lake into a eutrophic lake.

*Mesotrophic* lakes have moderate nutrient levels and can sustain plant and animal life.

**Ocean zones**

*Oceans* are bordered by continents, each situated on a *continental shelf.*

*Continental crust* extends under the water for some distance from the coast. After several hundred meters, the *continental crust* drops off rapidly, forming a steep, downward *continental slope.*

*Continental rise* follows the *continental slope;* contrary to the name, this region slops downward, albeit less steeply than the slope. The rise levels off into the vast *abyssal plain,* which is the bottom of most of the world's oceans. Large ridges and deep trenches mark it.

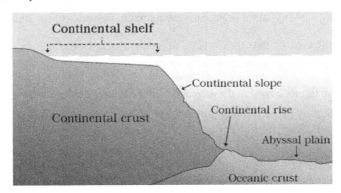

*Oceans are characterized by the continental shelf with the continental crust sloping downward*

*Ocean zones* are much larger and more complex than lake zones. Rather than the entire littoral zone, scientists typically refer to the *intertidal zone,* an area periodically covered and uncovered by water.

*Changing sea levels due to tides* presents a challenge to intertidal organisms. Organisms must anchor themselves to rocks, hide in crevices or burrow in the sediment to avoid desiccation and being swept away.

*Neritic zone* is where the water deepens past the intertidal zone, but the continental shelf continues below. The neritic zone is highly productive because sunlight and nutrients are relatively abundant. It is well-oxygenated and has stable conditions, suitable for most ocean life. Organisms from microscopic plankton to large fish are in the neritic zone and vast coral reefs.

*Coastal zone* marks the boundary between the shore and the open ocean.

*Oceanic zone* is when the continental shelf drops off into a slope; this marks the open seas. It is vast and sustains various sea life, though relatively minor compared to the neritic zone. The largest sea animals, whales, sharks, and giant fishes are in the oceanic zone. Smaller animals and plankton are in the surface waters.

*Pelagic zone* has waters of the ocean that are neither close to the bottom nor the shore. Pelagic waters are throughout the neritic and oceanic zones and are vertically stratified based on the light level.

*Photic zone* extends from the surface to about 1000 meters deep and is where photosynthesis occurs due to phytoplankton activity. Fish, jellies, dolphins, and seaweed live in the photic zone.

Apex predators in the upper waters of the photic zone include sharks, mackerels, and tunas. The bottom of this zone is poorly lit or *disphotic*; consequently, it is dominated by predators with excellent photoreceptors and adaptations to the low light. Prey organisms often have translucent or red coloring, well-disguised in dark waters.

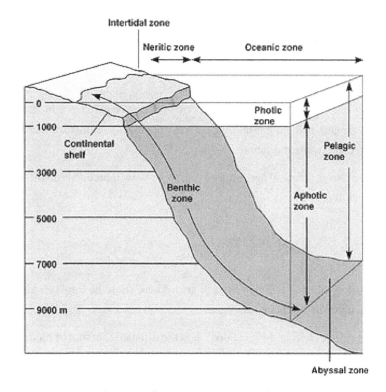

*Ocean with zones at respective depths*

Below the photic zone is the *aphotic zone,* where no photosynthesis occurs because it is dark. It extends to the abyssal plain 6,000 meters below and often deeper into massive ocean trenches. Familiar squids and sperm whales can be found in this zone, but most inhabitants are strange and poorly understood. Many animals release occasional flashes of light to communicate or attract prey at these depths. Animals in this area are carnivores, filter feeders, or scavengers who feed on dead organisms falling from above.

*Benthic zone* is the seabed, which may be completely exposed to air in the intertidal zone or thousands of meters below the surface at the abyssal plain of the oceanic zone. Benthic organisms are adapted to living on or in the sediment, often anchoring themselves to the underlying substrate.

*Sediment* may be sandy, rocky, muddy, or silty. In many areas, the seabed is covered in coral. As marine snow, benthic organisms rely on organic and inorganic nutrients falling from the water column above.

*Intertidal, littoral, and neritic zones* receive sunlight and support a varied food web with seaweed and filter feeders at the first trophic level. Starfish, crustaceans, mollusks, and bottom-dwelling fish occupy the upper trophic levels.

In the *oceanic zone*, the benthic zone receives little to no sunlight, and therefore no photosynthetic organisms can be found. Instead, filter feeders and scavengers feed on marine snow. Starfish, crustaceans, mollusks, and bottom-dwelling fish are common on the continental slope and rise.

There is much diversity of microbes but little *macrofauna* on the pitch-black abyssal plain. These include sponges, worms, sea lilies, and other invertebrates.; a few filter feeders, and scavengers (i.e., feed on dead organisms).

This is a region of extreme cold and intense pressure, except where hydrothermal vents expel superheated, sulfurous water. These vents support *chemosynthetic bacteria*, tube worms, and clams.

## Conservation Biology

### Biodiversity preservation

*Conservation biology* applies ecology and social sciences to preserving Earth's biodiversity. It stresses that biodiversity is vital for humans and organisms and strives to prevent extinction due to habitat destruction, pollution, invasive species, and overexploitation.

Conservation biology emphasizes practical applications, but there is an appreciable effort focused on the intrinsic value of nature to human cultures.

### Biodiversity

*Biodiversity* describes several concepts.

*Species diversity* is the variety of species living in each area. There could be 5 to 100 million species on Earth, and only a fraction of this diversity has been cataloged.

*Genetic diversity* describes alleles within the gene pool. It is the ultimate measure of biodiversity but challenging to assess. Genetic diversity maintains fitness and adaptability; threats to genetic variation pose extinction risks.

*Landscape diversity* is the interacting ecosystems in a region. Homogenous landscapes support a limited diversity of species, similar to isolated landscapes.

Biodiversity is not evenly distributed but is highest in the tropics and lowest at the poles. *Biodiversity hotspots* are regions with unusually high species concentrations. These regions are a fraction of Earth's area but estimate to contain 60% of all species; examples include the Mediterranean, the Amazon rainforest, and Madagascar.

*Biodiversity hotspots* are characterized by endemic species unique to that area alone. Biodiversity frontiers such as the deep sea likely have more species than was formerly suspected.

### Value of biodiversity

Benefits of biodiversity to humans are *ecological services,* which may be economical, scientific, aesthetic, or ethical. Diversity strengthens an ecosystem and makes it healthier, increasing the efficiency of these services.

For example, a greater diversity of crop plants increases their yield, while the greater diversity of fish keeps fisheries more stable and productive.

The importance of natural products in manufacturing material goods cannot be overstated. Economic benefits of diversity include food, oxygen, clothing, medicine, fuel, consumer products, and habitats. The rainforest contains up to $150 billion of potential medications, and many have been discovered.

For example, plastics, rubber, and lumber are a fraction of the materials derived from the environment. Fossil fuels, such as coal, oil, and natural gas, are generated by decomposed organisms.

Nature provides economically valuable services, such as pest control, pollination, soil maintenance, and biogeochemical cycles. Unless supplanted by technology, humans rely on the environment to purify water, break down pollutants, trap carbon dioxide, provide oxygen and recycle organic compounds into edible food.

Some ecosystem services are lifesaving. River and wetland ecosystems are natural buffers against flooding, storm surges, and extreme weather. Trees and plants hold the soil and prevent erosion that clogs reservoirs, creates landslides, chokes coastal ecosystems, and ruins fisheries. Trees are important because they are the largest providers of oxygen and remove atmospheric carbon dioxide. Deforestation worsens the issue of global warming by diminishing the carbon dioxide sink.

*Tourism of natural environments*, or "*ecotourism*," is a multibillion-dollar industry; many cities and countries base an entire economy on ecotourism. If these natural resources are threatened, it causes debilitating economic collapses. Humans are deeply impacted by aesthetic loss and ethical conflict. Erosion and extinctions threaten relationships with plants, animals, and natural habitats, thus human culture.

## Causes of extinction

The greatest threats to biodiversity cause species extinctions. Research shows that potent catalysts of extinction are habitat loss, introduced or invasive species, overexploitation of flora and fauna, and pollution.

*Habitat loss* may be caused by destruction, fragmentation, or degradation. The typical form is direct human destruction. Examples include clearing forests for agriculture, draining wetlands, diverting rivers and building dams, mining, trawling the ocean floor with fishing nets, and urbanization.

Unfortunately, biodiversity hotspots are often the most threatened by habitat loss. A classic example is the tropical rainforests, which are being cleared at an astonishing rate. Threatened biomes include grasslands, deciduous forests, wetlands, estuaries, and oceans.

*Habitat degradation* is an indirect habitat loss caused by pollution, climate change, and exotic species.

*Habitat fragmentation* usually results from urban sprawl and infrastructure, which can divide an area into fragments that are too small to support a species. Fragmentation hinders migration, which is crucial for the maintenance of diversity. For example, an invasive herbivore may weaken a grass population used as a habitat by native species.

Exotic species are introduced accidentally or deliberately into new ecosystems. Human circumvention of natural barriers has resulted in the transport of many alien species to new environments. Ecosystems evolve with their native organisms in balance, and introducing a new species often disrupts the food chain and lead to extinction.

*Overexploitation* is when harvesting wild populations become unsustainable.

For example, animals may be overexploited for food, hides, furs, ivory, pets, or sport.

Nearly one-third of fisheries have been overexploited, and tigers and elephants have been hunted nearly to extinction. Plants are typically overexploited for food, building materials, medicine, and agriculture.

Overexploitation hinders an ecosystem's ability to recover even decades after it ceases.

## Climate Change

### Pollution

*Pollution* is the introduction of harmful elements into an ecosystem. It results in the accumulation of greenhouse gases, acid deposition, disease, and other ill effects. For example, air pollution is caused mainly by exhaust from factories and motor vehicles.

*Soil and water pollution* typically result from agricultural, industrial, and sewage runoff, containing pesticides, heavy metals, oil, fertilizers, animal wastes, and toxic chemicals.

*Littering* of trash is physical pollution that affects the land and water.

However, pollution may take the abstract form of *light* and *noise pollution*.

*Noise pollution* interferes with natural communication between animals, particularly sonar. *Over-illumination* in cities disorients animals and impacts their circadian rhythms, migration patterns, and reproduction.

*Genetic pollution* is a recent phenomenon caused by human interference with the genetic diversity of a population. It can destabilize the population, decimate its fitness, and even decimate it.

For example, breeding or engineering hybrids, homogenizing the gene pool, or introducing new species affect the natural (i.e., wild-type or native) population.

### Climate change

Extinction is exacerbated by *climate change*.

For example, global warming melts ice caps, increasing sea levels and destroying coastal habitats. It warms the seas and increases pH, threatening many aquatic species adapted to certain conditions. The coral reefs are already suffering from temperature and acidity shock.

Global warming promotes the growth of pests and pathogens, increasing disease rates.

Climate change alters *global weather patterns*, causing extreme weather events which destroy habitats and kill wild populations.

Regions with a suitable climate shift rapidly, probably faster than organisms can migrate or adapt, allowing exotic species to outcompete native species in the changing environment.

### Biodiversity hotspots

Conservation biologists focus on *biodiversity hotspots* to maximize effectiveness.

Hotspots may be detected in various ways, including widespread field studies that provide accurate counts of species diversity but are labor-intensive.

A more straightforward but sometimes misleading method is to look for *indicator species,* highlighting certain conditions of an ecosystem that may otherwise go undetected.

For example, the presence of the spotted owl indicates a stable, old-growth forest, while the bleaching of corals indicates acidic waters.

*Indicator species* are often *keystone species*, which can be valuable targets for conservation since they prevent the extinction of several species.

Endemic, rare, and endangered species merit the primary attention of conservation efforts. Many of these organisms become *flagship species,* adored by humans for their looks or symbolism.

*Flagship species* are mostly mammals, such as polar bears and giant pandas, and can be a powerful tool for mobilizing conservation. Unfortunately, many vitally important invertebrate and plant species are disregarded in favor of flagship species.

*Umbrella species* spread over a range of habitats; they are often flagship, keystone, or indicator species. Because the umbrella species has a wide range and is easily observable, targeting conservation of the umbrella species undoubtedly assures conservation of species.

For example, protecting the spotted owl requires the protection of its habitat, old-growth forests in North America. These forests are home to hundreds of species that benefit from the spotted owl's conservation.

## Conservation techniques

*Conservation efforts* require *cost-benefit analysis*, statistical models, and detailed proposals to succeed.

For example, *population viability analysis* helps determine how much habitat a species needs to survive. This can guide conservationists to balance the costs of habitat preservation with the benefits for the species.

Governments take on conservation efforts if they are efficient and effective. One of the best ways to compel governments is to describe the practical, monetary advantages of acting. It is helpful to provide clear guidelines for what actions should take place.

*IUCN Red List* describes the conservation status of thousands of organisms, with categories such as "least concern," "vulnerable," "endangered," and "extinct."

For example, hunting and fishing laws, the creation of nature preserves, sustainable building practices, and development restrictions are conservation efforts for governments. Hunting, poaching, and fishing may be banned outright for species or only somewhat restricted.

*Sustainable hunting and fishing* practices aim to prevent the overexploitation of biodiversity.

Conservation aimed at *invasive* or *introduced species* often attempts to cull the populations of the problem species. This can be costly, difficult, and often requires an ongoing effort. Introducing a *new* exotic species which preys on the problematic one can be effective if done carefully, and scientists can be confident it will not exacerbate.

*Habitat loss* is the leading cause of extinction; *habitat preservation* is foremost for conservation biology. One challenging but essential way to protect biodiversity is to restore a degraded habitat to its former health.

## Habitat restoration

*Habitat restoration* falls under *restoration ecology*, which studies strategies to restore ecosystems.

*Planting vegetation* may reduce erosion; for example, controlled burns can clear species.

The goal of habitat restoration is to return the habitat to its natural state and ensure it can maintain this state without human intervention. This often takes the form of nature preserves, where species and their environment are protected from human interference.

*Wildlife corridors* are a recent technique used to connect habitats fragmented by land development.

*Preserves* and *corridors* are often selected using *gap analysis,* which overlays land-use maps with species maps to highlight areas where biodiversity is high but unprotected or fragmented.

For example, low impact development, reduction of logging and mining, and pollution control are ways habitat loss can be prevented. Of course, it is better to be proactive rather than reactive.

*Pollution control* is a facet of conservation that has received significant attention and international agreement in the *Kyoto Protocol* (1997). This treaty was drafted to target climate change, the critical frontier of conservation, primarily in reducing greenhouse gases and pollutants.

For example, pollution can be prevented or reversed by enacting an eco-friendly industry, better waste management, cleanup, recycling, and new technologies that reduce old, harmful substances.

The most effective conservation is *in situ,* occurring in the ecosystem in question.

*Ex-situ* conservation occurs outside the original ecosystem and may include relocating species to a new environment or breeding them in zoos and re-releasing them into the wild.

*Gene banks* are a focus of *ex-situ conservation*. Scientists maintain plant seeds, cuttings, and animal gametes, so these organisms may be reintroduced if the species become endangered or extinct.

# CHAPTER 2

# Populations and Community Ecology

- Ecology of Populations
- Population Growth Models
- Population Size Constraints
- Community Ecology
- Symbiosis
- Communities

## Ecology of Populations

### Ecology and habitats

Humans have been studying the natural world for hundreds of years, but the term *ecology* was coined in the 19th century by the German zoologist Ernst Haeckel (1834-1919).

*Ecology* studies the distribution and abundance of organisms and their interactions with one another and the environment. The field was significantly advanced by widespread acceptance of the theory of evolution.

Evolution allowed scientists to understand how ecological pressures such as natural selection shape the environment. Ecology has become modernized, with rigorous, comprehensive studies and sophisticated statistics. Modern ecology has applications in several fields, including conservation, agriculture, social science, etc.

Ecology is hierarchical, as it can be studied at many levels, from cellular to the *biosphere,* the entire region of Earth in which organisms reside. Most ecologists begin their study at the *organismal level*.

*Habitat* includes an organism's physical and biological surroundings, including nearby organisms.

Organisms of the same species often live in groups called *populations,* which occupy roughly the same region. *Community* includes the populations of all species in each locale.

For example, a freshwater lake is a community that may include algae, plants, fish, and microorganism populations. Organisms and their interactions are *biotic factors.*

*Ecosystem* includes all biotic factors as well as the physical environment. In the lake example, the ecosystem would include the populations described above and water salinity, temperature, pH, density, light level, soil composition, and other *abiotic factors*.

Ecosystems with similar abiotic factors make a *biome,* usually defined by its climate.

For example, the tropical rainforest is a biome that includes all hot, humid ecosystems supporting a high diversity of life. Collectively, biomes comprise the biosphere.

### Population size

*Population ecology* studies growth, abundance, and distribution. The size of the population is denoted as $N$, the total number of individuals. Population size in relation to living space is *population density* or the number of individuals per given area unit. How density is patterned over a range is *population dispersal*.

Populations may be spread uniformly, randomly, or clumped. Ecologists often study the changes in population distribution across space or time.

A population is densest near the center of its range and sparsest at the edge. This edge is the *zone of physiological stress* because it has suboptimal conditions for the species in question. Physiological stressors may include extreme temperatures, inadequate water, or pollution.

Species' theoretical range is determined by the multitude of physiological stressors it can tolerate. However, species may restrict this range due to biological stressors, such as competition and predation.

*Zone of intolerance* is beyond this, where no species can survive.

**Carrying capacity**

Biotic and abiotic resources are often in limited supply, and the environment can only support so many organisms, known as the *carrying capacity* (K).

When populations approach carrying capacity and deplete resources, they encounter *environmental resistance,* and growth slows.

*Carrying capacity* is determined by the available water, space, food, light, and other factors. It is density-dependent, becoming *restricted as growth increases.*

Stable populations do not attempt to maximize biotic potential but remain under carrying capacity.

However, overshooting carrying capacity can be a valuable strategy, provided the population can introduce new individuals before crashing.

Carrying capacity is an essential regulator of *population size* and a powerful driver of *evolution.* Populations respond to carrying capacity by *expanding their range* or *evolving adaptations*, which relieve them of some carrying capacity restrictions.

Populations cannot evade carrying capacity indefinitely, and *high mortality* results if it is overshot.

**Limiting factors**

Stressors are *limiting factors*, conditions that limit the growth or abundance of a population. Limiting factors may be *density-independent,* independent of population density (e.g., light availability and precipitation).

Limiting factors can be *density-dependent,* whereby the effect becomes severe as population density increases.

Density-dependent factors include competition, disease, parasites, and food scarcity. They typically fluctuate and drive a *population cycle,* a cyclic change in the population size.

The population size (N) over time can be predicted by *natality* (birth rate) and *mortality* (death rate).

Together, natality and mortality can be used to calculate the *intrinsic rate of natural increase* (r).

$$r = \frac{(\text{birth rate } - \text{ death rate})}{N}$$

However, population increase is usually subject to many factors. For example, population ecologists must consider the *immigration* of individuals into or the *emigration* of other individuals out of the population.

## Population Growth Models

### Population growth

Population growth typically exhibits one of two patterns.

*Discrete growth* (*discrete breeding* or *reproduction*) is when organisms breed at a particular time. They may breed once, as *semelparous,* or reproduce as *iteroparous* yearly. The former strategy produces *discrete generations,* in which the adult generation reproduces and soon dies, leaving behind the next generation. This results in a population with *one generation* at any given time.

*Iteroparity* (i.e., multiple reproductive cycles) produces *overlapping generations*, in which an elderly generation is living at the same time as a reproductive generation and a sexually immature generation. At any time, at least two generations can be observed.

*Continuous growth* is when organisms reproduce continuously without regard for a specific breeding season.

*Iteroparous* populations exhibit continuous growth and have overlapping generations.

Most organisms do not fit neatly into one of these two patterns and instead exhibit a combination of the two.

For example, plants may reproduce sexually at a specific time each year but reproduce asexually at any time.

### Exponential growth

*Exponential growth* often occurs in iteroparous (i.e., multiple reproductive cycles) populations with overlapping generations and is represented by a J-shaped *exponential growth curve.*

Populations enter exponential growth at a critical size when *growth accelerates rapidly.*

*Lag phase* is the first phase when growth is slow because the population is small.

*Biotic potential* considers the number of offspring produced by each reproductive event (clutch size), the frequency and a total number of reproductive events, offspring survival rate, and the age at which an individual reaches sexual maturity.

A population undergoing maximum growth fulfills its biotic potential with *no hindrance from limiting factors.*

Populations reach biotic potential when they have ample *space*, *resources*, and absence of *predation*.

**Growth curves**

S-shaped (*sigmoidal shaped*) *logistic growth curve* represents growth under environmental resistance. The first portion of the curve is *exponential*, with *lag* and *exponential phases*.

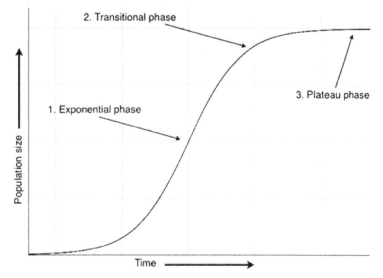

*S-shaped logistic growth curve of population growth with environmental resistance*

Populations enter a *stable equilibrium* phase with *minimal growth at carrying capacity*.

During stable equilibrium, *natality and mortality* are roughly *equal*.

Populations eventually reach a *transitional* or *deceleration phase* when the *birth rate falls* below the death rate due to resource competition, predation, disease, and other density-dependent factors. At this point, growth slows.

Logistic growth (*S*-shaped) curve: $\frac{\Delta N}{\Delta t} = rN \left(\frac{K-N}{K}\right)$

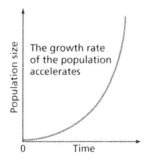 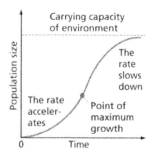

*Exponential (unrestricted) growth (left) and logistic (restricted) growth (right)*

## Age distribution graphs

*Age structure diagrams* represent the abundance of individuals of each gender and age group of a population.

*Horizontal bars* represent the number of individuals in each age group. A population with overlapping generations typically exhibits pre-reproductive, reproductive, and post-reproductive generations.

*Pyramid shape diagrams* indicate an expanding population with a high birth rate and exponential growth. The pre-reproductive generation is the largest because offspring are rapidly reproduced, while the reproductive generation is intermediate. The post-reproductive generation is the smallest as the elderly die.

*Bell shape diagrams* represent a relatively *stable population*, in which the pre-reproductive and reproductive generations are roughly equal, and the post-reproductive generation is smaller by a narrow margin.

*Urn-shaped diagrams* indicate a *declining population*. The post-reproductive generation is the largest because of few new individuals. Individuals from the reproductive generation enter the post-reproductive generation and continually die, while the pre-reproductive generation is too small to sustain growth.

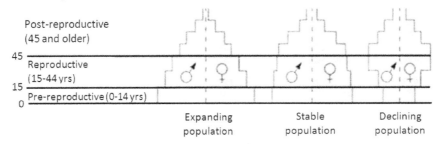

*Age structure diagrams: pyramid (left), bell-shaped (center), urn-shaped (right).*

## Mortality patterns

In demography, predictions ascertain the probability that an individual will die before their upcoming birthday based upon their age. The tool used to make these predictions is a *life table* (*mortality table* or *actuarial table*). This information signifies the survivorship of certain age-based populations.

| Region | 1990 | 1995 | 2000 | 2005 | 2010 | 2012 | MDG target 2015 | Decline (percent) 1990–2012 | Annual rate of reduction (percent) 1990–2012 | 1990–2000 | 2000–2012 |
|---|---|---|---|---|---|---|---|---|---|---|---|
| Developed regions | 15 | 11 | 10 | 8 | 7 | 6 | 5 | 57 | 3.8 | 3.9 | 3.8 |
| Developing regions | 99 | 93 | 83 | 69 | 57 | 53 | 33 | 47 | 2.9 | 1.8 | 3.8 |
| Northern Africa | 73 | 57 | 43 | 31 | 24 | 22 | 24 | 69 | 5.4 | 5.3 | 5.5 |
| Sub-Saharan Africa | 177 | 170 | 155 | 130 | 106 | 98 | 59 | 45 | 2.7 | 1.4 | 3.8 |
| Latin America and the Caribbean | 54 | 43 | 32 | 25 | 23 | 19 | 18 | 65 | 4.7 | 5.1 | 4.4 |
| Caucasus and Central Asia | 73 | 73 | 62 | 49 | 39 | 36 | 24 | 50 | 3.2 | 1.6 | 4.5 |
| Eastern Asia | 53 | 46 | 37 | 24 | 16 | 14 | 18 | 74 | 6.1 | 3.7 | 8.0 |
| Excluding China | 27 | 33 | 31 | 20 | 17 | 15 | 9 | 45 | 2.7 | −1.2 | 5.9 |
| Southern Asia | 126 | 109 | 92 | 76 | 63 | 58 | 42 | 54 | 3.5 | 3.1 | 3.9 |
| Excluding India | 125 | 109 | 93 | 78 | 66 | 61 | 42 | 51 | 3.3 | 3.0 | 3.5 |
| South-eastern Asia | 71 | 58 | 48 | 38 | 33 | 30 | 24 | 57 | 3.9 | 3.9 | 3.8 |
| Western Asia | 65 | 54 | 42 | 34 | 26 | 25 | 22 | 62 | 4.4 | 4.4 | 4.5 |
| Oceania | 74 | 70 | 67 | 64 | 58 | 55 | 25 | 26 | 1.4 | 1.0 | 1.7 |
| World | 90 | 85 | 75 | 63 | 52 | 48 | 30 | 47 | 2.9 | 1.7 | 3.8 |

*Life table, developed by the UN, indicates mortality levels and trends for children under five years*

Actuarial science uses two varieties of life tables.

*Period table* calculates mortality rates during a set period for a specified population.

*Cohort life table* (*generation life table*) represents a population's overall mortality rates.

*Cohort* is a group of individuals born at the same time aging together.

*Life tables* track cohorts over their lifetime.

**Survivorship curves**

*Survivorship* i to how many individuals remain alive at a given time.

The three general types of survivorship curves are:

*Type I survivorship curve* shows a long curve with a relatively short drop-off near the end in which most individuals survive until they die of old age (e.g., the human population).

*Type II survivorship curve*, which is negative and linear, shows individuals dying at a constant rate over their lifespan (e.g., some birds and lizards).

*Type III survivorship curve* is when most individuals in the population die at an early age.

However, those who survive tend to live for a relatively long time. It is the opposite of a Type I curve and is seen in many invertebrates, plants, and fish.

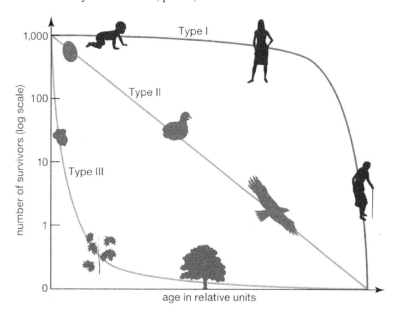

*Survivorship curves comparing type I, type II, and type III organisms*

## Population Size Constraints

### Regulation of population size

Populations are regulated by *density-dependent* and *independent factors*.

Factors may be *intrinsic* (i.e., within the population) or *extrinsic*. *Intrinsic factors* include the behavior and anatomy of the species, while *extrinsic factors* include climate, habitat, and other organisms.

*Exponential* and *logistic* growth curve models are a straightforward view of population growth that only considers classic limiting factors.

Natural populations may be affected by hundreds of complex and interrelated factors. These are usually *intrinsic factors* such as social behavior, influencing how competition proceeds and individuals immigrate or emigrate.

For example, populations may actively recruit or exclude members due to territoriality.

Straightforward models have *difficulty predicting randomness*. Populations deviate from expectations because of chance or unpredictable events, like natural disasters.

### Life history patterns

Ecologists have historically divided organisms into two major life-history patterns: *r-selection* and *K-selection*.

Most species are not strictly r-strategists or K-strategists; it is typical for a species to exhibit both characteristics.

Organisms may be able to shift strategy in response to environmental factors.

### r-selection

The r-selected species attempt to maximize their rate of natural increase. They typically overshoot carrying capacity, causing the population to crash suddenly. Therefore, population growth may show *severe fluctuations*.

*Opportunistic species*, typically r-strategists, rapidly seize the opportunity to proliferate. They are often the first to colonize a new habitat and do well in unstable environments subject to density-independent factors. They reproduce quickly and reach sexual maturity at an early age, maximizing reproduction before death. They may reproduce once; semelparity (single reproductive event) is a common characteristic of r-strategists. They must produce many offspring at one time because they cannot protect them from infant mortality.

r-selected organisms have a short lifespan and must quickly adapt to new environments.

### K-selection

K-selected species attempt to maintain their rate of natural increase. They exist near the carrying capacity at a state of equilibrium, making them an *equilibrium species*. Unlike r-strategists, K-strategists are specializers uniquely suited to their environment. This makes them successful but vulnerable to disturbances. They typically enter a new habitat after r-strategists have colonized it.

K-strategists reach sexual maturity slowly, but they can live long. They can reproduce several times throughout their lifespan, making them *iteroparous (multiple reproductive cycles during their lifetime)*. K-selected species are typically large and invest considerable energy in caring for their offspring, of which they rear one at a time.

**Human population growth**

*Human population* is in the *exponential phase of a J-shaped* growth curve.

*Global population* is currently increasing by about 80 million people per year. This tremendous growth has been fueled by technological advances, increased food supply, disease reduction, and habitat expansion.

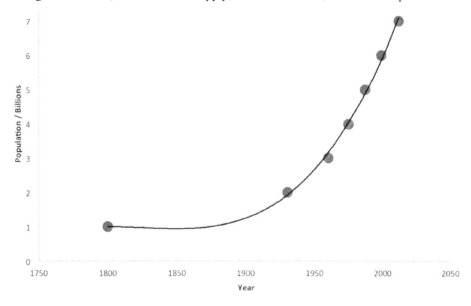

*Human population growth with exponential population growth between 1800 and 2020*

Estimates predict that the world population will level off this century at between 8 and 10 billion. Some claim this is a vast underestimate, and that the human population may reach 14 billion by the end of the 21st century

In the mid-20th century, the developed countries had a significant decline in mortality rate, soon followed by a decline in the birth rate. Currently, the growth rate in first-world nations is at about 0.1%. Their age structures are relatively stable, with some countries even exhibiting a declining population.

In the coming years, nearly all population growth will be seen in the less developed countries, especially in Africa, Asia, and Latin America. The growth rate in these countries is lower than at its peak of 2.5% in the 1960s.

Population growth is addressed by family planning, birth control, and encouragement to produce fewer children. However, due to cultural attitudes and a high infant mortality rate in underdeveloped nations, it is difficult to convince people to have fewer children or delay childbearing until later.

*This world map indicates the average population density per km$^2$*

## Ecological footprints

*Growing populations* of less developed countries and *high consumption* by developed countries put stress on the environment. Currently, the *ecological footprint* of developed nations is unsustainable.

*Ecological footprint* is the amount of land required to sustain an individual's lifestyle, including the area in which he or she lives, farmland required to produce food, factories required to produce material goods, and distances which these products must travel to reach the individual.

For example, an average American family consumes and produces waste for thirty people in India.

Developed countries account for *one-fourth of the world population* but provide 90% of the hazardous waste production. Intense resource consumption affects the cycling of chemicals and contributes to pollution and species extinction. Without drastic reductions in the collective ecological footprint, humans will overshoot carrying capacity and experience catastrophic disease, famine, and other density-dependent factors.

## Community Ecology

### Communities

*Community ecology* studies the composition, diversity, interactions, and relationships between populations and how these characteristics change.

*Community* includes all populations within an environment that interact. It may be large (entire forest) or small (bacterial community in an animal's gut). Because of this variability in scale, it is not easy to delineate the boundaries of a community.

*Composition of a community* is constantly in flux due to natural selection, migration, environmental changes, and random chance. Many communities fluctuate regularly with the seasons; for example, the tundra is inhospitable in winter but supports plant and animal life in the summer.

Communities may be transient, like an animal corpse, which supports a community until decay is complete.

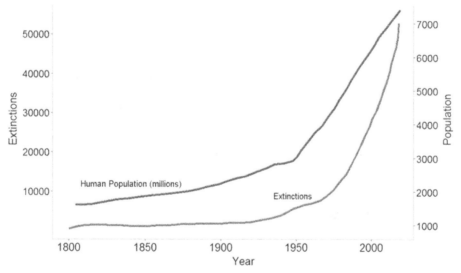

*Correlation between human population levels and the number of species lost to extinction*

### Community models

Models were proposed in the 20th century to articulate the concept of a community. American ecologist Frederic Clements (1874-1945) described a *holistic theory* in which the community acts together as a "superorganism."

Henry Gleason (1882-1975) proposed the *individualistic theory,* which states that each population can inhabit a community due to its unique adaptations. Under this model, a species' range is due to its tolerance to physiological stressors and is independent of the species' distribution.

Biodiversity is a product of chance and not of inherent characteristics of the species.

Stephen Hubbell's (b. 1942) *neutral theory* proposes that species can adapt, grow, and disperse at a basic level. Their differences are negligible, and the variation seen in communities is essentially due to randomness.

Likely, none of these models are precisely correct. It seems that communities are affected by biotic and abiotic factors, as well as by random chance.

## Community structure

*Species composition* (or *species richness*) is the number of species within a community without information about their relative abundances.

*Relative abundance* is species' evenness relative to the size of the community.

For example, a forest with 40 yellow poplars and 40 American elms has more species evenness than a forest with 70 poplars and 10 elms.

Together, evenness and richness describe the *species diversity* of a community. The most diverse communities have a high level of richness and evenness.

The structure of a community depends on abiotic factors and complex interactions between populations.

## Niche theory

*Niche theory* is essential to understanding how organisms and populations fit into the community.

*Ecological niche* is an organism's role in its community, including habitat, resources consumed, and interactions with other organisms. For example, two deer species may occupy the same geographic range but inhabit different niches because they feed on distinct species of plants.

*Fundamental niche* is the place an organism occupies without competition from other species.

Species typically have an area of niche overlap in the middle region where intense competition occurs.

Organisms are usually limited to a *realized niche* (or *restricted niche*) to avoid overlapping with other organisms. For example, one barnacle species may be able to live on rocks that are exposed to the full range of tides, making their fundamental niche the entire tidal area. However, a second barnacle species may be capable of outcompeting the first but can live in the lower tidal region where desiccation is minimal. This forces the first species into a niche that only includes the higher tidal region.

Generalists, such as humans, can occupy a variety of niches. They quickly adapt to a new niche if the current one is threatened. Organisms have developed strategies to maximize success under the constraints of niche theory.

*Specialists* become highly adapted to a single niche. Population interactions can be complex and include resource competition, predation, coevolution, and symbiotic relationships.

## Competition between populations

*Interspecific competition* is when species utilize a limited resource.

*Competitive exclusion principle* states that no two species can occupy the same niche simultaneously. Over time, one population replaces the other or evolves to occupy different niches.

*Natural selection* favors adaptations that minimize competition.

## Resource partitioning

*Resource partitioning* is when two species occupy the same habitat but pursue slightly different resources or secure resources differently, minimizing competition and maximizing success. This is commonly observed in birds, which may inhabit the same tree but spend time in different tree zones to avoid competition.

Studies show that when bird species are separated, they have intermediate beak sizes, but when forced together, they diversify and develop beaks of many sizes. This is *character displacement*, or a *niche shift*, and is a powerful form of evolution.

For example, flocks of swallows, swifts, and martins fly and eat the same insects but have different nesting sites.

**Predator–prey interactions**

*Predation* is a community interaction when one organism feeds on another. In a broad sense, this includes carnivores killing prey and filter feeders that strain microorganisms from the water, parasites that feed on a host, and herbivores that eat plants.

Herbivores that are *grazers* (grass eaters) and *browsers* (leaf eaters) are examples of animals that eat part of their prey, weakening it. This is similar to parasitic relationships.

Predator-prey relationships of the food web may fluctuate. Predator-prey population densities show peaks and valleys, with the predator population often lagging slightly behind prey. This may occur because the predator can overconsume the prey, which causes the prey population to decline, closely followed by the predator population.

It may be the opposite, in which the prey is unable to keep pace with the prey population, causing the prey to overshoot carrying capacity and crash. In many cases, several scenarios affect predator–prey cycling.

For example, the snowshoe hare and the Canadian lynx exhibit cycling, affected by predation and the hare's food supply. The grouse population cycles, perhaps because the lynx switches to grouse when the hare populations decline, evidence that predators and prey do not usually exist as simple two-species systems.

**Coevolution**

Predator-prey interactions drive *coevolution,* in which one species evolves in response to the adaptation of another. Prey has evolved several predator defenses.

*Crypsis* is a common adaptation that allows an organism to escape detection by predators. It may include camouflage, hiding behavior, or *mimicry* (imitation of another species).

*Batesian mimicry* is when one vulnerable species (the mimic) imitates another species (the model), which has successful antipredator defenses. For example, the harmless corn snake exhibits similar coloration to the venomous copperhead snake.

*Mullerian mimicry* is when several species, with some defense mechanism, coevolved to have similar coloration serving as a universal warning. This warning is *aposematic coloration.* Aside from toxicity, prey may have passive defenses that make the prey difficult, unpalatable, or fatal to eat. This may include large body size, sharp spines, tough skin or shells, and a foul odor.

Defenses against predation may be active, such as fleeing from, frightening, or fighting back against a predator.

*Active defenses* are more costly in energy but can be quickly adapted to a situation and are effective.

*Coevolution* need not be competitive, as many beneficial relationships result. For example, pollination involves millions of years of evolution between flowers and pollinators. Flowers have evolved energy-rich nectar and coloration and pheromones, attracting pollinators. The pollinators have evolved anatomy well adapted for nectar consumption and pollen transfer. This coevolution is an example of a *symbiotic relationship.*

## Symbiosis

### Symbiotic relationships

*Symbiosis* is a relationship between species involving three types: parasitism, commensalism, and mutualism.

*Symbiosis* is an intimate, often permanent, association between members of two populations that may (or may not) be beneficial or *obligatory*. One or both organisms cannot survive without the other.

### Parasitism

*Parasitism* is when an organism (the parasite) derives benefits to another's (the host) detriment. This relationship benefits the parasite at the host's expense and allows the parasite to live with minimal energy expenditure.

For example, tapeworms live in the intestines of animals, causing illness.

Parasites may be *ectoparasites*, which cling to the exterior of hosts using special appendages, or *endoparasites*, which live in the host.

Parasites occur in all kingdoms of life. Pathogenic bacteria and viruses are parasites.

Many parasites have several hosts. The primary host is the main source of nutrition, while the secondary host may serve as a vector to transport the parasite to other hosts.

*Parasitoids* invariably kill their host, unlike parasites, which usually permit the host to live.

### Commensalism

*Commensalism* is when one species benefits, and the other is neither benefitted nor harmed. It is challenging to determine commensalism because classification must determine that one organism is not affected. For example, barnacles on a whale could be considered commensalism, but this may be parasitism because they slow the whale.

Another example of commensalism is when plants disperse seeds by sticking to an animal's fur. The animal is neither harmed nor benefited, but the plant has the advantage of broader seed distribution.

Many ecologists argue that any relationship between the species has subtle parasitism or commensalism. Some relationships are so loose that it is difficult to classify as true commensalism. However, relationships that may be reasonably defined as commensalism include insects on animals for transport and crustaceans inhabiting the discarded shells of organisms.

### Mutualism

*Mutualism* is a cooperative relationship that benefits each, provided the relationship is balanced. The imbalance is commonly seen in mutualistic relationships, whereby one individual violates the terms of the relationship to gain an unfair advantage.

A classic mutualistic relationship is between fungi and algae. For example, mycorrhizae of plant roots and fungi are common mutualists, in which the fungus provides inorganic minerals to the plant in exchange for organic nutrients. The fungus provides anchorage and absorption for alga, while alga provides photosynthesis; together, they form a *lichen.*

Plant–fungus mutualism is often not obligatory because each organism can survive without the relationship.

By contrast, the relationship between ant colonies and the bullhorn acacia tree is necessary for the acacia's survival. The ants are protected within the tree and receive nutrients, while the ants defend against herbivores and plants that might block light to the tree. If the ants are killed, the tree is quickly overrun and dies.

*Cleaning symbiosis* is another common mutualism; crustaceans, fish, and birds clean ectoparasites from other animals, improving the "client's" health while providing the cleaner with food. However, cleaners may feed on the client's tissues, turning this into a case of parasitism.

Mutualistic relationships may involve the exchange of resources (e.g., *mycorrhizae*), a service for a resource (e.g., cleaning symbiosis, pollination), or the exchange of services (e.g., sea anemone and clownfish protecting one another from their respective predators).

## Communities

### Community development

*Ecological succession* is experienced by communities as they change. This process can be observed over years or vast periods of geologic time.

*Primary succession* occurs after an event creates or exposes a substrate that has never supported life. This may be bare rock left behind after a glacier moves or a lava flow after volcanic activity.

*Pioneer species* are the organisms first to colonize a newly exposed habitat. They are opportunistic, r-selected species that can tolerate harsh conditions. In primary succession, moss and lichens are the pioneer species, which die and leave behind organic matter that accumulates into the soil.

After soil is deposited, grasses grow, followed by shrubs and then trees. Herbivores enter the community, closely followed by their predators. As succession progresses, many K-selected species outcompete the pioneers.

If an existing community is sufficiently disturbed, all life will be destroyed, and the habitat will revert to a barren state. Everyday events are forest fires or abandonment of farmland. The habitat undergoes *secondary succession.*

Unlike primary succession, secondary succession is strongly influenced by the previous conditions of the habitat. The soil is already present and does not need to be built.

### Climax communities

Clements (1874-1945) popularized that species diversity and total biomass increase until a final equilibrium, or *climax community,* is reached. This is the stable state of the community, which remains relatively unchanged until a catastrophic event destroys it.

The stability of communities is *persistence through time*, *resistance to change*, and *recovery after disturbance*.

However, modern ecologists recognize that true climax communities are rare. Realistically, disturbances are so frequent that most communities are in succession and never truly reach a climax community.

Furthermore, the "steady" state of a community is dynamic. Many ecologists refer to the steady-state as the *mature* or *old-growth communities*. The transitional state is a *seral community* or *sere.*

Clements' ideas are summarized under the *climatic climax theory*, where each region has one climax community, determined by the climate. Other factors are negligible compared to climate.

Many ecologists subscribe to the *polyclimax theory*, which states that a region has multiple climax communities depending on climate plus environments such as topography and the nature of the disturbance.

*Climax pattern theory* proposes multiple climax communities but is influenced by the environment *and* the species present. This theory emphasizes how organisms respond to the *changing environment* and how *succession proceeds.*

Finally, many ecologists believe that succession is cyclical, with a habitat passing through several alternating climax communities.

**Succession models**

Three main models describe succession.

*Facilitation model* applies to species that alter the environment to make it hospitable to the following species. Soil building is a crucial example.

*Inhibition model* describes species that attempt to hold on to their place in the community and make it more difficult for new species to succeed. It assumes that each successional stage has a dominant species, which must be outcompeted or destroyed by a disturbance to allow the next species to establish itself.

*Tolerance model* describes species that neither help nor hurt succeeding species. This model assumes that the climax community is comprised of species that can co-exist.

All three models have been observed, but it is difficult to predict what an environment will experience.

**Community biodiversity**

*Intermediate disturbance hypothesis* states that a moderate level of disturbance yields the highest community diversity. Frequent disturbances may cause extinction, while few disturbances allow one species to grow dominant and outcompete others.

Occasional disturbances, however, periodically inhibit dominant species and dampen competition to allow new species to enter, maximizing biodiversity. Disturbances may alter the physical environment to favor different species than before. Many communities rely on disturbances to keep them healthy, so forest management personnel set controlled forest fires.

Competition must be at moderate levels to maintain diverse communities. r-strategists dominate communities that experience widespread, frequent disturbances are dominated by r-strategists, while undisturbed communities are dominated by K-strategists, which outcompete others.

**Keystone predators**

*Keystone predators* are essential species that regulate competition by controlling the population of species that would otherwise overrun a community. The starfish *Pisaster* is a classic example of a keystone predator that keeps the mussel *Mytilus* from outcompeting invertebrates and algae for space.

*Intermediate migration* best serves biodiversity when emigration is sufficient to offset mortality and immigration.

*The jaguar is an example of a keystone species that regulates competition*

*Island communities* may be on islands or isolated regions, such as a lake or forest patch surrounded by cropland.

Isolated communities have difficulty sustaining migration and may experience extinctions. Insular biogeography studies how isolation affects community structure.

*Insular biogeography* proposes that larger islands support high diversity, mainly because they include keystone predators.

Islands distant from other communities have the lowest migration rates and usually exhibit low diversity. They may experience extinction since individuals cannot easily emigrate and replenish the population.

## Heterogeneity

*Spatial heterogeneity model* is a concept in biogeography that explains why heterogeneous habitats can support higher diversity. The best habitats are patchy or heterogeneous, creating various niches.

Heterogeneity may be seen in the topography, soil, and climate.

Forests usually have vertical heterogeneity, or *stratification,* creating drastically different habitats at different forest heights.

*Spatial heterogeneity* is self-reinforcing since greater heterogeneity leads to more biodiversity, and diversity is a form of heterogeneity.

*Global biodiversity* has been on the decline because of humans.

For example, pollution, habitat destruction, and hunting cause extinctions, which have a domino effect that can collapse entire communities.

## Invasive species

*Invasive species* are rampant, which is a grave threat to diversity.

Invasive species often have *no natural predators* in the environment they are introduced to, allowing them to *outcompete* other species rapidly.

Many communities have become overrun by invasive species (within decades) and are now barren. The problem has been compounded by misguided efforts to introduce a more invasive species to cull the original invader. In many cases, the new invaders take the place of the old ones.

However, some efforts have successfully suppressed invasive species.

Ecologists continue to research methods to minimize the effects of human disturbances and interventions and preserve biodiversity.

# CHAPTER 3

---

# Evolution and Natural Selection

- Foundations of Evolution

- Natural Selection

- Observable Characteristics

- Speciation

- Environmental Factors of Speciation

- Population Growth Strategies

- Divergent, Parallel and Convergent Evolution

- Human Evolution

## Foundations of Evolution

### Historical context

The pre-Darwinian worldview was defined by deep-seated beliefs held to be intractable truths, namely that each species was specially designed and has not changed since Earth's creation. Variations among organisms of the same species were explained as circumstantial imperfections in a perfectly adapted creation.

However, Charles Darwin (1809-1882) lived during a time of profound change in the scientific and social realms. His ideas were part of a larger change in thought and perspective among scientists.

Georges Louis Leclerc (1707–1788), known by his title Count Buffon, was a French naturalist who wrote the 44-volume *Natural History of All Known Plants and Animals*. Buffon provided evidence of descent with modification and speculated on how environment, migration, geographical isolation, and competition influence the traits of organisms. His work was essential to developing the theory of evolution and natural selection, as he was among the first to assert that traits are *inherited from earlier descendants*. Paradoxically, Buffon's beliefs often directly contradicted his work, as he believed in a young Earth and the fixity of species.

Erasmus Darwin (1731–1802), the grandfather of Charles Darwin, was a physician and a naturalist whose writings on botany and zoology suggested the possibility of *common descent*, the theory that organisms descended from common ancestors. He based his conclusions on observations of embryonic development and the changes incurred in domestic plants and animals due to selective breeding by people. However, Erasmus Darwin offered *no mechanism* by which descent with modification might occur.

Jean-Baptiste Lamarck (1744–1829) was the first to propose *descent with modification* and that organisms adapt to their environments. Lamarck was an invertebrate zoologist who went against his contemporaries by embracing evolution. His assertion that organisms change proved correct, but the proposed mechanism was flawed.

### Evolutionary underpinnings

*Inheritance of acquired characteristics* was the Lamarckian belief that organisms adapt to their environment during their lifetime and pass on these adaptations to offspring. Lamarck suggested that body parts are enhanced by increased usage while unused parts are weakened.

Lamarck's theory of inheritance of acquired characteristics has been dismissed in favor of Darwin's theory of natural selection and modern additions to the Darwinian theory of evolution. Under this theory, a giraffe's neck would lengthen over its lifetime as it continually stretched to reach leaves, and the slightly lengthened neck would be passed onto the giraffe's offspring. Over time, these adaptations would accumulate in the long-necked giraffes of modern times.

At the time, however, Lamarck's ideas were fervently held by some scientists, while others, including naturalist Georges Cuvier (1769-1832), adamantly opposed his theory. The term "evolution" was not used; Lamarck referred to the changes of species as *transmutation*.

## Darwin's voyage to Galapagos Islands

In 1831, at the age of 22, English naturalist Charles Darwin (1809-1882) accepted a position aboard the ship *HMS Beagle*; this worldwide voyage provided Darwin with many observations that shaped his theories. He spent several weeks of his journey on the Galapagos Islands, volcanic islands off the South American coast. He observed many island species, which often varied drastically from mainland species and from island to island. The finches of the Galapagos are one such example of organisms experiencing natural selection.

Darwin noted that they resembled the mainland finch but varied in their nesting sites, beak size, and eating habits. These variations led Darwin to ruminate about the descent of these finches from the mainland species and how isolation on the islands may have contributed to their different traits.

After the *HMS Beagle* returned to England in 1836, Darwin waited over 20 years to publish his findings, as he knew the publication would be controversial. He used the time to publish research and gather further evidence on his grand theory of how life forms arise by descent from a common ancestor and change over time.

### *On the Origin of Species* publication

In 1859, Darwin felt compelled to publish *On the Origin of Species* when the English naturalist Alfred Russel Wallace (1823-1913) advanced a similar theory.

While Darwin developed his theories in the mid-1800s, Gregor Mendel (1822-1884) studied genetics. It is unclear whether Darwin ever read Mendel's work, but he did not include genetics in *On the Origin of Species.* Mendel's research went largely unnoticed until after his death, when early 20th century scientists realized the profound implications of his work.

The newly emerging wealth of knowledge about genetics provided an explanation and elaboration on natural selection that Darwin had not been able to describe. Scientists gradually understood that organisms have a genetic code (the genotype) working from the foundations he laid. The observable expression of the code (the phenotype) depends on gene variants known as *alleles* (i.e., alternative forms of a gene).

## Hardy–Weinberg equilibrium

*On the Origin of the Species* popularized *evolution* as the cumulative change of inheritable characteristics within populations, species, or groups. It occurs when *Hardy–Weinberg Equilibrium,* a central tenet of population genetics, is violated. This law states that *phenotypic* (*allelic*) and *genotypic* frequencies *do not change* between generations, provided: genes are unaffected by evolutionary forces (*no mutation*), the population is infinitely large and is not affected by *migration*, and *sexual selection* does not occur (i.e., mating is random).

In nature, these assumptions are often violated, resulting in evolution. Darwin described one mechanism of evolution, natural selection, but genetic drift, gene flow, and mutation violate the Hardy-Weinberg Equilibrium.

*Genetic drift* is random changes in allele frequency in a population and occurs by chance. Even if they are not the fittest of the population, some organisms may pass on more genes by the probability of chance.

*Gene flow* is the transfer of genes between two populations. This may occur by a migration when a population moves into a new habitat and encounters another population. Gene flow may be within a species or between two different species for hybridization.

**Genetic diversity**

*Hybrids* are offspring from two genetically dissimilar parents. Parents may be from the same species or different species. When species hybridize, genes flow between the groups, introducing genetic diversity.

*Mutations* are changes in an organism's DNA (genetic code) from damage or replication errors. Mutations are potent agents of evolution. Mutations can be fatal, harmless, or beneficial. When mutations introduce new traits that allow an organism to succeed, that organism may survive and pass on its mutated code.

**Phyletic gradualism and punctuated equilibrium**

*Microevolution* describes a change in allele frequency within a population. The population (known as *gene pool* or *deme*) is the arena of microevolution. Microevolution can be observed over short periods, especially in rapidly dividing organisms such as bacteria.

*Macroevolution* is a pattern of change in groups of related species over long geologic periods. In a sense, macroevolution is the sum of microevolution. The patterns of macroevolution determine *phylogeny*.

*Phylogeny* is the evolutionary relationship among species and groups of species.

*Phyletic gradualism* describes the constant, uniform accumulation of small changes, resulting in the gradual transformation of one species into a new species. Phyletic gradualism is generally disregarded as a model of macroevolution due to fossil evidence which indicates sudden, drastic speciation.

*Punctuated equilibrium,* which describes geologically long periods with little to no evolution, is the model supported by the fossil record where geologically short periods show rapid evolution.

**Evolutionary time measured by random changes in genomes**

*Random genetic* mutations not acted on by natural selection (i.e., environment favoring specific phenotypes) occur constantly. By measuring the amount of these neutral mutations, the amount of elapsed time can be determined.

*Genome differences* between species can be compared to determine how long ago they may have diverged.

*Molecular clock* dates time comparisons between species.

*Molecular clock estimates time based on genomic differences*

Genetic differences are measured by *phenomes* (i.e., a total of phenotypic traits) or DNA nucleotide sequences.

The simple molecular clock may indicate relative periods between organisms but cannot assign a numerical date.

Calibration of the molecular clock allows for precision *via* comparison against known fossil dates or evidence.

## Natural Selection

**Survival of the fittest**

*Natural selection* was proposed by Alfred Wallace (1823-1913) and Charles Darwin (1809-1882) as a driving mechanism of evolution. Wallace and Darwin theorized that environmental pressures select organisms adapted to make the fittest reproduce.

Three pre-conditions for natural selection:

*First condition* is that the population members have random but heritable variations. Individuals in a population differ due to *mutations and chromosomal recombination*; new adaptations arise.

*Second condition* is that in the population, more individuals are being produced in each generation than the environment can support. This creates *selective pressure to adapt* to survive in scarce resources.

*Third condition* relies on the first two conditions; some individuals have *adaptive characteristics to survive and reproduce*.

Natural selection results in *better-adapted individuals passing adaptations to their offspring*.

In contrast, the less-adapted individuals have their alleles eliminated from the gene pool, as they are likely to die before they can reproduce. An increasing proportion of individuals in succeeding generations have these adaptive characteristics. With time, the population may become a new species altogether.

Since the environment changes, there are no enduring perfectly adapted organisms. Over time, the fittest organisms may be poorly adapted to a changing environment.

*Extinction* occurs when the fitness of a population (or species) has declined, whereby in each generation, more individuals die than are born. This leads to a dwindling population and the elimination of the group.

**Fitness**

*Fitness* is the ability of an organism to pass genetic information on to future generations. Fitness is a measure of an organism's reproductive success. Evolutionary fitness differs from the colloquial term used to refer to a strong, healthy individual. Even the healthiest organism is considered "unfit" if it fails to reproduce.

*Relative fitness* compares the fitness of one phenotype to another.

Survival of the fittest is a component of the natural selection theory that describes *how* fitter individuals survive and pass on their traits while fewer fit individuals die out. Organisms whose traits enable them to reproduce to a greater degree have greater fitness.

For example, black western diamondback rattlesnakes are likely to survive on lava flows, while lighter-colored rattlesnakes survive on desert soil. Therefore, each species adapts to maximize its fitness to survive in its habitat.

**Selection by differential reproduction**

*Survival of the fittest* is misleading as it implies that the mere survival of the organism is the driving force of natural selection. Evolutionary success relies on *reproduction* to pass adaptations to subsequent generations. However, organisms may be well-suited for survival but fail to reproduce.

*Survival of the fittest* may be accurately termed *reproduction of the fittest* or *differential reproduction*.

*Differential reproduction* links *survival of the fittest* and how individuals have a *reproductive advantage*.

*Differential reproduction* occurs naturally, but humans have manipulated natural selection for thousands of years.

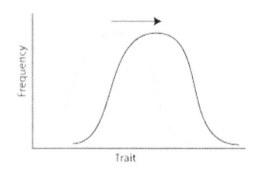

*Artificial selection* refers to selecting traits in plants and animals that humans prefer, otherwise known as breeding.

For example, dogs were bred by selecting wolves with friendlier, more domestic traits. Over time, this artificial selection compounded, producing domesticated dogs. Further selection for specific traits resulted in many breeds.

Domesticated animals and many crop varieties have been produced by artificial selection. Breeders of plants and animals try to produce organisms with desirable characteristics, such as high crop yields, resistance to disease, high growth rate, and many phenotypical characteristics that benefit people who consume or use these organisms.

*Selective breeding* often produces a hybrid between two parents with desirable traits.

*Hybrid offspring* possess the desirable traits of each parent. For example, one parent may possess dominant alleles for long life, while the other parent possesses dominant alleles for fast growth.

When *crossed* (or bred), hybrid offspring should be long-lived and fast-growing.

*Hybrid vigor* is the high fitness characteristic of hybrids.

*Hybridization* is when two groups with overlapping habitats mate at a geographic boundary in a *hybrid zone*.

## Observable Characteristics

### Phenotypic variations

*Natural selection* utilizes random variations (i.e., mutations); therefore, there is no directedness or anticipation of future needs. The organism is incapable of consciously picking and choosing the genome it desires.

Recessive alleles are expressed in diploid (2N) organisms with two copies (i.e., homozygosity). Only alleles causing *phenotypic differences* are subject to natural selection. Heterozygosity preserves recessive alleles, as heterozygotes carry rare recessive alleles that may otherwise be selected against.

For example, consider the preservation of two alleles encoding for hemoglobin: a dominant, normal, and recessive, defective allele. Homozygotes with both dominant alleles have typical hemoglobin. Heterozygous expression of one abnormal hemoglobin allele results in the sickle cell trait, while homozygous expression of both recessive alleles manifests anemia.

There is a high frequency of the sickle cell allele in Africa, with a high malaria incidence. A substantiated link has been made between those with sickle cell trait and immunity to the effects of malaria. The sickle cell trait is advantageous in areas where malaria has a higher incidence.

Therefore, a higher frequency of the sickle cell allele in Africa supports natural selection. There is a tradeoff, as a higher frequency of the allele results in a higher frequency of regressive heterozygosity, causing sickle cell anemia. Theoretically, anemia is an excellent defense against malaria, but severe health issues offset this.

### Favorable traits

Natural selection can be described in several ways.

*Directional selection* is when a trait at one extreme of a spectrum is favored while traits on the opposite end are selected against. Directional selection shifts the distribution toward favored traits. Over time, directional selection shifts the distribution curve of allele frequency towards the favored allele.

For example, natural selection leading to drug resistance in bacteria represents directional selection. Another example is in trees in the rainforest, competing for sunlight, and selection favors taller trees.

*Artificial selection* is mostly directional as humans progressively select traits. It allowed humans to increase the efficiency of livestock animals and crop plants, such as increasing milk yield from cows by continuously breeding cows with high milk production.

*Stabilizing selection* occurs when extreme phenotypes are eliminated and the intermediate phenotype is favored. Stabilizing selection favors alleles that produce *intermediate* clutch sizes.

For example, Swiss starlings' optimum number of eggs is four or five. If the female lays more or less than this number, fewer survive.

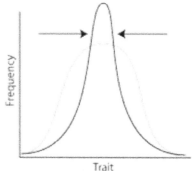

*Stabilizing selection favors a narrow range of phenotypes*

*Disruptive selection* occurs when the phenotypes at extremes are favored. Small beaks are selected for eating berries, while large beaks are selected for cracking seeds.

The intermediate phenotype (medium beaks) is selected against because a medium beak is not helpful for berries or seeds.

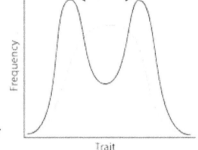

*Disruptive selection favors traits at the extremes*

## Group selection

*Group selection* is a natural selection that acts upon the group and not the individual.

Group selection is often provided as an explanation for altruism. Altruism is when an individual's fitness is sacrificed to benefit the group, usually family, as family shares similar genes. If altruism enables another family member to survive, the genes can be passed on; the individual may exhibit altruism even if sacrificing survival.

## Sexual selection

*Sexual selection* is the differential mating of males (or females) in a population. In most species, the females select superior males, which increases the fitness of their offspring. Females invest more energy in reproduction and thus attempt to maximize the quality of their mates. Males primarily attempt to maximize the number of their mates.

Male competition for mates leads to fights, with mating opportunities awarded to the most potent male. The genetically superior males exhibit traits that aid them in this competition and prove their strength (e.g., musculature, large stature, or bigger horns).

Sexual selection by females may lead to traits or behaviors in males that are not practical and do not increase the male's ability to survive. For example, colorful bird plumages make certain species easily identifiable by predators.

The pressure for males to attract females usually leads to *sexual dimorphism*, in which males and females are observably different.

## Adaptive radiation

*Adaptive radiation* is the rapid development and evolution of many new species from a single ancestral species. It occurs when the ancestral species is introduced into an area where diverse geographic or ecological conditions are available for colonization.

For example, the observations by Darwin of finches illustrate the adaptive radiation of several species from one founder species of mainland finch.

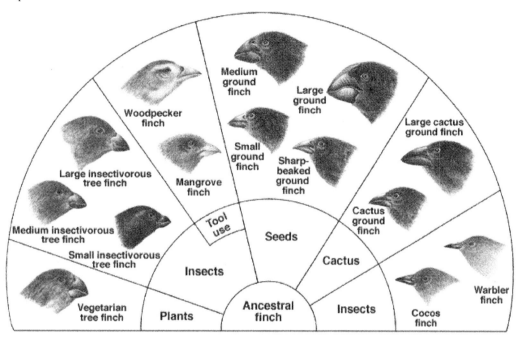

*Darwin's theory of finch evolution on the Galapagos Islands*
*illustrates adaptive radiation from differences in their environments*

## Evolutionary success increases gene pool

An increase in allele frequency represents evolutionary success for that allele. An increase in an individual's allele frequency is an evolutionary success for that individual.

For example, the peppered moth in European cities illustrates changes in allele frequency. Pre-industrialization, these moths were light-colored. However, as pollution increased in the 1800s, soot collected on the sides of buildings, making the light-colored peppered moth more visible to predators.

Mutations resulted in a new phenotype, darker than the white peppered moth. These new, darker peppered moths were favored over the lighter moths by natural selection, specifically directional selection.

Over time, the frequency of the dark allele increased in populations, reaching 95% in most industrial European cities. However, soot has been reduced in recent years, and most buildings are lighter than in the late 1900s.

Therefore, the allelic frequency of dark-peppered moths has decreased since, demonstrating directional selection back towards a light phenotype.

## Common Ancestry: Shared Conserved Features

### Common descent theory

*Common descent* theory is a central tenet of evolutionary biology. This theory states that any given group of organisms share a common ancestor from which they descended. It naturally follows that there is a common ancestor to every organism on Earth, called the *last universal common ancestor* (LUCA).

Darwin (1809-1882) and his contemporaries gathered much evidence about the foundation of this theory, but modern advances in molecular biology have provided many new insights.

In contemporary biology, life is divided into three domains of Archaea, Bacteria, and Eukarya. Archaea constitute a separate domain from Bacteria in recent years.

Although both are unicellular prokaryotes, archaea are too different from bacteria to be classified in the same domain.

It is proposed that LUCA first diverged into bacteria and archaea, with eukaryotes later developing from these.

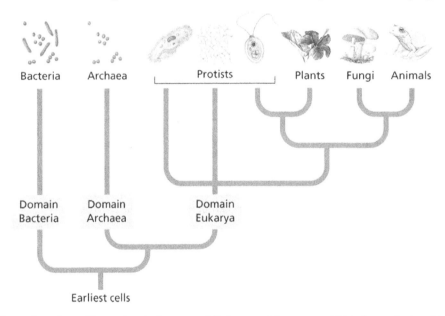

*Three domains of Bacteria, Archaea, and Eukarya with proposed kingdom relationships*

### Structural and functional relatedness of domains

*Archaea* live in a wide range of habitats, but the most well-known species are the extremophiles, which inhabit hostile environments like hot springs, salt lakes, and anaerobic swamps.

Bacteria and archaea exhibit common prokaryotic features, such as a cell wall (archaea lack peptidoglycan), but are different biochemically.

*Domain Eukarya* comprises a diverse array of unicellular to multicellular organisms, the most well-studied. It includes the kingdoms Animalia, Plantae, Fungi, and Protista.

Evidence from fossils, comparative anatomy, and other investigations have been underway since the 18th century.

Modern evidence comes from DNA and RNA sequencing, analysis of common enzymes and metabolic pathways, fundamental similarities in cell structure, and observation of ongoing evolution. While all three domains have unique differences, their underlying structure and function display undeniable similarities.

Organisms use fundamental building blocks, genetic codes, and metabolic pathways. Biochemical evidence is some of the most compelling. Specific genes are largely conserved across all domains of life, coding for proteins that can be remarkably similar or identical. Life forms use the biomolecules similarly.

For example, organisms use DNA and RNA as carriers of genetic information encoded in base nucleotides (A, T, G, C, and U). All organisms interpret these bases as triplet codes to synthesize proteins with twenty amino acids. This supports the hypothesis that all three domains descended from a common ancestor.

Furthermore, the code and method of interpretation are widespread. Many organisms share introns (noncoding mRNA sequences), which is notable because these are inoperative, and it is unknown why they are so similar.

**Structural evidence of eukaryotic relatedness**

The eukaryotes are the most well-researched domain on the Earth, as they are the most readily observable and of the most interest to humans. Consequently, there is a wide array of evidence for the relatedness of all eukaryotes.

Common structural features of eukaryotes include an extensive cytoskeleton and organelles such as mitochondrion, chloroplast, and nucleus. These organelles are part of the endomembrane system, a collective term for membranous sacs dividing a cell into its constituent parts.

In contrast to bacteria and archaea, Eukaryotes are the only organisms with this system of membrane-bound organelles. Notable similarities among eukaryotes include DNA-bound linear chromosomes and shared metabolic pathways, such as glycolysis.

The earliest evidence for the structural relatedness of eukaryotes comes from fossils. The fossil record is the history of life as recorded by remains from the past. Fossils may be skeletons, shells, seeds, imprints, and even soft tissues.

Unfortunately, the fossil record is often incomplete because most organisms decay before fossilization and soft-bodied organisms generally do not fossilize.

**Relative dating**

*Sedimentation* began when Earth formed; it accumulated particles forming a stratum, a recognizable layer in a sequence of strata.

*Relative dating* places it in the sequence indicating the age of a fossil; a stratum is older than the one above and younger than the one below. Most fossils are embedded in or recently eroded from sedimentary rock.

*Relative dating* does not establish the absolute age of fossils. For this, radioactive dating must be used. The technique is based on radioactive isotopes that have a quantifiable half-life, the time it takes half of a radioactive isotope to decay into a stable element.

Carbon-14 ($^{14}C$) is a radioactive isotope contained within organic matter. Half of carbon-14 decays to nitrogen-14 every 5,730 years. Therefore, comparing the carbon-14 radioactivity of a fossil to modern organic matter calculates the age of the fossil.

However, after 50,000 years, carbon-14 radioactivity is too low to measure age accurately. Paleontologists use potassium-40 and uranium-238, which have half-lives of billions of years.

Paleontologists use *strata* (i.e., flat layers of sedimentary rock) and *fossils* (*ossified* or *petrified* organisms) to study the history of life. It is an essential principle of fossil study (i.e., paleontology) that an organism most closely resembles a recent fossil in the line of descent.

Underlying similarities become fewer farther back in the lineage. Similar fossils can be used to construct a timeline showing changes from a common ancestor millions of years ago to a modern species.

For example, transitional forms such as bird-like dinosaur Archeopteryx establish birds descended from reptiles.

Fossils can reveal a wealth of information about an extinct animal, as in the case of the horse ancestor *Hyracotherium*, which was small with cusped, low-crowned molars, four toes on each front foot and three on each hindfoot. These adaptations for forest living were gradually replaced by larger size, grinding teeth, and reducing toes into hooves as the forests gave way to grasslands. Intermediate forms show this transition between *Hyracotherium* and the modern horse, genus *Equus*.

However, it can be challenging to identify the proper patterns in the fossil record and ignore misleading ones. Fossils are continually reclassified and reevaluated. For example, paleontologists have studied turtle fossils and proposed that they are closer to crocodiles than previously thought.

## Biogeographical evidence

*Biogeographical evidence* provides a valuable frame of reference for the fossil record.

*Biogeography* examines the distribution of organisms across the Earth, providing additional insight into evolutionary research. Physical factors, such as the location of continents, determine where a population can spread and greatly influence evolution. Related forms evolving in one locale and spreading to other accessible areas may explain the distribution of organisms.

*Biogeography*, as applied to evolution, is sometimes known as *phylogeography*.

For example, in the 19th century, Darwin observed that the Galapagos Islands had a variety of finch species, but the mainland had one. He concluded that the Galapagos finches had originated on the mainland and diversified once they reached the islands.

## Three domains of life

*Systematics* (or *classification*) is the study of the diversity of organisms using evidence from the molecular to the population level. It is often used synonymously with taxonomy, although it refers to nomenclature, a subset of broader classification.

*Phylogeny* of species reveals evolutionary relationships between organisms, past and present.

Systematics may be applied to modern species or extinct species included in the phylogeny.

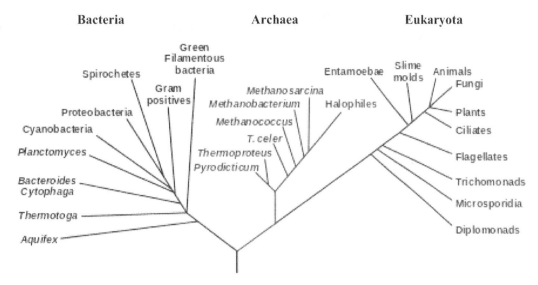

*Phylogenetic tree of life with three domains, nodes, and branches*

*Phylogenetic trees* visually indicate common ancestors and lines of descent.

*Common ancestor* is where two branches diverge at the node, while the tip of each branch is labeled with an individual taxon, usually a species. It is represented by a branching diagram that resembles a tree.

Often the tree includes an outgroup, which does not share the recent common ancestor of other groups on the tree. Outgroups provide a reference for the taxa of interest.

Phylogenetic trees can be constructed broadly or as narrowly as desired, from all life to a species' subforms. A traditional phylogenetic tree has branches corresponding to the relative length of evolutionary time.

*Plesiomorphy* and *symplesiomorphy* are synonyms for an ancestral character shared by all clade members, which does not distinguish a clade from other clades.

## Speciation

### Defining species

The definition of a species is controversial and inexact. At a particular stage of evolution, one population may become so genetically different from the other that it becomes a new species, the process of speciation. After enough changes in gene pool phenotypic and genotypic frequencies have amassed, speciation is an inevitable result. However, generally, different species cannot reproduce and produce viable and fertile offspring.

*Biogeography* is the study of the geographic distribution of life forms on Earth. Comparing the animals of South America and the Galápagos Islands led Darwin to conclude that adaptation to the environment can cause diversification, including the origination of new species. His conclusions were greatly influenced by Charles Lyell (1797-1875), a geologist who first presented the idea that geological variations were formed by slow, continuous processes such as erosion. This hypothesis contrasted with the prevailing belief that Earth's contours had been shaped by divine intervention and had only changed due to sudden, violent catastrophes. Lyell's theory of *uniformitarianism* supported what Darwin had observed while studying geology and fossils.

### Plate tectonics

Lyell and Darwin's conclusions were the precursors to *tectonic plate theory*, which describes the movement of Earth's crust. In 1920, German meteorologist Alfred Wegener (1880-1930) presented data supporting the highly controversial model of *continental drift*.

By the 1960s, the theory of continental drift was confirmed by overwhelming geologic and evolutionary evidence. For example, many of the same fossils have been found on different continents, indicating there was a time when the continents were united.

Continental drift explains why the coastlines of several continents mirror image each other, as in the outlines of the west coast of Africa and the east coast of South America. The same geological features are throughout the world in regions where the continents separated or collided.

The single ancestral supercontinent of Pangea separated over millions of years into land masses seen today. As the continents drifted apart, organisms were separated, resulting in great speciation. One example is the marsupials of Australia, who were isolated from other mammals, and therefore are different from mammals on other continents.

### Allopatric and sympatric speciation

*Allopatric speciation* is when a new species results from populations being separated by a geographic barrier. While geographically isolated, variations accumulate via natural selection, mutation, gene flow, and genetic drift until the two populations are reproductively isolated.

*Sympatric speciation* is when a single population member, without geographic isolation, develops genetic variations preventing reproduction with the original population.

For example, sympatric speciation is observed in polyploidy in plants.

*Polyploidy* is the possession of more than two sets (2N) of chromosomes (e.g., 3N, 4N). The failure to reduce the chromosome number produces polyploid plants that reproduce successfully only with other polyploid plants. Backcrosses with diploid plants are sterile. Polyploidy leads to new species of plants.

Aside from polyploidy, evidence for sympatric speciation is sparse. This issue is under intense research and debate in evolution. Researchers contend that sympatric speciation is a poorly understood subtype of allopatric speciation and that interbreeding makes true sympatric speciation impossible without a geographic barrier.

## Taxonomy

*Taxonomy* is the science of classifying organisms, an undertaking that humans have attempted for thousands of years. Carl Linnaeus (1707–1778), a Swedish naturalist, revolutionized the field of taxonomy when he introduced a streamlined, standardized taxonomic system that replaced hundreds of disorganized systems previously used. Linnaeus' system featured binomial nomenclature, in which a two-part name is given for each species (e.g., *Homo sapiens*).

Like other taxonomists, Linnaeus believed that each species had an "ideal" structure and held a fixed place in the *scala naturae*, the divine hierarchy of life. Linnaeus thought that classification should describe the fixed features of species and reveal God's plan and believed that the ideal form of each organism could be deduced and arranged according to the scala naturae. He was the first prominent scientist to propose that humans were closely related to other primates. This bold declaration clashed with the predominant belief that humans were fundamentally distinct from animals. However, his later work with hybridization suggested that species might change with time.

## Classifications

*Classification* establishes categories to assign species based on their relationship to other species. A *taxon* is a group of organisms in a classification category; *Homo* or *Felis* are taxa at a genus level, describing the genera of hominids and cats, respectively.

*Species* is a taxonomic category below the rank of *genus*. When a species has a wide geographic range, variant types may interbreed where they overlap; these populations may be named subspecies.

For example, *Canis lupus* contains around 40 subspecies, including *Canis lupus lupus* (Eurasian wolf) and *Canis lupus familiaris* (domestic dog). The addition of the subspecies makes for a trinomial or three-part name.

Previous taxonomic classifications separated organisms into two categories, Animalia, and Plantae. This is incorrect, as many new organisms were discovered that fit in both (and neither) categories.

These taxa are a kingdom, phylum, class, order, family, genus, and species from broadest to narrowest.

Super-, sub-, or infra prefixes add classifications to taxonomic levels; currently, at least seven classifications exist.

*Domain* is a taxon above kingdom and classifies organisms into Eukarya, Bacteria, and Archaea.

These domains and subsequent taxa are under revision, controversy, and debate.

## Environmental Factors of Speciation

### Adaptation and specialization

*Adaptation* is when an organism evolves to become suited to its environment. Because of natural selection, adaptive traits accumulate in each succeeding generation.

*Specialization* occurs as adaptations allow species to exploit a niche.

Organisms adapt in response to the evolution of other species within their habitat. Most environments change, and so organisms *adapt* or become *extinct*.

Organisms might adapt to an environmental change in their habitat (e.g., change in soil acidity or precipitation). They may adapt to a new habitat due to migration or an invasion from outside species.

*Co-adaptation* is when species evolve in response to another.

For example, pollinating insects and flowers continually co-adapt to maximize their mutualistic relationship.

Co-adaptation may be more threatening when a host species evolves into a hostile gut environment; the parasitic species must adjust to maintain its survival in the host species' gut.

*Exaptation* is when, over time, many traits are readapted for a new purpose.

*Maladaptation* is when traits are selected against because they become a distinct disadvantage.

### Ecological niches

*Niche* encompasses both physical and environmental conditions.

*Ecological niche* is the environment in which an organism lives and the role that it performs. The ecological niche is the organism's *habitat* (i.e., *area and resources used*) and its behavior and relationship with the habitat.

Organisms attempt to fill their niche by *maximizing resources*. This is accomplished by the specialization of the organism, as it adapts to its ideal niche.

### Competition

*Competition* is an intense *selection pressure* driving organisms to evolve and adapt to a different niche or better compete for resources in their current niche. Resources are best utilized when organisms occupy distinct niches, as they do not compete.

When niches overlap, resources become scarce, and the organisms threaten each other's survival. This results in competition, which can be interspecific and intraspecific.

*Intraspecific competition* is typical since members of the same species occupy similar niches.

Population growth is balanced by competition. Competition is minimal at a low population density, and population growth can occur rapidly. However, as the population grows, the available resources dwindle.

**Carrying capacity**

*Carrying capacity* describes the maximum population that the environment can support.

As a population approaches its carrying capacity, *intraspecific competition increases* and *slows population growth*.

Competition within a species can force members to occupy different niches, driving speciation.

Individuals may compete for mates, food, water, space, or other advantages. They compete indirectly by *depleting resources* that other organisms also utilize.

*Competitive exclusion principle* states that when species use the same resource in the same place, the species diverge into different niches by *niche differentiation*.

If this divergence does not occur quickly, one species outcompetes the other by pushing the species from the shared overlap of their niches. Exponential population growth is rare due to the pressures of competition.

However, humans exhibit exponential population growth by constantly finding and exploiting new resources.

## Population Growth Strategies

### r-selection *vs.* K-selection

Evolutionary ecology places species on a spectrum related to their population growth strategy.

*r-selected* species mature rapidly, reproduce early, and produce many offspring. A classic example of an r-selected organism is the mouse. Mice populations can grow exponentially due to their early reproductive capacity and large brood sizes. They reserve the energy that would otherwise be spent caring for their young by minimizing parental investment.

Of course, this results in a high offspring mortality rate. The mice population often quickly grows above the environment's carrying capacity, exhausting their resources. This results in sudden and intense competition (along with disease, overcrowding, and other threats), and the population dwindles. This fluctuation in population growth and subsequent decline is characteristic of r-selected organisms.

*K-selected* organisms, such as primates, tend to mature slowly. They usually maintain a steady population near their carrying capacity. Once at reproductive age, they produce few offspring but reproduce throughout life. They live longer and have a higher offspring survival rate but great energy investment.

Most organisms lie between r- and K-selection and shift strategy depending on environment and density.

Furthermore, organisms frequently exhibit r-selected traits in some areas and K-selected traits in others.

### Inbreeding

*Inbreeding* is mating between closely related individuals.

Inbreeding increases the frequency of homozygotes, decreases the frequency of heterozygotes, and decreases genetic diversity. Some organisms avoid inbreeding because it *increases disease rates* and other undesirable traits. However, inbreeding often occurs in nature, being unavoidable in small populations.

Inbreeding is a typical result of *artificial selection* by humans. Continuous inbreeding for selecting traits results in the *loss of specific genes* and *decreased genetic diversity* and can cause the *accumulation of genetic defects*.

*Inbreeding depression* is the loss of fitness resulting from inbreeding effects. In the long term, it is generally advantageous for organisms to promote genetic diversity, and present-day breeders strive to avoid inbreeding.

### Genetic diversity

*Genetic diversity* serves as a way for populations to adapt to changing environments. Variation in the gene pool may help a species be prepared for a wide range of scenarios such as food shortage or an epidemic of disease.

For example, an extremely contagious disease may threaten 99% of a species, but 1% possess an allele that provides disease resistance. With this allele, the population can survive when they would otherwise become extinct.

**Outbreeding**

*Outbreeding* (opposite of inbreeding) is when genetically dissimilar individuals are mated to increase genetic diversity. Generally, outbreeding increases the *fitness of a population*.

However, crossing individuals from different populations rarely results in less fit offspring than within the same population. This is *outbreeding depression*.

*Outbreeding depression* may result from disruptive selection when the *heterozygous genotype* is selected *against* in favor of the homozygous genotypes.

Outbred progeny display an intermediate phenotype that is not useful in the populations that its parents originated.

**Bottlenecks**

*Bottleneck* is a severe *reduction in population size*.

Bottlenecks can be deleterious to the population because the population is less able to adapt to environmental changes with a smaller, less diverse gene pool. For example, this can be caused by a natural disaster that eliminates most of a population.

Bottlenecks increase *effects of genetic drift* (i.e., random fluctuations in allele frequencies) because traits may be represented disproportionately when a population drastically decreases, especially if the decrease is random.

For example, in a population of white and brown rabbits in equal numbers, a natural disaster may kill mostly brown rabbits randomly. The bottlenecked population displays a disproportionate representation of the white rabbits' alleles. The population may grow in subsequent generations, but primarily white rabbits.

**Genetic drift**

*Genetic drift* is the random fluctuations in allele frequencies in a population.

*Genetic drift* is amplified when a small group migrates out of a large population.

*Founder effect*, as with a bottleneck, is when a small population has a limited gene pool that may not accurately represent the original population. Founders can profoundly affect the population's gene pool after generations.

Populations may diverge from genetic drift, mutations (i.e., *nucleotide sequence changes*), gene flow (i.e., *allele transfer between populations*), and natural selection (i.e., *environment favoring phenotypes*).

## Divergent, Parallel and Convergent Evolution

### Divergent evolution

*Divergent evolution* is when species from the same *lineage* (*common ancestor*) evolve to be increasingly different.

For example, bats and horses share a mammalian lineage, but the ancestral mammalian forelimbs became wings in bats and hooves in horses.

*Homologous structures* arose from the same common ancestor (e.g., bat's wings and horse's hooves).

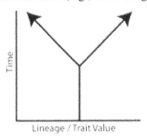

*Divergent evolution gives rise to homologous structures*

### Parallel evolution

*Parallel evolution* is when two related species of the same lineage evolve similarly.

For example, feeding structures of different crustacean species originated from ancestral leg mutations, evolving them into mouthparts.

Parallel evolution involves the same lineage, traits, and evolution from similar mechanisms or mutations.

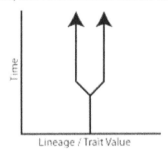

*Parallel evolution for two related species undergoing a similar evolution*

### Convergent evolution

*Convergent evolution* is when unrelated species of different lineage, by different mechanisms, evolve similarly.

For example, bats and butterflies have wings, but they came from different lineages and evolved through different mechanisms or mutations.

*Analogous structures* are similar but arose by convergent evolution.

Analogous structures can be deceptive, as they often seem to suggest common lineage when in fact, the structures are similar merely *by chance*.

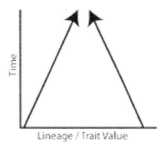

*Convergent evolution from unrelated species that become similar*

**Coevolution**

*Coevolution* is when species evolve in response to another; essentially, the accumulation of co-adaptations.

For example, a predator may develop a trait that aids in hunting prey. In response to this newly developed trait in the predator, the prey may evolve a trait allowing it to evade the predator more successfully.

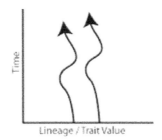

*Coevolution with an evolutionary relationship due to another species*

## Human Evolution

### Origin of humans

Scientific thought held Europe to be the birthplace of hominids due to the Eurocentric outlook and the discovery of some fossils in Europe. However, throughout the 20th century, archaeologists uncovered older australopithecine remains in Africa, with Africa acknowledged as the origin of humans.

Famous of these discoveries was *Lucy* in Ethiopia in the 1980s. She represents Australopithecus afarensis, meaning "*southern ape from afar*," which roamed the Earth 3 to 5 m.y.a.

*A. afarensis* is a direct ancestor to modern humans; that title may have belonged to other australopithecines.

Paleoanthropologists who discovered Lucy and other fossilized remains used skeletal features to map the subtle evolutionary changes in hominids. The pelvis and spine can determine whether an organism was bipedal and upright or walked on all fours. Lucy would have been bipedal, with stout stature and a relatively small cranium.

### Hominid fossils

The skull is one of the most critical skeletal features in hominid fossils. The development of a larger brain, and thus a larger skull, is one of the most prominent markers of human evolution.

DNA sequencing, genomics, and molecular biology help researchers map evolutionary relationships between humans and great apes.

Evidence suggests *Australopithecus africanus* superseded *A. afarensis* 2 to 3 m.y.a. due to critical adaptations.

Most notably, they had a larger cranium with more human-like facial features. They would have been taller and slimmer, and their hands better adapted for tool use.

*Africanus* evolved into *Australopithecus robustus* and *Australopithecus boisei,* once thought a direct ancestor of man. However, they became extinct, and other *A. africanus* evolved into the first members of the genus *Homo.*

### Homo habilis

*Homo habilis,* dated to 2.8 m.y.a. may mark the transition from the genus *Australopithecus* to *Homo.* These hominids exhibited evidence of intelligence comparable to modern man, most notably by using basic stone tools.

The *Quaternary Period,* which continues today, began 2.6 m.y.a. Early in the Quaternary Period, global cooling produced extensive glaciation, known as the *Ice Ages.*

Ice Ages spurred the evolution of mammals with significant capacity to retain heat, such as giant ground sloths, beavers, wolves, bison, woolly rhinoceroses, mastodons, and mammoths. Many of these species are now extinct, likely due to hunting by humans. While the other latitudes iced over, deserts developed in the tropics.

*H. habilis* diverged into several groups, which are still debated. The prevailing view is that *Homo erectus* evolved from *H. habilis* around 1.3 to 1.8 m.y.a. and migrated from Africa into Asia and Europe.

Earliest evidence of true humans has been dated to around 1.6 m.y.a.

*Archaic humans* included several groups, such as *Homo neanderthalensis* and *Homo heidelbergensis,* which are extinct. Whether these groups were subspecies of *Homo sapiens* or a different species is debated. There is little consensus, and it is impossible to draw clear lines between the *Homo* species and subspecies.

Archaic humans spread throughout Africa, Asia, and Europe over 1 million years. They developed wooden tools, like spears, and exhibited cranial capacity comparable to modern humans. Cognitive abilities allowed them to survive in hostile environments and dominate Earth. Humans would learn to control their environment and protect against many of the pressures of natural selection.

**Homo sapiens sapiens**

*Homo sapiens sapiens* is the subspecies representing modern humans, originating back 500,000 years and persisting. Intentional duplication of sapiens distinguishes them from their direct ancestor *Homo sapiens idaltu.*

*Neanderthals* are hypothesized to have common ancestry and co-existence with early man. They became widespread across Europe and Asia around 250,000 years ago.

Once a separate genus, some accept that Neanderthals were a species or subspecies of the genus *Homo.*

Neanderthals' robust and stocky nature made them well-suited to the cold, but *Homo sapiens* dominated deserts. Eventually, *Homo sapiens* prevailed even in the tundra.

Opinion divides on whether modern man outcompeted the Neanderthals or incorporated them via interbreeding.

Neanderthals vanished, and *Homo sapiens sapiens* became the sole humans around 40,000 years ago. They eventually inhabited all continents except Antarctica.

*Homo sapiens* characterizes the Quaternary Period as the "Age of Man." Many assert that a sixth mass extinction, driven by humans, signals the end of the Quaternary within the unknown future.

*Notes for active learning*

# CHAPTER 4

## Cell – the Basic Unit of Life

- Cell Theory
- Prokaryotic and Eukaryotic Cells
- Tissues Formed from Eukaryotic Cells
- Membrane-Bound Organelles
- Plasma Membrane
- Cytoskeleton
- Cell Cycle and Mitosis
- Cell Cycle Control

## Cell Theory

**Defining characteristics of cells**

*Cell theory*, the scientific theory which describes the morphological and biochemical properties of cells, is a fundamental doctrine of biology.

Classical cell theory includes three fundamental tenets derived from the research of early biologists:

1.  *All living organisms are composed of one or more cells.*

    Multicellular organisms are composed of many cells.

    Unicellular organisms (e.g., bacteria) are composed of one cell.

2.  *Cells are the smallest, basic units of life.*

    Cells are the smallest units of life because they are the smallest structures capable of carrying out the fundamental metabolic process (e.g., reproduce and divide, extract energy from their environment).

3.  *Cells arise from pre-existing cells and cannot be created from non-living material.*

    Creating new cells is cellular division and used in sexual and asexual reproduction.

As the modern understanding of biology evolved, so did the tenets of cell theory.

Modern cell theory adds the following concepts to classical cell theory:

4.  *Cells pass on the genetic material during replication in the form of DNA.*

5.  *The cells of organisms are chemically similar.*

6.  *Cells are responsible for energy flow and metabolism.*

The tenets of cell theory are somewhat dynamic, and as such, some scientists may omit some tenets or include others not mentioned here.

## Prokaryotic and Eukaryotic Cells

**Nucleus and other defining cellular characteristics**

Cells are divided into two taxa: *Eukarya* and *Prokarya*.

Prokaryotes are divided into the domains Bacteria and Archaea.

Prokaryotes and eukaryotes' salient difference is that prokaryotes lack a nucleus and membrane-bound organelles. A prokaryotic cell's main intracellular components are its single double-stranded circular DNA molecule, ribosomes, and cytoplasm.

Prokaryotic cells include a phospholipid plasma membrane and an outer peptidoglycan cell wall. They are usually smaller than eukaryotic cells with smaller ribosomes (30S and 50S subunits; 70S as assembled).

Eukaryotic cells have linear DNA enclosed in a membrane-bound nucleus and membrane-bound organelles.

Eukaryotic cells replicate via mitosis or meiosis, while prokaryotes replicate via *binary fission*, a form of asexual reproduction.

Many similarities exist between the two cell types.

Prokaryotes and eukaryotes contain cytoplasm, ribosomes, and DNA, and are unicellular or multicellular, although multicellular prokaryotes are rare.

Some eukaryotes are capable of asexual reproduction, albeit differently from prokaryotes.

Plants and fungi (eukaryotes) have cell walls like prokaryotes.

**Comparing prokaryotes and eukaryotes**

| Prokaryotes | Eukaryotes |
|---|---|
| Domains: Bacteria and Archaea | Domain: Eukarya |
| Cell wall present in all prokaryotes | Cell wall in fungi, plants, and some protists |
| No nucleus, circular strand of dsDNA | Membrane-bound nucleus housing dsDNA |
| Ribosomes (subunits = 30S and 50S; 70S) | Ribosomes (subunits = 40S and 60S; 80S) |
| No membrane-bound organelles | Membrane-bound organelles |

**Biochemistry considerations of surface-volume constraints**

The cell's metabolic activity describes the biochemical reactions within the cell.

Substances need to be taken into the cell to fuel these reactions, while the reactions' waste products need to be removed.

When the cell increases in size, so do its metabolic activity.

The cell's surface area is vital because it affects the rate at which particles can enter and exit, with a larger surface area resulting in a higher uptake and excretion rate.

The volume affects the rate at which biochemical materials are made (or consumed) within the cell; the chemical activity per unit of time.

As the volume (and associated chemical activity) of the cell increases, so does the surface area, but not to the same extent. When the cell gets bigger, its surface area-to-volume ratio gets smaller.

If the surface area-to-volume ratio decreases, substances cannot enter the cell fast enough to fuel reactions.

Waste products are produced faster than they can be excreted, and they accumulate inside the cell. Cells are not able to lose heat fast enough and may overheat.

The surface-area-to-volume ratio is important for a cell. The physical limitation of the area-to-volume ratio limits the size of cells.

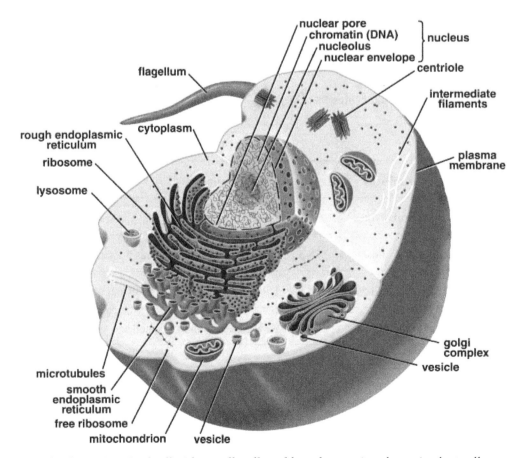

*A eukaryotic animal cell with no cell wall or chloroplasts as in eukaryotic plant cells*

**Nucleus compartmentalizes genetic information**

The *nucleus* is the largest membrane-bound organelle in the center of most eukaryotic cells. It contains the cell's genetic code—its DNA. The nucleus's function is to direct the cell by storing and transmitting genetic information.

Cells contain multiple nuclei (e.g., skeletal muscle cells), one, or rarely, none (e.g., red blood cells).

Inside the nucleus is the *nuclear lamina*, a dense network of filamentous and membranous proteins associated with the nuclear envelope and its pores.

The lamina provides mechanical support and is involved in crucial cell functions, including DNA replication, cell division, and chromatin organization.

The *nucleoplasm* is the nucleus's semifluid medium, analogous to the cell's cytoplasm. In the nucleoplasm, DNA and proteins interact to form *chromatin*.

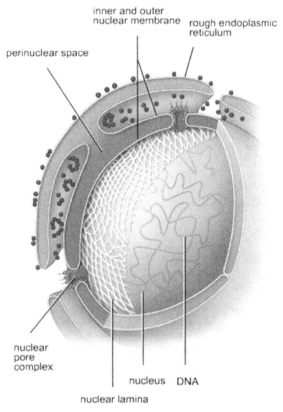

*A double membrane surrounds the nucleus of the cell with nuclear pores*
*for select transport of a substance in and out of the nucleus*

**Nucleolus location and function**

The *nucleolus* is a nonmembrane-bound region in the nucleus where ribosomal RNA (rRNA) is transcribed subunits assembled.

Chromosomal loci of the ribosomal RNA (rRNA) genes are known as nucleolar organizing regions (NORs). rRNA is essential for ribosome formation during protein synthesis (i.e., translation).

The rRNA subunits are exported from the nucleolus to the cytoplasm for assembly into ribosomes to translate mRNA into proteins. The nucleolus is the site of transcription and processing of rRNA subunits.

Thus, it has DNA, RNA, ribosomal proteins, including RNA polymerases, imported from the cytosol. Under the light microscope, the nucleolus is prominent in cells with high protein production.

**Nuclear envelope and nuclear pores**

The *nuclear envelope* (or *nuclear membrane*) is a double membrane system composed of an outer and inner membrane.

The nuclear envelope is analogous to the plasma membrane surrounding the cell.

The *perinuclear space* is between the two layers of the nuclear membrane.

*Nuclear pores* punctuate the nuclear double membrane for selective passage of specific biomolecules entering the nucleus.

Cell processes and communications require the segregation of biomolecules.

The number of nuclear pores is not static but changes based on the cell's needs.

Through the pores, signal molecules, nucleoplasm proteins, nuclear membrane proteins, lipids, and transcription factors can enter the nucleus, while mRNA, rRNA, and ribosomal proteins exit into the cytoplasm.

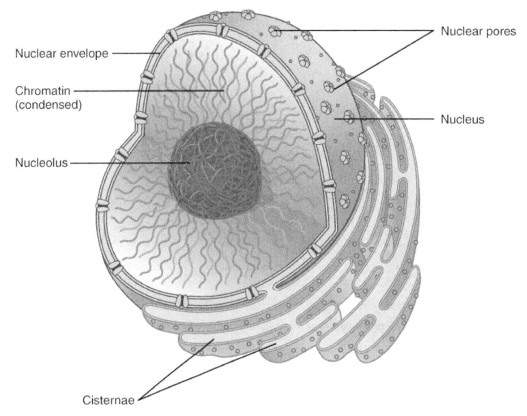

*The nucleolus is within the nucleus and assembles ribosomal subunits in eukaryotic cells*

## Tissues Formed from Eukaryotic Cells

**Simple and stratified epithelium**

*Epithelial cells* make up epithelial tissues, which line structures throughout the body, particularly organs and blood vessels. Several types of epithelial cells perform a variety of functions.

*Squamous epithelial cells* appear flat, *cuboidal epithelial cells* are cube-shaped, and *columnar epithelial cells* are column-shaped.

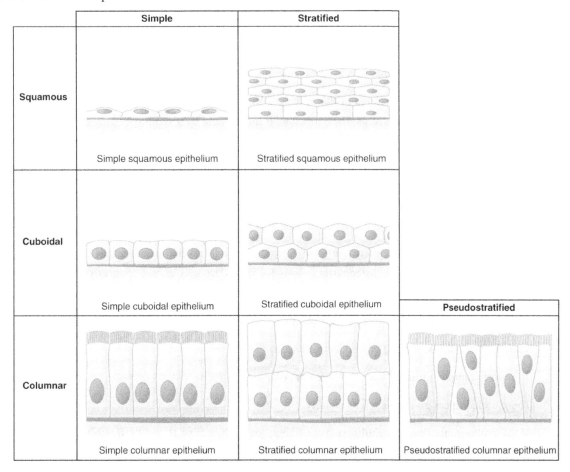

*Simple epithelium* is a single layer of epithelial cells connected by tight junctions. The simple epithelial layer's function is highly dependent on the types of epithelial cells involved.

*Simple squamous* layers are often involved in passive diffusion, lining surfaces such as the alveoli during oxygen exchange.

*Simple cuboidal* layers are involved in secretion and absorption (e.g., gland ducts, kidney tubules).

*Simple columnar* epithelial layers form a protective layer in the stomach and gut.

Layers as *stratified epithelium* protect and facilitate complex functions. For example, stratified columnar epithelium lines the vas deferens, protecting the glands and assisting in secretion. Stratified columnar and cuboidal epithelium are rare in human anatomy; stratified squamous epithelium covers the body as skin.

**Endothelial cells**

The *endothelium* is a layer of simple squamous cells that forms the interior lining of lymphatic vessels and blood vessels. It acts as a semi-selective barrier that controls the passage of materials.

*Lymphatic endothelial cells* are in direct contact with lymph.

*Vascular endothelial cells* are in direct contact with blood and line every part of the circulatory system, from the tiniest capillaries to larger arteries, veins, and the heart itself.

These endothelial cells have many functions, including blood clotting, the formation of new blood vessels, blood pressure control, and inflammation control. Endothelial cells have a strong cell division capacity and movement, proliferating quickly.

**Connective tissue, loose *vs.* dense fibers and the extracellular matrix**

*Connective tissue* holds structures of the body. It consists of specialized cells, ground substances, and fibers. The cells in connective tissue secrete the extracellular matrix held by ground substances.

The fibers, made mainly of collagen, give the matrix its strength.

Several connective tissue cells exist, making up bone, fat, tendons, ligaments, cartilage, and blood. For example, chondroblasts make cartilage, fibroblasts make collagen, and hematopoietic stem cells make blood.

The nomenclature of the numerous types of cells in connective tissue differentiates their function.

Cells with the suffix *blast* describe a stem cell that actively produces matrix, while the suffix *cyte* describes a mature cell. For example, osteoblasts (*osteo-* for bone) are specialized connective tissue cells that build the bone matrix.

Osteocytes are mature, immobile osteoblasts involved in bone maintenance.

Various types of fibers make up connective tissue.

The most common protein fiber is collagen or *collagenous fibers*.

These coiled fibers give collagen its rigidity.

Many collagenous fibers, including elastic fibers, give connective tissue its flexibility, and *reticular fibers*, which mainly join one connective tissue to an adjacent organ or blood vessel.

Connective tissue is "loose" or "dense."

The *loose connective tissue* has a higher concentration of ground substance and cells and fewer fibers. It provides protective padding around the internal organs, as well as fat.

The *dense connective tissue* has a higher concentration of collagenous fibers than loose connective tissue and is needed in anatomical structures that require great strength (e.g., ligaments and tendons).

*Cartilage* is a connective tissue that is produced and maintained by chondrocytes.

Cartilage absorbs shock and is on the ends of bones and in the spinal disks. Since it is more flexible than bone, cartilage is advantageous for structures that do not require much protection, such as the nose or ears.

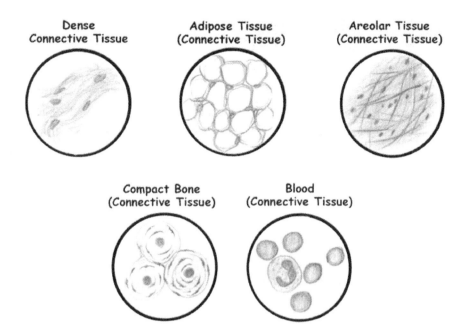

The *extracellular matrix* (ECM) exists outside of cells.

Cells secrete molecules that make up the matrix, including proteins and polysaccharides.

The ECM gives surrounding cells a physical and chemical support system in connective tissue.

## Membrane-Bound Organelles

**Cytoplasm and endomembrane system**

The cytoplasm is the cellular material outside the nucleus and within the cell's plasma membrane. It includes the *cytosol*, the cell's fluid medium, and the *organelles*, small, usually membrane-bound subunits with specialized functions (ribosomes are not membrane-bound). Among other functions, organelles structurally support the cell, facilitate cell movement, store and transfer energy, and exchange products in transport vesicles. Mitochondria in animal cells and chloroplasts in plant cells are organelles with genetic material and replicate independently of the nucleus.

The *endomembrane system* is a series of intracellular membranes that compartmentalize the cell. Vesicles bud from the endomembrane system as transport molecules within the cell. Products synthesized in the cell pass through at least some portion of the endomembrane system.

A typical pathway through the endomembrane system is:

1. Proteins produced in rough ER (endoplasmic reticulum) and lipids from smooth ER are carried in vesicles to the Golgi apparatus.

2. The Golgi apparatus modifies these products and sorts and packages them into vesicles transported to various cell destinations (e.g., organelles or exported from the cell).

3. Secretory vesicles transport products to organelles or the plasma membrane, secreted via exocytosis.

Aside from the Golgi apparatus, smooth and rough ER, and secretory vesicles, the endomembrane system includes the membranes of lysosomes, peroxisomes, and other organelles within the cell.

While most cells have the same organelles, their distribution may differ depending on the cell's function. For example, cells that require much energy for locomotion (e.g., sperm cells) have many mitochondria; cells involved in secretion (e.g., pancreatic islet cells) have many Golgi apparatuses; and cells that primarily serve a transport function (e.g., red blood cells) lack organelles.

**Structure of mitochondria**

*Mitochondria* (singular, *mitochondrion*) are responsible for aerobic respiration, converting chemical energy into ATP (adenosine triphosphate) using oxygen. ATP is used as the primary energy source within cells. Mitochondria vary in shape; they may be long and thin or short and broad. Mitochondria can be fixed in one location or form long, moving chains. They have a double membrane, with the outer membrane separating the mitochondria from the cytoplasm.

The inner membrane has folds as *cristae*, which project into the inner fluid, the *matrix* (analogous to the cytoplasm of the cell). Between the outer and inner membrane is the intermembrane space. This region is high in protons, creating a proton gradient, which drives ATP synthesis.

The cristae are dotted with *ATP synthase* protein complexes, powered by the proton gradient (used in the electron transport chain) to transform ADP into ATP. This process is essential to producing the energy that organisms require for metabolic functions. Thus, cells with higher energy needs require more mitochondria.

**Endosymbiotic theory of evolution**

Mitochondria are unique because they have their genome, distinct from the genome within the nucleus. They have circular DNA, inherited exclusively from the mother, containing genes for synthesizing some mitochondrial proteins.

Mitochondria can replicate their DNA independently from the nucleus. They have ribosomes, independent from the host cell's ribosomes in sequence and structure.

The unique characteristics of mitochondria support the *endosymbiosis theory* for the origin of eukaryotic cells. The endosymbiosis theory states that mitochondria were once free-living aerobic prokaryotes consumed by another cell about 1.5 billion years ago.

The prokaryote (likely a proteobacterium) became an endosymbiont within the cell, providing the anaerobic host cell with ATP via aerobic respiration. In return, the host cell provided the endosymbiont with a stable environment and nutrients.

Over time, the endosymbiont transferred most of its genes to the host nucleus, to the point that it became obligate (i.e., could no longer survive outside the host cell) and evolved into a mitochondrion.

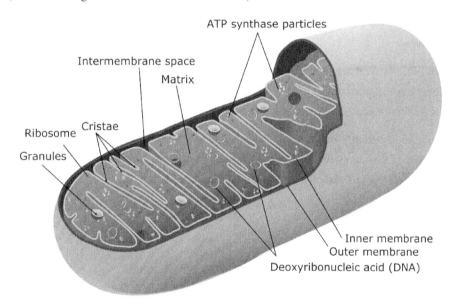

*Mitochondria have a double membrane enclosure with ATPase embedded in the inner membrane*

Biologists largely accept the endosymbiosis theory. One of the most compelling pieces of evidence is that mitochondrial DNA does not encode for its proteins.

Many of its genes are in the nuclear DNA; therefore, proteins must be imported into the mitochondria.

Mitochondrial DNA, ribosomes, and enzymes are similar to bacterial forms, and mitochondria replicate by a process similar to binary fission.

Additionally, some of the proteins within the mitochondria's plasma membrane are like prokaryotes, which are different from proteins in the eukaryotic plasma membrane.

**Lysosomes as vesicles containing hydrolytic enzymes**

*Lysosomes*, only in animal cells, are membrane-bound vesicles produced by the Golgi apparatus. These small organelles contain hydrolytic enzymes (low pH) for the digestion of macromolecules: proteins, nucleic acids, carbohydrates, and lipids. These macromolecules may originate from food, from the waste products of cells or foreign agents, such as viruses and bacteria. After these particles enter a cell in vesicles, lysosomes fuse with vesicles and digest their contents by hydrolyzing the macromolecules into their monomers.

Lysosomes are especially important in specialized immune cells. For example, white blood cells that engulf foreign agents use lysosomes to digest the invaders. *Autodigestion* is the process by which lysosomes digest parts of the body's cells due to disease or trauma or for immune purposes (e.g., programmed cell death).

Mutations in the genes that encode lysosomal enzymes cause *lysosomal storage disorders*. When a mutation renders certain lysosomal enzymes inefficient (or inoperable), waste products accumulate in the cells and cause severe, often incurable complications.

**Rough and smooth endoplasmic reticulum**

The *endoplasmic reticulum* (ER) is a system of membrane channels (or *cisternae*) continuous with the outer membrane of the nuclear envelope. The space enclosed within the cisternae, the *lumen*, is thus continuous with the perinuclear space.

The rough ER, so-called because of its rough appearance, is studded with ribosomes on the cytoplasmic side. Here, proteins are synthesized and enter the ER interior for processing and modification. Modifications may include folding the protein or combining multiple polypeptide chains to form proteins with several subunits.

The smooth ER is usually interconnected with the rough ER but lacks ribosomes, hence its smooth appearance. It is the site of various synthesis, detoxification, and storage processes, such as the synthesis of lipids and steroids and the metabolism of carbohydrates and other molecules.

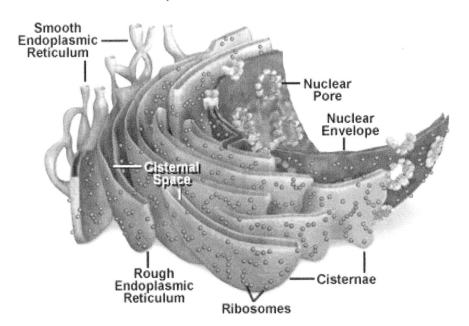

*The ER forms transport vesicles for trafficking particles to the Golgi apparatus*

**Ribosomes**

Ribosomes are organelles composed of proteins and ribosomal RNA (rRNA). They are either floating free in the cytoplasm, attached to the rough ER's surface, or within mitochondria and chloroplasts.

Ribosomes translate messenger RNA (mRNA) to coordinate the assembly of amino acids into polypeptide chains, which fold into functional proteins.

**Smooth endoplasmic reticulum for lipids biosynthesis**

The smooth ER and rough ER synthesize key membrane components. The smooth ER synthesizes the major lipids of a membrane: phospholipids, glycolipids, and steroids.

Some lipid products are already in the correct form for incorporation into a membrane once secreted by the smooth ER. Other lipids require modification by the Golgi apparatus.

Lipids synthesized in the smooth ER must pass through the Golgi apparatus before heading to their destination at the plasma membrane or membrane-bound organelles.

**Rough endoplasmic reticulum for transmembrane protein biosynthesis**

The rough ER synthesizes the protein components of cell membranes. This includes the plasma membrane, the membranes of the ER, Golgi apparatus, lysosomes, and other organelles.

Membrane proteins are divided into several classes (discussed later), but some of their functions include membrane transport, cell-to-cell adhesion, cell signaling, and catalysis.

Like lipids synthesized on the smooth ER, proteins synthesized on the rough ER follow a set pathway through the Golgi apparatus towards their destinations.

Proteins destined for the plasma membrane, Golgi apparatus membrane, ER membrane, or lysosomal membranes are inserted into the ER membrane immediately after synthesis on the cytosolic side of the rough ER membrane. These proteins are transported as membrane components rather than soluble proteins.

ER membrane proteins end their journey here, but the others proceed to the Golgi apparatus.

Upon post-translational processing, Golgi membrane proteins remain in the Golgi apparatus. The remaining proteins (secretory pathway) travel to the lysosome, the plasma membrane or undergo exocytosis to leave the cell.

Secretory proteins and proteins destined for the *lumen* of the ER or Golgi apparatus are released into the ER lumen following ER synthesis. ER lumen proteins remain in the ER lumen.

Golgi lumen proteins travel to the Golgi lumen, and secretory proteins travel to the Golgi and then the plasma membrane or are secreted by the cell.

Not all protein synthesis takes place on the rough ER. Free-floating ribosomes synthesize proteins designated for use in the cytosol and some organelles (e.g., nucleus, mitochondria, chloroplasts, peroxisomes) in the cytosol. After synthesis, cytosolic proteins are released directly into the cytosol.

Nuclear, mitochondrial, chloroplastic, and peroxisomal proteins are escorted to their destinations by receptor molecules.

Protein synthesis begins on free ribosomes. Therefore, proteins that need to be synthesized in the ER must be translocated there.

*Posttranslational translocation* to the ER occurs after a free-floating ribosome synthesizes a polypeptide.

*Cotranslational translocation* (common in mammalian cells) occurs as the polypeptide is synthesized.

**Organelles with double-membrane structures**

While most organelles of the eukaryotic cell are composed of a single bilayer membrane, three key organelles have a double membrane: mitochondria, chloroplasts, and the nucleus.

Mitochondria have a double membrane structure due to their proposed evolution from an endosymbiotic prokaryote. This double membrane is crucial for creating the proton gradient that drives ATP synthesis. The intermembrane space is high in proton concentration, while the matrix (like cytosol) within the mitochondria is relatively low in proton concentration. This proton gradient powers ATP synthases, with cytochrome proteins dotting the inner membrane's cristae, combining ADP with Pi and $O_2$ forming ATP by oxidative phosphorylation.

A sophisticated, double-membrane nuclear envelope surrounds the nucleus. The highly selective nuclear protein pores dotting the envelope regulate gene expression by controlling the passage of transcription factors, biomolecules, and mRNA into and out of the nucleus. Since the outer membrane is continuous with the rough ER, no vesicle transport is required to transport ER proteins into the nucleus. As a result, the cell's energy requirements are lower than if transport were required.

**Golgi apparatus modifies, packages and secretes glycoproteins**

The *Golgi apparatus*, named for the Italian 1906 Noble laureate Camillo Golgi, consists of a stack of flattened sacs. It acts as an intermediary in the secretion of biomolecules. The Golgi apparatus receives transport vesicles from the ER and may modify their contents before packaging the protein or lipid in vesicles for transport to their destination.

*Glycosylation* is when the Golgi apparatus modifies a protein by adding carbohydrates. Glycosylation affects a protein's structure and function and protects it from degradation. The Golgi apparatus glycosylates proteins (i.e., add sugar residues to a protein) and modifies existing glycosylations. The finished glycosylation product is a *glycoprotein* and is a protein with attached sugars or carbohydrates.

**Peroxisomes**

*Peroxisomes* are membrane-bound vesicles containing enzymes for a variety of metabolic reactions. They are involved in the catabolism (i.e., degradation) and anabolism (i.e., synthesis) of macromolecules, including fatty acids, proteins, and carbohydrates. When peroxisomes were first discovered, they were defined as organelles that produce hydrogen peroxide through oxidation reactions. Peroxisomes use catalase (enzymes end with ~*ase*) to degrade the produced hydrogen peroxide into water and oxygen or oxidize compounds.

Peroxisomes are abundant in the liver, where they are notable for producing bile salts from cholesterol and metabolizing alcohol. They participate in lipid biosynthesis. Peroxisomes' functions are vast and varied, making them a vital part of eukaryotic cells.

## Plasma Membrane

**Semi-permeable plasma membrane**

The *semi-permeable plasma membrane* separates cell contents from the extracellular environment and regulates the passage of materials into and out of the cell. The plasma membrane surrounds the cell, providing support, protection, and a boundary from the outside environment. It is primarily composed of lipids and proteins, forming a dynamic bilayer of lipids with membrane proteins. The function and composition of the two layers of a plasma membrane differ; therefore, the membrane is asymmetric.

**Phospholipid bilayer with embedded proteins and steroids**

Lipids are a large group of naturally occurring hydrophobic molecules. They are vital components of the plasma membrane. Lipids in the plasma membrane include phospholipids, steroids, and glycolipids. The foundation of the plasma membrane is the *phospholipid bilayer*. Phospholipids are molecules with a phosphate head and two long hydrocarbon tails. The head is hydrophilic and attracts water and other polar molecules, while the hydrocarbon tails are hydrophobic and repel water molecules.

The special dual nature of phospholipids, called *amphipathic*, allows them to align into a bilayer when placed in water spontaneously. In the bilayer, the hydrophilic phosphate heads point out towards the aqueous solution, while the hydrophobic tails point inward towards one another. Thus, the plasma membrane's extracellular and intracellular surfaces are hydrophilic, while the membrane's interior is hydrophobic. Hydrophobic interactions in the interior of the membrane hold the entire structure together.

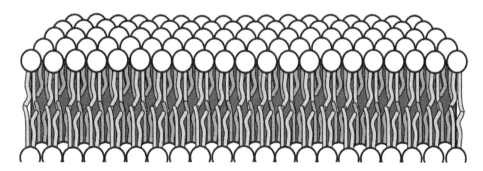

*Phospholipid bilayer (absent in the schematic are embedded proteins)*

The bilayer provides the plasma membrane with stability and with extraordinary flexibility. Lipids exhibit free lateral diffusion about the bilayer, resulting in varying lipid compositions across the membrane sections. Generally, cell membranes have a consistency like that of olive oil at room temperature.

Increasing the concentration of lipids with unsaturated hydrocarbon tails increases membrane fluidity; the addition of saturated hydrocarbon tails makes the membrane rigid.

Cells regulate membrane fluidity by lengthening phospholipid tails, altering the cytoskeleton, changing their protein composition, and adding steroids (e.g., cholesterol).

*Steroids* are a class of lipids that regulate membrane fluidity by hindering phospholipid movement. Cholesterol, a steroid in animal plasma membranes, plays a crucial role in maintaining membrane fluidity despite temperature fluctuation. At high temperatures, membranes become dangerously fluid and permeable unless cholesterol interferes with extreme phospholipid movement.

At low temperatures, membranes may freeze unless cholesterol prevents phospholipids from becoming stationary due to strong hydrophobic interactions.

Cholesterol molecules facilitate cell signaling and vesicle formation.

*Glycolipids* are lipids modified with a carbohydrate. In the plasma membrane, they assist in various functions and anchor the plasma membrane to the *glycocalyx*, a layer of polysaccharides linked to the membrane lipids and proteins.

Essentially, the glycocalyx is a carbohydrate coat present on the extracellular surface of the plasma membrane and the extracellular surface of the cell walls of some bacteria. The glycocalyx's carbohydrate chains face outwards, providing markers for cell recognition and adhesive capabilities to the cell.

**Fluid mosaic model and associated proteins of membranes**

In 1972, Garth L. Nicholson and Seymour J. Singer published the currently accepted *fluid-mosaic model*, which describes a plasma membrane as a phospholipid bilayer embedded with proteins. Electron micrographs of the freeze-fractured membrane (and other evidence) supported the fluid-mosaic model. The lipid portion of the plasma membrane gives it its "fluid" characteristic. Thus, fluidity describes the lipids that diffuse freely throughout the membrane and regulate consistency.

The membrane's protein components contribute to the "mosaic." Protein composition in the plasma membrane depends on the function of the cell. Some proteins are held in place by cytoskeletal filaments, but most migrate within the fluid bilayer.

The proteins embedded in a membrane are grouped into two classes by location.

*Peripheral membrane proteins* are on the membrane surface, mainly the intracellular side, interacting with cytoskeletal elements to influence cell shape and motility.

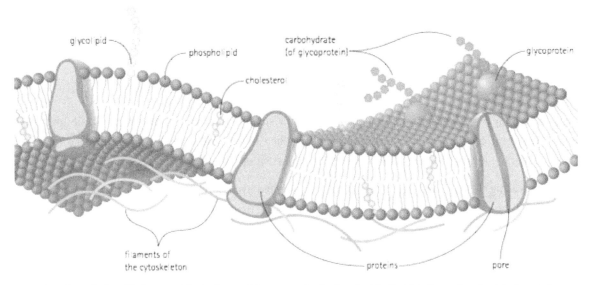

*The phospholipid bilayer with cholesterol between the hydrophobic lipid tails and embedded proteins*

These proteins are not amphipathic; they interact with the membrane's hydrophilic heads.

Peripheral membrane proteins are removed from the membrane with relative ease using high salt or high pH, and therefore are not permanently attached to the membrane.

*Integral membrane proteins* are permanently attached to the membrane and cannot be removed without disrupting the lipid bilayer. They possess hydrophobic domains anchored to hydrophobic lipids.

Most integral membrane proteins are *transmembrane* proteins, spanning the entire membrane.

Membrane proteins participate in cell signaling, cell-to-cell adhesion, transport through the membrane, enzymatic activity, and other biochemical activities.

## Functional classes of membrane proteins

*Receptor proteins* provide a binding site for hormones, neurotransmitters, and other signaling molecules. Receptor proteins are usually specific in that they bind to a single molecule or class of molecule. The binding of the signal molecule to the receptor triggers a cellular response corresponding to a specific biochemical pathway.

*Adhesion proteins* attach cells to neighboring cells for cell-to-cell communication and tissue structure. These proteins generally attach to one cell's cytoskeleton and extend through the plasma membrane to the extracellular environment, where they bind and interact with the adhesion proteins of another cell.

*Transport proteins* move materials into and out of the cell.

These include *channel proteins* and *carrier proteins.*

Channel proteins provide a passageway for large, polar, or charged molecules that cannot pass through the lipid bilayer without assistance.

The channel proteins facilitate the passive transport of molecules; they do not require ATP to operate.

However, carrier proteins may facilitate passive and active (energy-requiring) transport of molecules. They bind to specific molecules on one side of the cell membrane and changes conformation to release the molecule on the other side of the membrane.

*Enzymatic membrane proteins* carry out metabolic reactions at the cell membrane.

For example, enzymatic membrane proteins help digest membrane components for recycling. The mitochondrial membrane contains enzymatic proteins (e.g., protein complexes of the electron transport chain in aerobic cellular respiration).

*Recognition proteins* are glycoproteins that identify a cell to the body's immune system. They allow immune cells to recognize a substance as belonging to the body or as an invasive foreign agent to be destroyed.

Antigens are the basis for A, B, and O blood groups in humans.

Immune cells recognize the sugars attached to these proteins and attack any red blood cells with foreign sugars, so patients of blood groups cannot donate blood or receive blood from people with other blood groups.

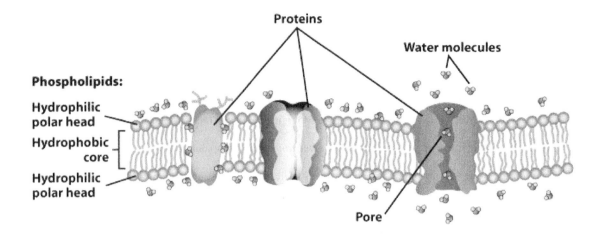

**Semi-permeable membranes produce osmotic pressure**

All fluids of the body are *solutions*: they contain dissolved substances (solutes) and a fluid (water) in which the substances dissolve (solvent).

*Diffusion* is the movement of solutes from an area with a higher to an area with a lower concentration.

*Osmosis* is the diffusion of water from a low solute concentration to an area of high solute concentration. Solutes diffuse to an area of lower solute concentration, while water (a solvent) diffuses to an area of higher solute concentration. The solute and solvent offset unequal solute concentration and restore equilibrium.

The natural inclination of solutes is to diffuse until they are evenly distributed. However, areas of the cell/tissue/organ/body require different solute concentrations. Separation areas are accomplished via the complex system of membrane compartmentalization in organs, tissues, and cells.

The body must prevent body compartments from reaching equilibrium but must allow the passage of certain atoms, ions, and molecules through membranes to the areas needed. Membranes are highly selective and tightly regulated.

*Osmolarity* is the total solute concentration of a solution measured in *osmoles*. Osmolarity considers penetrating and non-penetrating solutes and describes a single solution or compares different solutions.

A *hyperosmotic* solution has a higher osmolarity.

A *hypoosmotic* solution has a relatively low osmolarity.

*Isosmotic* solutions have the same osmotic pressure.

*Tonicity* describes the relative concentration of two solutions separated by a selectively permeable membrane and explains how diffusion occurs between them (e.g., between intracellular and extracellular fluid). Unlike osmolarity, tonicity refers to non-penetrating solutes (solutes that cannot cross a membrane) and describes how one solution compares to another.

A *hypertonic* solution has a relatively higher concentration of solute. Conversely, a *hypotonic* solution has a relatively lower concentration of solute. Therefore, a cell with a lower concentration of solute than the extracellular fluid is hypotonic to the fluid, while the extracellular fluid is hypertonic to the cell.

The reverse is true for a cell with a higher concentration of solute than the extracellular fluid.

A cell placed in a hypertonic solution shrinks through a process of *crenation* (i.e., shrinking of the cell) as water diffuses out of the cell to offset the high concentration of the outside solution. Conversely, a cell in a hypotonic solution swells as water rushes into the cell, causing *cytolysis* (i.e., bursting of a cell due to osmotic imbalance caused by excess water entering the cell.

Too much water can enter the cell, resulting in *lysis* (breakage of the cell).

An *isotonic* solution has an equal solute concentration to the solution it is being compared to. In this situation, there is no net water movement.

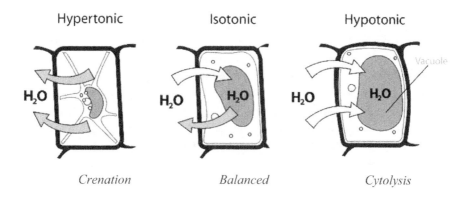

|            Hypertonic            |            Isotonic            |            Hypotonic            |
| :------------------------------: | :----------------------------: | :----------------------------: |
|            *Crenation*           |            *Balanced*          |            *Cytolysis*         |

**Passive transport, diffusion and osmosis**

The plasma membrane is selectively permeable; specific molecules can pass through. A molecule's ability to diffuse through the plasma membrane depends on the molecule's size, charge, and polarity. The greater the diffusing particle's lipid solubility, the easier it passes through the membrane.

Generally, smaller particles diffuse more rapidly than larger ones, and hydrophobic solutes diffuse faster than hydrophilic solutes.

Many particles cannot diffuse through the plasma membrane without assistance. Small, non-charged, or non-polar molecules pass through the membrane freely. Large, charged, or polar molecules usually require assistance to pass through the membrane.

Passive transport enables the movement of molecules across a membrane without energy expenditure by the cell. The methods include simple diffusion, osmosis, and facilitated diffusion. Passive transport utilizes a *concentration gradient*, whereby particles diffuse from an area of higher to an area of lower solute concentration.

*Simple diffusion* is the process for smaller, lipid-soluble molecules to diffuse through the phospholipid bilayer. For example, oxygen and carbon dioxide pass through the membrane via simple diffusion.

While water is a polar molecule, it is small enough to diffuse freely across a plasma membrane. *Osmosis* is the passive diffusion of water molecules.

Osmosis occurs when water moves from a region of lower solute concentration to a higher solute concentration region and is facilitated by *aquaporins* as channel proteins. Osmosis is classified as simple diffusion, despite requiring transport proteins like facilitated diffusion.

**Passive transport**          **Active transport**

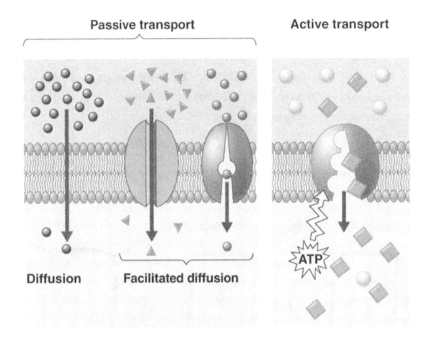

**Diffusion**      **Facilitated diffusion**

*Passive transport includes diffusion and facilitated diffusion with the*
*expenditure of energy as molecules move down the concentration gradient*

*Facilitated diffusion* allows larger, lipid-insoluble molecules that cannot freely pass through the phospholipid bilayer (e.g., sugars, ions, and amino acids) to get transported down their concentration gradient with the assistance of a carrier protein or channel proteins, often as a *uniporter*.

**ATP needed for primary active transport**

*Active transport* requires cellular energy to move solutes against their concentration gradient. Unlike passive transport, which exploits molecules' natural inclination to move down their concentration gradient, active transport requires energy expenditure to resist this opposing force. Carrier proteins are the transmembrane proteins that mediate molecules' movement too polar or too large to move across a membrane by diffusion, thereby governing active transport.

During this process, a solute (molecule to be transported) binds to a specific site on a transporter on one surface of the membrane. The transporter changes shape to expose the bound solute to the opposite side of the membrane. The solute dissociates from the transporter and is on the opposite side from which it started.

There are two types of active transport: primary and secondary.

*Primary active transport* utilizes energy generated directly from ATP. The carrier proteins for primary active transport are pumps. An example is a sodium-potassium pump, which works by moving 3 $Na^+$ ions out and 2 $K^+$ ions into a cell, resulting in a net transfer of positive charge outside the membrane.

Cellular sodium and potassium concentrations are maintained via active transport by the sodium-potassium pump ($Na^+$ / $K^+$ ATPase). When the intracellular $Na^+$ concentration is too high, and $K^+$ concentration is too low, the sodium-potassium pump must pump $Na^+$ out of the cell and $K^+$ into the cell to restore the appropriate concentration gradients.

**Energy coupling drives secondary active transport**

The energy for *secondary active transport* comes from an electrochemical gradient established by primary active transport. Secondary active transporters work via a mechanism of *cotransport.*

Cotransport occurs when one molecule moves with (down) its concentration gradient, while another molecule moves against (up) its concentration gradient.

The energetically favorable movement of the molecule moving with its concentration gradient powers the other molecule's movement against its concentration gradient.

*Antiporters* (e.g., sodium-calcium exchanger) move molecules in opposite directions, i.e., one is transported out while the other is transported into the cell.

*Symporters* move both molecules in the same direction.

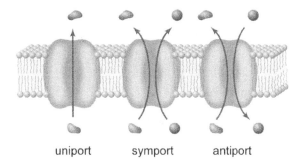

uniport     symport     antiport

**Membrane channels**

Membrane channels are transmembrane proteins that allow ions to diffuse across the membrane via passive transport.

Individual cells have different permeabilities, depending on their membrane channels.

The channel's diameter and the polar groups on the protein subunits forming channel walls determine the permeability of the channels for various ions and molecules.

*Porins* are channel proteins less chemically specific than many other channel proteins; generally, if a molecule can fit through the porin, it can pass through it.

*Ion channels* allow for the passage of ions.

Channel gating is the opening and closing of ion channels to the molecules they transport.

Changes in membrane potential modulate voltage-gated channels.

Ligand-gated channels are modulated by allosteric or covalent binding of ligands to the channel protein.

*Ligands* are small molecules that bind to a protein or receptor, usually to trigger a signal.

Mechanically gated channels are modulated by mechanical stimuli such as stretching, pressure, or temperature.

Several factors influence a single channel, and the same ion may pass through several channels.

**Electrochemical gradient produces a membrane potential**

The membrane potential is the electrical potential difference between the intracellular and extracellular environments. Nearly all eukaryotic cells maintain a non-zero membrane potential. The membrane potential is mediated by channels and pumps, altering electrochemical gradients as needed by the cell.

Whenever there is a net separation of electric charges across a cell membrane; a membrane potential exists for all cells. However, it is often the focus for neurons and depolarization with action potentials.

For a cell at rest, intracellular $K^+$ concentration is high, and $Na^+$ concentration is low, while extracellular $K^+$ concentration is low and $Na^+$ concentration is high. These concentration gradients facilitate transport across the plasma membrane and help the cell manage its *membrane potential*, the difference in electrical charge between the outside and inside the cell.

The concentration gradient influences molecules, but differences influence ions, creating the resting membrane potential. The *electrochemical gradient* is the combined forces of membrane potential and concentration gradient. These forces may oppose one another, work independently from one another, or work in conjunction.

**Membrane receptors and cell signaling pathway**

Cells must communicate with their neighbors as well as their environment.

*Cell signaling* is the system by which cells receive, integrate, and send signals to communicate information.

Signals are sent through the *extracellular matrix*, a collection of polysaccharides and proteins secreted by cells in multicellular organisms.

This matrix fills the space between cells, providing structure, facilitating cell signaling, and allowing cells to move and change their shape.

Membrane receptors may be on the plasma membrane or intracellular membranes.

Not all signal molecules bind to membrane receptors at the plasma membrane. For example, steroid hormones and gases diffuse across the plasma membrane and bind to intracellular receptors.

Other signal molecules enter the cell via endocytosis. In addition to hormones and gases, signal molecules include neurotransmitters, proteins, and lipids.

Membrane receptors are crucial in the cell-signaling pathways. When a signal molecule binds to a membrane receptor, it may initiate a metabolic response, change the membrane potential or alter gene expression.

*Signal transduction* is when one signaling molecule triggers a multi-step chain reaction, which indirectly transmits the initial signal to its destination. *Second messengers* are the molecules that relay the signal.

At steps in the signal transduction pathway, second messengers can greatly amplify the strength of the original signal by increasing the number of molecules they activate.

For example, one signal molecule at the membrane receptor may produce 10 second messengers, and these 10 second messengers may each produce another 10 second messengers, and so on, amplifying the signal significantly.

**Exocytosis and endocytosis**

The plasma membrane's fluidity allows it to change shape, pinch off, and reform. This fluidity enables substances to exit the cell via *exocytosis* and enter the cell via *endocytosis*.

Both processes require cellular energy and are therefore a form of active transport.

During exocytosis, membrane-bound vesicles in the cytoplasm fuse with the plasma membrane, and their contents are released outside the cell. The vesicle assimilates into the plasma membrane, replenishing portions of the membrane that would otherwise be lost.

The exocytosis process is triggered by stimuli, leading to an increase in cytosolic calcium concentration, which activates proteins required for the vesicle membrane to fuse with the plasma membrane. Exocytosis provides a route for releasing synthesized proteins as either extracellular secretions or proteins and lipids destined for the plasma membrane.

Endocytosis is essentially the opposite process of exocytosis. During endocytosis, extracellular molecules destined for the plasma membrane or the cytoplasm are imported into the cell.

In preparation for endocytosis, a region of the outer side of the plasma membrane invaginates to enclose the imported material. This indentation folds and pinches into a membrane-bound vesicle inside the cell.

*Pinocytosis* ("cell-drinking" or fluid endocytosis) is a form of endocytosis that cells use to import small amounts of extracellular fluid containing molecules absorbed by the cell. The process of pinocytosis may be non-specific or mediated by receptors on the plasma membrane.

*A few types of specialized cells perform phagocytosis.*

Phagocytosis (or *cell-eating*) involves importing larger particulate matter than imported by pinocytosis.

The particulate matter must be degraded before it is absorbed by the cell. As such, phagocytes digest bacteria, viruses, and cell debris as a function of our immune system.

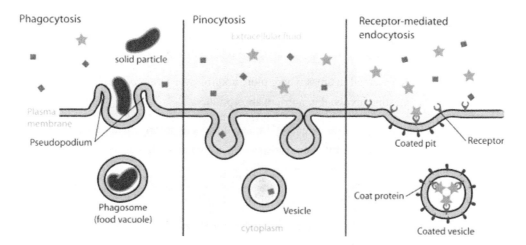

*Types of endocytosis with substrates taken into the cell*

**Gap junctions, tight junctions and desmosomes**

Cell junctions are points of contact that physically link neighboring cells.

Animal cells have three intercellular junctions: gap junctions, tight junctions, and anchoring junctions.

*Gap junctions* are protein channels that link the cytoplasms of adjacent cells. Gap junctions are communicating junctions because they allow for rapid cell-to-cell communication. They form by joining two membrane channels on adjacent cells, allowing small molecules and ions between cells while still preventing their cytoplasms from mixing.

Gap junctions are essential in cardiac muscle tissues, where electrical impulses must be transmitted through cells exceptionally rapidly so that the muscle fibers contract as a single unit.

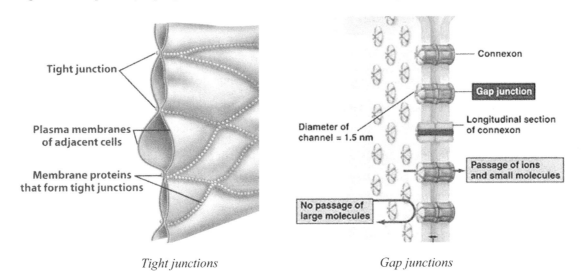

*Tight junctions*                    *Gap junctions*

The *tight junction* has plasma membrane proteins attach in zipper-like fastenings, holding cells so tightly that the tissues become barriers to molecules.

Tight junctions are formed by the physical joining of the extracellular surfaces of two adjacent plasma membranes, producing a seal that prevents the passage of materials between cells.

Materials must enter the cells by passive or active transport to pass through the tissue.

Tight junctions are essential in areas where more control over tissue processes is needed. For example, the epithelial cells in the intestine involved in nutrient absorption.

*Anchoring junctions* use proteins extended through one cell's plasma membrane and attached to another cell. Anchoring junctions are firm but still allow for spaces between adjacent cells.

*Desmosomes,* an anchoring junction, are created by dense protein patches on the plasma membranes of two cells. Internally, proteins anchor to the cell's cytoplasm, while the proteins adhere to one another.

The purpose and function of desmosomes are to hold adjacent cells firmly in place in tissue areas subject to stretching (e.g., bladder, skin, stomach).

## Cytoskeleton

### Cytoskeleton for cell support and movement

The *cytoskeleton* is a scaffold of flexible, tubular protein fibers extending between the nucleus to the plasma membrane in eukaryotes. This vast network of fibers maintains the shape of the cell, provides support, and facilitates vesicular transport.

The cytoskeleton is the cellular analogy to an animal's bones and muscles. It anchors organelles and enzymes to cell regions to keep them organized in the cytosol.

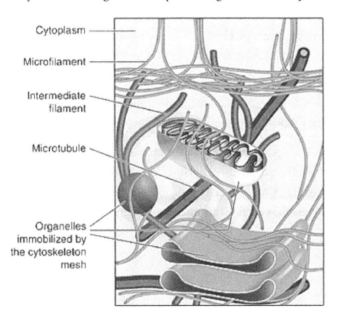

The cytoskeleton changes shape to facilitate contractility and movement, allowing the cell to divide, migrate or undergo endocytosis and exocytosis.

During cell division, the cytoskeletal elements rapidly assemble and disassemble, forming spindles for chromosomes' organization and cleaving the cell into two daughter cells.

The cytoskeleton's long fibers serve for intracellular transport, upon which vesicles and organelles move via motor proteins (e.g., dynein and kinesin).

*The cytoskeleton is a network of tubular proteins to provide shape and facilitate the transport of vesicles*

### Microfilaments for cleavage and contractility

*Microfilaments* (i.e., actin filaments) are the thinnest and abundant of the cytoskeleton proteins. They are contractile protein *actin* composed of long, thin fibers, about 7 nm in diameter, in bundles or mesh-like networks. Microfilament consists of two globular actin subunits chains twisted to form a helix.

Microfilaments assemble and disassemble quickly according to the needs of the cell. They are involved in cell motility functions, such as muscle cells' contraction, the formation of amoeba pseudopodia, and cleavage of the cell during cytokinesis.

While flexible, microfilaments are strong and prevent deformation of the cell by their tensile strength.

Microfilaments provide tracks for the movement of myosin. Myosin attaches to vesicles (or organelles) and pulls them to their destination along the microfilament track.

Additionally, the interaction between microfilaments and myosin is crucial to the cell's function.

## Intermediate filaments for support

*Intermediate filaments* are thicker than microfilaments but thinner than microtubules. Typically, they are 8 to 11 nm in diameter. These rope-like assemblies of fibrous polypeptides are found extensively in regions of cells subjected to stress. Most intermediate filaments are in the cytoplasm, supporting the plasma membrane and forming a cell-to-cell junction. However, *lamins*, a class of intermediate filaments, are responsible for structural support within the nucleus. Unlike microfilaments and microtubules, intermediate filaments cannot rapidly disassemble once assembled.

## Microtubules for support and transport

*Microtubules* (tubulin) are hollow protein cylinders about 25 nm in diameter and 0.2–25 μm in length. They are the thickest and most rigid of filaments. Microtubules are globular proteins of *tubulin* and β tubulin. The microtubule assembly brings these together as dimers, and the dimers arrange in rows.

Microtubule strength and rigidity make them ideal for resisting compression of the cell. However, these fibers serve functions similar to microfilaments. Microtubules act as tracks for intracellular transport, but they interact primarily with *kinesin* and *dynein* motor proteins rather than myosin.

Microtubules' transport function is crucial for trafficking neurotransmitters throughout nerve cells. Like microfilaments, microtubules are rapidly assembled or disassembled. Regulation of microtubule assembly is under the control of a *microtubule-organizing center* (MTOC). Microtubules radiate from the MTOC and extend throughout the cytoplasm. During cell division, the centrosome generates the microtubule spindle fibers necessary for chromosome separation.

## Eukaryotic cilia and flagella

*Cilia* and *flagella* are two types of microtubule complexes that protrude from the cell body and serve cell motility and sensory functions. In eukaryotes, they are membrane-bounded cylinders that enclose a matrix of nine pairs of microtubules encircling two single microtubules, a *9 + 2 pattern*. Movement occurs when these microtubules slide past one another. A basal body anchors the cilium (or flagellum) to the cell body at the plasma membrane. The basal body is derived from a centriole formed by nine pairs of microtubules without central microtubules, the *9 + 0 patterns*. Eukaryotic cilia and flagella grow by polymerizing (adding) tubulin to their tips.

Cilia are short, hair-like projections. Nearly every human cell has at least one cilium, *non-motile,* and functions as a sensory antenna important in cell signaling pathways. Non-motile cilia lack the 2 central microtubules and have a 9 + 0 pattern.

Many cells are covered with *motile* cilia, which undulates to transport particles across the cell surface. For example, motile cilia in the respiratory tract push mucus and irritants out of the lungs, trachea, and nose.

Essentially, eukaryotic flagella are structurally like eukaryotic cilia, so distinctions are often not drawn between them. Like cilia, they have sensory and motility functions. However, eukaryotic flagella tend to be longer and move with a whip-like motion. An example of a eukaryotic flagellum is the tail of a sperm cell.

Prokaryotic flagella are notably different from their prokaryotic cilia counterparts. Prokaryotic flagella are noted for their long, whip shape and functional differences from cilia.

**Centrioles and the microtubule-organizing centers**

The *centrosome* is the main microtubule-organizing center at the poles during mitosis and meiosis.

Centrosomes contain a pair of barrel-shaped organelles of *centrioles*.

The centrosome has a crucial role in mitosis when it divides into two centrosomes, interacting with chromosomes via microtubules to form the mitotic spindle.

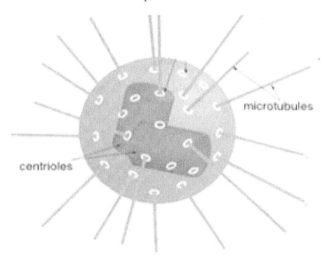

Centrioles are components of the centrosome. Microtubules radiate from these barrel-shaped structures, made of microtubules themselves. They are short cylinders with a ring pattern (9 + 0) of microtubule triplets.

In animal cells and most protists, a centrosome contains two centrioles oriented at right angles.

In mitosis, the terms centrioles and centrosomes are often used interchangeably because centrioles form the crucial parts of a centrosome.

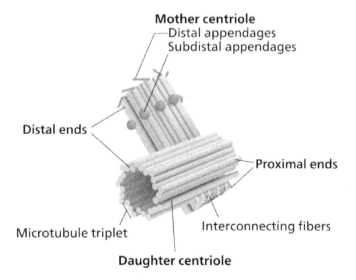

*Centrosome contains two centrioles oriented at right angles*

## Cell Cycle and Mitosis

**Methods for cell division**

The cell cycle describes a cell's lifetime, detailing the life stages from creating a cell to its division into two daughter cells.

Most of an organism's cells divide throughout their lifetime (i.e., an exception is nerve cells), as cell division is the process by which organisms grow, repair tissues, and reproduce.

Mitosis and meiosis are two types of cell division.

*Mitosis* is cell division when new *somatic* (or *body*) cells are added to multicellular organisms as they grow and when tissues are repaired or replaced.

As a cell prepares for mitosis, it grows larger, the number of organelles doubles, and the DNA replicates.

*Meiosis* produces gametes (reproductive cells of egg and sperm) by organisms that reproduce sexually. Meiosis is discussed separately.

Mitosis does not introduce genetic variations.

A daughter cell is identical in chromosome number and genetic makeup to the parent cell.

Mitosis distributes identical genetic material to two daughter cells.

What is remarkable is the fidelity with which the DNA is passed along, without dilution or error, between generations.

Eukaryotes divide by mitosis, but prokaryotes undergo *binary fission*, a form of asexual reproduction.

**Interphase as the common phase of the cell cycle**

*Interphase* is the stage before mitosis and represents most of the cell's life. This is not a static state but rather a progression towards mitosis.

However, in some cases, a cell halts its progress through interphase, either temporarily or permanently.

This may be because it is a non-dividing cell (e.g., nerve cell) or not healthy enough to perform growth and replicate interphase functions.

During interphase ($G_1 \rightarrow S \rightarrow G_2$), the cell prepares to divide by growing, replicating DNA and organelles, and synthesizing mRNA and proteins.

When it has completed interphase functions, the cell exits interphase and enters mitosis.

**Four stages of mitosis**

The four phases of mitosis: prophase, metaphase, anaphase, and telophase (PMAT).

1.  Prophase = *Prepare*: cell *prepares* for mitosis

2.  Metaphase = *Middle*: chromosomes align in the *middle* of the cell

3.  Anaphase = *Apart*: centromere splits

    The sister chromatids pull *apart* by microtubules to the opposite poles

4.  Telophase = *Two*: two daughter nuclei reform with separate nuclei

*Prophase*

*Prophase*, the first phase of mitosis, involves chromatin condensation, nucleolus dissolution, nuclear membrane fragmentation, and centrosome movement. *Chromatin condensation* is the process by which loose euchromatin condenses into chromosomes. Currently, the chromosomes have no fixed orientation in the cell.

Upon chromatin condensation, the nucleolus dissolves, and the nuclear membrane begins to fragment, exposing the chromosomes to the cytoplasm of the cell. Simultaneously, centrosomes begin to migrate to opposite sides of the cell. Microtubules start to extend from the centrosomes, forming the *spindle apparatus.*

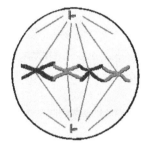

*Metaphase*

*Metaphase* follows prophase when nuclear fragmentation completes, and the centrosomes are at opposite poles of the cell. Microtubules emerge from the centrosomes and attach to the chromosomes.

Microtubules align chromosomes along an imaginary line in the center of the cell, the *metaphase plate* (or *equatorial plate*) completing the formation of the spindle apparatus. Chromosomes must be attached and aligned at the metaphase plate before the cell proceeds dividing.

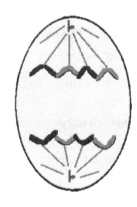

During *anaphase*, *sister chromatids* (i.e., chromatin strands replicated during the S phase of interphase but attached at the centromere) are pulled apart to opposite poles of the cell. The sister chromatids separate at their centromere and travel towards opposite centrosomes by the spindle microtubules. By the end of anaphase, equal numbers of sister chromatids are stationed by both centrosomes.

*Anaphase*

*Telophase* is the cell reverse action of prophase as it prepares to divide.

The spindle apparatus disassembles, and two daughter nuclei reform.

As spindle microtubules disassemble, two regions of identical chromatids are present.

A nuclear envelope develops around each region, forming two daughter nuclei.

Within the nuclei, chromosomal DNA uncoils into chromatin, and nucleoli form. The cell contains two identical daughter nuclei, and cell division proceeds.

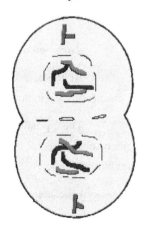

*Telophase*

**Cytokinesis divides the cytoplasm to produce two daughter cells**

*Cytokinesis* is the division of the cytoplasm to create two daughter cells. This usually coincides with the end of telophase but is *not* a phase of mitosis. Instead, it is a separate event that does not always occur.

When mitosis occurs but cytokinesis does not, multinucleated cell form; (often in plants, but in skeletal muscle cells of animals).

In animal cells, cytokinesis occurs by the process of *cleavage.*

First, a *cleavage furrow*, a shallow groove between the two daughter nuclei, appears. The cleavage furrow deepens as a microfilament band; the *contractile ring* constricts between the two daughter cells. A narrow bridge exists between daughter cells during telophase until constriction separates the cytoplasms.

The result is two daughter cells enclosed in their plasma membrane and their identical nuclei. Recall that the parent cell replicated its organelles before mitosis; thus, daughter cells contain a complete set of organelles smaller than the parent's cell size.

**Nuclear membrane reorganization during cell division**

Before mitosis begins, the cell's DNA is contained inside the nucleus, inaccessible to the mitotic spindle. During prophase and metaphase, the nucleolus disintegrates, chromatin condenses (i.e., heterochromatin), and the nuclear membrane breaks down.

This process exposes chromosomal DNA to the cell's cytoplasm and allows mitosis to divide the parental (original) cell into two identical daughter (new) cells.

The nuclear membrane does not reform until telophase, when the two daughter nuclei are each enclosed within nuclear membranes from fragments of the parental cell's nuclear membrane. Chromosomes then uncoil into relaxed chromatin (i.e., euchromatin), and the nucleoli reform, making nuclear reorganization complete.

**Centrioles, asters and spindles**

As discussed, centrioles are the microtubule-organizing centers of the cell. Centrioles replicate during interphase in preparation for mitosis.

During prophase, *polar microtubules* emerge from pairs of centrioles and centrosomes and push against each other and move the centrosomes to opposite sides of the cell.

*Astral microtubules* extend from the centrioles to assist in orienting the mitotic spindle apparatus.

At the end of prophase, kinetochore microtubules originate from the centrioles and attach to the chromosomes' kinetochores.

The spindle apparatus consists of two centrosomes (composed of two centrioles each), polar microtubules, astral microtubules (asters), and *kinetochore microtubules* (k-fibers) attached to the kinetochores on chromosomes.

Like animal cells, plant cells have a spindle apparatus, but many do not have centrioles or astral microtubules. Centrioles are not strictly necessary for mitosis, even in animal cells.

**Chromatids, centromeres and kinetochores**

As the cell enters metaphase, kinetochore microtubules extend from the centrosomes and attach to *kinetochores* on the chromosomes.

Kinetochores are assembled on the *centromere*, the chromosome region linking two sister chromatids.

There are two sections of the kinetochore: the inner kinetochore, which associates with the DNA of the centromere, and the outer kinetochore, which interacts with the kinetochore microtubules attached to the centriole.

During metaphase, microtubules pull on the chromosomes with tension, eventually aligning them at the metaphase plate. After successful attachment of chromosomes to the spindle via the kinetochore and microtubules, proteins are released from the kinetochore, which signals the end of metaphase and the beginning of anaphase.

**Mechanisms of chromosome movement**

In anaphase, the centromere holding the sister chromatids (S phase of interphase when the chromosome replicated to form two sister chromatids) dissolves, and the sister chromatids are released from their attachment point. The chromosomes are pulled to opposite sides of the cell by the shortening of kinetochore microtubules.

Shortening occurs when the motor protein attached to a kinetochore "walks" along the kinetochore-microtubule, dissembling the microtubule into tubulin subunits as it passes.

Polar microtubules assist the separation of chromosomes by lengthening the spindle. Wherever the ends of two polar microtubules from opposite poles overlap, motor proteins interact between the fibers and push them in opposite directions, thus pushing the entire spindle apart.

**Phases of the cell cycle ($G_0$, $G_1$, S, $G_2$, M)**

Interphase is divided into three phases: $G_1$, S, and $G_2$.

$G_0$ is another resting phase when the cell is not dividing nor preparing to divide. $G_0$ is the static state in which cells remain permanently (e.g., nerve cells) and others temporarily.

A cell exits $G_0$ and reenter the active cell cycle upon receipt of signals from *growth factor* proteins.

Under a microscope, a cell is recognized as being in interphase by the lack of visible chromosomes because the DNA is uncoiled as loose chromatin (i.e., euchromatin).

During the *$G_1$ phase* (*Gap phase 1*), the cell continues normal function as it grows larger and replicates its organelles, including ribosomes, mitochondria, and chloroplasts (if a plant cell).

The mitochondria generate sufficient storage of energy for the functions of mitosis.

In $G_1$, the cell synthesizes mRNA and proteins in preparation for the *S phase*.

In the S (*Synthesis*) phase, the cell replicates DNA and produces two sister chromatids attached at the centromere. During the S phase, DNA nucleotide damage must be detected and fixed before the cell proceeds.

*$G_2$ phase* (*Gap phase 2*) is where the cell grows and synthesizes proteins needed for mitosis.

Completing $G_2$ marks the end of interphase and the beginning of mitosis, abbreviated as M.

**Sequential phases of the cell cycle**

The sequential phases of the cell cycle are:

$G_0$ = no DNA replication or cell division

$G_1$ = making of organelles, increase in cell size (growth)

S = DNA replication, complete duplication of chromosomes (sister chromatids)

$G_2$ = making of organelles, increase in cell size (growth), cell committed to mitosis

M = mitosis (PMAT); prophase, metaphase, anaphase, and telophase

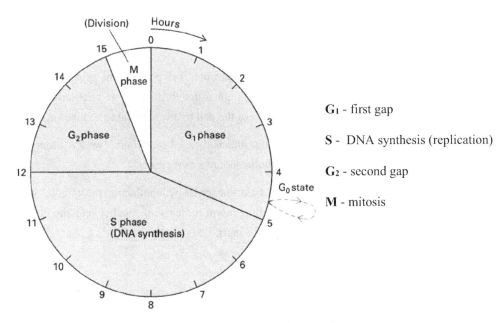

$G_1$ - first gap

S - DNA synthesis (replication)

$G_2$ - second gap

M - mitosis

*The cell cycle divided between interphase and mitosis*

Cell growth is *cell proliferation* (for populations of cells) or an individual cell's growth, whereby biomolecules are synthesized.

Cell proliferation is the goal of unicellular organisms.

However, in multicellular organisms, cell proliferation must be carefully monitored to prevent tumor formation and invasion into nearby tissues.

*Contact inhibition*, the tendency for cells to cease dividing when they come into physical contact with their neighbors, regulates this. Therefore, lack of free space signals growth arrest.

The growth of the individual cells regulates cell populations.

For individual cell development, growth arrest is *cellular quiescence* or *cell cycle arrest*.

During the cell cycle, the cell encounters checkpoints where the cell cycle is halted before proceeding.

## Checkpoints during cellular division

1. **The $G_1$ Checkpoint** – *Restriction Point*

   Partway through $G_1$, the cell reaches the restriction point.

   The cell checks for biomolecules, nutrients, and growth factors.

   If the cell is not sufficiently prepared for mitosis, the cycle halts, and the cell returns to $G_0$.

   Additionally, if DNA damage is detected, this triggers *apoptosis* (cell death) if the DNA is not repaired.

   If there are no inhibitory signals, the cell clears the checkpoint and proceeds toward DNA replication (S phase).

   $G_1$ is the checkpoint mediated by extracellular signals.

   After this point, intracellular signals direct the cell cycle to proceed or halt progress.

2. **The $G_2$ Checkpoint** – *DNA Damage Checkpoint*

   At the end of $G_2$, there is another checkpoint before the cell proceeds with mitosis.

   The cell checks for size and proper DNA replication.

   If the DNA has not finished replicating or damaged and requiring repair, it remains in $G_2$ until these issues are resolved.

3. **The M Checkpoint** – *Mitotic Spindle Checkpoint*

   After the cell has entered mitosis and has reached metaphase, a final checkpoint occurs.

   The M checkpoint ensures that the correct number of chromosomes are aligned at the mitotic plate and secured to the mitotic spindle.

   Errors during chromosome segregation (e.g., nondisjunction) can cause defects resulting in genetic conditions (e.g., Down syndrome).

   The M checkpoint reduces defects by arresting the cell in metaphase until the chromosomes are correctly attached to the spindle apparatus and aligned for anaphase.

## Cell Cycle Control

### Cyclin levels regulate cell division

The cell cycle is controlled by intracellular and extracellular signals that stimulate or inhibit metabolic events. Extracellular stimulatory signal molecules are growth factors; these are proteins or hormones that promote cell growth and differentiation.

*Extracellular inhibitory* signal molecules are growth suppressors or *tumor suppressors* because they prevent cancer cells' rampant growth.

Tumor suppressors inhibit growth by halting the cell cycle or directing the cell for apoptosis (i.e., cell death).

Intracellular signaling directs the cell cycle and involves the activation and inactivation of proteins; *cyclin-dependent kinases* (CDKs).

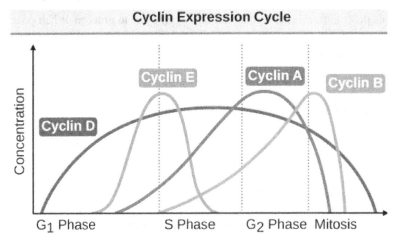

*Relative concentrations of cyclin proteins during phases of the cell cycle*

### Apoptosis as programmed cell death

*Apoptosis* is the programmed cell death that occurs in multicellular organisms. It occurs in developing tissue (e.g., embryonic development where parts of tissues are no longer needed) and adult tissue (i.e., cell death balances cell division).

Apoptosis destroys cells that threaten the organism, such as infected cells, cells with DNA damage, cancerous cells, and immune system cells no longer needed and are unnecessarily attacking other body cells.

While paradoxical, apoptosis is essential for growth. For example, cells must die to create spaces in the webbed hands of a fetus for the formation of separate digits.

When a cell dies by apoptosis, its cytoskeleton collapses, its nucleus fragments, and chromatin irreversibly condenses.

After apoptosis, specific neighboring cells (e.g., macrophages) recognize alterations in the surface of the dead cell and phagocytize the cell before its contents are leaked, allowing for efficient recycling of the cell's biomolecules.

Apoptosis usually begins in response to stress; nuclear receptors recognize stress factors, including nutrient deprivation, heat, viral infection, radiation, and lack of oxygen.

These stress factors lead to the release of intracellular apoptotic signals that cause proteins to initiate the apoptotic pathway.

Some internal or external pathways and signals cause cell death, but the morphological changes during apoptosis are consistent whatever the cause.

These changes include shrinkage and *blebbing* (bulging) of the plasma membrane and nuclear envelope and DNA fragmentation.

Engulfment by nearby phagocytic cells occurs as a result.

Apoptotic cells release signals which attract phagocytic cells.

The engulfment of the dying cell's fragments prevents viruses or other dangerous cell contents from spilling out of the damaged cell.

Mitochondria are the target of some apoptotic proteins.

These proteins may create pores in the mitochondrial membrane and cause swelling, or they may change the permeability of the mitochondrial membrane.

When the mitochondrial membrane is made more permeable, apoptotic effectors leak out and activate the apoptotic pathway's proteins.

**Cancer cells lose cell cycle controls**

Cancer cells are abnormal cells with various dangerous properties, making them a serious threat to the body. They invade and destroy normal tissue, causing serious illness and death.

Cancerous cells do not normally respond to the body's control mechanism. They no longer respond to inhibitory growth factors and do not require as many stimulatory growth factors.

Cancer cells may produce the required external growth factor (or override factors) or possess abnormal signal transduction sequences that falsely convey growth signals, thereby bypassing normal growth checks.

Due to their irregular growth cycles, if cancer cells' growth does occur, it does so at random points of the cell cycle.

Cancer can kill the organism because these cells can divide indefinitely (i.e., immortalized cells) if given a continual supply of nutrients.

DNA segments of *telomeres* form the ends of chromosomes and shorten with each cell division, eventually signaling the cell to stop dividing.

However, cancer cells produce telomerase (enzymes end with ~*ase*), which keeps telomeres long and allows cells to continue dividing as "*immortal.*"

Unlike normal cells, which differentiate, cancer cells are non-specialized.

Cancer cells do not exhibit contact inhibition; they do not avoid crowding neighboring cells but rather pile up and grow on one another. This behavior creates the characteristic tissue mass as a tumor.

Not all tumors are dangerous.

A *benign tumor* is encapsulated and does not invade adjacent tissue.

However, benign tumors can still compress and damage nearby tissue, and some benign tumors have the potential to become *malignant* (cancerous).

Malignancy occurs when new tumors are spread to areas distant from the primary tumor by *metastasis.*

## Angiogenesis, oncogenes and tumor suppressor genes

*Angiogenesis*, the formation of new blood vessels, is a process required for metastasis. Angiogenesis is triggered when cancer cells release a growth factor that causes nearby blood vessels to grow and transport nutrients and oxygen to the tumor.

Because of angiogenesis in metastasis, angiogenesis inhibitors are an important class of cancer drugs.

Cancer cells have abnormal nuclei that may be enlarged and have an abnormal number of chromosomes, as some chromosomes are mutated, duplicated, or deleted.

When the DNA repair system fails to correct mutations during DNA replication, damage to crucial genes may occur.

*Oncogenes* encode growth factor proteins such as Ras, which stimulates the cell cycle (analogous to a *gas pedal* in a car).

In contrast, *tumor-suppressor genes* encode proteins such as p53 that inhibit the cell cycle (analogous to the *brake pedal* in a car).

Mutations of oncogenes or tumor suppressors can cause cancer.

Mutation of *proto-oncogenes* may convert them into *oncogenes*, which are cancer-causing genes.

An oncogene can cause cancer by coding for a faulty receptor in the stimulatory pathway, for an abnormal protein, or for abnormally high levels of a normal product that stimulates the cell cycle.

More than 100 oncogenes have been identified; the *ras* gene family includes variants associated with lung cancer, colon cancer, pancreatic cancer, leukemia, and thyroid cancers.

Mutation of tumor-suppressor genes results in unregulated cell growth.

For example, the *p53* tumor-suppressor gene is frequently mutated in human cancers than other known genes; it usually functions to trigger cell cycle inhibitors and stimulate apoptosis.

However, if it malfunctions due to mutation, cell growth is not suppressed, and cancer may result.

*Editor's note: Nomenclature in molecular biology uses an italicized lower-case abbreviation for the gene (e.g., p53), while the protein (e.g., Ras) begins with a capital letter but is not italicized.*

# CHAPTER 5

# Enzymes and Cellular Metabolism

- Cell Metabolism

- Cellular Respiration Reactions

- Mitochondria and Oxidative Stress

- Principles of Metabolic Regulation

## Cell Metabolism

### Metabolism for energy production

*Energy* is the capacity to do work. Cells continually use energy to develop, grow, reproduce, and perform biochemical functions.

*Kinetic energy* is the energy of motion. Examples of kinetic energy include the beating of cilia, a contracting muscle, and the pumping of ions across a plasma membrane.

*Potential energy* is stored energy. The food contains *chemical energy* within bonds as potential energy.

Chemical energy can be transformed into other forms of energy through chemical reactions. For example, when a living organism digests food through a series of chemical reactions, the energy it obtains from the food moves its body; chemical energy is converted to kinetic energy.

*Metabolism* is the sum of the biochemical reactions in a cell. Metabolism consists of *anabolism* (synthesis) and *catabolism* (breakdown) of organic molecules required for cell structure and function.

Energy obtained from catabolism drives anabolism. The *metabolic pool* is molecules of biosynthesis.

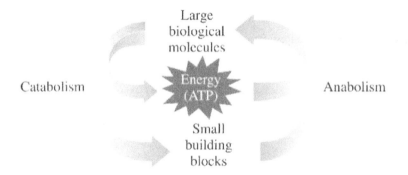

*Metabolism includes catabolism (breakdown) and anabolism (synthesis)*

### Metabolic pathways

A *metabolic pathway* is an orderly sequence of linked reactions; a specific enzyme catalyzes each step in the pathway. Metabolic pathways begin with a *reactant* (a substance that participates in a reaction) and end with a *product* (a substance formed by the reaction). A and B are reactants in a reaction $A + B \rightarrow C + D$, and C and D are products. Since pathways often use the same molecules, one pathway can lead to several others.

Metabolic pathways are compartmentalized into sections of the cell. Within organisms, energy must be transferred in small amounts to minimize the heat released in the process.

Reactions producing energy (i.e., exergonic) are coupled with reactions requiring energy (i.e., endergonic), thereby helping thermoregulation maintain constant body temperature for homeostasis.

*Thermodynamics* studies energy transformation and is an important concept in chemical reactions. Chemical reactions involve: 1) the breaking of chemical bonds in the reactants, which requires energy, and 2) the making of new chemical bonds to form products, releasing energy in the form of heat.

## Glycolysis as the first step of cellular respiration

In *cellular respiration*, cells release the energy in chemical bonds of food molecules and transfer this energy to ATP molecules, which allows for efficient use of an organism's energy. The ATP generated during cellular respiration is used for life's essential processes.

Cellular respiration is *aerobic* (with oxygen) or *anaerobic* (without oxygen).

*Glycolysis* (*glycol* for sugar, *lysis* for breaking) is the first step in cellular respiration and the same in aerobic and anaerobic cells because glycolysis does not require oxygen. Glycolysis occurs in the cytosol of the cell and catabolizes a six-carbon glucose molecule into two three-carbon pyruvate molecules.

During glycolysis, energy is transferred through phosphate groups undergoing hydrolysis reactions (breaking) and condensation (joining).

Glycolysis yields two ATP molecules and two NADH molecules per molecule of glucose.

While it consists of ten steps, the summary of the steps is:

1. The glucose molecule undergoes several enzymatically regulated reactions and becomes a double-phosphorylated fructose molecule.

2. The 6-carbon fructose molecule is cleaved into two glyceraldehyde 3-phosphates (3-carbon molecules with a phosphate group), abbreviated GA3P (or PGAL). Transformation requires 2 ATP.

3. Hydrogen and water are removed from the two PGAL, leaving two pyruvate molecules. This creates 2 NADH and 4 ATP (net ATP production is 2 ATP).

Glucose is not always immediately available, as it is stored in skeletal muscles and the liver as the polysaccharide glycogen. Hormones control whether glucose enters the anabolic pathway to form glycogen or the catabolic pathway to undergo glycolysis to form pyruvate. If the catabolic pathway signals are initiated, cellular respiration begins (glycolysis → Krebs → electron transport chain).

## Fermentation produces lactic acid or ethanol

Glycolysis produces two pyruvate molecules, two NADH molecules, and two ATP molecules. At this point, it is possible to begin the aerobic part of cellular respiration (Krebs Cycle) or continue with anaerobic respiration. *Fermentation* is the next step in anaerobic (i.e., without oxygen) cellular respiration, which occurs in the cytoplasm. It occurs in yeast and bacteria but occurs in oxygen-starved muscle cells of vertebrates.

The goal of fermentation reactions is to oxidize NADH produced in glycolysis into $NAD^+$ by reducing the pyruvate. The $NAD^+$ molecules are used in another round of glycolysis to produce two more ATP and two more NADH. Fermentation is a slow and inefficient method of making ATP since only two ATP are produced in each cycle (compared to ~36 ATP produced in each aerobic respiration cycle).

*Lactic acid fermentation* produces two molecules of lactate (or lactic acid as the acidic form of the molecule) and occurs in bacteria and some fungi. It is used to produce some foods (e.g., yogurt). Lactic acid fermentation occurs in humans and other mammals' muscle cells during demanding physical activities (e.g., sprinting) when energy demands are high; lactic acid fermentation provides a quick burst of energy via ATP synthesis needed for the muscular activity.

Lactic acid is toxic to mammals; this is the "burn" felt when undergoing strenuous activity. When blood cannot remove lactate from muscles, this decreases the pH, causing muscle fatigue. *Oxygen debt* is the oxygen that the body needed but is not delivered to the cell. Oxygen is needed to restore ATP levels and rid the body of lactate ("repaying" the oxygen debt), which is why a person might breathe harder after exercise. Recovery occurs after lactate is sent to the liver, converted into pyruvate; some pyruvate is expired or converted into glucose.

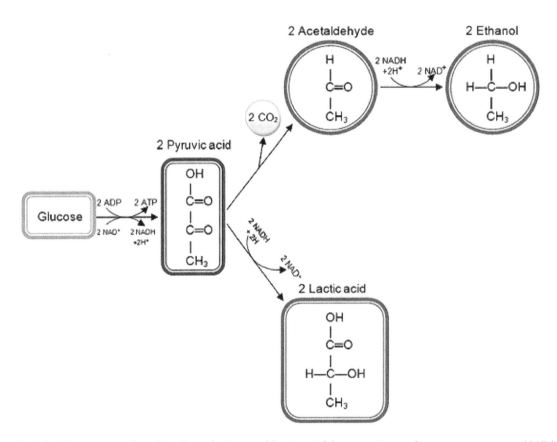

*Alcoholic fermentation for ethanol production and lactic acid fermentation pathways to regenerate NAD⁺*

**Gluconeogenesis**

In addition to catabolizing glucose, many organisms produce it from non-carbohydrate substances, as *gluconeogenesis*. Gluconeogenesis occurs in the mitochondria and cytoplasm of many organisms, including animals, plants, fungi, and bacteria. For vertebrates, gluconeogenesis occurs primarily in the liver and, to a limited extent, in the kidneys. This process maintains the glucose concentration in the blood.

A variety of non-carbohydrate carbon substrates, including pyruvate, glycerol, lactate, and certain amino acids, are used as the starting molecule in gluconeogenesis. If the starting molecule is not pyruvate, the first step in gluconeogenesis is to convert the precursor (e.g., lactate) to pyruvate. An amino acid precursor enters the gluconeogenesis metabolic pathway at oxaloacetate or later in the pathway (for glycerol).

In addition to building up glucose from carbon substrates (i.e., gluconeogenesis), organisms derive glucose by breaking down stored energy sources, such as the polysaccharides of starch and glycogen, with hormones controlling these processes.

## Cellular Respiration Reactions

### Acetyl-CoA production

Aerobic cellular respiration includes the anaerobic process of glycolysis and the aerobic processes in the mitochondria of eukaryotes.

Three processes within the mitochondria are pyruvate decarboxylation, the Krebs cycle (the citric acid cycle or TCA), and oxidative phosphorylation via the electron transport chain (ETC).

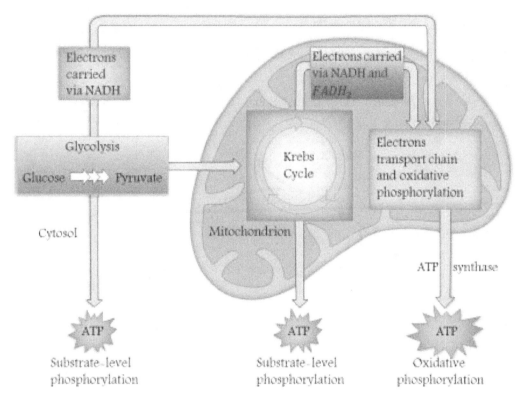

*Cellular respiration for glycolysis, Krebs cycle, and electron transport chain*

*Pyruvate decarboxylation* follows glycolysis in aerobic respiration.

Pyruvate decarboxylation is a link reaction as the intermediate step after glycolysis and before the Krebs cycle, thereby linking the two metabolic pathways.

In eukaryotes, pyruvate decarboxylation occurs in the mitochondrial matrix (cytosol of mitochondria).

### Krebs cycle substrates and products

The *Krebs cycle* occurs in the fluid matrix of the mitochondria's cristae compartments. The cycle is named after Sir Hans Krebs, who received the 1953 Nobel Prize for identifying these reactions.

The Krebs (or *citric acid*) cycle is the tricarboxylic acid cycle (TCA) cycle because of intermediate acids.

The Krebs cycle removes energy, carbon dioxide, and hydrogen from acetyl-CoA via enzyme-mediated reactions of organic acids. It begins by joining acetyl-CoA (2 carbons) with oxaloacetate (4 carbons), producing citric acid (6 carbons).

Citric acid undergoes several oxidations, decarboxylation, dehydrogenation, and hydration, yielding two $CO_2$, one GTP, three NADH, and one $FADH_2$ for each turn.

One glucose yields four $CO_2$, two GTP, six NADH, and two $FADH_2$.

GTP readily converts to ATP in the cell.

The cycle regenerates oxaloacetate to begin again. Glucose splits into two pyruvates during glycolysis; one glucose undergoes two turns of the Krebs cycle.

The oxidations release energy stored by the nucleotide carriers (NADH and $FADH_2$) when they accept the hydrogen electrons.

Cytochromes use this stored energy in NADH and $FADH_2$ in the electron transport chain to produce ATP by oxidative phosphorylation.

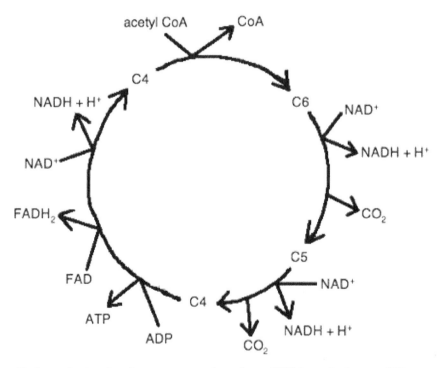

*Krebs cycle showing the reactants and products. GTP is equivalent to ATP*

To summarize, the Krebs cycle degrades two-carbon acetyl groups from acetyl CoA into $CO_2$, and the carbon dioxide is released in two reactions (as a waste product exhaled in animals).

GTP is produced in one of the reactions and is converted into ATP.

Hydrogen is removed in four reactions. $NAD^+$ accepts two electrons and the proton in three reactions, creating three NADH.

FAD accepts two electrons and the proton in one reaction, creating one $FADH_2$.

**Krebs cycle regulation**

The Krebs cycle must be carefully regulated to generate the proper amount of ATP. Although oxygen is not directly used in the Krebs cycle, the cycle can only occur under aerobic conditions because FAD and $NAD^+$ can be regenerated when oxygen is present. If oxygen is drastically reduced, respiration may drop to the point where it may lead to death.

Low oxygen concentrations divert aerobic cellular respiration from the Krebs cycle to anaerobic fermentation.

The Krebs cycle is mainly regulated by substrate availability, product inhibition, and competitive feedback inhibition. During the cycle, ADP (a substrate) is converted to ATP, and a decreased amount of ADP reduces the cycle rate.

**Oxidative phosphorylation and the electron transport chain**

*Oxidative phosphorylation* is the next step in aerobic cell respiration, including the electron transport chain (ETC). This step produces the majority of ATP. This is done by the oxidation (loss of electrons) by high-energy intermediates (NADH and $FADH_2$), causing $H^+$ to be pumped into the intermembrane space (between inner and outer membranes) of the mitochondria.

The electron transport chain reactions occur at the *cristae*, which are the folds of the inner mitochondrial membrane that increase the surface area for the electron transport chain. During this process, a gradient across the mitochondrial membrane is created to drive ATP production.

Depending on cell conditions and if involving a prokaryotic or eukaryotic organism, about 32 to 34 molecules of ATP are produced by oxidative phosphorylation per glucose molecule.

The *electron transport chain* uses the NADH and $FADH_2$ from the Krebs cycle for a series of protein complexes that extract energy and pump protons across the inner mitochondrial membrane.

Energy is released as the hydrogen and electrons from the $NAD^+$ and $FAD^+$ carrier molecules flow into the system.

When the electrons reach the end of the chain, they are accepted by oxygen (the final electron acceptor), and water is released when oxygen combines with the electrons and protons.

**Molecules and energy produced by cellular respiration**

During aerobic cellular respiration, glucose breakdown provides energy for a hydrogen ion gradient across the mitochondria's inner membrane, coupling proton flow with ATP formation.

At the end of cellular respiration, glucose is oxidized to carbon dioxide and water, and ATP is produced.

The overall chemical equation for aerobic respiration is:

$$C_6H_{12}O_6 + 6\ O_2 \rightarrow 6\ CO_2 + 6\ H_2O + \text{energy (ATP)}$$

It is the reverse of the equation for photosynthesis (e.g., plants), which uses carbon dioxide ($CO_2$), water, and energy from sunlight to create glucose and oxygen.

## Mitochondria and Oxidative Stress

### Mitochondria for energy production

*Mitochondria* are organelles involved in energy production. A mitochondrion (or *cell's powerhouse*) has a double membrane with an intermembrane space between the outer and inner membrane. The *matrix* is a watery substance containing ribosomes and enzymes. Enzymes in the matrix and inner membrane catalyze the oxidation of carbohydrates, fats, and amino acids. These enzymes are vital for the link reaction and the Krebs cycle.

The inner membrane is where the electron transport chain and ATP synthase are located and where oxidative phosphorylation occurs. The space between the inner and outer membranes is a small volume space that protons are pumped into. Due to its small volume, a high concentration gradient is reached quickly, vital for chemiosmosis.

The outer membrane is a membrane that separates the contents of the mitochondrion from the rest of the cell, creating the ideal environment for cell respiration. The cristae are tubular projections of the inner membrane that increase the surface area for oxidative phosphorylation.

The parts of aerobic cellular respiration occurring in the mitochondria are 1) the link reaction (i.e., pyruvate converts to acetyl-CoA), 2) the Krebs cycle (matrix of mitochondria), and 3) oxidative phosphorylation (proton gradient within the intermembrane space of mitochondria).

During these processes, the pyruvate from glycolysis is broken down to $CO_2$ and $H_2O$, which is why aerobic respiration is considered as glucose breakdown.

$CO_2$ and ATP are transported from the mitochondria to the cytoplasm. $CO_2$ enters the bloodstream for transport to the lungs for expiration. $H_2O$ remains or enters the blood for excretion by the kidneys.

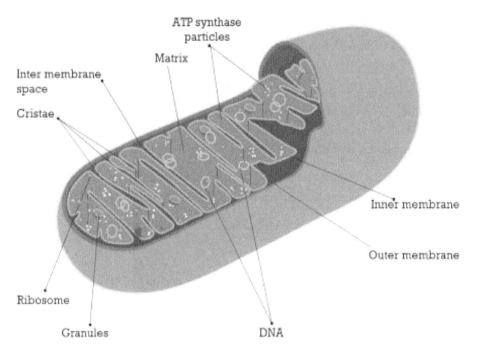

*Mitochondrion with cellular compartments and select biomolecules*

**Free radicals and oxidative stress**

*Oxidative stress* is an imbalance between reactive oxygen species (i.e., free radicals) and the organism's ability to detoxify harmful substances.

*Free radicals* are atoms or molecules with an unpaired electron (single dot for an unpaired electron in the molecule). They have an odd number of electrons.

Free radicals, such as the hydroxyl radical (HO•), are highly reactive, and if they react with important cellular components such as the cell membrane or DNA, the cell can be severely damaged.

The extent of the damage can be extensive because when a free radical abstracts an electron from a cell component, the cell component must take an electron from another cell component, leading to a chain of free radical reactions.

The creation of free radicals disrupts cellular signaling if the original molecule were a cellular messenger.

Oxidative stress is involved in many diseases, including cancer, Alzheimer's disease, and Parkinson's disease. However, oxidative stress can be beneficial (e.g., when it attacks pathogens rather than the host's cells).

*Antioxidants* are molecules that donate electrons to free radicals without becoming destabilized, and they are the primary method by which the reactive oxygen species are counteracted.

Oxidative stress is caused by a decrease in antioxidant levels, increased free radical levels, or both.

Sometimes, oxidative stress can trigger apoptosis or necrosis (cell injury leading to premature cell death).

## Catalysts and Enzyme Catalysis

**Catalysts increase the reaction rate**

*Catalysts* are substances in a chemical reaction that increase the reaction rate by lowering the activation energy (often through an alternative pathway) needed to proceed.

A catalyst participates in a chemical reaction but remains chemically unchanged and used repeatedly.

For a reaction mechanism separated into elementary steps, a catalyst appears at the start and reappears at the end of the reaction. A catalyst is neither a reactant nor a product in the reaction.

Acids, bases, and metal ions often act as catalysts.

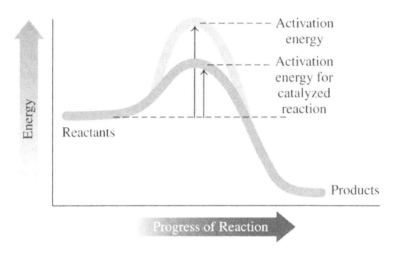

There are homogeneous catalysts and heterogeneous catalysts.

*Homogeneous catalysts* are in the same phase as the reactants.

A *heterogeneous catalyst* is in another phase than the reactants.

Catalysts often immobilize reactants near each other, increasing the probability of a collision and, therefore, the corresponding reaction rate.

A heterogeneous catalyst is dissolved acid catalyzing esters' hydrolysis in an aqueous solution.

Most heterogeneous catalysts are solids, and the reactants are often gases or liquids.

Modern cars have *catalytic converters* in their exhaust systems.

These heterogeneous catalysts provide a solid surface for exhaust molecules to bind and react.

Catalytic converters reduce pollutants such as carbon monoxide (CO), nitrogen oxide (NO), and hydrocarbons (e.g., octane as $C_8H_{18}$).

## Enzyme Structure and Function

**Enzymes catalyze biological reactions**

Enzymes (e.g., proteins) are biological catalysts that increase the reaction rates of biochemical reactions.

Biological enzymes are more efficient than chemical catalysts; enzymes can increase a reaction rate by a factor of greater than ten million $(1 \times 10^7)$.

Enzymes assist almost all chemical reactions that occur in living organisms.

Enzymes are biological molecules that act as catalysts by increasing the rate of chemical reactions.

Although RNA molecules (e.g., ribozymes) can catalyze reactions, most enzymes are proteins.

An enzyme cannot force a reaction to occur if it would not usually occur (i.e., products are less stable than reactants); it makes a reaction occur faster.

Enzymes are highly specific in their action and catalyze a single reaction or class of reactions.

Enzymes are not consumed in a reaction, so small amounts of enzymes are needed in a cell. They form enzyme-substrate complexes with the reactants.

A *substrate* is a molecule on which the enzymes act.

**Enzyme shape dictates function**

The overall 3D shape (i.e., tertiary or quaternary structure) of an enzyme is vital to its function.

Enzymes are often named for their substrates by adding the suffix "-ase."

For example, ribonuclease, abbreviated as RNase, is an enzyme that catalyzes the degradation of ribonucleic acid (RNA) into smaller components.

For example, the enzyme hexokinase is written above or below the reaction arrow. The reactants (starting material) upon which an enzyme acts, written to the left of the reaction arrow, are substrates.

An enzyme may bind to one or more substrates (a molecule that enzymes act upon).

In the example below, there are two substrates: glucose and adenosine triphosphate (ATP). The products (to the right of the reaction arrow) are glucose-6-phosphate and adenosine diphosphate (ADP).

Intermediates (not pictured) are temporarily formed between initial reactants and final products.

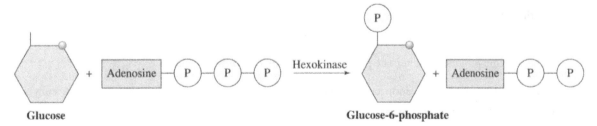

The substrates glucose and ATP are catalyzed by hexokinase to form glucose-6-phosphate and ADP. The hexokinase is not consumed in the reaction and continues the process with new substrates.

**Enzymes reduce the energy of activation**

Reactants must reach a certain energy level before the reaction can convert substrates into products.

The energy is the *activation energy* ($E_a$) needed to break bonds within the reactants and form products.

At a later stage in the reaction, energy is released as new bonds form within the product.

Enzymes decrease the activation energy of a reaction by lowering the energy of the transition state.

The *transition state* (bond making and bond breaking) is when the reactants are in an activated complex.

As shown below, the transition state corresponds to the highest energy level—the activation energy.

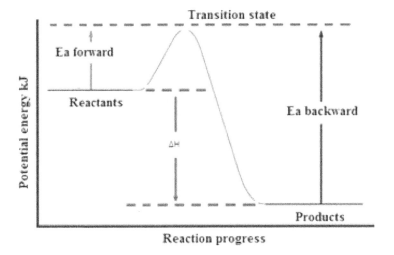

*The energy is on the y-axis, and time on the x-axis. The products are lower in energy than reactants, and the reaction is spontaneous. The enzyme speeds the rate of spontaneous reactions*

Activation energy is an energy barrier to the reaction, which the reactants must overcome before they are converted into products. This is accomplished non-enzymatically by increasing the temperature, increasing molecular collisions between reactants.

Homeostasis means the body temperature is maintained within narrow ranges in many organisms.

The same enzyme may lower the activation energy barrier for the forward and reverse reaction, increasing both reaction rates, or another enzyme catalyzes each reaction separately.

**Enzymes do not affect Δ*G***

In the graph, the enzyme makes it easier for reactions to occur by lowering the required activation energy, but it does not alter the net energy release, Δ*G* (Gibbs free energy).

The enzyme provides an alternate pathway for reactants to form products.

The lowering of the activation energy, which is accomplished during the formation of the enzyme-substrate complex, occurs in several ways:

*Proximity*: When the enzyme-substrate complex forms, the substrates are nearby, and therefore do not have to find each other as in a solution, thereby lowering the entropy (i.e., the disorder) of the reactants.

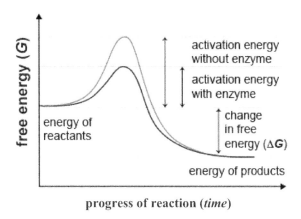

**progress of reaction (*time*)**

*Optimizing orientation*: The enzyme holds the substrates in the correct alignment and at the appropriate distance, usually by aligning active chemical groups. This lowers the entropy of the reactants.

*Modifying bond energy*: While binding to the substrate, the enzyme may stretch or distort a bond and weaken them so that less energy is needed to break the bond.

*Electrostatic catalysis*. Acidic or basic amino acids in the enzyme's active site (i.e., a portion of the enzyme where the substrate binds) may form ionic bonds with the intermediate, which stabilize the transition state and lower the activation energy.

**Biochemical conditions affect enzyme activity**

Many factors can affect enzyme activity, including substrate concentration, pH, temperature, and the presence of modulators.

At a constant enzyme concentration, an increase in the substrate concentration increases the enzyme's activity by increasing the number of random collisions between the substrate and the active site on the enzyme.

However, at some point, available active sites are bound, and increasing the substrate concentration does not affect enzyme activity, a state of *saturation*.

The substrate in a cell is regulated by an organism's diet, absorption rates in the intestine, the permeability of the plasma membrane, or changes in the substrate's intracellular breakdown and synthesis.

Enzymes have an optimum pH at which they work most efficiently. The enzyme maintains its tertiary structure and its active site at this pH. As the pH diverges from the optimum, enzyme activity decreases or ceases.

Additionally, changes in pH may change the nature of an amino acid side chain.

If an enzyme requires a carboxylate ion ($COO^-$), lowering the pH could convert the carboxylate ion to a carboxylic acid ($\sim COOH$), causing enzyme activity to decrease.

An enzyme's pH optimum depends on the location of the enzyme. Enzymes in the stomach function at a lower pH because of their acidic environment.

**pH and temperature influences enzyme activity**

| Enzyme | Location | Substrate | pH Optimum |
|---|---|---|---|
| Pepsin | Stomach | Peptide bonds | 2 |
| Sucrase | Small intestine | Sucrose | 6.2 |
| Urease | Liver | Urea | 7.4 |
| Hexokinase | All tissues | Glucose | 7.5 |
| Trypsin | Small intestine | Peptide bonds | 8 |
| Arginase | Liver | Arginine | 9.7 |

Sometimes, an enzyme's active site functions as a microenvironment more conducive to the reaction, such as providing a pocket of low pH in an otherwise neutral cell.

There is a temperature optimum at which an enzyme exhibits peak activity. Like the pH optimum, it is dependent on the environment in which the enzyme operates typically. For example, a human DNA polymerase has a lower temperature optimum than a thermophilic bacterium's DNA polymerase. For most human enzymes, the optimum temperature is body temperature (37 °C).

As temperature increases, molecules move faster, with more random collisions between enzymes and substrates. Within the upper-temperature limit range, enzyme activity may double with every 10-degree increase.

However, as with pH, the temperature gets too high at a certain point, and bonds maintaining the 2°, 3° and 4° structure of the protein dissociate. This causes the enzyme's active site to become unstable, leading to a loss of function.

A *denatured* protein changes its three-dimensional shape. Denaturation alters an enzyme or another organic molecule structure so that the enzyme cannot carry out its intended function. The enzymes in bacteria are often denatured by high temperatures in processes like boiling contaminated drinking water and heat-sterilizing medical and scientific equipment.

Enzyme activity is decreased by low temperatures, as when food is stored in a refrigerator or freezer. Enzymes are major food spoilage agents, but low temperatures can significantly slow the spoilage process.

**Modulator affect enzyme activity**

*Modulators* are compounds that modify the binding site of an enzyme, inhibiting or enhancing the enzyme's activity. Modulators can strongly affect enzyme activity through covalent (irreversible) or non-covalent (reversible) interactions between modulators and enzymes.

Modulators are products of other chemical reactions or are activated by chemical signals. If modulators are required for enzymes to catalyze the reaction, they are cofactors.

Modulators that increase an enzyme's catalytic activity are enzyme *activators*, *enhancers*, or *inducers*; modulators that decrease or eliminate an enzyme's catalytic activity are enzyme *inhibitors*.

## Principles of Metabolic Regulation

### Homeostasis as a dynamic steady state

Metabolism refers to the biochemical reactions occurring in living organisms' cells, including the reactions that allow the cell to grow, reproduce, and function.

Because organisms are usually in environments continually changing, metabolism must be tightly regulated so that the cell's internal conditions remain constant.

This is *homeostasis* and establishes a "dynamic steady-state."

Homeostatic processes act at multiple levels, from the cell or the tissue to the whole organism. Examples include the regulation of pH, blood glucose, and internal body temperature.

Catabolic (breaking down) and anabolic (building up) pathways are extensively regulated.

During the metabolic reactions in steady-state conditions, the substrate is converted to the product as efficiently as possible.

Metabolic *regulation* is the changes that signaling molecules cause on enzyme activity for catalyzing reactions in metabolic pathways.

Metabolic *control* is how changes in enzyme activity control flux (i.e., the overall rate) of the pathway.

These two concepts are intricately linked with multiple levels of metabolic control.

### Intrinsic and extrinsic control of metabolism

*Intrinsic control* occurs when the reactions in metabolic pathways are self-regulated by responding to changes in the levels of products and substrates.

For example, the product of glycogen phosphorylase is glucose-6-phosphate, and it is inhibited by glucose-6-phosphate (feedback inhibition or negative feedback). Positive feedback occurs when a reaction's product amplifies the reaction rate (e.g., blood clotting).

*Extrinsic control* occurs when a cell in a multicellular organism alters its metabolism according to a signal sent from another cell. These signals are usually hormones or growth factors.

They are detected by receptors on the affected cell's surface, leading to the transmission of signals within the cell (second messenger system). An example of extrinsic control is the hormone-triggered phosphorylation cascade that reduces the rate of glycogen synthesis (described earlier).

Extrinsic control systems allow for the maintenance of homeostasis at the whole-organism level.

There are three components to homeostatic control mechanisms that enable this to happen.

The *receptor* is the first component, which senses environmental stimuli.

The receptor sends a signal to the second component, the *control center* (e.g., brain).

The control center sends a signal to the third component, the *effector*, which responds to the stimuli.

*Notes for active learning*

# CHAPTER 6

# Photosynthesis

- Photosynthetic Organisms
- Photosynthetic Structures
- Photosynthetic Reactions
- Calvin Cycle
- Types of Photosynthesis

## Photosynthetic Organisms

### Photosynthesis

*Photosynthesis* converts solar to chemical energy to assemble organic molecules and fuel metabolic activities.

Photosynthesis includes the 1) *light-dependent reactions* when solar energy is captured and 2) *Calvin cycle* (light-independent or *dark* reactions) when carbohydrates (sugars) are produced.

Photosynthesis is a *backbone process* crucial for life. Only plants, algae, and certain bacteria can perform photosynthesis, but all organisms perform cellular respiration (i.e., the breakdown of nutrients into energy).

Photosynthesis is a complex metabolic pathway, expressed as:

light energy + carbon dioxide + water → carbohydrate + oxygen + water

light energy + 6 $CO_2$ + 12 $H_2O$ → $C_6H_{12}O_6$ + 6 $O_2$ + 6 $H_2O$

In eukaryotes, photosynthesis occurs in *chloroplasts*, while cellular respiration occurs in *mitochondria*.

### Cellular respiration

Cellular respiration breaks down carbohydrates (e.g., glucose) produced from photosynthesis into energy (ATP) to fuel metabolic activities:

carbohydrate + oxygen → carbon dioxide + water + energy

$C_6H_{12}O_6$ + 6 $O_2$ → 6 $CO_2$ + 6 $H_2O$ + ~34 ATP

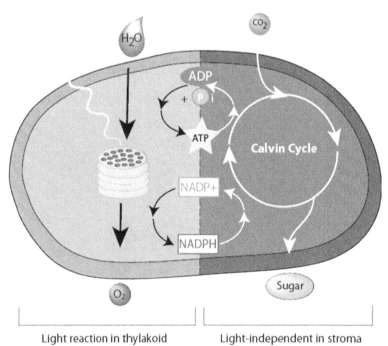

| Light reaction in thylakoid | Light-independent in stroma |

*Light-dependent reactions produce ATP and NADPH, while the light-independent reactions produce sugars*

**Solar energy**

*Solar radiation* is composed of a range of wavelengths, most of which are filtered out as they pass through the atmosphere. The ozone layer filters the high-energy wavelengths (e.g., gamma rays, x-rays, UV radiation). Many low-energy wavelengths (e.g., radio waves, microwaves, and some infrared radiation) are filtered. 42% of the light from the sun hitting the Earth's atmosphere reaches the surface.

*Visible light* is most of the solar radiation reaching Earth's surface.

*Photons* are discrete particles (or *packets*) of light named by Einstein. A photon is *both* a particle and a wave, exhibiting both properties. The energy of photons varies inversely with wavelength. Longer wavelength light has lower energy, while shorter-wavelength light has higher energy.

*Excitation* is when a molecule absorbs light energy, and the energy levels of its electrons are elevated.

*Light energy* may be converted into many forms, a property exploited by photosynthesis.

*Fluorescence* is when energy is emitted upon absorption.

*Phosphorescence* is when energy is emitted after delay.

**Photosynthetic autotrophs**

*Primary producers* (or *autotrophs*) transform inorganic elements of their surroundings into organic compounds. Nearly all primary producers are *photosynthetic autotrophs,* using light energy to create carbohydrates.

*Chemosynthetic autotrophs* are producers using inorganic chemical reactions to create organic compounds. Food chains rely on photosynthesizing organisms (except for rare life based on chemosynthetic autotrophs).

Organic molecules created by photosynthesis fuel *primary producers* and organisms *above them in the food chain.*

*Rate of photosynthesis* by an organism can be determined by measuring oxygen ($O_2$) production and carbon dioxide ($CO_2$) uptake or indirectly by an increase in biomass. Measuring the uptake of carbon dioxide ($CO_2$) is more complex and is usually done indirectly.

For example, oxygen ($O_2$) bubbles released by aquatic plants during photosynthesis determine ($O_2$) production. When plants absorb carbon dioxide from water, water pH rises, so measuring pH levels indicate CO2 uptake.

**Abiotic factors of photosynthesis**

Four *abiotic* (or *nonliving*) factors are necessary for photosynthesis: carbon dioxide ($CO_2$), water ($H_2O$), light, and temperature. These components influence the efficiency of photosynthesis. Usually, only one is the *limiting factor* for a plant at a given time.

Earth's atmosphere contains approximately 78% nitrogen and 21% oxygen, with the remaining 1% being a mixture of gases such as carbon dioxide. $CO_2$ in the atmosphere reaches photosynthetic tissues via *stomata* (openings) on the underside of plant leaves. The carbon dioxide dissolves in a thin film of water covering the outside leaf cells and diffuses through the cell walls to reach the chloroplasts.

The rate of photosynthesis increases with $CO_2$ concentration but levels off at high concentrations.

*Water* is an *abiotic factor* that may or may not be plentiful at the location of an individual plant. In hot, dry climates, plants often close their stomata to conserve water, reducing $CO_2$ supply to the chloroplasts. Less than 1% of the water that plants absorb is used in photosynthesis; the remainder is *transpired* (evaporated from leaves) or incorporated into cellular components. Water in photosynthesis is the source of the $O_2$ gas byproduct.

**Visible light spectrum**

Light is a crucial component of photosynthesis. Light wavelengths within the visible light spectrum, ranging from red light at 780 nm to violet light at 390 nm, are forms of solar radiation useful for photosynthesis.

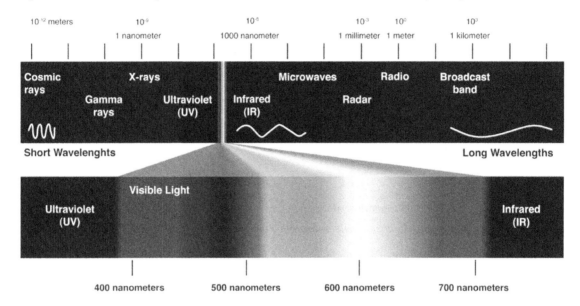

*Electromagnetic spectrum includes visible light, with blue light having the most energy*

Mnemonic ROY G BIV (red, orange, yellow, green, blue, indigo, violet) describes the order of colors by decreasing wavelength (or increasing energy). Wavelength and energy are inversely proportional. Therefore, red has the longest wavelength but the lowest energy in the visible spectrum.

Photosynthetic pigments utilize the visible light spectrum, with photosynthesis rates varying by wavelength. Light intensity varies widely depending on the time of day, temperature, season, altitude, latitude, and atmospheric conditions. Of the visible light reaching a leaf, approximately 80% is absorbed.

Violet-blue light (400 to 525 nm) and orange-red light (625 to 700 nm) are the wavelengths most often absorbed for photosynthesis. Light intensity is a limiting factor because if there is no sunlight, *photolysis* (splitting of water by photons) cannot occur during the light-dependent reactions. This results in a shortage of ATP and NADPH, products of the light-dependent reactions necessary for the Calvin cycle.

At low and medium light intensity, the rate of photosynthesis is proportional to light intensity. However, high-intensity light is not necessarily beneficial for plants, as it can decrease photosynthetic efficiency.

Temperature, like abiotic factors, has an optimum range. The enzymes involved in photosynthesis work slowly and, therefore, less efficiently at low temperatures.

As temperature increases, the rate of photosynthesis increases steeply until the optimum temperature is reached. If the temperature increases beyond this point, then the rate of photosynthesis decreases rapidly.

**Plant anatomy**

Plant photosynthesis requires the intake of $CO_2$ and $H_2O$. Water absorption is primarily by roots that move the water up through vascular tissue in the stem until it reaches the leaves.

*Mesophyll cells* within the leaves are specialized, where photosynthesis takes place.

The exchange of $O_2$ and $CO_2$, and some water, occurs through the *stomata*.

*Guard cells* open and close stomata pores. The density of stomata depends on ecological conditions like humidity and $CO_2$ concentration.

The plant's leaves, composed of the *lamina* (blade) and the *petiole* (stalk), are its primary photosynthetic organs and typically have a large surface area to maximize light harvesting.

*Simple leaf* has one lamina, while a *compound leaf* has many distinct laminae.

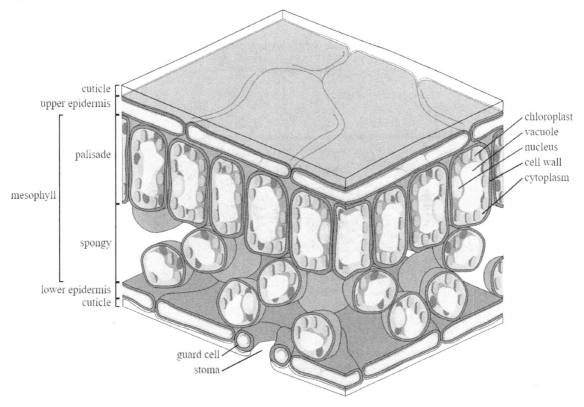

*Cross-section of a typical C$_4$ plant leaf anatomy with guard cells regulating stomata aperture*

Leaves are highly variable in shape and usually thin, so light penetrates to cells on the underside. The underside of leaves is often covered with hairs called *trichomes*, which catch water, reduce airflow, and produce wax. The waxy cuticle covers the outer epidermis of leaves, preventing water loss but limiting gas exchange.

The upper and lower epidermises of the leaf feature the stomata and serve a protective function, while loosely arranged *spongy mesophyll* tissue creates air spaces.

*Palisade mesophyll* is more tightly packed and contains the highest concentration of chloroplasts which usually remain near the cell wall for optimal use of light.

## Photosynthetic Structures

### Chloroplasts

$CO_2$ and $H_2O$ entering a mesophyll cell diffuse into the chloroplasts, the site of the light-dependent reactions and the Calvin cycle. A chloroplast is a double-membraned organelle known as a *plastid*. Each has ribosomes and identical copies of a double-stranded, circular DNA molecule unique to the cell's DNA.

*Chloroplast membrane structures* include an outer plasma membrane, an intermembrane space, and an inner plasma membrane. Within the inner membrane, a fluid-filled space called *stroma* is the site of the Calvin cycle.

*Thylakoids* are flattened *disc-like sacs* organized into stacks as *grana* within the stroma. These structures have a large surface area for light absorption and an inner lumen where protons ($H^+$) accumulate. The accumulation of protons ($H^+$) in the thylakoid lumen creates an electrochemical gradient for photosynthesis. Light-dependent reactions occur in the thylakoids.

Chlorophyll and pigments for the absorption of solar energy are embedded in thylakoid membranes.

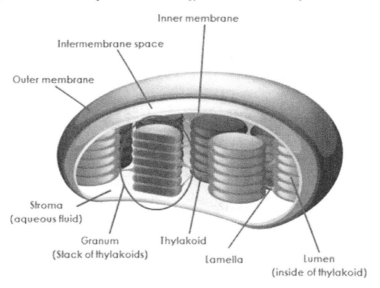

*Chloroplast is a double-membered structure with stroma as the site of the Calvin cycle*

### Photosynthetic pigments

Pigment molecules have a distinctive *light absorption spectrum;* graphing *percent light absorbed vs. wavelength.*

*Action spectrum* graphs plot photosynthetic activity *vs.* wavelength of light.

*Action spectrums* (resembles absorption spectrums) indicate chlorophyll is the primary pigment in photosynthesis.

It is the abundant photosynthetic pigment in plants, so the rate of photosynthesis is highest at the low wavelengths of visible light (400 to 525 nm). These wavelengths, which comprise violet and blue light, are the most readily absorbed by chlorophyll.

Chlorophyll absorbs an appreciable portion of red and orange light, which is why significant photosynthetic activity is found there.

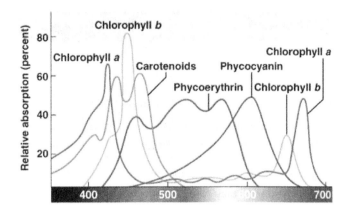

*Relative absorption of visible light wavelengths (nm) by plant photosynthetic pigments*

Little light is absorbed by chlorophyll at wavelengths of yellow and green light (525 to 625 nm), and most are reflected, giving plants their green color.

Photosynthetic organisms that are not green utilize alternate photosynthetic pigments.

For example, red algae use *phycobilins,* which absorb blue, yellow, and green light and reflect red light.

## Chlorophyll, carotenoids and accessory pigments

Chlorophyll exists in several forms which differ slightly in molecular structure. Chlorophyll molecules have a long lipid tail that anchors them in the lipid layers of thylakoid membranes, a *porphyrin ring* of alternating double and single bonds, and a single atom of magnesium in the center.

Chlorophyll is analogous to *heme,* the iron-containing pigment in hemoglobin protein within the red blood cells which transports $O_2$.

*Chlorophyll a* and *chlorophyll b* are the common forms, with chlorophyll *a* generally three times as abundant as chlorophyll *b*. Chlorophyll *a,* a bluish-green pigment, has the formula $C_{55}H_{72}MgN_4O_5$, while chlorophyll *b*, which is yellow-green, is $C_{55}H_{70}MgN_4O_6$.

Chlorophyll *b* broadens the spectrum of light available for photosynthesis. It absorbs light energy and transfers the energy to a chlorophyll *a* molecule. Green plants contain other pigments contributing to photosynthesis.

*Carotenoids* are yellow-orange pigments that absorb light in the violet, blue and green ranges of the spectrum. When chlorophyll decomposes in autumn, plant leaves turn yellow, orange, and red as carotenoids become visible.

Even though carotenoids are present in lesser amounts, they allow a low rate of photosynthesis at wavelengths of light that chlorophyll cannot absorb.

*Accessory pigments* (antenna pigments) are the light-absorbing pigments that aid chlorophyll *a*, including chlorophyll *b, c, d,* and carotenoids.

## Photosynthetic Reactions

### Light energy conversions

*Light-dependent reactions* require solar energy for energy-capturing reactions. The primary function of the light-dependent reactions is to trap solar energy and store it as chemical energy as ATP or NADPH. These reactions begin with light striking chlorophyll molecules. Subsequent reactions convert light energy to chemical energy.

When solar energy excites electrons in the antenna complex, it is *photoactivated*. The energized electrons pass from one pigment molecule to the next until they reach the special chlorophyll *a* pair at the reaction center.

### Electron transport chain

*Electron transport chain* (ETC) is when reaction centers pass excited electrons to the first in a series of electron carriers. Excited electrons in the chlorophyll are unstable and re-emit absorbed energy as they migrate along the electron transport chain. The result is the production of ATP and NADPH.

*Light reactions* comprise events from the initial photoactivation of a photosystem to ATP and NADPH synthesis. This process is constant during daylight hours as the plant produces ATP and NADPH for the Calvin cycle.

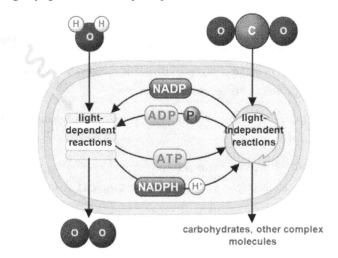

*Light-dependent and light-independent (Calvin cycle) reactions during photosynthesis*

### Photosystems I and II

Two photosystems play critical roles in the light-dependent reactions of photosynthesis. Photosystem I (PS I) is best excited by light at about 700 nm, while photosystem II (PS II) cannot use photons of wavelengths longer than 680 nm. Each photosystem has an antenna complex composed of chlorophyll, carotenoids, accessory proteins, and cofactors such as magnesium and calcium.

*Oxidation-reduction reactions* occur throughout photosynthesis and cellular respiration. Photosynthesis proceeds to the Calvin cycle reactions in the stroma, where the NADPH and ATP created by the light-dependent reactions are used to reduce CO2 into carbohydrates. Oxidation results in the net loss of an electron or electrons, while reduction results in the net gain of an electron or electrons. Mnemonic "OIL RIG" for Oxidation Is Loss and Reduction Is Gain.

## Light-dependent and light-independent reactions

*Photosynthesis* occurs in two stages.

*Light-dependent reactions* capture the energy of light and use it to make the energy storage and transport molecules ATP and NADPH.

*Light-independent reactions* (Calvin cycle) use the energy from short-lived electronically excited electron carriers to convert carbon dioxide and water into organic compounds used by the organism (and animals that feed on it). This set of reactions is *carbon fixation*.

Calvin cycle has four steps: carbon fixation, reduction phase, carbohydrate formation, and regeneration phase. ATP and NADPH provide energy for the chemical reactions in this sugar-generating process.

Sunlight provides the energy for the reaction:

ATP + NADPH + carbon dioxide ($CO_2$) → sugar

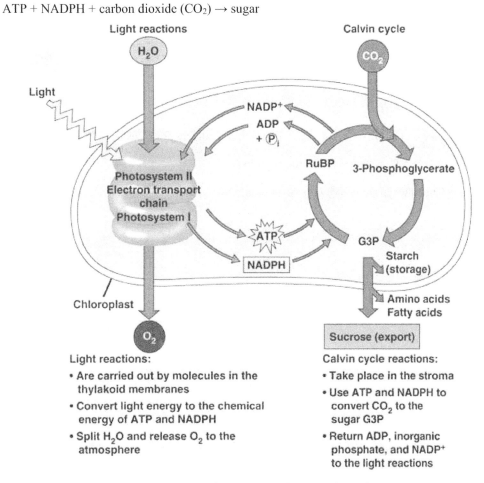

*Products of light-dependent (ATP and NADPH) and light-independent reactions (sugars)*

**Oxidation–reduction reactions**

Photosynthesis uses oxidation-reduction reactions:

- Overall, photosynthesis is a redox reaction: water is oxidized to oxygen and $CO_2$ is reduced to sugar and water

- During photolysis, water is oxidized by *solar energy* transferred by photons into oxygen, protons, and electrons

- During the electron transport chain (ETC), each molecule in the chain is reduced (gains an electron) as it receives an electron and oxidized (loses an electron) as it passes the electron

- At the end of the electron transport chain, $NADP^+$ is reduced to NADPH

- During the Calvin cycle, $CO_2$ is reduced into sugar (carbohydrates) and water

**Light-dependent reactions**

There are two sets of light-dependent reactions in the thylakoid membrane:

*noncyclic electron pathway* and

*cyclic electron pathway.*

Each pathway produces ATP, but only the noncyclic electron pathway produces NADPH.

*Photophosphorylation* is ATP production via photosynthesis.

*Cyclic* and *noncyclic* pathways are *photophosphorylation.*

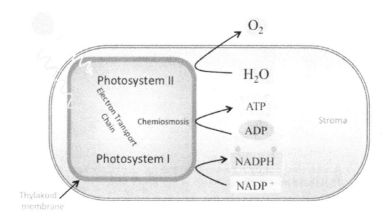

*Light-dependent reactions include photosystems II and I that produce $O_2$, ATP, and NADPH*

## Calvin Cycle

### Carbon-fixing reactions

*Carbon-fixing reactions* have emerged as an apt description of the Calvin cycle. The reactions that accomplish this have historically been light-independent (or dark) reactions. ATP and NADPH are essential products of light-dependent reactions and used to synthesize carbohydrates from atmospheric $CO_2$.

Despite their names, these reactions *do not* typically occur at nighttime. They indirectly require light because they rely on light-dependent reactions that require daylight. The term "dark reactions" is less common, and some claim that "light-independent" is a misnomer.

These reactions occur in the stroma of chloroplasts and occur if the end products of the light-dependent reactions are available. Depending on the plant, the carbon-fixing reactions may progress differently. Commonly, atmospheric $CO_2$ combines with the 5-carbon sugar *ribulose-1,5-bisphosphate* (RuBP).

$CO_2$ and RuBP convert into a 6-carbon sugar such as glucose via several steps. Some sugars combine into polysaccharides (e.g., starch) for storage within the plant.

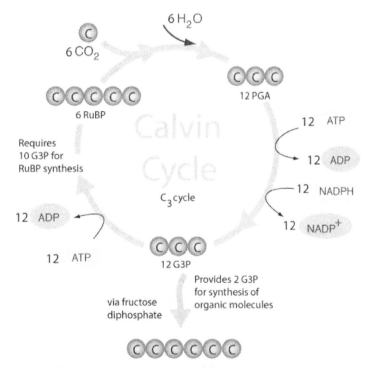

*Calvin cycle reaction (light-independent) synthesizes sugars from $CO_2$*

### Calvin cycle reactions

Calvin cycle has three stages: 1) carboxylation, 2) reduction, and (3 regeneration.

1)  Carboxylation or Fixation of Carbon Dioxide:

$$CO_2 + RuBP \Rightarrow PGA$$

*Carboxylation* is the attachment of $CO_2$ to 5-carbon RuBP, forming an unstable 6-carbon intermediate.

*Ribulose-1,5-bisphosphate carboxylase/oxygenase* (RuBisCO) catalyzes this reaction. RuBisCO comprises 20–50% of the protein content of chloroplasts.

Its ubiquity makes it the most common protein in nature. When the 6-carbon intermediate is formed, it splits to form two molecules of the 3-carbon compound *3-Phosphoglyceric acid* (3-PG, 3-PGA, or PGA).

3-Phosphoglyceric acid is *glycerate 3-phosphate*.

2) Reduction of 3-Phosphoglyceric acid:

$$PGA + ATP + NADPH \Rightarrow G3P + ADP + Pi + NADP+$$

PGA is phosphorylated to form an intermediate using ATP produced by light-dependent reactions. The intermediate is reduced by NADPH, the other product of light-dependent reactions, to form *glyceraldehyde 3-phosphate*. This is a 3-carbon compound, like PGA.

Glyceraldehyde 3-phosphate (G3P, GP, GA3P, or GAP) is *triose phosphate* (TP) and *3-phosphoglyceraldehyde* (PGAL).

Along with each G3P, the reduction produces ADP, inorganic phosphate (Pi), and $NADP^+$.

G3P can be converted into useful molecules, such as glucose. Glucose is the starting point for synthesizing polysaccharides (i.e., starch and cellulose). Glucose can be combined with fructose to form sucrose, a vital plant carbohydrate.

3) Regeneration of RuBP:

$$G3P + ATP \Rightarrow RuBP + ADP + Pi$$

However, only one G3P can be used for conversion into glucose.

The remaining G3P regenerates RuBP, which is essential for continuing carbon fixation.

These G3P are met with a carbon acceptor and undergo a series of reactions, requiring energy from ATP, which converts them into RuBP. At this point, the cycle begins again. While this description followed the fate of one original RuBP molecule, the process uses six RuBP and six $CO_2$ for each cycle.

Carboxylation converts six 5-carbon RuBP and six $CO_2$ into six 6-carbon unstable intermediates. The six intermediates break down into twelve 3-carbon PGA.

$$6 \ RuBP + 6 \ CO_2 \rightarrow 12 \ PGA$$

During reduction, 12 PGA plus 12 ATP and 12 NADPH are converted into 12 3-carbon G3P, 12 ADP, 12 Pi, and 12 $NADP^+$. Two of the G3P create *glucose phosphate*.

$$12 \ PGA + 12 \ ATP + 12 \ NADPH \rightarrow 12 \ G3P + 12 \ ADP + 12 \ Pi + 12 \ NADP^+$$

During regeneration, the 10 G3P, using 6 ATP, are remade into 6 RuBP, producing 6 ADP and 4 Pi.

$$10 \ G3P + 6 \ ATP \rightarrow 6 \ RuBP + 6 \ ADP + 4 \ Pi$$

## Types of Photosynthesis

**C₃, C₄ and CAM plants**

$C_3$, $C_4$, and CAM describe how plants perform photosynthesis.

$C_3$ and $C_4$ refer to the carbon length of the first photosynthetic carbohydrate product. $C_3$ plants produce a 3-carbon molecule, 3-phosphoglyceric acid (PGA), and $C_4$ plants produce a 4-carbon molecule, oxaloacetate (OAA). Some plants do not undergo the Calvin cycle.

Like $C_4$, CAM (crassulacean acid metabolism) plants produce oxaloacetate but undergo photosynthesis differently.

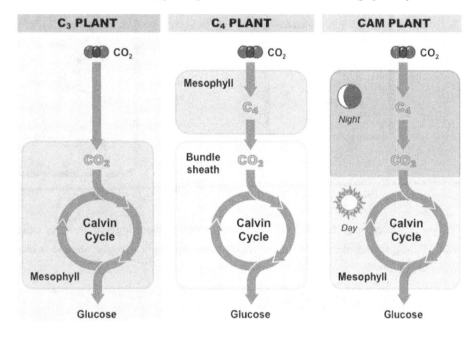

*$C_3$, $C_4$ and CAM plants comparing glucose synthesis with mesophyll and bundle sheath cells*

**C₃ photosynthesis**

More than 90% of angiosperms are $C_3$ plants. In $C_3$ plants, the Calvin cycle proceeds as described, in which $CO_2$ is fixed into the 3-carbon molecule PGA.

In hot weather, stomata close to conserve water, decreasing $CO_2$ concentration in leaves while increasing $O_2$ concentration. High $O_2$ concentration is a disadvantage because RuBisCO can use $O_2$ in the Calvin cycle rather than $CO_2$.

Using $O_2$ in this way is *photorespiration* because it intakes $O_2$ and produces $CO_2$, like cellular respiration.

**Photorespiration**

RuBP reacts with $O_2$ to create $CO_2$ during photorespiration, in contrast to photosynthesis, when RuBP reacts with $CO_2$ to form carbohydrates. The former is an oxygenation reaction, while the latter is a carboxylation reaction.

RuBisCO performs oxygenation rather than carboxylation around 25% of the time, which may be promoted by low $CO_2$, high $O_2$, or elevated temperatures.

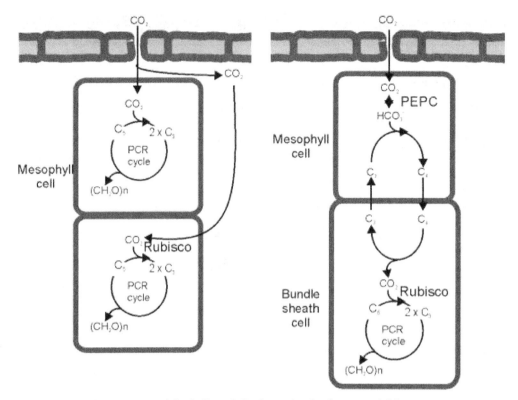

*Comparison of $C_3$ (left) and $C_4$ plants for the fixation of $CO_2$*

*Photorespiration* produces one PGA and one *phosphoglycolate*. Phosphoglycolate is of little use in plants. It inhibits carboxylation, so the plant must spend energy converting phosphoglycolate to a useful molecule and reclaim two carbons.

*Peroxisomes* break down the products of this process.

Photorespiration is a wasteful and inefficient process that results in a net energy loss for the plant. Plants expend up to 40% of the energy stored in sugars for the inevitable damage created by oxygenation reactions.

Photosynthesis evolved billions of years ago when the concentration of atmospheric $O_2$ was low, making photorespiration rare. Photorespiration grew to be a great inconvenience to plants. The oxygenation reaction developed as an adaptation to Earth's early atmosphere.

Plants evolved mechanisms to *reduce damage caused by $O_2$* in the Calvin cycle.

Humans have attempted to circumvent issues created by the oxygenation reaction. Molecular genetics has been used to modify the properties of RuBisCO to eliminate the oxygenation reaction while retaining the carboxylation reaction. The two reactions have not been separated because modifications in RuBisCO reduce oxygenase and carboxylase activity. Nature developed a system to avoid photorespiration.

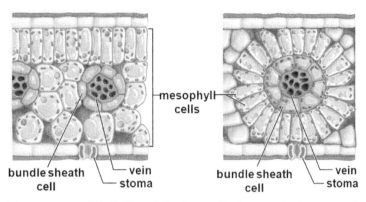

*The comparison of the anatomy of C₃ (left) and C₄ plants. C₄ photosynthesis uses carbon concentration to improve the efficiency of photosynthetic carbon fixation. The leaves of most C₄ plants have a Kranz leaf anatomy consisting of bundle sheath and mesophyll cells.*

## C₄ photosynthesis

*C₄ photosynthesis* is in less than 5% of plants, mostly in hot, dry climates. It is exceptionally well represented in the grasses. Corn and sugar cane, two of the most important crops, are C₄ plants. Because C₄ plants avoid photorespiration, their net photosynthetic rate may be 2 to 3 times more than C₃ plants.

C₄ photosynthesis evolved from C₃ plants independently many times in the evolutionary timeline. The enzymes co-opted for C₄ photosynthesis were already present in the C₃ plants from which they evolved.

However, in moist or cold environments, C₃ plants are more efficient. Researchers attempt to artificially convert certain C₃ plants into C₄ plants to maximize crop yields and allow agriculture in hostile environments.

While C₃ plants have chloroplasts in their mesophyll cells, C₄ plants have additional chloroplasts in special *bundle sheath cells*. These cells surround the veins of the leaves, an arrangement called *Kranz anatomy.*

In the leaves of a C₄ plant, mesophyll cells are arranged concentrically around the bundle sheath cells.

Light-independent reactions are split between cell types, with preliminary carbon fixation in mesophyll cells and the Calvin cycle in bundle sheath cells. RuBisCO is in bundle sheath cells. Rather than RuBisCO, the mesophyll cells have an alternate phosphoenolpyruvate (PEP) enzyme.

When $CO_2$ enters the leaves of a C₄ plant, it is first absorbed by mesophyll cells, as in a C₃ plant. However, rather than being fixed by RuBisCO into PGA, the $CO_2$ is combined with PEP to form 4-carbon *oxaloacetate* (OAA).

*PEP carboxylase* (PEP-C or PEPCase) catalyzes this reaction. PEPCase assimilates carbon more efficiently while avoiding photorespiration. PEPCase has no affinity for $O_2$, unlike RuBisCO, and has a higher affinity for $CO_2$ at high temperatures than RuBisCO.

*Oxaloacetate* is usually converted to *malate,* a reduced form of oxaloacetate, and pumped into the bundle sheath cells. Some plant species reduce oxaloacetate to aspartate rather than malate, and many do not alter oxaloacetate before shuttling it to the bundle sheath cells.

In bundle sheath cells, *malate* is converted to *oxaloacetate* and *decarboxylated* ($CO_2$ is removed) to form 3-carbon *pyruvate*. $CO_2$ remains in the bundle sheath cells to begin the Calvin cycle. Pyruvate is returned to the mesophyll cells to be regenerated into PEP using ATP, and its efficiency is lost in cooler temperatures.

The initial fixed carbon form, whether oxaloacetate, malate, or aspartate, does not substitute for any of the carbon compounds of the Calvin cycle, such as RuBP or PGA. These acids merely serve as sources of $CO_2$ for the conventional Calvin cycle in the bundle sheath cells. $CO_2$ is fixed into RuBP as normal and proceeds throughout the cycle. In this regard, $C_4$ plants fix carbon twice: once in the mesophyll and once in the bundle sheath.

## CAM photosynthesis

*CAM photosynthesis* is an alternative to the $C_3$ strategy, found almost exclusively in plants from dry environments.

CAM (*crassulacean acid metabolism*) plants include cacti, stonecrops (family Crassulaceae, the strategy is named), orchids, bromeliads, and succulents.

Like $C_4$ plants, CAM plants use PEPcase to fix $CO_2$ into *oxaloacetate* and separate this step from the Calvin cycle.

While $C_4$ plants separate them spatially, with the former in mesophyll cells and the latter in bundle sheath cells, CAM plants separate them temporally. Both steps proceed in the *mesophyll cells*, but initial $CO_2$ occurs at night, while the Calvin cycle is during the day.

In CAM plants, *stomata* are opened only at night when $CO_2$ is taken up into the plant and incorporated into the *mesophyll*. They use PEPCase to react with $CO_2$ and PEP to form *oxaloacetate*, which they convert into *malate* and store as the malic acid in large vacuoles in the mesophyll cells.

During the day, malic acid is returned to the chloroplasts for conversion into oxaloacetate, then decarboxylated into pyruvate and $CO_2$. The $CO_2$ is introduced into the Calvin cycle, while pyruvate is used to regenerate PEP.

CAM strategy evolved to avoid transpiration rather than reduce effects of photorespiration, although a benefit. The advantage of CAM over a C4 strategy is conserving water by closing stomata during the day.

There is no $CO_2$ intake during daytime, as stomata are closed to avoid transpiration. Photosynthesis in a CAM plant is minimal due to the limited amount of $CO_2$ fixed at night, allowing them to live in stressful conditions.

# CHAPTER 7

# Microbiology

- Virus Structure

- Viral Infection and Replication

- Viral Life Cycles

- Prokaryotic Cell: Bacteria Classifications

- Prokaryotic Cell: Bacteria Structure

- Bacterial Cell Walls

- Prokaryotic Cell: Growth and Physiology

- Prokaryotic Cell: Genetics

- Gene Expression Control in Prokaryotes

## Virus Structure

### Discovery of viruses

In 1884, French microbiologist Louis Pasteur (1822-1895) suspected that an infectious agent smaller than bacteria caused rabies. In 1892, Russian biologist Dimitri Ivanovsky (1864-1920) confirmed Pasteur's hypothesis about the existence of such agents while working with the tobacco mosaic virus. He showed that passing crushed leaf extracts from infected tobacco plants through a filter with pores smaller than bacteria resulted in a filtered, still infectious solution. With modern technologies, such as the electron microscope (developed in the 1930s), these infectious agents could be visualized. The term *virus* (Latin term for "poison") names these microscopic agents.

Viruses are hypothesized to have originated from the cells they infect, implying that their nucleic acids originated from host cell genomes. This hypothesis implies that viruses emerged after cells came into existence. Viruses can mutate and evolve, so a vaccine specific to a virus may not always be effective.

For example, the flu virus (influenza) mutates regularly and requires new vaccines for protection each year.

### Viral transmission

Viruses are spread between organisms in several ways. *Airborne transmission* occurs when viruses in the air infect an organism. *Blood-borne transmission* occurs when viruses in foreign blood or bodily fluids enter an organism's circulatory system and cause infection.

Additionally, contamination of an organism's water or food supply with viruses can cause transmission.

### Structural characteristics

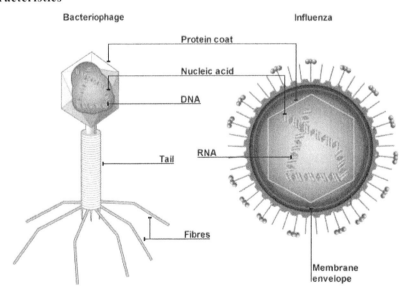

*Common elements for viruses are an outer protein coat and nucleic acid (RNA or DNA) as the genetic material*

*Bacteriophages* (or *phages*) are viruses that infect bacterial cells.

The *head* stores the genetic material, the fibers of the *tail* attach to the host bacterium, and the *sheath* provides a passageway for the genetic material to be injected into the host bacterium.

---

**Nucleic acid and protein composition**

Viruses are small particles containing as few as three or several hundred genes. They are host specific and can infect virtually any cell type as a class of particles. Viruses have at least two parts: an *outer capsid* composed of protein subunits and an *inner core* containing genetic (DNA or RNA) material.

Genetic material and structure classify viruses. Their nucleic acid may be DNA or RNA and can exist as single-stranded (ssRNA or ssDNA) or double-stranded (dsRNA or dsDNA).

Viruses do *not* contain organelles or nuclei. Genetic (RNA or DNA) material is packed inside the protein capsid.

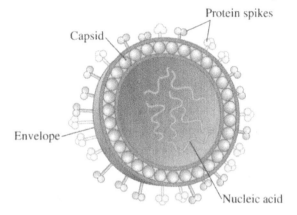

*Structure of an enveloped virus with protein spikes for host specificity*

**Enveloped and nonenveloped viruses**

Viruses vary in size and shape. Some viruses include an envelope as an additional layer outside the protein capsid. Enveloped viruses are generally less virulent and more sensitive to degradation than nonenveloped viruses.

Viruses can have surface extensions, molecules extending from the capsid that allow the virus to interact with host cells (cells infected with a virus), such as protein spikes.

**RNA or DNA genomes**

Viruses cannot replicate their nucleic acid (DNA or RNA) or synthesize their proteins. They use host cell machinery for replication, transcription, and translation. Their single-stranded or double-stranded DNA or RNA encodes for proteins necessary to make new viruses. The viral genome has several hundred genes at most, whereas a human cell contains about 20,000 protein-coding genes.

Although the host cell provides the synthetic machinery needed for viral activity and replication, the viral genomes of some viruses may encode the proteins they require. For example, a special RNA replicase (RNA-dependent RNA polymerase) replicates viral RNA genomes directly from the RNA template.

**Relative size**

A virus is similar to a large protein and is usually under 200 nm in diameter (although some are larger). Viruses are roughly 100 times smaller than bacteria and 1,000 times smaller than most eukaryotic cells.

## Viral Infection and Replication

### Obligate intracellular parasites

The prime directive of organisms is to reproduce and survive, which applies to viruses. Viruses are tiny nucleic acid carriers surrounded by various proteins and a membrane. Due to their size and simplicity, they cannot replicate outside a living cell. Thus, viruses are *obligate intracellular parasites*. Viruses have living and non-living characteristics but are not considered "*living organisms*." They are noncellular and cannot metabolize or respond to stimuli.

Viruses need to reproduce within a host before it dies for the infection to propagate. By altering the genetic makeup, viruses hijack the host cell's synthetic machinery to replicate their genetic material and synthesize their proteins. Viruses multiply inside the cell, spreading to cells to repeat the process.

Viruses cause infectious diseases in plants and animals, including humans. Some viruses are specific to human cells (e.g., human papillomavirus, hepatitis B virus). Some are cancer-producing because they contain *oncogenes*, which are normal genes that mutate to cause cells to undergo repeated divisions.

*Antibiotics* are chemicals derived from bacteria or fungi harmful to microorganisms. Antibiotics are effective for bacteria but cannot treat viral infections because viruses use host cell enzymes, not their enzymes, and interfering with the host cell's enzymes would harm the infected organism. In humans, viral diseases are controlled by preventing transmission, administering vaccines, and using antiviral drugs.

### Virus specificity

Over one thousand disease-causing viruses infect plants. These viral infections are difficult to distinguish from nutrient deficiencies, and plants generally propagate in a way to avoid viral infection.

Viruses are *specific to a type of cell or species* because they bind to host cell receptors.

*Host range* is the host organisms that a virus can infect. For example:

- Tobacco mosaic virus infects certain plants

- The rabies virus infects mammals

- The AIDS virus (HIV-1) infects white blood cells in humans

- Hepatitis virus invades liver tissues

- Poliovirus only reproduces in spinal nerve cells

### Viral infections

During *attachment*, portions of the viral capsid adhere to specific sites on the host cell surface. If the virus is enveloped, glycoprotein spikes often serve as ligands for attachment. The attachment step is the basis for host cell specificity (i.e., why viruses that infect one cell type cannot infect another with distinctive characteristics and surface receptors).

Viruses may use an enzyme to digest the rigid peptidoglycan cell wall of bacteria to allow penetration.

Teichoic acids, which provide rigidity in the cell walls of Gram-positive bacteria, are common binding sites.

*Penetration* is one of many methods genetic material can enter a host cell. Bacteriophages use a syringe-like mechanism to inject genetic material; the head and the rest of the protein body remain outside the host cell.

*Nonenveloped viruses* often enter the cell through *endocytosis*, an engulfing process where the entire virus enters the cell. Enveloped viruses often enter similarly, but they first allow their envelope to fuse with the host membrane before their genetic material and protein coat enter the cell.

**Viral replication**

*DNA viruses* use typical DNA-dependent DNA polymerases to replicate their DNA. DNA can be transcribed to mRNA, then translated for viral proteins. The replicated DNA and translated proteins assemble into virions (i.e., complete virus particles).

*RNA viruses* do not have to be immediately transcribed as DNA viruses do. However, they use RNA-dependent RNA polymerase encoded in their genome to replicate their RNA.

RNA serves as the mRNA transcript, translated into viral proteins. This replicated RNA and the translated proteins assemble into new virions.

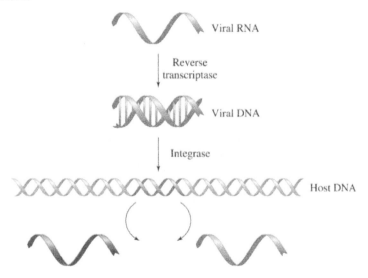

*RNA viruses undergo reverse transcription before integrating into the host genome*

*Biosynthesis* stage of viral infection involves the synthesis of viral components. After the virus enters the host cell, the cell is altered to start transcribing the viral genetic material and translating the mRNA into viral protein.

The viral genome replicates to form the genetic material of each new virus. The virus relies on host cell machinery, using the host's polymerases, ribosomes, tRNA, ATP, deoxyribonucleotide triphosphates (dNTP), and amino acids.

Some viruses encode special enzymes (e.g., reverse transcriptase for RNA → DNA) required for their replication. Additionally, the expression of host genes unnecessary for viral replication is decreased.

## Viral Life Cycles

### Lytic *vs.* lysogenic life cycles

Viruses have two life cycles: the lytic and lysogenic cycles.

*Lytic cycle* involves attachment to and penetration of the host cell, followed by replication of genetic material, the synthesis of proteins, and the release of newly-assembled viruses. After attachment and penetration, the viral genome integrates into the host genome as a *provirus* (or *prophage* if the host is a bacterium). It remains inactive for a period, passing to daughter cells (or lysogenic cells) as the host cell divides.

*Lysogenic cycle* is a dormant (or *latent*) stage connected to the lytic cycle. Stimuli (e.g., UV radiation or nutritional stress) trigger the virus to exit the lysogenic cycle and begin replication and protein synthesis of the lytic cycle.

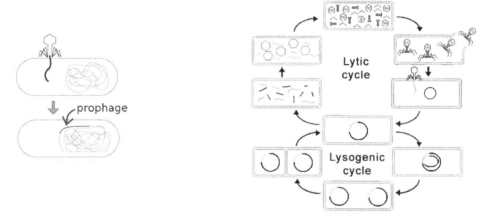

*Formation of a prophage: the virus is shown on the left image at the top, attached to the bacterial cell, before injection of the viral genome. The lytic cycle results in the cell rupture releasing prophages while lysogenic phase viruses replicate along with the host cell.*

*Viral life cycles* depend on the nucleic acid (ssRNA, dsRNA, ssDNA, or dsDNA), influencing how replication, transcription, and translation proceed.

### Self-assembly and release of virions

Newly-produced capsid proteins and viral genetic material assemble into new viruses spontaneously within the host cell; this assembly is the *maturation* of the new viruses.

Viruses are released in two major ways.

*Nonenveloped viruses* often exit using *lysis*, destroying the host cell membrane.

*Enveloped viruses* generally exit by budding, which involves coating the interior of the host cell membrane with viral proteins and passing through the membrane. As the virus exits, it takes a piece of the host membrane and becomes enveloped. Therefore, viral envelopes are derived mainly from the host cell's membrane. If the host has a cell wall, the virus may use an enzyme (lysozyme) encoded in its genome to break it down.

Viruses are *obligate intracellular parasites* and spread extracellularly to find new host cells to infect. Many viral envelope components, such as lipids, proteins, and carbohydrates, are obtained from the host cell's plasma or nuclear membranes. The typical model of a phage is a nonenveloped virus released by lysis, and the standard animal virus model is an enveloped virus that exits by budding.

After exiting, the viruses may infect other cells, and the cycle is renewed.

**Transduction transfers genetic material**

*Transduction* transfers DNA from one bacterium to another using a bacteriophage.

First, the bacteriophage introduces viral DNA into the bacterium. When viral DNA is assembled into new viruses during the lytic cycle, a portion of bacterial (*host*) DNA is assembled into a new virus with viral genetic material.

When this phage infects another host, the bacterial DNA it carries is introduced. This bacterial DNA in the new host is incorporated by *recombination* with its homologous counterpart in the host cell's DNA.

**Retroviruses and reverse transcriptase**

*Retrovirus* is a single-stranded RNA virus that uses a DNA encoded intermediate in its life cycle. However, not all single-stranded RNA viruses are retroviruses. Once the RNA of a retrovirus enters the cell, it uses its reverse transcriptase to make a DNA complement of its RNA genome. Newly synthesized double-stranded DNA (*complementary* or *cDNA*) is transcribed to mRNA and translated into the viral proteins.

cDNA is randomly integrated into the host genome by a virally-encoded enzyme (integrase). This begins a lysogenic cycle, where the integrated DNA is replicated along with the host DNA. External stimuli and factors cause this retroviral DNA to be transcribed, producing new viruses in a lytic cycle.

Prophages often exit the host chromosome and reform into virions when they exit the lysogenic cycle. However, integrated retroviral DNA is typically transcribed like other genes in the host genome during the lysogenic cycle.

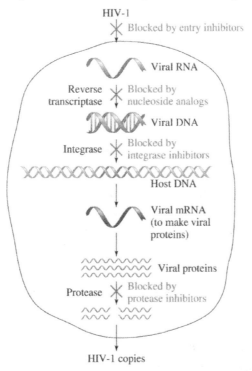

*HIV-1 is a retrovirus that uses reverse transcriptase to propagate the infection*

## Prokaryotic Cell: Classifications

### Prokaryotic domains: Bacteria and Archaea

Prokaryotes include *Bacteria* and *Archaea* domains of life. They were likely the first cells in evolutionary history; fossils of prokaryotes that date 3.5 billion years ago have been found. These fossils indicate that prokaryotes were alone on Earth for 2 billion years, evolving diverse metabolic capabilities and pathways.

Bacteria are encountered every day—they live inside and on humans and animals. A single spoonful of soil can contain 1010 prokaryotic organisms; bacteria are the most numerous life form.

Bacteria were discovered in the *seventeenth century* when Dutch naturalist Antonie van Leeuwenhoek (1632-1723) examined scrapings from his teeth under a microscope. He labeled these organisms "*little animals*." It was believed that organisms could arise spontaneously from inanimate matter.

Around 1850, Louis Pasteur (1822-1895) refuted the *theory of spontaneous generation* by demonstrating that contamination was necessary for the growth of microbes.

### Classification criteria

*Classification of bacteria* was based initially on metabolism and nutrition, among other characteristics.

However, work done by Carl Woese (1928-2012) in the 1980s has revised the bacterial taxonomy based on similarity with 16S rRNA (genes encoding for the 30S small subunit of the prokaryotic ribosome).

Bacteria were classified into 12 lineages based on *16S rRNA sequences*, but phyla have increased to around 52.

Bacteria display a wide range of morphologies and live almost everywhere on the planet, including soil, water, hot springs, and deep portions of the Earth's crust, and are vital for the recycling of many nutrients. They often live in symbiotic relationships with plants and animals, but some are pathogens that cause disease and even death.

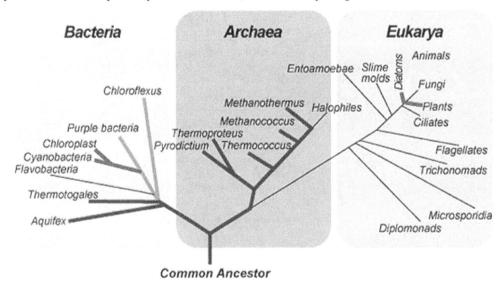

*Phylogenetic tree of the three domains of life: Bacteria, Archaea, and Eukarya, and the lineage of their relationships based on 16S rRNA genes*

**Archaea**

*Archaea* are prokaryotes with molecular characteristics that distinguish them from *bacteria* and *eukaryotes*.

Archaea inhabit *extreme environments*, such as those with high salt, elevated temperature, or harsh chemicals.

Archaea and bacteria are hypothesized to have diverged from a common ancestor about 3.7 billion years ago. Archaea and eukaryotes initiate transcription in the same manner and have similar types of tRNA.

Eukaryotes likely split from archaea, as suggested by archaea and eukaryotes sharing some ribosomal proteins, not in bacteria.

Archaea are *spherical, rod-shaped, spiraled, lobed, plate-shaped,* or *irregular-shaped*.

DNA and RNA sequences in archaea are closer to eukaryotes than bacteria. Archaeal cell walls have polysaccharides but no peptidoglycan, as in bacteria.

Additionally, archaea may have unusual lipids in their plasma membranes (glycerol linked to hydrocarbons rather than fatty acids) that allow them to function at elevated temperatures.

Most archaea are chemoautotrophs, and none are photosynthetic, suggesting that chemoautotrophs evolved first.

Some exhibit mutualism or commensalism, but none are parasitic or known to cause disease.

**Methanogens, halophiles and thermoacidophiles**

There are many types of archaea, including *methanogens*, *halophiles*, and *thermoacidophiles*.

*Methanogens* live under anaerobic environments (e.g., marshes), producing methane. Methane is produced from hydrogen gas and carbon dioxide, and its production is coupled with ATP formation. Methane released into the atmosphere contributes to the greenhouse effect.

Methanogenic archaea produce about 65% of the methane found in Earth's atmosphere.

*Halophiles* require high salt concentrations (e.g., Great Salt Lake). Their proteins use halorhodopsin (light-gated chloride pump) to synthesize ATP in the presence of light. They usually require salt concentrations of 12-15%; in comparison, ocean water is 3.5%.

*Thermoacidophiles* thrive in hot, acidic environments (e.g., geysers) at temperatures around 80 °C, although this varies depending on the species. The metabolism of sulfides forms acidic sulfates, and they generally thrive at a pH between 2–3.

## Prokaryotic Cell: Bacteria Structure

**Bacilli (*rod-shaped*), spirilla (*spiral-shaped*) and cocci (*spherical*)**

Most bacteria, on average, are 1–1.4 μm wide and 2–6 μm long, making them visible with light microscopes.

Three basic shapes:

- *Bacillus* is elongated or rod-shaped.

- *Spirillum* is spiral-shaped.

- *Coccus* is spherical.

Cocci and bacilliform clusters and chains vary in size between species.

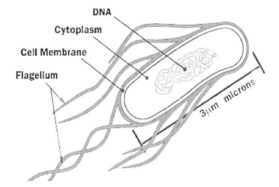

*Escherichia coli (E. coli) bacterium with a peptidoglycan cell wall and circular DNA genome*

As cells get larger, the *ratio of surface area relative to volume* decreases, limiting how large an actively metabolizing cell can become. An adequate surface area is required for vital processes, such as nutrient exchange across the plasma membrane.

If there is a disproportionate cell *volume* and insufficient *surface area*, the *exchange rate* does not support metabolism. Cells needing a greater surface area-to-volume ratio use modifications, such as folding or microvilli (small membrane projections), to increase the surface area while minimizing the additional volume associated with these modifications.

**Lack of nuclear membrane and mitotic apparatus**

Unlike eukaryotes, prokaryotic cells lack a *nucleus* (prokaryote means "*before a nucleus*"). However, prokaryotes have a dense area where their DNA is concentrated, called the *nucleoid region*. It is irregularly shaped, dense with nucleic acid, and not enclosed by any membrane.

Prokaryotic DNA is a *single, circular, double-stranded DNA chromosome* without histones or associated proteins like eukaryotes. Bacterial cells may have *plasmids*. These plasmids, which are smaller than genomic DNA, may confer additional abilities or characteristics (e.g., genes to encode proteins for antibiotic resistance).

Prokaryotes lack a mitotic apparatus used in eukaryotes to separate chromosomes during mitosis. Instead, prokaryotes use their cytoskeleton to pull replicated DNA apart during *binary fission* resulting in cell division.

**Lack of eukaryotic organelles**

Prokaryotic cells *lack membranous organelles* of eukaryotic cells. They do not have the Golgi apparatus or endoplasmic reticulum, nor do they have mitochondria or chloroplasts. Their cytoplasm is a semifluid solution with the enzymes needed for essential chemical reactions. Some may have *inclusion bodies*, which are granules that store various substances.

Prokaryotes have thousands of ribosomes for protein synthesis, but they are *smaller* (the 30S, 50S subunits; 70S assembled) than eukaryotic (40S, 60S subunits; 80S assembled) ribosomes. *S* is Svedberg units for density.

**Prokaryotic cell walls**

Like eukaryotes, prokaryotes have a typical plasma membrane with a *phospholipid bilayer*. Prokaryotic plasma membranes form internal pouches (i.e., *mesosomes*), increasing the *surface area for metabolic processes*.

Outside the plasma membrane of bacteria, fungi, and eukaryotic plant cells is a rigid *cell wall* that keeps the cell from bursting or collapsing due to osmotic changes.

Bacterial cell walls have *peptidoglycan*, a polysaccharide-protein molecule that gives the wall much strength (archaea have cell wall polysaccharides but *no peptidoglycan*).

The cell wall protects the cell from the outside environment and maintains cell shape. Some prokaryotes (e.g., Gram-negative bacteria) have an outer membrane (lipopolysaccharide) outside their peptidoglycan cell wall.

Plant cell walls are *cellulose* (polysaccharides of glucose monomers), and fungi cell walls have *chitin*.

Some prokaryotes have another layer of polysaccharides and proteins outside their cell walls, a *glycocalyx* or *capsule*. The capsule is not easily washed off during experiments. Some prokaryotes may have a *slime layer*, a loose gelatinous sheath conferring some protection from environmental assaults (e.g., antibiotics or dehydration). Slime layers or capsule coverings benefit parasitic prokaryotes as protection from host defenses.

**Antibiotics**

Bacteria continuously remodel their *peptidoglycan cell walls* as they divide, making the cell wall a drug to target. β-lactam antibiotics (e.g., penicillin) *prevent peptidoglycan cross-links* in a bacterium's cell wall by inhibiting the enzyme that catalyzes the formation of these cross-links. This creates an imbalance in cell wall degradation and production, causing the bacterium to lose its cell wall and become susceptible to rupture from osmotic pressure.

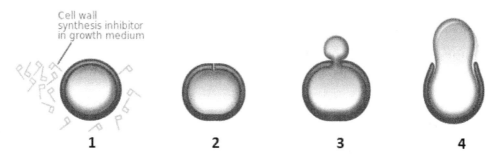

*Penicillin's mechanism of action on peptidoglycan cell wall during cell division. Initially, (1) cell wall synthesis is inhibited, (2) cross-linking is blocked, (3) blebbing of plasm membrane, (4) lysis of plasma membrane, and subsequent release of bacterial cellular contents.*

## Bacterial Cell Walls

### Gram staining

*Gram staining* (developed in the 1880s by Hans Christian Gram; 1853-1938) differentiates bacteria by cell walls.

*Gram-positive* bacteria stain *purple*, while *Gram-negative* bacteria stain *pink*.

Gram staining procedure involves staining bacterial cells with crystal violet dye, washing away the dye, and recoloring them with a pink counterstain dye.

*Gram-positive bacteria* have a *thick peptidoglycan* layer and *no outer membrane*. Their thick peptidoglycan readily takes up the purple dye.

*Gram-negative bacteria* have a *thin peptidoglycan* layer surrounded by *an outer membrane*. They take up the purple dye, but their outer membranes degrade in the washing step (typically alcohol), *removing the purple color*.

The washing step does not affect the thick peptidoglycan of the Gram-positive bacteria, leaving them *purple*.

*Recoloring* with a pink dye visualizes the *Gram-negative bacteria*.

Pink dye does not affect the *purple color of the Gram-positive bacteria*.

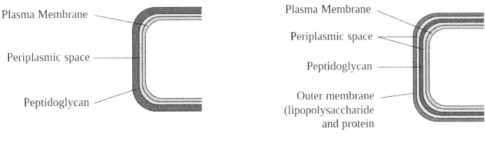

*Gram-positive cell wall stain purple*          *Gram-negative cell wall stain pink*

Gram-negative bacteria have a special *lipopolysaccharide* (LPS) in their outer membrane, absent in Gram-positive bacteria. This is an *endotoxin* and invokes an immune response in humans. This outer membrane provides

Gram-negative bacteria with some protection from antibiotics, while Gram-positive bacteria are generally more vulnerable to antibiotics.

### Flagellar propulsion in bacteria

Some bacteria have *flagella* and are motile. The flagellum is a filament composed of three strands of the flagellin protein wound in a helix and inserted into a hook anchored by a *basal body*.

*Basal body* is an organelle formed from a centriole and an array of microtubules. It is capable of 360° rotation, causing the cell to spin and move forward. A motor powered by a proton (or sodium) gradient provides the energy.

Eukaryotic flagella are composed of *microtubules* with motion powered by ATP hydrolysis.

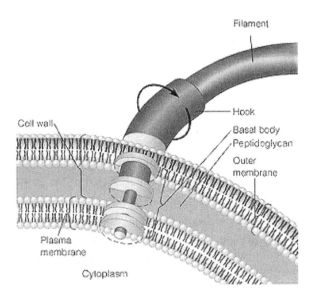

*Flagellum for a Gram-negative bacteria passing through the outer membrane*

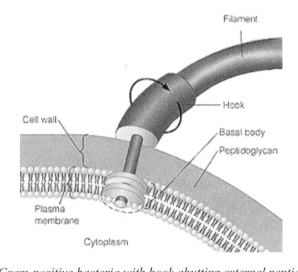

*Flagellum for a Gram-positive bacteria with hook abutting external peptidoglycan cell wall*

## Fimbriae and pili

Prokaryotes may have short, hair-like filaments or appendages called *fimbriae* extending from their surface, attaching to cells or inanimate objects.

Fimbriae of *Neisseria gonorrhoeae* allow it to attach to human host cells and cause gonorrhea.

*Pili* are similar appendages to fimbriae, but they are thicker and fewer in number. They help bacteria adhere to one another for motility or the exchange of genetic material.

## Prokaryotic Cell: Growth and Physiology

**Binary fission**

Prokaryotes reproduce by *binary fission*, a form of *asexual reproduction* which results in offspring with genetically identical chromosomes.

*Binary fission* in prokaryotes is similar to *mitosis in eukaryotes* because each process results in daughter cells identical to the parental cell. However, cell division is a routine part of the growth process that produces and repairs cells in multicellular fungi, plants, and animals. In contrast, binary fission is the method of prokaryotic reproduction. Eukaryotic cells have a spindle apparatus required for distributing chromosomes to daughter cells during mitosis, while prokaryotes divide without microtubules, spindles, or centrioles.

*E. coli* bacteria divide in about 20 minutes, while eukaryotic cells may require an hour or a day.

Binary fission follows the sequence:

1.  Before division, the single, circular DNA chromosome is replicated and attached to a special site tethered to the plasma membrane.

2.  The two chromosomes separate as the cell enlarges and pulls them apart.

3.  When the cell is approximately twice its original length, the plasma membrane grows inward. A new polysaccharide cell wall (cell plate) bisects the cell, and the plasma membrane forms, dividing the cell into two roughly equal-sized daughter cells.

**Genetic adaptability and antibiotic resistance**

*Prokaryotes* evolved to live in various environments because they have a high degree of genetic adaptability, allowing species to differ in acquiring and utilizing energy. There are many sources for *genetic variation* in prokaryotes. Mutations are rapidly generated and distributed through a population because prokaryotes have a short generation time (e.g., 20-minute intervals).

Prokaryotes are haploid (1N, single copy of a gene), so mutations are immediately subjected to natural selection.

Additionally, plasmids (extrachromosomal circular pieces of DNA) can carry genes for antibiotic resistance and transfer them between bacteria (e.g., transformation and conjugation).

**Exponential growth**

The growth of bacteria can be modeled with phases.

*Lag phase* is when bacteria adapt to their environment; the cells are maturing but not yet dividing.

*Log phase* is when bacteria grow exponentially by binary fission in a medium with adequate space and nutrients. The *rate of population growth doubles* with each consecutive period (e.g., 20-minute intervals). However, this cannot continue indefinitely.

*Stationary phase* is when food and space become scarce, *growth slows*, and *plateaus*.

*Death* or *decline phase* is when there is a lack of nutrients or improper conditions, and bacteria perish.

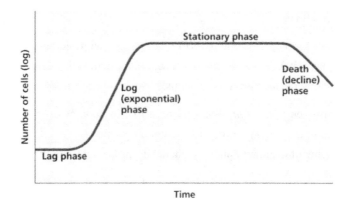

*Bacterial growth with a log phase before reaching a stationary phase*

**Anaerobic and aerobic organisms**

Bacteria species differ in their need for and tolerance of oxygen ($O_2$).

*Obligate anaerobes* cannot grow in the presence of $O_2$; this includes the species of anaerobic bacteria of the *Clostridium* genus that cause botulism, gas gangrene, and tetanus.

*Obligate aerobes* must have $O_2$ for growth and die without it.

*Facultative anaerobes* can grow in the presence or absence of gaseous $O_2$, although they grow better with $O_2$.

*Autotroph* (i.e., a "producer") is an organism capable of self-nourishment; autotrophic prokaryotes include photoautotrophs and chemoautotrophs.

*Photoautotrophs* are photosynthetic and use light energy to assemble the organic molecules required. Although the most well-recognized photoautotrophs are plants, many bacteria are in this category.

*Primitive photosynthesizing bacteria* (green sulfur bacteria and purple sulfur bacteria) use bacteriochlorophyll and hydrogen sulfide ($H_2S$) as proton and electron donors instead of $H_2O$, so they *do not* release $O_2$.

*Advanced photosynthesizing bacteria*, such as cyanobacteria, use bacteriochlorophyll and chlorophylls found in plants. $H_2O$ is used as the proton and electron donor, releasing $O_2$.

*Chemoautotrophs* make organic molecules by using energy derived from the oxidation of inorganic compounds in the environment. Deep ocean hydrothermal vents provide $H_2S$ and allow for the growth of chemosynthetic bacteria. Methanogens (archaea) include chemosynthetic bacteria that produce methane ($CH_4$) from hydrogen gas and $CO_2$. ATP synthesis and $CO_2$ reduction are linked to this reaction, and methanogens can decompose animal wastes to produce electricity as an environmentally-friendly energy source.

*Nitrifying bacteria* oxidize ammonia to nitrites ($NH_3$ to $NO_2$) and nitrites to nitrates ($NO_2$ to $NO_3$).

*Heterotrophs* cannot synthesize their food. Most free-living bacteria are *chemoheterotrophs* that take in pre-formed organic nutrients. There is likely no organic molecule that some prokaryotic species cannot break down with numerous aerobic *saprotrophs* (i.e., organisms that feed on the dead organic matter and use oxygen).

*Decomposers* recycle substances in the ecosystem by degrading dead organic matter and making it available to photosynthesizers.

**Parasitic and symbiotic bacteria**

Some bacteria are *symbiotic*, forming close, long-term relationships with members of other species, including *mutualistic* (each organism benefits), *commensalism* (one benefits, and the other is unaffected), and *parasitic* (one organism benefits while the other is harmed) relationships.

- Mutualistic nitrogen-fixing *Rhizobium* bacteria live in nodules on the roots of soybean, clover, and alfalfa, reducing nitrogen to ammonia, which the plant requires. *Rhizobium* bacteria use some of the plant's photosynthetically-produced organic molecules in return.

- Mutualistic bacteria that live in the intestines of humans benefit from partially-digested material and release vitamins K and $B_{12}$, which humans use for blood components.

- Mutualistic prokaryotes, in the stomachs of cows and goats, digest cellulose, which the animal cannot do by itself, and release nutrients that the cow or goat can use. The bacteria get a warm, moist environment and a constant food supply.

- Mutualistic cyanobacteria provide organic nutrients to fungi, and the fungus protects and supplies inorganic nutrients to the bacteria. This composite symbiotic organism is a *lichen*.

- Commensalistic bacteria live in (or on) organisms of other species and cause them no harm and no benefit, such as some bacterial species that live on the skin of humans.

- Parasitic bacteria (e.g., chlamydia, Cryptosporidium) are responsible for infectious plant and animal diseases.

**Chemotaxis**

Cells can engage in mechanical activities: they can move, and the organelles within them can move.

*Cell migration* is the movement of cells from one location to another and is often the response to stimuli.

*Chemotaxis* is movement in response to chemicals.

For example, bacteria may swim toward the highest concentration of food molecules (*positive chemotaxis*) and flee from the poisons they detect in their environment (*negative chemotaxis*). They can do this by sensing chemical gradients through transmembrane receptors that bind attractants (or repellents), and these receptors stimulate the rotation of flagella, causing the bacteria to move.

Prokaryotes may engage in *phototaxis*, which is movable in response to light. Additionally, some prokaryotes can move in response to physical forces in their environment. This ability to respond to force is *mechanotaxis*.

## Prokaryotic Cell: Genetics

### Plasmids as extragenomic DNA

*Plasmids* are DNA apart from the genomic DNA in some prokaryotes. Plasmids are generally circular, although examples of linear plasmids are known. They usually carry beneficial genes but are not always essential for growth and survival. They range from less than one kilobase (i.e., a thousand nucleotides) to several megabase.

Plasmids replicate independently of the genomic DNA, are inherited, and can be extracted in genetic engineering procedures as vectors to carry foreign DNA into bacteria.

*Episomes* are plasmids that can incorporate themselves into the bacterial chromosome.

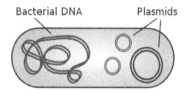

*Bacterium with double-stranded, circular chromosomal DNA and extranuclear plasmids*

### Conjugation

*Conjugation* transfers genetic material between bacteria via a temporary *sex pilus* joining a recipient bacterium.

*Conjugative pili* (sex pili) are the tubes used by bacteria during conjugation to pass replicated DNA between cells. A plasmid is sent from donor to recipient through the sex pilus, where it can be incorporated through recombination. Plasmids can contain antibiotic resistance genes so that conjugation may transfer that resistance.

The most well-studied example is the sex pilus of *E. coli,* which possesses an *F plasmid,* an *episome* (e.g., plasmid) that contains the "fertility factor."

Since an F plasmid is an *episome*, genomic DNA may be transferred. If the F plasmid is transferred to an F⁻ recipient and integrated successfully, the recipient becomes F⁺ and creates its sex pili. Conjugation can occur between bacteria of the same species, closely related species, or distantly related species.

Conjugation is an important mechanism of horizontal gene transfer, contributing to the genetic diversity of prokaryotes.

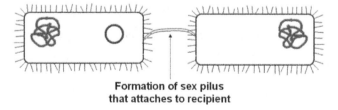

**Formation of sex pilus
that attaches to recipient**

*Bacterial conjugation: donor (with plasmid) is on the left, and the recipient is on the right*

**Transformation of bacterial genomes**

*Transformation* is the process of bacteria taking up DNA fragments from outside the cell and incorporating them into their genomes. There are two major sources of these fragments:

DNA secreted by live bacteria and DNA released from a bacterium that dies.

DNA spills into the environment when cells lyse (i.e., rupture).

Transformation of DNA fragments containing an antibiotic-resistant gene (i.e., plasmid) confers antibiotic resistance to the recipient bacterium.

**Transposons**

*Transposons* (*transposable elements* or *jumping genes*) are segments of chromosomal DNA that can insert into another region in the genome.

Transposons were proposed by cytogeneticist Barbara McClintock (1902-1992) during her research on maize (*corn*) during the 1940s and 50s. Established scientists criticized and shunned her data interpretations. She received an *unshared* Nobel Prize in 1983 for discovering transposons and elucidating mechanisms for genetic changes influencing protein expression.

Transposons exist in prokaryotes and eukaryotes and move within or between chromosomes.

Changes in the genome caused by transposon relocation can be advantageous (e.g., phenotypic advantage), disadvantageous (e.g., proto-oncogenes → oncogenes), or neutral (e.g., intron mutations).

Some transposons make copies inserted into other locations in the genome ("*copy and paste*").

Other transposons excise and migrate from the original location in DNA and insert into another ("*cut and paste*").

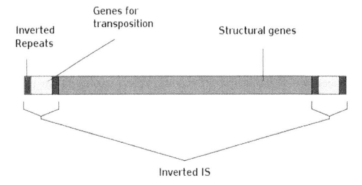

*Bacterial DNA transposon flanked by inverted repeats as breakpoints on the DNA*

## Gene Expression Controls in Prokaryotes

**Gene expression**

*Gene expression* involves *transcription* (DNA → RNA) and *translation* (RNA → proteins).

Gene expression is different in eukaryotes and prokaryotes. Eukaryotes regulate gene expression at several levels, including *transcription, post-transcription, translation*, and *post-translation*.

Prokaryotes regulate gene expression predominantly at the *transcription level*.

Eukaryotes have *transcription factors*, but much regulation of gene expression occurs at other levels.

In prokaryotes, gene regulation primarily consists of actions by transcription factors, which are proteins with *DNA-binding domains* that affect transcription.

For example, *RNA splicing* of the mRNA transcript, which occurs in eukaryotes, can alter the RNA in ways (alternative splicing) to translate a different protein. RNA splicing does *not* occur in prokaryotes because prokaryotes do not have introns.

However, prokaryotes do have some regulations at the translation level. In prokaryotes, mRNA transcripts with a more accurate *Shine-Dalgarno sequence*, which attracts ribosome binding, are translated readily.

Eukaryotes, however, make *modifications to mRNA* (primary transcript → mRNA) to regulate translation, such as the 5' cap or 3' poly−A tail (which do not occur in prokaryotic mRNA).

**Transcription and translation coupling**

*Transcription-translation coupling* in prokaryotes occurs during translation as the mRNA is being transcribed. It does not occur in eukaryotes because the modification of the RNA transcripts into mature mRNA occurs in the nucleus and translation in the cytoplasm, requiring transport of the mRNA out of the nucleus before translation.

Prokaryotes do not have these physical restrictions since they have no membrane-enclosed nucleus and RNA processing, so transcription and translation can occur concurrently.

**Attenuation**

*Attenuation* is a form of *gene regulation* in prokaryotes using *transcription-translation coupling*.

*Attenuator* is a chromosomal nucleotide sequence that can cause *premature termination* of transcription of a gene based on ribosome activity.

One example of attenuation is the *trp* operon, a collection of genes encoding components used to synthesize the amino acid tryptophan. The attenuation mechanism causes transcription to *terminate when tryptophan levels are high*, allowing the bacterium to conserve resources.

Early in the *trp* operon, a unique sequence is exceptionally high in codons specifying tryptophan.

When tryptophan levels are *low*, the ribosome stalls the translation of RNA high in tryptophan codons since there is insufficient tryptophan amino acids for polypeptide synthesis.

When tryptophan levels are high, the ribosome quickly translates along this RNA. Once it translates a certain distance, interactions in the mRNA transcript cause a stem-loop to form, including the attenuator sequence. This loop acts as a *stop signal*; it interacts with the RNA polymerase, causing it to *terminate transcription*.

Because the ribosome stalls, a different stem-loop forms—one without the attenuator sequence. This stem-loop does not act as a stop signal and allows RNA polymerase to transcribe the operon without being terminated.

### High level of tryptophan

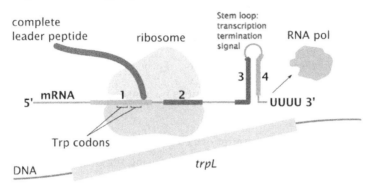

*Attenuation in the trp gene; stem-loop formation depends on tryptophan levels. High levels of tryptophan inhibit gene expression, and polypeptide transcription is terminated.*

### Low level of tryptophan

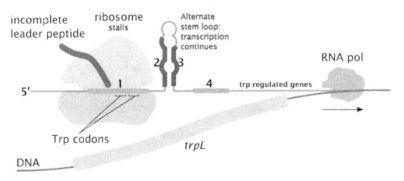

*Attenuation in the trp gene; stem-loop formation depends on tryptophan levels. Low levels of tryptophan induce gene expression, and the complete polypeptide is transcribed.*

## Jacob–Monod *lac* operon

Bacteria do not always require the same enzymes, and they produce enzymes as needed. In 1965, Nobel Prize microbiologists Francois Jacob (1920-2013) and Jacques Monod (1910-1976) were recognized for their *operon model* for regulating gene expression in prokaryotes.

*Operons* are a functional collection of DNA regulatory sequences and genes collectively to regulate transcription.

In the operon model, several genes encoding for enzymes in a metabolic pathway are a nucleotide sequence on a chromosome; the expression of structural genes is controlled by the same regulatory genes, including a single promoter.

Operons have:

- *Promoter*: DNA sequence where RNA polymerase binds to initiate transcription

- *Operator*: a sequence of DNA blocking RNA polymerase when repressor protein is bound

- *Structural genes*: DNA sequences encoding for related proteins; operons typically encode for *enzymes* (i.e., proteins acting as catalysts) in their structural genes

- *Regulatory genes* (or *regulators*): regions within (or outside) the operon that encodes for repressor proteins or activator proteins, regulating the attachment of RNA polymerase to the promoter.

  Repressor proteins bind to the operator to block RNA polymerase from attaching to the start site of transcription. Activators and repressors are *transcription factors*.

*Transcription factors* are proteins that bind to DNA sequences (*enhancers* or *silencers*) to affect transcription.

*Activator transcription factors* bind to *enhancers* to increase transcription, while *repressor transcription factors* bind to silencers to decrease transcription.

*Enhancers* and *silencers* in prokaryotes are near the core promoter (i.e., a minimal portion of promoter required for transcription initiation). They are part of the extended promoter (a sequence upstream of the gene with additional regulatory elements).

*Operator* in an operon is essentially a silencer because it decreases transcription when a repressor binds it.

The terms *co-repressor* and *co-activator* describe molecules that bind to activators and repressors, changing their shape to affect how well they can bind DNA and thus affect transcription. They function by activating inactive proteins or inactivating active proteins. They are named for their effect on transcription: *co-repressors* decrease transcription, and *co-activators* increase transcription.

In *lac* operons, lactose works as a co-activator by *inactivating* a repressor. When a co-repressor binds to its target, the resulting complex becomes an active repressor *or* an inactive activator, decreasing transcription.

When a co-activator binds to its target, the resulting complex becomes an active activator or inactive repressor, which increases transcription.

In this example, the lactose molecule is an *inducer*, and the inducer-repressor complex is a *co-inducer*.

*Notes for active learning*

# CHAPTER 8

# Biological Molecules

- Water

- Macromolecules

- Proteins

- Lipids as Organic Molecules

- Metabolism of Fatty Acids

- Carbohydrates

- Nucleotides and Nucleic Acids

## Water

### Molecular formula of water

Water is vital for life on Earth but is an inorganic molecule due to its lack of carbon.

A molecule of water contains one oxygen atom covalently bonded to two hydrogen atoms in a bent conformation because of the two lone pairs of electrons on the oxygen atom.

$$\overset{\delta^-}{O}$$
$$\overset{\delta^+}{H} \quad \overset{\delta^+}{H}$$

Due to oxygen's electronegativity, bonding electrons are concentrated near this central atom, giving oxygen a partial negative charge on oxygen and a partial positive charge on hydrogen.

This unequal sharing of electrons makes water a polar molecule.

### Significance of water for living systems

The first cells evolved in water and incorporated water into their living systems; today, organisms are 70–90% water.

Water is liquid between 0 °C and 100 °C, which is critical since it serves as the solvent of living organisms.

The polarity of waters allows it to dissolve ionic, polar, or semi-polar molecules.

This solubility allows substances such as nutrients to be carried in the blood and is a suitable medium for metabolic reactions.

The evaporation of water cools plants and animals. These organisms allow heat (i.e., energy) to break hydrogen bonds as water molecules evaporate and release energy into the air.

### Hydrogen bonding between water molecules

Water can form four hydrogen bonds: one at each hydrogen atom and two at lone pairs of electrons on the oxygen atom.

When water molecules form hydrogen bonds, they create strong intermolecular forces that give water characteristic properties.

*One hydrogen bond (dash line) between water molecules. Two hydrogen bond acceptors from each lone pair of electrons on partial negative oxygen and two hydrogen bond donors from each partial positive hydrogen*

Hydrogen bonds are responsible for water's cohesive and adhesive properties.

*Cohesion* is water's tendency to stick due to hydrogen bonding. The strong cohesion between water molecules produces a high *surface tension*, measured by breaking a liquid's surface. Water's high surface tension helps cell membranes from collapsing and allows insects to walk on water.

*Adhesion* is water's ability to attract other polar molecules. Adhesion and cohesion work together so water can "climb" against gravity up a thin glass tube, the vascular tissues of a plant, or an animal's blood vessels.

This *capillary action* of adhesion is an essential process of life.

The oxygen of water ($H_2O$, shown below) has two bonding and two non-bonding domains. The water molecule experiences electron repulsion from the two lone pairs on its bonds.

The water molecule adopts a bent shape (see the previous chart) to minimize the van der Waals repulsion of the negatively charged electrons.

*A water molecule ($H_2O$) is bent due to the two lone pairs of $e^-$ on oxygen*

## Physical properties of water

*Physical properties* are quantitative measures of a substance that can be determined without permanently altering the substance.

For example, the boiling point of water is a physical property because the water condenses (i.e., the reverse process of boiling) to form a liquid.

Water has a high *heat capacity*, as the degree to which a substance changes the temperature in response to the gain or loss of heat.

The temperature of a large body of water is stable in response to temperature (average kinetic energy of a molecule) changes of the surrounding air.

Since water can hold more heat, its temperature falls slower than other liquids; this moderates Earth's surface temperature and protects organisms from rapid temperature changes.

Heat capacity is reflected in the *heat of vaporization,* the amount of energy required to boil a substance (change from liquid to a gaseous state).

Water has an unusually high boiling point due to the many strong intermolecular hydrogen bonding.

At standard pressure, water boils at 100 °C because a high amount of heat is needed to break the hydrogen bonds. The high boiling point of water is vital for life on Earth.

If the water boiled at a lower temperature, the water in organisms would boil, and they would not survive.

Water has a high *heat of fusion*, the energy required to melt from its solid state.

This makes Earth's ice caps resistant to sudden and frequent melting. Unlike most other substances, the solid (ice) exhibits a density lower than the liquid (water).

As water freezes, its hydrogen bonds become rigid and push apart, expanding the water and settling it into a crystal pattern at 0 °C.

The large air spaces between molecules lower the density of ice and allow it to float in liquid water. Because of this property, bodies of water freeze from the top down.

If ice were denser than water, it would sink, and ponds would freeze solid.

Water becoming less dense as it freezes is beneficial to organisms; as ice forms at the surface, it insulates the water underneath, maintaining a hospitable environment for aquatic organisms. The ice does not sink and remains deep in the body of water, which, over time, would pose an issue for organisms as the ambient temperature decreases.

**Chemical properties of water**

*Chemical properties* are not observable without altering a substance in a chemical reaction.

Water is a universal solvent that dissolves a great number of solutes.

This is possible because of water's polarity, causing it to attract charged (or polar substances), associating around the individual molecules, and breaking the aggregation of the solute.

Ionized or polar molecules attracted to water are *hydrophilic.*

Non-ionized and nonpolar molecules that cannot attract water are *hydrophobic*.

Water is a reactant and product in many chemical reactions, outside of and within living systems.

Water is an *amphoteric* substance; it can act as an acid or a base.

A water molecule acts as a base by accepting a hydrogen ion; a second water molecule acts as an acid.

## Macromolecules

### Biomolecules

*Biomolecules* are the molecules of life on Earth. Except for trace minerals, biomolecules are *organic molecules*, compounds containing carbon. *Inorganic molecules* such as water and salts are not classified as biomolecules but are significant components in life processes.

Carbon is the essential element of life because of its bonding capabilities and versatility. It has four valence (outer shell) electrons in the highest energy level of the electron shells surrounding the nucleus, allowing it to form up to 4 bonds with other atoms. Other elements can form 4 (or more) bonds, but they are larger and cannot fit into the incredible variety of configurations that carbon atoms can.

Along with carbon, the abundant elements in living organisms are hydrogen, nitrogen, and oxygen.

Together these elements comprise 95% of the weight of the body. Elements sulfur, calcium, and potassium make up the remaining 5%.

### Monomers and polymers

*Monomers* are small organic molecules. They are assembled into *polymers,* repeating chains of monomer subunits. Polymers are characterized as *macromolecules,* large organic molecules.

Polymers are formed by a *dehydration synthesis* (condensation reactions).

Monomers are joined by removing $H_2O$ by a hydroxyl group (–OH) from one molecule and hydrogen from the other. Therefore, water is a byproduct of dehydration synthesis reactions.

*Hydrolysis* disassembles polymers into monomers, which involves the addition of water to cleave the long-chain molecule.

There are four classes of macromolecules: proteins (comprised of amino acids), nucleic acids (comprised of nucleotides), lipids (often comprised of glycerol and fatty acids), and carbohydrates (comprised of sugars).

### Organic macromolecules

| Polymer | % Dry weight (liver cell) | Monomer | Examples | Function |
|---------|---------------------------|---------|----------|----------|
| Proteins | 72% | Amino acids | Enzymes, antibodies, peptide hormones | Catalysis, signaling, structure, transport, motility, immunity |
| Nucleic Acids | 8% | Nucleotides | DNA, RNA | Storage and expression of heredity |
| Lipids | 13% | Glycerol and fatty acids | Fatty acids, fats, oils, steroids | Energy, signaling, membranes, insulation |
| Polysaccharides | 7% | Monosaccharides | Simple sugars, carbohydrates | Energy, cell structure |

## Proteins

### General functions of proteins in living systems

Proteins are the most abundant macromolecules in living organisms and serve various functions. This includes structural support of cells and tissues, transport of molecules across cell membranes and throughout the body, hormone signaling, movement, and immune defense.

Many proteins are *enzymes,* which act as organic catalysts to speed up chemical reactions within cells.

### Amino acids as the building blocks of proteins

*Amino acids* are the organic monomers from which proteins are constructed. There are 20 different amino acids common in living organisms. Like organic molecules, amino acids have a carbon backbone. The *alpha carbon* is bonded to four other groups: a hydrogen atom, a *carboxyl group* (–COOH), an *amino group* (–NH₂), and an *R group.* The R group, or *side chain*, differentiates the amino acids.

Amino acids join via dehydration condensation (or dehydration synthesis), when the *amino terminus* (–NH₂) of one amino acid joins with the *carboxyl terminus* (–COOH) of the other, forming a *peptide bond.* Several amino acids linked by peptide bonds create a polymer, the *polypeptide.* A protein may consist of one or several polypeptides arranged together.

### Peptide bond is rigid for protein conformation

The peptide bond has the carbonyl O and H pointed in opposite directions (i.e., up and down).

The peptide bond is rigid due to a partial double bond character with the lone pair of electrons on N resonating for the carbonyl carbon.

Peptide bond

### Protein shape determines function

A protein molecule contains carbon, hydrogen, oxygen and nitrogen, and sometimes other elements such as sulfur.

Proteins are often structured around other molecules and ions, which help them function or maintain their overall shape.

A functional protein consists of one or more polypeptides that have been twisted, folded, and coiled into a unique shape. The order of the amino acids guides the three-dimensional conformation of the protein.

Protein shape is an essential component of the protein's function in the organism.

## Protein classification

Globular proteins and fibrous proteins are the two main structural classes of proteins. *Globular proteins* fold into a compact, roughly spherical shape. They are somewhat water-soluble since they have polar amino acid side chains on their surface. Nonpolar side chains are arranged in the interior of the protein, away from water. Globular proteins may act as enzymes, hormones, membrane proteins, transporters, and immune responders. Some globular proteins are assembled into larger protein complexes with a structural function.

*Fibrous proteins* are structural proteins with long, thread-like structures strong and durable. Fibrous proteins are elongated rather than spherical and, unlike globular proteins, are not water-soluble. They provide structure, strength, and flexibility to intracellular and extracellular components. For example, fibrous proteins are used in cell walls and connective tissue between organs.

*Membrane proteins* interact with biological membranes, and they are extremely important for the survival of organisms. They move molecules across the membrane or relay signals between the intra and extracellular environment.

*Integral* membrane proteins span the membrane and are permanently attached, while *peripheral* membrane proteins are on one side or the other and are temporarily attached. Pumps, channels, and receptors are examples of membrane proteins.

Protein modifications

Proteins may be modified into *conjugated proteins* by adding non-protein molecules. For example, a *lipoprotein* is a lipid-bound to protein, while a *glycoprotein* is a carbohydrate bound to protein.

Proteins may be bound as *chromoproteins* (pigment molecules), *nucleoproteins* (nucleic acids), *metalloproteins* (metal ions), and many others.

*Cofactors* are non-protein molecules.

Organic cofactors are *coenzymes,* while inorganic cofactors tend to be metal ions.

A *prosthetic group* is a cofactor that is tightly bound to the protein. For example, *heme proteins* (e.g., hemoglobin) are transporter proteins that require a prosthetic group such as *heme.* This small metalorganic compound helps hemeproteins bind molecules such as oxygen. Because metal is involved, hemeproteins are classified as metalloproteins.

## Primary structure of proteins

The *primary structure* (1°) of a protein is the linear sequence of amino acids. This is determined by the DNA sequence of the gene that encodes the protein. A change of a single amino acid alters the primary structure and often the function of the protein. For example, sickle cell anemia is caused by the mutation of a single amino acid (substituting valine for glutamic acid at position 6) in hemoglobin.

## Secondary structure of proteins as motifs

The *secondary structure* (2°) involves the interactions between nearby amino acids in the primary structure. It describes how initial three-dimensional patterns such as coiling and folding arise from these interactions. The secondary structure is dependent on hydrogen bonding between portions of the amino acid backbone. It does not involve covalent or ionic bonds and excludes interactions between the side chains.

The two major secondary structures are alpha helices and beta-pleated sheets. These result from hydrogen bonds between regions of the peptide chain.

The *alpha helix* is a coiling, cylindrical pattern formed from hydrogen bonds between the partially positive carbonyl (−C=O) of one amino acid and the partially negative amine (−N−H) of another, four positions away. The number and positioning of the hydrogen bonds give the α-helix strength and flexibility. The peptide backbone coils around the axis of the helix, while the amino acid side chains (R groups) project outwards.

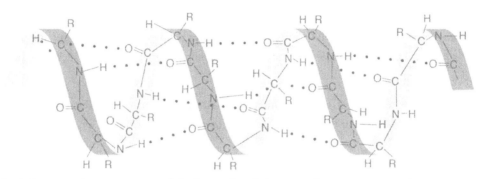

*Alpha helix secondary structure with hydrogen bonds between the amino group of one amino acid and the carbonyl group of another four residues (amino acids) away*

The *beta-pleated sheet* (β sheet) is a pleated ribbon of amino acids. It is planar rather than cylindrical.

Hydrogen bonds form between peptide bonds in adjacent polypeptide chain regions as *β strands*. This forms an organized network that folds into pleats.

Adjacent β strands may be running in the same direction (e.g., moving from the amino end to the carboxyl end), which are *parallel.*

However, β-pleated sheets can be *antiparallel* if the β strands are aligned in opposite directions.

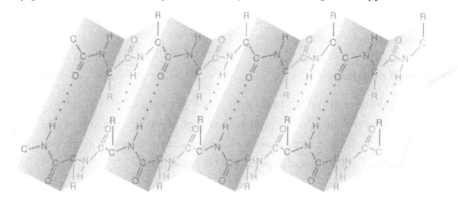

*β-pleated sheets as antiparallel with hydrogen bonds between the sheets*

When ionic bonds form between side chains and interrupt repetitive hydrogen bonding, irregular regions of *loop conformations* may occur.

**Tertiary structure with proline, cysteine and hydrophobic bonding**

*Tertiary structure* arises when secondary structures interact and form a three-dimensional conformation.

Unlike a secondary structure, tertiary structure is due to interactions between side chains of amino acids rather than the peptide backbone.

These interactions may be ionic bonds, covalent bonds, hydrophobic interactions, hydrophilic interactions (hydrogen bonds), or van der Waals' forces. The aqueous environment strongly influences the tertiary structure since it affects hydrophobic and hydrophilic interactions.

Most forces stabilizing tertiary structures are relatively weak except the *disulfide bridges* (covalent bonds). These bonds form between two cysteine side chain*s,* one of the 20 amino acids.

Cysteine has a sulfhydryl group that bonds with another cysteine's sulfhydryl and create a covalent disulfide bridge (−S−S−).

*Proline*, an amino acid with a ring structure, is another significant tertiary structure component. This amino acid is rigid and does not bend to accommodate other amino acids, causing kinks in the protein chain.

**Quaternary structure of proteins**

All proteins have a primary structure, and most have a secondary structure and tertiary structure.

However, specific large proteins have a *quaternary structure,* arranging multiple protein polypeptide chains into a multi-unit complex. For example, *collagen* is a fibrous protein of three polypeptides supercoiled like a rope. This provides structural strength for collagen's role in connective tissue.

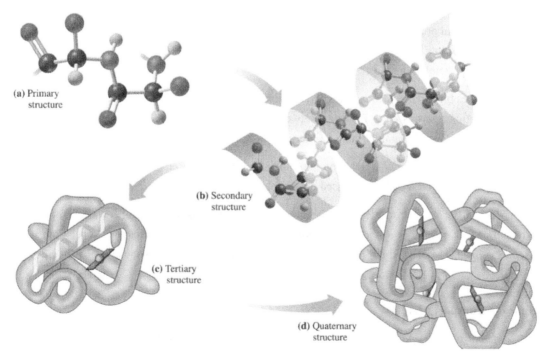

*Hemoglobin: an example of a four-subunit protein. Proteins have primary, secondary, and tertiary structures. Proteins can have 2 or more polypeptide chains (e.g., hemoglobin has 2 alpha and 2 beta chains)*

In quaternary structure, protein subunits are held by the same interactions (i.e., hydrophobic, ionic, or covalent disulfide bridges) that stabilize the tertiary structure of a single protein.

A protein with two subunits is a *dimer*, a protein with three is a *trimer,* and a protein with four is a *tetramer*. The naming of quaternary structures proceeds in this way.

Protein polypeptide chains may be identical or different, as in hemoglobin, a tetramer of two alpha chains and two beta chains.

### Denaturation of proteins disrupts their function

*Denaturation* is a process that disrupts the attractive stabilizing forces in the secondary, tertiary, or quaternary structure (but not the covalent bonds between individual amino acids or disulfide bonds of −S−S−) of a protein. When a protein is denatured, its primary structure does not change, but its overall structure is unraveled, and it becomes dysfunctional.

Changes in pH, salt concentration, temperature, or other conditions may denature a protein.

For example, proteins become denatured if they are transferred to an organic solvent such as urea or acetone. This is because organic solvents are hydrophobic, inducing the protein to refold so that its hydrophobic regions now face the organic solvent.

Heat denatures proteins because it imparts energy to break the weak hydrogen bond interactions that maintain the conformation, so organisms strive to maintain stable body temperature. Changes in pH can change the R groups' polarity (ionization), disrupt an enzyme's function, or unravel it entirely.

### Protein function by binding to receptors

An essential property of proteins is the ability to bind to other molecules. A *binding site* is a position on a protein that binds to a ligand (molecule associated with the protein). The ligand is generally small and binds specifically to a protein's shape.

Enzymes bind to ligand *substrates* and convert them into products. Proteins may utilize binding for non-enzymatic functions. In this case, the bond between the ligand and the protein is typically non-covalent and reversible. The binding of a ligand usually initiates a conformational change in a protein.

*Affinity* is the degree to which a protein binds a particular ligand. Proteins often exhibit high *selectivity* and bind one ligand or class of ligands based on complementary shapes.

*Receptor proteins* are typically on the outer surface of the plasma membrane, where they bind to ligands. The ligand acts as a *signal molecule.* The binding of a ligand induces the release of other molecules (second messengers) inside the cell, which relay the signal and produce a cellular response to the ligand (e.g., peptide hormone).

### Membrane transport proteins

*Membrane transport proteins* are transmembrane proteins that coordinate the passive or active movement of specific molecules across the membrane. These proteins allow a particular molecule (or class of molecules) to pass through, contributing to the *selective permeability* of the plasma membrane.

Membrane transport proteins may be *channel proteins* or *carrier proteins.*

*Ligand-gated ion channels* are a group of channel proteins that utilize non-enzymatic binding to open their gates. Ligand-gated ion channels are similar to receptor proteins in that they bind a signal molecule, causing a conformational change in the protein. This change opens the channel and allows ions to pass through the plasma membrane.

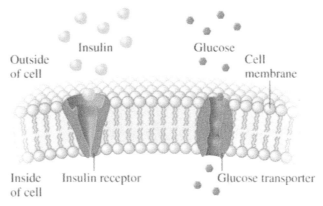

*Transmembrane proteins*

*Carrier proteins*, unlike channel proteins, do not form a continuous pore through the membrane but are open on one side at a time.

For example, a ligand that binds at the extracellular side of the carrier protein induces a conformational change that moves the ligand to the intracellular side and closes the extracellular side. The ligand can be released into the cytoplasm of the cell.

Some transport proteins are free-floating and travel between cells. Hemoglobin, for example, transports oxygen from the lungs to other tissues in the body.

*Cytochromes* (often loosely associated with the inner membrane of the mitochondria and chloroplasts) are another group of hemeproteins that carry electrons for various metabolic processes.

**Proteins as antibodies in the immune system**

*Antibodies* are globular proteins involved in the adaptive immune system, a specialized subset of the immune system which responds to pathogens and antigens (molecules that stimulate an immune response).

Antibodies, *immunoglobulins* (Ig), recognize foreign substances (e.g., viruses) and target them for destruction. They bind to an *antigen* (Ag), a molecule on the invader that signals its identity.

An antibody's secondary structure consists of β-pleated sheets bound tightly. These are arranged into a quaternary structure of four polypeptide subunits.

The structure is held through disulfide bridges between the polypeptide chains as a Y shape.

The stem of the Y is similar in antibodies and can bind to receptors on various cells in the body.

Antibodies bind antigens at the top of each arm of the Y. These antigen-binding sites are specific to the antibody and depend on the individual amino acids within the antibody protein.

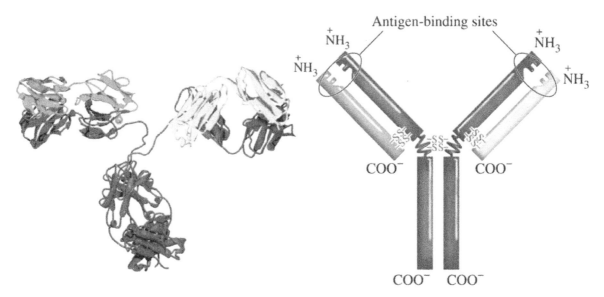

*Antibody structure with ribbon diagram on the left and detailed view of the four polypeptide chains on the right. Each antibody has a similar shape with two heavy chains and two light chains. The binding site for an antigen is in the variable region at the ends (arms of Y shape)*

**Motor proteins transport vesicles within the cell**

*Motor proteins* convert chemical energy into mechanical work and allow cellular motility by generating forces and torque in the cell.

Motor proteins typically have a complex quaternary structure.

*Myosin* and *actin* are motor proteins in muscle cells where they drive muscle contraction.

*Kinesins* and *dyneins* are two common classes of motor proteins, used for transporting materials within a cell and orchestrating chromosome separation during mitosis and meiosis.

Dynein transports towards the negative (−) end.

Kinesin transports toward the positive (+) end of the microtubule.

Dyneins generate the movement of cilia and flagella.

Motor proteins are commonly associated with the *cytoskeleton*, the fibrous network within the cell. They transport molecules by progress along filaments of the cytoskeleton, pulling along vesicles or other proteins. This guided movement is more rapid and targeted than simple diffusion of the substance within the cytoplasm.

**Dietary protein and cellular metabolism of amino groups**

When carbohydrates and fats are unavailable, proteins are used as an energy source. Proteins are the least desirable energy source for the body because a large amount of energy is required for protein breakdown.

*Proteolysis* (protein catabolism) requires proteases to break the peptide bonds of proteins via hydrolysis to release smaller polypeptides or amino acids.

Amino acids can provide intermediates for a variety of other molecules.

Most amino acids are deaminated (the amino group is removed) in the liver and are converted into pyruvate, acetyl-CoA, or other Krebs cycle intermediates. Depending on the amino acid, these intermediates enter cellular respiration at various points.

From dietary intake, protein digestion begins in the stomach, where proteins are denatured (unfolded) by the acidic digestive juices. Digestive enzymes like pepsin, trypsin, and chymotrypsin hydrolyze covalent peptide bonds. Amino acids are absorbed in the small intestine into the bloodstream for delivery to the tissues.

## Keto acids for ATP synthesis

Amino acids can produce ATP when other fuel supplies are low, and the cell does not require other nitrogen-containing compounds.

To produce ATP, the amino acid group must be removed by oxidative deamination to produce a keto acid and $NH_3$ or transferred to a keto acid by *transamination* (transfer of an amino acid group to an organic acid).

The keto acid enters the glycolytic pathway or the synthetic pathways for glucose and fat. The amino group's nitrogen is used to synthesize critical nitrogen-containing molecules such as purines and pyrimidines.

The toxic $NH_3$ (ammonia) passes into the bloodstream through the plasma membrane. It is transported to the liver, linked with $CO_2$ to form, in mammals, the relatively non-toxic urea, excreted by the kidneys. In fish, insects, and birds, ammonia is converted to uric acid rather than urea.

Amino acids may replenish the intermediates in the Krebs cycle.

Three-carbon amino acids (e.g., alanine) enter the pathways as pyruvate.

Four-carbon amino acids (e.g., aspartate) are converted to oxaloacetate.

Five-carbon amino acids (e.g., valine) are converted to α-ketoglutarate.

Some amino acids can enter at more than one point, depending on cellular requirements.

## Essential amino acids

Plants synthesize amino acids as needed; animals lack some enzymes needed to make some amino acids.

Humans synthesize eleven of the twenty necessary amino acids.

The diet must provide the remaining nine amino acids as *essential amino acids*.

The total free amino acid pool in the body is derived from:

1) ingested protein degraded to amino acids during digestion,

2) synthesis of non-essential amino acids from keto acids, and

3) the breakdown of body proteins.

The amino acids in these pools are used for protein biosynthesis.

## Lipids as Organic Molecules

### Lipids include fats, steroids, oils and waxes

*Lipids* are a class of organic molecules that include fats, steroids, oils, and waxes.

Unlike other macromolecules, they are not polymers because they are made of subunits arranged in various configurations, not necessarily chains. Their subunits vary widely and are not classified as monomers.

Because lipids are almost exclusively made of nonpolar covalent bonds, they are hydrophobic and have low reactivity.

### Lipid structure and function

Lipids have a variety of functions in the body. Animals and other mammals use them for high capacity energy storage by packing specialized adipose cells with *fats*.

These *adipose cells* swell and shrink as fat is taken in and discharged. Fat is used for protection and temperature regulation by cushioning organs and insulating the body against heat loss.

*Steroids* are a class of lipids used as hormones, the body's chemical messengers.

*Oils* and *waxes* are mixtures of lipids and chemicals. Many plants and animals secrete them to waterproof and protect cells in the epidermis.

Oil produced by mammals lubricates the hair and provides immune defense.

### Phospholipids in cell membranes

Like proteins, lipids can be conjugated with other groups.

Lipids with a phosphate group are *phospholipids* in cell membranes in conjunction with proteins.

Membranes include *sphingolipids,* lipids with an amino alcohol.

These elements are responsible for the shape and fluidity of membranes.

*Glycolipids,* with a carbohydrate group, are arranged outside on cell membranes for cell recognition.

Other lipid conjugates are important for recognition and signaling.

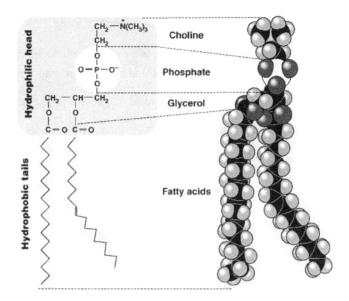

*Phospholipids contain a hydrophobic tail and hydrophilic head. The tail may be saturated or unsaturated. The polar head is often modified (i.e., contains phosphate, carbohydrates or choline) with groups attached to one carbon in the three-carbon glycerol backbone*

## Saturated and unsaturated fatty acids

*Fatty acids* are lipids with a carboxyl group attached to (often) a 16 to 18 carbon skeleton. Fatty acids differ in length based on the number of carbons they contain and the number and locations of double bonds.

If the fatty acid contains no double bonds, it is a *saturated* fatty acid because the carbons are saturated with the maximum number of hydrogens. If any of the carbons form double bonds, the fatty acid becomes *unsaturated*. Saturated fatty acids are straight chains, while unsaturated fatty acids have kinks wherever double bonds are present.

*Saturated fatty acids contain single bonds are often solids at room temperature because the chains pack tightly*

*Unsaturated fatty acids contain double bonds, and the chain becomes "kinked" at the double bond*

**Fatty acids for ATP production**

Free fatty acids are found throughout the body as an energy source since they yield ATP when broken down. However, large quantities of fatty acids are assembled into fats for long-term storage.

In a typical fat molecule, three fatty acids are linked to *glycerol* (three-carbon alcohol).

The glycerol is the backbone of the fat, linked to the three fatty acids by ester linkages.

This structure is a *triglyceride*.

*Glycerol and three fatty acid chains form a triglyceride*

**Steroids as essential molecules**

*Steroids* are cyclic lipids containing a carbon skeleton of four fused rings. The hundreds of steroid classes are differentiated by various functional groups on the rings.

*Sterols* are steroid alcohols widely found in animals, plants, and fungi.

*Cholesterol* is a sterol in animal cell membranes, regulating membrane fluidity.

Despite its infamous association with cardiovascular disease, cholesterol is vital for building and maintaining cell membranes and is an essential precursor to *steroid hormones.*

**Lipids as signals and cofactors**

Many lipids are intra and extracellular signals, which bind to particular proteins.

Steroid hormones travel throughout blood as cell-to-cell messengers.

Receptors on a cell membrane may receive a hormonal signal and release *second messengers* inside the cell to relay the message. Derivatives of sphingolipids are commonly used as second messengers and as cell recognition.

*Phosphatidylinositol* is another class of lipids that act as intracellular signals.

Some lipids act as cofactors for enzymes (e.g., *fat-soluble vitamins*). Humans must intake these vitamins from food or synthesize them from endogenous lipids.

**Fat-soluble vitamins**

There are four fat-soluble vitamins (A, D, E, and K). Vitamin A has many interconverted forms, such as retinol and beta-carotene. These have anti-inflammatory, antioxidant, and immune functions; they function in eye and skin health and are precursors to certain hormones.

Vitamin D has several forms and regulates the uptake of minerals in the small intestine, especially calcium and phosphate.

Vitamin D is limited in edible foods; it is synthesized from cholesterol in the skin or catalyzed by UV radiation. It is vital for the skeletal and immune systems' health and functions as a precursor for hormones.

Vitamins E and K are oxidation-reduction cofactors.

Vitamin E is an antioxidant that protects other vitamins, cell membranes, and free fatty acids from oxidative stress damage (i.e., free radical damage).

Vitamin K catalyzes the production of blood clotting factors and other essential proteins in the bones and kidneys.

**Steroid hormones**

Steroid hormones bind to receptors and trigger gene expression and metabolism changes. Sex hormones (testosterone, estrogen, and progesterone) are examples of steroid hormones.

Another steroid is *cortisol,* produced by the brain's adrenal cortex in response to stress and inflammation.

Cortisol digests macromolecules, regulates electrolyte and water balance and promotes glucose synthesis in response to low blood sugar.

*Aldosterone* is a steroid hormone that regulates kidney function.

**Prostaglandins act as hormones**

*Prostaglandins* are 20-carbon fatty acid derivatives with hormonal functions.

They operate within the *paracrine* and *autocrine* systems, signaling between adjacent cells and signaling within a single cell.

They are produced locally in response to specific signals and may initiate inflammation, clotting or anti-clotting, vasodilation or vasoconstriction, and smooth muscle movement in the gastrointestinal tract and uterus.

Additionally, they affect the wake-sleep cycle (circadian rhythm), the fever response, and the responsiveness of specific tissues to various hormones like glucagon and epinephrine.

## Metabolism of Fatty Acids

### Fatty acids as an energy source

When glucose supply is low, the body uses other energy sources: other carbohydrates, fats, and then proteins. First, these molecules are converted to glucose or glucose intermediates; they are degraded in glycolysis or by the Krebs cycle.

Fatty acids are an essential energy source because they are reduced and anhydrous (hydrophobic), which allows for a higher energy yield. Carbohydrates are hydrated, so the amount of energy stored per unit mass is much lower than fatty acids.

For this reason, it is ideal for an organism to store energy as fat in the adipose tissue when a large quantity of energy needs to be kept in reserve for later use (e.g., hibernating bear).

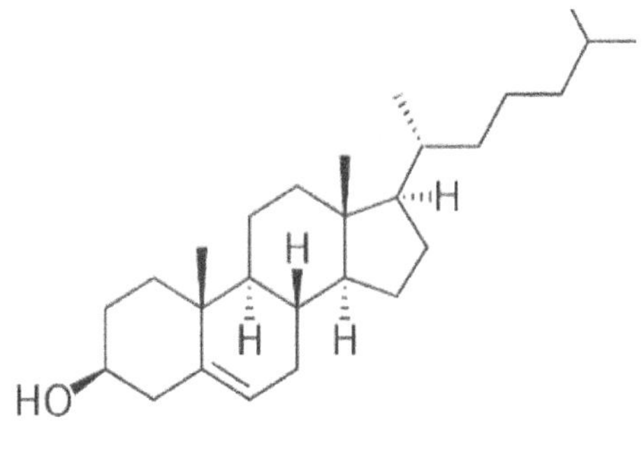

*trans*-Oleic acid

*cis*-Oleic acid

*Cholesterol is a four fused ring structure* 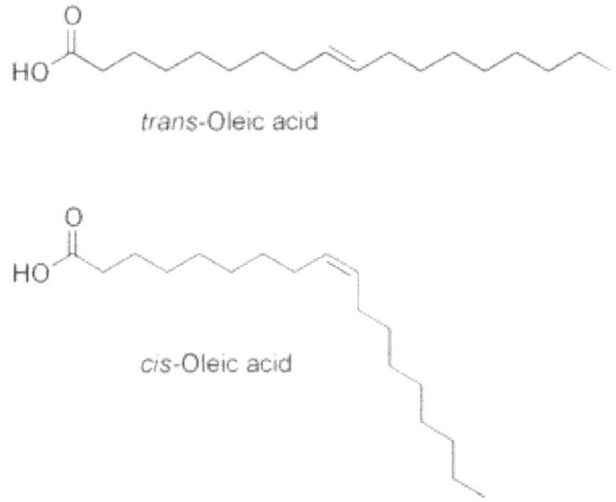          *Cis and trans unsaturated fatty acids*

### Digestion, transport and storage of fats

The pancreatic enzyme lipase breaks down triglycerides into free fatty acids and monoglycerides. Once across the intestinal wall, free fatty acids and monoglycerides are reassembled as triglycerides, while the cholesterol is linked to another free fatty acid, forming a cholesterol ester.

These are repackaged as chylomicrons, lipoproteins that transport triglycerides in the bloodstream and the tissues, where they are used for energy production or are stored. The liver is an essential organ for fatty acid metabolism.

*Adipocytes* are cells where most body fat is stored, as the entire cytoplasm is filled with a single fat droplet. Adipocytes synthesize and store triglycerides during food uptake and cluster to form adipose tissue beneath the skin and around internal organs.

### Beta oxidation of fatty acids

Fatty acids are degraded to produce ATP when glucose supplies are low.

Any duplication (copies, uploads, PDFs) is illegal.

The molecule undergoes β oxidation (beta carbon of the fatty acid is oxidized to a carbonyl group).

In this process, fatty acyl-CoA undergoes oxidation by repeatedly cleaving two-carbon molecules, each time producing a new fatty acyl-CoA that is two carbons shorter, along with one molecule of acetyl-CoA.

β oxidation works best for even-numbered saturated fatty acids due to the repetitive cleaving of two carbons from the chain. Saturated fatty acids produce one NADH and one $FADH_2$ for every two carbons.

The acetyl-CoA produced during β oxidation enters the Krebs cycle, and the typical progression of aerobic cellular respiration occurs. A short eight-carbon fatty acid can produce four acetyl-CoA.

Each acetyl-CoA yields 12 ATP (3 NADP, 1 $FADH_2$, and 1 ATP).

Therefore, this eight-carbon fatty acid nets 48 ATP, and fat with three chains of this length produces 144 ATP, illustrating why fats are an excellent source of energy.

Fats provide 9 calories per gram, while carbohydrates and proteins provide 4 calories per gram each.

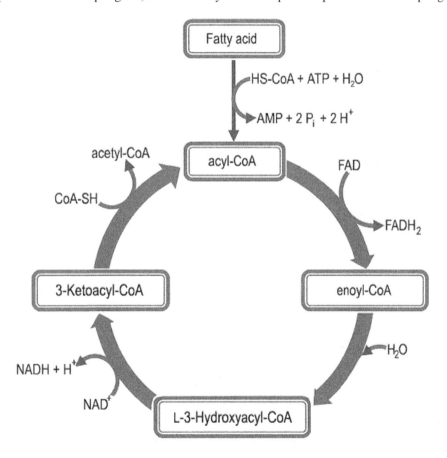

*Each turn of β oxidation produces one NADH and one $FADH_2$,*
*used in the electron transport chain to produce ATP*

## Ketogenesis

Sometimes there is an insufficient supply of glucose in the body (e.g., during fasting). Once the cellular carbohydrate stores have been depleted, the organism must find another way to obtain energy.

*Ketogenesis* is the production of ketone derivatives of acetyl-CoA groups as another form of fatty acid breakdown and occurs in the mitochondria of the liver.

The oxidation of large amounts of fatty acids can cause acetyl-CoA to accumulate in the liver.

If the quantities of acetyl-CoA are high, it may exceed the Krebs cycle's processing capacity. This can occur when excess deaminated ketogenic amino acids are degraded, causing acetyl-CoA buildup. In cases of high acetyl-CoA accumulation, the ketogenesis pathway is initiated.

## Oxidation of fatty acids

In ketogenesis, the two-carbon acetyl units condense in the liver, forming the following four carbon ketone molecules: β-hydroxybutyrate, acetoacetate, and acetone. These are collectively referred to as *ketone bodies.*

These ketone bodies are transferred from the liver to the heart, brain, and muscles. In these organs, β-hydroxybutyrate and acetoacetate are reconverted to acetyl-CoA for entry into the Krebs cycle.

Acetone is converted to pyruvate, lactate, and acetate or excreted as waste if it is not used quickly.

*Ketosis* is when an excessive amount of ketone bodies is present. In this metabolic state, energy comes from ketone bodies in the blood. It occurs during fasting or low-carbohydrate diets and is "fat-burning mode."

If the body fails to regulate ketone production properly, the excessive formation of ketone bodies can cause *ketoacidosis* or *metabolic acidosis* since acetoacetate and *β*-hydroxybutyrate are acidic. In this condition, blood pH is drastically decreased and can sometimes be fatal.

## Lipogenesis and essential fatty acids

When there are excess dietary carbohydrates, the molecules must be converted to fat for storage.

The anabolism of fats primarily occurs in the cytoplasm and the endoplasmic reticulum of liver cells, in contrast with the fatty acid breakdown, which occurs in the mitochondria.

*Lipogenesis* is when fats are produced from acetyl-CoA and malonyl-CoA precursors by fatty acid synthases that polymerize and reduce acetyl groups.

Lipogenesis is stimulated by insulin. The synthesized fatty acids are esterified with glycerol to create triglycerides, and the triglycerides are packaged into lipoproteins and secreted from the liver.

To synthesize an unsaturated fatty acid, a desaturation reaction introduces a double bond into the fatty acyl chain (usually requiring a desaturase enzyme).

*Essential fatty acids* cannot be synthesized in mammalian tissue and are required in the diet.

The essential fatty acids are linolenic acid (omega-3 fatty acid) and linoleic acid (omega-6 fatty acid). If these are not consumed in the diet causing deficiency of essential fatty acids, health problems may develop.

## Carbohydrates

### Classification of carbohydrates

*Carbohydrates* (saccharides, from the Greek word for sugar) are molecules made of carbon, hydrogen, and oxygen. This composition of elements is different from *hydrocarbons,* the main components of lipids that contain carbon and hydrogen.

The empirical formula for carbohydrates is $C_NH_{2N}O_N$ (e.g., glucose is $C_6H_{12}O_6$).

monosaccharide (glucose)

disaccharide (sucrose)

polysaccharide (amylose starch)

*Comparison of a monosaccharide (e.g., glucose), disaccharide (e.g., sucrose), and polysaccharide (e.g., amylose starch). Glycosidic (alpha or beta) bonds link the monomers*

### Monosaccharides

*Monosaccharides* are classified by the number of carbons they contain and the monomers for carbohydrates (simple sugars), from which all carbohydrates are made.

They serve as energy and may be used to modify a vast array of other molecules.

Monosaccharides are the raw material for synthesizing monomers, including amino acids and fatty acids.

Monosaccharides have the empirical formula of $CH_2O$. They have a carbonyl group (C=O) and multiple hydroxyl (O−H) groups.

The location of the carbonyl group classifies monosaccharides; a carbonyl at one of the terminal carbons is an *aldose*, while a carbonyl at a middle carbon is a *ketose.* They are classified by the amount of carbon.

For example, six-carbon sugars are *hexoses*, five-carbon sugars *pentoses*, and three-carbon sugars *trioses.*

Monosaccharides are *chiral,* or asymmetrical, with a "right-handed" and "left-handed" isomer.

**D-glucose as the primary sugar**

Organisms use D-glucose (right-handed glucose), not L-glucose.

Glucose ($C_6H_{12}O_6$) is the most abundant monosaccharide in animals and references blood sugar because it is the primary monosaccharide in blood. In animals, glucose is an important energy source for the body.

Other natural monosaccharides include galactose, fructose, ribose, and deoxyribose (~*ose* for sugars).

Monosaccharides are metabolized quickly by cells as energy for cellular respiration (produces ATP). However, the cells might not need the energy at once and therefore stores it.

Monosaccharides are stored by polymerizing them into larger carbohydrates (e.g., glycogen).

**Disaccharides**

*Disaccharides* are two monosaccharides joined by dehydration synthesis.

*Lactose* (~*ose* for sugars) is composed of the monosaccharides galactose and glucose and is in milk. It is broken into these individual monomers by *lactase* (~*ase* for enzymes).

However, some people lack this enzyme and cannot break down lactose, leading to lactose intolerance.

Disaccharides are soluble in water but are too large to pass through cell membranes by diffusion and must be digested into monosaccharides.

*Maltose* (~*ose* for sugars) is composed of two glucose molecules and forms in the digestive tract of humans during the digestion of polysaccharides.

*Sucrose* (~*ose* for sugars) is glucose and fructose and is used primarily by plants to transport sugars.

*Maltose is a disaccharide of two glucose monomers joined by the β-glycosidic bond*

**Polysaccharides for structure and energy storage**

*Polysaccharides* are polymers of monosaccharides that have structural and energy storage functions. *Starch* is a straight chain of glucose molecules with few side branches formed by plants as carbohydrate storage.

*Glycogen* is a highly branched polymer of glucose with many side branches; it is "animal starch" because it is the carbohydrate storage of animals.

Glycogen is a short-term energy source rapidly mobilized to break into glucose as needed. It is stored in muscles and the liver, but for less than 24 hours, since it takes up a large space. Excess glycogen must be broken down and excreted as waste.

*Cellulose* is a straight chain of glucose similar to starch, but with glucose, monomers arranged by *beta linkages* (strong cross-linkages). This strength makes cellulose tough, durable, and fibrous; it is the primary constituent of plant cell walls.

Humans cannot digest cellulose due to the lack of an enzyme to cleave the strong β-linkages. However, grazing animals have specially adapted digestive systems and symbiotic bacteria, which assist the process.

**Carbohydrates as a source of energy**

Humans ingest carbohydrates (or "carbs") as mono-, di-, and polysaccharides.

During digestion, polymers are broken into monosaccharides and absorbed by the body. These may be used by the body moments after eaten or polymerized into glycogen for storage.

Carbohydrates are soluble in water, making them easy to transport within the body.

Monosaccharides are digested more rapidly than lipids, used when the body requires a surge of energy.

When an animal requires glucose, it uses blood glucose until exhausted. It may degrade glycogen into glucose or synthesize glucose from other biomolecules, such as amino acids.

In animals, the breakdown of carbohydrates begins with digestion into individual *glucose* monomers.

Glucose is oxidized by *glycolysis,* forming ATP and other products.

Glycolysis is followed by aerobic (i.e., Krebs cycle and electron transport chain) or anaerobic (i.e., fermentation) respiration.

Aerobic respiration is most efficient, but in the absence of oxygen, as during high-intensity exercise, organisms utilize anaerobic respiration to produce ATP.

**Ribose and deoxyribose**

Ribose and deoxyribose are five-carbon sugars (pentoses) as the backbones of RNA and DNA.

Ribose, in RNA, is sugar with one hydroxyl group (~OH) attached to each carbon atom.

Deoxyribose, in DNA, is a modified sugar that lacks one hydroxyl absent at the 2' position.

This difference of one oxygen atom is important for the enzymes that recognize DNA and RNA because it allows the two molecules to be differentiated and identified.

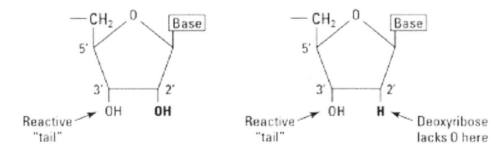

*Ribose (RNA) sugar is on the left with the hydroxyl at the 2' position.*
*Deoxyribose (DNA) sugar is on the right, whereby hydrogen replaces the 2' OH.*

## Nucleotides and Nucleic Acids

### Structure and function of nucleosides and nucleotides

*Nucleotides* are the monomers of nucleic acids: *deoxyribonucleic acid* (DNA) and *ribonucleic acid* (RNA). A nucleotide has three components: a nitrogenous base, a pentose sugar, and a phosphate group.

*Nitrogenous bases* are single or double rings made of carbon, nitrogen, and oxygen. P*entose sugar* is a five-carbon molecule bonded to the nitrogenous base. In RNA, the pentose sugar is *ribose,* hence the name ribonucleic acid. In DNA, the sugar is devoid of oxygen at the 2' position (*deoxyribose).*

Together, the pentose and nitrogenous bases are a *nucleoside.* Adding a *phosphate group* makes it a *nucleoside monophosphate,* the full name for a nucleotide. If three phosphate groups are added, the nucleoside becomes a *nucleoside triphosphate.*

These molecules are not used in nucleic acids but rather for metabolic processes; *adenosine triphosphate* (ATP) is a well-known example.

*A nucleoside has a nitrogenous base and a pentose sugar (i.e., ribose or deoxyribose).*
*A nucleotide is formed when one or more phosphate groups are added to the nucleoside.*

### Sugar-phosphate backbone of nucleic acids

Nucleotides join to form nucleic acids using dehydration synthesis by linking them with *phosphodiester bonds*. The free 3' hydroxyl group of one nucleotide forms a bond with the 5' phosphate group on the sugar of the next nucleotide.

Alternating sugars and phosphate groups form the backbone of nucleic acids. At the ends of the nucleic acid is a sugar group and (at the other) a phosphate group. These terminal groups determine the directionality of the molecule: the sugar is at the *3' end*, and the phosphate is at the *5' end.*

During DNA or RNA synthesis, polymerization elongates the molecule from the 5' to 3' end (always adding the following monomer to the 3' end of the growing polymer).

A linear nucleic acid begins to twist into a helical shape as it elongates. It may remain single-stranded (RNA) or be joined to another strand (DNA).

**Pyrimidines and purines hydrogen bond between the sugar-phosphate backbones**

Nitrogenous bases are purines or pyrimidines and extend from the sugar-phosphate backbone.

*Purines* have a six-membered ring joined to a five-membered ring. The two purines are adenine and guanine. Adenine contains carbon, nitrogen, and hydrogen, while guanine includes double-bonded oxygen.

*Pyrimidines* are smaller because they have a single six-membered ring. There are three pyrimidines: cytosine, thymine, and uracil.

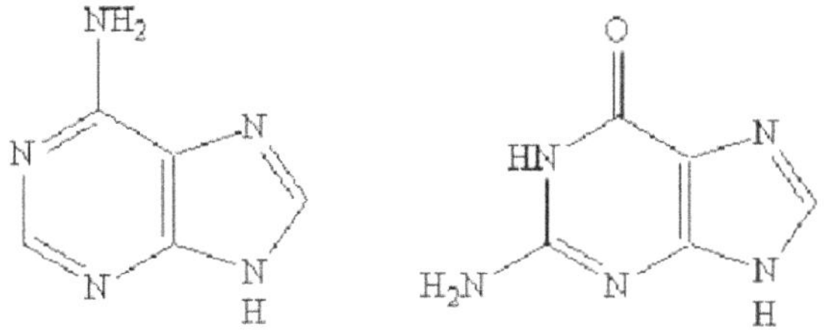

Adenine          Guanine

Purines

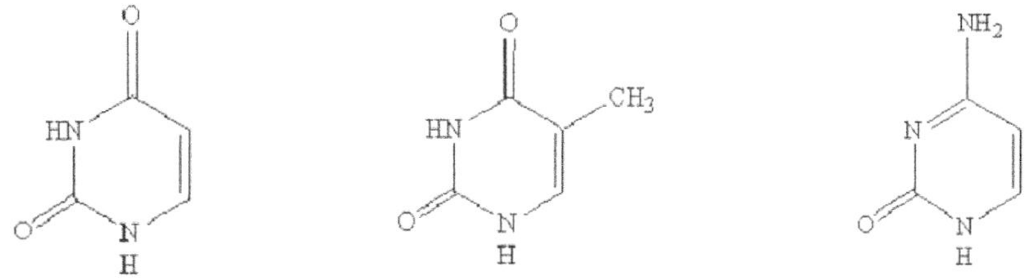

Uracil          Thymine          Cytosine

Pyrimidines

In double-stranded nucleic acids, purines and pyrimidines are paired by hydrogen bonds.

Guanine pairs with cytosine ($G\equiv C$) for DNA and RNA.

However, in DNA, adenine is paired with thymine (A=T), while in RNA, it is paired with uracil (A=U). Thymine is only in DNA, and uracil only in RNA.

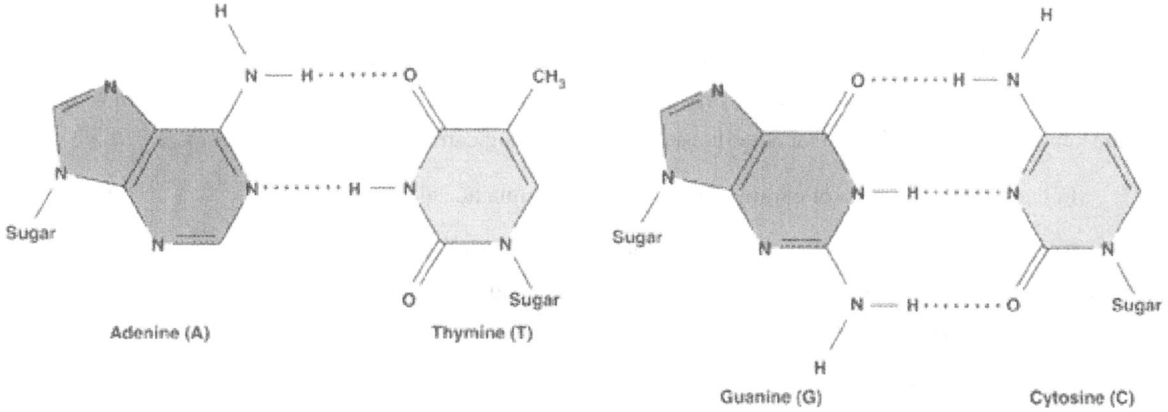

Adenine (A)          Thymine (T)          Guanine (G)          Cytosine (C)

*Adenine and thymine are paired with two hydrogen bonds, while guanine and cytosine*

*are paired with three hydrogen bonds. A purine (A or G) pairs with a pyrimidine (C, T or U)*

**Deoxyribonucleic acid as a base-paired double helix**

The DNA molecule is responsible for encoding the information that gives rise to the cell's day-to-day activities. DNA controls the direction of its replication, controls RNA synthesis, and influences protein synthesis.

DNA is double-stranded, formed from two separate nucleic acid chains oriented in opposite directions (antiparallel). The 3' end of one strand is aligned to the 5' end of the other.

The helices are intertwined and give rise to DNA's shape: the *double helix.*

Each nitrogenous base of one strand is paired with a nitrogenous base on the other, *complementary base pairs.* The double helix is held by hydrogen bonding between their nitrogenous bases.

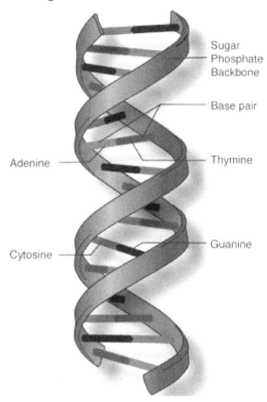

*DNA double helix with two antiparallel strands of DNA. The outside is the sugar-phosphate backbone; bases (A, C, G, T) project inwards with hydrogen bonds to hold the structure as a double helix*

**DNA is the genetic code**

DNA is the genetic code of life due to its chemical and physical properties. The backbone is negatively charged, which allows it to react with positively charged histone proteins and become "supercoiled" into compact chromosomes. This is why DNA that is millions of base pairs long can fit into the nucleus of a cell.

In humans, the 23 pairs of chromosomes are in each somatic cell's nucleus.

Repulsion forces between stacked base pairs give DNA stability and make it relatively resistant to denaturation. However, a hydrogen bond linking bases is weak and easily broken. This is important because DNA strands must be separated to replicate (during the *S* phase of the cell cycle) new DNA before cell division.

Each strand is the template for the synthesis of a new strand.

The complementary nature of the strands ensures that each strand carries the same information and serves for the hereditary propagation of the genetic material unique to an organism.

**RNA for transcription and gene regulation**

*Transcription* is the synthesis of RNA from a DNA template.

M*essenger RNA* (mRNA) is transcribed from a template strand of DNA. The mRNA is *translated* into a protein. After mRNA is encoded with the genetic information by DNA, it relays the message to *ribosomal RNA* (rRNA). rRNA is unusual because it has enzymatic properties as an enzymatic protein. rRNA molecules aggregate into a *ribosome,* binds to mRNA, and initiates protein synthesis (translation) in the cytoplasm.

*Transfer RNA* (tRNA) molecules assist with translation by adding amino acids as dictated by the genetic code carried by the mRNA molecule.

Other RNAs regulate gene expression, splice noncoding (introns) information from mRNA before it is translated, and otherwise modify RNA.

**Introns, exons, telomeres and centromeres**

*Noncoding* DNA sequences have an essential role.

The majority of DNA is made of *intron* sequences rather than *coding* sequences or *exons.*

Introns and exons are transcribed into mRNA, but the introns are spliced out during mRNA processing and before export from the nucleus into the cytoplasm for translation into proteins.

*Telomeres* are repetitive sequences of noncoding DNA that protect the ends of DNA from inevitable degradation with each replication of DNA during mitosis.

Noncoding regions of DNA regulate gene expression by promoting or inhibiting transcription into RNA.

*Centromeres* (involved in DNA replication) are other noncoding regions with a structural function in chromosomes.

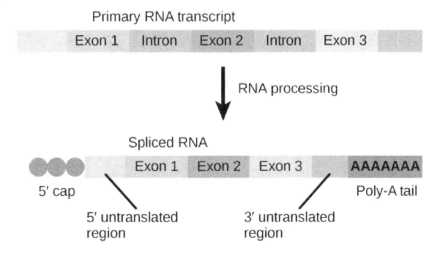

*The DNA encodes for a primary transcript complementary to the DNA sequence.*
*The mRNA undergoes three steps: removal of introns and joining of exons, the addition of a 5' cap,*
*and a 3' poly-A tail while in the nucleus. The processed mRNA is exported to the cytoplasm*
*as the template for protein synthesis during translation*

*Notes for active learning*

# CHAPTER 9

# Chromosomes, Genes and DNA

- Deoxyribonucleic Acid (DNA) Structure and Function

- DNA Replication Mechanism and Required Biomolecules

- Genetic Code

- Transcription of DNA into mRNA

- Translation Synthesizes Proteins from mRNA

- Eukaryotic Chromosome Organization

- Control of Gene Expression in Eukaryotes

## Deoxyribonucleic Acid (DNA) Structure and Function

**Nucleotide composition**

*Deoxyribonucleic acid* (DNA) is the sequence of paired nucleotides that stores the genetic code necessary for replicating and determining the sequence of amino acids in proteins.

The transcription process uses DNA as a template to form a *ribonucleic acid* (RNA), which serves as a temporary transcript of hereditary genetic information.

*Ribosomes* translate the information from mRNA into a sequence of amino acids to form polypeptides, folding into proteins.

DNA contains four nucleotides (adenine, cytosine, guanine, and thymine).

*Nucleotides* consist of 1) at least one phosphate group, 2) a pentose sugar, and 3) a one or two-ringed structure containing carbon and nitrogen (i.e., nitrogenous base). The term "base" relates to its ability to accept hydrogen ions (protons). First, glycosidic bonds link the sugar to the nitrogenous base, creating a *nucleoside* (sugar and base only), as shown below.

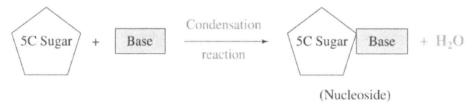

(Nucleoside)

*Nucleoside formation by a condensation reaction that joins the ribose*
*to the adenine to form adenosine (lacking the phosphate group of a nucleotide)*

**Nucleic acids assemble from nucleotides**

These nucleotides form a long strand with phosphodiester bonds in the sugar-phosphate DNA backbone.

A nucleotide polymer comprises a *nucleic acid*, and its acidity is due to the phosphate groups.

Nucleic acids (i.e., RNA and DNA) store, transmit and express genetic information in cells.

DNA has two nucleic acid strands combined to form the double-stranded DNA molecule.

Strands are joined when the bases of each strand (i.e., A = T and C ≡ G) form *base pairs*.

The DNA in a single human cell contains about 3 billion base pairs.

Because DNA has a helical twist, the coiling of the DNA strand makes the DNA compact.

The 3 billion base pairs in one human cell would stretch to about 6 feet in length.

The sequence of base pairs encodes the genetic information of the cell.

In nucleic acids, the genetic code determines the sequence of amino acids in the synthesized proteins.

**Purine and pyrimidine nitrogenous bases**

Early researchers knew that the genetic material must have a few necessary characteristics. It must store information used to control the development and the metabolic activities of cells, it must be stable to be accurately replicated during cell division and be transmitted for many cell cycles and between generations of offspring (i.e., progeny), and it must be able to undergo mutations, providing the genetic variability required for evolution.

The two types of nucleic acids were soon discovered: deoxyribonucleic acid (DNA) and ribonucleic acid (RNA). In the early twentieth century, researchers discovered that nucleic acids contain four types of nucleotides, the repeating units that make up the long DNA molecule.

There are four bases in DNA nucleotides. *Adenine* (A) and *guanine* (G) are purine bases and consist of two nitrogen-containing rings, while *thymine* (T) and *cytosine* (C) are pyrimidine bases and consist of one nitrogen-containing ring.

*Purines with a double ring structure*          *Pyrimidines with a single ring structure*

**Deoxyribose and ribose**

*Deoxyribose* is a pentose (5-carbon) sugar in DNA.

By convention, the carbons of the sugar are numbered.

The phosphate group of DNA is attached to the 5' carbon.

Deoxyribose has a hydroxyl group (OH) at the 3' carbon (as does the ribose sugar in RNA).

RNA has a similar but not identical structure to DNA.

The pentose sugar in RNA is *ribose*, which has the same structure as deoxyribose, except RNA has a hydroxyl group instead of hydrogen at the 2' position.

Because deoxyribose is missing this hydroxyl group, it is *deoxy* (without oxygen).

RNA contains the *uracil* pyrimidine instead of thymine (uracil replaces thymine in RNA). These two pyrimidine bases have similar structures, except for a methyl group ($CH_3$) present in thymine but not in uracil.

Although DNA and RNA's primary structures are similar, their structures in three-dimensional space (tertiary structure) are distinct. RNA molecules are single-stranded, so base pairs can form between sections of the same molecule, resulting in shapes such as stem-loops.

Double-stranded DNA is a double helix with two strands bonded in an anti-parallel orientation held by hydrogen bonds between the bases (C≡G and A=T).

**Sugar-phosphate backbone of DNA**

*Single-stranded DNA with negatively charged sugar-phosphate backbone and bases projecting inwards*

*when the second strand of DNA hydrogen bonds with it to form a double helix*

**Chargaff's rule**

In the 1940s, Austrian-born biochemist Erwin Chargaff analyzed the base content of DNA using chemical techniques.

Chargaff discovered that for a species, DNA has the *constancy* required of genetic material.

This constancy is *Chargaff's rule*, which states that the number of pyrimidine bases (T and C) equals the number of purine bases (A and G).

The bases make hydrogen bond base pairs in the same way: purine A uses a double bond with the pyrimidine T. The purine G uses a triple bond with the pyrimidine C. This is a *complementary base pairing*.

Chargaff's rule states that the number of adenines in a DNA molecule equals the number of its base pair, thymines, and the number of guanines equals the number of its base pair, cytosines. Hence, A = T and G $\equiv$ C.

**Complementary base pairing bonds A/T and G/C**

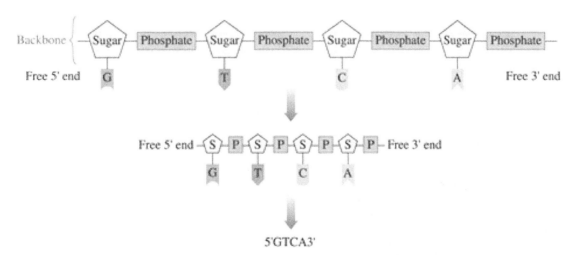

Adenine has 2 hydrogen bonds to Thymine          Guanine has 3 hydrogen bonds to Cytosine

Despite the restriction of base-pair bonding, the G/C content relative to A/T content differs among species while adhering to Chargaff's rules.

Because G/C pairs have three hydrogen bonds instead of the two hydrogen bonds in A/T pairs, the strands in DNA molecules with higher G/C content are tightly bound than those with higher A/T content.

G/C base pairs have a higher $T_m$ (melting temperature when ½ bonds are broken) than A/T base pairs.

Although there are four bases (A, C, G, T) and two types of base pairs (A/T, C/G) in DNA, the base sequence variability is enormous. A human chromosome contains about 140 million base pairs on average.

Since any of the four possible nucleotides are present at each nucleotide position, the number of possible nucleotide sequences in a human chromosome is $4^{140,000,000}$, or 4 raised to 140,000,000.

Use this mnemonic for which bases are purines or pyrimidines:

CUT the PIE (Cytosine, Uracil, and Thymine are pyrimidines)

PURe As Gold (purines are Adenine and Guanine)

*Chargaff's rule identifies the amount of all bases when one purine (A or G) and one pyrimidine (C or T) are hydrogen-bonded in a complementary-paired double-stranded DNA molecule*

---

**Watson–Crick model of DNA structure**

During the 1950s, English chemist Rosalind Franklin produced X-ray diffraction photographs of DNA molecules. Rosalind Franklin's work provided evidence that DNA has a helical conformation, specifically, as two strands of DNA wind together in a double helix. A double helix can be envisioned as a twisted ladder.

American James Watson, and Englishman Francis H. C. Crick, received the Nobel Prize in 1962 for their model of DNA. Using information gathered by Chargaff and Franklin, Watson and Crick built a model of DNA in a double helix secondary structure.

Sugar-phosphate molecules form a backbone on the outside of the helix, while bases point toward the middle and form base pairs with the complementary strand. Their model was consistent with Chargaff's rules and the DNA polymer dimensions provided by Franklin's x-ray diffraction photographs of DNA.

**Structure of complementary base-paired helical DNA**

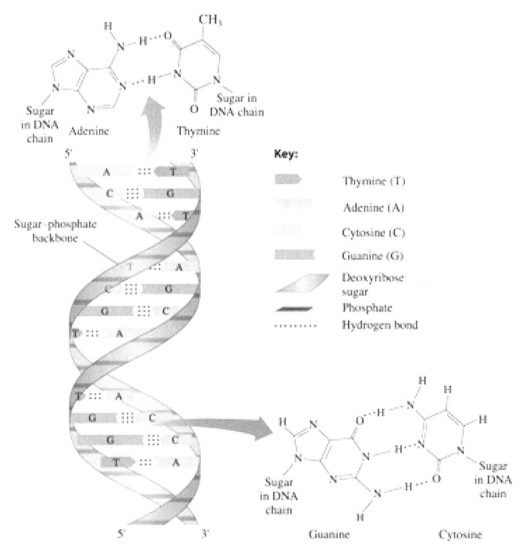

*Antiparallel strands of DNA with phosphodiester bonds between the sugar-phosphate backbone.*
*Hydrogen bonds hold the complementary base pairs*

**Antiparallel strands use complementary bonding**

Each strand in DNA has a direction relative to the numbering on the pentose ring. In a free nucleotide, the phosphate is attached to the 5'–phosphate of deoxyribose, while the 3'–OH of deoxyribose is exposed.

When phosphodiester bonds form, a 3' hydroxyl of one deoxyribose sugar attaches to a 5' phosphate of an incoming sugar. Thus, DNA strands have a distinct polarity, with a 5' end and a 3' end.

Two strands bound in double helix orient in opposite directions and the two strands are *antiparallel*.

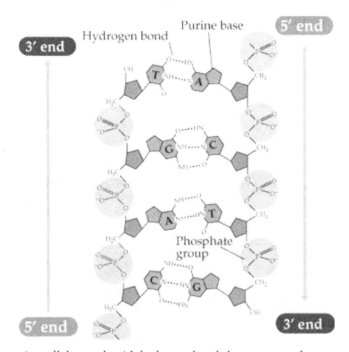

*DNA as two antiparallel strands with hydrogen bonds between complementary base pairs*

**Griffith's experiments for transforming factor**

In 1931, bacteriologist Frederick Griffith experimented with *Streptococcus pneumonia,* a pneumococcus bacterium that causes pneumonia in mammals. He first injected two sets of mice with different pneumococcus strains: a virulent strain with a mucous capsule (S strain) due to the colonies' smooth appearance and a non-virulent strain without a capsule (R strain) due to the colonies' rough appearance.

Mice injected with the S strain died, while mice injected with the R strain survived.

Griffith performed two more sets of injections to determine if the capsule alone was responsible for the S strain's virulence. In one set of mice, he injected S strain bacteria that had been first subjected to heat ("heat-killed bacteria"). These mice survived.

In another set of mice, he injected a mixture of the heat-killed S strain and the live R strain.

These mice died, and Griffith recovered living S strain pneumococcus from the mice's bodies, despite only heat-killed S strain being injected into the live mice.

Griffith concluded that the R strain had been "transformed" by the heat-killed S strain, allowing the R strain to synthesize a capsule and become virulent.

The phenotype (virulent capsule) of the R strain bacteria must have been due to a change in genotype (genetic material), which suggested that the transforming substance must have passed from the heat-killed S strain to the R strain.

This passing of this unknown substance is *transformation*.

**Avery, MacLeod, and McCarty experiment uses enzyme degradation**

In 1944, molecular biologists Oswald Avery, Colin MacLeod, and Maclyn McCarty reported transforming substance in the heat-killed S strain was DNA.

This conclusion was supported by evidence showing purified DNA resulted in transformation.

Enzymes that degrade proteins (proteases) and RNA (RNase) do not prevent a transformation.

However, using enzymes that digest DNA (DNase) does prevent transformation. Additionally, the transforming substance's molecular weight appeared great enough for genetic variability.

These results support DNA as the genetic material controlling the biosynthetic properties of a cell.

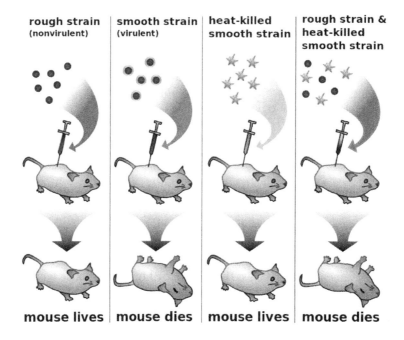

**Hershey and Chase radiolabel DNA, RNA and protein**

In 1952, researchers Alfred Hershey and Martha Chase performed experiments with bacteriophages (i.e., virus that infects bacteria) to confirm that DNA was the genetic material.

A *bacteriophage* (phage) is a virus that infects bacteria and consists only of a protein coat surrounding a nucleic acid core.

They used the T2 bacteriophage to infect the bacterium *Escherichia coli*, a species of intensely studied bacteria that lives within the human gut.

The purpose was to observe which bacteriophage component—the protein coat or the DNA—entered the bacterial cells and directed the reproduction of the virus.

In two experiments, they radiolabeled the bacteriophage protein coat with $^{35}$S and the DNA with $^{32}$P.

Each aliquot of phages infected the bacterial cells. The separate populations of bacterial progeny were lysed (blender experiment) and analyzed for the presence of isotope-labeled sulfur or phosphorus.

The progeny became labeled with $^{32}$P, while the sulfur of the progeny was unlabeled, confirming that DNA (contains P), not protein (contains S), is the transmissible genetic material.

**Genes and genome**

*Genes* are sequences of DNA nucleotides that contain and transmit the information specifying amino acid sequences for protein synthesis.

DNA molecules contain many genes.

The *genome* refers collectively to the genetic information encoded in a cell.

Human cells contain 23 pairs of bundled DNA as chromosomes in the nucleus, totaling 46 chromosomes per cell except for reproductive (germline) and red blood (erythrocyte) cells.

**RNA as the messenger molecule**

RNA molecules transfer information from DNA in the nucleus to protein synthesis in the cytoplasm.

RNA molecules are synthesized during transcription according to template information encoded in the hereditary molecule of DNA.

These RNA molecules are processed, and ribosomes translate mRNA to synthesize proteins.

DNA→ replication during S phase → DNA chromosome with sister chromatids

DNA → transcription → mRNA → translation → protein

## DNA Replication Mechanism and Required Biomolecules

### DNA replication mechanism

DNA replication is the copying of a DNA molecule. During the S (synthesis) phase of the cell cycle, DNA replicates when the strands of the double helix separate, and exposed strands act as a template for DNA synthesis.

Free deoxyribonucleoside triphosphates (dNTPs) are base-paired to form new, complementary strands.

Errors in the base sequence during replication may be corrected by a mechanism of *proofreading* or DNA repair.

Replication of linear DNA in eukaryotes starts at multiple points of origin (circular DNA in prokaryotes has a single origin).

Once replication is initiated, the DNA strands separate at these points of origin as *replication bubbles*.

### Replication forks

The two V-shaped separating ends of the replication bubble are the sites of DNA replication or *replication forks*.

Once a strand of DNA is exposed, the enzyme *DNA polymerase III* for prokaryotes (pol γ for eukaryotes) incorporates free deoxyribonucleoside triphosphates (dNTPs), which are nucleotides with three phosphate groups, into the complementary strand by catalyzing the exergonic loss of phosphate.

The two phosphate groups cleaved in the process become nucleotides and release energy ($-\Delta G$), making the overall polymerization reaction thermodynamically favorable, thus driving the reaction forward.

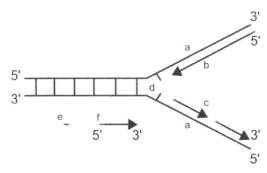

*DNA replication: a: template strands, b: leading strand, c: lagging strand, d: replication fork, e: RNA primer, f: Okazaki fragment*

Polymerization occurs on both strands and ends of the replication bubbles until the entire DNA is replicated, a process that results in two complementary DNA molecules.

Eukaryotes replicate their DNA at a relatively slow pace of 500 to 5,000 base pairs per minute, taking hours to complete replication.

In comparison, prokaryotes can replicate their DNA at a faster rate of 500 base pairs per second.

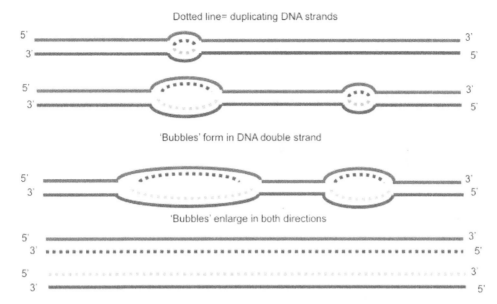

*The time sequence of DNA replication process with 'bubbles' joining to form complementary DNA*

## Stages of DNA replication

The process of DNA replication is divided into three steps:

1.  *Unwinding*—the enzyme *DNA helicase* unwinds the double helix, pulling the DNA strands apart and breaking hydrogen bonds between base pairs. Each separated strand is now a template for synthesizing a new (daughter) strand of DNA.

2.  *Complementary base pairing*—free dNTPs form hydrogen bonds with their complementary base pair. Adenine pairs with thymine, and guanine pairs with cytosine.

3.  *Joining*—DNA polymerase (III or γ) catalyze nucleotides into the new strand. Incoming dNTPs cleave two phosphate groups, becoming nucleotides (one phosphate group). *T*hey are incorporated in a 5' to 3' direction, and the deoxyribose sugar and phosphate are covalently added.

## DNA replication is semiconservative

In 1958, Matthew Meselson and Franklin Stahl provided evidence for the model of DNA replication. They first grew bacteria in a medium with heavy nitrogen ($^{15}$N) and then switched the bacteria to light nitrogen ($^{14}$N) for further divisions.

When they measured the density of the replicated DNA using centrifugation, they observed that the density of the replicated DNA was intermediate—less dense than a molecule made entirely with $^{15}$N, but denser than a molecule made entirely with $^{14}$N.

After one division, these hybrid DNA molecules (1 light and 1 heavy strand) were present in the cells.

Half the DNA molecules were light after two divisions, and half were hybrid.

These results support the *semiconservative model,* one of three main theoretical models originally proposed in DNA replication.

---

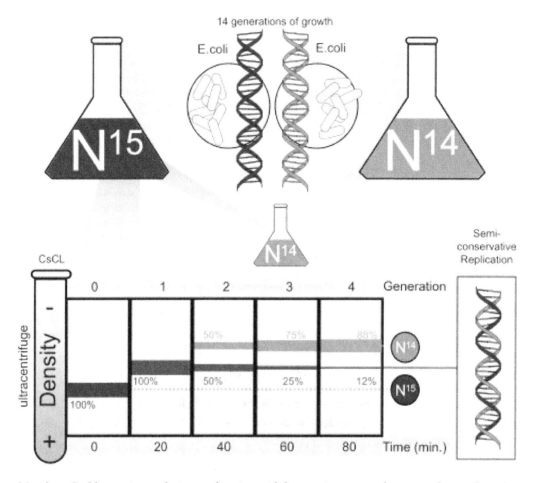

*Meselson-Stahl experiment during replication with heavy nitrogen as the original growth medium*

DNA replication is semiconservative because the daughter double helix consists of one parental strand and one new strand, meaning that half of the double helix is conserved from material in the parent generation.

**Three competing models for DNA replication**

In a *conservative model*, one entire double strand acts as the template, while the new double strand is composed entirely *de novo* (i.e., from the beginning, new).

If this model were accurate, Meselson and Stahl's experiment would produce only heavy and light DNA molecules in the daughter cells, with no hybrid strands of intermediate density.

In a *dispersive model*, the parent double-strand is made into two new strands, with daughters containing a mixture of old and newly-incorporated nucleotides.

The two densities in the DNA of the cells in the second generation of the Meselson and Stahl experiment were inconsistent with the dispersive model.

That model would have resulted in DNA of a single density.

**Multiple origins of replication and Okazaki fragments**

The average human chromosome contains 140 million nucleotide pairs, and the replication forks proceed at a rate of about 50 base pairs per second.

At this rate, the replication process takes about a month, but since there are many replication origins on the eukaryotic chromosome, the process takes hours.

Replication begins at some origins earlier than others, but as replication nears completion, the replication bubbles meet and fuse to form two new DNA molecules.

DNA replication occurs in the S phase of interphase and must be completed before a cell can divide (e.g., mitosis or meiosis). Drugs with molecules similar to the four nucleotides (i.e., nucleotide analogs) are used by patients to inhibit cell division of rapidly dividing cancer cells.

There are many origins of replication in linear DNA of eukaryotes, and several replication forks are formed simultaneously, forming several replication bubbles.

Accordingly, the Okazaki fragments in eukaryotes are shorter (100 – 200 nucleotides), while Okazaki fragments in prokaryotes are longer (1,000 – 2,000 nucleotides). Replication occurs twenty times faster in prokaryotes than in eukaryotes, which undergoes more proofreading during DNA replication.

**Telomeres as repeating ends of DNA molecules**

DNA polymerase adds nucleotides to a 3' –OH end of a preexisting polynucleotide, i.e., it cannot synthesize *de novo*. This is not an issue for circular DNA in prokaryotes, but it is a problem for synthesizing the lagging strand at the ends of linear DNA in eukaryotes.

Although primase can add an RNA primer to the end of the DNA molecule on the lagging strand, DNA polymerase I cannot replace DNA without RNA primers cannot perform *de novo* synthesis.

The RNA segment, as well as its complementary DNA on the opposite strand, would be degraded since chromosomes are regulated to consist of complementary DNA. This leads to degradation of the RNA nucleotides of about 8-12 nucleotides at the ends of DNA strands after each round of replication, eventually encroaching on essential genes on chromosomes and leading to cell death.

*Telomeres* are the end pieces of each chromosome. There are two telomeres on each of the 46 human chromosomes, which adds up to 92 telomeres in total. Their repetitive sequences and associated proteins protect the ends from degradation and provide a way for DNA ends to be replicated without loss of important sequence when the RNA primer initiates replication along the leading strand.

In the 1980s, telomeres were proposed to create special segments of DNA synthesized by the telomerase enzyme. This enzyme essentially lengthens the ends of DNA with repeating sequences, usually TTAGGG in humans and other vertebrates.

The problem with terminal degradation of DNA still occurs, but since extra sequences have been added during embryogenesis and in stem cells, no essential information is lost. In healthy adult cells, telomerase is off.

**Telomerase extends the chromosome ends**

The telomerase enzyme carries an internal RNA template. It attaches to the end of the DNA molecule and extends the 3' end with additional DNA. The new DNA added is complementary to the internal RNA template on the enzyme.

This new DNA is added during embryogenesis, leading and lagging strand synthesis takes place as normal. A portion of the telomere is lost with each replication cycle during the organism's lifetime.

Since a double-stranded break is indicative of DNA damage, telomeres have developed associated proteins that inhibit the cell's ability to recognize DNA damage, thereby preventing the unwanted activation of repair mechanisms, cell-cycle arrest, or apoptosis.

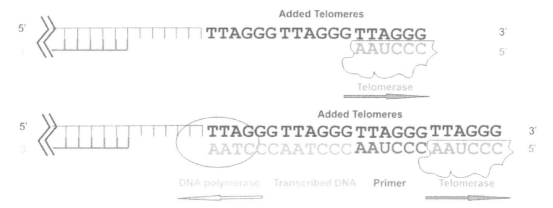

*Telomerase has an internal RNA template to which complementary DNA*
*is synthesized to extend the ends of the chromosomes*

**DNA repair mechanisms during replication**

The accuracy of DNA replication cannot be attributed solely to base-pairing specificity, which has an error rate of 1 out of $10^5$ base pairs. This rate is not consistent with the observed error rate of 1 in $10^9$ base pairs. To arrive at this fidelity, errors during replication must be repaired, the first of which is *proofreading* and performed by DNA polymerases.

DNA polymerase is an aggregate of subunits that combine to form an active *holoenzyme* complex. These aggregates often catalyze more than one reaction. When polymerases inevitably make polymerization errors, DNA polymerase I and III use proofreading to make corrections.

DNA polymerase I and III have 3' to 5' exonuclease activity. When these polymerases incorporate an incorrect nucleotide into the strand (does not base pair correctly with the complementary strand), the exonuclease subunit breaks the phosphodiester bond at the 5' end, excises the nucleotide, and the polymerase subunit inserts the correct nucleotide.

Since polymerases synthesize in the 5' to 3' direction, this excision is named for the complementary strand's 3' to 5' direction.

In addition to 3' to 5' exonuclease activity, DNA polymerase I (but not III) has a 5' to 3' exonuclease. This enzymatic activity allows DNA polymerase I to remove nucleotides ahead of it while synthesizing a new strand simultaneously (5' to 3' polymerization).

This is the basis by which DNA polymerase I excises ribonucleotides in the RNA primers and replaces them with DNA.

This coupling of 5' to 3' exonuclease activity with 5' to 3' polymerization is *nick translation* since a single-stranded cut (nick) essentially translates along the strand as the sequence is replaced with new nucleotides.

Ligase must seal the nicks with phosphodiester bonds in the backbone when repairs are made.

## DNA mismatch repair mechanisms

In addition to proofreading, mismatch repair and excision repair are two standard systems that correct errors in DNA.

In *mismatch repair*, a group of enzymes detects a mismatched base pair in a double-stranded DNA molecule that the DNA polymerase proofreading mechanism has missed.

The repair enzyme decides which DNA strand is the template (parent) strand of the new (daughter) DNA molecule by recognizing methylation sites.

Newly synthesized DNA is unmethylated; therefore, the base on the unmethylated strand must be the mismatched base. Since complete methylation is eventually reached after a period, mismatch repair is most accurate immediately after DNA synthesis.

## Base-excision and nucleotide excision repair

*Base-excision repair* (BER) and *nucleotide-excision repair* (NER) act on bases with a mutated structure rather than mismatched base pairs.

BER generally works on small mutations. The excision of the damaged base occurs through breakage of the phosphodiester backbone at the resulting abasic site, and gap-filling by DNA polymerase replaces the base.

*Nucleotide-excision repair* is similar, but it for mutations that seriously affect the helical structure.

NER usually replaces a larger DNA region rather than a single nucleotide or a small patch as in BER.

For example, DNA exposure to UV light may distort the DNA structure, potentially causing problems during replication, resulting in a pre-cancerous state.

This is why UV (i.e., sunlight) exposure is linked to higher occurrences of skin cancer.

NER recognizes the damage, removes the offending stretch of single-stranded DNA, and polymerizes new DNA using the remaining sequence as a template.

## Genetic Code

**The central dogma of molecular biology**

The *central dogma* of molecular biology (i.e., DNA → RNA → protein ) describes the flow of genetic information in living systems. It states that information flows from DNA to mRNA to protein. DNA is *transcribed* by RNA polymerase to create mRNA molecules, and ribosomes translate mRNA to produce the polypeptide chains comprising proteins.

The central dogma identifies DNA and RNA as information intermediates; information can flow back and forth between DNA and RNA (exemplified by retroviruses, where reverse transcriptase catalyzes DNA formation from RNA) but identifies the protein as a pathway product.

A protein sequence does not act as a template for the synthesis of DNA or RNA.

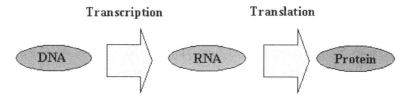

*The central dogma of the flow of genetic information*

**Genes encode proteins**

Classical geneticists classify a gene as any of the particles of inheritance on a chromosome. Molecular biologists describe a gene as a sequence of DNA nucleotide bases that encodes for a protein. DNA is responsible for the genotype or genetic makeup of an organism.

Protein is responsible for the phenotype or observable characteristics (e.g., the organism's physical, physiological, developmental, or behavioral traits). Phenotypes result from the actions of enzymes, biological catalysts (mostly proteins) that regulate biological functions. Any alteration of the processes in the central dogma of molecular biology may affect proteins' formation and affect the phenotype.

The two strands of DNA are named by their relationship to the RNA and protein that their sequences lead to. The *template strand* is used as the template for RNA synthesis and has a complementary sequence to the coding strand. The *coding strand* has an identical sequence to the transcribed RNA but substitutes thymine for uracil. The template strand is the *antisense strand* or *anticoding strand*, and the coding strand is the *sense strand*.

**Messenger RNA is complementary to DNA**

RNA (ribonucleic acid) is a nucleic acid that carries a complimentary copy of the genetic code of DNA and is translated into the amino acid sequence of proteins.

Unlike DNA, RNA a 2'−OH sugar on the ribose instead of deoxyribose (2'−H), and the pyrimidine base uracil replacing thymine. RNA generally does not form helices.

*Messenger RNA* (mRNA) is a single-stranded piece of RNA containing the bases complementary to the original DNA strand.

The mRNA transcript is synthesized in the nucleus, but after *processing,* it is transported into the cytoplasm where ribosomes are located. The ribosomes *translate* the mRNA sequence into amino acids and synthesize the polypeptide chains of proteins.

RNA, like DNA, can be replicated in special cases. However, a single-stranded RNA template must be used to synthesize a complementary strand. The new strand must serve as a template for another round of synthesis to create an additional RNA molecule identical to the first template.

**Codon-anticodon relationship**

Ribosomes read the RNA containing information to synthesize protein as a series of base triplets known as *codons*. The three bases of each codon determine the amino acid incorporated into the growing polypeptide as the ribosome moves along the mRNA transcript.

Each amino acid is added to the polypeptide chain, linked by peptide bonds between the amino acids. After the completed polypeptide dissociates from the ribosome, special modifications and three-dimensional folding occur (in the ribosome for eukaryotic cells) to form the functional protein.

From the four types of ribonucleotide bases (adenine, cytosine, guanine, uracil), there are $4^3 = 64$ codons possible from a series of three ribonucleotides. However, with few exceptions, 20 naturally-occurring amino acids make up an organism's proteins.

In this way, the code is *degenerate;* more than one codon may specify the same amino acid.

In 1961, Marshall Nirenberg and J. Heinrich Matthaei assembled the initial relationships between naturally occurring amino acids and the codons that specify them. They found that an enzyme is used to construct synthetic RNA in a cell-free system.

By translating three ribonucleotides at a time and observing the amino acid incorporated, they began to decipher the triplet code. This demonstrated the role of nucleotides in protein synthesis.

Three nucleotides (codon) specify a single amino acid.

**Initiation and termination codons**

The 64 codons include 4 special codons. AUG (start codon) codes for methionine and signals the start of translation on an RNA transcript, forming the first amino acid in the nascent polypeptide.

Three other codons, UAG, UGA, and UAA, do not encode for any amino acid but signal a ribosome to terminate translation.

Although the code is degenerate (a single amino acid is specified by more than one codon), it is *unambiguous*: each nucleotide triplet encodes a single amino acid.

The amino acid sequence of a peptide encoded by a nucleotide sequence can be determined from the genetic code.

For example, AUG–CAU–UAC–UAA encodes for: Met–His–Tyr–Stop.

Additionally, the degeneracy of the genetic code is observed in the table.

For example, CCC, CCU, CCA, and CCG encode for the amino acid proline.

**Second letter**

| | U | C | A | G | |
|---|---|---|---|---|---|
| **U** | UUU } Phe<br>UUC<br>UUA } Leu<br>UUG | UCU<br>UCC<br>UCA } Ser<br>UCG | UAU } Tyr<br>UAC<br>**UAA Stop**<br>**UAG Stop** | UGU } Cys<br>UGC<br>**UGA Stop**<br>UGG Trp | U<br>C<br>A<br>G |
| **C** | CUU<br>CUC<br>CUA } Leu<br>CUG | CCU<br>CCC<br>CCA } Pro<br>CCG | CAU } His<br>CAC<br>CAA } Gln<br>CAG | CGU<br>CGC<br>CGA } Arg<br>CGG | U<br>C<br>A<br>G |
| **A** | AUU<br>AUC } Ile<br>AUA<br>AUG Met | ACU<br>ACC<br>ACA } Thr<br>ACG | AAU } Asn<br>AAC<br>AAA } Lys<br>AAG | AGU } Ser<br>AGC<br>AGA } Arg<br>AGG | U<br>C<br>A<br>G |
| **G** | GUU<br>GUC<br>GUA } Val<br>GUG | GCU<br>GCC<br>GCA } Ala<br>GCG | GAU } Asp<br>GAC<br>GAA } Glu<br>GAG | GGU<br>GGC<br>GGA } Gly<br>GGG | U<br>C<br>A<br>G |

*First letter* (left axis) · *Third letter* (right axis)

*Genetic code with 3 nucleotides specifying an amino acid*

**Mutations change the deoxyribonucleic acid (DNA) sequence**

A genetic mutation is a permanent change in the sequence of DNA nucleotide bases, evading proofreading and repair mechanisms.

Major types of mutations include *point mutations*, in which a single base is replaced; *additions*, in which sections of DNA are added; and *deletions*, in which sections of DNA are deleted. The result is the potential for a misread in the DNA nucleotide code or the loss of a gene.

Mutations are categorized by their effect; *nonsense* mutations, *missense* mutations, *silent* mutations, *neutral* mutations, and *frameshift* mutations.

Mutations have consequences that range from no effect to inactivation of a protein's function.

At some point mutations, the corresponding change in the RNA causes a change in the resulting polypeptide. For example, a DNA sequence <u>C</u>CA mutated to <u>T</u>CA causes the RNA codon <u>G</u>GU for glycine to be changed to the <u>A</u>GU codon for serine. In this case, a single nucleotide change has caused a single amino acid change.

*Missense mutations* cause codons to specify different amino acids.

*Nonsense mutations* cause a codon that specifies for an amino acid to change to a stop codon, which results in a truncated (often nonfunctional) protein.

Mutations can result in nonfunctional proteins, and a single nonfunctioning protein can have dramatic effects. However, not all DNA mutations lead to changes in the resulting protein.

For example, a DNA sequence <u>G</u>AT mutated to <u>G</u>AA causes the RNA codon <u>C</u>UA to change to <u>C</u>UU; both codons translate the same amino acid, leucine.

A *silent mutation* cannot be observed in the organism's phenotype (i.e., protein sequence).

A *neutral mutation* neither benefits nor inhibits the function of an organism. For example, a mutation leading to an amino acid change from aspartic acid to glutamic acid, which has negatively-charged side chains, may not cause a major structural or functional change in a protein. In this example, the organism may be unaffected by the amino acid change. Silent mutations are essentially neutral mutations unless some mechanism is affected, depending specifically on the DNA or corresponding amino acid sequence.

There are several ways a mutation may not negatively affect the organism. For example, mutations within introns (segments excised when mRNA is processed) may not affect the functional protein. Proteins may be unaffected by an amino acid change, especially if the new amino acid has similar properties.

If a gene is damaged, there may be no adverse effect on the organism if the paired chromosome's homologous gene can produce an intact protein. Damage to genes that synthesize amino acids may not affect the organism if that amino acid is obtained from an external source, such as the medium a bacterium is growing on.

A *frameshift mutation* alters the triplet reading frame so that codons downstream from the mutation are out of register and not read correctly. They occur when one or more nucleotides are inserted or deleted, resulting in a new sequence of codons and nonfunctional proteins; it may affect the position of the stop codon.

For example, if there is a mRNA sequence GAC CCG UAU corresponding to aspartic acid, proline, and tyrosine, deletion of the first amino acid causes a frameshift mutation. The mutated mRNA sequence would be ACC CGU AU, and it now encodes for threonine and arginine. The human transposon *Alu* causes hemophilia when a frameshift mutation leads to a premature stop codon in the gene for clotting factor IX.

*Spontaneous mutations* occur randomly but are rare due to imperfections in the replication machinery.

*Mutagens* are environmental agents that produce changes in DNA. Proofreading and other repair mechanisms lower the likelihood of mutation to one out of a billion base pairs replicated, but high exposure to mutagens may increase this rate. Many mutagens are *carcinogens* or cancer-causing agents.

If a mutation occurs in a somatic cell (cell other than an egg or sperm), it affects the individual organism and can cause cancer conditions. Future generations can inherit mutations in germ cells (sperm or egg cells) and cause genetic diseases; more than 4,000 genetic diseases have been identified.

## Exogenous mutagens and transposons

Radiation is a common mutagen. X-rays and gamma rays are ionizing radiation that creates dangerous free radicals (i.e., atoms with unpaired electrons), and ultraviolet (UV) radiation can cause pyrimidines (thymine or cytosine) to form covalent linkages as pyrimidine dimers. Cellular repair enzymes must remove it. A lack of these enzymes causes xeroderma pigmentosum, which leads to a higher incidence of skin cancer.

Organic chemicals can act directly on DNA. The mutagen 5-bromouracil pairs with thymine, so the A–T base pair becomes a G–C base pair. Other chemicals may add hydrocarbon groups or remove amino groups from DNA bases. Tobacco smoke contains chemical carcinogens.

A chemical mutagen is sodium nitrite ($NaNO_2$), a preservative in processed meats. In the presence of amines, sodium nitrite forms nitrosamines, which assist in the conversion of the base cytosine into uracil.

*Transposons* are DNA sequences that can move within and between chromosomes and cause mutations when they change the DNA sequence. These "jumping genes" were proposed by Barbara McClintock and first detected in maize (corn). Now transposons have been observed in bacteria, fruit flies, and other organisms.

## Transcription of DNA into mRNA

### mRNA structure and function

Messenger RNA (mRNA) is the single-stranded RNA transcript comprising the nucleotide sequence information to synthesize polypeptides. It is different from tRNA or rRNA because it has a modified guanine (7-methylguanosine) base 5' cap and a series of adenine nucleotides as a 3' poly-A tail. 5' capping occurs early before the RNA polymerase is finished transcribing RNA.

The cap is used by a ribosome for attachment to begin translation; it provides stability for the mRNA molecule. The polyadenylation at the 3' end of the transcript creates the poly-A tail of approximately 150-200 adenine (A) nucleotides.

This is *template-independent* because it does not require a template strand for the polymerization to occur. This tail inhibits the degradation of mRNA in the cytoplasm by hydrolytic enzymes.

Delay of degradation allows the mRNA to remain in the cell cytoplasm for longer, leading to more polypeptides translated from the same transcript. Polyadenylation can occur in prokaryotes, but it instead promotes degradation.

The region between the 5' cap and the mRNA start codon is the 5' untranslated region (5'−UTR). Similarly, the region between the mRNA stop codon and the poly-A tail is the 3'−UTR. Although UTRs are not translated, they function for stability and localization of the pre-processed mRNA (pre-mRNA, heterogeneous nuclear RNA, or hnRNA).

*mRNA structure, including the untranslated regions (UTRs)*

### mRNA processing in eukaryotes

In eukaryotes, the newly-formed RNA (*primary transcript RNA* or *pre-RNA*) are processed before leaving the nucleus as a *mature RNA*. Processing involves capping and polyadenylation (described above).

Additional processing that must occur during the formation of the mature RNA molecule is the splicing of the *introns*, the non-coding RNA regions that must be excised. The *exons* are the coding regions that remain in the final transcript.

After the introns are excised, the exons are joined in the process of *RNA splicing*.

The mRNA exons are eventually translated into polypeptides after leaving the nucleus. The organization of genes into introns and exons is of evolutionary importance.

Exons generally represent functional protein domains, so splicing and exon composition changes allow the easy shuffling of protein domains to create new proteins.

Splicing differs during developmental (i.e., fetus, adult) or tissue-specific (e.g., lung, heart).

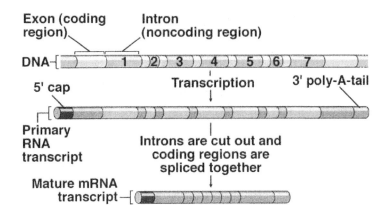

*mRNA with introns removed and exons ligated*

An exception for RNA processing involves mitochondria, which have the complete set of machinery needed to produce their proteins, and their circular DNA molecules (like prokaryotes) lack introns.

DNA is not always transcribed into mRNA; it produces other types of RNA such as *transfer RNA* (tRNA) or *ribosomal RNA* (rRNA). tRNA molecules travel out of the nucleus after transcription, where they are "activated" when a tRNA synthetase enzyme attaches the corresponding amino acid.

rRNAs (synthesized in the nucleolus within the nucleus), along with various proteins, form the subunits of ribosomes before the subunits migrate out of the nucleus into the cytoplasm.

**Histones and mechanism of transcription**

Transcription (DNA → RNA) transforms the information in stable DNA into dynamic mRNA, a necessary component for protein production.

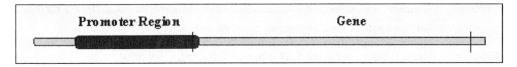

*A segment of DNA with upstream promoter region where RNA polymerase binds to initiate transcription*

Transcription takes place in the nucleus, where DNA to be transcribed adopts an "open" conformation, uncoiling and thus exposing the template strand.

DNA is usually tightly bound to histones, but the binding of histone deacetylases causes a conformational change in the DNA-histone complex, allowing the association to become loose and open. In an open conformation, exposed DNA promoter regions are likely to be recognized by transcription factors.

The *promoter* is regions on DNA where the RNA polymerase binds to begin transcription of mRNA. Promoters are often 30, 75, and 90 nucleotide base pairs upstream (towards the 5' end) from the *transcription start site* (TSS), where transcription begins.

RNA polymerase uncoils DNA to expose the template strand and processes from 3' to 5' along the DNA, incorporating free ribonucleotide triphosphates (NTPs) into the growing mRNA strand NTPs (i.e., ATP, CTP, GTP, or UTP) become ribonucleotides. Since RNA polymerase moves from the 3' to the 5' end of a DNA template sequence, the RNA transcript is synthesized in a 5' to 3' direction (same as in DNA synthesis), which requires a free 3'−OH end.

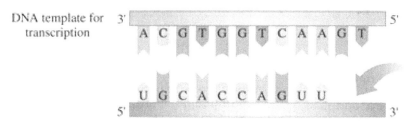

*The direction of transcription with bases added to 3' end of mRNA*

The mRNA strand is complementary to the DNA template and the same as the DNA coding strand (except uracil replaces thymine).

Phosphodiester bonds link ribonucleotides as is DNA, but with ribose instead of deoxyribose in DNA.

## RNA polymerase catalyzes mRNA formation

RNA polymerization creates transcripts that must dissociate from the template DNA. A short portion of the RNA is base-paired with the DNA for the correct sequence to be polymerized, but otherwise, the 5' end of the RNA transcript is not hydrogen-bonded to the template strand of the DNA double-strand. The DNA strands reform their double helix once the newly synthesized RNA dissociates from the DNA.

Unlike DNA polymerase III, RNA polymerase does not require a primer to initiate synthesis; the stretch of DNA template strand that encodes for a single RNA transcript is the *transcription unit* (i.e., promoter, RNA-coding sequence, and terminator).

In addition to the promoter and TSS, eukaryotes can contain a *TATA box* (or *Hogness box*) in their promoter, specialized thymine, and adenine nucleotides sequence. Eukaryotic transcription requires particular proteins, or *transcription factors*, to control and enable transcription.

Many transcription factors bind at the TATA box to regulate transcription.

Not all genes have a TATA box.

The *transcription initiation complex* is the complete assembly of transcription factors and RNA polymerase bound to the DNA.

## Termination of transcription

Termination of transcription occurs when RNA polymerization ends, and the RNA transcript is released from the DNA coding strand. Termination in prokaryotes occurs when the RNA polymerase transcribes the *terminator* sequence. Termination is not well understood in eukaryotes, but it includes various protein factors that interact with the DNA strand and the RNA polymerase.

Transcription in eukaryotes usually proceeds at least 30 base pairs after the RNA stop codon, and termination usually occurs in two ways.

*Intrinsic termination* is where specific sequences, the *termination sites* create a stem-loop in the RNA that causes the RNA to dissociate from the DNA template strand.

The second mechanism is *rho (ρ) dependent termination*, where the ρ protein factor travels along the synthesized RNA and dislodges the RNA polymerase off the DNA template strand.

**Multiple RNA polymerases transcribe the same template**

Cells produce thousands of copies of the same RNA transcripts. Since many transcripts are available for translation, protein synthesis occurs more quickly than if translation occurs along a single mRNA.

In prokaryotes and eukaryotes, multiple RNA polymerases transcribe the same template simultaneously.

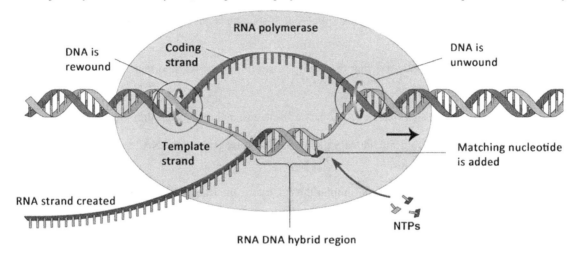

*RNA polymerase synthesizes a single strand of RNA complementary to the DNA template strand*

**Summary of transcription**

1. RNA polymerase binds to the promoter region on the DNA, initiating transcription.

2. RNA polymerase uncoils and separates the DNA strands as it synthesizes the RNA strand in a 5' to 3' direction.

3. One DNA strand is used as a template (antisense strand). The other strand (coding strand) is not used but has the same sequence as the RNA transcript (sense strand), except with thymine (in DNA) instead of uracil (in RNA).

4. Free nucleoside triphosphates (NTP) are incorporated, losing two of their phosphates. The new RNA nucleotides temporarily form base pairs with the template DNA.

5. The terminator sequence causes the RNA polymerase to stop transcription and separate from the DNA, and the DNA rewinds.

6. RNA destined for protein translation is messenger RNA (mRNA).

7. mRNA processes in the nucleus with splicing (remove introns and join exons), adding 5' G−cap and 3' poly−A tail.

8. Processed mRNA migrates through nuclear pores into the cytoplasm for protein translation.

**Functional and evolutionary significance of introns**

The role of RNA non-coding (intronic) regions of the genome is still contested.

Molecular biology is moving to understand that these regions are important in regulating gene products.

Intron sequences often contain short stretches of RNA, known as small interfering RNA (siRNA), which significantly affect regulating gene expression.

The evolutionary importance of the noncontinuity of the genome is controversial.

Some researchers assert that because spliceosome-splicing is not conserved in prokaryotes, it has limited importance to species' origin.

However, others hypothesize that the ability to shuffle genes is important to the evolution of unique phenotypes within a population.

Introns can provide significant evolutionary advantages, mainly because they enable alternative splicing.

For example, the thyroid and pituitary glands use the same primary mRNA transcript, but via alternative splicing, produce different proteins.

Investigators have found that the simpler the eukaryote, the less likely is the presence of introns.

Though introns are mostly restricted to eukaryotes, an intron has been discovered in the gene for a tRNA molecule in the cyanobacterium *Anabaena*; this intron is *self-splicing* (like a ribozyme) and capable of splicing itself out of an RNA transcript.

## Translation Synthesizes Proteins from mRNA

### mRNA and ribonucleases

Messenger RNA (mRNA) molecules containing information transcribed from DNA are transported into the cytosol from the nucleus after processing (i.e., 5' cap, 3' poly-A tail, and splicing – the removal of introns and ligation of exons). The mRNA contains the information necessary for ribosomes to assemble amino acids into polypeptides, the building blocks of proteins.

*Translational control* occurs in the cytoplasm after mRNA leaves the nucleus, but before there is a protein product. The life expectancy of mRNA molecules and their ability to bind ribosomes can vary.

The longer an active mRNA molecule remains in the cytoplasm; the more proteins are synthesized. mRNAs may need additional changes before they are translated.

*Ribonucleases* are enzymes that degrade RNA (e.g., mRNA). Mature mRNA molecules contain a 5'−cap and 3'−poly-A tail, non-coding segments that influence how long the mRNA can avoid being degraded by ribonucleases.

### Translational controls

An example of translational control in mature mammalian red blood cells that eject their nucleus but synthesize hemoglobin protein for several months, so the mRNAs in red blood cells must persist during this time since no additional RNA is transcribed.

Another example of translational control involves frog eggs with mRNA as "masked messengers" not translated until fertilization occurs. When fertilization of the frog egg occurs, the mRNA is "unmasked," and there is a rapid synthesis of proteins.

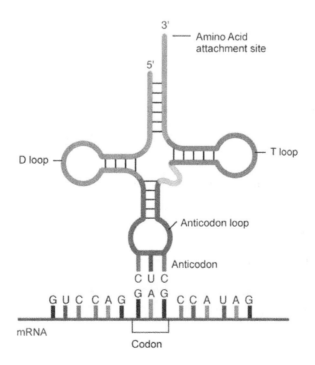

**Transfer RNA interprets codons**

Transfer RNA (tRNA) is the interpreter of the codons on the mRNA. tRNA associate each three-nucleotide anticodon with amino acids and transfer the corresponding amino acid to the growing polypeptides.

tRNA carries a single amino acid on its 3' end and has an anticodon segment.

An *anticodon* (contained within the *anticodon loop*) is a special three-nucleotide sequence on the tRNA molecule that base-pairs with a complementary three-nucleotide codon on the mRNA.

After a tRNA activated with amino acid base pairs (*via* hydrogen bonds) with a codon, the ribosome incorporates the amino acid into the growing polypeptide.

The tRNA, now free from the amino acid, which is part of the growing polypeptide, dissociates and returns to the cytoplasm, ready to become charged by binding another specific amino acid at its 3'− end.

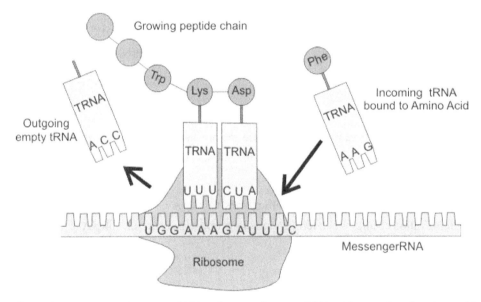

*Peptide synthesis using codons on mRNA and anticodons on tRNA with associated amino acids*

**tRNA as anticodons**

There are many tRNAs with anticodons complementary to codons.

A tRNA-activating enzyme (aminoacyl tRNA synthetase) charges the 3'−end of a tRNA with the correct amino acid, an *aminoacylation* process.

Twenty tRNA-activating enzymes corresponding to each of the 20 unique amino acids.

The chemical properties and three-dimensional structures of each tRNA allow the tRNA-activating enzymes to recognize their tRNA.

When the amino acid is attached to the tRNA molecule, a high-energy bond is created using ATP.

The energy stored from this high-energy bond transfers and binds the amino acids to the growing polypeptide chain during translation.

**Wobble position of mRNA**

The third base of an mRNA codon is the *wobble position* because of "flexibility" in the third position of codon-anticodon (hydrogen bonding) base pairing. For example, the base U of a tRNA anticodon in the third position can base pair with A or G. The most versatile tRNA have the modified base inosine (I) in the wobble position because inosine forms hydrogen bonds with U, C, or A.

Wobble explains why degenerate (synonymous) codons for an amino acid differ in the third position.

It allows a tRNA holding an amino acid to potentially bind to multiple codons with a different third base, each encoding for the same amino acid specific to that tRNA.

**Ribosomal RNA**

Ribosomal RNA (rRNA) is synthesized from a DNA template in the nucleolus (organelle in the nucleus).

Many proteins are transported from their site of synthesis in the cytoplasm into the nucleus, where rRNA and proteins form the small subunit (the 30S for prokaryotes and 40S for eukaryotes) the large subunit (50S for prokaryotes and 60S for eukaryotes) of the complete ribosome.

These two subunits travel out to the cytoplasm through the nuclear pores, where they join to form the complete ribosome (the 70S for prokaryotes and 80S for eukaryotes) when translation occurs.

Each ribosome is composed of dozens of associated proteins.

The "S" stands for Svedberg units, which measures the density and corresponds to the sedimentation value from the particles' configuration.

**Ribosomes structure and function**

The ribosome is composed of a few rRNA molecules and many proteins.

The ribosome consists of a small subunit and a large subunit. Prokaryotic ribosomes are the 70S (30S small subunit + 50S large subunit), while eukaryotic ribosomes are 80S (40S small subunit + 60S large subunit).

The Svedberg values for the subunits do not add sedimentation coefficients for the assembled ribosome due to differences in density of the complete structure compared to the individual subunits.

In ribosomes, the ribonucleotides of mRNA are interpreted and synthesized into an amino acid sequence.

The mRNA strand fits into a groove on the small subunit, bases pointing toward the large subunit.

The ribosome acts as a "reader," and when it reaches a termination sequence in the mRNA, the link between the synthesized polypeptide chain and tRNA is broken.

The completed polypeptide is released from the ribosome.

Prokaryotic cells contain about 10,000 ribosomes, and eukaryotic cells contain many more.

Ribosomes have binding sites for mRNA and tRNA molecules.

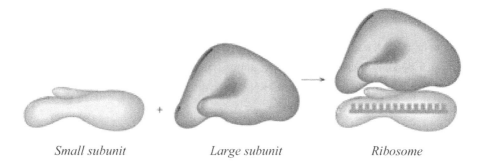

| *Small subunit* | *Large subunit* | *Ribosome* |

**Free *vs*. bound ribosomes**

Ribosomes can float freely in the cytosol or attach to the endoplasmic reticulum (ER); the *rough ER* is due to its appearance caused by the ribosomes studding its surface.

*Free ribosomes* synthesize proteins primarily used within the cytosol of the cell.

As small proteins emerge from the ribosome, they undergo folding.

Larger proteins fold within the recess of small, hollow chambers in proteins known as *chaperones*.

*Bound ribosomes* on the rough endoplasmic reticulum usually synthesize proteins used for the secretory pathway (e.g., secreted from the cell, embedded into membranes, or targeted for organelles).

Multiple ribosomes can simultaneously translate the same mRNA with elongating polypeptides of different lengths in relation to the ribosomes' progress.

A group of ribosomes on a single RNA is a *polyribosome* (polysome).

However, mRNA molecules cannot be translated indefinitely and are eventually degraded into ribonucleotides by cytoplasmic enzymes.

A ribosome has three sites holding a tRNA: the *E* (exit) *site*, *P* (peptidyl) *site,* and *A* (aminoacyl) *site.*

The E site is the 5' of the mRNA held by the ribosome and the A site on the 3'−side.

The E site holds a discharged tRNA that is ready for dissociation, the P site tRNA holds the growing polypeptide, and the A site tRNA holds the following amino acid to be added to the polypeptide chain.

**Post-translational modifications of protein**

*Post-translational control* regulates the activity of the protein in the cell after translation. For a polypeptide product of translation to become a functional protein, post-translational modifications are made.

These modifications include bending and twisting the chain into the correct three-dimensional shape (protein folding), sometimes facilitated by chaperone molecules.

The growing polypeptide folds into its tertiary structure, forming disulfide links, salt bridges, or other interactions that make the polypeptide a biologically-active protein.

Other changes include additions to the polypeptide chain, such as carbohydrate or lipid derivatives that may be covalently attached when the functional protein is folded.

The initial amino acid methionine is often removed from the beginning of the polypeptide. Some molecules are composed of multiple polypeptide chains that must be joined to achieve the functional protein (quaternary structure).

Post-translational control may involve degradation to "activate" a protein.

For example, the bovine protein proinsulin is inactive when first translated.

After a sequence of 30 amino acids is removed from the middle of the chain and disulfide bonds join the two pieces, the protein becomes active.

In other cases, proteins are degraded to cause deactivation.

**Proteasomes and signal sequence**

Proteasomes degrade misfolded, ubiquitinated proteins for amino acid protein recycling

*Proteasomes* (enzymes that target proteins) are large protein complexes that carry out this task.

For example, cyclins that control the cell cycle are present temporarily and degraded.

Proteins to be secreted from a cell have a signal sequence that binds to a specific membrane protein on the surface of the rough endoplasmic reticulum.

During translation, the protein is fed into the lumen of the rough ER; the signal sequence is removed.

Once the protein is folded correctly in the rough endoplasmic reticulum, portions of the endoplasmic reticulum bud off, forming vesicles with the properly folded protein.

The vesicles migrate to the Golgi apparatus and fuse with the Golgi membrane.

Within the Golgi, carbohydrates and other groups are added or removed according to the destinations of the proteins (most secreted proteins are glycoproteins).

The proteins are packaged into vesicles that bud off the surface of the Golgi membrane and may travel to the plasma membrane (secretory pathway), where they fuse and release their contents in the extracellular fluid through *exocytosis*.

## Eukaryotic Chromosome Organization

### Histone proteins and supercoiling

Histones are positively charged chromosomal proteins responsible for the compact packing and winding of chromosomal negatively charged DNA. A histone protein octamer and a histone H1 protein (nucleosome) form a protein core around which DNA winds to achieve a compact state.

Nonhistone chromosomal proteins are associated with the chromosomes. They have various functions, such as regulatory and enzymatic roles. An active research area is chromatin remodeling via histones to regulate gene expression within cells.

A chromosome consists of a single DNA molecule wound tightly around thousands of *histone* proteins. The basic unit of compact DNA is a *nucleosome* consisting of negatively charged DNA wound around a positively-charged histone octamer core and held in place by an additional histone H1.

A nucleosome consists of two H2A, two H2B, two H3, two H4, and one H1 histone.

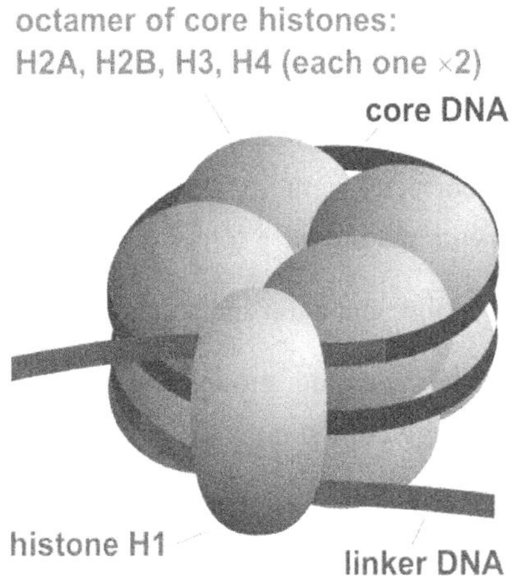

octamer of core histones:
H2A, H2B, H3, H4 (each one ×2)

core DNA

histone H1

linker DNA

*Nucleosome consists of an octomer and a histone H1*
*between the linked regions of the chromosome*

### Chromatin and nucleosomes

*Chromatin* is a strand of nucleic acid and associated protein.

A nucleosome is a bead-like unit made of DNA wound around a complex of histone proteins.

When DNA is wrapped around several nucleosomes, the resulting structure looks like beads on a string.

*Nucleosomes* form the basic unit of coiling in DNA.

In turn, these nucleosomes form higher-order coils, as *supercoils*.

The level of supercoiling influences transcription, decreasing transcription levels for compacted DNA.

Human DNA is separated into 46 compact, supercoiled pieces (organized into 23 pairs) with nucleosomes and other proteins. These separate pieces of nucleic acid comprise the chromosomes.

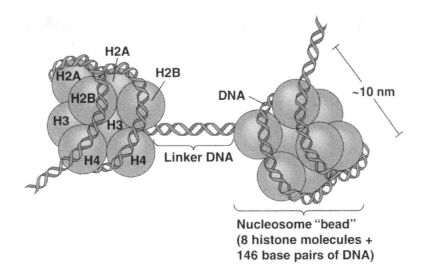

**Nucleosome "bead"**
**(8 histone molecules +**
**146 base pairs of DNA)**

### Centromeres hold sister chromatids during replication

A *centromere* is a heterochromatin (i.e., tightly coiled DNA) region on the chromosome at the center (metacentric) or near one of the ends (telocentric).

After replication, sister chromatids are attached at the centromere.

During mitosis, spindle fibers (comprised of tubulin) are attached to the centromere (via the kinetochore) and pull the sister chromatids apart during anaphase.

During anaphase of mitosis, the centromere splits, and the sister chromatids become chromosomes in the daughter cell during cell division.

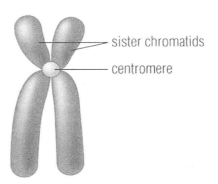

*One chromosome with two sister chromatids attached at the centromere*

## Control of Gene Expression in Eukaryotes

**Transcriptional control by DNA binding proteins**

*Transcriptional control* in the nucleus determines which structural genes are transcribed and the rate of transcription. It includes the organization of chromatin and the protein transcription factors initiating transcription. Regulatory proteins include repressors and activators, and they influence the attachment of RNA polymerase to the promoter region on the DNA.

*Transcription factors* are positively charged proteins with DNA-binding domains that allow them to bind to the promoter, enhancer, and silencer regions of DNA to regulate transcription. *Enhancers* increase transcription when bound, while *silencers* decrease it.

Transcription factors are influenced by intracellular or extracellular signals, accounting for the wide variation in gene expression in cell types. Pathways and types of signals exist to influence transcription factors, including the allosteric regulation of proteins and covalent modifications by kinases, phosphatases, and other enzymes. The DNA-binding domains themselves are varied in how they interact with the DNA double helix.

Common domains include helix-turn-helix (HTH), zinc finger, and basic region leucine zipper (bZIP).

*Pre-initiation complex* forms when transcription factors gather at the promoter region (segment of DNA where RNA polymerase binds) adjacent to a structural gene. The transcription factor complex leads to activation (or repression) of the gene. The complex attracts and binds RNA polymerase or promotes the separation of DNA strands. However, transcription may (or may not) begin at this point, depending on which transcription factors (activators or repressors) are bound.

While promoters are generally close to the affected gene in prokaryotes and eukaryotes, eukaryotic regulatory elements (i.e., enhancers and silencers) can be far from the promoter – even thousands of nucleotides away along the DNA strand that bends to stabilize the structure. This is not true for prokaryotic regulatory elements.

Since the enhancers and silencers must interact with the promoter to influence transcription, eukaryotic DNA can loop back on itself. The transcription factor bound to the enhancer or silencer can contact the promoter or RNA polymerase. Intermediate proteins between the transcription factors and RNA polymerase are often involved in the process.

**Gene amplification and duplication**

*Gene duplication* (gene amplification or chromosomal duplication) is a mechanism by which genetic material is duplicated and serves as a molecular evolution source. There are many ways gene duplication occurs.

*Ectopic recombination* occurs during unequal crossing over between homologous chromosomes (during meiosis) due to the DNA sequence similarity at duplication breakpoints.

*Replication slippage* arises from an error in DNA replication; the DNA polymerase dissociates and re-attaches to the DNA at an incorrect position and mistakenly duplicates a section.

*Aneuploidy* (an abnormal number of chromosomes, often harmful) is another example of gene duplication, as is *polyploidy* (whole genome duplications), due to *nondisjunction*, the failure of sister chromatids (i.e., mitosis) or homologous chromosomes (i.e., meiosis) to separate properly during cell division.

Gene duplication is evolutionarily advantageous because it creates genetic redundancy.

A mutation in the second copy of a gene may not have harmful effects on the organism because the original gene can still function to encode functional protein products.

Since mutations of the second copy of a gene are not directly harmful, mutations accumulate rapidly (in the duplicated region) than usual. The second copy of the gene can develop a new function.

Therefore, gene duplication is believed to have played an essential role in evolution.

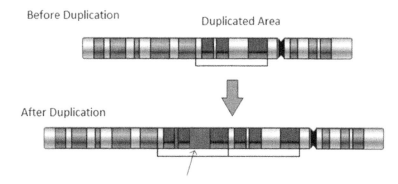

*Point mutations are common in duplicated regions and accelerate the evolution of new proteins*

## Post-transcriptional control and mRNA splicing

*Post-transcriptional control* occurs in the nucleus after DNA has been transcribed and mRNA has formed. In this regulation, the RNA strands are processed before leaving the nucleus with certain variations.

Timing is one form of control. The speed at which mRNAs leave the nucleus affects the amount of gene product available per unit of time.

Various mRNA molecules differ in the rate they travel through the nuclear pores.

Additionally, mRNA must eventually be degraded, and the rate and timing of mRNA degradation, controlled by the cell, affect how much protein is translated. Modifications, such as adding a 5' cap and a 3' poly-A tail, affect control by protecting the mRNA from ribonuclease degradation.

Post-transcriptional control affects the sequences present in the RNA products.

Alternative splicing is the process by which introns are removed (cut from the transcript), and exons are ligated (rejoined) in different ways, forming mRNA products from the same initial hnRNA transcript.

The hypothalamus and thyroid gland contains the gene that encodes for the peptide hormone calcitonin, but the mRNA that leaves the nucleus, therefore the translated protein, is not the same in both types of cells.

Alternative splicing of the calcitonin gene occurs in the hypothalamus, leading to the production of a calcitonin gene-related peptide (CGRP). The thyroid gland produces regular calcitonin. Radioactive labeling experiments show different splicing in these strands.

Alternative splicing has been observed in cells that produce neurotransmitters, muscle regulatory proteins, and antibodies.

Additionally, experiments indicate that alternative splicing occurs at various development stages (i.e., embryogenic *vs.* adult cells).

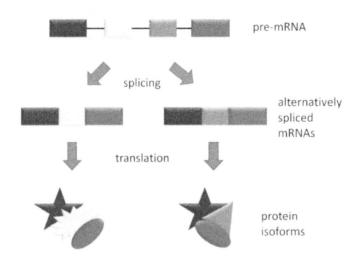

RNAs are subject to post-transcriptional control. For example, special modifications to nucleotides are made to control the structure of tRNA and rRNA.

## Cancer

Cancer is a disorder that arises from mutations in the somatic cells and results from the failure of the control system that regulates cell division, which leads to uncontrolled growth.

Cancer may develop in tissues and has terminology depending on the location and the way it develops.

*Carcinomas* are cancers in epithelial cells, *sarcomas* are cancers in muscle cells, and *lymphomas* are cancers involving white blood cells. The lungs, colon, and breasts are the organs commonly affected by cancer.

The incidence of cancer increases with age due to the accumulation of defective mutations (i.e., mutagen exposure or errors during DNA replication).

## Oncogenes and tumor suppressor genes

*Oncogenes* are dominant cancer-producing genes encoded for irregular forms of cell surface receptors that bind growth factors, producing a continuous growth signal. Oncogenes cause cancer when they are activated. The products of many oncogenes are involved in increased cell division.

Before an oncogene is activated, it may be a harmless *proto-oncogene*. Researchers have identified several proto-oncogenes whose mutation to an oncogene cause increased growth and leads to tumor formation.

The *ras* (italicized, lowercase for the gene and capitalized for the corresponding protein) family of genes is the common group of oncogenes implicated in human cancers.

The alteration of one nucleotide pair converts a normal functioning *ras* proto-oncogene to an oncogene.

*Tumor suppressor genes* are recessive cancer-producing genes with mutated forms. Tumor suppressor genes protect cells from becoming cancerous by inhibiting tumor formation through cell division control.

Mutations in tumor suppressor genes alter the protective proteins encoded by these genes and disrupt their function, leading to cancer. A *tumor* is an abnormal replication of cells that form a tissue mass. If the cells remain localized, the tumor is *benign* (i.e., remains localized), but if the tumor invades the surrounding tissue because it undergoes metastasis, it is *malignant*.

Tumor-suppressor gene, *p53*, is frequently mutated in cancers compared to other known genes. The p53 protein acts as a transcription factor to turn on the expression of genes whose products are cell cycle inhibitors.

The p53 can stimulate *apoptosis* (i.e., programmed cell death), the ability of cells to self-destruct by autodigestion with endogenous enzymes. In apoptosis, the plasma membrane is kept intact, and the digested contents are not released; instead, phagocytic cells engulf the whole cell to eliminate these undesirable cells.

Cancer cells continue to grow and divide in situations where normal cells would not (lack contact inhibition); they fail to respond to cellular controls and signals that halt growth in normal cells. Cancer cells avoid the apoptosis (self-destruction) that normal cells undergo when extensive DNA damage occurs.

Cancer cells stimulate angiogenesis (the formation of new blood vessels) to nourish the cancer cell, and they are immortal (divide for generations after a normal cell). In contrast, normal cells die after some divisions.

Cancer cells can *metastasize* (relocate) and grows in another location.

## Heterochromatin *vs.* euchromatin

DNA exists as euchromatin and heterochromatin within the cell.

*Euchromatin* is a looser conformation of DNA and histones than the tightly-condensed *heterochromatin*. Euchromatin appears lighter than the darker heterochromatin when viewed under an electron microscope.

DNA sequences in heterochromatin are generally repressed, while those in euchromatin are available and actively transcribed when the RNA polymerase binds to the single-stranded DNA.

Much of the satellite DNA (large, tandem repeats of noncoding DNA) appears in heterochromatin.

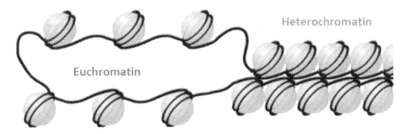

*Euchromatin is transcribed while heterochromatin is not transcribed*

When DNA is transcribed, activators known as remodeling proteins can push aside the histone portion of the chromatin, allowing transcription to begin.

During interphase ($G_1$, S, and $G_2$ phase), chromatin exists as either of the two types, but it condenses to supercoiled heterochromatin during mitosis.

**Chromatin remodeling**

The form of compactness that the DNA adopts depends on the cell's cellular needs and is regulated by covalent *histone modifications* by specific enzymes.

Examples of modifications are *histone methylation*, causing tighter packing that prevents transcription.

*Histone acetylation* uncoils DNA and promotes transcription.

There are other types of histone modifications, such as ubiquitination and phosphorylation.

As an active area of investigation, the *histone code hypothesis* states that DNA transcription is partly regulated by these histone modifications, especially on the unstructured ends of histones.

*Chromatin remodeling complexes* are another mechanism for regulating chromatin structure. These protein complexes are ATP-dependent and thus have a common ATPase domain.

ATP hydrolysis gives these domains the energy to reposition nucleosomes and move histones, creating uncoiled DNA regions available for transcription.

**DNA methylation regulates gene expression**

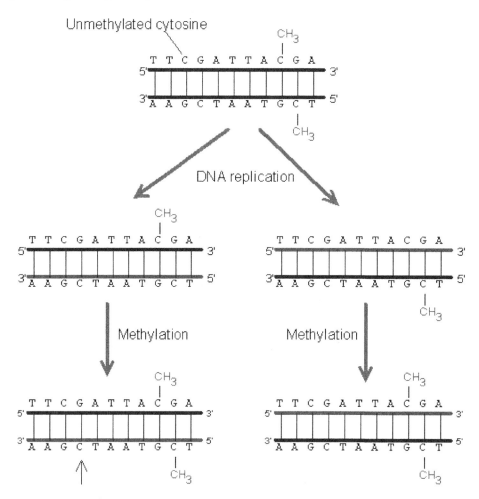

*Modifications such as methylation facilitate proper DNA repair*

*DNA methylation*, which reduces the transcription rate, is another method that the cell uses to regulate gene expression. DNA methyltransferase enzymes add a methyl ($-CH_3$) group to the cytosine bases of DNA, converting them to 5-methylcytosine.

The methylated cytosine residues are usually adjacent to guanine, which results in methylated cytosines diagonal from each other.

DNA methylation patterns are heritable to daughter cells, as it is passed on during cell division.

*Epigenetics* studies potential transcriptional changes (such as DNA methylation and histone modification) that do not involve DNA sequence changes.

## Non-coding RNA for regulatory control

*Non-coding RNA* (ncRNA) is functional RNA not translated into proteins. They have an essential role in many cellular processes, including RNA splicing, DNA replication, and the regulation of gene expression.

ncRNA can participate in histone modification, DNA methylation, and heterochromatin formation.

The majority of ncRNA are *long ncRNA* (over 200 nucleotides) that form a complex with chromatin-modifying proteins and function in chromatin remodeling.

There are three classes of *short ncRNA* (less than 30 nucleotides), including microRNA (miRNA), short interfering RNAs, and piwi-interacting RNA.

*microRNAs* (miRNA) are folded RNA molecules with hairpin loops that bind to target mRNA sequences through complementary base pairing. miRNA can induce degradation of the mRNA by shortening its poly-A tail, which destabilizes the mRNA, or they can cleave the mRNA into pieces. This silences the mRNA and prevents translation from occurring.

A single miRNA molecule can target and repress several mRNAs.

*Short interfering RNAs* (siRNAs) are double-stranded RNA molecules often created through catalysis by the Dicer enzyme, which produces siRNAs from longer double-stranded RNAs. siRNAs function similarly to miRNAs, as they interfere with the expression of genes with complementary sequences.

siRNA degrades mRNA, blocks translation, induces heterochromatin formation, and blocks transcription.

*Piwi-interacting RNAs* (piRNA) form RNA-protein complexes with the piwi family of proteins, and they are the largest class of short ncRNA in animal cells. They suppress transposon activity in germline cells by forming an *RNA-induced silencing complex*. piRNAs do not have any known secondary structure motifs.

## Senescence and aging

*Senescence* is the gradual deterioration of function in an organism, eventually leading to death. Except for a few with remarkable properties of immortality, all organisms undergo senescence.

One of the most puzzling questions humans currently face is *why* they age.

Some have suggested that senescence results in avoiding cancer, while others blame environmental factors such as radiation and oxidative agents, causing DNA damage and cellular damage. The reasons for senescence are likely a combination of these and other factors.

At the cellular level, senescence refers to a cell that is no longer able to divide.

Generally, cells are limited to 50 to 70 divisions, a threshold of the *Hayflick limit.*

A senescent cell is not dead; instead, it actively continues its metabolic functions. The condition may be initiated by activation of oncogenes or by the cell's recognition of its DNA damage.

*Oncogenes* signal abnormal cells to avoid senescence or undergo apoptosis to avoid tumor development.

**Factors damaging DNA**

Causes of DNA damage include radiation, oxidation (free radical damage), and telomeres' shortening.

*Telomeres* are nonsensical DNA sequence repeats added to the 3' ends of DNA strands by the enzyme *telomerase.*

Replication inevitably incurs shortening of the DNA, leading to DNA damage so severe that the cell cannot continue dividing.

Telomeres act as fodder for the inevitable losses from DNA replication to protect the encoding regions from destruction.

Telomerase allows cells to proliferate for incredibly long periods because they are not affected by the loss of DNA incurred by replication.

Most cells are subject to the Hayflick limit, but embryonic cells and specific adult cells contain high telomerase levels to divide continually.

The shortening of telomeres is associated with various diseases involving premature aging, such as pulmonary fibrosis (scarring of the lungs).

Shortened telomeres prevent the cells from dividing without losing genes, leading to cellular senescence.

The lack of sufficient telomeres may cause chromosomes to fuse, corrupting the genetic blueprint, making the chromosomes appear broken.

The cell eventually recognizes what appears to be DNA damage and thus enters apoptosis.

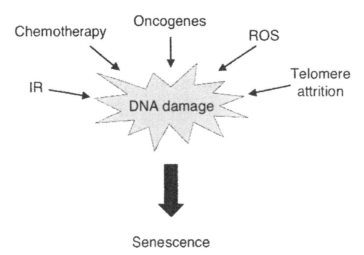

*Environmental and biochemical factors contributing to senescence*

# CHAPTER 10

# Heredity

- Mendelian Concepts of Inheritance

- Meiosis and Genetic Variability of Offspring

- Experimental Methods of Genetics

## Mendelian Concepts of Inheritance

### Mendel established the field of genetics

Gregor Mendel (1822-1884) was an Austrian monk whose experiments with plant breeding in the mid-1800s formed the basis of modern genetics. Mendel was a friar at the monastery of St. Thomas in Brunn, Austria, while teaching part-time at a local secondary school. Mendel's goal was to have firm scientific evidence for how genetic information is passed from parents to offspring. He focused on how plant offspring acquired traits from their parents. He traced the inheritance of individual traits and kept careful records of numbers, then used his understanding of probability to interpret the results.

Mendel chose to study the *Pisum sativum* (garden pea), as it was easy to cultivate, had a short generation time, and could be cross-pollinated by hand. Mendel chose 22 of the many pea varieties for his experiments. Concerning certain traits, the plants used in the experiment had to be *true-breeding* (progeny identical to parents). He chose this approach to ensure accuracy and simplicity in his studies.

Inbreeding genetically similar individuals obtain true-bred organisms for several generations. Pea plants can be *self-pollinated*, an effective form of inbreeding. The process eliminates genetic variation from the gene pool and results in a strain with certain identical traits in all individuals.

Mendel studied seven traits: seed shape, seed color, flower position, flower color, pod shape, pod color, and plant height. He correctly hypothesized that the inheritance pattern between generations was because the genetic information was being passed from their parents. He terms these *hereditary factors.*

### Particulate theory of inheritance

The *particulate theory of inheritance* proposed by Mendel stated that factors, or "discrete particles," do not blend.

This contrasts with the *blending theory of inheritance*, discredited, which stated that offspring have traits blended from the parents. For example, red and white flowers would produce pink flowers. This is observed in nature, but the pink offspring self-fertilize and produce several all-red and all-white offspring. Proponents of the blending theory dismissed this as mere instability in genetic material.

Charles Darwin wanted to develop a theory of evolution based on hereditary principles, but the blending theory did not account for genetic variation and species diversity.

Mendel's particulate theory properly accounts for Charles Darwin's theory of evolution, although he never knew this because he did not live to see Mendel's work rediscovered. A *particulate inheritance theory* is essential for Darwin's theory of *natural selection*. Otherwise, any selectively favored trait would be blended away when the selected individual reproduced with one of a different trait.

Mendel's explanation of heredity was remarkable since it was based solely on the interpretation of breeding experiments, and it was done long before scientists understood cell division and molecular biology.

During the early part of the 20th century, the processes of mitosis and meiosis were discovered by the microscopic examination of cells. Researchers found that Mendel's hereditary factors were not free-floating particles but instead were on chromosomes in the nucleus. The hereditary factors were given the name genes.

**Genes, autosomes and diploidy**

A *gene* is a stretch of DNA encoding for a trait (or characteristic). Genes encode for a protein that produces a trait on a molecular level. An organism's *genome* includes its entire set of genes.

The *chromosomal theory of inheritance* states that genes are on chromosomes, and inheritance patterns are explained by the locations of genes on chromosomes.

Chromosomes are classified as autosomes and allosomes.

*Autosomes* are non-sex chromosomes with the same number and kind in all sexes. *Allosomes* are sex chromosomes (e.g., X or Y). Humans have 22 pairs of autosomes (44 total) and 1 pair of allosomes (2 total).

*Diploidy* is the characteristic of having pairs of chromosomes. One member of each pair is from the mother, and the other is from the father. *Homologous chromosomes* are similar but not identical copies.

**Loci, genotype and phenotype**

A *locus* is the location of a gene or segment of DNA on a chromosome. Loci are mapped by their physical position on the chromosome or by their relative distance from each other.

The loci of two homologous chromosomes are identical in their placement and align during meiosis.

Loci are identical, but the gene at a locus may be in different forms (e.g., brown eyes or blue eyes) as *alleles*. An allele is an alternative form of the gene and differs from another allele by one or more nucleotide bases that encode a specific protein.

Diploid organisms have two similar versions of each chromosome so that an individual can have a maximum of two alleles for each gene, one on each chromosome. One allele comes from the mother, and one comes from the father. Traits exhibited by an organism are determined based on the alleles an individual has inherited.

**Alleles for blood types**

A diploid organism inherits two alleles, but there are usually more than two alleles of each gene.

*Multiple alleles* are when more than two alleles encode for a characteristic. A classic example is blood type in humans. There are three blood group alleles: $I^A$, $I^B$ and i.

Each can have two alleles, so the possible combinations are $I^A I^A$, $I^A i$, $I^B I^B$, $I^B i$, $I^A I^B$ and ii. An organism's combination of alleles is its *genotype.*

| Genotype | Blood type (phenotype) |
|:---:|:---:|
| $I^A I^A$ or $I^A i$ | A |
| $I^B I^B$ or $I^B i$ | B |
| $I^A I^B$ | AB |
| ii | O |

**Homozygosity and heterozygosity**

*Zygosity* is the similarity of the alleles at any given locus.

An individual is *homozygous* for a gene when the two alleles that the individual carries are identical.

For blood types, people with the genotype $I^AI^A$, $I^BI^B$ and ii are homozygous with two identical alleles.

A *heterozygous* individual has two different alleles, as the genotypes $I^Ai$, $I^Bi$, and $I^AI^B$.

**Wild-type and recessive phenotypes**

The *wild-type allele* is the most prevalent and dominant version of the allele, with exceptions.

*Mutant alleles* are the product of changes in the nucleotide sequence within DNA (mutation) and are generally less common in a population.

For example, red eyes are a wild-type trait in Drosophila (fruit fly), while white eyes are the mutant trait. However, alleles often do not fit into these categories with an additional variation.

When an allele is *recessive,* the individual must inherit two copies of this allele to express the trait. The *dominant* allele is when a single copy is needed for it to be observed. A dominant allele masks (or hides) the expression of a recessive allele.

For example, the allele for attached earlobes in humans is recessive, and the allele for unattached earlobes is dominant. An individual must inherit two attached earlobe alleles to express this trait. If she inherits one attached allele and one unattached allele, the unattached allele dominates the other, leading to unattached earlobes.

By convention, the dominant allele is an uppercase letter, and the recessive allele is a lower-case letter. The letter is the first letter of the dominant or recessive allele (by convention).

For example, in Mendel's pea plants, the alleles for seed shape are named R for the dominant round allele. The recessive allele, wrinkled, is denoted *r.* However, in fruit flies, the wing size alleles are named for the recessive allele, vestigial wings.

Therefore, the dominant allele (normal wings) is denoted V and the recessive allele as v. In many cases, the locus is given one letter. The alleles are superscripts of the letter.

For example, with sex chromosomes (e.g., $X^AX^a$). Complex naming schemes are seen for multiple alleles (e.g., blood types) and co-dominant or incompletely dominant alleles (discussed later).

**Genotype and phenotype**

*Genotype* is the alleles received when an organism is conceived.

The *phenotype* describes the observable traits which are expressed. Due to recessiveness and dominance, zygosity cannot be deduced by observation of phenotype.

Two organisms with different allele combinations can have the same phenotype.

For example, if a homozygous individual has the alleles $I^AI^A$ and a heterozygous individual has the alleles $I^Ai$, they have different genotypes but the same phenotype, and both exhibit blood type A since $I^A$ is a dominant allele. Its presence overshadows the i allele in the heterozygous individual.

Mendel inferred genotype from observable phenotype by performing breeding experiments that revealed how traits emerge, disappear, and re-emerge over generations.

Traits are *characters,* and their expression in an individual is a *character state.*

Mendel streamlined his experiments by using *discontinuous* character state*s* (i.e., no intermediates).

Discontinuous traits have discrete, distinct categories; the trait is either there or not. Mendel could quantify his results by counting the two phenotypes among the offspring of each experimental cross.

Mendel's knowledge of statistics enabled him to recognize that his results followed theoretical probability calculations, even though his small sample size resulted in slight deviations from expected ratios.

**Probability of inheritance**

*Probability* is the likelihood that a given event occurs by random chance.

With a coin flip, there is a 50% chance of heads and a 50% chance of tails. In Mendelian genetics, the chance of inheriting one of two alleles from the parent is 50%.

The *multiplicative law of probability* states that the chance of two or more independent events occurring together is the product of the probability of the events occurring separately.

If two parents heterozygous for unattached earlobes (genotype Ee) have a child, the probability of the child's genotype is calculated.

In half (½) of cases, the mother passes an E allele to the child, and in the other half, she passes an e allele. The same is true for the father.

The possible combinations for the child's genotype, where one allele is inherited from the mother and another from the father:

$$EE = ½ × ½ = ¼, \quad eE = ½ × ½ = ¼ \quad Ee = ½ × ½ = ¼ \quad ee = ½ × ½ = ¼$$

The *additive law of probability* calculates the probability of an event that occurs in two or more independent ways; it is the sum of individual probabilities of each way an event can occur.

In the example, the chance that the child is a heterozygote is the sum of the probability of having the genotype eE (¼) or Ee (¼) = ½, or a 50% chance.

The probability of having unattached earlobes is the sum of the probabilities of inheriting at least one E (dominant) allele. This sum is ¼ + ¼ + ¼ = ¾, or a 75% chance.

**Punnett square for probabilities of inheritance**

These laws of probability were used in creating a method that predicts the genotypic results of genetic crosses: the *Punnett square,* introduced by R. C. Punnett.

For example, in a Punnett square, all types of alleles from the father's gametes may be aligned vertically.

All possible alleles from the mother's gametes may be aligned horizontally; possible combinations of offspring are placed in squares.

The Punnett square predicts the chance of each child's genotype and corresponding phenotype.

In genetics, probability depends on independent, mutually exclusive events.

For example, the odds of a couple having a boy or a girl is 50%.

Using the multiplicative law of probability, it is overall unlikely that a couple has 5 boys:

$$\frac{1}{2} \times \frac{1}{2} \times \frac{1}{2} \times \frac{1}{2} \times \frac{1}{2} = 1/32, \text{ or } 3.125\%.$$

However, this probability has no bearing on each event.

If the couple has four boys, there is a 50% chance their fifth child is a boy or a girl.

Each fertilization is an independent event.

In the Punnett square below, note that the mother has two copies of the X allele, while the father has one X allele and one Y allele.

In 50% of cases, the child inherits an X from the mother and an X from the father, while in the other 50% of cases, the child inherits an X from the mother and a Y from the father.

Mother

|  |  | X | X |
|---|---|---|---|
| Father | X | XX (Girl) | XX (Girl) |
|  | Y | XY (Boy) | XY (Boy) |

*Punnett square for the probability that parents have a girl (XX) or boy (XY); probability is 50%.*

**Monohybrid cross**

Mendel began his experiments by creating true-breeding plants and *crossing* (mating) two true-breeding strains for alleles of the same trait.

An example is to cross a true-breeding pea plant with round seeds with another plant with wrinkled seeds; these two individuals constitute the *parental (P) generation.*

Crossbreeding is accomplished by removing the pollen-producing male organs from a "father" plant and using them to fertilize the ovary of another.

Because pea plants are *monoecious* (both male and female reproductive organs), Mendel removed the male organs from the "mother" plant to prevent self-pollinating.

The *first filial* (F1) generation is the hybrid offspring produced by this cross.

These individuals breed with one another to produce the *second filial* (F2) generation.

This is a *monohybrid cross* because it is between two individuals heterozygous for a single trait (e.g., Rr × Rr). This produces F2 offspring in a phenotypic ratio of 3:1 round to wrinkled seeds.

Example using true-breeding plants with round seeds and true-breeding plants with wrinkled seeds.

Compare results to genotype to observed phenotype ratios.

**Test cross**

Proportions of a test cross with a homozygous dominant

| P generation: | homozygous round (RR) × homozygous wrinkled (rr) |
|---|---|
| F1 generation: | 100% heterozygous round (Rr) |
| F2 generation: | 25% homozygous round (RR) |
| | 50% heterozygous round (Rr) |
| | 25% homozygous wrinkled (rr) |
| | Genotypic ratio: 1:2:1 RR to Rr to rr |
| | Phenotypic ratio: 3:1 round-seeded to wrinkle-seeded |

The F2 offspring ratio is conceptualized using a Punnett square of the F1 generation cross, Rr × Rr:

|  | | **Parent 1 gametes** | |
|---|---|---|---|
| | | **R** | **r** |
| **Parent 2 gametes** | **R** | RR | Rr |
| | **r** | Rr | rr |

When Mendel performed this experiment with the six other traits for pea plants, he obtained similar results.

He recognized a pattern of 3:1 phenotypic ratio in the F2 generation.

Mendel extended his experimental results by inductive reasoning to claim that discontinuous traits would follow the same pattern no matter the animal or plant studied. This was how he developed the notion that each distinct phenotypic trait in an individual is controlled by two "hereditary factors" (now termed alleles).

The alternative hypothesis that each trait is controlled by one factor was not a viable explanation because it could not explain the reappearance of wrinkled seeds in the F2 generation.

These observations led him to develop the principles of dominance and recessiveness since he understood that the factor for round seeds masked the factor for wrinkled seeds.

He could have hypothesized that there are more than two hereditary factors in each. However, he used the principle of *parsimony*, which states that the simplest explanation for an observation is likely accurate.

**Mendel's law of segregation**

From these conclusions, Mendel was able to deduce his first law of inheritance: *the law of segregation*.

Organisms have two alleles for each trait, segregating during gamete formation for one allele per gamete.

During fertilization, gametes from two individuals are united, giving the offspring a complete set of alleles for each trait.

Although Mendel did not understand meiosis when he formulated his theories, he correctly outlined its principles in this law. He understood that if two alleles control each distinct phenotype, it follows that one is passed to the offspring by each parent. Otherwise, the number of alleles doubles with every generation.

Mendel's law of segregation is consistent with the particulate theory of inheritance because individual "discrete particles" of inheritance are passed on from generation to generation.

### Dihybrid crosses

Mendel performed a *dihybrid cross* between two organisms heterozygous for two traits rather than one.

A dihybrid cross is achieved by first crossing parent organisms true-breeding for different forms of two traits; it produces F1 offspring heterozygous for both traits (dihybrids).

Mendel performed a dihybrid cross of the F1 individuals with one another.

He expected the dihybrids to produce two types of gametes: dominant (RY) and recessive (ry) gametes.

He thought he would see a phenotypic ratio of 3:1 in the F2 generation, as with his monohybrid crosses.

This means that 75% of the F2 would be round and yellow, and 25% would be wrinkled and green.

Mendel's expected Punnett square for his F1 dihybrid cross:

|      | RY   | ry   |
|------|------|------|
| RY   | RRYY | RrYy |
| ry   | RrYy | rryy |

| | |
|---|---|
| P generation: | homozygous round yellow (RRYY) × homozygous wrinkled green (rryy) |
| F1 generation: | 100% heterozygous round yellow offspring (RrYy) |
| F2 generation: | 25% homozygous round, homozygous yellow (RRYY) |
| | 50% heterozygous round, heterozygous yellow (RrYy) |
| | 25% homozygous wrinkled, homozygous green (rryy) |
| | Genotypic ratio: 1:2:1 RRYY to RrYy to rryy |
| | Phenotypic ratio: 3:1 round yellow to wrinkled green offspring |

However, Mendel observed the following results from the dihybrid cross.

Parents' genotype                      RRYY   ×   rryy

Parents' gametes                          RY        ry

F1 generation                                    RrYy

F1 gametes                                RY  rY  Ry  ry

Punnett square of gametes produced

|      | RY   | Ry   | rY   | ry   |
|------|------|------|------|------|
| RY   | RRYY | RRYy | RrYY | RrYy |
| Ry   | RRYy | RRyy | RrYy | Rryy |
| rY   | RrYY | RrYy | rrYY | rrYy |
| ry   | RrYy | Rryy | rrYy | rryy |

☐ Round and yellow phenotype            ▨ Wrinkled and yellow phenotype
▨ Round and green phenotype             ☐ Wrinkled and green phenotype

## Mendel's law of independent assortment

The offspring from that cross produced a phenotypic ratio of 9:3:3:1 (of round and yellow, round and green, wrinkled and yellow, and wrinkled and green). It was not predicted that the offspring could have the dominant form of one phenotype and the recessive form of the other.

He deduced that dihybrids produce not two types of gametes (RY and ry) but *four:* RY, Ry, rY, and ry.

He realized that dominant alleles do not have to be shuffled into the same gametes as other dominant alleles, nor do recessive alleles.

*Mendel's law of independent assortment* states that alleles assort independently from other alleles and that a parent's gametes contain all possible combinations of alleles. This leads to a phenotypic ratio of 9:3:3:1 in dihybrid crosses. However, the ratio often breaks down in complex cases, patterns of *non-Mendelian inheritance* (do not follow Mendel's laws), for reasons that would not be understood until the 20ᵗʰ century.

Humans cannot be bred like pea plants, so their genetic relationships are studied using pedigrees.

## Pedigree analysis

*Pedigrees* are charts that portray family histories by including phenotypes and family relationships. In a pedigree chart, squares represent males, circles represent females, and diamonds represent individuals of unspecified sex. If an individual displays a trait studied, their shape is filled.

Heterozygotes are half-filled (if the disorder is autosomal) or have a shaded dot inside the symbol (if the disorder is sex-linked). If the trait of interest is a disease, heterozygotes are *carriers*.

However, it is not known if an individual is heterozygous since this may not be visible phenotypically.

Lines between individuals denote relationships. Horizontal lines connect mating couples, and a vertical line connects to their offspring.

Siblings are grouped under a horizontal line that branches from this vertical one, with the oldest sibling on the left and the youngest on the right.

If the offspring are twins, they are connected by a triangle. If an individual dies, its symbol is crossed out. If it is stillborn or aborted, it is indicated by a small circle.

The generations are shown with Roman numerals (I, II, III), and each from the same generation is indicated by Arabic numbers (1, 2, 3). The pattern of inheritance of a trait is determined by analyzing pedigrees.

Often, the trait in question is a genetic disease. These are typically recessive traits seen by the way the disorder skips generations, passed by carriers.

The first family member to seek treatment for the disease is the *proband* and indicated by an arrow.

The proband serves as the starting point for the pedigree, and researchers may work backward and forward from there.

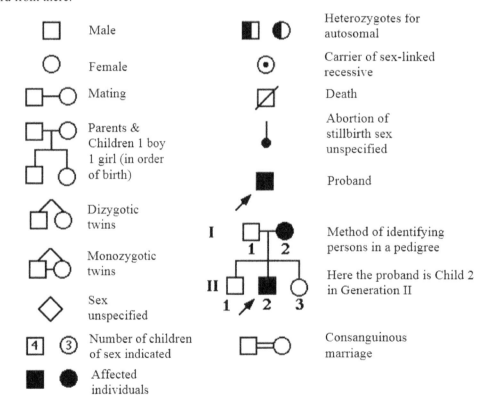

*Pedigree chart convention specifying relationships and observed phenotypes*

**Phenotypes for complete dominance**

Dominance is a relationship between alleles of one gene, in which one allele is expressed over a second allele at the same locus. Thus far, only *complete dominance* of alleles has been discussed. This occurs when only one dominant allele is needed to express a trait since it masks the recessive allele.

The traits of Mendel's pea plants had complete dominance, with a round seed shape dominating the wrinkled seed shape.

| Genotype | Phenotype |
|---|---|
| *RR* | Dominant - round |
| *Rr* | Dominant - round |
| *rr* | Recessive - wrinkled |

The homozygous dominant and heterozygous individual exhibit the "dominant phenotype," but the heterozygote has a recessive allele, though not observed.

**Phenotypes for co-dominance**

In *co-dominance*, two or more alleles are equally dominant, so a heterozygote expresses the phenotypes associated with both alleles. A famous example in humans is the ABO blood type system, a multiple allele system.

The locus is named "I." A person with genotype $I^AI^A$ or $I^Ai$ expresses the A blood type; a person with $I^BI^B$ or $I^Bi$ expresses the B blood type; and a person with $I^AI^B$ expresses roughly equal amounts of both "A" and "B" antigens, giving the blood type AB.

Thus, $I^A$ and $I^B$ are co-dominant.

The allele i represents the absence of any antigens.

Therefore it is recessive and must be homozygous to express type O blood.

Blood groups with genotype and phenotype:

| Genotype | Phenotype |
|---|---|
| $I^AI^A$ | *A* |
| $I^AI^O$ | *A* |
| $I^AI^B$ | Both *A* and *B* |
| $I^BI^B$ | *B* |
| $I^BI^O$ | *B* |
| $I^OI^O$ | *O* |

**Phenotypes for incomplete dominance and pleiotropy**

Mendel dismissed the notion that traits "blend."

*Incomplete dominance* (partial dominance) occurs when the phenotype of a heterozygote is an intermediate of the phenotypes of the homozygotes.

For example, true-breeding red and white-flowered four-o'clock plants produce pink-flowered offspring.

The red allele is partially dominant to the white allele, so its effect is weakened and pink.

This does not support a blending theory of inheritance since the red and white parental phenotypes reappear in the F2 generation.

P                 true-breeding red × true-breeding white; $(C^R C^R) \times (C^W C^W)$

F1                All pink offspring; $(C^R C^W)$

If these F1 individuals are crossed, the results are:

pink × pink; $(C^R C^W) \times (C^R C^W)$

F2                1 red: 2 pink: 1 white; $1(C^R C^R) \times 2(C^R C^W) \times (C^W C^W)$

Another example of incomplete dominance is *sickle-cell anemia*, a blood disorder controlled by incompletely dominant alleles. Homozygous dominant individuals $(Hb^A Hb^A)$ are asymptomatic and healthy.

Homozygous recessive individuals $(Hb^S Hb^S)$ are afflicted with sickle-cell anemia. Their red blood cells are irregular in shape (sickle-shaped) rather than biconcave due to abnormal hemoglobin. Sickle-shaped red blood cells clog vessels and break down, resulting in poor circulation, anemia, low resistance to infection, hemorrhaging, damage to organs, jaundice, and pain in the abdomen the joints.

This is an example of *pleiotropy,* where one gene affects many traits.

Incomplete dominance is heterozygous individuals $(Hb^A Hb^S)$ since they do not have the full-blown disease but have some sickled cells and minor health problems. This is the *sickle-cell trait.* In regions prone to malaria (e.g., Africa), being heterozygous for the sickle-cell allele confers an advantage because the malaria parasite dies as potassium leaks from sickle cells.

*Heterozygote advantage* describes when the heterozygote has an advantage over the homozygote.

**Penetrance and expressivity**

*Penetrance* is the frequency by which a genotype results in a corresponding phenotype.

For example, Mendel's pea plants had 100% penetrance for seed color. A plant with genotype Yy or YY had yellow seeds, and a plant with genotype yy had green seeds.

However, many genes have *incomplete penetrance.*

For example, the BRCA gene (breast cancer) for women with this mutation has an 80% lifetime risk of developing cancer. Certain people have a gene that predisposes them to lung cancer, but they may never develop cancer due to their lifestyle habits and random chance.

This means that a genotype does not guarantee that the expected phenotype is expressed in some cases.

Phenotypes can exhibit *expressivity* (variation in the presentation). This is different from penetrance (i.e., whether the phenotype is expressed). Expressivity refers to varying degrees of phenotype expression.

In *constant expressivity*, individuals with the same genotype have the same phenotype. For example, if pea plants are homozygous recessive for flower color (pp), they are approximately the same shade of white.

Discontinuous traits typically exhibit relatively constant expressivity.

However, a trait like polydactyly (i.e., extra digits) in humans is prone to *variable expressivity* when a phenotype is expressed to different degrees from the same genotype. Although a single gene controls polydactyly, afflicted individuals have extra fingers or toes. The expressivity varies from person to person.

Crossing individuals with different alleles of a continuously varying phenotype does not produce the discrete ratios that enabled Mendel to discover the laws of inheritance.

## Continuous variation

The genetics of *continuous variation* is more complex than discontinuous variation (e.g., pea plants).

Such traits follow a bell-shaped curve when the number of individuals is plotted against the range of the variable trait.

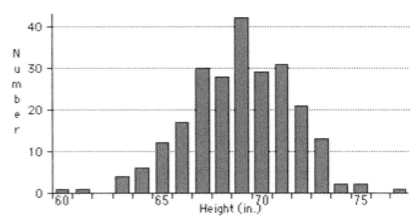

*Continuous variation for height distribution in a population*

With continuous variation, there is a phenotype between two chosen for comparison because the distribution of phenotypes varies along a continuum; individuals differ by small degrees.

Mendel's theory explains discontinuous and continuous patterns of individual variation.

However, with continuous variation, many different genes typically influence the same trait, not one, as Mendel proposed.

Traits such as height and weight are not due to variable expressivity of a single gene but due to *polygenic inheritance*. Polygenic inheritance is when two or more genes govern one trait.

Often, the genes have an additive effect, with each dominant allele adding to the "intensity" of the phenotype. The more genes involved, the more continuous the phenotypic variation, with a bell-shaped curve.

A human example of polygenic inheritance is skin color. Many genes control skin pigment and the more dominant alleles that an individual has, the darker their skin.

Parents with intermediate skin color can have offspring with light or dark skin.

Albinism, a condition where the eyes, skin, and hair have little to no color due to lack of pigment production, is an example of *epistasis*, a phenomenon where one gene interferes with other genes in the expression of a phenotype.

It does not matter if an individual has other genes that would otherwise give her dark skin; if the individual is homozygous recessive for the albinism gene, this shuts off pigment production and prevents the other genes from being expressed.

Traits such as height and weight have a polygenic component but are heavily influenced by outside factors, such as environment, exercise, and nutrition (nature *vs.* nurture).

## Hybrids and viability

*Leakage* is gene flow from one species to another, which occurs when individuals of two related species mate and produce *hybrid* offspring.

The hybrid now has genetic information from both species and may mate with either one, causing genes to "leak" from each gene pool and flow into the other.

A hybrid is the product of parents true-breeding for forms of one trait.

The parents may be of different breeds of a single species or a different species.

When hybrids are created from two species, they may not always be *fertile* (capable of producing offspring). This may be because the hybrid is infertile or dies before reproductive age.

If the hybrid is fertile and able to reproduce, the offspring may prove not viable (able to survive until reproduction), known as a *hybrid breakdown.*

*Hybrid vigor* (heterosis) is when the hybrid has the best qualities of both species or strains.

The hybrid's superior quality is due to the suppression of recessive alleles and the increase in heterozygotic traits, leading to heterozygote advantage.

Hybrids are bred to create new breeds that are healthier or more desirable than either parent breed.

## Outbreeding, population genetics and gene pool

*Outbreeding* is the mating of genetically dissimilar individuals and a powerful agent of genetic diversity.

Inbreeding promotes harmful recessive alleles and decreases the number of alleles in the population.

*Population genetics* studies the variation of alleles within a population.

The *gene pool* is the total genetic information in the population, described by gene frequencies.

Modern biologists view individuals as temporary vessels housing a small fraction of the gene pool.

Thus, the concept of a gene pool is an abstract pooling of genetic variation in the population; it does not exist apart from the individuals themselves.

*Demes* are local gene pools consisting of individuals likely to breed.

A great deal of evolutionary change occurs in these groups.

## Meiosis and Genetic Variability of Offspring

**Meiosis for genetic variability**

There are several sources of genetic variability in nature, some random, while others result from selective processes. These include mutation, sexual reproduction, diploidy, outbreeding and balanced polymorphisms.

Meiosis is essential to sexual reproduction, diploidy, and genetic diversity.

Asexual organisms produce offspring as genetic clones of themselves, but sexual reproduction creates offspring similar to and unique from either parent.

Meiosis creates haploid gametes that fuse and form a diploid zygote.

Meiosis provides several opportunities to promote variability in the gene pool and allow for new combinations of alleles.

**Sister chromatids and tetrads**

Mitosis and meiosis begin similarly with a somatic cell in G1 of interphase, 46 chromosomes.

Chromosomes have a homologous structure that originated from the other parent; there are 23 homologous pairs, and each chromosome is scattered randomly within the nucleus. During the S phase, each chromosome duplicates.

Each duplicate is renamed a sister chromatid, and together, two sister chromatids comprise one chromosome. Sister chromatids are chromatin strands attached at the centromere, identical copies (except for low-frequency mutations of nucleotides) of the same chromosome (not homologous).

One chromosome (a pair of sister chromatids) has another chromosome, its homolog.

During prophase / metaphase of mitosis, the chromosomes do not attempt to locate their homolog. Chromosomes align along the metaphase plate individually. During anaphase, each chromosome's sister chromatids are separated so that one chromatid (resulting as a single strand separated at centromere) is partitioned into a daughter cell. The result is two diploid daughter cells with identical genetic makeup.

However, during prophase I and metaphase I of meiosis, homologs do pair into a *tetrad* (bivalent). The tetrad consists of two homologous chromosomes or four sister chromatids.

Tetrads line up on the metaphase plate so that one homologous chromosome is on one side, and the other homolog is on the other side of the midline.

During anaphase I, the tetrad is separated, and one chromosome is pulled into one pole, while the second is pulled toward the other pole. The result of meiosis I is that two daughter cells have different genetic compositions; one has half of the organism's genome and the second cell has the other half.

A key difference is that mitosis involves one set of cell divisions, in which the chromatids of each chromosome separate. In meiosis, there are two sets of cell divisions.

During the first division, the chromosome of each tetrad separates (the chromosome has 2 strands attached at the centromere). In the second division, the centromere splits, and the sister chromatids separate.

**Comparing mitosis and meiosis**

| Mitosis | Meiosis |
|---|---|
| One set of divisions | Two sets of divisions |
| Occurs in body (somatic) cells | Occurs in the testes or ovaries (gametes) |
| Two identical daughter cells | Four unique daughter cells (four sperm cells or one egg with up to three polar bodies) |
| Daughter cells are diploid 2N → 2 cells with 2N | Daughter cells are haploid 2N → 4 cells with 1N |
| No crossing over occurs | Crossing over (tetrad) during prophase I creates genetic variability |

**Mendelian segregation of genes**

When the homologous pairs are arranged into tetrads during meiosis, their ends overlap and cause *recombination* (i.e., exchange of genetic material).

Homologous chromosomes exchange DNA, so once separated, the maternal chromosome has some paternal DNA, and vice versa.

Gametes are unique from the organism's genome.

Mendel understood that different genes are segregated into gametes despite being unaware of meiosis.

His first *law of segregation* supports the conclusion diploid individuals have two alleles but pass one to their offspring. Segregation of genes and diploidy are important concepts for explaining genetic variability.

**Independent assortment**

Mendel's second law, the *law of independent assortment*, states that any gamete may have any combination of alleles. In the era of molecular biology, this occurs during meiosis.

During metaphase I of meiosis, homologous chromosomes pair as tetrads along the metaphase plate in a random orientation. They have pulled apart so that some homologous chromosomes from each parent end up in one daughter cell or another.

The law of independent assortment requires that homologous chromosomes line up randomly during metaphase. The segregation of alleles of one gene does not affect the segregation of alleles of another gene.

Mendel initially thought that a dihybrid (e.g., AaBb) produces the gametes AB and ab.

However, he realized that the A alleles and the B alleles are not linked; they can segregate into gametes in four combinations: AB, aB, Ab, and ab. He noted that these gametes are produced in equal numbers; no one combination is favored over another.

Mendel's research was based on simplistic traits of pea plants. He sometimes encountered puzzling phenotypic ratios, which suggested that some allele combinations were frequent.

If Mendel chose two phenotypic traits controlled by two tightly linked loci for his dihybrid cross, he would have obtained two types of gametes due to the *linkage.*

## Gene linkage

Mendel's law of independent assortment does not apply to linkage, whereby some genes are on the same chromosome and inherited together. His law is applied to chromosomes rather than genes; chromosomes assort independently, but alleles do not.

*Linked genes* are close on the same chromosome, while those far apart or on different chromosomes are *unlinked genes.*

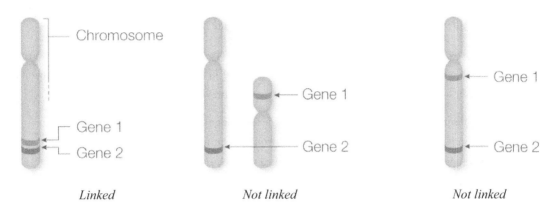

*Linked*          *Not linked*          *Not linked*

Genes on separate chromosomes are unlinked and can segregate independently, but genes on the same chromosome are often inherited together as a *linkage group.* However, this is not always true.

## Crossing over and recombination

*Crossing over* allows genes on the same chromosome to become unlinked due to the probability that the genes undergo recombination in the region between them.

*Genetic recombination* introduces genetic diversity into the gametes during meiosis. It includes independent assortment and crossing over. Crossing over occurs during prophase I of meiosis when homologous chromosomes are paired into tetrads.

The pairing of tetrads is *synapsis* and is facilitated by a protein structure of the *synaptonemal complex.* It is thought that the synaptonemal complex functions primarily as a scaffold to allow interacting chromatids to complete their crossover activities.

During prophase I, synapsis links the four sister chromatids (4 strands with 2 chromosomes) of a homologous chromosome pair. The ends of separate chromatids often overlap and make contact at sites, as *chiasmata*, between loci.

Both chromatids cut at the same locus, allowing them to bind where they are cut (chiasma) and swap their DNA. In this way, an individual can create gametes with some chromatids different from the chromatids they inherited.

*Recombinants* are chromatids that have undergone recombination, and those which did not are *parental.*

Once crossing over is finished, the homologous chromosomes are no longer tightly linked, and the homologous chromosomes are independent. However, the recombinant chromatids remain connected by their chiasma until anaphase, when the centromeres divide and liberate each sister chromatid strand, which becomes a chromosome.

## Sex-linked characteristics

In a human, the usual chromosome complement is 46, two of which are sex chromosomes. A human female has two X chromosomes, while a human male has an X and a Y chromosome.

The sex chromosomes carry genes that determine the sex of an organism and various unrelated traits that are *sex-linked*. Because the Y chromosome is small, the X chromosome essentially carries all sex-linked traits as X-linked traits. The alleles are designated as superscripts to the letter X.

In females, one of the duplicate X chromosomes is deactivated during embryonic development, resulting in an unused chromosome, a *Barr body*. This is random in cells, so in one cell, the paternal X chromosome may become the Barr body, while in another, the maternal X chromosome becomes the Barr body.

In males, chromosomes X and Y do not make a homologous pair since they are of various sizes and contain different genes. The X chromosome in humans is longer than the Y chromosome and contains many genes. The smaller Y chromosome has no opposing alleles to those on the X chromosome in a male.

Males are *hemizygous* for X-linked traits, meaning they have one allele since they have one X chromosome. In the pairing seen below, genes on the X chromosome with an arrow pointing to them are dominant because they have no opposition from the Y chromosome. There are genes with loci on the X and Y chromosomes.

Males are prone to certain genetic diseases due to this characteristic. A female inheriting a sex-linked recessive allele encoding for a genetic disease may inherit the other X chromosome's dominant allele. She is unafflicted (i.e., complete dominance) or has minor afflictions (incomplete or co-dominance). However, a male has no such mitigating protection and is affected by the single x-linked trait.

## Y chromosome genes and sex determination

The Y chromosome is significantly smaller than the X chromosome and contains a lower density of genes, perhaps 50 to 60. However, these few genes have an important impact on sex determination and male characteristics.

Genes on the Y chromosomes that do not recombine are passed from father to son and are not present in females. The lack of recombination weakens natural selection effectiveness to reduce the frequency of disadvantaged variants and select for favorable ones.

Humans have an *XY sex-determination system*. Most other mammals, along with some insects and fish, follow this. Females produce gametes with a single X chromosome, while sperm from the male can contain a Y chromosome or an X chromosome.

There is a 50% chance that a gamete contains either chromosome. Therefore, when the gametes fuse during fertilization, there is a 50% chance of a female (or male) sex.

The maternal gamete is *homogametic* because its cells possess the XX sex chromosomes. Sperm gametes are the variable factor and are thus *heterogametic* because around half contain the X chromosome, and the other half possess the Y chromosome.

In the absence of a Y chromosome, genes on the X chromosomes direct a fetus to produce female sex hormones and develop internal and external female sex organs. However, if a Y chromosome is present, its *SRY gene* inhibits female sex organs' development and promotes male sex organs.

The SRY gene is powerful since it controls other genes' activity, directing the development of internal and external male characteristics. Gene mutations can cause the fetus to develop nonfunctional testes or ovaries.

In some cases, errors during the male production of gametes attach the SRY gene to an X chromosome. This results in a female fetus developing male phenotypic characteristics.

**DNA nucleotide sequence mutations**

*Mutations* are changes in the DNA nucleotide sequence that arise by means other than recombination. Mutant genes may produce abnormalities in structure and function, leading to disease.

Cystic fibrosis, sickle-cell anemia, hemophilia, and muscular dystrophy are *single-gene diseases* because they arise from mutations in a single gene.

*Polygenic diseases,* such as diabetes, cancer, cleft lip, and schizophrenia, result from several defective genes that have little effect on their own but collectively can have significant effects. The environment greatly influences many genetic disorders, physical features, and behavioral traits.

Genetic mutations can be beneficial, neutral, or harmful.

Beneficial or *advantageous mutations* provide an improvement to the fitness of the organism.

*Deleterious mutations* disrupt gene function and result in a harmful effect on the fitness of the organism. Mutations can be harmful in one situation but advantageous in another.

*Neutral mutations* have a negligible effect on fitness, neither harmful nor beneficial. Mutations may not affect the phenotype as *silent mutations,* or the effect does not arise until later generations.

*Random mutations* are changes in the DNA sequence due to radiation, chemicals, replication errors, or other chance events.

*Transcription errors* occur specifically during the transcription of DNA into mRNA. This results in mRNA with some RNA nucleotide sequences that do not accurately correspond to the original DNA code.

*Translation errors* occur during the translation of mRNA into a protein by a mutant amino acid sequence.

**Classifying mutations**

*Base substitutions* are when another replaces one or more nucleotides. They range from advantageous to fatal (as with many mutations), but most base substitutions are minor.

Nucleotide base substitutions may cause a stop codon to halt transcription, a *nonsense mutation.*

Substitutions could cause a different amino acid to be transcribed in the protein, causing a *missense mutation.* A single amino acid change may change the protein's function or render it inoperable.

However, since some mRNA codons can encode for the same amino acid (i.e., code is degenerative), sometimes base substitutions may not result in a different amino acid sequence.

*Silent mutations* do not affect the phenotype.

*Deletions* involve a base (or several bases) being removed from the DNA or mRNA sequence, while *insertions* involve adding one (or more) bases.

One or two insertions (or deletions) result in *frameshift mutations* by shifting the reading frame of the three-base codons.

For example, the mRNA sequence AUGUUGACUGCCAAU is meant to be read:

AUG - UU<u>G</u> - ACU - GCC – A …

Met  - Leu  - Thr  - Ala  - …

If the 6th base (guanine) is deleted, a frameshift mutation changes the transcribed amino acids.

AUG - UUA - CUG - CCA - …

Met  - Leu  - Leu  - Pro  - …

The first codon is unaffected and still encodes for methionine. The second codon *is* changed, but since this codon encodes for the same amino acid (leucine), it is a silent mutation.

However, the third and fourth codons are changed to encode different amino acids. It is assumed that many other amino acids in the sequence are changed. This is a severe mutation rendering the protein inoperable.

However, deletions and insertions of nucleotides that involve multiples of threes do not cause a frameshift since they remove an entire codon (i.e., three nucleotides that encode an amino acid). The reading frame remains intact, but the absence of a single amino acid may be a serious issue.

**Repetitive sequences and gene duplication**

*Slipped-strand mispairing* is a mutation that occurs during transcription, translation, or DNA replication. After DNA strands are denatured during replication, the template or replicated strand may slip (become temporarily dislodged) and cause incorrect pairing of complementary bases. This is believed to have led to the evolution of many repetitive DNA sequences in the human genome.

Portions of the chromosome are subject to deletion, especially during meiosis. Chromosomal deletion may be severe and renders the gamete incapable of fertilization or spontaneous abortion.

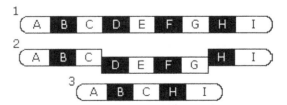

*Chromosomal deletion where sections D, E, F, and G are absent after deletion*

---

## Chromosomal inversions and translocation

Along with base mutations, the chromosome's entire structure is subject to rearrangement, especially during meiosis. Chromosomal mutations may be severe or fatal, terminating the fetus before birth.

*Inversions* involve a stretch of DNA breaking and reattaching in the opposite orientation.

Two types of inversions are paracentric and pericentric.

*Paracentric inversions* do not involve the centromere; they occur when a piece of the arm of chromosome breaks, inverts and reattaches.

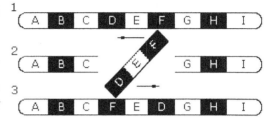

A *pericentric inversion* includes the centromere; the breakpoint is on either arm of the chromosome.

The organism experiencing the newly inverted sequence may not be viable if it includes a necessary chromosome region. The mutation could be advantageous. However, inversions usually do not affect the organism's phenotype and go undetected. Their greatest impact is on the production of gametes since they are often marked by loops in the chromosome that affects recombination.

An individual with a chromosomal inversion may generate gametes with altered linkage relationships or abnormal chromatids. The former case is likely harmless, while the latter usually yields inviable gametes.

*Translocation* is when a segment of one chromosome separates and binds to the other. This is a drastic rearrangement that is often lethal. An individual inheriting a chromosome that has been altered due to translocation has extra alleles or too few alleles, leading to a variety of defects. This may occur in autosomal and sex chromosomes, leading to infertility issues and other genetic disorders.

*XX male syndrome* occurs when the portion of the Y chromosome containing the SRY gene is translocated to an X chromosome during a male's gamete production. If the sperm cell containing the mutant X chromosome fertilizes an egg, a female fetus develops male secondary sex characteristics and genitalia.

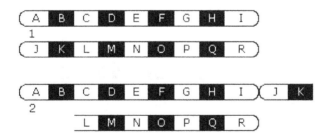

*Chromosomal translocation where section J and K join the other chromosome*

## Nondisjunction and nontypical karyotypes

Although safeguards are in place to ensure chromosomes are properly separated during meiosis, these checks sometimes fail.

Failure of proper chromosome separation causes *nondisjunction errors,* in which three chromosomes of a tetrad are pulled to one side of the spindle, and one is pulled to the other side. This results in gametes having an extra chromosome and gametes lacking a chromosome.

A chromosome with three copies is *trisomy*, while a chromosome with one copy is *monosomy*. Both examples of gamete formation by nondisjunction usually lead to an inviable zygote.

*Down syndrome* is a common nonlethal autosomal trisomy involving chromosome 21. In general, the chance of a woman having a Down syndrome child increases with age. This disorder leads to faster aging, moderate to severe developmental issues, and a higher risk of health complications.

Many nonlethal nondisjunction errors involve the sex chromosomes.

Females with *Turner syndrome* have one X sex chromosome. This results in nonfunctional ovaries and the absence of puberty. Afflicted females have somewhat masculine characteristics and sterile but usually have no cognitive issues using hormone therapy.

*Klinefelter syndrome* occurs when a zygote receives one Y chromosome and two (or more) X chromosomes. The Y chromosome makes affected individuals identifiably male, but they have underdeveloped sex organs and are sterile.

The extra X chromosomes cause the development of breasts, lack of facial hair, and cognitive delay.

Males with Klinefelter syndrome have one or more Barr bodies due to the extra X chromosomes.

**Karyotypes**

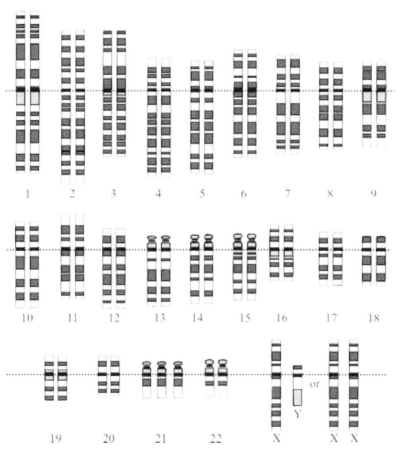

*Karyotype of a male patient with Down syndrome (three chromosomes, 21) and an extra set of X chromosomes (XXXY) as a variant of Klinefelter syndrome (XXY)*

Females with *Poly-X syndrome* have extra X chromosomes and extra Barr bodies. They do not exhibit enhanced feminine characteristics and appear physically normal. Some experience menstrual irregularities, but most have regular menstruation and are fertile. Females with three X chromosomes are not developmentally delayed but have impaired cognitive skills. However, four X chromosomes cause severe cognitive impairment.

*Jacob's syndrome* is one X chromosome and two Y chromosomes. Although it was previously believed that individuals with Jacob's syndrome were likely to be aggressive, this claim is refuted.

Males with Jacob's syndrome are taller than average, suffer from persistent acne, and tend to have speech and reading problems.

Many genetic disorders, especially from nondisjunction, can be detected during pregnancy. Chorionic villi sampling testing, amniocentesis, and karyotyping are prenatal testing methods.

*Karyotyping* (visual examination of chromosomes) determines the gender of a fetus and surveys for chromosomal abnormalities.

The sex chromosome structure deduces the gender since Y chromosomes are markedly smaller than X chromosomes. Missing or extra chromosomes visualize nondisjunction. If there are two of each chromosome, the 23 chromosome pairs result in 46 chromosomes. Deviations from this, such as three copies of chromosome 21, signifies a nondisjunction.

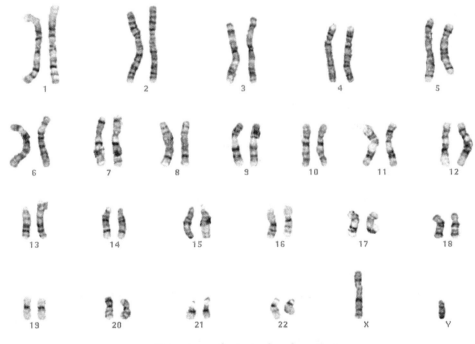

*Karyotype of a typical male patient*

## Inborn errors of metabolism

*Inborn errors of metabolism* are genetic disorders that cause mild to severe metabolic issues. These diseases are caused by a mutant gene that results in abnormal enzyme production, affecting the gastrointestinal system, the circulatory system, the nervous system, or any area of the body.

They are typically rare and have severe health implications.

However, benign inborn errors of metabolism, such as lactose intolerance, arise from an inability to produce the digestive enzyme lactase.

Unlike many genetic disorders, inborn errors of metabolism are caused by a single gene mutation.

**Autosomal recessive disorders**

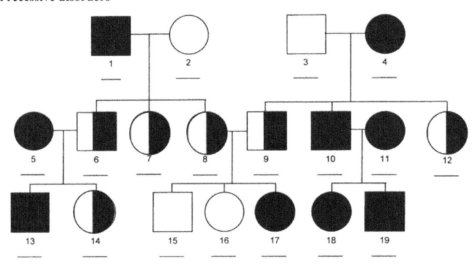

*Pedigree for autosomal recessive: squares denote males, circles denote females; shaded figures are afflicted, while half-filled figures are carriers*

*Autosomal recessive* disorders are discerned from pedigrees by establishing the presence of specific patterns of inheritance. The first observation is that affected children usually have unaffected carrier parents since recessive alleles are statistically rare in the general population.

Two homozygous dominant parents produce unaffected children.

However, if one parent is affected, the children are unaffected carriers. If one parent is affected and the other is a carrier, they have a 50% chance of producing a carrier child or affected child as in the pedigree chart. Note the many carriers (half-filled circles or squares) due to their affected parents.

Individuals 15 and 16 (third generation) may be homozygous dominant or carriers. Genetic testing reveals if they inherited two dominant alleles from each carrier parent or a dominant allele from one and a recessive allele from the other parent.

*Tay-Sachs disease* is an autosomal recessive disorder rare in the general population but afflicts approximately 1 in 3,600 Ashkenazi Jews at birth. Tay-Sachs results in death by about age three due to progressive neurological degeneration. A genetic mutation prevents the production of the enzyme hexosaminidase A (Hex A), leading to accumulations of its substrate, glycosphingolipid, in lysosomes of brain cells. Tay-Sachs is one of many *lysosomal storage disorders* caused by abnormal lysosomal function.

*Cystic fibrosis* is a common lethal genetic disease in Northern European ancestry. About 1 in 20 Caucasians in the U.S. is a carrier for cystic fibrosis, and about 1 in 3,000 is afflicted. The disease is caused by a mutation of chromosome 7 that prevents chloride ions from passing into some cells. Since water normally follows Cl⁻, a lack of water in lung cells causes viscous mucus and subsequent respiratory issues. This disease has gastrointestinal, kidney, and fertility effects.

*Phenylketonuria* (PKU) is a common inherited disease of the nervous system, occurring once in about 15,000 births. A mutant gene on chromosome 21 results in a lack of enzymes that metabolize the amino acid phenylalanine. The absence of the enzyme causes the accumulation of phenylalanine in nerve cells and impairs the CNS. From neonatal diagnosis, children are placed on low-phenylalanine diets that prevent severe neural degeneration.

**Sex-linked recessive disorders**

*Sex-linked recessive disorders*, like autosomal recessive disorders, results in all children affected if the parents are both affected. Two unaffected parents can bear affected offspring (male only) if the mother is a carrier.

She has a 50% chance of donating a recessive allele to a son, afflicting him with the disease. If the mother is homozygous recessive, this results in 100% of male offspring as affected.

Female offspring are unaffected as the father donates a dominant X-linked allele; but, all are carriers.

If an affected male mates with a homozygous dominant female, offspring are unaffected. However, if the father is affected and the mother is a carrier, 50% of their children, regardless of sex, are affected.

*Color blindness* is an X-linked recessive disorder involving mutations of genes coding for green-sensitive pigment or red-sensitive pigment; the gene for blue-sensitive pigment is autosomal. About 8% of Caucasian men have red-green color blindness.

*Duchenne muscular dystrophy* is the common form of muscular dystrophy and is characterized by the wasting (atrophy) of muscles, eventually leading to death. It affects 1 in 3,600 male births. This X-linked recessive disease involves a mutant gene that fails to produce the protein dystrophin. The lack of dystrophin promotes an enzyme that dissolves muscle fibers. Affected males rarely live to be fathers; the allele survives in the population due to transmission by carrier females.

About 1 in 10,000 males is a hemophiliac with an impaired blood clotting ability. This is a classic example of an X-linked recessive disorder, famously seen in the royal families of Europe throughout the 19th and 20th centuries.

Queen Victoria was a carrier of the disease and passed it on to many of her descendants. Due to diplomatic marriages within a small subpopulation, it was transmitted to royal families in Russia, Germany, and Spain. The issue was exacerbated by incest, not uncommon, to keep power and assets within the family.

**Autosomal dominant disorders**

*Autosomal dominant* disorders are discerned from pedigrees by establishing the presence of certain patterns. The first is that affected children must have an affected parent. Two affected parents can have an unaffected child if both parents are heterozygous.

However, two unaffected parents cannot have a child that is affected.

As with autosomal disorders, males and females are affected with equal frequency.

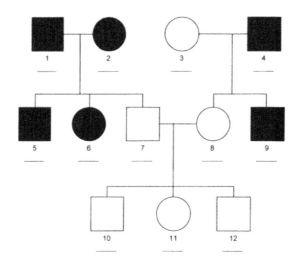

*Pedigree for autosomal dominant: circles denote females, squares denote males;*
*filled shapes are affected individuals, while unfilled shapes are not carriers of the disorder*

*Neurofibromatosis* is an autosomal dominant disorder in about 1 in 3,500 people. It is caused by an altered gene on chromosome 17 that controls the production of the neurofibromin protein, which normally inhibits cell division. When this gene is mutated, neurofibromin is nonfunctional, and affected individuals develop neurofibromas, benign skin tumors. In most cases, symptoms are mild, and patients live healthy lives but can be severe.

Since the severity of symptoms varies, this is an example of *variable expressivity*.

*Huntington's disease* is an autosomal dominant disorder that, while fatal, usually does not onset until middle age, after an afflicted individual may already have children. Therefore, the disease continues to pass through the generations. The gene for Huntington's disease is on chromosome 4.

This gene encodes the *huntingtin protein* as extra glutamine in the amino acid sequence, causing the mutant huntingtin protein to form clumps inside neurons.

*Achondroplasia* is a form of dwarfism caused by defective bone growth in about 1 in 25,000 people. People with achondroplasia have short limbs, a deformed spine, and an average torso and head. Like many genetic disorders, being homozygous dominant for achondroplasia is lethal; afflicted individuals are heterozygotes.

### Sex-linked dominant disorders

*Sex-linked dominant disorders* have characteristics distinguished from other inherited genetic disorders, which is discerned by analyzing a pedigree.

If a male is affected, his female offspring are affected because he donates an affected X chromosome to his female offspring. Since the allele is dominant, offspring are affected.

By contrast, male offspring are affected if the mother has the disease because the father donates a Y chromosome (does not carry the gene) to his male offspring.

Unlike autosomal genetic disorders, sex-linked genetic disorders affect the sexes disproportionately, as in the pedigree below. There are no carriers since having one dominant allele signifies affliction. Like autosomal dominant disorders, dominant sex-linked disorders are not common in the population since they lead to health problems that reduce the reproduction frequency. This makes the alleles rarer in the gene pool, a self-fulfilling cycle that keeps them at a low frequency.

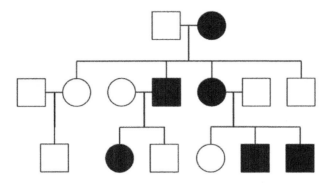

*Pedigree for dominant sex-linked disorder: squares denote males, circles denote females; filled shapes are afflicted individuals, while unfilled are healthy individuals*

The *fragile X syndrome* is an X-linked dominant disorder in which the *FMR1* gene is mutated. This causes a deficiency of the protein FMRP protein, affecting neural and physical development. The mutation is found among both sexes, though it is prevalent in females. Affected children often have hyperactive behaviors, intellectual disabilities, and autism spectrum disorders. Although about one-fifth are unaffected due to incomplete penetrance, these symptoms are severe in males.

**Pedigrees and test crosses**

Pedigrees must determine sex-linked traits in humans since it is not ethical to orchestrate human mating, while other organisms are bred to determine patterns of inheritance.

In non-humans, a *reciprocal cross* involves two sets of parents, in which the male and female have opposite traits. For example, in one set, a female pea plant has white flowers, and the male has purple flowers, and in another, the female has purple flowers, and the male has white flowers. This determines the inheritance of sex-linked traits.

If the trait is autosomal, both crosses produce the same results; if not, they produce different results.

*Test cross* uses the homozygous recessive to mate with an organism of known phenotype but unknown genotype. If progeny resemble the known phenotype parent, the parent is homozygous dominant.

A 50:50 ratio means that the parent is heterozygous for the phenotypic trait.

For example, AA × aa = Aa and Aa × aa = Aa and aa.

**Mutagens and carcinogens**

The genetic component of cancers is the leading cause of death in developed nations and the second leading cause in developing nations. Most cancers are caused by a genetic predisposition and by carcinogens.

*Carcinogens* are any physical, chemical, or biological agents that cause cancer.

The majority of carcinogens are *mutagens,* harmful agents that cause DNA mutations.

Toxic chemicals, radiation, free radicals, viruses, and bacteria are possible mutagens.

*Exogenous mutagens* come from an external event, like smoking a cigarette or exposing one's skin to UV radiation.

*Endogenous mutagens* arise internally as byproducts of metabolic processes. *Reactive oxygen species* (ROS) are a class of endogenous mutagens containing oxygen and are highly reactive (e.g., $H_2O_2$ and $O^{-2}$).

*Mitogens* are another class of carcinogens that trigger an increase in mitosis rate. While carcinogens are mutagens or mitogens, there are mutagens and mitogens that do not lead to cancer.

### Genetic drift, founder effect and inbreeding

*Genetic drift* refers to random changes in allele frequencies of a gene pool over time. This occurs in large and small populations, but the effect is magnified in small populations. Isolated gene pools can quickly diverge from the parent population. Over time, large populations may speciate (organisms cannot reproduce to produce viable and fertile offspring).

Genetic drift causes alleles to be lost and others to become *fixed,* meaning they are the only allele for a gene in the population. Variation among populations can often be attributed to the random effects of genetic drift.

The *founder effect* is an example of genetic drift, whereby a handful of founders leave a source population and establish a colony. The new population contains a fraction of the total genetic diversity of the original population. Over time, the founders' alleles may occur at high frequencies in the new population, even if they are rare in the original population. For example, cases of dwarfism are high in the Pennsylvania Amish community because a few German founders were dwarfs.

The *bottleneck effect* may occur after excessive predation, habitat destruction, or a natural disaster rather than a founding event. After the catastrophe, there is a major decrease in the total genetic diversity of the original gene pool.

Purely by chance, alleles are lost, and this affects the future genetic makeup of the population. Today, relative infertility is found in cheetahs due to a bottleneck in earlier times. Small populations suffer low genetic variation due to the high rates of inbreeding.

Genetic drift is a random process, greatly enhanced when other genetic diversity agents are random. Random mating, in which individuals pair by chance and not by any selection, is one example. However, most populations practice nonrandom mating, which inhibits genetic diversity.

*Inbreeding*, where relatives mate, can occur as nonrandom mating because they are near others.

*Assortative mating* occurs when individuals mate with those that have similar phenotypes. This may divide a population into two phenotypic classes with reduced gene exchange.

Phenotypes can be selected due to *sexual selection* when males compete for the right to reproduce, and (often) the females select males based on phenotype.

### Gene flow and genetic variation

*Gene flow* is the introduction (or removal) of alleles from populations when individuals leave (emigration) or enter the population (immigration).

Gene flow increases variation within a population by introducing novel alleles from another population.

Continued gene flow decreases variation between populations, causing their gene pools to become similar. Because of this, gene flow is a powerful opposing force in speciation.

**Balanced polymorphisms and frequency-dependent selection**

*Balanced polymorphisms* add to genetic variability by maintaining two different alleles in the population rather than encouraging homozygosity. Balanced polymorphisms are maintained by heterozygote advantage, hybrid vigor, and frequency-dependent selection.

*Frequency-dependent selection* is when the frequency of one phenotype affects the frequency of another.

For example, a prey animal population may have several coloring phenotypes in the population (e.g., gray, brown, black fur). When the gray phenotype becomes frequent in the population, predators become familiar with this phenotype and can identify prey by their gray fur.

Natural selection makes it so that the rarer phenotypes (brown and black fur) have an advantage.

Prey evolve these phenotypes until one becomes common, with frequency-dependent selection changes.

This is *minority advantage* when the rarest phenotype has the highest fitness (i.e., chance of survival).

Phenotypes can have a positive frequency-dependent relationship from safety in numbers.

For example, individuals of a poisonous species may evolve coloring that signals their toxicity. Predators learn this signal and avoid individuals with this phenotype.

In this example, it is a disadvantage to have a unique phenotype that is not identifiable as poisonous because these individuals have an increased probability of being eaten by predators.

**Summary of essential genetics terms**

*Carrier* - an individual that has one copy of a recessive allele (i.e., gene variant) that causes a genetic disease in individuals homozygous for this allele.

*Codominant alleles* - pairs of gene variants affecting phenotype when present in a heterozygote.

*Dominant allele* - a gene variant (i.e., allele) with the same effect on the phenotype, whether it is present in the homozygous or heterozygous state.

*Genotype* - the gene variant of an organism.

*Heterozygous* - with two *different* alleles of a gene.

*Homozygous* - with two *identical* alleles of a gene.

*Locus* - the position of a gene on a chromosome.

*Phenotype* - the characteristics of an organism.

*Recessive allele* - a gene variant effecting the phenotype in the homozygous state.

## Experimental Methods in Genetics

**Testcross determines parental genotype**

A *test cross* is the mating of an individual with an unknown genotype against an individual with a homozygous recessive genotype. This may be done for one or more traits. Mendel used this to ensure his plants were true-breeding.

For example, Mendel may have had a plant with white flowers (a recessive trait), so he knew it was homozygous recessive for white flowers; genotype pp.

Another plant may have had purple flowers, but he could not be sure whether it was Pp or PP since this is the dominant phenotype.

He crossed the purple (known phenotype but unknown genotype) plant with the white plant.

The phenotypic results of a test cross indicate the presence of the genotypes even though the genotypes (PP or Pp) could not be observed phenotype is observed.

Example: A white-flowered pea plant (genotype pp) and an unknown, purple-flowered pea plant (genotype P) are test-crossed to determine the genotype (PP or Pp) of the purple parent.

To analyze a test cross of a white plant and an unknown purple plant, establish the possible gametes.

**Probability used for testcross analysis**

Since the white parent is a homozygote (pp), there is a 100% probability that it contributes a p allele and a 0% probability that it contributes a P allele; every gamete contains a p allele.

If the purple parent is a homozygote (PP), there is a 100% probability that it contributes a P allele to its offspring and a 0% probability of contributing a p allele.

The likelihood that their offspring are genotype Pp is $1.0 \times 1.0 = 1.0$ (or 100%) from probability.

The probability of genotype PP is 0%, and the probability of genotype pp is 0%; offspring are Pp to exhibit the phenotype of a purple flower.

However, if the purple parent is a heterozygote (Pp), there is a 50% probability that it contributes a p allele and a 50% probability that it contributes a P allele.

Therefore, the probability that they have offspring with genotype Pp is $1.0 \times 0.5 = 50\%$.

The probability of genotype pp is $1.0 \times 0.5 = 50\%$.

The probability of genotype PP is 0%. Half of their offspring are Pp and exhibit a purple flower phenotype, and half are pp and exhibit a white flower phenotype.

Its offspring with the white plant determine the purple plant genotype.

If the offspring are purple, the unknown parent must be genotype PP.

If the offspring is half purple, half white, the unknown parent must be genotype Pp.

**Testcross, Punnett square and observed phenotypes**

This test cross (homozygous recessive with unknown genotype) is summarized:

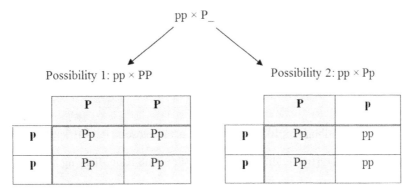

*100% purple offspring indicated a purple a homozygous parent*

*50% purple offspring, and 50% white offspring indicates a purple parent that is heterozygous*

**Two-trait test cross and backcross**

For a two-trait test cross (e.g., seed color), the results are an extension of the single trait test cross.

If a double homozygous recessive parent (rryy) is crossed with a round-seeded yellow parent of an unknown genotype, the unknown parent has four possible genotypes: RRYY, RrYY, RRYy, RrYy.

| Known parent genotype | Possible parent genotype | Possible parent gametes | Offspring phenotype ratio |
|---|---|---|---|
| rryy | RRYY | RY, RY, RY, RY | 1 round yellow |
| rryy | RrYY | RY, RY, rY, rY | 1 round yellow : 1 wrinkled yellow |
| rryy | RRYy | RY, RY, Ry, Ry | 1 round yellow : 1 round green |
| rryy | RrYy | RY, rY, Ry, ry | 1 round yellow : 1 wrinkled yellow : 1 round green : 1 wrinkled green |

After creating hybrid F1 individuals from a parental generation, a *backcross* is performed by breeding the offspring with the parents (or an individual with the same genotype as the parents).

This conserves desirable traits in the F2.

Backcrosses are used for a "knock out" (i.e., inactivate the gene) to study the function of a specific gene.

Backcrossing occurs naturally in small populations, especially among plants.

Artificial backcrossing is done in genetic research to study the function of specific genes by eliminating them and observing the effect when absent.

**Gene mapping, crossover frequencies and map units**

The rate of "unlinking" of genes maps the *physical distances* between two genes on the same chromosome.

The further apart two genes are, the more likely they become unlinked during crossing over.

The frequency of recombination is an estimate of linkage because it indicates the distance between loci.

The maximum frequency of recombination is 50%. For example, genes undergoing recombination 50% of the time are unlinked.

Genes undergoing recombination 10% of the time must be close as it is difficult for them to be separated.

Frequencies are calculated by dividing the number of recombinant offspring by the number of offspring.

Recombinants are identified by their rarity amongst offspring since parental-type offspring are frequent.

If more than two genes are studied, different types of crossing over can occur, and the recombinants are divided into two-, three-, or four-stranded crossovers.

Two-stranded crossovers occur more frequently than three-stranded crossovers; four-stranded crossovers are rarest.

A 1% recombination frequency equals 1 map unit, measured in *centimorgans* (cM) as an arbitrary, relative unit and not physical distances.

Suppose crosses are performed for three genes, and recombination frequencies are calculated.

The genes can be ordered (arrange by relative distance) since one map relationship explains the distances between them.

Biochemical methods map the physical distances between loci by the number of DNA nucleotide bases.

Human chromosomes must be mapped this way since it is impossible to measure recombination frequency among a person's offspring due to the small sample size and lack of control over reproduction.

**Biometry and statistical methods in genetics**

Mendel's knowledge of statistics, a new branch of mathematics at the time, greatly aided his work.

Today, statistics is an integral field of life sciences.

*Biometry,* or *biostatistics,* applies mathematical models and statistics to a vast array of biological fields.

Biometry is used for biological experiments, the collection, summarization, analysis of data, and interpretation of and inferences from the data.

Problem-solving in genetics usually relies on statistics.

Allelic, genotypic, and phenotypic frequencies are calculated using statistics to determine the characteristics of a family (or population).

Models are applied that describe genetic inheritance, even for complex non-Mendelian patterns.

# CHAPTER 11

# Biotechnology in Life Sciences

- Recombinant DNA and Biotechnology

- Targeted Nucleotide Amplification

- Molecular Biology Techniques Analyze DNA, RNA and Protein

- Analyzing Gene Expression from RNA Levels

- Application of Biotechnology

## Recombinant DNA and Biotechnology

### Genetic engineering

*Recombinant DNA* refers to a genetic material that has been artificially "recombined" from disparate sources. The recombination of these DNA segments can occur through viral transduction, bacterial conjugation, transposons, or artificial recombinant DNA technology.

Crossing over during meiosis prophase I produce recombinant chromosomes.

Recombinant DNA plays a significant role in contemporary society. For example, genetically modified crops and many meat sources rely on recombinant DNA technologies.

Additionally, several important pharmaceuticals are assembled using recombination technologies. As the techniques available to manipulate genetic material become sophisticated, recombinant technologies become a larger part of everyday life.

### Gene cloning

A *clone* is a genetically identical organism (or a group of genetically identical cells) derived from a single parental cell.

*Gene cloning* refers to the production of identical copies of the same gene.

When a gene is cloned, the first step is to extract and purify the DNA from the organism of interest.

The gene of interest is introduced into the nucleotide sequence of another organism.

Restriction enzymes (i.e., extracted from bacterial cells) cut double-stranded DNA at specific nucleotide sequences to generate DNA fragments (some with sticky ends).

These fragments are incorporated into commercially available bacterial vector plasmids (circular pieces of DNA) that are cut by the same restriction enzymes to hybridize the sticky ends.

The plasmid is the vector.

The foreign gene is sealed into the vector DNA by the enzyme DNA ligase, and the plasmids are introduced into bacteria by transformation.

Before this, the bacteria must be "made competent" to take up the plasmid; this is done through *electroporation*, where an electric field increases the cell membrane's permeability, or *heat shock*, which increases the fluidity of the membrane, allowing plasmids to pass through the membrane more easily.

*Subcloning* moves a gene of interest from a parent (i.e., source) vector to a target vector.

This multi-step process is shown in the following diagram.

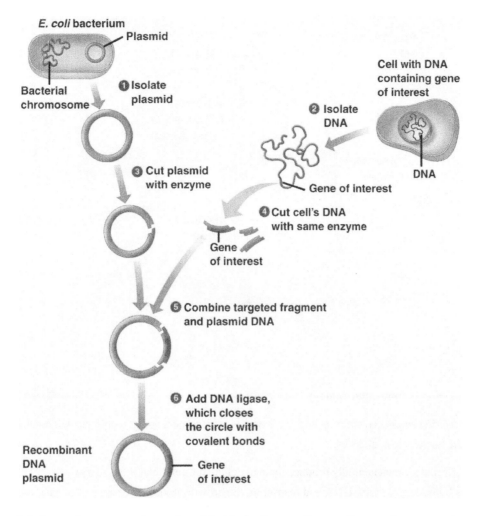

*Subcloning by constructing a plasmid with the "gene of interest" to synthesize proteins*

**Transformation**

Transformation is the update of DNA by bacterial cells.

A screening method, such as incorporating an antibiotic-resistant gene on the plasmid and cultivation on an antibiotic-containing medium, inhibits the growth of the colonies without the recombinant DNA.

The transformed bacteria are allowed to grow at optimum conditions, thus creating copies (i.e., cloning) of the gene of interest. See diagram below.

If a eukaryotic gene is to be expressed in a bacterium, it must be accompanied by the regulatory regions unique to bacteria.

The eukaryotic gene cannot contain introns because bacteria do not have the cellular mechanisms necessary to remove introns and ligate the remaining exons.

If a prokaryotic gene is to be cloned into a mammalian cell, a poly-A tail must be added to the mRNA.

The protein is expressed within the recombinant cells to study the gene's functionality.

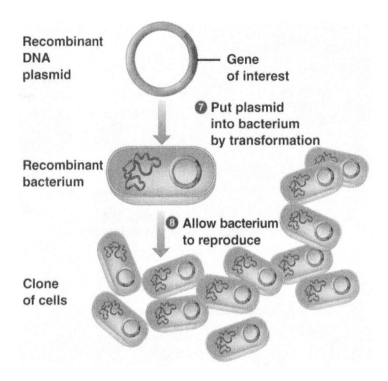

**Restriction enzymes in molecular biology**

A *restriction enzyme* (restriction endonuclease) is an enzyme that can recognize and cut double-stranded DNA at specific nucleotide sequences.

Bacteria and archaea naturally produce them to defend the cell (analogous to a primitive immune system) against viruses by destroying viral DNA and restricting the growth of viruses: "restriction" enzymes.

The restriction enzymes synthesized by a strain of bacteria do not recognize "self" and therefore do not cut the endogenous DNA. Therefore, a bacterium is unaffected by its restriction enzymes.

Restriction enzymes are usually named for the species from which they were isolated; for example, *Bam*HI was isolated from *Bacillus amyloliquefaciens* strain H, and *Eco*RI was isolated from *E. coli* strain RY13.

Recombinant DNA technology uses restriction enzymes as molecular scissors, cleaving DNA pieces at specific nucleotide palindrome sequences.

*Palindrome sequences* read the same from 5' → 3' of one strand and 5' → 3' of the other strand.

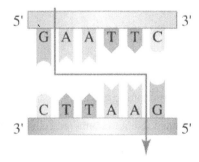

*The restriction enzyme cuts DNA along the sequence shown by the arrow to generate sticky ends*

**Hybridizing restriction fragments with plasmids**

*Restriction fragments* are the resulting DNA fragments after cleavage by restriction enzymes.

Some restriction enzymes cut to make *blunt ends*, which cannot hybridize.

Other restriction enzymes cut at staggered locations to make short single-stranded segments with *sticky ends*, which hybridize.

*Hybridization* anneals (i.e., joins) plasmid and restriction fragment DNA by forming hydrogen bonds.

The "sticky ends" allow for directional insertion of foreign DNA into vector DNA (catalyzed by DNA ligase, creating phosphodiester bonds between DNA pieces).

An example of a blunt end, where N represents one of the four unspecified nucleotides:

```
5'    NNNNNNNATT          AATNNNNNNNNN  3'
3'    NNNNNNNTAA          TTANNNNNNNNN5'
```

An example of a sticky end:

```
5'   NNNNNNNNNNNNNNNG          AATTCNNNNNNNNN  3'
3'   NNNNNNNTTAA          CNNNNNNNNNNNNNNNNNN5'
```

The nucleotides at the cut's location must be the nucleotides specified as the target sequence recognized and cut by a restriction enzyme.

**DNA libraries screen for genes**

After DNA is extracted from an organism, a *DNA library* (gene library) is constructed to organize an organism's DNA.

A DNA library represents, stores, and propagates a collection of genes using live populations of microorganisms; populations contain a different restriction fragment inserted into a cloning vector.

There are several types of DNA libraries.

A *genomic library* contains a set of nucleotide clones representing the entire genome of an organism.

The number of clones in a genomic library can vary, depending on the size of the genome of that organism and the size of the DNA fragment that is inserted into the cloning vector used in the library.

Genomic libraries are useful for studying the function of regulatory sequences, introns, untranscribed regions of DNA and for studying genetic mutations that may occur in disease or cancer tissues.

A *cDNA library* represents the genes from an organism actively expressed.

The cDNA (complementary DNA) is reverse transcribed from expressed mRNA isolated from the cell. This is usually less than 1% of the genome in an organism.

cDNA libraries are useful for studying the mRNAs expressed in specific cells or tissues and detecting alternative splicing of genes.

A *randomized mutant library* is created by the *de novo* synthesis of a gene.

While the DNA is synthesized in the laboratory, alternative nucleotides are added into the sequence at various positions, resulting in a mix of DNA molecule variants of the original gene.

These variants are cloned into vectors, creating the library.

Randomized mutant libraries are used to screen for proteins with favorable properties, such as improved binding affinity, enzyme activity, or stability.

## cDNA for expressing desired proteins

cDNA can be synthesized by the enzyme *reverse transcriptase*, which synthesizes a DNA copy of processed mRNA.

Reverse transcriptase is generally associated with *retroviruses*, which use this enzyme to reverse-transcribe their RNA genome into DNA when infecting a host (e.g., HIV).

Reverse transcriptase can naturally be in viruses, prokaryotes, and eukaryotes. This enzyme is utilized for the mRNA-template synthesis of cDNA, which is necessary for biotechnology for several recombinant techniques.

As of 2021, there are six known retroviruses (i.e., viruses using reverse transcriptase).

cDNA does not contain introns. Bacteria are transfected with the cDNA of human genes to produce large quantities of human proteins.

For example, mRNA encoding for insulin is extracted from a human pancreatic cell that produces insulin. cDNA copies are made from this mRNA by using reverse transcriptase.

A selected plasmid is cut using the same restriction enzymes.

The plasmid and the gene are combined, and the DNA (gene and plasmid) fragments hybridize.

Bacterial host cells are transformed with recombinant plasmids with the integrated human insulin gene.

The bacteria cell translates the insulin protein.

It must be collected and purified. cDNA, rather than genomic DNA, must be used because bacterial DNA does not have the cellular proteins to undergo splicing (i.e., a mechanism to excise introns and ligate exons).

## DNA denaturation, reannealing and hybridization

Double-stranded DNA is reversibly *denatured* into single-stranded DNA when subjected to heat or extreme pH, causing the hydrogen bonds linking A–T and C–G complementary nitrogenous bases to disassociate.

*Annealing* is the opposite process, where subsequent cooling, or return to physiological pH in the presence of salt, the hydrogen bonds to re-associate, forming double-stranded DNA from single-stranded DNA.

During *hybridization*, which is an important part of many biotechnology techniques, complementary base pairs anneal by hydrogen bonding.

**Expressing cloned genes to harvest therapeutic proteins**

Genes are cloned into an expression vector (i.e., plasmid or a virus) and are inserted into a host (usually bacteria, but may be yeast, fungi, or eukaryotes).

*Expression* of that gene is when the host cells with the donor DNA produce protein from the gene of interest (recombinant) as they undergo normal protein synthesis.

When cloned genes are expressed in industrial settings, the goal is to make a large quantity of the protein, so the expression is at an extremely high level as *overexpression*.

The *recombinant protein* is the targeted protein that is subsequently isolated and purified.

Eukaryotic host cell lines (host cells) are used to produce proteins that require significant post-translational modifications or RNA splicing because prokaryotic cells lack the necessary machinery for these processes.

However, using bacteria for protein expression has a distinct advantage because bacterial cells allow for large-scale protein production (due to short replication times for bacterial cell growth).

Because of the ease of growth, low cost to maintain the cells, and short replication cycles, *E. coli* is among the frequently used hosts for expressing cloned genes.

## Targeted Nucleotide Amplification

### Polymerase chain reaction (PCR) amplifies target DNA

*Polymerase chain reaction* (PCR) was developed in 1983 by Kary Mullis.

PCR exponentially generates millions of copies of a piece of DNA in a test tube.

PCR is specific, so the targeted DNA sequence is less than one part in a million of the DNA sample.

A single gene can be amplified.

There are several components necessary for PCR.

One component is the DNA template (e.g., forensic sample) containing the DNA region to be amplified.

Additionally, two primers (short strands of DNA, usually between 14 and 20 nucleotides) complementary to the 3' ends of the coding and template strand of the DNA target are needed ("forward" and "reverse" primer, respectively).

The enzyme *DNA polymerase* replicates the DNA and requires nucleotide primers to initiate synthesis.

PCR uses high temperatures, so the DNA polymerase enzyme must withstand heat without denaturing.

*Taq* polymerase from *Thermus aquaticus* (bacterium lives in hot thermal springs) is frequently used.

PCR components include deoxynucleoside triphosphates (dNTP – dATP, dGTP, dCTP, and dTTP); the four "building blocks" used by DNA polymerase while synthesizing a complementary strand of DNA.

These dNTPs lose two phosphate groups when incorporated into the growing strand and become adenine, guanine, cytosine, and thymine.

PCR uses a buffer solution containing cations (often $Mg^{2+}$), required to stabilize the DNA polymerase as it binds to the complementary strand of the negatively charged DNA sample to be amplified.

### PCR uses three steps to amplify DNA

PCR involves three steps. First is denaturation, where heat is applied (about 94 °C) to separate the double-stranded DNA template.

Annealing is when the mixture is cooled (about 54 °C) for primers to hybridize (anneal) to the now single-stranded DNA template.

Excessive primers are added to outcompete in re-annealing of the parent DNA strands that were separated during the initial heating.

The last step is elongation (about 72 °C), where heat-stable DNA polymerase extends the primers along the respective target DNA strands.

20 to 30 rounds of PCR are performed to create large quantities of amplified DNA fragments.

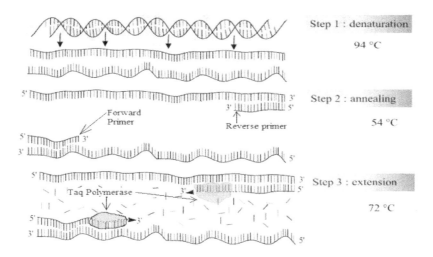

*Polymerase Chain Reaction: temperatures depend on DNA sample and primers*

## PCR amplification for sample analysis

PCR amplification and subsequent DNA analysis are often used to detect viral infections, genetic disorders, and cancer.

It determines the nucleotide sequence of genes (e.g., Human Genome Project, forensics, identification).

PCR can use DNA from many sources, including blood, semen, and various tissues, so it is useful in forensics when a small amount of DNA is available.

If a DNA fragment undergoes 30 PCR cycles, the result is $2^{30} \approx 1.02 \times 10^9$ copies of the DNA fragment.

A limitation of PCR amplification is fidelity.

The heat-resistant bacterial DNA *Taq* polymerase, unlike eukaryotic polymerases, does not perform "proofreading" during replication.

Therefore, mistakes are expected at about one mutation per million nucleotides replicated during mismatching between the newly synthesized and parental strand.

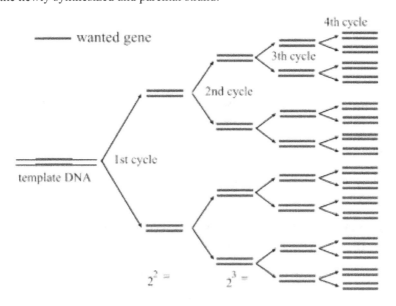

## Molecular Biology Techniques Analyze DNA, RNA and Proteins

### Gel electrophoresis to resolve fragments

In *gel electrophoresis*, macromolecules such as DNA, RNA, and proteins are separated (resolved) by size or charge. The macromolecules move through an agarose or polyacrylamide gel due to an applied electric field consisting of a negative charge and a positive charge at the other end.

DNA is negatively charged, so it moves away from a negative cathode toward a positive anode. Electrophoresis uses an electrolytic cell, so the charge of the cathode is negative, and the anode is positive. Based on resistance within the gel, larger DNA fragments migrate less than shorter fragments.

During gel electrophoresis, the DNA molecules are resolved according to size, resulting in a visible pattern of bands. The same separation based upon size is observed for RNA, proteins, or macromolecules.

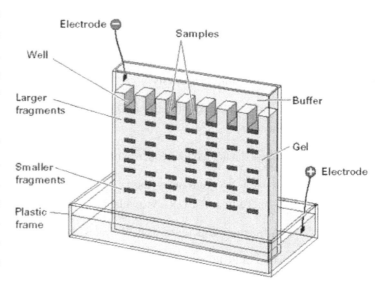

A *molecular weight ruler*, or *DNA ladder*, containing a mixture of DNA fragments of known sizes is run on the gel along with the DNA fragments. The unknown sizes of the resolved fragments are measured by comparing them to the known sizes of the ladder (i.e., reference values) once electrophoresis is complete.

Proteins are separated by polyacrylamide gel electrophoresis (PAGE). Before electrophoresis, they are denatured (i.e., unfolded) with sodium dodecyl sulfate (SDS), which imparts a distribution of negative charge per unit mass on the proteins. The procedure is referred to as SDS-PAGE.

The migration of proteins in SDS-PAGE (similar to DNA) is inversely proportional to the macromolecules' molecular weight (i.e., smaller molecules move further than larger molecules due to resistance).

### Southern blotting targets DNA fragments

*Southern blotting* identifies target DNA fragments in a large sample of DNA.

The DNA is cut into fragments by restriction enzymes, and fragments are resolved (i.e., separated) by gel electrophoresis.

The double-stranded DNA is denatured in an alkaline environment, separating the DNA into single strands for later hybridization.

The single-stranded DNA is transferred to a nitrocellulose membrane by applying pressure, and capillary action transfers the DNA from the gel to the membrane.

The membrane is baked (i.e., fixed) at high temperatures so that the DNA becomes permanently attached.

The hybridization probe (a single radioactively-labeled or fluorescently-labeled DNA fragment) with the predetermined sequence is added to the solution containing the nitrocellulose membrane.

This labeled probe hybridizes to the nitrocellulose membrane to identify the location of the sequence of DNA (resolved by gel electrophoresis).

After hybridization, the excess probe is washed away, and autoradiography (or fluorescence) visualizes the hybridization pattern on the radioactively-labeled (via x-ray film) or fluorescent sample (via spectroscopy).

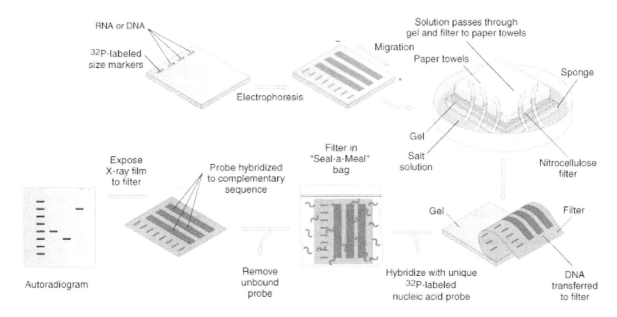

*Southern blot method where gel electrophoresis and the fragment resolves DNA is located by hybridization of the labeled probe with a complementary sequence to the target gene*

**Northern and Western blotting for RNA and proteins**

*Northern blotting* is similar to Southern blotting but uses RNA instead of DNA.

*Western blotting* is the equivalent technique used for proteins, where antibodies bind to the protein of interest and mark it for visualization.

Use the mnemonic SNoW DRoP and match the letters.

S -    Southern - DNA    - D
N -    Northern - RNA    - R
o -                      - o
W -    Western - Protein - P

**DNA sequencing to determine the gene structure**

*DNA sequencing* determines the precise nucleotide sequence in a DNA molecule.

The most popular method for DNA sequencing is the *dideoxy method*, known as the *chain termination method* or "Sanger sequencing."

It was created by Fredrick Sanger, awarded the 1980 Nobel Prize in chemistry for this discovery.

DNA is synthesized from four deoxynucleotide triphosphates (dNTPs), each contains a 3' OH group.

The Sanger sequencing method uses fluorescently-tagged synthetic dideoxynucleotides (ddNTP) that lack the 3'−OH group.

When a dideoxynucleotide is randomly added to a growing DNA strand, the strand cannot be elongated because there is no 3'−OH for the next nucleotide to attach.

The ddNTPs are present in limited quantities. A dNTP may add depending on probability, allowing the growing DNA strand to continue elongation, or a ddNTP may get added, terminating the strand.

This results in various DNA strands of various lengths, separated by gel electrophoresis.

An instrument identifies the fluorescent ddNTPs, and since the four ddNTPs are labeled a unique color, the DNA sequence are read by an automatic scanner.

Sanger sequencing works well for DNA fragments of up to 900 nucleotides.

**Shotgun sequencing for genome structure**

For longer pieces of DNA (e.g., entire genomes), *shotgun sequencing* is used.

In shotgun sequencing, a long piece of DNA is randomly cut into smaller fragments, cloned into vectors, and sequenced individually by the dideoxy method.

A computer analyzes the sequences to search for overlapping sequences and reassembled them into the proper order. This yields the full sequence of the original piece of DNA.

*Pairwise-end sequencing* is a variety of shotgun sequencing that analyzes the ends of DNA fragments for overlap as an ideal method for longer genomes.

Several high-throughput sequencing methods do not use Sanger sequencing; they are *next-generation sequencing* and have been developed to meet the high demand for low-cost sequencing (e.g., ancestry analysis).

These sequencing techniques utilize parallel processing and generate millions of sequences concurrently.

## Analyzing Gene Expression from RNA Levels

**mRNA levels for quantifying gene expression**

Different cells in the body express various combinations of genes that encode for distinct products.

In addition to quantifying gene expression, analyzing the location of expression (cell type or stages of development) are useful. There are methods to quantify the level at which genes are expressed, and the information obtained from these gene expression analysis methods is useful.

For example, the expression levels of an oncogene (growth factor promoting gene) can determine a person's susceptibility to cancer.

Genes are transcribed into mRNA and then translated into proteins, so mRNA and protein are gene products. Depending on the study's intent, expression levels of mRNA or proteins are quantified.

One approach for measuring mRNA levels is the Northern blot, mentioned earlier.

Another approach is using *reverse transcriptase PCR* (RT-PCR). In RT-PCR, a primer anneals to a specific mRNA strand, and the enzyme reverse transcriptase synthesizes a cDNA copy of the mRNA.

Standard PCR protocol replicates this cDNA, followed by gel electrophoresis to separate the resulting DNA fragments. If the DNA fragment with the suspected molecular weight appears on the gel, the mRNA sequence of interest is present in the sample, and it may be concluded that the gene of interest is being expressed.

Gel electrophoresis of the RT-PCR product is performed along with standardized samples of known mRNA amounts. By comparison, the expression level is calculated from how much mRNA is expressed by the gene.

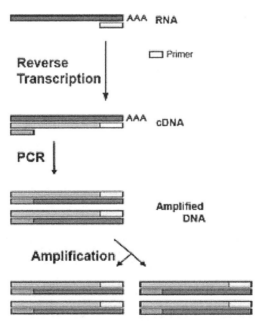

*RT-PCR identifies expressed genes from mRNA*
*containing a poly-A tail as the original template*

**DNA microarrays for gene expression**

*DNA microarrays* evaluate gene expression using small glass chips containing many DNA fragments to probe for specific genes. DNA microarrays allow for the simultaneous analysis of thousands of gene products.

To use a DNA microarray, mRNA must be extracted from the cells being studied and reverse transcribed (RT-PCR) into cDNA labeled with a fluorescent probe.

The cDNA is combined with the microarray so it can base pair with the attached DNA fragments. An automated microscope scans the DNA microarray to determine which DNA fragments have bound. This analysis provides a complete and precise profile of gene expression.

For protein quantification, a Western blot is performed, which gives information about the protein's size (i.e., its location on the gel) and its identity (antibody bound). Although modifications to the protein (e.g., ubiquitination) can easily be identified because this method is sensitive to protein size changes, quantifying the level of protein expression is not accurate.

*Quantitative mass spectrometry* (MS) is a reliable method to determine the amount of protein expressed. In quantitative MS, isotopic tags distinguish the proteins.

When viewing the mass spectrum, the peak intensities of isotope pairs indicate the abundance of corresponding proteins.

DNA microarrays determine changes in the level of gene expression. This can lead to an evaluation of the genes' functions.

For example, DNA microarrays with probes for all 6,000 yeast genes have been used to monitor gene expression as the yeast is made to shift from growing on glucose to growing on ethanol. About 1,000 genes increase in activity during this change, while about 1,000 other genes decrease in activity. More than 2,000 genes are involved when yeast switches from metabolizing glucose to metabolizing ethanol.

**Determining gene function**

One of the direct methods to determine a gene's function is to study mutant organisms with changes in their nucleotide sequence that disrupt the gene.

Spontaneous mutants may be in populations, but it is more efficient to generate mutations with DNA-damaging mutagens.

Besides exposing the organism to mutagens, *insertional mutagenesis* is another method to create interruptions in the genetic code by inserting exogenous DNA into the genome.

Although humans are not used in these processes for ethical reasons, model organisms such as Drosophila flies, zebrafish, and yeast are used.

After a collection of mutants has been created, a *genetic screen* determines the altered phenotypes.

Suppose the phenotype of interest is a metabolic deficiency (e.g., organism that cannot grow without a specific nutrient). The genetic screen is simple to perform, but screening for subtle phenotypes is challenging. The next step is to identify the gene causing the altered phenotype.

If insertional mutagenesis was used, the DNA fragments containing the insertion could be amplified via PCR, sequenced (e.g., Sanger sequencing), and searched in a DNA database to find homologous genes.

However, if mutagens were used, the process of locating and identifying the gene is laborious.

## Chromosomal location of genes

One method to determine the gene's chromosomal location is by estimating the distance between genetic loci by calculating the recombination frequency, a technique of *linkage analysis*.

Once the gene is located, it is searched on a database to find homologous genes and ascertain function.

In 2007, the Nobel prize was awarded for creating a *knockout organism*, where the gene of interest was "knocked out" (i.e., inactivated) in a mouse.

Knockout organisms are often made by inserting DNA with the altered gene into target vectors, transformed into embryonic stem cells, and inserted into early embryos of the organism.

By studying the phenotype of the resulting organism and comparing it to the wild type (i.e., the most common phenotype in nature), the knock-out gene's function is determined.

*Mutant libraries* are created as collections of organisms of a species that have genes systematically deleted. These are extremely valuable tools for studying the roles of various genes.

In addition to knockouts, mutants are generated that overexpress a gene or express it at the wrong time or in the wrong tissue. These studies provide essential information about a gene's function.

## Application of Biotechnology

### Stem cells in human therapy

*Stem cells* are not fully differentiated (i.e., morphologically or biochemically distinct) and renew themselves through cell division and divide and differentiate into specialized cell types.

For example, a single stem cell may differentiate into a blood cell, liver cell, or kidney cell. In many tissues, *somatic stem cells* (adult stem cells) function as an internal repair system and can replace damaged cells or tissues by differentiating into tissue-specific cells. Since different types of cells in the adult organism originate from a single zygote, *embryonic stem cells* are necessary for embryonic development.

*Stem cell therapy* uses stem cells to treat diseases. A bone marrow transplant is the common therapeutic use of stem cells. Stem cells in the bone marrow give rise to red blood cells, white blood cells, and platelets. When a patient has cancer and is given high doses of chemotherapy, it targets the intended cancer cells.

However, chemotherapy destroys noncancerous cells in the bone marrow, which prevents the patient from producing blood cells. To avoid this, before the patient is treated with chemotherapy, she can undergo a bone marrow harvest where stem cells are removed from the bone marrow by using a needle inserted into the pelvis (hip bone).

Alternatively, if the patient's stem cells cannot be used, they are harvested from a matching donor.

After chemotherapy, the patient undergoes a bone marrow transplant in which the stem cells are transplanted into the patient through a drip, usually via a vein in the chest or the arm.

These transplanted stem cells migrate to the bone marrow and produce healthy blood cells.

Therefore, the therapeutic use of stem cells in bone marrow transplants allows cancer patients to undergo high-dose chemotherapy treatment. Without this therapeutic use of stem cells, patients would be able to take low doses of chemotherapy to avoid destroying bone marrow cells needed for replenishing blood cells. Their chances of recovering from cancer are reduced.

Several ongoing studies are testing the use of stem cells for the regeneration of brain tissue, heart tissue, and other tissue to treat diseases such as Alzheimer's, diabetes, heart disease, and Crohn's disease.

Different stem cells are being studied, including adult stem cells, amniotic stem cells (from the fluid of the amniotic sac where the fetus develops), induced pluripotent stem cells (created by reprogramming adult cells), and embryonic stem cells.

Embryonic stem cells are taken from the inner cell mass of a blastocyst, a structure formed in the early stages of embryo development.

### Disadvantages of stem cell therapy

If stem cells are harvested from a donor with a different major histocompatibility complex (MHC), the patient's immune system will target the stem cells (i.e., antibodies mount an immune response) and reject them. Therefore, a well-matching donor must be identified for stem cell transplantation to be effective.

Additionally, the stem cells' ability to differentiate into a specific cell type may pose a problem if they do not differentiate into the cell type needed for treatment.

Stem cells pose the risk of forming tumors (uncontrolled cell growth).

## Practical applications of DNA technology

Recombinant DNA technologies have many practical applications, especially in medicine and in the development of pharmaceuticals. For example, medical products (e.g., insulin) are expressed in *E. coli* cells. Large quantities of the protein are cultured and used to treat diseases (e.g., diabetes, cancer, and viral infections).

Recombinant DNA is utilized to create vaccines. The outside protein shell of an infectious virus is combined with a harmless host so that the surface proteins activate the patient's immune system but are not infected with the virus.

*Gene therapy* involves introducing healthy patient genes to compensate for defective ones, helping to treat genetic diseases and other illnesses.

Gene therapy is classified into *ex vivo* (cells are modified outside the body) and *in vivo* (cells are modified inside the body). Gene therapy is still being developed for use in the clinic.

Treatment of adenosine deaminase (ADA) deficiency may involve manipulating stem cells for *ex vivo* gene therapy.

ADA deficiency is a severe combined immunodeficiency (SCID), in which the lack of functional ADA enzyme causes inhibition of DNA synthesis as well as toxicity to immune cells, leading to immunodeficiency.

In this treatment, bone marrow stem cells are removed, infected with a retrovirus that carries a normal gene for the ADA enzyme, and returned to the patient.

Because the genes are replaced in the stem cells, the genes are spread into many cells during cell division, leading to greater production of the functional enzyme. Patients have shown significant improvement.

In *ex vivo* gene therapy for familial hypercholesterolemia, a condition where liver cells lack a receptor for removing cholesterol from the blood is treated. High cholesterol leads to fatal heart attacks at a young age.

During treatment, a small portion of the liver is surgically removed and infected with a retrovirus with a normal gene for the receptor. The cells infected with the gene are reintroduced into the patient, leading to lowered cholesterol levels in the patients receiving this treatment.

Potential *in vivo* gene therapy treatment for cancer involves making cancer cells vulnerable to chemotherapy and making normal cells resistant.

Injecting a retrovirus containing a normal *TP53* gene that promotes apoptosis of cells into tumors may inhibit their growth.

In another *in vivo* gene therapy, a gene for a vascular endothelial growth factor (VEGF) can be injected alone (or within a virus) into the heart to stimulate branching of coronary blood vessels (i.e., angiogenesis), helping to treat heart disease.

**Medical applications from The Human Genome Project**

To properly utilize gene therapy treatments, it is important to understand the genetic basis of disease.

The Human Genome Project, launched in the 1980s by the National Institutes of Health (NIH, Bethesda, MD) and assisted by other research teams such as Craig Venter, was a major help with these efforts.

The Human Genome Project aimed to map the nucleotide base pair sequences along the 23 human chromosomes. It took 15 years to learn the sequence of the three billion base pairs along the length of human chromosomes.

The cost to sequence a genome of the human (or a person) has decreased from $2.7 billion to approximately $1,000, making sequencing for medical applications more affordable through advances in technology.

The Human Genome Project found few differences between the sequence of bases within humans and many other organisms with known DNA sequences.

Since complex organisms (e.g., humans) share such a large number of genes with simpler organisms, the uniqueness of a complex organism may be due to the regulation of these genes. For example, about 97% of human DNA does not encode for protein product and includes noncoding DNA, regulatory sequences, introns, and untranscribed repetitive sequences.

*Tandem repeats* (*satellite DNA*) are abnormally long stretches of contiguous repetitive sequences within an affected gene and cause disease in some instances (e.g., Huntington's disease). The Human Genome Project helped to elucidate the identity and relative amounts of different types of DNA sequences.

Additionally, the Human Genome Project studied mitochondrial DNA sequences, which provided information on the origins, evolution, and migration of ancestral humans.

With the sequencing of the complete human genome, it is now easier to study how genes influence human development and identify many genetic diseases.

Sequencing of the human genome allows for new pharmaceuticals based on DNA sequences of genes or the structure of proteins encoded by these genes.

**Forensics and paternity tests**

Information about the human genome is useful in *forensic science,* analyzing physical evidence by crime investigators and presented in court during a trial.

The genome of humans differs roughly once per 1,000 nucleotides; these differences are *single nucleotide polymorphisms* (SNPs).

Short tandem repeats (STR) have 2 to 5 nucleotides, which differ except for identical twins.

*Restriction fragment length polymorphisms* (RFLPs) are the differences in fragment lengths after restriction enzymes cut the DNA sequences from different samples.

The genetic sequences that give rise to RFLPs are inherited in a Mendelian fashion.

Forensic scientists use RFLP analysis to compare the DNA at the crime scene (e.g., in traces of blood or semen) with the suspect's DNA.

For a paternity test, the child's DNA is compared with that of the putative father.

These are *DNA fingerprinting* examples, using DNA to identify individuals since no two individuals share identical genomes.

DNA fingerprinting and PCR can identify deceased individuals from skeletal remains.

## Applications of genetic engineering

*Genetic engineering* is the manipulation of the genome of an organism.

An important aspect of genetic engineering is the ability to move a gene from one organism to another.

This process first involves splicing out a gene of interest by a restriction enzyme.

This gene is placed into another organism by cutting the target chromosome and sealing the new sequence with DNA ligase.

The target organism now has a gene sequence for polypeptide production.

*Transgenic organisms*, or organisms with a foreign gene that has been inserted, are genetically engineered to produce specific protein products.

Some products include enzymes used in chemical synthesis for substances that may otherwise be expensive to produce.

For example, phenylalanine, used in aspartame sweeteners, is produced by transgenic bacteria.

Transgenic bacteria have been used to protect the health of plants from environmental issues.

Ice-minus bacteria have been created by removing genes encoding a specific protein on the outer cell wall of *Pseudomonas syringae* that facilitates ice formation.

The introduction of this genetically modified bacteria protects vegetative plant parts from frost damage.

Root-colonizing bacteria with inserted insect toxin genes protect corn roots from damage by insects.

Cleanup of various substances can utilize genetic engineering.

For example, transgenic bacteria can be optimized for oil degradation or formed into a bio-filter to reduce the number of chemical pollutants flowing into the air.

Some bacteria remove sulfur from coal before it is burned to clean up toxic dumps.

These bacteria are given "suicide genes" that cause them to die after doing their job.

Bacteria can be engineered to process minerals. Genetically engineered "bio-leaching" bacteria extract copper, uranium, and gold from low-grade ore.

Many major mining companies already use bacteria to obtain various metals.

In addition to bacteria, transgenic plants and animals can be engineered.

*Protoplasts* are plant cells with their cell wall removed. An electric current makes tiny holes in the plasma membrane through which genetic material enters the cell. The protoplasts develop into mature plants.

Foreign genes now give cotton, corn, and potato strains to produce an insect toxin. Crops are made resistant to certain herbicides so that the crop plants are sprayed with the herbicide and not be affected by it.

Plants are engineered to produce human proteins (e.g., hormones, clotting factors, antibodies) in seeds.

Antibodies made by corn can deliver radioisotopes to tumor cells, and a soybean-engineered antibody can treat genital herpes. Mouse-eared cress has been engineered to produce biodegradable plastic in cell granules.

**Cloning organisms**

The creation of transgenic animals requires methods to insert genes into animals' eggs.

Foreign genes can be manually microinjected into the eggs, or a vortex mixing is used.

Vortex (mixing) involves placing the eggs in an agitator with DNA and silicon-carbide needles that make tiny holes through which the DNA can enter the egg.

Many types of animal eggs have been injected with bovine growth hormone (bGH) to produce larger fish, cows, pigs, rabbits, and sheep using this technique.

It may be possible to use genetically engineered pigs to serve as a source of organs for human transplant.

*Gene pharming* uses transgenic farm animals to produce pharmaceuticals; the product is obtainable from the milk of females.

One example is the transfer of the gene for factor IX, a blood clotting factor, from humans into sheep so that this factor is produced in the sheep's milk.

Clones are cells identical to the parent and arise in nature by organisms that reproduce asexually.

An underground stem or root sends up new shoots as clones of the parent plant.

Members of a bacterial colony on a petri dish are clones as they came from the division of the same cell.

For many years, it was believed that adult vertebrate animals could not be cloned.

In 1996, the first cloned mammal, Dolly, a sheep, was born. Since then, other animals have been cloned.

Dolly was cloned by taking udder cells (i.e., somatic – not germline cells) from a donor sheep.

These cells were cultured in a low-nutrient medium to switch the genes off and make the cell dormant (i.e., not undergoing cellular activities as in the adult cell).

An unfertilized egg was taken from another sheep, and its nucleus was removed using a micropipette.

The egg cell was fused with the udder cells using an electric pulse.

The fused cells developed like normal zygotes and became an embryo, implanted into a "surrogate mother" sheep.

One lamb was born and named Dolly. This lamb was genetically identical to the sheep from which the udder cells were taken.

Dolly survived for almost seven years, but due to somatic cells—not germline cells—she survived for about half the average life expectancy of a sheep.

## Safety and ethics of DNA technology

Genetic engineering is becoming common due to the numerous applications involved.

The advances in DNA technology have allowed for the detection of people, plants, or animals genetically prone to hereditary diseases.

Preparation for the effects of the disease or the passing of the normal gene to offspring minimizes disease.

Within the realm of bioethics, if an abnormality is detected while a fetus, it can sometimes be treated.

However, abortion is an option in these circumstances, which adds to this issue's ethical aspects.

Organisms are engineered to exhibit desirable characteristics (e.g., bacteria producing human insulin).

Infectious diseases are treated by introducing genes that encode antiviral proteins specific to an antigen.

However, there are ethical considerations.

Nature is a highly complex, interrelated chain consisting of many species linked in the food chain.

Some scientists believe that creating genetically modified organisms may have irreversible effects with unknown and potentially undesirable consequences.

Governments have produced legislation to control what experiments are performed and therapies developed that involve genetic engineering.

In some countries, strict laws prohibit any experiments involving manipulating genetic content or the cloning of humans.

People feel that it is unethical to create transgenic animals with an increased potential for suffering (e.g., a pig with no legs).

Despite the ethical issues and legal restrictions, several experimental breakthroughs have been made possible by genetic engineering.

Scientists successfully manipulated the genetic sequence of a rat to grow a human ear on its back.

This was unusual but was done to reproduce human organs for medical purposes.

Therapeutic cloning of human cells (i.e., production of human embryos) could help harvest pluripotent embryonic stem cells to treat diseases.

However, there are many unresolved ethical issues involved.

**Arguments for and against therapeutic cloning in humans**

*Arguments for*

Embryonic stem cells can be used for therapies that save lives and reduce pain for patients. A stem cell can divide and differentiate into cell types to replace tissues or organs required by patients.

Cells can be taken from embryos that have stopped developing, so these embryos would have died anyway.

Cells are taken at a stage when the embryos have no nerve cells and cannot feel pain.

*Arguments against*

Every human embryo is a potential human being and should be given a chance to develop.

More embryos are generally produced than are needed, so many are needlessly destroyed.

The risk of embryonic stem cells developing into tumor cells.

**Genetic modifications of crops**

For example, the transfer of a gene encoding the Bt toxin protein from the bacterium *Bacillus thuringiensis* to maize crops.

Maize crops are often destroyed by insects that eat the corn; adding the Bt toxin gene kills the insects. This is controversial. The table below summarizes the benefits and possible harmful effects of genetically modifying the maize crops.

*Benefits*

Since there is less damage to the maize crops, there is a higher crop yield, which may lessen food shortages for populations.

Since there is a higher crop yield, less land is needed to grow more crops. Instead, the land can become an area for wildlife conservation.

There is a reduction in pesticides, expensive and harmful to the environment, wildlife, and farmworkers.

*Harmful Effects*

The consequences of consuming modified crops are unclear. Consumer advocates have raised concerns. The bacterial DNA or the Bt toxin gene could be harmful to human or animal health.

Other insects not harmful to the crops could be destroyed. The maize pollen contains the toxin, and so if it is blown onto nearby plants, it kills insects feeding on the plants.

Cross-pollination occurs, resulting in some wild plants being genetically modified with the Bt gene. These plants have an advantage as they are resistant to certain insects, causing wild plants to become endangered.

As these technologies develop, ethical issues become important to society.

# CHAPTER 12

# Respiratory System

- General Structure and Function of the Respiratory System

- Structure of Lungs and Alveoli

- Breathing Mechanisms

- Thermoregulation by Evaporation and Panting

- Alveolar Gas Exchange

## General Structure and Function of the Respiratory System

### Gas exchange

The human *respiratory system* includes the structures that conduct air to and from the lungs. Its purpose is to supply the body's tissues with oxygen.

The pathway of oxygen in the respiratory system involves cooperative transport and diffusion within the circulatory system.

Oxygen is taken in from the environment by the lungs. Here, the circulatory system's red blood cells meet the lung's alveoli, and oxygen diffuses into the cells.

Red blood cells carry the oxygenated blood towards the body's tissues. Carbon dioxide follows a reverse path, traveling in deoxygenated blood from the tissues and back to the lungs. It is expelled through the nose (or mouth) into the external environment.

*Cellular respiration* involves the breakdown of organic molecules (e.g., glucose) to produce ATP. A sufficient supply of oxygen is required for aerobic respiration of the Krebs cycle and the electron transport chain to convert potential energy within food into the energy of ATP efficiently.

Carbon dioxide is generated by aerobic cellular respiration and must be removed from the cell. There is an exchange of gases, where carbon dioxide leaves the cell and oxygen enters. Animals have organ systems involved in facilitating respiration and regulating gas transport between the environment and the body's cells.

Breathing involves inspiration (bringing air into the lungs) and expiration (moving air out of the lungs). In general, gas exchange exchanges one gas for another. External respiration involves gas exchange with the external environment at a respiratory surface.

### Oxygen and carbon dioxide exchange at the alveoli

Internal respiration is complex in animals and involves a gas exchange between blood and tissue fluid. The process occurs in the lungs' alveoli (i.e., small air sacs). Oxygen diffuses into the capillaries surrounding the alveoli. Carbon dioxide diffuses out of the capillaries and into the alveoli.

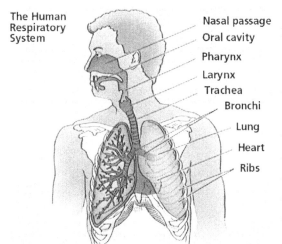

The Human Respiratory System

Nasal passage
Oral cavity
Pharynx
Larynx
Trachea
Bronchi
Lung
Heart
Ribs

The lungs are deep within the thoracic cavity to protect from desiccation. The pathways in the respiratory system connect the lungs to the outside environment. Human lungs have at least 50 times the skin's total surface area.

Air enters through the nose (or mouth). It is warmed, filtered, and passed through the nasal (or oral) cavity. Air passes through the *pharynx* into the upper part of the trachea containing the *larynx*. The larynx is held open by cartilage that forms the *laryngeal prominence* (Adam's apple).

The *vocal cords* are two bands of tissue that extend across the opening of the larynx. As air passes, these tissues vibrate, creating sounds. The walls of the *trachea* are reinforced with C-shaped rings of cartilage.

As the food is swallowed, the larynx rises, and the *glottis* is closed by a flap of elastic, cartilaginous tissue, the *epiglottis*. The soft palate's backward movement covers the nasal passage entrance; this movement directs food downward.

**Airways enter the lungs**

Airways beyond the larynx are divided: the *conducting zone* and *respiratory zone*.

The trachea divides into two *bronchi*. After passing the larynx, the air moves into the bronchi that carry air to the lungs.

Bronchi are reinforced to prevent their collapse and are lined with ciliated epithelium and mucus-producing cells. The C-shaped rings of cartilage diminish as bronchi branch within the lungs.

The *conducting zone* has no gas exchange and consists of the tracheal tube, which branches into two bronchi before entering the lungs and branching.

The walls of the trachea and the bronchi contain cartilage for support. *Terminal bronchioles* are the first branches without cartilage.

Each bronchus branches into numerous smaller tubes within the lungs as *bronchioles* that conduct air to *alveoli*, grape-like sac clusters.

The *respiratory zone* is where gas exchange occurs and consists of the respiratory bronchioles with alveoli attached.

The respiratory bronchioles with capillaries and alveoli for gas exchange are shown above.

Oxygen moves from the alveoli to the red blood cell, while carbon dioxide moves from the red blood cell (or dissolved in the plasma) to the alveoli for expiration by the lungs.

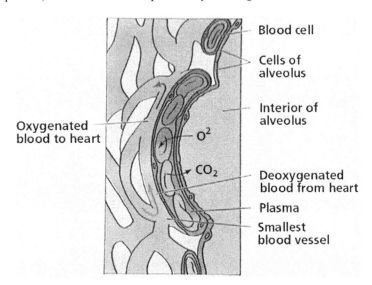

**Protection against disease and particulate matter**

The respiratory system has several mechanisms to protect against disease and particulate matter.

The nasal cavity contains visible hairs as *vibrissae*. Nostril hairs filter out coarse particles.

The *paranasal sinuses* secrete mucus, making its way through the mucous glands into the lamina propria and into the respiratory mucosa, where the mucous traps foreign particles pathogens.

The respiratory mucosa's epithelial cells secrete *defensins*, natural antibiotics that aid in defense against invading microbes.

*Serous glands* supply the *lamina propria* with water fluid containing lysozyme (antibacterial enzyme). Macrophages, which engulf pathogens, are present.

The respiratory mucosa is a part of the nasal cavity's ciliated epithelial lining.

Cilia on the mucous lining of the respiratory tract sweep pathogens and particles out of the body by creating a slight current.

The nasal cavity wall contains three projections: superior, medial, and inferior turbinate (or conchae). These projections increase the surface area of the nasal mucosa.

As air passes, the heavier non-gaseous components tend to be deflected into the mucosal surfaces.

The entire respiratory tract has a warm, wet, mucous membrane lining exposed to environmental air.

The airways and pressure difference between the lungs and atmosphere are important factors in the flow of air in and out of the lungs. Many diseases can affect the condition of the airways.

## Structure of the Lungs and Alveoli

**Thoracic cavity**

The *lungs* are two large, lobed organs in the chest. The *thorax* is a closed compartment, bound at the neck by muscles and separated from the abdomen by the *diaphragm*, a sheet of skeletal muscle. The thorax wall comprises ribs, *sternum* (breastbone), and intercostal muscles between ribs.

Lungs are ingrowths of the body wall and connect to the outside by a series of tubes and small openings. The *pleura* (a thin sheet of cells) separates the inside of the chest cavity from the lungs' outer surface. The *pleural sac* (closed sac) surrounds each lung. The pleural surface coating the lung is the *visceral pleura* attached to the lung by connective tissue.

The *parietal pleura* (outer layer) is attached to the thoracic wall and diaphragm. A thin layer of intrapleural fluid separates the two layers of the pleura. Changes in the hydrostatic pressure of the intrapleural fluid (the intrapleural pressure $P_{ip}$, the intra-thoracic pressure) cause the lungs and thoracic wall to move together during breathing.

Lung breathing evolved about 400 million years ago. Lungs are not solely in the domain of vertebrates. Some terrestrial snails have gas exchange structures like those in frogs. The lungs are composed of alveoli, the air sacs where gas exchange with blood occurs. Lungs have a non-respiratory function and release biologically active substances into the blood and remove them. They trap and dissolve small blood clots.

**Alveoli as the site of gas exchange**

*Alveoli* are open-ended, hollow sacs as continuous lumens of airways. Their inner walls are lined with a single layer of flat epithelial cells called *type I alveolar cells*, interspersed by thicker, specialized *type II alveolar cells*. Alveolar walls contain capillaries and a small interstitial space with interstitial fluid and connective tissue. Alveolar wall cells secrete a fluid that keeps the inner surface of the alveoli moist, allowing gases to dissolve.

*Surfactant*, a natural detergent, prevents the alveoli sides from sticking. Blood within an alveolar-capillary wall is separated from the air within an alveolus by a thin barrier of 0.2 μm thick. Pores in the walls permit the flow of air. The extensive surface area and thin barrier permit the rapid exchange of large quantities of oxygen and carbon dioxide by diffusion.

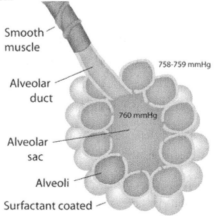

Smooth muscle
758-759 mmHg
Alveolar duct
760 mmHg
Alveolar sac
Alveoli
Surfactant coated

*Gas exchange of oxygen and carbon dioxide occurs at the alveoli in the lungs*

## Breathing Mechanisms

**Measuring respiration rates and lung capacity**

*Tidal volume* is the amount of air entering the lungs during a single, regular inspiration or leaving the lungs in a single expiration.

The *inspiratory reserve volume* is the amount of air above the tidal volume during deepest inspirations.

The *functional residual capacity* the volume of air remaining in the lungs after expiring the tidal volume.

The *expiratory reserve volume* is the additional volume of air after expiring the resting tidal volume. It is the volume expired via actives contraction of the expiratory muscles.

The *residual volume* is the air remaining in the lungs after maximal expiration.

The *vital capacity* is the maximal volume of air expired after a maximal inspiration.

*Minute ventilation* is the volume of gas inhaled (or exhaled) from a person's lungs per minute.

Minute ventilation (ml/min) = Tidal volume (ml/breath) × Respiration rate (breaths/min)

*Anatomic dead space* is space within the airways that do not permit gas exchange with the blood.

*Alveolar ventilation* is the volume of air entering the alveoli per minute.

Ventilation (ml/min)

= [Tidal volume (ml/breath) – anatomic dead space (ml/min)] × respiratory rate (breaths/min)

Since a fixed volume of tidal volume is dead space, increased depth of breathing elevates alveolar ventilation *more than* increased breathing rate.

*Alveolar dead space* is the volume of inspired air not used for gas exchange from reaching the alveoli.

*Physiologic dead space* is the sum of the anatomic and alveolar dead space.

**Diaphragm and rib cage**

The *diaphragm* is a muscle that pulls down when contracting, which increases chest volume, decreases air pressure, and stimulates inspiration.

The *rib cage* expands outward during inspiration. Intercostal muscles help this expansion. At rest, the rib cage maintains lung volume, prevents the lungs from collapsing, and forms a cage around the lungs for protection.

The volume of the lungs is dependent on two factors.

*Trans-pulmonary pressure* is the difference in pressure between the inside and outside of the lungs, and *lung compliance* is the lung's ability to stretch.

Muscles used in respiration are attached to the chest wall. When they contract (or relax), they change the chest dimensions, changing the transpulmonary pressure, lung volume, and alveolar pressure, causing air to flow in (or out) of the lungs.

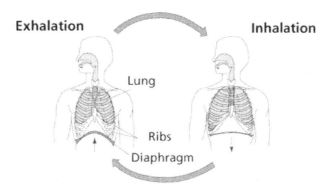

*Diaphragm contraction during inspiration and relaxation during expiration*

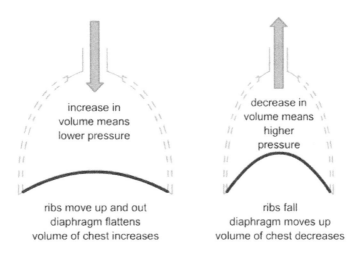

*Inspiration when diaphragm contracts (air in, on the left) and expiration when the diaphragm relaxes (air out)*

When a person inhales, muscles in the chest wall contract, lifting the ribs and pulling them outward.

The diaphragm contracts and moves downward, enlarging the chest cavity. The reduced air pressure in the lungs causes air to enter the lungs. Exhaling reverses these steps.

**Pressure differences facilitate breathing**

*Intrapulmonary pressure* is the atmospheric pressure because the lungs are open to the atmosphere and therefore have the same pressure as the outside environment. If the intrapleural pressure is less than the atmospheric pressure, it sucks on the lungs and prevents them from collapsing. During inspiration, intrapleural pressure decreases and causes the lungs to expand.

*Differential pressure* is the difference between intrapulmonary (i.e., inside the lungs) and intrapleural (i.e., outside the lungs) pressure.

Like other mammals, humans breathe through a *negative pressure* mechanism; akin to sucking.

During inhalation, lowering the diaphragm and raising the ribs forms negative pressure by increasing the thoracic cavity volume. The air, which is under greater outside pressure, flows into the lung.

Increases in the $[CO_2]$ and $[H^+]$ in the blood are the primary stimuli that increase the breathing rate.

## Regulation by nervous control

The *vagus nerve* exercises influence the respiratory system, heart, and viscera. This is an involuntary control, so breathing cannot be consciously stopped for long periods. The body breathes when able and needed.

The *diaphragm* and *intercostal muscles* are skeletal muscles.

Therefore, breathing depends on the cyclical excitation of these muscles.

Control of this neural activity resides with *medullary inspiratory neurons* in the medulla oblongata.

Peripheral chemoreceptors (carotid bodies) and aortic bodies in close contact with arterial blood are stimulated by a steep decrease in arterial $pO_2$ and an increase in $H^+$ concentration.

The medullary inspiratory neurons receive inputs from apneustic and pneumotaxic centers in the pons.

Negative feedback from pulmonary stretch receptors controls respiration, known as the *Hering-Breuer reflex*. This reflex is triggered to prevent over-inflammation of the lung.

Protective reflexes (e.g., coughing, sneezing) protect the respiratory system from irritants.

Receptors for sneezing are in the nose or pharynx, while those for coughing are in the larynx, trachea, and bronchi. These reflexes are characterized by a deep inspiration followed by a violent expiration.

The descending pathways accomplish voluntary control of breathing from the cerebral cortex. It cannot be maintained when involuntary stimuli are high.

*Tachypnea* (rapid breathing) is a reflex effect from the J receptors in the lungs. It is stimulated by an increase in interstitial lung pressure due to the occlusion of a pulmonary vessel as a pulmonary embolus.

## Thermoregulation by Evaporation and Panting

**Conchae exchange heat and moisture**

One of the functions of the nose and the nasal cavity is to warm and moisten the inspired air, along with retrieving moisture and heat from the expired air.

The high-water content of the mucus film humidifies inhaled air. A bed of capillaries and thin-walled veins lie under the nasal epithelium. The capillaries and thin veins are involved in warming the incoming air.

If the air is very cold, the *plexus* (a network of veins and capillaries) work to fill with blood. The heat-intensifying process is amplified.

Heat and moisture are exchanged from expired air. The conchae have been cooled by incoming inspired cold air. As warm air leaves, it precipitates moisture on the conchae, which extracts heat from the humid air flowing over them.

The surfaces involved in respiratory evaporation must be kept moist, as water is continuously evaporating from them.

On a cold day, people see water vapor in their breath; water evaporated from the lungs.

Water is a product of cellular respiration, and it, along with carbon dioxide, is expired during breathing.

Thermal panting is caused by a buildup of body heat, resulting from an increase in the environmental temperature or additional activity and increased metabolic rates.

Appropriate chemical receptors perceive oxygen and carbon dioxide levels.

When the oxygen levels are too low (or carbon dioxide levels are too high), the respiratory system responds by increasing the overall rate of respiration.

The overall panting rate increases at high altitudes (due to low $pO_2$ levels).

## Alveolar Gas Exchange

### Diffusion

Even though alveoli are tiny, their abundance in the lungs results in a large surface area for gas exchange.

The alveoli walls have a single layer of thin cells, creating a short diffusion distance for the gases.

*Diffusion* is the passive movement of materials from a higher to a lower concentration.

A short diffusion distance allows for rapid gas exchange.

*Ventilation* is the mechanism of breathing. It is the process of bringing fresh air into the alveoli and removing stale air.

Ventilation maintains the concentration gradient of carbon dioxide and oxygen between the alveoli and capillaries of the blood.

Partial pressures measure the differences between oxygen and carbon dioxide concentrations (i.e., $[CO_2]$). The greater the difference in partial pressure, the higher the diffusion rate.

The body must expel $CO_2$, the product of cell respiration.

The body needs to take in oxygen for cellular respiration to make ATP.

There must be a low concentration of carbon dioxide in the alveoli so that carbon dioxide can diffuse out of the blood in the capillaries (where it exists in a high concentration) and into the alveoli.

### Differential partial pressures of $O_2$ and $CO_2$

There must be a high concentration of oxygen in the alveoli compared to a low concentration of oxygen in the capillaries so that oxygen can diffuse into the blood of the capillaries from the alveoli.

The $O_2$ in the alveoli flows down its partial pressure gradient from the alveoli into the pulmonary capillaries. Here, $O_2$ binds to hemoglobin for transport.

The $CO_2$ flows down its partial pressure gradient from the capillaries into the alveoli for expiration.

Blood entering pulmonary capillaries is the venous blood of systemic circulation. This blood has a high $pCO_2$ and a low $pO_2$.

Differences in partial pressures of $O_2$ and $CO_2$ on the two sides of the alveolar-capillary membrane result in net diffusion of oxygen from the alveoli to the blood and carbon dioxide from the blood to the alveoli.

With this diffusion, capillary blood $pO_2$ rises, and $pCO_2$ falls, net diffusion of these gases ceases when partial pressures in the capillaries become equal to the alveoli.

Diffusion improves with vascularization (i.e., more blood vessels); $O_2$ delivery to cells is promoted by erythrocytes (i.e., red blood cells) with the $O_2$-binding protein hemoglobin.

*Diffuse interstitial fibrosis* is a disease where the alveolar walls thicken with connective tissue and reduce gas exchange.

Ventilation-perfusion inequality can result from ventilated alveoli with no blood supply or blood flow through the alveoli with no ventilation, resulting in reduced gas exchange.

In a steady-state, the volume of oxygen consumed by body cells per unit of time equals the volume of oxygen added to the blood in the lungs.

The *rate of expiration* is the volume of carbon dioxide produced by cells.

*Respiratory quotient* (RQ) is the ratio of $CO_2$ produced / $O_2$ consumed and nutrients used for energy.

Ventilation is the exchange of air between the atmosphere and the alveoli.

Air moves by bulk flow from high pressure to low-pressure regions.

During ventilation, air moves into the lungs from changing alveolar pressure by changes in lung dimensions.

*Hypoventilation* is an increase in the ratio of carbon dioxide production to alveolar ventilation.

*Hyperventilation* is a decrease in the ratio of carbon dioxide production to alveolar ventilation.

*Notes for active learning*

# CHAPTER 13

# Circulatory System

- Circulatory System Overview

- Arterial and Venous Systems: Arteries, Arterioles, Venules and Veins

- Composition of Blood

- Blood Types and Rh Factor

- Oxygen and Carbon Dioxide Transport by Blood

## Circulatory System Overview

### Network for transporting gases, nutrients, hormones

The circulatory system is responsible for *thermoregulation* (i.e., regulating body temperature), transport, fluid balance, and immune system function. It transports $O_2$, $CO_2$, nutrients, waste products, and hormones.

Blood components direct fluid retention or excretion maintain appropriate blood volume and composition. They affect how materials move out of or into the bloodstream from surrounding tissues.

Gases are taken in or released via respiration, and nutrients are absorbed from the small intestine and distributed to tissues via the bloodstream.

Blood filtration is at the kidneys and liver; waste products and poisons are metabolized and removed.

Steroid and peptide hormones are circulated throughout the body via the bloodstream, allowing for cellular communication.

The circulatory system protects the body from disease by facilitating immune system cell movement.

The circulatory system maintains core body temperature by redirecting blood flow to the skin and extremities.

When temperatures drop, the body initiates *vasoconstriction* of the blood vessels to the skin, reducing blood flow near the surface and thus limiting heat loss to the air.

Conversely, high temperatures cause *vasodilation* of blood vessels, increasing blood flow to the skin and promoting heat loss to the surroundings.

### Four-chambered heart structure and function

The heart is a cone-shaped, muscular organ about the size of a fist located between the lungs and directly behind the sternum. It circulates blood throughout the body by a rhythmic pumping action.

The heart's chambers are lined with epithelial tissue in the *endocardium*

The outermost tissue is the *epicardium*.

The *myocardium* (i.e., cardiac muscle) is the thick middle layer as the bulk of the heart.

The cardiac muscle is entirely under the control of hormones and involuntary control by the autonomic nervous system. Unlike skeletal muscle, it has branching bands of muscle fibers connected by *intercalated disks*.

These disks allow electrical signals to travel through the cardiac muscle cells, which contract as a unit.

Cardiac muscle cells have a single nucleus, unlike the multi-nucleated skeletal muscle cells.

The heart is surrounded by a double-layered sac of the *pericardium*, cushioned by the *pericardial fluid*.

Connective tissue separates the four chambers of the heart.

The *septum* is an internal wall that divides the heart into its right and left halves.

Each half of the heart contains an upper, thin-walled *atrium* and a lower, thick-walled *ventricle*.

**Atria and ventricles**

The four chambers function as a double-sided pump.

The atria are thinner and weaker than the muscular ventricles but hold the same blood volume.

Each atrium receives blood from the veins (i.e., blood flowing towards the heart) of the cardiovascular system and delivers it to its respective ventricle through a valve.

The ventricles pump blood to the body through arteries (i.e., blood flowing away from the heart), also regulated by a valve.

The valves between the atria and ventricles are the *atrioventricular valves,* and the valves between the ventricles and arteries are the *semilunar valves* for their half-moon shape when closed.

Heart valves are supported by *chordae tendineae* (i.e., strong fibrous tendons) attached to muscular projections of ventricular walls to prevent valves from inverting.

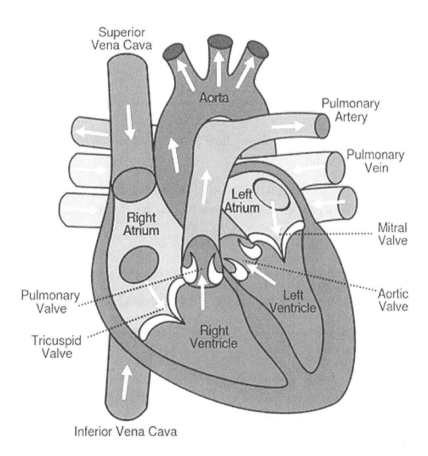

*The heart has four chambers, blood vessels, valves, and the route of blood through the heart*

Deoxygenated blood returning from the body enters the *right atrium* through two major veins: the *superior vena cava* and the *inferior vena cava.*

**Tricuspid and semilunar valves**

The right atrium sends blood through the right atrioventricular (or *tricuspid*) valve to the *right ventricle.*

The *tricuspid valve* has three flaps, which snap shut when the right ventricle contracts so that blood does not flow back into the right atrium.

The right ventricle ejects the blood through the *pulmonary semilunar valve* into the *pulmonary arteries.*

The pulmonary arteries are the only arteries carrying deoxygenated blood; other arteries carry oxygen-rich blood.

The pulmonary semilunar valve prevents backflow into the right ventricle from the pulmonary arteries.

The pulmonary arteries deliver the deoxygenated blood to the lungs.

Oxygenated blood returns from the lungs through *pulmonary veins* and is delivered to the *left atrium.*

The left atrium pumps this newly oxygenated blood through the left atrioventricular valve (*bicuspid* or *mitral valve*) to the *left ventricle.*

Blood is ejected into the aorta (largest artery) through the aortic semilunar valve in the left ventricle.

The left ventricle is the strongest and thickest chamber of the heart since it must pump blood throughout the body. This blood delivers oxygen to the body tissues and returns deoxygenated blood to the right atrium to restart the cycle.

The right atrium and ventricle are separated from the left atrium and ventricle so that oxygenated blood does not mix with deoxygenated blood.

Blood is pumped out of the heart through one set of vessels and returns to the heart via another set. This structure ensures appropriate blood pressure and gas concentrations in different areas of the circulatory system.

**Endothelial cells in the heart and blood vessels**

The interior of the heart and blood vessels are lined with *endothelium,* a thin layer of *endothelial cells.*

This semi-permeable layer controls the passage of cells and molecules in and out of the bloodstream.

Endothelial cells help prevent blood clots and plaque formation and facilitate an inflammation response to invasive agents and damaged cells.

*Basal muscle tone* is a muscle's passive, baseline resistance to stretching, which varies throughout the body. Endothelial cells can rapidly change a blood vessel's smooth muscle tone from its basal level. Hormones and nerve signals regulate this vasoconstriction and vasodilation.

Endothelial cells control blood pressure by producing nitric oxide (a potent vasodilator) and *endothelial-1* (i.e., a potent vasoconstrictor). The controlled production of nitric oxide is essential to maintaining basal tone and therefore balanced blood pressure.

Endothelial cells are involved in *angiogenesis*, the formation of new capillaries. This process is vital to wound healing and the formation of collateral vessels, which provide alternate routes for blood flow during a circulatory system blockage.

**Systolic and diastolic blood pressure**

*Blood pressure* is the pressure blood exerts on the walls of the blood vessels. It is usually measured in the arteries since blood pressure is strongest.

*Systolic pressure* is measured as the ventricles contract, and blood is forcefully ejected from the heart.

*Diastolic pressure* is the blood pressure when blood is not being pumped since the ventricles are relaxing. Systolic pressure is the maximum blood pressure and is higher than diastolic blood pressure. Reference blood pressure is 120 (systolic) over 80 (diastolic).

Both measurements of blood pressure represent a stage of a single heartbeat. *Systole* is the phase of contraction and blood ejection. When the term systole is used alone, it only refers to the ventricles. During ventricular systole, the atria are relaxed (i.e., in *diastole*).

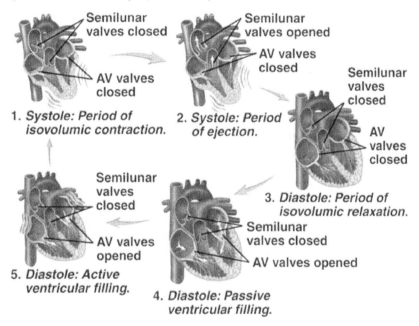

*Valves of the heart open and close during rhythmic contractions of the atria and ventricles*

**Heart disease**

Heart issues can be diagnosed by observing irregularities in the cardiac cycle. During heart failure, the heart does not pump an adequate volume of blood. This may be due to diastolic dysfunction when a ventricle wall has reduced compliance and cannot fill adequately, resulting in reduced EDV and reduced SV.

Heart failure may be caused by systolic dysfunction, which results from myocardial damage that impairs cardiac contractility and therefore decreases SV. Adaptive reflexes to counter the reduced SV strive to maintain blood pressure by retaining fluid to increase blood volume or constricting vessels.

Unfortunately, excess fluid retention can impair respiration, and vasoconstriction makes it difficult for the heart to pump. If the heart does not quickly recover from heart failure, it becomes weaker.

**Pulse rate**

A *pulse* is measured in arteries far from the heart since it is a wave effect that passes down the arterial blood vessels' walls. The pulse occurs when the aorta expands and immediately recoils following ventricular systole. Since there is one arterial pulse per ventricular systole, the arterial pulse rate determines the heart rate. For adults, a normal pulse rate (resting heart rate) is between 60 and 100 beats per minute (bpm); children have high resting pulse rates.

Generally, bradycardia, a lower heart rate, implies an efficient heart function and better cardiovascular fitness (e.g., a well-conditioned athlete may have a pulse rate closer to 40 bpm). Bradycardia refers to a low heart rate (less than 60 bpm), while *tachycardia* refers to a heart rate greater than 100 bpm.

**Pulmonary and systemic circulation**

The cardiovascular system has two major circulation pathways.

*Systemic circulation* includes the loop between the heart and nearly all arteries, capillaries, and veins of the body.

*Pulmonary circulation* includes the path from the heart to the pulmonary arteries, pulmonary capillaries, pulmonary veins, and the heart. This is the only part of the circulatory system in which the arteries transport deoxygenated blood, and the veins transport oxygenated blood.

Blood pressure is lower in the pulmonary circulation since the blood vessels are shorter and have less *vascular resistance* to blood flow.

Pulmonary circulation begins when deoxygenated blood from systemic circulation enters the right atrium and drains to the right ventricle through the right atrioventricular (tricuspid) valve. The blood is ejected through the pulmonary semilunar valve into the right and left pulmonary arteries.

The pulmonary arteries branch many times to form hundreds of thousands of *pulmonary capillaries* in the lungs.

These capillaries surround *alveoli,* the tiny sacs in which gas exchange occurs.

Carbon dioxide and water from the blood diffuse through the alveoli and are exhaled, while oxygen is inhaled and diffuses from the alveoli into the blood.

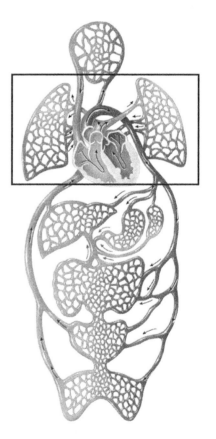

*Pulmonary (enlarged) between heart and lungs and systemic circulation between heart and body*

The oxygenated blood returns to the heart's left atrium via the pulmonary vein.

Once oxygenated, blood returns to the heart, delivered through the left atrioventricular (bicuspid or mitral) valve into the left ventricle. It is pumped out of the left ventricle into the aorta via the aortic semilunar valve.

Systemic circulation begins as oxygenated blood travels through the body.

**Arteries, capillaries and veins**

The aorta is the body's largest and thickest artery. It arches and branches into the upper body's major arteries before descending through the diaphragm, where it branches into arteries supplying the lower parts of the body.

Arteries diverge into capillaries around organs and tissues to exchange gases, nutrients, and wastes.

The capillaries merge into venules and veins as the blood returns toward the heart. Veins of the lower body coalesce into the inferior vena cava, while those of the upper body coalesce into the superior vena cava.

These two vessels empty into the heart's right atrium so that the blood may enter pulmonary circulation and be re-oxygenated.

When oxygen levels are low, systemic capillaries that feed tissues in need of oxygen undergo vasodilation to deliver more blood to where it is needed most.

By contrast, pulmonary capillaries, which feed low-oxygen alveoli, undergo vasoconstriction so that blood is diverted to alveoli where gas exchange (uptake of $O_2$) is efficient.

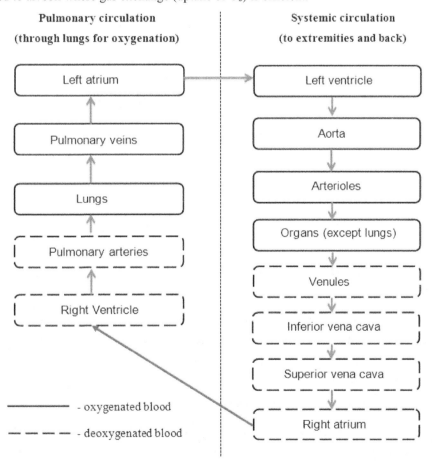

*Coronary circulation* supplies blood to the heart itself. *Coronary arteries* originate from the aorta and feed into capillaries that cover the heart and nourish myocardial cells. Deoxygenated blood from the coronary capillaries drains into the *cardiac veins,* which merge directly into the right atrium.

Blocked flow in coronary arteries can result in chest pain and heart attacks.

## Arterial and Venous Systems: Arteries, Arterioles, Venules and Veins

**Structural and functional differences**

The circulatory system is divided into the arterial, capillary, and venous portions.

The arterial system carries blood away from the heart.

Systemic arteries carry oxygenated blood from the heart to the body. Pulmonary arteries carry deoxygenated blood from the heart to the lungs.

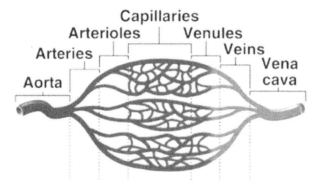

*Blood is received from the arteries, and gas exchange occurs at the capillaries*
*before the blood returns to the heart through the veins*

Arteries are large, thick, and elastic, with multi-layered connective tissue walls, smooth muscle, and endothelium. The outermost layer is made of longitudinal collagen and elastic fibers to avoid leaks and bulges (an aneurysm).

Within the connective tissue layers are circular smooth muscle and elastic fibers, which maintain muscle tone and contract to force blood through vessels. An inner layer of endothelium lines the narrow lumen.

The strong, elastic arterial walls can maintain high blood pressure in the arterial system and aid in pumping blood throughout the body. During systole, contraction of ventricles ejects blood into arteries, distending the arterial walls.

During diastole, the walls recoil elastically and force blood through. There is always blood in the arteries to keep them semi-inflated, which is why diastolic blood pressure is not zero (averages 80 mmHg).

**Three artery types**

The three major arteries are elastic, muscular, and coronary arteries.

The *elastic arteries* include the aorta and its major branches. They are the largest, thickest, and most elastic of the arteries, providing an elastic pipe for blood directly out of the heart. Elastic arteries are not able to undergo vasoconstriction.

*Muscular arteries* (distributing arteries) distribute blood to specific organs. They contain a large amount of smooth muscle to direct blood flow and are involved in vasoconstriction.

*Coronary arteries* directly supply and nourish the heart. They originate from the base of the aorta above the aortic semilunar valve and branch across the heart's outer surface, the epicardium.

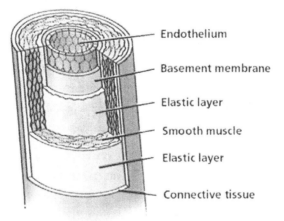

*Cross-section of distributing arteries*

*Arterioles* are smaller vessels that branch from the arteries. They have walls of an endothelium, smooth muscle, and connective tissue, but these layers are thin.

Arterioles are active in vasoconstriction and vasodilation, allowing the body to redirect and control blood flow and pressure.

**Capillaries as the site of diffusion**

Small arterioles branch into a network of *capillary beds.*

The capillary beds surround the body's organs and tissues and connect the arterial and venous systems.

Capillaries are microscopic blood vessels that contain no muscle or connective tissue, a single layer of endothelial cells across which gases, nutrients, enzymes, hormones, and wastes diffuse.

After blood from the systemic arterial system exchanges nutrients and wastes with the capillaries of organs and tissues, deoxygenated blood leaves the capillaries and flows into the systemic *venous system*.

The venous system vessels (e.g., venules, veins) are thinner, porous, and less elastic. They contain an outer layer of fibrous connective tissue, a middle layer of smooth muscle and elastic tissue, and an endothelium inner layer. Vasoconstriction and dilation occur in the venous system.

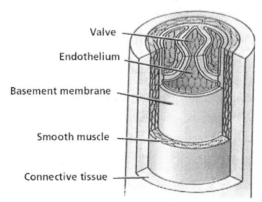

*Veins with valves and without a thick layer of smooth muscle, as in arteries*

**Venules and veins return blood to the heart**

*Venules*, thin and porous, are analogous to arterioles. They gather blood from capillary beds and merge into the larger veins. The veins have thicker and resistant walls but are still weaker than arteries. Their thin walls and wide lumens make venous blood pressure lower than arterial blood pressure.

Unlike arteries, veins collapse when they contain little blood and are compressed by neighboring skeletal muscles. The squeezing action of skeletal muscles helps the low-pressure, slow-moving blood travel to the heart. Veins depend on the action of the diaphragm and their smooth muscle walls to deliver blood to the heart. Larger veins have valves that prevent blood's backflow when moving against gravity.

Arteries are the thickest and strongest of the blood vessels, followed by the veins, arterioles, venules, and finally, the capillaries. The sympathetic nervous system innervates the walls of arteries, arterioles, veins, and large venules.

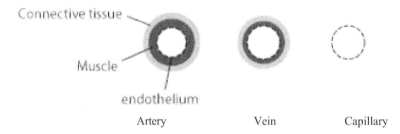

*Cross-sectional comparison of the three main vessels of the circulatory system*

Not all blood received from the capillaries is immediately delivered to the heart. Blood from the gastrointestinal capillary beds, for example, is first delivered to the liver to process and filter nutrients via the *hepatic portal vein.* The hepatic vein leaves the liver and enters the inferior vena cava. Blood below the diaphragm returns through the *inferior vena cava*, while blood from the upper body returns through the *superior vena cava.*

**Cardiac output**

The pressure differential between the high-pressure arteries and low-pressure veins facilitates blood flow throughout the circulatory system.

The resistance to flow is the opposing force that blood counteracts to move through the circulatory system.

*Total peripheral resistance* (TPR) is resistance throughout the circulatory system. TPR is a function of blood vessel diameter, blood vessel length, and viscosity.

*Cardiac output* (CO) measures the rate of blood flow from the heart; equals stroke volume (SV) per minute:

$$CO = HR \text{ (heart rate)} \times SV$$

CO is increased by a large increase in heart rate, resulting from increased sinoatrial node (SA) activity. A small increase in SV is caused by increased ventricular contractility mediated by sympathetic activity. The Frank-Starling mechanism accounts for an increase in end-diastolic volume.

*Blood velocity* describes the speed at which blood moves through a vessel. Since the blood volume flow rate (or *cardiac output*) is approximately constant, blood velocity depends on the total cross-sectional area.

*Bernoulli's principle* states that velocity is inversely proportional to cross-sectional area and is calculated by dividing cardiac output by the vessel's cross-sectional area.

Blood pressure is highest in arteries and decreases as it travels to arterioles, capillaries, venules, and veins. It is dependent on cardiac output, resistance to flow, total blood volume, vessel elasticity, and other factors.

Systemic arterial blood pressure is measured in most cases, but systemic venous blood pressure is of interest. Additionally, the pressure in the pulmonary circulation is measured.

The difference between systolic and diastolic pressure is *pulse pressure* (PP), while the average of the two is *mean arterial pressure* (MAP).

The MAP is calculated by multiplying cardiac output by *total peripheral resistance* (TPR).

$$MAP = CO \times TPR$$

Blood pressure is highest in the arteries for several reasons; arteries are closest to the heart's forceful ejections, have a small cross-sectional area, and high resistance. Arterioles have the greatest resistance to flow since they are most capable of vasoconstriction, but the aorta has the highest pressure since it is closest to the heart.

**Valves regulate blood flow in veins**

The veins have the lowest blood pressure because the force of cardiac output diminishes over time, and a larger cross-sectional area provides less resistance. Veins require the *skeletal muscle pump* (skeletal muscle contraction), the *respiratory pump* (diaphragm), and valve action to maintain flow.

Blood volume is an important determinant of venous pressure. At any given time, most of the blood is in veins. Walls of veins are less elastic; they can stretch to accommodate large volumes of blood without recoiling (i.e., resisting flow).

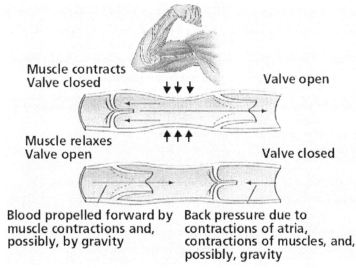

Muscle contracts
Valve closed                    Valve open

Muscle relaxes
Valve open                      Valve closed

Blood propelled forward by      Back pressure due to
muscle contractions and,        contractions of atria,
possibly, by gravity            contractions of muscles, and,
                                possibly, gravity

Consequently, veins have low blood pressure, and vasoconstriction is necessary to increase pressure in the veins and drive blood towards the heart.

*Varicose veins* are abnormal distention developing when veins' valves become weak and ineffective. Commonly, they are in the back of legs and pool blood under gravity's pressure.

Capillaries have slow, and even blood flow due to their high total cross-sectional area. Capillaries are the narrowest vessels, but the total cross-sectional area is higher than other vessels.

While systemic circulation is a high-pressure system, the pulmonary circulation is low pressure.

Therefore, the right ventricle is weaker than the left ventricle since it does not need to work as hard.

The pulmonary circulation has shorter blood vessels and does not need as much force to work against gravity. The elasticity and lack of smooth muscle in pulmonary vessels decrease resistance.

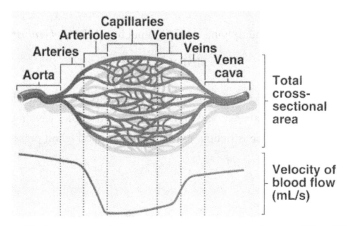

*The relationship between total cross-sectional area and velocity of blood flow*

**Blood volume and pressure**

Human blood pressure is usually measured at the upper arm's brachial artery, reflecting systemic arterial pressure due to the contraction and relaxation of the right ventricle.

A *sphygmomanometer* is an instrument with a pressure cuff to measure blood pressure. Healthy young adults have a systolic pressure of about 120 mmHg and a diastolic pressure of 80 mmHg (millimeters of mercury).

*Hypotension* is low blood pressure due to low blood volume, excessive vasodilation, anemia, or heart conditions. If prolonged, hypotension can lead to *arrhythmia* (irregular heartbeat), dizziness, and fainting.

*Shock* is severe hypotension that may cause tissue or organ damage due to reduced blood flow.

*Hypovolemic shock*, in which blood volume is reduced, may be caused by severe external bleeding (i.e., hemorrhage), dehydration, diarrhea, or vomiting.

Blood volume refers to the dissolved substances in the blood and not the fluid itself; therefore, a person can have a healthy 5 liters of blood but experience hypovolemia due to a lack of electrolytes.

*Low-resistance shock* is a consequence of excessive vasodilation, which may occur due to endocrine or nervous system malfunction, weakened blood vessels, and various drugs.

*Cardiogenic shock* is when heart conditions reduce cardiac output to dangerous levels. Severe cardiogenic shock may be due to a heart attack and cardiac arrest.

When the body detects hypotension, it activates the sympathetic nervous system, which promptly increases stroke volume, heart rate, and total peripheral resistance to raise mean arterial pressure. Interstitial fluid enters the bloodstream due to reduced capillary pressure.

Over time, fluid ingestion and kidney excretion are altered, and erythropoiesis is stimulated to replace blood volume. Usually, the body can rapidly offset hypotension, but it is fatal if it is severe and long-lasting.

**Hypertension**

*Hypertension* occurs when there is increased arterial pressure, generally due to an increased peripheral resistance resulting from the reduced arteriolar radius.

*Renal hypertension* results from renin's increased secretio*n,* which generates the vasoconstrictor *angiotensin II.*

Prolonged hypertension results in an increase in the left ventricle's muscle since it pumps against increased arterial pressure. This could decrease contractility and lead to heart failure.

Hypertension may be caused by stress, obesity, high salt intake, or smoking, along with a genetic predisposition.

Two genes are involved in hypertension for some individuals; they produce angiotensin. Persons with this form of hypertension may be cured by gene therapy in the future.

Hypertension is often not detected until a stroke, or heart attack occurs but is monitored by blood pressure.

Pressure higher than 160 / 95 mmHg in women or  130 / 95 mmHg in men is indicative of hypertension.

**Cardiovascular disease**

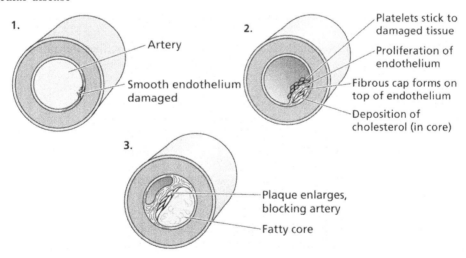

*Progressive degeneration of the arterial lumen due to atherosclerosis and obstruction by cholesterol plaque*

Hypertension is seen in people with *atherosclerosis* (or *arteriosclerosis*). This condition occurs when soft masses of fatty materials, mainly cholesterol, accumulate beneath the inner linings of arteries.

As this *plaque* accumulates, it protrudes into a vessel and interferes with blood flow. The thickened wall reduces blood flow and releases vasoconstrictors, exacerbating the problem.

Platelets may detect the plaque as a vascular irregularity and adhere to it, forming a clot.

**Blood clots, myocardial infarction and stroke**

A *thrombus* is a clot that remains stationary.

An *embolus* is a clot that dislodges into the bloodstream, which is deadly if it reaches the heart or brain. Atherosclerosis can develop in early adulthood, but symptoms may not appear until age 50 or older.

In families, atherosclerosis is inherited as *familial hypercholesterolemia*.

Atherosclerosis of a coronary artery may cause occasional chest pain, *angina pectoris*, which flares during periods of stress or physical exertion. Nitroglycerin and related drugs dilate blood vessels and relieve pain.

Hypertension and atherosclerosis are significant contributors to heart disease, the leading cause of death in the US. Angina indicates oxygen demands are greater than the capacity to deliver it and is a warning sign of heart disease.

If atherosclerosis and clotting in the coronary arteries create insufficient blood flow (i.e., *ischemia*), some heart muscle may die due to the lack of oxygen. This leads to *myocardial infarction* (MI), a *heart attack*.

Damaged myocardial cells may create abnormal impulses that cause *ventricular fibrillation,* uncoordinated ventricular contractions. If ventricular fibrillation severely impairs the heart's ability to deliver blood to the systemic circulation, it results in *cardiac arrest*.

A *stroke* is insufficient blood flow to the brain, which may occur if an embolus blocks a small cranial arteriole or bursts; it can result in paralysis, severe neurological impairment, or death.

A stroke is a *cardiovascular accident* (CVA). Warning symptoms that foretell stroke include numbness in the hands or face, difficulty speaking, and blindness in one eye.

If a cerebral artery is partially blocked, it is a temporary and less serious impairment as a *transient ischemic attack.*

**Three types of capillaries**

Capillaries in the body span approximately 60,000 miles in total, permeating every tissue in the body to exchange nutrients, gases, and metabolic byproducts.

Capillaries concentrate around organs such as the liver and intestines, which undergo high metabolic activity levels.

Blood velocity decreases as blood flows through capillaries because the total cross-sectional area of capillaries is relatively large. Narrow, water-filled spaces often separate the endothelial cells of a capillary as *intercellular clefts.*

The three capillaries are continuous capillary, fenestrated capillary, and sinusoidal capillary.

*Continuous capillaries* contain no pores on endothelial cells, but many have clefts at cell boundaries. They exchange materials through their clefts or via endocytosis and exocytosis. Continuous capillaries are predominantly in skin and muscles and in the cranium, where their tight junctions seal the blood-brain barrier.

*Fenestrated capillaries* contain small pores large enough for molecules to leak through but not blood cells. They are predominantly in the small intestine (facilitate nutrient absorption), in the endocrine glands (allow passage of hormones), and in the kidneys (filter blood).

*Sinusoidal capillaries* contain pores large enough for blood cells to pass through. They are mostly in lymphoid tissues, the liver, and bone marrow. They facilitate lymphocyte travel and blood cell modifications.

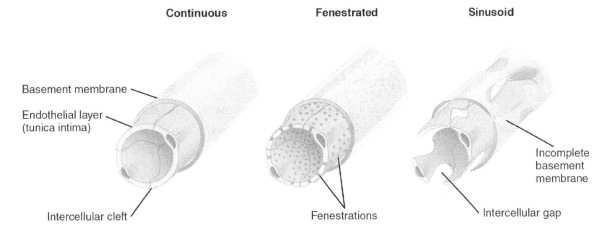

Capillary beds have two kinds of vessels: *true capillaries* (involved in the exchange between cells and blood) and *metarterioles* (which allows some blood to bypass the capillary bed).

Metarterioles directly connect the arteriole and venules on opposite sides of the bed.

Capillaries branch from the arterial side of the metarteriole; where they connect is a muscular sphincter.

Contraction of the sphincters shuts blood flow to the bed and causes blood to pass directly to the venule.

During exercise, metarterioles divert blood from the capillary beds of the skin and digestive organs, so it is directed to the muscles.

*Autoregulation* permits constant blood flow in capillary beds because arterioles reflexively stretch and constrict to counteract pressure changes.

## Angiogenesis

Angiogenesis of capillaries is continuous to respond to growth, injury, and changing metabolic activity. This process is activated by growth factors that direct partial digestion of an existing capillary to split in two or "sprout" a new capillary.

Angiogenesis is active in wound repair, muscle development, fat deposition, and tumor formation since these processes require an increased blood supply to the new tissues.

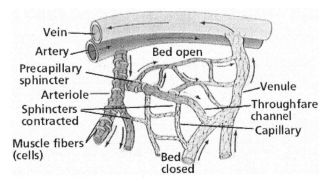

*Capillary beds with metarterioles shown*

**Gas and solute exchange mechanisms**

Capillaries are so narrow that only single red blood cells can pass. Some capillaries have small pores between the capillary wall cells, allowing white blood cells and other substances to flow in and out of capillaries by *paracellular* transport.

There are three basic mechanisms by which substances move across capillary walls to enter or leave the interstitial fluid: diffusion, vesicle transport, and bulk flow.

*Diffusion* is the passive movement of substances through the plasma membrane. Small molecules such as glucose and oxygen leave the capillaries and diffuse into the tissues, while carbon dioxide and small wastes leave the tissues and enter the capillaries.

*Vesicle transport* allows for the passage of materials via endocytosis and exocytosis. Larger, hydrophobic molecules typically travel through capillary walls by vesicle transport.

*Bulk flow* results from *hydrostatic pressure* and causes fluid to move from capillaries to the tissue fluids. It is higher in sinusoidal and fenestrated capillaries and lowers in continuous capillaries.

Bulk flow is opposed by *osmotic pressure*, which moves fluid from tissues to the capillaries due to differences in protein concentration. Both forces are described in the *Starling equation*, which explains how fluid and dissolved solutes either leave the capillaries (filtrate) or enter the capillaries (reabsorb).

At the arterial end of a capillary, hydrostatic pressure is higher than the osmotic pressure, so water leaves the capillary and enters the tissues. Midway along with a capillary, there is no net movement of water.

At this point, oxygen and nutrients diffuse into the tissue fluid, while carbon dioxide and other metabolic wastes diffuse into the capillaries.

At the venous end of a capillary, osmotic pressure is higher than hydrostatic pressure, so water is reabsorbed in the bloodstream.

**Heat exchange mechanisms**

The hypothalamus is responsible for monitoring blood temperature at about 37 °C. If there are significant fluctuations from this set point, the hypothalamus sends nerve signals to the blood vessels to restore proper body temperature. When external conditions are hot, vasodilation allows blood to flow near the skin's surface so that heat is lost through convection and radiation.

The opposite process occurs when external conditions are cold. Blood is kept away from the skin's surface through the mechanism of vasoconstriction. Blood flow is most reduced in the extremities, where the high surface-area-to-volume ratio causes heat to dissipate rapidly.

Humans and other animals use *countercurrent heat exchange* to conserve heat. Major veins and arteries run parallel deep in the arms and legs' muscles, with blood flowing in the opposite directions. When heat loss is not a concern, most blood returns from the skin through surface veins not parallel to the deep arteries. However, in cold conditions, blood returns through deep veins to exchange heat with the arteries.

Blood moving through the warm arteries cools as it travels toward the extremities. By the time it reaches the body's surface, it is closer to the outside air temperature, minimizing the temperature gradient and reducing heat loss. As the cold blood returns through the deep veins, it is reheated by the nearby warm arterial blood.

**Peripheral resistance impedes blood flow**

Resistance to flow (i.e., peripheral resistance) is the impedance of blood flow in the arteries caused by blood entering the arteries faster than it can leave, resulting in vessels stretching from increased pressure.

The elastic walls of the arteries contract during the diastole phase, but the heart contracts before enough blood flows into the arterioles to relieve the pressure in the arteries.

Peripheral resistance is a function of blood viscosity, blood vessel length, and blood vessel diameter.

A higher concentration of blood cells and plasma proteins increases viscosity and creates a higher resistance to flow.

Diseases that cause an increase in the number of blood cells are problematic due to increased resistance, which forces the heart to work harder.

Blood vessel length may impact flow resistance.

An overweight individual with additional blood vessels to service fat cells has greater resistance, partly why they are prone to increased heart problems.

Blood vessel diameter is important as well.

Vasoconstriction increases resistance, and vasodilation decreases resistance.

Obstruction from plaque (i.e., atherosclerosis) inside blood vessels increases resistance by reducing the diameter for blood flow.

Total peripheral resistance is the sum of resistance to flow by systemic blood vessels, although the primary determinant is resistance in the arterioles.

Because TPR affects blood pressure, deviations from normal blood pressure elicit homeostatic reflexes that alter TPR to offset the difference.

Hypertension causes blood vessels to dilate to relieve resistance, while hypotension causes vasoconstriction to increase resistance.

## Composition of Blood

### Plasma, chemicals and blood cells

There are 4 to 6 liters of blood in the average person.

Blood is connective tissue; mammalian blood contains up to 60% *plasma* (a liquid matrix) and 40% cellular components suspended in the plasma.

Plasma is 90% water and 10% dissolved organic and inorganic substances such as salts, gases, metabolic wastes, nutrients, proteins, and hormones. Salts and proteins in the plasma act as buffers maintaining the blood near a pH of 7.35. They maintain blood osmotic pressure to regulate osmosis into and out of the bloodstream.

*Albumin* is the primary protein in plasma, partially responsible for maintaining osmotic pressure and carrying steroid hormones and fatty acids.

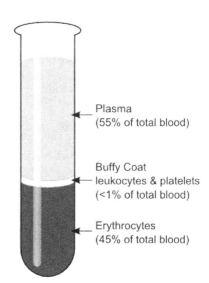

Plasma
(55% of total blood)

Buffy Coat
leukocytes & platelets
(<1% of total blood)

Erythrocytes
(45% of total blood)

*Fibrinogen* and its derivative *fibrin* are other important plasma proteins to form blood clots. Plasma contains *bilirubin*, a hemoglobin breakdown product excreted in bile, urine, and feces.

*Globulins* are another class of plasma protein with various functions; *immunoglobulins* are antibodies produced by the immune system.

The *serum* is the plasma from which fibrinogens and other clotting factors have been removed. This is a non-clotting fluid important in the medical field.

*Erythrocytes* (i.e., red blood cells) are flattened biconcave cells about 7 μm in diameter. The disk shape of mature erythrocytes is due to a lack of a nucleus. They are the most abundant blood cells, with 4 to 6 million in 1 cubic millimeter of blood.

Each cell contains about 200 million red-colored hemoglobin molecules used to transport $O_2$ and $CO_2$. Erythrocytes catalyze the conversion of $CO_2$ and $H_2O$ to $H_2CO_3$.

### Leukocytes and cells of the immune system

*Leukocytes* (or white blood cells) are larger, have an irregularly-shaped nucleus, and lack hemoglobin. They make up less than 1% of the blood's volume. Leukocytes are essential components of the immune system and, like erythrocytes, are generated from stem cells in the bone marrow. They may be in the bloodstream, lymphatic system, body tissues, or stored in the spleen.

The five types of leukocytes have specific functions.

*Neutrophils* are the most abundant leukocytes, which travel throughout the bloodstream. Neutrophils and other white blood cells enter interstitial fluid tissues by slipping through capillary walls by *diapedesis.*

Neutrophils engulf pathogens such as bacteria and fungi, making them *phagocytes.* They are the first responders to infection and initiate the early inflammation response.

*Eosinophils* respond to parasites, cancer cells, and allergic irritants.

*Basophils* are involved in allergies, as they release the chemical histamine to promote vasodilation, part of the inflammation response. Both leukocytes are in the blood and the tissues.

*Monocytes* in the bloodstream differentiate and become *macrophages,* upon which they enter the tissues and consume dead cells, damaged cells, and pathogenic agents. Monocytes regulate the chemical signals which other leukocytes respond to inflammation.

*Lymphocytes* are a class of white blood cells primarily in the lymphatic system rather than the blood.

*B lymphocytes* differentiate in the bone marrow and produce antibodies in response to antigens. They are stored after infection for future use if the same pathogen recurs.

*T lymphocytes* mature in the thymus and have a variety of roles.

Some T cells directly attack virus-infected and cancerous cells, while others assist other leukocytes in their functions. An important group of T cells inhibits an immunological response when it is no longer needed.

*Platelets* are enucleated cell fragments, which bud off from large bone marrow cells as *megakaryocytes.*

Platelets carry clotting factors and adhere to damaged tissues and blood vessels to stop uncontrolled bleeding. They survive for ten days before being removed by the liver and spleen.

## Erythrocytes, spleen and bone marrow

In children, most bones produce blood cells, while in adults, only the bones of the upper body do so.

Blood cells are descended from a single population of bone marrow cells, the *pluripotent hematopoietic stem cells*.

The pluripotent hematopoietic stem cells divide into two lineages, the *lymphoid stem cells*, which give rise to lymphocytes, and the *myeloid stem cells*, which give rise to other leukocytes and erythrocytes.

Protein hormones and paracrine agents regulate cell division and differentiation, collectively the *hematopoietic growth factors* (HGF).

*Erythropoiesis* (erythrocyte production) is stimulated by the *erythropoietin* hormone, secreted mainly by the kidneys. Erythrocytes are continuously manufactured from stem cells in the bone marrow of the long bones, ribs, skull, and vertebrae.

Iron, folic acid, and vitamin $B_{12}$ are important constituents of the blood absorbed in the small intestine from food. Folic acid and vitamin $B_{12}$ stimulate the process of erythropoiesis, and iron is necessary for the structure and function of hemoglobin.

*Polycythemia* results from excess erythrocyte production, leading to a condition with extra erythrocytes resulting in sluggish blood flow through the capillaries.

*Anemia* results from insufficient production (or excessive degradation) of erythrocytes.

Since erythrocytes have no nucleus, they cannot generate proteins and gradually degrade over time.

After about 120 days, erythrocytes are destroyed by phagocytes in the liver, spleen, and bone marrow.

*Heme,* the iron-containing cofactor of hemoglobin, undergoes chemical degradation by the liver and becomes bilirubin, secreted as the pigment in bile.

*Globin* is the protein component of hemoglobin and is degraded into amino acids.

Each second, two million erythrocytes are produced to replace those taken out of circulation.

Iron released from degraded erythrocytes may be immediately incorporated into the hemoglobin of new erythrocytes or stored for later use in the liver and spleen as *ferritin.*

**Liver produces clotting factors for wound healing**

*Hemostasis* is the stoppage of bleeding from blood vessels. Venous bleeding leads to less rapid blood loss because veins have lower blood pressure.

*Hematoma* (bruise) is the accumulation of blood in tissue from bleeding. When a blood vessel is severed, it constricts, and the opposite endothelial surfaces of the vessel stick to slow the outflow. Other processes such as clotting follow this.

*Coagulation* (clotting) occurs when liquid blood becomes gel-like to repair an injury. Platelets contain enzymes and chemicals involved in the clotting process.

The liver produces clotting factors (e.g., fibrinogen) circulating in the plasma.

Platelets sense blood vessel abnormalities (usually a tear) and bind to the exposed connective tissue. They partially seal the leak via an intermediary is the *von Willebrand factor* (vWF), a plasma protein secreted by endothelial cells and platelets.

The binding of platelets to collagen triggers them to secrete substances that change the surface platelet proteins' shape for *platelet activation.* Activation attracts other platelets to form an aggregation as a *platelet plug.*

As the wounded blood vessel repairs itself, the clot begins to contract and becomes compact. When repair is complete, the clot is dissolved by the *fibrinolytic* or *thrombolytic* system, which activates plasmin to digest the fibrin network.

*Hemorrhagic disorders* are mostly hereditary and nonhereditary diseases in which the affected individual's blood cannot clot. Minor cuts and bumps cause uncontrolled external and internal bleeding, which can be deadly.

*Hemophilia* is a hereditary disorder in which the liver cannot produce one of the clotting factors.

Non-genetic forms of hemorrhagic disorders can be caused by liver disease or vitamin K deficiency.

## Blood Types and Rh Factor

**The Rh factor antigen on red blood cells**

The Rh factor is an antigen in human blood types. Rh-positive (Rh⁺) has the Rh factor on red blood cells (RBC); Rh negative (Rh⁻) lacks the Rh antigen on the RBC. Rh-negative persons do not have antibodies to the Rh factor but begin to make them when exposed to Rh positive blood. Rh-positive is a genetically dominant trait.

*Hemolytic disease* may occur if the mother is Rh-negative and the father is Rh-positive. During pregnancy, the Rh factor is important; an Rh-negative mother and an Rh-positive father pose an Rh conflict. The child's Rh-positive RBC can leak across the placenta into the mother's circulatory system when the placenta breaks down. The presence of the "foreign" Rh-positive antigens causes the mother to produce anti-Rh antibodies.

Anti-Rh antibodies pass across the placenta and destroy the RBC of the Rh-positive child. The Rh issue has been solved by giving Rh negative women an Rh immunoglobulin injection (Rho-Gam) either during the first pregnancy or within about 72 hours after the birth of an Rh-positive newborn. The injection includes anti-Rh antibodies that attack a child's RBCs before they trigger the mother's immune system. The injection is not effective if the mother has already produced antibodies; hence, timing is important.

**Blood types and transfusions**

*Blood types* (blood groups) are classified by the presence (or absence) of inherited antigens on erythrocytes' surface. These antigens include proteins, carbohydrates, glycolipids, or glycoproteins. There are no O antigens. Type A⁻ (A negative) blood has A antigens present on the erythrocyte, but no Rh factor (Rh⁻) and no B antigens. Type A⁻ blood produces anti-B antibodies bind to B antigens, and antibodies bind to the Rh antigen.

RBC with a particular antigen agglutinate when exposed to corresponding antibodies. *Agglutination* is the clumping of red blood cells due to a reaction between antigens on red blood cells. To receive blood, the recipient's plasma must not have an antibody that causes donor cells to agglutinate.

Patients with type AB blood can receive any type of blood; they are a universal recipient.

Patients with type O blood cannot receive A, B, or AB, but they are universal donors.

Patients with type A blood cannot receive B or AB blood.

Patients with type B blood cannot receive A or AB blood.

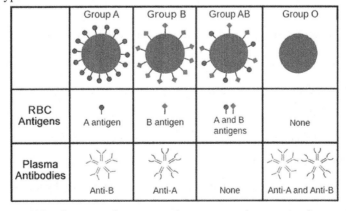

*Overview of blood types with associated antigens and corresponding antibodies*

## Oxygen and Carbon Dioxide Transport by Blood

### Hemoglobin and hematocrit

Vertebrates utilize the red-colored pigment hemoglobin to increase the blood's oxygen-carrying capacity. Hemoglobin includes a tetrameric *globin* protein that surrounds a *heme* group. Heme is an iron-containing molecule that loosely binds to a single $O_2$ molecule.

*Hematocrit* is the percentage of blood volume made of erythrocytes. It is a useful measure of a person's ability to transport oxygen. Low hematocrit indicates *anemia,* a reduced ability to carry oxygen in the blood.

### Sickle cell anemia

Anemia causes constant fatigue and weakness due to the decreased circulation of oxygen. It may be due to an abnormally low concentration of healthy, functional erythrocytes, insufficient hemoglobin, or a combination. These issues can occur due to blood loss, iron, vitamin $B_{12}$ deficiency, abnormal erythrocytes, insufficient erythrocyte production, or excessive erythrocyte destruction.

*In sickle cell anemia, the red blood cells are shaped like sickles (a crescent moon) and become rigid and sticky. Due to their irregular shape, these cells can get stuck in small blood vessels (capillaries), slowing or blocking blood flow to parts of the body.*

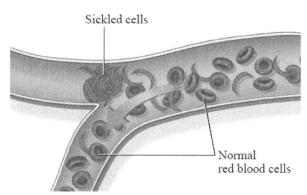

Sickled cells

Normal red blood cells

### Oxygen content of blood

Because hemoglobin is a tetramer, there are four heme groups per hemoglobin and four $O_2$ binding sites.

With millions of hemoglobin molecules per erythrocyte, the blood can carry 70 times more oxygen than if it was dissolved in plasma.

Oxygen in the blood is measured by partial pressure (i.e., $pO_2$), saturation, or total content.

*Partial pressure* describes oxygen's contribution to the total pressure of gases in the blood.

*Saturation* refers to how many heme-binding sites are bound to oxygen in the blood.

Content is calculated by saturation, partial pressure, and hemoglobin concentration to determine the number of oxygen molecules in the blood.

Oxygen consumption increases in proportion to the magnitude of physical exercise up to the point of maximal oxygen consumption – *VO₂ max.*

After VO₂ max is reached, an increase in exertion is sustained briefly by anaerobic metabolism.

Typically, $VO_2$ max is determined by cardiac output. It may be limited by carbon monoxide content, the respiratory system's ability to deliver oxygen to the blood, and the muscles' oxygen use.

## Oxygen affinity and dissociation curves

Inhaled oxygen diffuses into alveolar capillaries and binds to hemoglobin in erythrocytes. It is transported to tissues for cellular respiration. A small amount of blood oxygen is carried as dissolved $O_2$ in plasma, but the majority is reversibly combined with hemoglobin molecules in erythrocytes.

Hemoglobin with no bonded oxygen is *deoxyhemoglobin* (Hb).

Hemoglobin bonded to oxygen is *oxyhemoglobin* ($HbO_2$).

The fraction of Hb as $HbO_2$ is the *percent of hemoglobin saturation.*

$$\% \text{ hemoglobin saturation} = \frac{O_2 \text{ bound to Hb} \times 100}{\text{Maximal capacity of Hb to bind } O_2}$$

When $pO_2$ is high, hemoglobin binds to oxygen to form oxyhemoglobin. Blood is fully saturated with oxygen when erythrocytes contain oxyhemoglobin. This occurs in the lungs, where oxygen content is highest. In body tissues deprived of oxygen, $pO_2$ is low, and erythrocytes release oxygen from oxyhemoglobin. Oxygen diffuses into the plasma and tissue cells.

An *oxygen dissociation curve* shows the percent of oxyhemoglobin and non-bonded hemoglobin at various partial pressures of oxygen. Usually, a curve is labeled with the value at which the erythrocytes are fifty percent saturated with oxygen, the *p50 value.*

Hemoglobin has a sigmoidal oxygen dissociation curve because oxygen binding to one subunit somewhat relaxes the other subunits' conformation, resulting in easier binding for additional oxygen. This is *cooperative binding.*

When one $O_2$ molecule binds, the others bind with less difficulty.

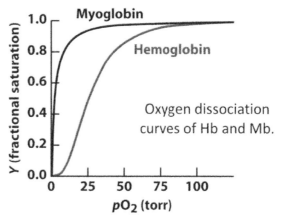

*Myoglobin (hyperbolic) and hemoglobin (sigmoidal) dissociation curves*

Likewise, when one $O_2$ is released, the remaining $O_2$ are released with ease. Thus, oxygen has the highest affinity to hemoglobin when three of its four polypeptide chains are already bound to oxygen.

*Myoglobin* is a single-chain protein subunit similar to hemoglobin, responsible for carrying oxygen in muscle tissue. It saturates quickly and is released in emergencies of low oxygen when a burst of muscle movement is needed under reduced $pO_2$ conditions (e.g., swimming to the surface of a body of water after being submerged).

Myoglobin binds to oxygen tighter than hemoglobin, as it has a greater affinity towards oxygen but can bind one $O_2$ molecule. This does not allow for cooperative binding, giving myoglobin an oxygen dissociation curve that is hyperbolic. The myoglobin curve does not change over a wide range of pH. Myoglobin in the bloodstream after muscle injury must be removed since it is toxic to the kidneys.

## Bohr effects on the oxygen dissociation curves

The oxygen dissociation curve is not static and can shift to the right or the left. A shift to the right means that for a given $pO_2$, less $O_2$ is bound to hemoglobin.

Several conditions can produce a right shift, including increased temperature, increased $pCO_2$ or decreased pH. Increasing the temperature denatures the bond between oxygen and hemoglobin, which naturally decreases oxyhemoglobin concentration.

*The Bohr Effect* describes how the oxygen dissociation curve is altered by pH and $CO_2$. It was proposed in 1904 to explain how $H^+$ and $CO_2$ affect the affinity of $O_2$ for hemoglobin.

The affinity of $O_2$ for hemoglobin is inversely related to acidity ($\uparrow H^+$) and $pCO_2$ levels.

Although $CO_2$ does not directly compete with $O_2$ for hemoglobin binding sites, it binds to specific areas of the hemoglobin molecule and encourages the release of $O_2$ molecules.

A decrease in pH is an increase in $H^+$ molecules, which bind to hemoglobin and promote the $O_2$ release.

Both factors result in a Bohr shift, in which the $O_2$ dissociation curve shifts to the right.

High temperature, high $CO_2$, and low pH are conditions observed during exercise since temperature and $CO_2$ level rise due to increased metabolism, and pH is decreased due to lactic acid buildup.

Under normal physiology, the oxygen dissociation curve predictably shifts to the left in the lungs to maximize $O_2$ loading.

## Oxygen loads in the lungs and dissociates at the tissue

As seen in the curve, as $pO_2$ increases, the $O_2$ saturation of hemoglobin increases.

The lungs' alveoli are $O_2$ rich, causing hemoglobin of deoxygenated blood to be saturated with $O_2$.

The diffusion gradient favoring oxygen movement from alveoli to blood is maintained because oxygen binds to Hb and keeps the plasma $pO_2$ low since only dissolved oxygen contributes to $pO_2$.

In tissues, the procedure is reversed.

The low $pO_2$ and high $pCO_2$ in the body tissues cause hemoglobin in the bloodstream to release $O_2$.

There is a net diffusion of oxygen from the blood into cells and a net diffusion of carbon dioxide from cells into the blood.

*Fetal hemoglobin* binds to oxygen more tightly than adult hemoglobin to attract $O_2$ from maternal blood.

Due to its higher binding affinity, the fetal hemoglobin curve shifts to the left of the adult curve.

**Carbon monoxide binds hemoglobin with high affinity**

*Carbon monoxide* (CO) is lethal since it can bind to hemoglobin around 200 times more tightly than oxygen. It interferes with the $O_2$ transport function of blood by combining with Hb to form *carboxyhemoglobin* (COHb).

Due to the high binding affinity, small amounts of CO can occupy a large proportion of the Hb in the blood, making it unavailable for transporting $O_2$.

If this happens, the Hb concentration and dissolved oxygen in the blood are typical, but $O_2$ concentration is dangerously reduced.

The presence of COHb shifts the $O_2$ dissociation curve left, thus interfering with the unloading of $O_2$ into oxygen-deprived tissues.

*Bohr effect shifts hemoglobin dissociation curve to the right*

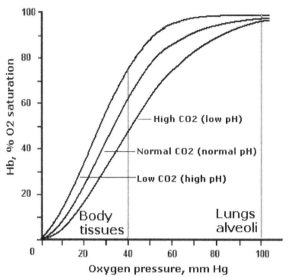

**Carbon dioxide levels and transport by the blood**

Carbon dioxide is transported in the blood in three forms:

> 1) dissolved in plasma as $CO_2$,
>
> 2) dissolved in plasma as the bicarbonate ion ($HCO_3^-$), and
>
> 3) combined with hemoglobin.

As CO2 diffuses from the tissues into the blood, about 5% remains dissolved in plasma as $CO_2$.

10–20% combines with hemoglobin as *carbaminohemoglobin* (HbCO$_2$).

As with oxygen, this complex can be unbound so that $CO_2$ is released into the plasma.

Unlike $O_2$, $CO_2$ binds to amino groups on hemoglobin rather than the iron heme group.

$$CO_2 + Hb \leftrightarrow HbCO_2$$

75 to 85% of $CO_2$ enters erythrocytes and combines with water to form carbonic acid ($H_2CO_3$), dissociating into $HCO_3^-$ and $H^+$. This reaction is catalyzed by *carbonic anhydrase* (enzymes end with ~*ase*).

The ions are released into the plasma to continue transport.

The bicarbonate and hydrogen ions create a bicarbonate buffer system that maintains blood pH.

$$CO_2 + H_2O \leftrightarrow H_2CO_3 \leftrightarrow HCO_3^- + H^+$$

Some $H^+$ atoms remain in erythrocytes and bind oxyhemoglobin, releasing oxygen. This is an important process for oxygen transport and prevents fluctuations in pH since excess $H^+$ is removed from the blood.

## Cardiac control of heart rate

Intrinsic and extrinsic stimulation controls the circulatory system. The intrinsic stimulation comes from the *sinoatrial* (SA) node's pulses as the "pacemaker" of the heart, in the upper dorsal wall of the right atrium; it initiates the heartbeat.

The cardiac muscle cells in the SA node are self-exciting and capable of initiating contraction in nearby cells. The SA node's capacity for spontaneous, rhythmical self-excitation results from gradual depolarization, the *pacemaker potential*, of the cells.

When the node spontaneously generates an excitatory impulse, depolarization quickly spreads to the left atrium, and the two atria contract simultaneously.

After a slight delay, the action potential spreads through the *atrioventricular* (AV) *node* located at the right atrium base close to the septum. The delay in the action potential allows atrial contraction to be completed before the ventricles contract.

*AV bundles* extend from the node toward the ventricles and carry the signal to the bottom of the heart, branching into *Purkinje fibers.* These fibers cause rapid contraction of the ventricles.

The long refractory period of cardiac muscle cells limits the re-excitation of neurons. It ensures that there is time for the chamber to fill with blood before the next contraction occurs.

*Tetanus* is when skeletal muscle remains contracted and cannot relax. The heart may experience many arrhythmias (i.e., abnormal heart rate patterns) due to disruptions in the heart's electrical conduction system.

*Tachycardia* (high heart rate) and *bradycardia* (low heart rate) are two such arrhythmias.

## EKG and fibrillation

*Fibrillation* is a rapid, abnormal heartbeat that can affect the atria and ventricles. Atrial fibrillation is concerning but typically not an emergency, while ventricular fibrillation is an emergency that usually accompanies a cardiac arrest. With the application of a strong electric current, the SA node may reestablish a coordinated beat.

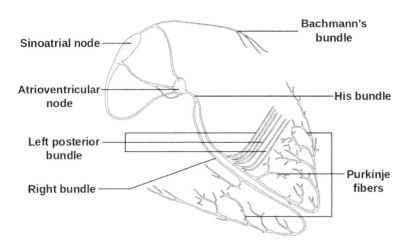

An *electrocardiogram* (ECG or EKG) diagnoses arrhythmias and heart abnormalities by recording the electrical changes in the myocardium during a cardiac cycle.

These contraction pulses generate currents in extracellular fluids recorded at the skin's surface. An EKG typically consists of five major deflections: P wave, Q wave, R wave, S wave, and T wave.

*The innervation of the heart. Heartbeat originates in SA node → AV node → bundle of His → Purkinje fibers for ventricular contraction. Electrocardiogram illustrates the electrical charges during a cardiac cycle*

**Neural and hormonal control of heart rate**

Stimulation of the sympathetic fibers increases heart rate and force of contraction. These neurons release *norepinephrine*, which binds to receptors on the SA node's cardiac muscle cells, increasing calcium ion uptake.

Higher intracellular calcium levels allow the cells to rapidly reach the threshold voltage, increasing heart rate and contractility. Sympathetic responses are activated during exercise; blood flow is redirected to muscles, cardiac output increases, and constriction occurs in the veins to help return blood to the heart.

The kidney's adrenal medulla releases *epinephrine* (i.e., adrenaline) in response to stress and other stimuli. This acts similarly to norepinephrine and causes a sympathetic heart rate increase.

Circulatory responses occur in the heart and throughout the systemic and pulmonary circulation.

Various receptors monitor conditions throughout the circulatory system.

The receptors may be *peripheral* (in blood vessels) or *central* (in the brain itself). Peripheral receptors often transmit the signal to the brain to carry out responses. However, blood vessels can respond to stimuli with a local reflex. For example, the walls of arterioles automatically constrict in response to stretch.

**Chemoreceptors and baroreceptors**

*Chemoreceptors* monitor pH, oxygen, and carbon dioxide levels.

Peripheral chemoreceptors are in the aorta and carotid arteries and transmit signals to the *cardiovascular control center* (CVCC) in the medulla oblongata of the brain.

Central chemoreceptors are in the medulla, where they measure gas levels and pH in the brain.

If these receptors detect that oxygen levels are low, carbon dioxide levels are high, or pH is low, the body attempts to increase gas exchange to compensate. This occurs due to exercise.

The sympathetic nervous system stimulates an increase in heart rate and stroke volume, resulting in higher cardiac output. This causes more rapid blood flow through the lungs, the rapid release of excess carbon dioxide, and oxygen uptake.

Selective vasoconstriction delivers oxygen to the tissues that need it most. In the long term, angiogenesis ensures these tissues receive greater oxygen.

*Baroreceptors* are in the carotid arteries, the aorta, and the medulla. They work with chemoreceptors to control blood pressure by continually adjusting vasoconstriction and vasodilation.

A drop in arterial pressure causes the carotid and aortic baroreceptors to signal the medulla to immediately initiate a sympathetic response of vasoconstriction and higher cardiac output.

In the long term, the kidneys retain fluid to maintain blood volume.

By contrast, a rise in arterial pressure stimulates the carotid baroreceptor reflex to initiate vasodilation.

The medulla decreases sympathetic activity and increases parasympathetic activity, lowering cardiac output to reduce the pressure. Over time, the kidneys increase urination to lower blood volume.

*Notes for active learning*

# CHAPTER 14

# Immune System

- Lymphatic System
- Immune System: Non-Specific and Specific Immunity
- Innate Immune System
- Adaptive Immune System
- Immune System Tissues and Organs
- Antigen and Antibody

## Lymphatic System

### Lymph nodes, lymphatic vessels and capillaries

The lymphatic system is an open, unidirectional, secondary circulatory system. It contains a network of *lymph nodes, lymphatic vessels,* and *lymphatic capillaries.*

The lymphatic system usually transports excess *interstitial fluids,* known as *lymph.* However, lymph can be moved by autonomic, smooth muscle contraction in larger lymph vessels.

The lymph functions to return proteins to the bloodstream, redistribute body fluid, remove foreign bodies from the bloodstream, and maintain tissues' structural and functional integrity. Lymph monitors blood for bacterial or viral infection.

The lymph system is associated with the cardiovascular system and has three main functions.

### Lymphatic system equalizes fluid distribution

If the interstitial fluid pressure is greater than the lymphatic pressure, the lymph vessel opens. When the lymph vessel opens, interstitial fluid enters the lymphatic capillaries. Lymphatic circulation eventually merges with venous circulation, returning the lymph fluid to the blood. However, if the interstitial fluid pressure is less than the lymphatic pressure, the lymph vessel closes, preventing lymph from leaking out.

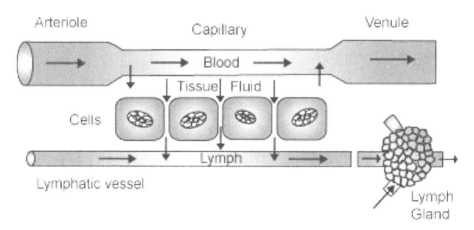

*Relationship of fluid exchange between the circulatory and lymphatic systems*

The movement of fluid is dependent upon skeletal muscle contraction. When muscles contract, fluid is squeezed past a valve that closes, preventing backflow.

### Lymph transports substances

The lymphatic system is responsible for transporting oxygen and carbon dioxide gas and chemical substances such as amino acids, glucose, and fats.

The lymphatic system transports other nutrients and cellular compounds. Lymph contains various clotting factors, including fibrinogen, globulin, various chemical elements (including calcium and iron), and some waste material (such as uric acid).

The lymphatic system provides a pathway by which fat absorbed in the gastrointestinal tract can reach the blood. Fats are absorbed into the small intestine's lacteals (lymphatic capillaries in the small intestine).

Lacteals receive lipoproteins at the intestinal villi. The lymphatic vessels transport these absorbed fats into the bloodstream. The lymph in the lacteals (chyle) has a milky appearance due to its high-fat content. Proteins and large particles that capillaries cannot absorb are removed by lymph.

**Lymph returns substances to the blood**

The lymphatic system takes up fluid that has diffused out of the blood capillaries and has not been reabsorbed. Lymphatic vessels carry interstitial fluid to the cardiovascular system. This compensates for the net filtration out of the blood capillaries.

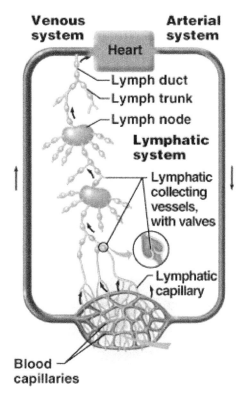

*Interstitial fluid moves from the lymphatic to the cardiovascular system*

The lymphatic capillaries collect cells and plasma proteins that leak out of the blood capillaries and transport them to the venous system.

Lymph is a clear, colorless liquid with a similar composition to blood plasma; however, lymph has a higher protein content (e.g., lymphocytes) than blood plasma. Lymph is mostly water, plasma proteins, chemicals, and white blood cells.

*Lymph* is the tissue fluid that enters the lymphatic capillaries. Lymph, a fluid derived from interstitial fluid, runs through the lymphatic vessels, lymphatic nodes, and other lymphatic organs. Lymph tissue contains *lymphocytes* (cells involved in immune response), cleans, and filters the fluid.

**Diffusion of lymph from capillaries by differential pressure**

Lymphatic capillaries have a single layer of endothelial cells resting on a basement membrane.

Their water channels are permeable to interstitial fluid components, including protein molecules. Interstitial fluid enters these capillaries by bulk flow.

The fluid flows through the lymph nodes into two lymphatic ducts that drain into subclavian veins in the lower neck.

The basic flow of lymph is through the blood plasma from the capillaries into the interstitial fluid, where it becomes lymph and is returned to the blood.

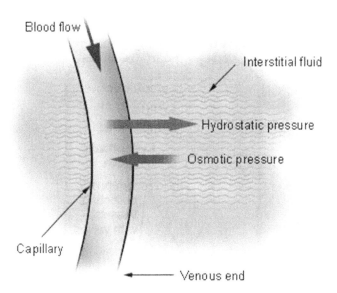

*Blood becomes lymph due to a higher hydrostatic pressure forcing plasma into the interstitial space*

**Lymph nodes anatomy and function**

*Lymph nodes* are small (about 1–25 mm), ovoid or spherical masses of lymphoid tissue located along lymphatic vessels.

Lymph nodes filter the lymph before it is returned to the blood.

Lymph nodes are concentrated with phagocytic white blood cells.

Lymph nodes are absent in the central nervous system.

A lymph node has two regions: the *outer cortex* and the *inner medulla*.

A typical lymph node is surrounded by connective tissue compartments, known as *lymph nodules*.

The cortex contains nodules where lymphocytes and macrophages congregate to fight pathogens.

Macrophages are concentrated in the medulla and cleanse the lymph.

Lymph sinuses separate the macrophages and lymphocytes.

**Afferent and efferent lymphatic vessels**

*Afferent lymphatic vessels* (only in the lymph nodes) enter the lymph nodes periphery.

After branching and forming a dense plexus in the capsule's substance, the afferent lymphatic vessels open into the cortical lymph sinuses.

Many afferent lymphatic vessels carrying lymph to the nodes enter via the convex side.

The lymph travels through the lymph sinuses and eventually enters an efferent lymphatic vessel.

The *efferent lymphatic vessels* (in the lymph nodes, the spleen, and tonsils) carry the lymph away from the node.

They begin at the medullary part of the node's lymph sinuses in the lymph node and leave the nodes for the veins or greater nodes.

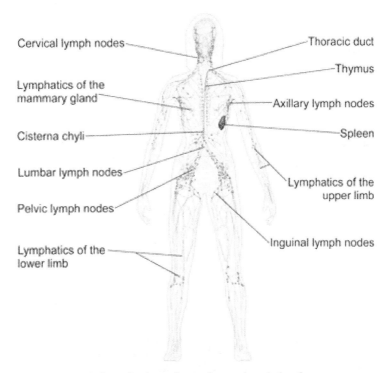

*Lymphatic nodes and associated glands*

**Lymph nodes and lymphocytes**

Lymph nodes cluster in certain regions of the body, including the inguinal nodes in the groin, the axillary nodes in the armpits, and the cervical nodes in the neck.

Lymphatic capillaries join as *lymphatic vessels* that merge before entering one of two ducts.

The structure of the larger lymphatic vessels resembles veins, including the presence of valves.

The *thoracic duct* is larger than the right lymphatic duct.

It serves the lower extremities, abdomen, the left arm, the left side of the head and neck, and the left thoracic region.

The thoracic duct delivers lymph to the left subclavian vein of the cardiovascular system.

The *right lymphatic duct* serves the right arm, the right side of the head and neck, and the right thoracic region. It delivers lymph to the right subclavian vein of the cardiovascular system.

*Lymphocytes* produced in the red bone marrow by the differentiation of progenitor cells are the primary immune response agents.

When pathogens or foreign antigens enter a lymph node, local lymphocytes are released into the bloodstream towards the invasion site.

Once the lymphocytes are activated, they release chemicals that stimulate an immune response for proliferation, antibody production, and cytokine release.

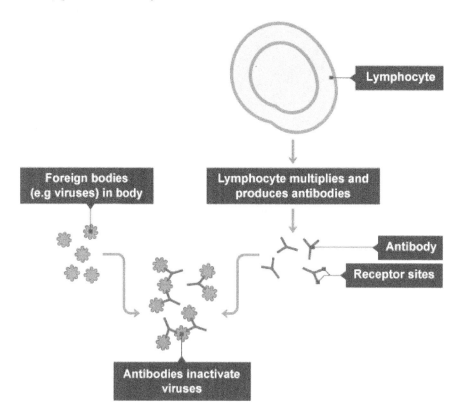

*Immune response from pathogen to antibody production specific to the antigen*

## Immune System: Non-Specific and Specific Immunity

### Active and passive immunity

*Immunity* defends against infectious agents, foreign cells, and abnormal cancer cells. Immunity usually lasts for some time, and individuals do not ordinarily get the same illness twice. Immunity is acquired naturally through infection or artificially by medical intervention (e.g., vaccination).

The two types of *induced immunity* are active immunity and passive immunity.

*Active immunity* is when an individual produces their antibodies.

*Passive immunity* is when an individual receives prepared antibodies.

*Active immunity* can develop naturally after a person is infected. However, active immunity is induced when a person is healthy to prevent future infection. An example of induced active immunity is a vaccine.

### Vaccination and antibody titer

Vaccinations are used to expose bodies to a particular antigen. These antigens are usually destroyed or severely weakened before they are administered to decrease their potency.

After a vaccine, the immune response is measured by the antibody level present in the serum, known as the *antibody titer*.

After the first exposure, a *primary response* occurs, going from no antibodies present to a slow rise in titer. After a brief plateau, a gradual decline follows as antibodies bind to antigens or degrade. After a second exposure to the same antigen, a *secondary response* occurs, and the antibody titer rises rapidly to a level much greater than before; this is a "booster."

The high antibody titer is now expected to prevent any disease symptoms if the individual is infected.

Active immunity depends on memory B and memory T cell responses (see adaptive immunity section).

Active immunity is usually long-lasting, although a booster may be required every few years.

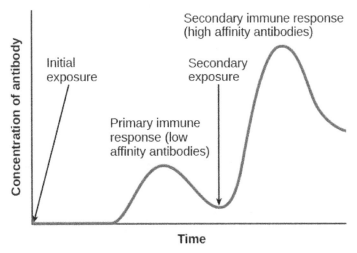

*Antibody production profile comparing primary and secondary responses*

*Passive immunity* defends against antigens by using antibodies from a foreign source.

For example, an infant receives antibodies through the placenta or the mother's breast milk, rendering the child immune to a specific pathogen.

If in immediate danger of an infectious agent, a patient can receive antibodies from another individual with medical intervention.

However, the effects of this passive immunity are short-lived because antibodies are not made by an individual's B cells.

For example, a patient receives a gamma globulin injection (a serum containing antibodies against the agent) taken from another or animal previously exposed to the antigen.

If antibodies are derived from animals, individuals may become ill with *serum sickness*, an inflammatory response from the individual's hypersensitivity to animal proteins due to detecting the animal's proteins as potentially harmful antigens.

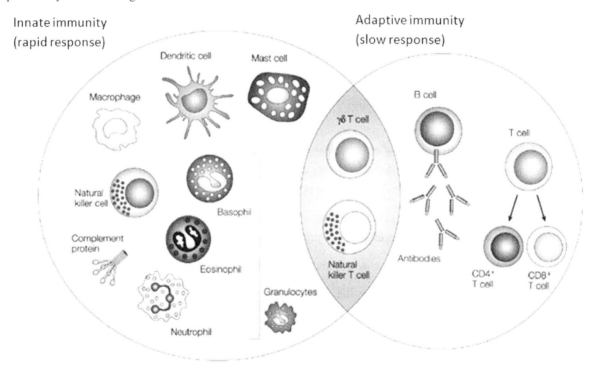

*Innate immunity (rapid response) compared to adaptive immunity (slow response) on the right*

**Major histocompatibility complex**

The *major histocompatibility complex* (MHC) comprises genes encoding specific proteins on cells' surfaces. These complexes, which are in highly evolved vertebrates, help the immune system recognize foreign substances.

These molecules are enclosed in many gene layers in humans, clustered on the same chromosome region. Human MHC proteins are the HLA (human leukocyte antigens).

There are two major classes of MHC molecules. Class one MHC molecules are along the membranes of all cell types. Class two MHC molecules are only in the immune system's macrophages and lymphocytes. No two individuals have the same MHC molecules because genes have many alleles (i.e., alternative gene forms).

These molecules are collectively the tissue type.

The MHC molecules contain various genes that encode for other proteins, including complement proteins, chemical messengers of cytokines, and enzymes, sometimes called the third class of MHC molecules.

MHC molecules were recognized as antigens that stimulate an organism's immunological response to transplanted organs and tissues. After skin graft experiments on mice in the 1950s, it was found that graft rejection was an immune reaction mounted by the host organism against foreign tissue.

The host recognized the MHC molecules as foreign and attacked them. The importance of the major histocompatibility complex (MHC) proteins was recognized to contribute to the difficulty of transplanting tissues from one organism (or person) to another.

**Recognition of self *vs.* non-self and autoimmune disease**

Each virus, bacteria, or other foreign body has molecular markers that make it unique. Host lymphocytes (i.e., those in the body) can recognize and differentiate *self-molecules*, which belong to the body and are not foreign.

*Non-self molecules* are targeted by lymphocytes. An example of a non-self molecule is an antigen, which triggers B and T lymphocytes' mitotic activity.

When a pathogen invades a body, MHC markers on the cells' plasma membranes distinguish between self and non-self cells.

The pathogen displays a combination of self and non-self markers, and T cells interpret this as non-self.

Cancer cells or tissue transplant cells are often recognized as non-self by T cells.

When T cells encounter non-self cells, they divide and produce four kinds of cells: cytotoxic T cells, helper T cells, suppressor T cells, and memory T cells.

MHC molecules are vital parts of the immune system because they allow T lymphocytes to detect macrophages that have ingested a foreign microorganism. The partially digested microorganism displays a distinctive peptide bound to an MHC complex on the macrophage's surface.

The T lymphocyte recognizes this foreign fragment attached to the MHC molecule and consequently initiates an immune response.

In an adaptive immune system, an antigen-specific response is initiated. This requires the identification and recognition of non-self antigens during antigen presentation.

*Autoimmune diseases* are when cytotoxic T cells or antibodies mistakenly attack the body's cells as a foreign antigen. Under these conditions, the differentiation between self and non-self molecules is lost.

Autoimmune diseases may be genetic (i.e., heritable) or caused by bacteria, viruses, drugs, or chemical agents.

**Endogenous immunity *vs.* autoimmune disease**

| Typical Immune Response | Autoimmune disease |
|---|---|
| Antigens invade<br>↓<br>Antibodies form<br>↓<br>Antibodies remove invading antigens<br>↓<br>Antibodies remain and protect | Immune system forms antibodies<br>to self-antigens<br>↓<br>Antibodies attack self-antigens<br>↓<br>Inflammation and tissue damage |

Some examples of autoimmune diseases are myasthenia gravis, multiple sclerosis, systemic lupus erythematosus, rheumatic fever, and type I diabetes.

In myasthenia gravis, the neuromuscular junctions do not work correctly, and muscular weakness results.

In multiple sclerosis (MS), the myelin sheaths of nerve fibers are attacked.

Many symptoms are elicited in systemic lupus erythematosus resulting in further disease.

While there are no cures for autoimmune diseases, they are managed by therapeutics.

## Innate Immune System

### Nonspecific immune responses

The first line of defense in the body is *surface coverage*. The skin and mucous membranes protect the body from pathogens. The skin is composed of a dry, acidic, dead cellular layer that allows for optimal, non-specific surface protection.

The mucous membranes contain lysozymes, which are enzymes that break down bacteria. Other cells in the mucous membranes contain cilia that filter the pathogens and particulates.

*Nonspecific* responses are generalized responses to pathogen infection and do not target specific cell types. Individuals do not ordinarily become immune to their cells; the immune system can distinguish self from non-self cells. In this manner, the immune system aids, rather than counters, homeostasis.

Lymphocytes recognize antigens because they have antigen receptors; the protein shape allows the receptors and antigens to combine like a *lock and key*.

During maturation, differentiation occurs, so there is a lymphocyte for various antigens.

The non-specific response consists of white blood cells (WBCs) and plasma proteins. The four nonspecific defenses include a barrier to entry, inflammatory reaction, natural killer cells, and protective proteins.

The *barrier to entry* is the first non-specific response. Skin and the mucous membrane lining the respiratory, digestive, and urinary tracts are mechanical barriers. Oil gland secretions inhibit the growth of bacteria on the skin.

Ciliated cells line the upper respiratory tract to sweep mucus and particles up into the throat to be swallowed. The stomach has a low pH (between 1.2 and 3) that inhibits bacteria's growth.

Harmless bacteria in the intestines and vagina inhibit pathogens from colonizing.

The *inflammatory reaction* is the second non-specific response, which is the series of events that occur if the tissue is damaged. The inflamed area often has four symptoms: redness, pain, swelling, and heat.

Aspirin, ibuprofen, and cortisone are anti-inflammatory agents that counter the chemical mediators of inflammation.

*Natural killer cells* are the third non-specific response. Natural killer cells are a class of lymphocytes that recognize abnormal cells like cancerous cells. They attach to these abnormal cells and release chemicals that eventually destroy them.

*Protective proteins* are the fourth non-specific response. These proteins protect the cell nonspecifically.

### Complement proteins

*Complement proteins* are plasma proteins, which have a role in non-specific and specific defenses. The complement system contains plasma proteins and is designated by the letter C and a subscript.

One activated complement protein activates another protein in a set series of domino reactions. In this way, a limited number of proteins can activate other proteins, "complementing" specific immune responses.

Additionally, the complement system amplifies an inflammatory reaction by attracting phagocytic cells to the site of infection.

Complement proteins bind to antibodies already on the surface of pathogens, increasing the probability of neutrophil or macrophage phagocytize pathogens.

Complement proteins form a *membrane attack complex* that produces holes in bacterial cell walls and plasma membranes; from osmotic pressure, fluids and salts enter the bacterium to the point where the cell bursts.

**Lymphocytes produce antibodies**

*Lymphocytes* are leukocytes that produce antibodies. They are any of the three subtypes of white blood cells in a vertebrate's immune system.

The white blood cells include the natural killer cells, T cells, and B cells.

Each lymphocyte makes one specific antibody. Different lymphocytes are needed so the body can produce specific antibodies.

Antibodies are on the surface of the plasma membrane of lymphocytes, with the antigen-combining site projecting outwards.

Pathogens have antigens on their surface, which bind to a specific lymphocyte's antibodies at the antigen-combining site (i.e., the epitope on the antigen for antibody binding).

When this happens, the lymphocyte becomes active and starts to make clones by dividing via mitosis. These clones start to make antibodies to defend the body against the pathogen.

**Macrophages digest foreign material**

In general, *macrophages* are involved in engulfing foreign objects. A macrophage engulfs a pathogen and acts as an antigen-presenting cell.

When monocytes enter tissues, they differentiate into macrophages to ingest the pathogens. Connective and lymphoid tissues have resident macrophages that devour old blood cells and debris.

Macrophages trigger an explosive increase in leukocytes by releasing colony-stimulating factors; these chemicals diffuse into the blood and are transported to the red bone marrow to stimulate the production of white blood cells (WBC).

Inflammation promotes macrophage (i.e., phagocytic white blood cell) activity.

Macrophages secrete *interleukins*, communication proteins among WBC.

*Interleukin-1* increases body temperature, causing fever. The fever causes drowsiness and reduces the body's energy usage and stress, enhancing the WBC's ability to protect against infection.

A *mast cell* is an example of a macrophage.

Mast cells, which resemble basophils, reside in the connective tissue and mucous membranes.

During an allergic response, they release histamine, bringing about inflammation.

With tissue damage, tissue cells and mast cells release chemical mediators, such as histamine and kinins.

Histamine and kinins caused vasodilation and increased capillaries' permeability to white blood cells.

Enlarged capillaries produce redness and a local increase in temperature.

The swollen area and the kinins stimulate free nerve endings, causing pain.

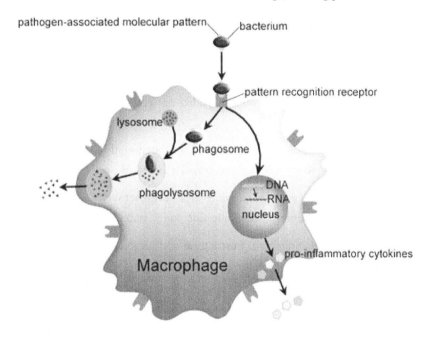

**Phagocytes**

*Phagocytes* are formed from *stem* (i.e., undifferentiated) cells in the bone marrow and digest foreign material to destroy it. They do this by recognizing pathogens and engulfing them by endocytosis.

Enzymes (lysosomes) within the phagocytes digest the pathogens.

Phagocytes can ingest pathogens in the blood and body tissue since they can pass through the pores of capillaries and into these tissues.

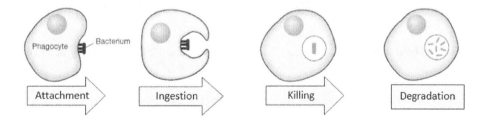

*Stages of phagocytosis from attachment to degradation*

**Neutrophils**

Neutrophils phagocytize bacteria.

*Eosinophils* are phagocytes that secrete enzymes to kill parasitic worms.

*Basophils* secrete histamine to enhance inflammation.

*Neutrophils* are granulocytes due to the presence of granules in their cytoplasm. They are polymorpho-nuclear (PMN) leukocytes because of their unique, lobed nuclei. PMN leukocytes phagocytize pathogens and destroy them.

Neutrophils and monocytes migrate by the amoeboid movement to the injury site and escape from the blood by squeezing through the capillary wall.

They contain various toxic substances that kill or inhibit various bacteria and fungi growth. Like macrophages, they activate a respiratory burst.

These respiratory burst products are strong oxidizing agents like hydrogen peroxide, free oxygen radicals, and hypochlorite.

Neutrophils are the most abundant phagocytes, and they are usually the first cells that go into action at the site of infection. Pus is the accumulation of dead neutrophils and tissue, cells, bacteria, and living WBC.

*Dendritic cells* are phagocytic cells present in tissues in contact with the external environment, mainly the skin, and the nose's inner mucosal linings, small intestine, lungs, and stomach.

Dendritic cells are essential in antigen presentation and serve as the connection between innate and adaptive immunity systems.

## Plasma cells secrete antibodies

*Plasma cells* (a type of B cell) secrete antibodies. They originate in bone marrow but leave the bone marrow to differentiate into plasma cells in the lymph nodes.

Plasma cells are transported by the blood plasma and the lymphatic system.

When a B cell in a lymph node of the spleen encounters an appropriate antigen (i.e., foreign substance), it is activated to divide.

B cells act as antigen-presenting cells and internalize various offending antigens taken by the B cell through receptor-mediated endocytosis and processed.

The antigenic peptides (pieces of the antigen) are on the surface of various MHC molecules and are presented to the T cells.

The T cells bind to the MHC antigen molecule and activate the B cell, usually occurring in the spleen and lymph nodes.

The B cell starts differentiating into specialized cells. For example, *germinal center B cells* differentiate into memory cells or plasma cells.

This process of differentiation for B cells is affinity maturation. These B cells become plasmablasts (immature plasma).

Eventually, they begin producing large volumes of antibodies in the lymph nodes and spleen. Once the threat of infection has passed, new plasma cell development ceases, while those present die.

**Inflammatory response to infection**

There is an inflammatory response during an infection's early stages, which is a nonspecific attack. Phagocytes become active and digest the pathogen. It causes localized redness, swelling, heat, and pain.

White blood cells are more active at higher temperatures, and inflammation recruits white blood cells to the infection site by sending out chemical signals.

Changes in the capillary wall structure (higher permeability) allow more interstitial fluid and white blood cells to leak into the tissues.

Neutrophils, lymphocytes, and monocytes are the cells involved in the inflammatory response.

*Neutrophils* are the first white blood cells that go to the injury site during acute inflammation. They are anti-bacterial cells that break down bacterial cells by releasing various lysosomal enzymes.

The neutrophils recognize the bacterial cells as foreign agents by the antibody molecules attached to the bacteria's surface.

These antibody molecules are in the blood's plasma and interstitial fluid. Here, they bind to one specific antigen or foreign agent that the body has seen before.

*Lymphocytes* start to accumulate during the inflammatory response process.

If their presence is prolonged or is large in number, it may suggest that the antigen is still present and an infection has formed.

The lymphocytes are responsible for producing large numbers of antibodies. These antibodies are unique to each lymphocyte. These antibodies recognize foreign molecules and differentiate between self and non-self.

*Monocytes* are phagocytic cells that circulate in the blood along with macrophages. They are in the connective tissue.

The monocytes and macrophages engulf and digest foreign microorganisms, tissue debris, and various dead cells. With lymphocytes, they recognize and destroy foreign substances.

**Allergies**

An *allergic reaction* is a hypersensitive immune response mechanism. It can cause itching, inflammation, or tissue injury.

Allergies are hypersensitivities to foreign substances (e.g., pollen). A response to these antigens, *allergens*, usually involves tissue damage.

Immediate and delayed allergic responses are two of the four possible responses.

An *immediate allergic response* occurs within seconds of contact with an allergen, and cold-like symptoms are common.

*Delayed allergic responses* are initiated by sensitized memory T cells at the allergen's site in the body.

The tuberculin skin test is an example: a positive test shows prior exposure to TB bacilli but requires time to develop tissue reddening.

**Natural killer cells use cell-to-cell contact**

*Natural killer cells* use cell-to-cell contact to destroy virus-infected cells and tumor cells; they lack specificity or memory. They do not directly attack the invading microbes but instead destroy the host cells, such as the tumor cells.

This concept is predominantly related to cells with an abnormally low level of major histocompatibility complex markers, resulting in viral infections of various host cells.

The natural killer cells are activated when the MHC markers are altered, have the condition of "missing self," and are involved in the adaptive immune system.

Many experiments show that natural killer cells can readily adjust to the immediate environment and form an antigen-specific immunological memory vital for secondary infections with the same antigen.

The natural killer cell's role in innate and adaptive immunity is essential in cancer therapy research.

## Adaptive Immune System

**Specific immune responses**

Adaptive immunity is highly specified for a pathogen or antigen.

Antigen-presenting cells have foreign antigens on their surface, and the antigens are recognized by T and B cells.

Dendritic cells are an example of an antigen-presenting cell.

*Specific defenses* are physical, chemical, and cellular defenses against the invasion of viruses, bacteria, and other agents of disease. Pathogens have antigens that can be components of foreign or cancer cells.

The *specific response* is activated when nonspecific methods are insufficient, and the infection spreads.

The *specific immune response* reacts to unique antigens and is primarily the result of the B and T lymphocytes. Some lymphocytes entrap antigens on their surface.

B lymphocytes (B cells) produce and release antibodies.

T lymphocytes (T cells) produce antibodies on their surface.

When lymphocytes attach to antigens, they encode unique antibodies that recognize these antigens.

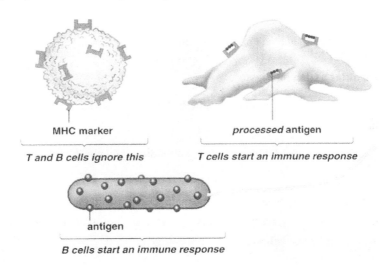

MHC marker

*T and B cells ignore this*

*processed* antigen

*T cells start an immune response*

antigen

*B cells start an immune response*

*Molecular cues that stimulate lymphocytes to create an immune response*

A *humoral response* (antibody-mediated response) responds to antigens circulating in lymph or blood (e.g., bacteria, fungi, parasites, viruses, and blood toxins).

The humoral response is a form of adaptive immunity. An example of humoral response is a bacterial infection. Initially, inflammation persists, and macrophages and neutrophils engulf the bacteria.

The interstitial fluid flushes into the lymphatic system, where lymphocytes are in the lymph nodes.

Macrophages process the foreign organism and present the bacterial antigen to the B lymphocytes.

With assistance from helper T cells, the B cells differentiate into plasma and memory cells.

Plasma cells produce antibodies released into the blood to attack the antigen, while memory cells prepare for the same event if the antigen attacks again (i.e., elicits a secondary response).

## Clonal selection initiated by specific antigens

*Clonal selection* is the response of lymphocytes to specific antigens. Clonal selection theory states that the antigen selects the B cell to produce many clones of the corresponding plasma cells.

The selection portion is the B cell lymphocytes activating specific antigens.

B cells are in the blood and lymphoid tissues and are produced from lymphoid stem cells. The clonal portion of this concept deals with the multiplication of antibodies, which occurs in particular cells.

B cells present a specific antibody on the surface. The appropriate antigen forms a complex with the antibody on the cell, thereby activating the cell's development.

The cells not meeting specific criteria are not activated.

Antigen-antibody interaction occurs, and the complexes populate on the surface. These complexes are internalized and begin to swell and divide rapidly.

The B cells differentiate into plasma and memory cells.

*Plasma cells* produce specific antibodies.

*Memory cells* circulate but actively produce no antibodies.

## T lymphocytes, interleukins and cytokines

*T cells* (T lymphocytes) arise from stem cells in the bone marrow. They travel to the thymus, where they differentiate and mature.

T cells have antigen receptors but do not make antibodies; they check molecules displayed by non-self cells.

At maturity, T cells acquire receptors for self-markers, such as the major histocompatibility complex (MHC) molecules and antigen-specific receptors. They are released into the blood as "maiden" T cells. T cells ignore cells with MHC molecules, as well as free-floating antigens.

The antigen must be presented to them by an *antigen-presenting cell* (APC).

When an antigen-presenting cell presents a viral or cancer cell antigen, the antigen is linked to an MHC protein; together, they are presented to a T cell. This binding promotes rapid cell division and differentiation into effector cells and memory cells (all with receptors for the antigen).

Cytotoxic T cells and helper T cells are responsible for cell-mediated immunity.

When a donor and recipient are histocompatible, a transplant is likely successful.

*Interleukins* improve T cells' ability to fight cancer. Interleukin antagonists help prevent skin or organ rejection, autoimmune diseases, and allergies to vaccine adjuncts (e.g., suspension solution).

Cancer cells with altered proteins on their cell surface should be attacked by cytotoxic T cells.

Cytokines (e.g., interleukins, interferon, growth factors) may awaken the immune system and lead to the destruction of cancer. Clinicians withdraw T cells from a patient and culture them in the presence of interleukin.

The T cells are re-injected into the patient. The remainder of the interleukins maintains the killer activity of the T cells. They have storage vacuoles containing *perforin molecules*, which perforate a plasma membrane and cause water and salts to enter, ultimately causing the cell to burst.

*Effector helper T cells* secrete interleukins that stimulate T cells and B cells to divide and differentiate. Helper T cells stimulate the activation of B cells, cytotoxic and suppressor T cells. They improve response to other immune cells. When exposed to an antigen, they enlarge and secrete cytokines.

*Cytokines* stimulate the helper T cells to clone and stimulate immune cells to perform their functions.

Cytokines stimulate the macrophages to perform phagocytosis and stimulate B cells to become antibody-producing plasma cells. For example, the human immunodeficiency virus (HIV), which causes an autoimmune deficiency syndrome (AIDS), infects helper T cells primarily and inactivates the immune response.

*Memory T cells* remain in the body after an encounter with an antigen and save time for an immune response to the same antigen. Like B cells, memory T cells have unique antigen receptors.

*Suppressor T cells* (*regulatory T cells*) use negative feedback in the immune system. They generally suppress the proliferation of effector T cells.

The cell-mediated response is effective against infected cells, mainly using T cells to respond to a non-self cell, including cells invaded by pathogens.

A non-self cell binds to a T cell, which starts clonal selection. This initiates a series of events, including the production of cytotoxic T cells and helper T cells, the binding of helper T cells to macrophages that engulf pathogens, and the production of interleukins by the helper T cells, which stimulate the proliferation of T cells, B cells, and macrophages.

Tissue rejection occurs when cytotoxic T cells cause the disintegration of foreign tissue. This is a correct differentiation between self and non-self.

The selection of compatible organs and the administration of immunosuppressive drugs prevent tissue rejection. Transplanted organs should have the same type of HLA antigens as the recipient.

Cyclosporine and tacrolimus are immunosuppressants that inhibit the response of T cells to cytokines.

## Roles of B cells and T cells in immunity

*B lymphocytes* (B cells) arise from stem cells in the bone marrow and mature in the spleen.

They give rise to plasma cells that produce and secrete antibodies. Antibodies are released from plasma cells and are specific for an antigen. A single B lymphocyte produces one antibody type.

*Memory B* cells are long-lived B cells that do not release antibodies in response to antigen invasion; instead, they circulate in the body, proliferate, and respond quickly (via antibody synthesis) to eliminate a subsequent invasion by the same antigen.

These cells have a similar function to memory T cells.

*Antibody-mediated immunity* is the defense by B cells.

It is *humoral immunity* because antibodies are present in the *humor*, bodily fluid (i.e., blood and lymph).

The plasma membrane of B cells contains *antigen receptor-antibodies* (immunoglobulins).

*Immunoglobulins* are proteins specific to each antigen.

There are five classes (IgA, IgD, IgE, IgG, and IgM) of immunoglobulins based on variation in the Y-shaped protein-constant region and variable regions of the antibody protein.

Each B cell carries its antibody as a membrane-bound receptor on its surface. A B cell does not clone until its antigen is present, recognizing the antigen directly. Helper T cell secretions stimulate them to clone.

Some cloned B cells do not produce antibodies but remain in the blood as memory B cells.

Antibodies are proteins that recognize antigens (i.e., foreign substances).

The undifferentiated B cell produces antibodies that move to the cell surface and protrude.

The B cell circulates in the blood, and when it encounters the antigen, it becomes primed for replication.

The B cell must receive an interleukin signal from a helper T cell, which has already become activated by a macrophage with an MHC-antigen complex. This promotes rapid cell division.

The B cell population differentiates into effector and memory B cells.

The effector B cells produce a staggering number of free-floating antibodies.

When these free-floating antibodies encounter an antigen, they tag it for destruction by phagocytes and complementary proteins.

These responses occur for extracellular toxins and pathogens; antibodies cannot detect pathogens or toxins inside cells.

When mitosis occurs, the daughter populations become subdivided.

Effector cells (or plasma cells), when fully differentiated, seek and destroy foreign cells.

Making memory cells is efficient because it does not necessitate T cells' activation in proliferating antibodies if the same antigen is present.

Memory cells allow the body to mount a greater, sustained response against the same pathogen during a secondary response.

Thus, a secondary response usually takes less time.

Immunological specificity and memory involve three events, including recognizing an invader, repeated cell division that forms huge lymphocyte populations, and the differentiation into subpopulations of effector cells and memory cells.

**Interferons**

*Interferon* is a protein that is produced by a virus-infected animal cell. Interferons bind to the receptors of non-infected cells, producing substances interfering with viral reproduction.

Interferons are specific to species (e.g., human interferons for humans).

## Immune System Tissues and Organs

### Lymphocytes originate from lymphoid tissue

Lymphoid tissue is in the lymph nodes, thymus, and various organs. It is where lymphocytes reside, proliferate, and differentiate.

Lymphoid tissues are where white blood cells (WBC) reside and proliferate.

### Bone marrow and blood cell production

Human bone marrow consists of red marrow and yellow marrow.

Red marrow contains mostly hematopoietic tissue; yellow bone marrow is predominantly fat cells.

Red and yellow marrows contain blood vessels and capillaries.

*Red marrow* is the origin of blood cells, including leukocytes, platelets, and red blood cells.

At birth, bone marrow is red. However, with age, a portion of the red marrow is converted to yellow marrow, and by adulthood, about half of the bone marrow is red.

In adults, red marrow is in the flat bones, including the skull, sternum, ribs, clavicle, pelvic bones, and vertebrae, and in the cancellous ("spongy") material at the epiphyseal ends of long bones (e.g., femur and humerus). Red marrow consists of reticular fibers produced by reticular cells packed around thinly-walled sinuses.

Differentiated blood cells enter the bloodstream at these bone sinuses.

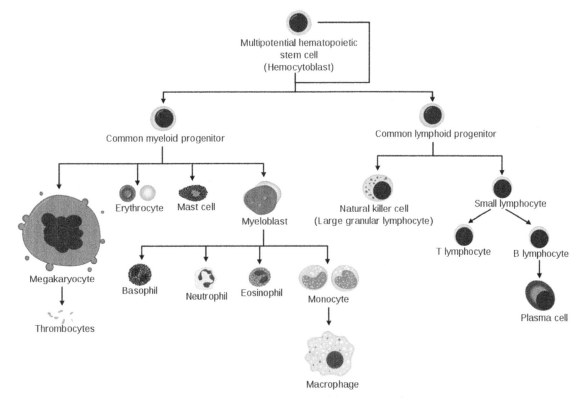

*Blood stem cells give rise to cells of the immune system*

*Yellow bone marrow* is in the medullary cavity (i.e., hollow interior in the center of long bones). When the body is exposed to trauma like extreme blood loss, the body converts the yellow bone marrow into the red bone marrow to increase red blood cell (i.e., erythrocyte) production.

## Spleen filters the blood

The *spleen* is in the upper left abdominal cavity below the diaphragm. The spleen is similar to a lymph node but is larger (nearly the size of a fist).

Lymph nodes cleanse the lymph, while the spleen cleanses the blood.

A capsule divides the spleen into nodules containing sinuses filled with blood. A *spleen nodule* has red pulp and white pulp.

The *red pulp* contains red blood cells, lymphocytes, and macrophages. It purifies the blood that passes through by removing microorganisms and worn-out or damaged red blood cells.

*White pulp* mainly contains lymphocytes. If the spleen ruptures due to injury, it can be removed, as other organs assume its functions. However, a person without a spleen is susceptible to infections and may require antibiotic therapy.

## Thymus produces T cells

The *thymus* is involved in the immune response.

The *thymus gland* is along the trachea behind the sternum in the upper thoracic cavity. It is larger in children than in adults and may disappear in old age.

The thymus is divided into lobules by connective tissue.

The lobules are the site of T lymphocyte maturation.

Each lobule's *medulla* (i.e., inner region of an organ or tissue) consists mainly of epithelial cells producing thymic hormones (thymosin).

Secreted *thymosins* stimulate lymphocytes to differentiate into T cells, identifying and destroying infected body cells.

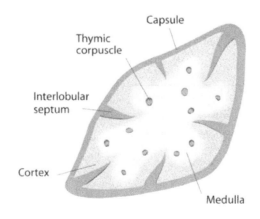

*Structure of the thymus with cortex and medulla*

## Antigen and Antibody

### Antigen-antibody complex

An *antigen* is a non-self molecule that triggers an immune response. Antigens are foreign substances, usually, proteins or polysaccharides, which stimulate the immune system to react, consequently stimulating antibody production.

*Antibodies* are molecules that bind to antigens so that lymphocytes recognize the antigens. The antigen binds with a specific antibody at the *antigen-binding site*.

The *antigen-antibody complex,* or immune complex, marks the antigen for destruction via phagocytosis by neutrophils, macrophages, or complement activation. When antibodies bind to antigens, they bring about neutralization, where a pathogen cannot adhere to the host cell.

This *opsonization* (i.e., a pathogen targeted for destruction by phagocytes) enhances phagocytosis-complement activation, where the antibody destroys the infected cell by creating holes in the cell membrane.

Additionally, the antibodies mark macrophage or natural killer cell phagocytosis by complement proteins, agglutination of antigenic substances, or chemical inactivation (if a toxin).

### Structure of the antibody molecule

*Antibodies* are large globular proteins that defend the body against pathogens by binding to antigens on the pathogen's surface and destroying them.

Antibodies are secreted into the blood, lymph, and bodily fluids and usually bind to a specific antigen.

Antibodies consist of two light chains and two heavy chains linked by disulfide bonds.

Antibodies are Y-shaped proteins, with each tip of the "Y" binding to an antigen.

The "Y" tips are hypervariable regions because they are unique for antigen-specific antibodies.

Each antibody arm has a "heavy" and a "light" polypeptide chain.

*Heavy chains* have constant regions and variable regions.

*Light chains* have constant and variable domains.

The *constant regions* have amino acid sequences that remain constant but differ among antibodies.

The *variable regions* have portions of polypeptide chains with amino acid sequences that change, allowing for antigen specificity.

The variable region forms the antigen-binding sites of antibodies (i.e., tips of the "Y"), where their shape is specific to an antigen.

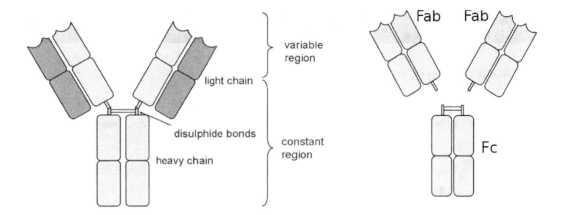

*Antibody Fab (fragment antigen-binding) region binds to antigens. The Fc (fragment crystallizable) region interacts with cell surface receptors, allowing antibodies to activate the immune system*

**Five classes of immunoglobulins**

There are five classes of circulating antibodies, or immunoglobulins (Igs):

- ***IgG antibodies*** contain two Y-shaped structures and are the primary antibodies in the blood and extracellular fluids.

  They are not common in the lymph and tissue fluid.

  IgG antibodies protect the body from infection by binding to many pathogens and toxins.

- ***IgM antibodies*** are pentamers (i.e., five Y-shaped structures).

  They appear in blood soon after infection and disappear before it is over.

  They are useful activators of the complement system.

- ***IgA antibodies*** contain two Y-shaped structures that attack pathogens before reaching the blood.

  They are the primary antibody in bodily secretions.

- ***IgD antibodies*** contain two Y-shaped structures that are receptors for antigens on immature B cells.

- ***IgE antibodies*** contain two Y-shaped structures and are involved in immediate allergic reactions.

  They are attached to the plasma membrane of mast cells (in tissues) and basophils (in the blood).

  When an *allergen* attaches to IgE antibodies on these mast cells, they release large amounts of histamine and other substances, causing cold symptoms or anaphylactic shock.

**Anaphylactic shock**

*Anaphylactic shock* is a severe systemic reaction causing symptoms such as throat swelling, an itchy rash, and a sudden drop in blood pressure.

Allergy shots may prevent the onset of allergic symptoms.

Injections of an allergen cause the body to build up high quantities of IgG antibodies because they do not cause allergy.

The IgG antibodies combine with allergens received from the environment before reaching IgE antibodies on mast cells and basophils plasma membranes.

**Monoclonal antibodies**

Every plasma cell derived from the same B cell secretes the same antibody against the same antigen; these are *monoclonal antibodies.*

Monoclonal antibodies can be produced in vitro. B lymphocytes (usually harvested from mice) are exposed to a particular antigen.

Activated B lymphocytes are fused with myeloma cells (malignant plasma cells that divide indefinitely).

*Hybridomas* are two different cells fused—hybrid cells and cancerous cells (suffix *-oma*).

Monoclonal antibodies are used for rapid, reliable diagnoses of various conditions (e.g., pregnancy).

Monoclonal antibodies identify infections, distinguish cancerous cells from normal cells, and transport radioisotopes or toxic drugs to target tumors.

**Antigen presentation stimulates antibodies**

A pathogen enters an antigen-presenting cell (APC). Pieces of the pathogen are displayed at the surface of APCs.

The T cell receptors recognize the presented antigen and activate various immune responses.

When a macrophage engulfs an extracellular pathogen, pieces of the pathogen become the antigen, and they are presented at the macrophage's cell surface.

Helper T cells recognize the presented antigen and activate macrophages to destroy the pathogen.

Helper T cells activate B cells to produce antibodies against the pathogen.

When an intracellular pathogen invades a host cell, pathogen pieces are presented on the host cell surface.

Cytotoxic T cells recognize the presented antigen and signal the infected cell to self-destruct.

*Notes for active learning*

# CHAPTER 15

# Nervous System

- Neuron

- Organization of Vertebrate Nervous System

- Major Functions of the Nervous System

- Sympathetic and Parasympathetic Nervous Systems

- Reflexes and Feedback Mechanisms

- Perception of Sensations

- Sensory Receptors of the Nervous System

- Hearing and the Perception of Sound

- Visual Perceptions

- Senses of Touch, Taste, Smell and Balance

## Neuron

### Neuron structure and function

*Neurons* (nerve cells) generate electric signals that pass from one end of the cell to another. Neurons release chemical messengers, *neurotransmitters*, to communicate with other cells. A neuron conducting signals toward a synapse (the junction where a neuron communicates with a target cell) is a *presynaptic neuron*.

A neuron conducting signals away from a synapse is a *postsynaptic neuron*.

*Neurotrophic factors* are proteins that guide the development of neurons.

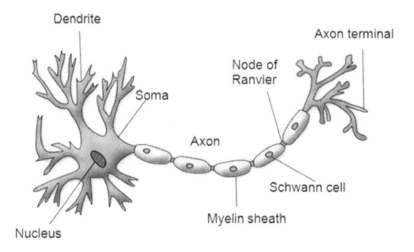

*Neurons contain dendrites to receive signals that propagate along the axon toward the axon terminal*

Neurons outside the central nervous system (CNS) can repair themselves, but neurons within the CNS cannot. In the autonomic nervous system, the transmission of an impulse involves the interaction between at least two neurons.

The first neuron is the *preganglionic neuron*, and the second is the *postganglionic neuron*. Neurons vary in size and shape but have three parts: cell body, dendrites, and axon.

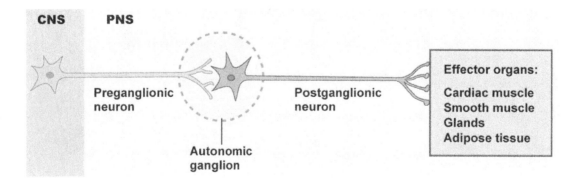

*A motor neuron relays signals from the brain or spinal cord to a muscle or gland*

## Cell body as the site of nucleus and organelles

Because nerve cells are specialized for signal transmission and pathway-formation, the form of neurons reflects their function. The cell body contributes to a neuron's density. The cell body houses the neuron's organelles, such as the nucleus and mitochondria. The cell body has a well-developed, rough endoplasmic reticulum and a Golgi apparatus to synthesize and modify essential proteins for proper neuronal function. This part of the neuron is similar in form to most somatic cells, except for the dendrites.

## Dendrite and axon structure and function

*Dendrites* are the branched receptive areas of a neuron that extend from the cell body. They receive information and conduct impulses toward the cell body. The branching of dendrites increases the surface area for receiving signals (e.g., neurotransmitter).

The number of dendrites depends on the function of the neuron. For example, *unipolar neurons* have one dendrite.

The *axon* differentiates neurons from other cells. The axon is crucial in the neuron's impulse generation and is responsible for carrying outgoing messages from the cell.

A long axon is a *nerve fiber*. A nerve fiber is a single axon, while a nerve is a bundle of axons bound by connective tissue. This axon can originate from the CNS and extend to the body's extremities. This effectively provides a pathway for messages from the CNS to the periphery.

Axons conduct impulses away from the cell body to stimulate or inhibit a neuron, muscle, or gland.

*Axon terminals*, secretory regions of the nerve, are at the end of the axon, away from the neuron's cell body. Other names for the axon terminal are the synaptic knob or synaptic bouton.

The neuron's axon terminal is the signal transmission site toward the receptor of another cell.

## Neuroglia, glial cells and astrocytes

Nervous tissue is made of neurons and neuroglia.

*Neuroglia* support and nourish the neurons.

*Glial cells* are nervous tissue support cells capable of cellular division. Oligodendroglia and Schwann cells are glial cells that support neurons physically and metabolically.

*Astroglia* regulates the composition of the extracellular fluid in the CNS.

*Microglia* perform immune functions.

Glial cells include ependymal cells (use cilia to circulate cerebrospinal fluid), satellite cells (support ganglia), and astrocytes (provide physical support to neurons of CNS; maintain the mineral and nutrients balance).

## Myelin sheath, Schwann cells, oligodendrocytes

The *myelin sheath* is a phospholipid layer that surrounds a neuron's axon. The myelin sheath insulates the axon, increasing the conductivity of the electrical messages sent through a nerve cell.

Myelin is an excellent insulator because it is fatty and does not contain channels.

By preventing leakage of charge, myelin increases the speed of propagation, enabling axons to be thinner. It is formed by the membranes of highly-specialized, tightly-spiraled *neuroglia cells*. These neuroglia cells are Schwann cells or oligodendrocytes.

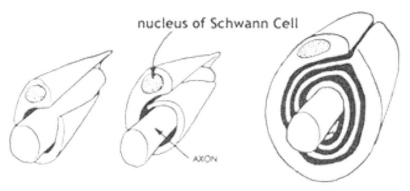

*Schwann cell sheath is a phospholipid coat growing around a nerve axon*

In the peripheral nervous system (PNS), the *Schwann cells* produce myelin for nerve cells. Many specialized cells wrap myelin around the neuron's axon, providing an insulating sheath that prevents signal transmission loss.

*Oligodendrocytes* are the central nervous system analog of Schwann cells. They make myelin sheaths (insulation) around CNS axons. Insulation occurs at intervals, punctuated by openings known as *nodes of Ranvier*, exposing the axon's plasma membrane, causing an action potential to jump along the nodes of Ranvier.

Only vertebrates have myelinated axons.

Myelinated axons appear as *white matter*, while neuronal cell bodies appear as *gray matter*.

Many neurodegenerative autoimmune diseases result from a lack of myelin sheath. For instance, in multiple sclerosis, the lack of insulation from a myelin sheath slows or leaks the conductivity of signals across neural pathways, severely decreasing the efficiency of the patient's nervous system.

**Nodes of Ranvier**

The spaces between adjacent sections of myelin where the axon's plasma membrane is exposed to extracellular fluid are *nodes of Ranvier* (neurofibril nodes). The myelin sheath prevents the flow of ions between intracellular and extracellular compartments.

Therefore, action potentials occur at the non-insulated nodes of Ranvier; *saltatory conduction* is this jump of action potentials from one node to another.

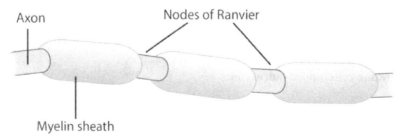

*Nodes of Ranvier for saltatory conduction occurring at exposed sections of plasma membrane*

**Synapse and neurotransmitters for impulse propagation between cells**

*Synapse* is the space between the axon bulb and the next neuron's dendritic receptor. A synapse is a junction between two neurons that permits a neuron to pass an electrical (or chemical) signal to another cell.

A synapse consists of a *presynaptic membrane*, a *synaptic cleft*, and the *postsynaptic membrane*.

In a synapse, the presynaptic neuron's electrical activity influences the electrical activity in the postsynaptic neuron. The influence may be excitatory (positive response) or inhibitory (negative response).

There is a narrow fluid-filled space of the synaptic cleft between the presynaptic membrane and the postsynaptic membrane. Neurotransmitters are released into synaptic vesicles from the presynaptic neuron's axon terminal and into the synaptic cleft. The vesicles migrate the synaptic cleft and travel toward the postsynaptic neuron, binding to postsynaptic receptors.

In *convergence*, presynaptic neurons affect a single postsynaptic neuron. This allows information from many sources to influence the activity of one cell.

In *divergence*, a single presynaptic nerve cell affects several postsynaptic nerve cells, allowing one information source to affect multiple pathways.

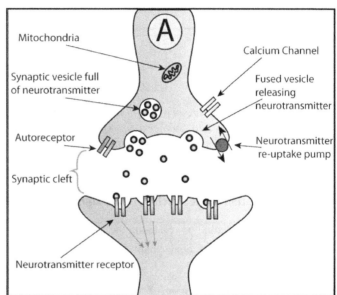

*The synaptic cleft between two neurons*

The nervous system uses several types of synapses to create complex pathways for relaying information. *Axodendritic synapses* exist between the axon terminal of one presynaptic neuron and one dendrite of the postsynaptic neuron. An *axosomatic synapse* resides between the axon terminal of the presynaptic neuron and the cell body of the postsynaptic neuron. *Axoaxonic synapses*, while rare, can exist between the presynaptic and postsynaptic axon terminal.

**Classifying electrical and chemical synapses**

At *electric synapses*, the presynaptic and postsynaptic cells are joined by *gap junctions*, allowing action potentials to flow directly across the junction. Due to the short distance and the direct, physical link between the two neurons, these junctions provide high-speed transmission signals. Since chemical synapses are usually fast enough for signal transmission, electrical synapses are relatively rare.

At a *chemical synapse*, the axon of the presynaptic neuron ends in a swelling as the axon terminal.

The synaptic cleft's extracellular space separates the presynaptic and postsynaptic neurons, preventing a direct propagation of current.

Chemical synapses are unidirectional; a signal can only be transmitted from the presynaptic to the postsynaptic neuron.

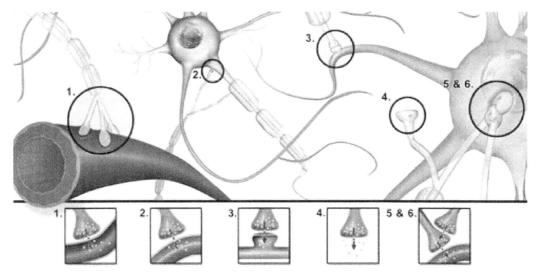

*Synapse types: 1) axosecretory – axon terminal secretes directly in the bloodstream, 2) axoaxonic – axon terminal secretes into another axon, 3) axodendritic – axon terminal ends in a dendritic spine, 4) axoextracellular – axon with no connection secretes into the extracellular fluid, 5) axosomatic – axon terminal ends on soma and 6) axosynaptic – axon terminal ends on another axon terminal*

**Synaptic propagation between cells without signal loss**

An action potential travels along the axon and reaches the end of the presynaptic neuron. Depolarization of the presynaptic membrane opens the voltage-gated calcium channels.

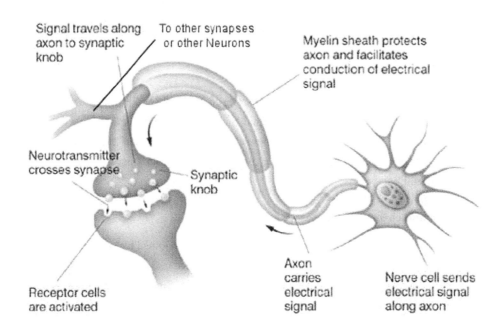

*Dendrites receive stimuli, propagate impulse without diminution along the axon and release neurotransmitter into the synaptic cleft toward the postsynaptic neuron*

Calcium ions flow into the presynaptic neuron, causing vesicles with neurotransmitters inside the neuron to fuse with the plasma membrane. The $Ca^{2+}$ ions induce reactions allowing neurotransmitter vesicles to fuse with the plasma membrane. Membrane fusion releases the neurotransmitter into the synaptic cleft by exocytosis. These synaptic vesicles store neurotransmitters that diffuse across the synapse towards the postsynaptic membrane.

When an action potential arrives at the presynaptic axon bulb, synaptic vesicles merge with the presynaptic membrane. When vesicles merge with the neuron's plasma membrane, neurotransmitters are discharged into the synaptic cleft.

Neurotransmitter molecules diffuse across the synaptic cleft to the postsynaptic membrane, binding with specific receptors.

### Neurotransmitters, presynaptic and postsynaptic membranes

The neurotransmitters are released into the synaptic cleft via exocytosis. These neurotransmitters diffuse via *Brownian* motion (i.e., random and irregular motion) and bind within the synaptic cleft to specific receptors on the postsynaptic plasma membrane.

The receptors are ligand-gated ion channels, which open and let sodium and other positively charged ions into the postsynaptic neuron.

As these positively charged ions enter the postsynaptic neuron, they cause the neuron's membrane to depolarize, resulting in an action potential moving along the postsynaptic neuron.

The calcium ions are pumped into the synaptic cleft from inside the presynaptic neuron. The neurotransmitters are degraded and recycled by enzymes in the synaptic cleft.

*Neurotransmitters* are chemicals that cross the synapse between neurons or neurons and a muscle or gland. After an action potential has traveled down the axon, it induces neurotransmitters' release from the presynaptic neuron's axon terminal into the synapse. The axon terminal, or synaptic knob, contains vesicles of neurotransmitters waiting to be exocytosed.

An action potential reaching the synaptic knob causes an influx of calcium, which signals the vesicles to fuse with cell membranes (exocytosis) to release the neurotransmitters into the synaptic cleft.

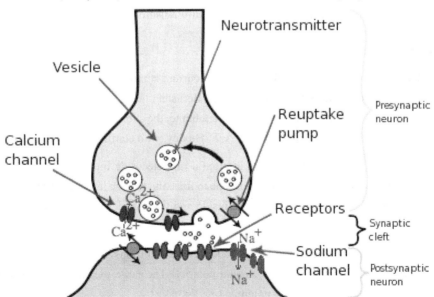

*Synaptic transmission with Ca⁺ causing the release of neurotransmitter from the presynaptic membrane into the cleft*

**Postsynaptic neurons and graded potentials**

Once the postsynaptic membrane receives the neurotransmitter, the chemicals bind to a receptor (usually on the dendrite) and open ion channels. This changes the membrane potential of the postsynaptic neuron.

If this *graded potential* stimulus is large enough, it triggers an *all-or-none response*, inducing the propagation of the signal down the axon of the postsynaptic neuron. Enzymes quickly degrade these neurotransmitters, or it is taken up by the presynaptic terminal so that they do not persistently stimulate the postsynaptic neuron.

**Classifying neurotransmitters**

More than 200 neurotransmitters have been identified. *Acetylcholine* (ACh) and *norepinephrine* (NE) are two common neurotransmitters. *Cholinergic fibers* release ACh. In some synapses, the postsynaptic membrane contains enzymes that rapidly inactivate the neurotransmitter. For example, acetylcholinesterase degrades acetylcholine. Once a neurotransmitter is released into a synaptic cleft, it initiates a response and is removed from the cleft.

*Biogenic amines* are neurotransmitters containing an amino group such as *catecholamines* (e.g., dopamine, norepinephrine, epinephrine, serotonin). Nerve fibers that release epinephrine and norepinephrine are adrenergic and noradrenergic fibers, respectively. Amino acid neurotransmitters are prevalent neurotransmitters in the CNS. These include glutamate, aspartate, GABA (gamma-aminobutyric acid), and glycine.

*Neuropeptides* are composed of two or more amino acids. Neurons that release neuropeptides are peptidergic (e.g., beta-endorphin, dynorphin and enkephalin groups). Nitric oxide, ATP, and adenine act as neurotransmitters. Many PNS neurons end at neuroeffector junctions on muscle and gland cells. Neurotransmitters released by these efferent neurons activate the target cell.

In other synapses, the presynaptic membrane reabsorbs neurotransmitters for repackaging in synaptic vesicles or for the molecular breakdown. The short existence of neurotransmitters in a synapse prevents continuous stimulation (or inhibition) of postsynaptic membranes. Several drugs affect the nervous system by interfering with (or potentiating) the action potentials by neurotransmitters.

**Resting potential and electrochemical gradient**

Luigi Galvani discovered in 1786 that an electric current stimulates a nerve. An impulse is too slow to be caused merely by an electric current in an axon. Julius Bernstein proposed that the impulse is the movement of unequally distributed ions on either side of an axon-membrane, the axon's plasma membrane. The 1963 Nobel Prize went to British researchers A. L. Hodgkin and A. F. Huxley, who confirmed this theory.

Hodgkin, Huxley, and other researchers inserted a tiny electrode into the giant axon of a squid. The electrode was attached to a voltmeter and an oscilloscope to trace the change in voltage. The voltmeter measured the difference in the electrical potential between the inside and the outside of the membrane. The oscilloscope indicated any changes in polarity.

Since the plasma membrane is more permeable to potassium ions than to sodium ions, there are more positive ions outside the cell; this accounts for some polarity. The large, negatively charged proteins in the cytoplasm (e.g., $Cl^-$) contribute to the resting potential of $-70$ mV.

When an axon is not conducting an impulse, an oscilloscope records a membrane potential of –70 mV; the inside of the neuron is negative compared to the outside.

*Resting potential* is the electrical potential across the plasma membrane of a cell's axon that is not conducting an impulse. This polarization is due to the difference in electrical charge on either side of the axon membrane.

## All-or-none action potentials, depolarization and repolarization

*Action potentials* are large, rapid alterations in the neuron's plasma membrane potential. It is the reversal and restoration of the electrical potential across the plasma membrane as electrical impulses pass (i.e., depolarization and repolarization) that use the $Na^+/K^+$ pump. Membranes capable of producing action potentials are excitable membranes (e.g., membranes of nerve and muscle cells).

When the membrane becomes depolarized, sodium channels open, and positive sodium ions rush inside.

During *depolarization*, the ion concentration is opposite from the resting potential. Sodium ions dominate the inside, while potassium ions dominate the outside. In response, the membrane potential moves in a positive direction. The membrane potential goes from about –70 mV at resting potential to +30 mV in the depolarization phase.

During *repolarization*, potassium channels open and sodium channels close. The positive potassium ions rush outside, and the membrane potential drops down. Now, sodium ion concentration is higher on the inside, while potassium ion concentration is higher on the outside. This is the opposite of the resting state. Thus, the membrane potential returns to its resting value, and the potential returns to –70 mV in the repolarization phase.

A *hyperpolarization* is an event in the all-or-none axon propagation where potassium channels do not close fast enough. The membrane potential briefly drops below the standard resting potential of around –80 mV.

An action potential is all-or-none. If neurotransmitters cause the postsynaptic cell to reach the threshold, an action potential is induced in the postsynaptic cell by the presynaptic action potential.

Propagation between neurons involves no transmission loss. The postsynaptic action potential is as large as the presynaptic.

## Interneurons integrate and transmit signals

*Interneurons* are typically within the central nervous system structures (i.e., the spinal cord and brain) and account for about 99% of neurons in the body.

Interneurons are multipolar with many dendrites for receiving information and a single axon sending the collected information toward the synapse.

Interneurons form complex brain pathways throughout the central nervous system, transmit signals to the periphery via motor neurons and act as integrators to evaluate impulses for the appropriate response.

Generally, the term interneuron refers to small neurons that connect to other nearby neurons (as opposed to *projection neurons* that can connect over long distances).

Interneuron pathways play essential roles in human survival and advancement, accounting for memory and language. Interneurons are usually inhibitory, although excitatory interneurons do exist.

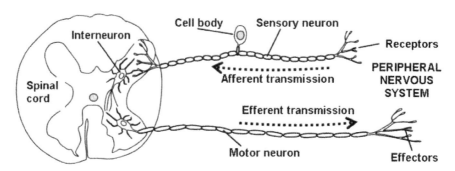

*CNS and PNS structures with the direction of propagation shown for afferent sensory neurons*
*(receptors → CNS) and efferent motor neurons (CNS → effectors)*

**Sensory and effector neurons**

*Afferent neurons* (i.e., sensory neurons) send impulses from the PNS towards the CNS. Afferent neurons are unipolar, as a single dendrite collects information and transmits it through one axon. A sensory receptor at a dendrite of an afferent neuron conveys signals from tissues and organs to the brain and spine.

Receptors are specialized endings of afferent neurons or separate cells that affect the ends of afferent neurons. They collect information about the external and internal environment in various energy forms. This stimulus energy is first transformed into a graded potential (receptor potential).

*Stimulus transduction* is the process by which a stimulus is transformed into an electrical response. The initial depolarization in afferent neurons is achieved by a *receptor potential* (in receptors) or by a spontaneous change in the neuron membrane potential as a *pacemaker potential*.

*Efferent neurons* (i.e., motor neurons) carry signals away from the CNS to cells of muscles or glands in the peripheral system. In total, 43 main nerves are branching off the CNS to the peripheral nervous system. Efferent neurons are structurally multipolar and stimulate *effectors*, which are target cells that elicit a response. For example, neurons may stimulate effector cells in the stomach to secrete gastrin.

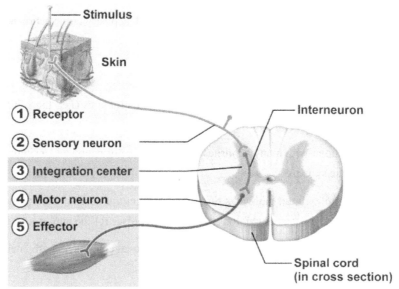

*A stimulus is processed through a sensory neuron to the spinal column.*
*An interneuron communicates the information to a motor neuron for a response at the effector*

## Organization of Vertebrate Nervous System

**High-level control and integration of body systems**

The three functions of the nervous system are:

- receiving sensory input

- transferring and interpreting impulses

- generating motor output to muscles and glands

The nervous system is a highly organized arrangement of neural pathways that extends to nearly every part of the body.

*Neurons* are cells specialized to quickly transmit electrical impulses by forming pathways toward or away from the brain.

The nervous system is organized so the brain uses these neural pathways to interpret stimuli from the environment and subsequently direct the appropriate response to the body.

These responses involve other bodily systems (e.g., the endocrine, muscular and cardiovascular systems).

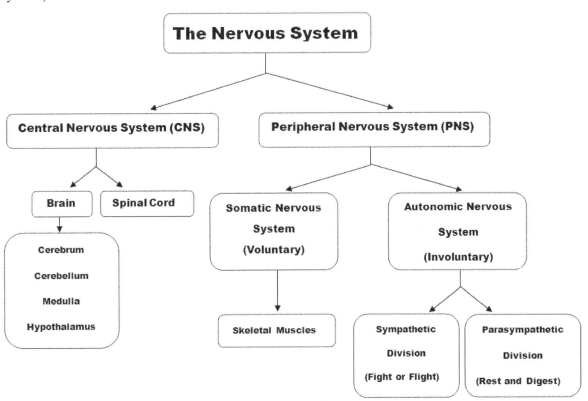

*The nervous system divides into the central and peripheral nervous system*

**Central nervous system *vs.* peripheral nervous system**

The central nervous system (CNS) consists of the brain and the spinal cord, while the peripheral nervous system (PNS) consists of other nerves and ganglia (collections of cell bodies).

The PNS contains the *somatic nervous system*, including the pathways of voluntary control over our skeletal muscles and the involuntary *autonomic nervous system*, including the *sympathetic* (fight or flight) and *parasympathetic* (rest and digest) branches.

The PNS sends signals from sensory neurons toward the CNS.

The CNS sends signals to muscles and organs via effector neurons to cause specific actions.

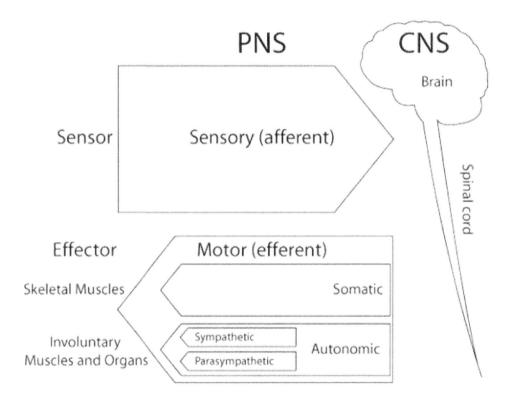

*The nervous system is divided into the central nervous system (CNS) and peripheral nervous system (PNS), with afferent and efferent responses to stimuli.*

## Major Functions of the Nervous System

### Adaptive capability to external stimuli

The nervous system's highly adaptive capability helps the brain interpret external influences efficiently.

The brain's interpretation of the environment begins at the sensory receptor. The brain communicates the corresponding response using other bodily systems.

A *stimulus* is energy that activates a receptor. Stimulus energy is first transformed into graded or receptor potentials. S*timulus transduction* is when a stimulus is transformed into an electrical response.

Each receptor is specific to a stimulus type; it is an *adequate stimulus*.

Receptors respond to a specified intensity range of that stimuli.

However, the nervous system has adapted so that receptors can still be activated when stimuli are not specified for a receptor. This adaptation allows the nervous system to communicate with the rest of the body if a receptor does not appropriately respond to the environment.

This is an example of *nonspecific stimuli* and occurs when the nonspecific stimulus is of high intensity.

### Threshold, all-or-none responses and efferent control

The *threshold potential* is when a membrane is depolarized to generate an action potential.

A stimulus strong enough to depolarize the membrane is the threshold stimulus.

A stimulus greater than threshold magnitude elicits an action potential of the same amplitude.

This reaction occurs because once the threshold is reached, membrane events are no longer dependent upon the strength of the stimulus.

Action potentials, therefore, occur maximally or do not occur at all, generating an *all-or-none* response.

A single action potential cannot convey information about the magnitude of the stimulus that initiated it.

*Efferent neurons* (or *motor neurons*) stimulate *effectors* or target cells that elicit a specific response.

Effectors include muscles, sweat glands, and stomach cells secreting gastrin.

Motor neurons have many dendrites and a single axon. They conduct impulses from the central nervous system (CNS) to muscle fibers or glands.

The efferent system is divided into a somatic and an autonomic system.

### Somatic and autonomic nervous systems

The *somatic nervous system* innervates skeletal muscles.

It consists of myelinated axons without any synapses. The activity of these neurons leads to excitation (e.g., contraction) of skeletal muscles; therefore, they are motor neurons. Motor neurons are never inhibitory.

The somatic fibers are responsible for voluntary movement.

The *autonomic nervous system* innervates smooth and cardiac muscles and consists of two neurons connecting the CNS and effector cells.

The synapse between these two neurons is the autonomic ganglion.

The nerve fibers between the CNS and the ganglion are pre-ganglionic fibers.

The post-ganglionic fibers are between ganglion and the effector cells.

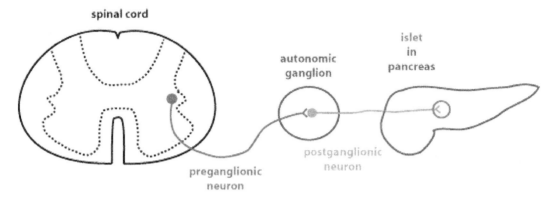

*An autonomic nervous system with information traveling from spinal cord to effector cell via pre-ganglionic and post-ganglionic fibers*

**Negative feedback to achieve homeostasis**

Within the autonomic nervous system, impulses are involuntary.

Examples of involuntary impulses include respiratory system control and heart rate.

The autonomic nervous system can be divided into the *sympathetic* (fight or flight) and *parasympathetic* (rest and digest) systems.

Both systems use negative feedback mechanisms, whereby high levels of a compound inhibit its production.

For example, the alternating release of the antagonistic hormones insulin and glucagon is essential for homeostatic blood sugar regulation.

The *ganglia* (i.e., collection of cell bodies) of sympathetic neurons are close to the spinal cord and are arranged to act as a single unit.

The parasympathetic ganglia neurons are close to the organs and are arranged so that the parts can act independently.

The sympathetic system is involved in responses to stress.

Many organs and glands receive a dual innervation from sympathetic and parasympathetic fibers.

The two systems generally have opposite effects and work to regulate a response.

**Sensory input by the peripheral nervous system**

*Afferent neurons* have sensory dendritic receptors conveying signals from tissues/organs into the CNS.

The *somatic system* has two main pathways in opposite directions. One pathway uses *nerves* (i.e., bundles of axons) to carry sensory information from the peripheral skeletal muscles back to the CNS.

The other pathway works in the opposite direction, allowing humans to consciously use their muscles by sending impulses from the CNS to skeletal muscles.

The receptor is the site of stimulation. Once the receptor receives the stimuli, the sensory neuron carries the impulse to the *integration center*. The integration center connects sensory neurons to motor neurons via synapses inside the CNS. Integration is monosynaptic or polysynaptic.

There are no *interneurons* (i.e., neurons that link sensory and motor neurons) involved in *monosynaptic* integration. Monosynaptic integration involves a direct synapse from the sensory to a motor neuron.

*Polysynaptic* integration requires at least one interneuron. Once the signal reaches the motor neuron, it is carried toward the effector, the site of response to the stimulus.

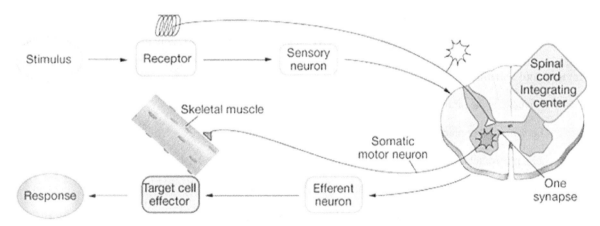

*A monosynaptic reflex has a single synapse between the afferent and efferent neurons.*

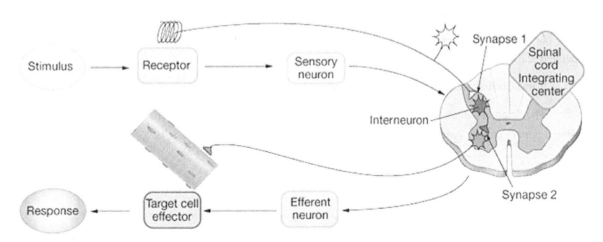

*A polysynaptic reflex has two (or more) synapses (i.e., interneurons) between the afferent and efferent neurons*

## Limbic system structures and purpose

The *limbic system* is a complex network of tracts in the brain.

The limbic system incorporates multiple brain areas such as the medial portions of cerebral lobes, subcortical nuclei, and the diencephalon.

The two major structures of the limbic system are the *hippocampus* and the *amygdala*.

The limbic system's coordination of multiple areas of the brain allows us to interpret stimuli from the environment and act accordingly.

The *hippocampus* delivers sensory input to the prefrontal area of the brain. People are aware of past experiences because the hippocampus stores this information in designated association areas.

The *amygdala* is the area of the brain that associates emotions with thoughts or experiences.

After the amygdala and the hippocampus process sensory information, the highly developed prefrontal cortex allows reasoning, preventing humans from acting purely upon basic emotion.

A general interpretation area receives information from the sensory association areas, allowing to quickly integrate signals and send them to the prefrontal area for immediate response.

The prefrontal area in the frontal lobe receives input from other association areas and reasons and plans.

## Memory and learning

*Memory* is the brain's ability to retain and recall information.

*Learning* takes place when a person retains and utilizes memories.

The prefrontal area in the frontal lobe is active in *short-term memory* (e.g., telephone numbers).

*Long-term memory* is a mix of semantic (e.g., numbers, words) and episodic memory (e.g., events).

*Skill memory* is the ability to perform motor activities, commonly referred to as "muscle memory."

The *hippocampus* serves as an intermediary between processed memories and the prefrontal cortex.

The amygdala is responsible for fear conditioning and associates danger with certain sensory stimuli.

*Long-term potentiation* (LTP), the strengthening of neural pathways in the hippocampus following associated learning, is essential for memory storage.

Some excited postsynaptic cells may die due to excessive amounts of glutamate neurotransmitter.

The death of neurons in the hippocampus may be the underlying cause of Alzheimer's disease, gradually causing a person's memory to deteriorate.

## Sympathetic and Parasympathetic Nervous Systems

### Sensory and motor branches of the nervous system

The PNS consists of the sensory and motor branch. It lies outside the CNS and contains the cranial and spinal nerves. The PNS transmits signals to and from the CNS using sensory and motor neurons. 12 pairs of cranial nerves connect to the brain, and 31 pairs of spinal nerves connect to the spinal cord.

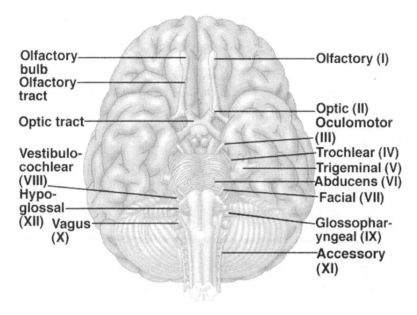

*Twelve pairs of cranial nerves labeled with the number and common name*

*Cranial nerves* mostly connect to the head, neck, and facial regions, and *spinal nerves* lie on either side of the spinal cord. Nerves are made from many parallel nerve fibers containing axons and myelin sheaths. S*pinal roots* are the paired spinal nerves that leave the spinal cord by two short branches. The *dorsal root* (or sensory root) contains fibers of sensory neurons conducting nerve impulses to the spinal cord. The *ventral root* contains the axons of motor neurons that conduct nerve impulses away from the spinal cord.

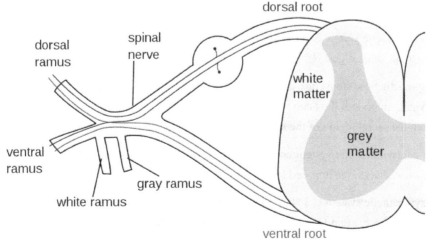

*Dorsal root carries impulses to the spinal cord, while the ventral root carries impulses away*

*Spinal nerves* are mixed nerves that conduct impulses to and from the spinal cord. Spinal nerves contain sensory and motor fibers, with each type of fiber serving its region. *Sensory nerves* contain sensory nerve fibers. *Motor nerves* contain motor nerve fibers. The cell bodies of neurons are in the CNS or ganglia.

The PNS is divided into the somatic and autonomic systems. The *somatic system* is responsible for the voluntary movement of skeletal muscles.

**Sympathetic division of the autonomic nervous system**

The *autonomic system* controls involuntary movements of cardiac muscle, smooth muscle, and glands.

There are two divisions: the sympathetic and parasympathetic systems.

Both systems function in an involuntary manner, innervate internal organs and utilize two neurons and one ganglion for each impulse. The first neuron has a cell body within the CNS and a preganglionic fiber. The second neuron has a cell body within the ganglion and a postganglionic fiber.

Breathing rate and blood pressure are regulated by reflex actions to maintain homeostasis.

The *sympathetic system* is responsible for fight or flight responses, generally raising blood pressure and heart rate. Most preganglionic fibers of the sympathetic system arise from the *thoracic-lumbar* (middle) portion of the spinal cord and almost immediately terminate in ganglia that lie near the spinal cord.

The preganglionic fiber is short, while the postganglionic fiber that contacts an organ is long.

The sympathetic system is vital during emergencies (the "fight or flight" response). To defend itself or flee, the body activates the sympathetic system to accelerate the heart rate and dilate the bronchi.

These responses require a supply of glucose and oxygen.

The sympathetic system inhibits digestion to divert energy from less necessary digestive functions. It increases blood pressure, dilates the pupils to allow more light into the eye, and breaks down glycogen to release glucose into the blood.

The neurotransmitter released by the postganglionic axon is mainly norepinephrine, similar to epinephrine (adrenaline).

**Parasympathetic division of the autonomic nervous system**

The *parasympathetic system* is responsible for rest and digest responses, lower heart rate, and promote non-emergency functions (e.g., digestion, relaxation, sexual arousal).

The parasympathetic system consists of a few cranial nerves and nerves exiting the spinal cord, including the vagus nerve (which innervates the heart and branches to the pharynx, larynx, and some internal organs) and fibers that arise from the sacral region of the spinal cord.

Since the parasympathetic system contains efferent nerves from the cranial and the sacral regions, the efferent nerves are *craniosacral* (as opposed to the thoracic-lumbar sympathetic nerves).

The parasympathetic system is a "housekeeper system," which promotes internal responses resulting in a relaxed state. It causes the eye pupil to constrict, promotes digestion, and slows the heartbeat.

*Acetylcholine* is the neurotransmitter released by the parasympathetic system.

## Reflexes and Feedback Mechanisms

### Reflex arcs as a survival mechanism

Reflexes involve the spinal cord and do not require the brain's participation.

There are two advantages to this. First, the brain is continuously working, and any additional tasks for the brain result in precious resources being diverted. Second, reflexes are designed to be fast responses.

For instance, if someone puts their hand on a hot stove, they probably would not analyze the pain before removing their hand from the heat. As a result of bypassing the brain, the reaction time to these stimuli is faster.

*Reflex arcs* use negative feedback. They are rapid, involuntary responses to stimuli involving two or three neurons, but the brain does not integrate sensory and motor activities.

Instead, the reflex arcs synapse in the spinal cord. Even though the reflex arc bypasses the brain, the brain is aware that the response took place. One example of a reflex arc is immediate withdrawal from a painful stimulus. Another example is the knee-jerk reaction. Tapping the knee-tendon causes a sudden stretching of the muscle, and the reflex leads to contraction of that muscle, creating the knee-jerk (negative feedback).

### Feedback loops affect flexor and extensor muscles

Feedback loops occur when a system's outputs are fed back into the system as inputs, leading to a change. The two types are positive and negative feedback loops.

*Positive feedbacks* are mechanisms that encourage the continuation of a cycle. An example of positive feedback is uterine contractions when one contraction leads to oxytocin release and subsequently more contractions. Another example is blood clotting when platelets are activated at the wound site and attracts platelet activation and clumping. Positive feedbacks are not common because they disrupt homeostasis.

*Negative feedbacks* are mechanisms that counteract the continuation of a cycle. For example, a drop in blood pressure causes ADH release, increasing blood pressure. Conversely, an increase in blood pressure causes a drop in ADH.

Another example is in the Golgi tendon reflex, a sudden contraction of the quads (extensor muscles) causes negative feedback that relaxes the quads and contracts the hamstrings (flexor muscles).

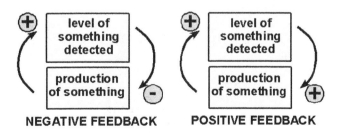

**Reflex arc**

The mechanism of a *reflex arc* occurs in the following sequence:

1. Sensory receptors generate an impulse in a sensory neuron that moves along sensory axons toward the spinal cord.

2. Sensory axons enter the cord dorsally and pass signals to interneurons.

3. Interneurons pass the signals to motor neurons.

4. Impulses travel along motor axons to an effector.

5. The effector causes an effect (e.g., muscle contracting) to withdrawal from a pain stimulus.

The reflex response occurs because the sensory neuron stimulates interneurons. Some impulses extend to the cerebrum. When this occurs, a person becomes conscious of the stimulus and the reaction.

Reflexes often affect flexor and extensor muscles. During the knee-jerk reflex, the extensors of the quads are contracted while the flexors of the hamstrings are relaxed.

**Spinal cord function and meninges**

The CNS, in the midline of the body, consists of the brain and the spinal cord. It integrates sensory information and controls the body. The CNS is vital because it controls biological processes and conscious thought. Because of the spinal cord and brain's critical importance, these organs are safely encased within bones.

The *cranium* protects the brain, and the *spine* protects the spinal cord. Both are wrapped in three connective tissue coverings as *meninges*.

The spaces between the meninges have *cerebrospinal fluid* to nourish and protect the CNS. The cerebrospinal fluid is within the central canal of the spinal cord, produced by the *ventricles* of the brain.

The meninges in the CNS have three layers: the outermost *dura mater*, the middle *arachnoid,* and the inner *pia mater*. The space between the pia and the arachnoid, the *subarachnoid space*, is filled with *cerebrospinal fluid* (CSF), acting as a shock absorber for neural tissue. Because the brain cannot store glycogen, it depends on a continuous supply of glucose and oxygen from the bloodstream.

The exchange of substances between the blood and extracellular fluid in CNS is highly restricted via a complex group of blood-brain barrier mechanisms. The CSF and the brain's extracellular fluid are in diffusion equilibrium but are separated from the blood.

A group of nerve fibers traveling in the CNS is a *pathway* (or tract). A band of nerve fibers that connects the left and right halves is a *commissure.*

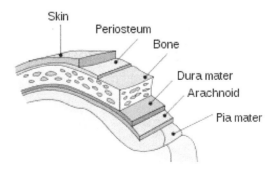

---

**Dorsal and ventral horns for information propagation**

Information in the CNS passes along two types of pathways:

1) *Long neural pathways*, in which neurons with long axons carry information directly between the brain and spinal cord or between regions of the brain.

   There is no diminution in the transmitted information.

2) *Multineuronal* (or *multisynaptic*) *pathways* have many neurons or synapses.

   New information is integrated into the transmitted information.

Neuron cell bodies have similar function clusters as ganglia in the PNS and nuclei in the CNS.

The spinal cord has two main functions. It provides communication between the brain, the spinal nerves, and the synapse (or synapses if it is polysynaptic) for the reflex arc.

Sensory information enters through the *dorsal horn* in the spinal cord.

Sensory information exits through the *ventral horn* as motor information moves toward the periphery.

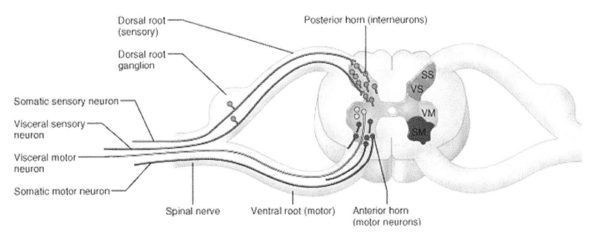

*Sensory neuron (dorsal root) and a motor neuron (ventral root)*

**Gray and white matter of the brain and spinal cord**

The spinal cord and brain are composed of gray and white matter.

These areas of matter have unmyelinated or myelinated neurons, whether the neuron's axons have been covered with myelin. This phospholipid substance allows for a faster propagation of axon potentials in neurons.

*Gray matter* is composed of interneurons, cell bodies, dendrites, and glial cells. Unmyelinated cell bodies and short fibers give gray matter its color. In a cross-section, the gray area looks like a butterfly (or the letter H). It contains portions of sensory neurons, motor neurons, and the short interneurons that connect them.

Multiple nuclei make up the *basal ganglia* gray matter in the brain.

Common malfunctions in this area lead to conditions such as Huntington's and Parkinson's disease.

In *white matter*, the long myelinated fibers of interneurons run in tracts, giving the white matter its color.

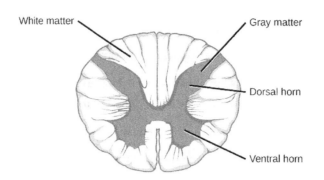

*Comparison of gray (unmyelinated) matter and white (myelinated) matter*

**Descending and ascending tracts connect the brain and spinal cord**

Tracts conduct impulses between the brain and the spinal nerves; ascending tracts are *dorsal*, and descending tracts from the brain are *ventral*.

*Ascending tracts* of the lower brain centers relay sensory information to the primary somatosensory area.

*Descending tracts* from the primary motor area communicate with the lower brain centers.

Near the brain, tracts cross over from one side of the body to the other; therefore, the left side of the brain controls the right side of the body.

*Afferent fibers* enter from the peripheral system on the dorsal side of the spinal cord *via* dorsal roots (containing the dorsal root ganglia).

*Efferent fibers* leave the spinal cord on the ventral side via the ventral roots. The two roots combine to form a spinal nerve on each side of the spinal cord.

There are 31 pairs of spinal nerves, designated by 4 levels of exit: cervical (8), thoracic (12), lumbar (5), sacral (5), and coccygeal (1).

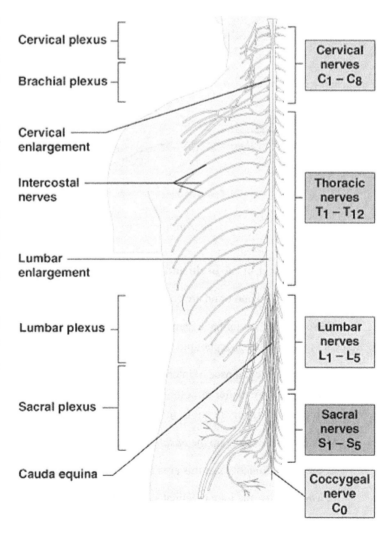

## Perception of Sensations

### Psychophysics and experimental psychology

The field of psychophysics was founded in the mid-1800s by Gustav Theodor Fechner, a German physicist, psychologist, and philosopher. His experiments started the field of psychophysics and the broader field of *experimental psychology*.

*Psychophysics* is the quantitative study of the relationship between physical and psychological events. Specifically, it refers to the study of stimuli and the resulting sensations and perceptions of an organism.

The main areas of study within psychophysics are a threshold, Weber's law, signal detection theory, and sensory adaptation.

### Threshold and detecting stimuli

The threshold is the intensity that must be exceeded for a reaction or phenomenon to occur.

*Sensory threshold* refers to the weakest stimulus that can be detected by an organism 50% of the time.

*An absolute threshold* is the weakest stimulus that can be detected at a certain percentage (often 50%) of the time when there is initially no stimulus present.

A typical hearing test, for example, plays beeps at increasing volume levels.

The test-taker is instructed to indicate when first hearing a beep. A hearing test of this variety seeks to measure the absolute threshold for hearing, which is why there is initially no sound.

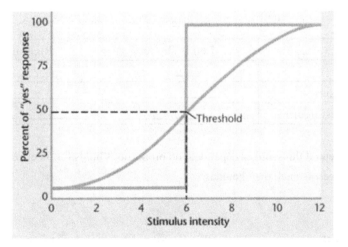

*Sensory threshold plotting perception vs. stimulus intensity*

*Differential threshold* is the level at which an organism can perceive a change in an already-detected stimulus and detect it half of the time.

An example is when one notices an increase in a room's temperature.

The point at which this temperature difference is detected subtracted by the original temperature is the differential threshold.

The differential threshold is the magnitude of the intensity between the original and the final stimuli.

*Terminal threshold* refers to the upper limit at which a stimulus can no longer be detected.

For example, if a person touches a hot stove, the pain would be felt instead of heat because the terminal threshold for temperature has been exceeded.

The highest pitch that a person can hear is the terminal threshold for pitch.

**Weber's law of just noticeable differences**

Initially proposed for weightlifting, *Weber's law* (named after German physician Ernst Heinrich Weber, founder of experimental psychology) posits that the differential threshold for an individual is dependent on proportion, not the amount.

For example, if a weightlifter notices when one pound is added to the ten-pound weight that he was lifting, then according to Weber's law, he noticed that when two pounds are added to a twenty-pound weight.

For this reason, Weber's law is the *law of just noticeable differences*.

Weber's law was later applied to sensations. Although it does not hold entirely true for sound or high or low-intensity stimuli, Weber's law is generally accurate for sight, touch, taste, and smell.

One typical experiment in which Weber's law is generally supported involves having a test subject judge two lines, with one line longer than the other. This is repeated with a longer set of lines.

Findings show that the difference in these larger lines must be proportional to the smaller lines for participants to notice that one is longer. The proportion of change necessary to notice a difference varies.

Weber's law for detecting proportional differences

|  | Left is shorter | Right is longer |
|---|---|---|
| Obvious | ____ | ____ |
| Less obvious | _____ | _____ |
| Hard to distinguish | _____ | _____ |

The same differential threshold as dependent on proportions holds for other senses. A dog, for example, detects more subtle changes in smell than humans.

**Signal detection theory**

*Signal detection theory* aims to uncover the internal and external mechanisms that contribute to sensation and perception.

It posits that the detection of a given stimulus is partly dependent on the intensity of the stimulus.

For example, a loud noise is more likely to be detected than a soft noise, and a temperature change of 10 °F is more likely to be detected than a change of 2 °F.

Signal detection theory proposes that the psychological state of experiencing the stimuli affects how it is perceived. For example, someone walking alone at night in an unsafe neighborhood likely experiences a soft noise as subjectively louder than the same noise during the day.

This theory is significant because it notes that past experiences and expectations influence perceptions.

Signal detection theory has applications for researchers seeking to understand sensation by lab experiments. These researchers often begin perception experiments with a *signal detection test*.

In each trial of the test, a stimulus is either presented to or withheld from a participant. The participant is instructed to indicate whether he perceived a stimulus at each trial.

Through repeated trials, a *receiver operating characteristic* curve is plotted, providing information to the researchers on detecting various stimuli. This curve provides a unique baseline for each participant and allows researchers to study perception accurately. Sensory systems are constantly recalibrating based on the environment.

**Sensory adaptation**

*Sensory adaptation* is the ability to recalibrate when a constant stimulus persists over time as receptors respond by decreasing their sensitivity to the stimulus. This ability of receptors to adapt is found in all sensory receptors, apart from pain receptors.

A person does not generally notice the sensation of clothes on the skin because skin receptors have adapted to this constant stimulus by reducing their sensitivity. Similarly, a friend's house may have a specific smell associated with it. However, the people living in the house often cannot detect it because their olfactory receptors have adapted.

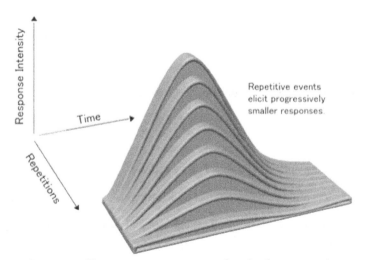

*Sensory adaptations illustrate receptors responding by decreasing their sensitivity*

Sensory adaptation can be observed in the visual system. When in the dark, the concentration of the light-sensing chemical in the rods and cones in the eye increases. This leads to increased sensitivity and the ability to see with acuity.

Dark adaptation occurs in cones within about ten minutes, while rods can take up to thirty minutes to become fully adapted.

## Sensory Receptors of the Nervous System

### Sensation by intensity, location, duration and adaption

Sensory systems encode for four aspects of a stimulus. *Type* (or modality) is the first aspect of a stimulus.

The stimulus is primarily encoded by the kind of receptor it activates. For example, taste is encoded by taste receptors, while smell is encoded by odor receptors.

*Intensity* is the second aspect of a stimulus. An increased stimulus results in a larger receptor potential, leading to a higher frequency of action potential.

Stronger stimuli affect a larger area and recruit more receptors.

*Location* is the third aspect of a stimulus encoded by the stimulated receptor site.

*Acuity* is the precision of location, negatively correlated with convergence in ascending neural pathways, the receptive field's size, and overlap with adjacent receptive fields. The response is highest at the center of the receptive field since receptor density is highest.

*Lateral inhibition* increases acuity when excited neurons reduce the activity of neighboring neurons.

*Duration* is the fourth aspect of a stimulus encoded by two types of receptors: rapid adapting receptors and slow adapting receptors.

*Rapid adapting receptors* respond quickly at the onset of a stimulus but slow down gradually during the remainder of the stimulus.

*Slow adapting receptors* maintain responses at or near the initial firing level for the stimulus's duration.

Rapid adapting receptors are critical for signaling rapid change, while slow adapting receptors are essential for signaling slow changes.

### Sensory classifications by receptor, location or stimulus detected

*Sensory receptors* are nerve endings that respond to an internal or external stimulus.

Three methods classify sensory receptors: 1) receptor complexity, 2) location, and 3) stimulus detected. An example of complex receptors is the encapsulated nerve endings with a physical specialization.

Less complex receptors are free nerve endings of dendrites as terminal ends without specialization.

*Exteroceptors* are at or near the skin's surface and respond to stimuli occurring on the body's surface. Exteroceptors encode for tactile sensations and vision, hearing, smell, and taste.

*Interoceptors* respond to stimuli occurring inside visceral organs and blood vessels. For example, receptors within the GI tract carry signals to the brain relating to feelings of hunger. Interoceptors are associated with the autonomic nervous system.

*Proprioceptors* respond to internal stimuli occurring in skeletal muscles, tendons, ligaments, and joints and can detect the position of a body part in space.

**Categorical types of sensory receptors based on stimuli**

When classifying receptors by the stimuli they detect, receptors are grouped into five categories.

*Mechanoreceptors* respond to touch and pressure and can rapidly adapt or slow adapting receptors.

*Photoreceptors* respond to light.

*Thermoreceptors* respond to temperature and temperature changes. One thermoreceptor responds to increases in temperature, while another responds to decreases.

*Chemoreceptors* respond to taste, smell, and changes in blood chemistry. Chemoreceptors are in animals, and chemoreception is the most primitive sense.

*Nociceptors* respond to pain and tissue damage.

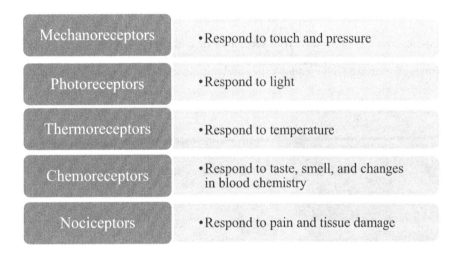

The skin contains receptors close to the surface (the boundary between the dermis and the epidermis). However, mechanoreceptors that respond to pressure are deeper in the dermis.

Proprioceptors, mechanoreceptors, photoreceptors, thermoreceptors, chemoreceptors, and nociceptors are *somatic sensors* and are part of the *somatosensory system.*

**Sensory pathways in the brain and spinal column**

A *sensory unit* is made of a single neuron and its receptor endings. When stimulated, a sensory unit brings about activity in its neuron's receptive field within the brain.

For example, when the retina cells' receptive field is stimulated, associated neurons in the visual cortex of the occipital lobe are activated so that the sensory input is interpreted.

Specific pathways are needed for each of the senses and types of stimuli. Sensory information is carried through the spinal cord to higher levels of the brain through *ascending pathways*. Via these pathways, information from taste cells is transmitted to the parietal lobe.

Information from the eyes is transmitted to the occipital lobe, and information from the ears is transmitted to the temporal lobe.

Ascending pathways for touch are the posterior column, anterolateral, and spinocerebellar pathways.

- The *posterior column pathway* carries fine touch, vibration, pressure, and proprioceptive (position of body parts) sensations from the skin and joints.

  Information is transmitted to the cerebral cortex's postcentral gyrus via first-order, second-order, and third-order neurons.

- The *anterolateral pathway* (or *spinothalamic tract*) carries sensations of pain, temperature, and poorly localized touch.

  Information travels from the skin through the ventral posterolateral nucleus in the thalamus to the somatosensory cortex of the postcentral gyrus. The spinothalamic tract consists of two adjacent pathways: an anterior and a lateral pathway. The anterior pathway carries poorly localized touch sensations, while the lateral pathway carries information about pain and temperature.

- The *spinocerebellar pathway* carries sensations of limb and joint position.

  Information from the Golgi tendon organ and muscle spindles is conveyed to the cerebellum.

| Posterior column pathway | • Carries fine touch, vibration, pressure, and proprioceptive sensations<br>• Information is sent to the postcentral gyrus of the cerebral cortex |
|---|---|
| Anterolateral pathway | • Carries sensations of pain, temperature, and poorly localized touch<br>• Information is sent to the somatosensory cortex of the postcentral gyrus |
| Spinocerebellar pathway | • Carries sensations concerning limb and joint position<br>• Information is sent to the cerebellum |

## Hearing and the Perception of Sound

**Ear structure and function**

The human ear has three main parts: the *outer ear*, the *middle ear,* and the *inner ear*. The outer ear is what most people think of when they think of an ear. The outer ear consists of the pinna and the auditory canal.

The *pinna* (or *auricle*) is the visible region outside the head. Its role is to direct and amplify sound waves.

The *auditory canal* is the opening of the ear, lined with fine hairs that filter the air. The auditory canal contains modified sweat glands that secrete earwax (cerumen) to guard against foreign matter.

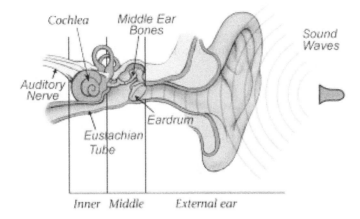

*Anatomy of the human ear with external (outer), middle and inner ear*

The *middle ear cavity* is filled with air and contains three tiny bones known collectively as *ossicles*.

These bones of the middle ear cavity are the *malleus* (or hammer), *incus* (or anvil), and *stapes* (or stirrup).

Ossicles convert vibrations of the *eardrum* (or *tympanic membrane*) into waves of fluid in the inner ear.

The *auditory tube* (or *eustachian*) extends from the middle ear to the pharynx equalizing the outer ear.

The *oval window* (or *vestibular window*) is a membrane-covered opening separating the middle and inner ear.

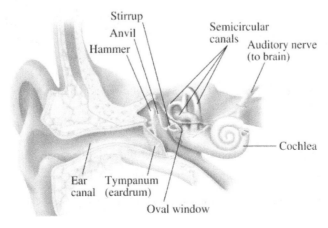

*Human ear showing ossicles, semicircular canals and cochlea*

**Inner ear structure and function**

The inner ear contains the *bony labyrinth*, a hollow cavity in the skull's temporal bone.

The bony labyrinth has two main functional parts: the cochlea and the vestibular system.

The *cochlea* is spiral-shaped and houses the cochlear duct containing the *organ of Corti*.

The organ of Corti has *stereocilia* hair cells.

Afferent neurons from these hair cells form the *cochlear nerve*.

The cochlea's upper compartment is the *scala vestibuli*, a fluid-filled cavity that conducts sound vibrations to the *cochlear duct*.

The cochlear duct transforms this vibrational energy into electrical energy and sends signals to the brain.

The *vestibular system* of the bony labyrinth is composed of three perpendicular semicircular canals and critical for the sense of balance.

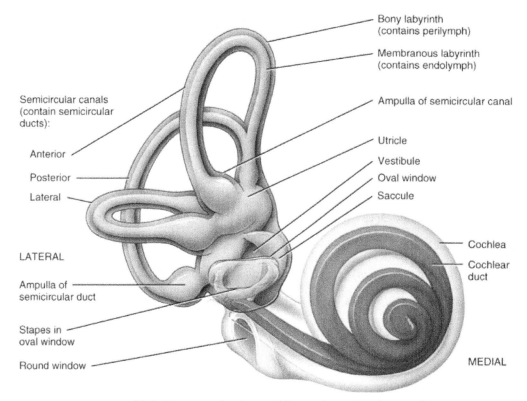

*Right inner ear showing cochlea and semicircular canals*

**Hearing process**

The hearing process begins when sound waves enter the auditory canal, hitting the tympanic membrane (eardrum) and causing it to vibrate. These vibrations move to the ossicles.

The sound is amplified about twenty times by the size difference between the tympanic membrane and the oval window.

The stapes strike the oval window's membrane, passing pressure waves to the fluid in the cochlea.

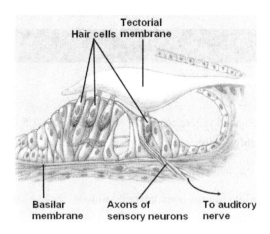

*Anatomy of the human ear with hair cells and tectorial membrane relationship*

When the stapes strikes the membrane of the oval window, pressure waves move from the vestibular canal to the tympanic canal and across the *basilar membrane*, the base for these hair cells, causing the round window to bulge.

This excites the stereocilia, which bend from the vibration of the basilar membrane. This bending of the stereocilia generates nerve impulses in the cochlear nerve that travels to the brain stem.

**Measuring sound and auditory pathways in the brain**

| Source | Sound Level (dB) | Intensity (W/m²) |
|---|---|---|
| Nearby jet airplane | 150 | 1000 |
| Machine gun | 130 | 10 |
| Siren, rock concert (**Threshold of Pain**) | 120 | 1 |
| Subway, power mower | 100 | $1 \times 10^{-2}$ |
| Busy traffic | 80 | $1 \times 10^{-4}$ |
| Vacuum | 70 | $1 \times 10^{-5}$ |
| Normal conversation | 50 | $1 \times 10^{-7}$ |
| Mosquito buzzing | 40 | $1 \times 10^{-8}$ |
| Whisper | 30 | $1 \times 10^{-9}$ |
| Rustling leaves | 10 | $1 \times 10^{-11}$ |
| **Threshold of hearing** | 0 | $1 \times 10^{-12}$ |

*Perception of sound by human ear*

When nerve impulses traveling from the cochlear nerve into the brainstem reach the auditory areas of the cerebral cortex, the information is interpreted as sound.

This occurs via the *primary auditory pathway*, which starts in the cochlea and moves through the vestibulocochlear nerve to the superior olivary complex.

A neuron carries the message to the *mesencephalon*, which forms a major component of the midbrain. The primary auditory cortex receives the message.

The organ of Corti is varied in structure, so areas are sensitive to different pitches. The organ of Corti's narrow base detects high pitch, while the wide tip detects low pitch. The nerve fibers from these regions lead to slightly different activations in the brain, producing the sensation of pitch.

The magnitude of vibrations detects sound volume. Increased stimulation of receptors is interpreted as louder, while decreased stimulation is interpreted as softer.

The brain detects the tone based on the distribution of the hair cells stimulated, allowing a person to differentiate the sound of a piano from that of a violin, even if the two instruments are playing the same tune at the same volume.

## Visual Perception

### Eye structure and function

The human eye is an elongated sphere measuring approximately 2.5 cm in diameter. Although similar to a camera, the eye is a considerably complex network of interconnected parts.

The eye is contained by the *orbit*, a pear-shaped structure that is formed by several bones.

The *sclera* is the outer, white fibrous layer covering most of the eye for protection.

The *cornea* is the transparent part of the sclera at the front of the eye. It is conceptualized as the "window of the eye." The cornea focuses light on the retina and acts as a protective covering.

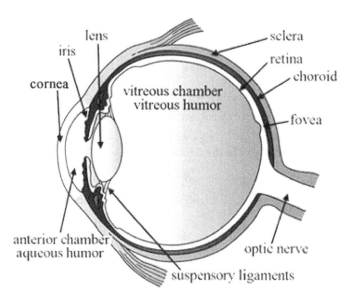

*Anatomy of the human eye*

The *pupil* is the black circle in the middle of the eye that dilates and constricts in response to changing light levels. The size of the pupil determines the amount of light that can enter the eye.

The dark brown inner layer of the eye is the *choroid* containing blood vessels and pigments that absorb stray light rays. The choroid thickens to form a ring-shaped ciliary body, which becomes the *iris*.

The iris is the pigmented area of the eye that surrounds the pupil. The iris controls the amount of light allowed into the eye by dilating and constricting the pupil using the *papillary sphincter* and *dilator muscles*.

Stimulation of the sympathetic nerves dilates the pupil to let in more light when the environment is dark. In contrast, stimulation of the parasympathetic nerves constricts the pupil to allow in less light when the environment is bright.

The *lens* sits behind the iris and aids in focusing refracted light onto the retina. It divides the eye into two chambers: aqueous humor and vitreous humor.

The *aqueous humor* nourishes the cornea and fills the anterior cavity. Blocking outflow of the aqueous humor results in increased pressure in the eye or *glaucoma*.

The *vitreous humor*, which is jelly-like and protects the shape of the eye, fills the posterior cavity.

The lens focuses light onto the retina by thickening (for nearby objects) and thinning (for distant objects).

The *retina* is a thin layer of tissue that sits behind the lens and is responsible for interpreting visual stimuli. The retina contains blood vessels and cells that sense light.

The retina contains the *fovea centralis*, which produces color vision in daylight. Considerable processing occurs in the retina before an impulse is sent to the brain.

**Visual acuity and image perception**

*Myopia* (nearsightedness) is when people see objects well when close but not when they are far away. This is often due to an elongated eyeball that focuses a distant image in front of the retina. A new treatment of radial keratotomy surgically cuts and flattens the cornea to correct this issue.

*Hyperopia* (farsightedness) is when people see objects well when they are far away but not close. This is often due to a shortened eyeball that focuses images behind the retina.

*Astigmatism* occurs when the cornea or lens is uneven, causing images to blur.

*Cataracts* occur when the lens becomes opaque due to new cells forming within it. Light can no longer enter through the lens. If (due to age) the lens loses its elasticity and can no longer assume a spherical shape, near vision is lost. This type of vision loss is *presbyopia*.

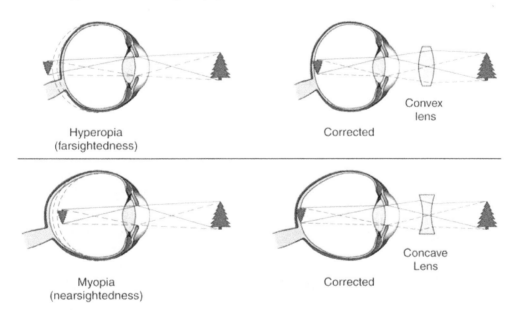

*Conditions associated with visual perception*

**Cones and rods for light and color perception**

Vision begins when light becomes focused on photoreceptors in the retina.

*Photoreceptors* are cells that sense light by detecting the presence and intensity of light. Photoreceptors are on the back of the retina, which picks up photons of light via the 130,000,000 rods and cones situated on it.

Photoreceptors sense light because they contain *photopigments*, which absorb light. There are four types of photopigments: rhodopsin, blue-sensitive pigment, green-sensitive pigment, and red-sensitive pigment.

These photopigments are contained within two types of photoreceptors: rods and cones. Rods and cones have an outer segment joined to an inner segment by a stalk. The outer segment contains stacks of *lamellae*, membranous disks with molecules of rhodopsin.

*Rhodopsin* molecules contain the protein *opsin* and the pigment molecule *retinal*, the chromatophore molecule, derived from vitamin A.

*Cones* are responsible for sharp vision and color vision. They are primarily located in the *macula*, an extremely sensitive retina area. They are contained in the *fovea*, an area within the macula. There are three kinds of cones containing blue, green, or red pigment.

These pigments are composed of rhodopsin and opsin, with varying opsin structures allowing for the absorption of different wavelengths of light. Intermediate colors stimulate combinations of cones; the brain interprets the combined nerve impulses as one of 17,000 hues. Humans and other primates are animals having color vision.

*Rods* are responsible for peripheral and night vision. Rods are more sensitive to light than cones but do not provide detailed images or detect color.

When a rod absorbs light, rhodopsin splits into opsin and retinal, leading to the closure of ion channels in the rod cell plasma membrane. This produces signals that result in impulses to the brain.

Rods are grouped outside of the macula in the periphery of the retina.

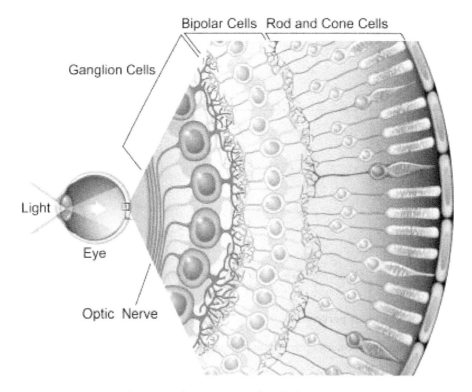

*Anatomy of structures within the human eye*

## Visual image processing

Light rays enter the eye through the cornea, which bends them due to its curved surface to freely pass through the pupil (the opening in the center of the iris with the ability to dilate and constrict depending on how much light is passing through). Light rays pass through the lens.

The shape of the lens is controlled by the *ciliary muscle*, which relaxes when viewing distant objects, causing the lens to flatten.

The lens becomes rounder when viewing near objects where light rays must bend to a greater degree. This change is *visual accommodation*.

Once light rays have passed through the lens, they pass through the vitreous humor.

Light rays focus on the retina.

Due to refraction, the retina image is inverted 180 degrees, corrected in the brain.

Once rods and cones have sensed the light within the retina, this sensory information needs to be transmitted to the brain to translate into vision.

The retina has three layers of neurons transmitting this information by rods and cones near the choroid, *bipolar cells,* and *ganglion cells.*

Since only rod and cone cells are sensitive to light, light must penetrate through the ganglion cells.

When a rod absorbs light, rhodopsin splits into opsin and retinal, leading to a cascade of reactions and the closure of ion channels in the rod cell plasma membrane. This stops the release of inhibitory molecules from the rod's synaptic vesicles, which starts signals that result in impulses to the brain.

Rods and cones synapse with bipolar cells, creating a hyperpolarization that activates the retinal (the pigment molecule) and causes it to change its shape.

After the retinal is activated, it changes to its resting shape, and the photoreceptor cell is depolarized.

## Integration of signals by ganglion cells

Bipolar cells pass the information to ganglion cells. Through this process, integration occurs.

Many rods can synapse with a single ganglion cell, resulting in indistinct vision.

However, each cone synapses with one ganglion cell, resulting in clear vision.

There are more rods and cones than nerve fibers leaving ganglionic cells.

If rod cells in a receptive field are stimulated, the ganglion cell is weakly stimulated or remains neutral.

If the center of the receptive field is lit, the ganglion cell is stimulated.

If only the edges of the receptive field are lit, the cell is inhibited.

Historically, visual perception was believed to encompass only what was seen by the eye externally. It was believed that these external stimuli directly produce a perception in the brain.

However, from the discoveries of science, it is now known that this is not accurate. Information from the eye is a physiological process; significant processing of the signals that the eye receives occurs in the brain.

To reach the brain, the ganglion cells produce an action potential. This is the first step in the pathway from the eye to the brain.

Axons from the ganglion cells form the optic nerve.

The *optic nerve* is a pathway that crosses to the opposite side of the brain at the *optic chiasm*.

Thus, information stemming from the right side of the visual field is sent to the left half of the brain, and information stemming from the left side of the visual field is sent to the right half of the brain.

**Optic nerve and parallel processing**

A *blind spot* is an area where the optic nerve passes through the retina that lacks rods and cones.

The brain combines information from both eyes to compensate for this blind spot.

Information from the optic nerve travels through the optic tract and terminates in the thalamus's lateral geniculate nucleus. This information is sent from the thalamus to the occipital lobe's visual cortex.

Here, a visual association area compares new visual information with old information.

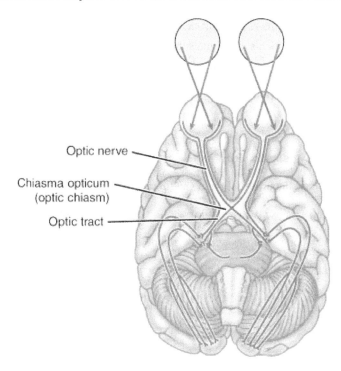

*Perception of sight and processing by the brain*

Once visual information has been transmitted through this pathway, the brain processes the inverted image from the retina and makes it appear upright. The brain combines the two images from each eye to form a 3D image, which judges distance.

*Parallel processing* is the brain's ability to process differing quality stimuli simultaneously. This helps a person to perceive the world in a unified way rather than in disjointed pieces.

In vision, information is divided into color, motion, shape, and depth.

Each component is analyzed individually by the brain. This new information is compared with stored memories to identify the stimuli better.

These four components (color, motion, shape, and depth) are integrated to form a complete image without analyzing each component individually.

Some researchers hypothesize that before these separate processes become integrated, they are stored as memories to help the brain recognize the image.

*Feature detection* is the brain's way of filtering visual information for important objects.

Feature detection can be conceptualized as focusing on common elements across instances of an object.

For example, if someone sees ten cats, each a different size and color, they still know that they are cats.

Similarly, one can identify the letter "a" below, regardless of the font.

**a a *a* a a a a**

*Example of feature detection*

It is hypothesized that this process is via *feature detectors*, specialized neurons in the visual cortex that encodes certain features such as lines, angles, and movements.

## Senses of Touch, Taste, Smell and Balance

**Sensation of touch**

*Somatosensation* is the comprehensive sensory system of touch, specifically pain, temperature, vibration, and body position; the types of receptors part of the somatosensory system include nociceptors, thermoreceptors, proprioceptors, and mechanoreceptors.

**Taste bud anatomy and function**

The sense of taste is useful from an evolutionary perspective. Potentially harmful foods tend to taste bitter, while high-calorie foods tend to taste sweet, increasing an organism's chance of survival. The sensation of taste begins with *taste buds*, as they contain the receptors for taste.

Taste buds are primarily on the tongue, specifically along the walls of *papillae*, small elevations on the surface of the tongue.

Isolated taste buds are on the hard palate, pharynx, and epiglottis surfaces and contained by *epithelium*.

Taste buds contain multiple taste cells, which open at a taste pore. Particles of food dissolved in saliva encountering taste receptors.

Taste receptors detect five elements of taste: sweet, sour, salty, bitter, and umami (i.e., savory). Taste buds for these elements are concentrated regions of the tongue, and these elements are organized into independent pathways. The brain appears to take an overall weighted average of taste messages to form the perceived taste.

Taste is a form of *chemoreception* because chemical signals are transduced into action potentials.

Elongated taste cells contain hair-like *microvilli* that bear receptor proteins.

These receptor proteins sense certain chemicals. Microvilli release neurotransmitters to send signals to the brain.

Primary sensory axons for taste run through the facial, glossopharyngeal, and vagus nerves. This information is primarily transmitted to the gustatory cortex in the neocortex.

Taste information moves through the thalamus and is received by two frontal lobe regions: the insula and the frontal operculum cortex.

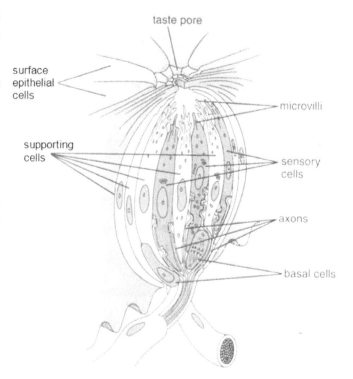

*Taste buds and neural processing*

**Olfactory cells process smells**

*Olfactory cells* are modified bipolar neurons in the *epithelium* (mucous membrane) on the nasal cavity roof. Olfactory cells are a form of chemoreceptor because they detect chemicals.

Humans have about 40 million olfactory cells that can detect over one trillion odors. Olfactory cells are covered in tufts of long, non-motile cilia containing receptor proteins for an odor molecule.

Olfactory cells contain one type of odor receptor. There are approximately 400 types of olfactory receptors in human.

When chemicals enter the nostrils, they become trapped in the nasal cavity's mucus, where they dissolve. These molecules bind to the cilia receptors, causing cell depolarization and creating an action potential.

Information is passed to the olfactory cortex within the limbic system through a pathway in the brain.

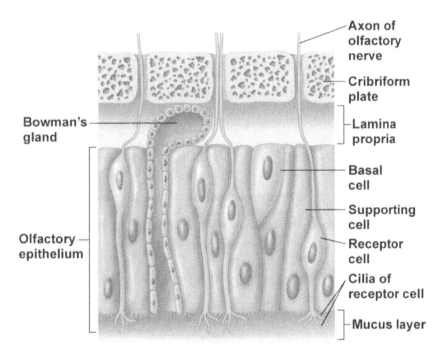

*Cells involved in the sense of smell*

The sense of smell is supplemented by taste, as the same substances often stimulate the receptors for taste and smell.

A person loses the sense of taste while sick with a cold, often due to olfactory deficiencies.

**Pheromones influence behavior**

*Pheromones* are chemicals secreted in sweat and other bodily fluids and influence the body of the organism secreting them.

In many animals, pheromones play a crucial role in behavior, particularly for sex, fear, and food.

Pheromones play a role in mate attraction; some organisms can release pheromones that attract potential mates from over two miles away.

Pheromones mark territories; dogs and cats spray their pheromone-filled urine on objects.

There is research to suggest that pheromones influence human behavior. A widely known study conducted by Martha McClintock suggested that women's menstrual cycle could be altered, depending on what pheromones the women were exposed to. The methodology of this study has, however, been questioned.

It has been hypothesized that women prefer the smell of men who have genetically encoded immunity (i.e., innate immunity) different from theirs because this results in disease-resistant children.

Pheromones in non-humans are detected by olfactory membranes, as well as by the *vomeronasal organ*.

In adult humans, the vomeronasal organ appears shrunk or absent, suggesting that it is through the normal olfactory process if humans can sense pheromones.

**Olfactory pathways in the brain**

The olfactory pathway is not yet well understood; however, it is known that once the cilia have detected sensory information, it is transferred to the olfactory bulb through openings in the *cribriform plate*, a part of the skull at the top of the nasal cavity.

The *olfactory bulb* is at the base of the brain and is in direct contact with the limbic system.

The limbic system is involved in adrenaline flow, emotion, behavior, and long-term memory.

It is hypothesized that the olfactory bulb's connection with the limbic system is why smells are associated with strong emotions and memories.

Input in the olfactory bulb is transferred through the lateral olfactory tract to the primary olfactory cortex.

The information travels through the thalamus, where interneurons communicate this information to the orbital frontal cortex, where conscious smell perception occurs.

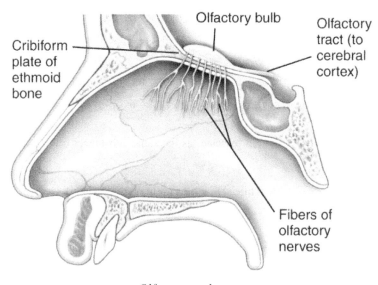

*Olfactory pathways*

## Kinesthetic and vestibular sense

The *kinesthetic sense* is the body's perception of its position, including the movement of joints, muscles, and tendons. Even when one's eyes are closed, the brain can sense where parts of the body are.

*Proprioception* (kinesthetic sense) provides constant feedback to the brain of the muscles in the body. Much of this information is subconscious.

Proprioceptors provide sensory information about joint angle, muscle length, and muscle tension. Information from the body is transmitted from these proprioceptors to the brain's parietal cortex, where information about the position of body parts is interpreted.

The channel through which this transmission of information occurs is still being studied, although it is hypothesized to be a similar pathway to touch.

The *vestibular sense* refers to the awareness of balance and spatial orientation. Sensory information for this sense primarily originates in the inner ear, but visual and proprioceptive information is used.

## Dynamic and static equilibrium

The sense of balance is divided into dynamic equilibrium and static equilibrium.

*Dynamic equilibrium* is the rotational movement of the head and utilizes the semicircular canals. The enlarged bases of the canals are *ampullae* (ampulla, singular). Fluid within the canals causes the stereocilia of the hair cells to bend. The vestibular nerve carries this information to the brain.

*The vestibular sense assists in balance and spatial orientation*

*Static equilibrium* involves vertical and horizontal movement and is detected when the head moves with reference to gravity. Static equilibrium utilizes the utricle and the saccule by the *maculae* (specialized mechanoreceptors) within them.

The *utricle* and the *saccule* are small membranous sacs with hair cells. The utricle is sensitive to horizontal movements, while the saccule is sensitive to vertical movements. Small carbon granules that rest on a gelatinous membrane containing hair cells are displaced when movement occurs. This bends the hair cells and indicates the direction of movement.

Information from static equilibrium and dynamic equilibrium hair cells is transmitted to the parietal lobe. There, it is integrated with sensory information stemming from other areas of the body to provides a sense of movement and balance.

*Notes for active learning*

# CHAPTER 16

# Skeletal System

- Skeletal System Structure and Function
- Skeletal Structure
- Bone Structure and Composition
- Endocrine Control of the Skeletal System

## Skeletal System Structure and Function

### Structural rigidity and support

The bones provide a rigid framework for the body and allow the movement of muscles anchored to them.

For example, the large leg bones support the body against the pull of gravity.

The leg and arm bones permit flexible body movement, pelvis bones support the trunk, and the atlas (i.e., 1$^{st}$ vertebra) supports the skull.

### Bones store calcium under hormonal influence

Bones store essential minerals needed to sustain life (e.g., calcium, phosphorus, and others). Bones are critical in maintaining calcium homeostasis. When blood calcium is low, parathyroid hormones (PTH) signals the osteoclasts of bone to break down the bone matrix and release calcium.

Most of the Ca$^{2+}$ in the body is stored in the bone matrix as *hydroxyapatite*.

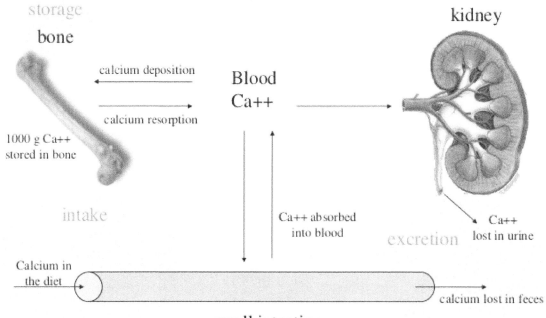

*Calcium homeostasis with calcium stored in bone*

### Skeleton provides physical protection

One of the skeletal system functions is to protect the internal organs.

The rib cage protects delicate internal organs, including the heart and the lungs.

The skull protects the brain, and the spine protects the spinal cord.

Many large bones shelter bone marrow, which contains stem cells needed to produce blood.

## Skeletal Structure

### Basic anatomy of the skeletal system

The skeletal system has three main components: bone, cartilage, and joints. *Bone* is a tough, rigid form of connective tissue that gives the human skeleton its strength.

*Cartilage* is a form of connective tissue but is not rigid and tough compared to the bone.

*Joints* are where bones connect, allowing the skeletal system to be mobile.

The human vertebrate skeletal system divides into the axial (midline) and appendicular skeletons.

The *axial skeleton* at the body's midline consists of the skull, vertebral column, sternum, and rib cage.

The cranium and the facial bones form the skull.

Additionally, newborns have membranous junctions as *fontanels* that usually close by the age of two.

The bones of the cranium contain *sinuses*, air spaces lined with mucous membranes that reduce the skull's weight. Sinuses give a resonant sound to the voice.

Two mastoid sinuses drain into the middle ear; *mastoiditis* is an inflammation of sinuses that can lead to deafness.

The cranium comprises eight bones: one frontal, two parietal, one occipital, two temporal, one sphenoid, and one ethmoid bone.

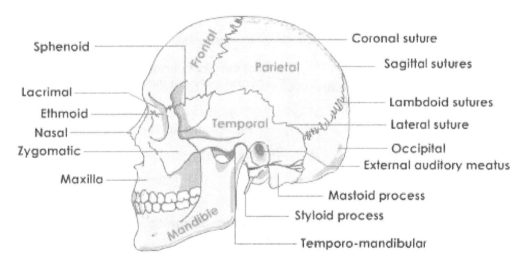

The spinal cord passes through the *foramen magnum*, an opening at the skull base in the *occipital bone*.

Each *temporal bone* has an opening that leads to the middle ear.

The *sphenoid bone* completes the skull's sides and forms the floors and walls of the eye sockets.

The *ethmoid bone*, in front of the sphenoid, is part of the orbital wall and part of the nasal septum.

**Facial bones**

There are fourteen facial bones, including one mandible, two maxillae, two palatines, two zygomatic, two lacrimal, two nasal, and one vomer.

The *mandible* bone (lower jaw) is the movable portion of the skull; it contains tooth sockets.

The *maxilla* bone forms the upper jaw and the anterior of the hard palate; it contains tooth sockets.

The *palatine* bones make up the posterior portion of the hard palate and the floor of the nasal cavity.

The *zygomatic* bone gives the prominence of the cheekbones. *Nasal* bones form the bridge of the nose.

Other bones make up the nasal septum, which divides the nasal cavity into two regions.

The ears are elastic cartilage and lack bone, whereas the nose is a mixture of bone, cartilage, and fibrous connective tissue.

**Vertebral column anatomy**

The *vertebral column* supports the head and trunk and protects the spinal cord and roots of the spinal nerves. The vertebral column serves as an anchor for the other bones of the skeleton.

There are seven *cervical vertebrae* in the neck.

The twelve *thoracic vertebrae* are in the thorax (or chest).

The *lumbar vertebrae* are in the small of the back.

One *sacrum* is formed from five fused *sacral vertebrae.*

One *coccyx* is formed from four fused *coccygeal vertebrae.*

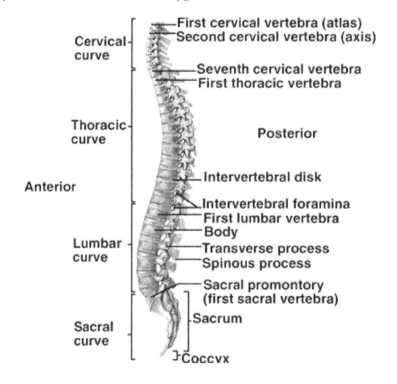

Typically, the spinal column has four normal curvatures that provide strength and resiliency in posture.

*Scoliosis* is a sideways curvature; *hunchback* and *swayback* are conditions of the spinal column.

*Intervertebral discs* between the vertebrae act as padding to prevent the vertebrae from grinding against each other and absorb physical shock. Intervertebral discs weaken with age.

In contrast, *vertebral discs* allow for motion between vertebrae for movement, such as bending forward.

The *rib cage* protects the heart and lungs yet is flexible enough to allow breathing. Twelve pairs of ribs connect directly to the *thoracic vertebrae* in the back; seven pairs of ribs attach directly to the sternum.

Three pairs connect to the sternum indirectly via cartilage at the front of the sternum.

There are two pairs of ribs (floating ribs) unattached to the sternum and attach to the vertebrae.

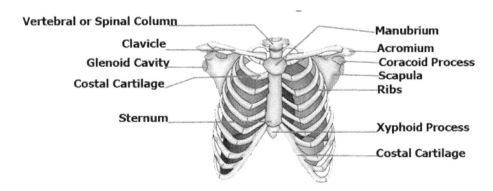

*Rib cage with twelve pairs of ribs*

## Appendicular skeleton

The *appendicular skeleton* consists of the bones within the pectoral girdle, the pelvic girdle, and the upper and lower limbs.

The *pectoral girdle* is specialized for flexibility and built for strength. Ligaments loosely link the components of the pectoral girdle. The *clavicle* (collarbone) connects with the *sternum* in the front and the *scapula* in the back. The scapula is held in place by muscles and can move freely.

The *humerus* is the long bone of the upper arm; its rounded head fits into a socket of the scapula.

The *radius* is lateral of bone in the lower arm (i.e., the forearm); it articulates with the humerus at the elbow joint (a hinge joint), and the radius crosses in front of the ulna for easy twisting.

The *ulna* (elbow bone) is the medial of the two bones in the lower arm. The larger end of the ulna joins with the humerus to make the elbow joint.

The flexibility of the hand is attributable to the presence of many bones.

The wrist has eight *carpal bones* that look like small pebbles.

Five *metacarpal bones* fan out to form the framework of the palm.

The *phalanges* are the bones of the fingers and thumb.

The *pelvic girdle* consists of two heavy, large coxal (hip) bones.

The *coxal bones* are anchored to the *sacrum*; together with the sacrum, they form a hollow cavity that is wider in females than in males. It transmits weight from the vertebral column via the sacrum to the legs.

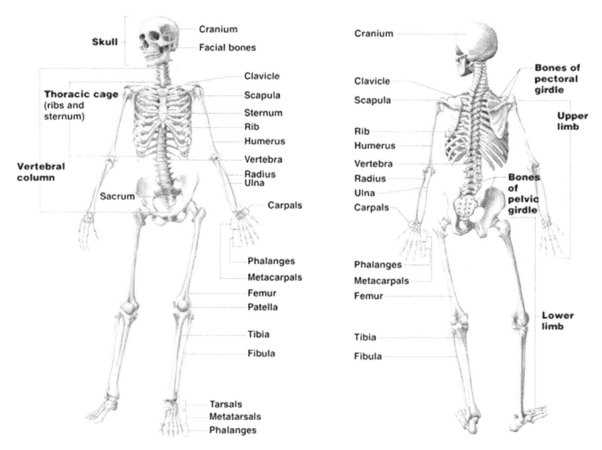

*Human adult skeletal system: anterior view (left) and posterior view (right)*

The *femur* is the largest, longest, and strongest bone of the body; however, it is limited in the amount of weight it can support.

The *patella* is the kneecap and is a thick, roughly triangular bone that allows for knee extension.

The *tibia* has a ridge called the "shin"; its end forms the inside of the ankle. The shin bone is strong.

The *fibula* is the smaller of the two bones; its end forms the outside of the ankle.

There are seven *tarsal bones* in the ankle. In standing or walking, tarsal bones receive the weight and pass it to the heel and ball of the foot.

The *metatarsal bones* form the arch of the foot and provide a springy base.

The *phalanges* are the bones of the toes, which are stouter than those of the fingers.

## Bone structure and function

Bones are classified by their shape.

*Long bones* consist of a *diaphysis* (shaft) with two ends shaped like rods.

Examples include the thigh (femur), upper arm (humerus), and finger bones (phalanges).

The *diaphysis* of the bone consists of a central medullary cavity filled with *fatty tissue* (yellow bone marrow), which is surrounded by a thick collar of compact bone. Yellow marrow in the shaft of long bones has fat molecules and serves as a vital energy reservoir.

The *epiphysis* (expanded end of the bone) consists mainly of spongy bone surrounded by a thin layer of compact bone.

*Spongy bone* has numerous plates separated by irregular spaces. Spongy bone is lighter but designed for strength. The solid portions of the bone follow the lines of stress. Bone spaces are often filled with *hematopoietic tissue* (red bone marrow), a specialized tissue that produces blood cells.

The epiphysis contains *articular cartilage*, which is a pad of hyaline cartilage. This is where long bones articulate (i.e., a joint) and act as a "shock absorber."

The *epiphyseal line*, or the remnant *epiphyseal disc* or *plate*, is cartilage at the diaphysis junction, and the epiphysis is the growth plate.

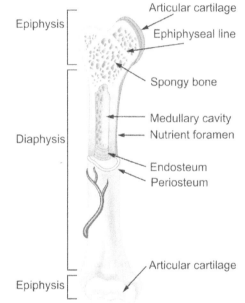

*Long bone with central diaphysis and terminal epiphysis*

The *periosteum* (outer fibrous) protective covering of the diaphysis is richly supplied with blood vessels, lymph vessels, and nerves. It allows for the insertion of tendons and ligaments into the bone. The *nutrient foramen* is a perforating canal that allows blood vessels to travel in and out of the bone.

*Osteons* are the functional unit of *compact bone*. The bone cells are in small chambers of lacunae, arranged in concentric circles around central canals.

*Lacunae* are separated by a matrix with protein fibers of collagen and mineral deposits.

The *osteogenic layer* contains the *osteoblasts,* the bone-forming cells, and the *osteoclasts*, the bone-destroying cells. The *endosteum layer* is the inner lining of the medullary cavity and contains a layer of osteoblasts and osteoclasts.

*Short bones* are cube-like. The outer surface is a thin layer of compact bone and internally contains spongy bone. The short bones are in the hands and feet. They are predominantly made of spongy bone.

They contain a tubular shaft and articular surfaces at each end but are smaller than a long bone. The articulations that they are joined by allows for increased flexibility and decreased mass. These bones provide stability and strength. Examples include wrist (carpals) and bones (tarsals) bones.

*Flat bones* are thin and usually curved with an outer layer of periosteum-covered compact bone surrounding an inner core of endosteum-covered spongy bone. The spongy bone is essentially sandwiched between two layers of thin, compact bone.

The spongy bone within the epiphyses of flat bone and long bone contains hematopoietic tissue (red marrow). Their structure provides a flat and broad surface area for tendon attachment.

The strong structure of bones offers protection to internal organs [e.g., most skull bones, breastbone (sternum), shoulder blades (scapulae), and the ribs].

*Irregular bones* are not long, short, or flat. Their complicated shape is due to their specialized function of providing mechanical support for the body and protecting the spinal cord. Their structure consists of a thin layer of compact bone with an internal component of spongy bone (e.g., the vertebrae, hips, auditory ossicles).

*Sesamoid bones* develop within a tendon. Since they act to hold the tendon away from the joint, the angle of the tendon is increased, and thus the force of the muscle is increased (e.g., patella and pisiform).

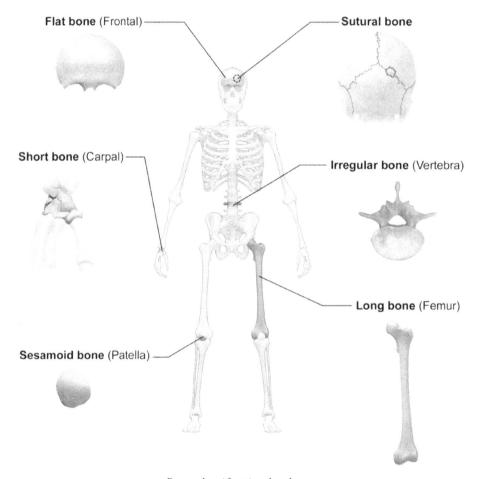

*Bone classification by shape*

*Wormian bones* (sutural bones) are small bones that lie within the major skull bones. These are irregular isolated bones that appear in addition to the usual centers of ossification of the cranium. They are predominantly in the lambdoid suture (posterior aspect of the skull), which is more tortuous than other sutures.

## Cartilage structure and function

*Cartilage* is an avascular connective tissue with a dense matrix of collagen and elastic fibers embedded in a rubbery ground substance. The matrix is produced by *chondroblasts* cells that become embedded in the matrix as *chondrocytes* (mature cartilage cells). They occur individually or in groups, within spaces of *lacunae* (sing. *lacuna*) in the matrix. Three types of cartilage are hyaline cartilage, fibrocartilage, and elastic cartilage.

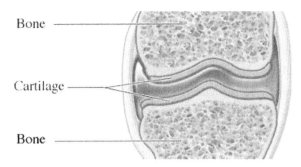

Bone ——

Cartilage ——

Bone ——

*Cross section of a joint with cartilage cushioning the apposition of two bones*

The cartilage cells secrete into the extracellular matrix, containing fiber meshwork that gives the cartilage its characteristic flexibility and resilience properties.

The surface of most cartilage in the body is surrounded by a membrane of dense, irregular connective tissue as *perichondrium*.

Unlike other connective tissues, cartilage contains no blood vessels or nerves.

Cartilage is softer and more flexible than bone.

For example, the ear, nose, larynx, trachea, and joints are made of cartilage. It possesses the properties of compressibility and resilience (ability to resume its original shape after deformation), which is important in locations such as the ends of bones in joints, knees, and between vertebrae.

*Hyaline cartilage* is the most abundant of the three types. Hyaline cartilage consists of a bluish-white, shiny, ground elastic material with a chondroitin sulfate matrix into which fine collagen fibrils are embedded.

Mesenchyme tissue initiates the formation of chondrocytes, which produce collagen.

Collagen is present in tissue as a triple helix with hydroxyproline and hydroxylysine, ground substance, and elastin fibers.

Hyaline cartilage covers the surface of bones at joints (especially in osteoarthritis-prone areas vulnerable to damage due to wear), including the ends of long bones and the anterior ends of the ribs. It facilitates smooth movements at joints, provides flexibility and support, reduces friction, and absorbs shock in joints.

Hyaline cartilage in the embryonic skeleton provides smooth surfaces, enabling tissues to move and slide easily over each other.

For example, hyaline cartilage is in bronchi, bronchial tubes, costal cartilages, the larynx (voice box), the nose, and the trachea.

## Fibrocartilage

*Fibrocartilage* (meniscus) is a tough form of cartilage that consists of chondrocytes scattered among clearly visible dense bundles of collagen fibers within the matrix.

Fibrocartilage lacks a perichondrium. Fibrocartilage tissue provides support and rigidity to attached and surrounding structures and is the strongest of the three cartilage types.

A fibrocartilage is *calli*, the tissue formed between the end of bones at the healing fracture site.

When there is a blood clot, granulation tissue forms into cartilage and eventually into full-fledged bone.

Other examples include intervertebral discs (between the vertebrae of the spine), the menisci (cartilage pads of the knee joint), the pubic symphysis (hip bones join at the front of the body), and in the portions of the tendons that insert into cartilage tissue, especially at the joints.

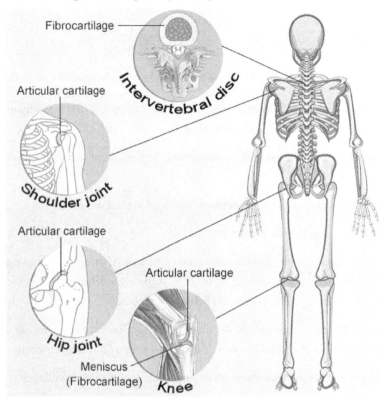

Knee bones are a capped crescent-shaped piece of meniscus cartilage.

The knee joint contains 13 fluid-filled sacs as *bursae*, which ease the friction between the tendons, ligaments, and bones. Inflammation of the bursae (*bursitis*) is the cause of "tennis elbow."

*Elastic cartilage* is yellowish with cartilage cells (chondrocytes) in a threadlike network of elastic fibers within the cartilage matrix. A perichondrium is present.

Elastic cartilage provides support to surrounding structures and defines and maintains the shape of the area in which it is present (e.g., external ear). Other examples include the auditory (Eustachian) tubes, external ear (the auricle), and epiglottis (flap on the larynx).

**Joint structure and function**

A *joint* is where bones meet. Joints connected to bones are synovial, fibrous, or cartilaginous.

*Synovial joints* (mobile joints) have a fluid-containing cavity that lubricates bone movement. They are usually involved with bones that move relative to each other.

Most joints are synovial joints, with the two bones separated by a cavity (e.g., the carpals, wrist, elbow, humerus and ulna, shoulder, hip joints, and knee joints). Synovial joints are subject to arthritis.

In osteoarthritis, the cartilage at the ends of bones disintegrate, and the bones become rough and irregular from mechanical "wear and tear." In rheumatoid arthritis, the synovial membrane becomes inflamed and thickens. The joint degenerates and becomes immovable and painful. An autoimmune reaction likely causes this.

Types of synovial joints include ball and socket (e.g., shoulder and hip), hinge (e.g., fingers, elbow), gliding (e.g., scaphoid, and lunate bones of the wrist), and immobile (e.g., plates of the skull and rib-to-sternum connection). The ball and socket joint allows the most freedom of motion.

*Fibrous joints* (immovable) connect bone to bone with cartilage (or fiber). An example of an immovable joint is a suture, usually holding the bones of a skull; includes the skull, pelvis, spinous process, and vertebrae.

*Cartilaginous joints* (slightly moveable) include joints between the vertebrae, spine, and ribs. For example, the two hipbones are slightly movable because they are ventrally joined by cartilage and respond to pregnancy hormones.

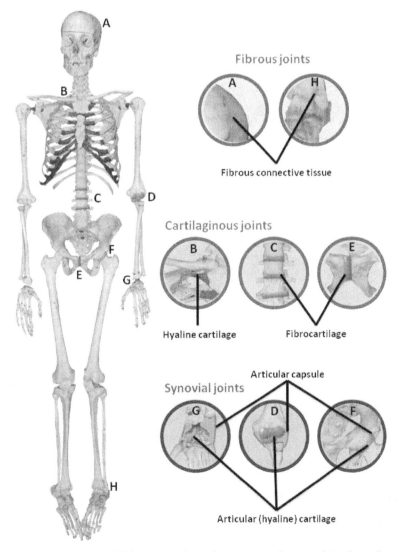

*The three types of joints are synovial, fibrous, and cartilaginous, with examples of cartilage and connective tissue are shown. Note the reference to examples and locations on the skeletal structure*

**Hierarchical structure of ligaments and tendons**

Ligaments and tendons are soft collagenous tissues.

*Ligaments* connect bone to bone, while *tendons* connect muscle to bone. Ligaments and tendons play a significant role in musculoskeletal biomechanics, and they represent an important area of orthopedic treatment in which medical challenges remain.

A challenge is restoring the normal mechanical function of these tissues.

Ligaments and tendons have a hierarchical structure that affects their mechanical behavior. Ligaments and tendons can adapt to changes in their mechanical environment due to injury, disease, or exercise.

Unlike bone, there are not quantitative structure-function relationships for ligaments and tendons.

Firstly, the hierarchical structure of ligaments and tendons is more difficult to quantify than bone.

Secondly, the ligaments and tendons exhibit both nonlinear and viscoelastic behavior even under physiologic loading, which is more difficult to analyze than bone's linear behavior.

The largest structure for these soft collagenous tissues is the ligament (or tendon). The ligament (or tendon) splits into smaller entities as *fascicles*.

The fascicle contains the basic *fibril* of the ligament (or tendon) and the *fibroblasts*, the biological cells of the ligament (or tendon). There is a structural characteristic at this level that plays a significant role in the mechanics of ligaments (and tendons): the crimp of the fibril.

The *crimp* is the waviness of the fibril; this contributes significantly to the nonlinear stress-strain relationship for ligaments, tendons, and essentially all soft collagenous tissues.

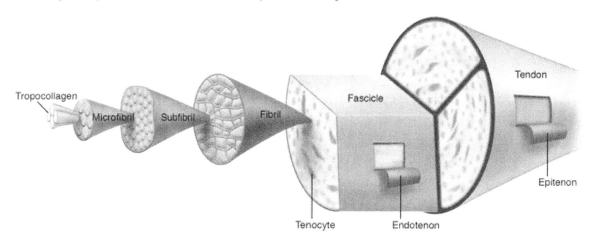

*Ligaments and tendons have a hierarchical structure*

**Anatomy and functions of ligaments and tendons**

*Ligaments* connect bone to bone, forming a *joint capsule*, which stabilizes and strengthens the joints.

The joint capsule is lined with a synovial membrane that produces lubricating synovial fluid.

Ligaments are made of dense bundles of connective tissue made of collagenous fibers, surrounded and protected by dense irregular connective sheaths.

Blood is supplied to ligaments through microvascularity from insertion sites to supply the nutrition needed for growth, matrix synthesis, and repair.

*Capsular ligaments* are a part of the articular capsule that surrounds synovial joints. They act as mechanical reinforcements.

*Extra-capsular ligaments* join with other ligaments and provide joint stability.

*Intra-capsular ligaments* are less common and promote stability but allow a larger range of motion.

*Cruciate ligaments* occur in pairs of three.

The collagen fibrils in ligaments have slightly less volume and organization than fibrils in tendons.

Ligaments have a higher percentage of proteoglycan matrix than tendons.

Fibroblasts are present in ligaments.

In "double-jointed" individuals, the ligaments are unusually loose, allowing them to stretch their ligaments more than average.

A *tendon* is a tough band of fibrous connective tissue that can withstand tension. Tendons connect muscle to bone at moveable joints and anchor the muscle.

Tendons contain collagen fibrils (Type I), a proteoglycan matrix, and fibroblasts arranged parallel.

Type I collagen constitutes about 86% of dry tendon weight; glycine (~33%), proline (~15%), and hydroxyproline (~15%, to identify collagen because it is almost unique to it).

Tendons carry tensile forces from muscle to bone, and they carry compressive forces when wrapped around bone like a pulley.

The tendons procure blood through the vessels in the *perimysium*, a sheath of connective tissue that covers the tendon, through the periosteum, the membrane covering the bone's outer surface

*Origin* is the point of attachment of the muscle to stationary bone, and *insertion* is a point of attachment of the muscle to a bone that moves.

## Mechanical properties of ligaments and tendons

*Viscoelasticity* is another vital aspect of ligament and tendon behavior, indicating time-dependent mechanical behavior.

The relationship between stress and strain is not constant but depends on displacement (or load).

There are two major types of behavior characteristic of viscoelasticity.

*Creep* is increasing deformation under constant load. This contrasts with an elastic material that does not exhibit increased deformation no matter how long the load is applied.

*Relaxation stress* is the second significant behavior, as the stress is reduced or relaxes under a constant deformation.

Ligaments are viscoelastic as they gradually strain under tension and return to their original shape when the tension is released. However, a joint cannot retain its original shape when extended past a certain point or extended for a prolonged period.

A joint becomes *dislocated* when this occurs, often due to trauma.

Once a joint has become dislocated, it must be manually moved back to its original position as soon as possible. If the ligaments are lengthened for a prolonged period, the joint is weakened, making it susceptible to future dislocations.

*Hysteresis* (energy dissipation) is a characteristic of the viscoelastic material.

If a viscoelastic material is loaded and unloaded, the unloading curve does not follow the loading curve.

The difference between the curves represents the amount of energy dissipated (or lost) during loading.

**Stress *vs.* strain for tendons and ligaments**

There are three major regions of the stress-strain curve: 1) toe region, 2) linear region, and 3) yield and failure region. During physiological activity, most ligaments and tendons exist in the toe and somewhat in the linear region. These constitute a nonlinear stress-strain curve since the slope of the toe region is different from the linear region.

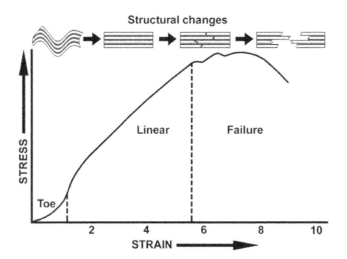

For structure-function relationships, the toe region represents "un-crimping" in the collagen fibrils. Since it is easier to stretch out the collagen fibrils' crimp, this part of the stress-strain curve shows a low stiffness.

As the collagen fibrils become uncrimped, the collagen fibril backbone becomes stretched, giving rise to a stiffer material.

As individual fibrils within the ligament or tendon begin to fail, damage accumulates, stiffness is reduced, and the ligaments and tendons begin to fail.

Thus, ligaments and tendons' overall behavior depends on the individual crimp structure and the failure of the collagen fibrils.

## Bone Structure and Composition

### Chemical composition of bone

The bone's chemical composition is organic components (~25% by weight), inorganic components (~70% by weight), and water (~5% by weight). Bone is connective tissue and is characteristically hard, strong, elastic, and lightweight.

Bones are made from a combination of compact and spongy bone.

Macroscopically, bone is a solid structure with internal canals where blood vessels run and holes where cells can reside. The structure is surrounded by membranes containing stem cells, including osteoblast (bone-building) and osteoclast (bone degrading) cells.

Microscopically, bone is composed of cells, with the extracellular matrix arranged in cylinders as *osteons*, which contain blood vessels and nerves running through the middle.

### Four types of bone matrix cells

Four types of cells make up the bone matrix.

*Osteoprogenitor* cells are derived from mesenchyme and may undergo mitosis and differentiate into osteoblasts.

*Osteoblasts* are stem cells that form the bone matrix by secreting collagen and organic compounds from which bone is formed. They cannot undergo mitosis.

As the collagenous matrix is released around them, they are enveloped by the matrix and differentiate into osteocytes. Osteoblasts secrete a matrix material of osteoid.

*Osteoids* are primarily made of collagen, which gives bone its high tensile strength. They contain glycolipids and glycoproteins.

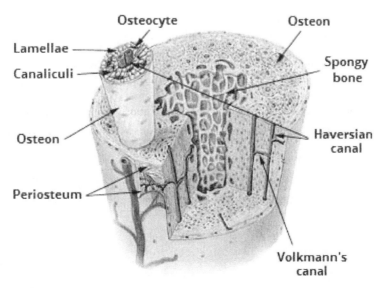

*Bone cross-section with structure highlighted*

*Osteocytes* are mature bone cells derived from osteoblasts. They are principal bone cells that cannot undergo mitosis. They maintain daily cellular activities to exchange nutrients and waste with blood.

Osteoclasts are multinucleated cells functioning in bone resorption, including the destruction of the bone matrix, and are essential in developing, growing, maintaining, and repairing bone. They develop from monocytes.

**Compact and spongy bones**

*Compact bone* is a highly organized, solid, smooth, dense type of bone that does not appear to have cavities from the outside. In compact bone, osteoclasts burrow tunnels, as *Haversian canals*.

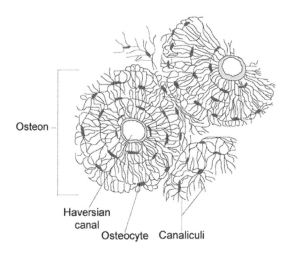

*Compact bone from a transverse section of a long bone's cortex*

The Haversian system is comprised of osteocytes, the star-shaped bone cells that lie in the *lacunae*.

The osteoblast secrets the matrix of collagen and calcium salts in concentric *lamellae* (layers) around the central Haversian canal, containing blood vessels and nerves. The elongated cylinders are bonded to form the long axis of a bone.

The *canaliculi* are a communication canal within the bone that connects the lacunae of the osteons.

*Volkmann's canals*, small channels that run perpendicular to the bone's surface, connect adjacent Haversian canals' blood and nerve supplies.

*Spongy bone* (cancellous) is less dense and consists of poorly-organized *trabeculae*, small, needle-like pieces of bone with much open space between them. Spongy bone is nourished by diffusion from nearby Haversian canals.

Spongy bone supports soft tissue, protects internal organs, assists in body movement, mineral storage, blood cell production, and energy storage in the form of adipose (fat) cells in the marrow.

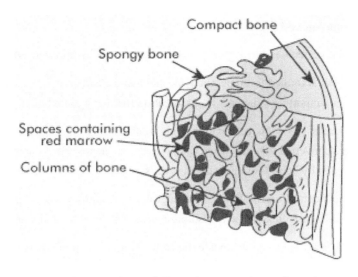

*Bone with spongy bone in the medulla and compact bone along the cortex*

**Calcium–protein matrix of bones**

Calcium is the most abundant mineral in bone and the most abundant mineral in the body. Calcium is an element that cannot be produced by any biological processes and must enter the body through diet.

Bones act as a storage site for calcium. The extracellular matrix of bone consists of calcium salts, primarily calcium phosphate [$Ca_3(PO_4)_2(OH)_2$], which gives bone its hardness (or rigidity), collagen fibers, and ground substance (glue).

Calcium ions are vital for physiology and are needed for bone mineralization, tooth health, regulation of the heart rate, blood coagulation, contractions of smooth and skeletal muscle cells, and regulation of nerve impulse conduction.

The calcium level in the blood is highly regulated at about 9-10 mg/dL. When the body cannot maintain this level, a person experiences hypocalcemia (or hypercalcemia), as described below.

Bone has a mineral content of roughly 50% by volume. The mineral content of the matrix consists mostly of calcium phosphate, hydroxyapatite, with minimal amounts of magnesium, carbonate, and acid phosphate. Hydroxyapatite bone crystals are tiny and are soluble and vital in mineral metabolism.

The organic matrix of bone is composed of about 90% collagen protein.

Collagen is formed through chains that resemble short threads that twist into triple helices (resembling strings). They line up and bind, forming fibrils. The fibrils are arranged in layers, and the mineral crystals deposit between the layers.

Matrix maturation expresses alkaline phosphatase and noncollagenous proteins (i.e., osteocalcin, osteopontin, and sialoprotein). Calcium and phosphate-binding proteins aid in the ordered deposition of minerals by regulating the amount and size of the hydroxyapatite crystals formed.

The mineral portion of the matrix provides for the mechanical rigidity and strength of the bone. The organic portion of the matrix contributes to the flexibility and elasticity of the bone.

**Bone ossification, formation and growth**

The human fetal skeleton is cartilaginous that serves as scaffolds for bone construction.

The fetal skeleton is formed from mesenchyme and hyaline cartilage that is loosely shaped like bones. This "skeleton" provides supporting structures for ossification (hardening into bone).

At about 6-7 weeks' gestation, ossification begins and continues throughout adulthood. The cartilaginous models are converted to bones when calcium salts are deposited in the matrix, first by cartilaginous cells and later by bone-forming osteoblast cells.

The main components of ossification are cartilage cells (chondrocytes), precursor cells (osteoprogenitor cells), bone deposition cells (osteoblasts), bone resorption cells (osteoclasts), and mature bone cells (osteocytes).

During ossification, blood vessels invade the cartilage and transport osteoprogenitor cells to the center of ossification. At the center of ossification, the cartilage cells die, forming small cavities. Osteoblast cells form progenitor cells, which begin depositing bone tissue outwards from the center. From this process, spongy textured calcaneus bone and smooth outer compact bone form.

*Endochondral ossification* is the conversion of cartilaginous scaffolds to bones. Some bones, such as facial bones, form without a cartilaginous scaffold and is *intramembranous ossification*. The replacement of preexisting connective tissue with bone occurs through intramembranous and endochondral ossification.

Endochondral ossification occurs when a bone is formed from hyaline cartilage. Most bones in the skeleton are formed in this manner. There is a primary ossification center at the middle of a long bone; secondary centers later form at the ends.

*Primary ossification centers* harden in a fetus and during infancy.

*Secondary ossification centers* develop in a child and harden during adolescence and early adulthood. A cartilaginous growth plate forms between the primary and secondary ossification centers. As the growth plate remains between the two centers, bone growth continues.

The perichondrium becomes the periosteum, containing layers of undifferentiated cells, including osteoprogenitor cells that later develop into osteoblasts.

*Appositional growth* is when osteoblasts secrete osteoid against the shaft of the cartilage scaffold to provide support for the new bone.

*Hypertrophy* occurs when chondrocytes in the primary ossification center begin to grow. They stop secreting collagen and other proteoglycans and begin secreting alkaline phosphatase and other enzymes essential for mineral deposition.

After the calcification of the matrix, hypertrophic chondrocytes start to die off to form cavities within the bone. The hypertrophic chondrocytes start to secrete vascular endothelial cell growth factors that induce the sprouting of blood vessels from the perichondrium.

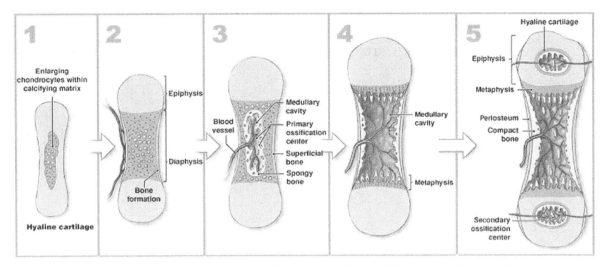

*1) Enlargement of chondrocytes, 2) formation of a superficial layer of bone, 3) production of spongy bone at primary ossification center, 4) growth in length and diameter, 5) formation of secondary ossification centers*

**Hematopoietic cells**

Blood vessels forming in the periosteal bud invade the cavity left by the chondrocytes and branch in opposite directions along the length of the shaft. These blood vessels carry hematopoietic cells, osteoprogenitor cells, and various other cells within the cavity. The hematopoietic cells eventually form the bone marrow.

Osteoblasts, differentiated from the osteoprogenitor cells that enter the cavity via the periosteal bud, use the calcified matrix as a scaffold and begin to secrete osteoid, forming the bone *trabecula.* The osteoclasts formed from macrophages break down spongy bone to form the medullary (or bone marrow) cavity.

*Hematopoiesis* is blood cell formation. Blood cells are formed in the red marrow of certain bones. The flat bones of the skull, ribs, and breastbone (i.e., sternum) contain red bone marrow that manufactures blood cells.

During intramembranous ossification, a bone forms on (or within) a fibrous connective tissue membrane.

The connective tissue membrane eventually forms the periosteum, made of fibers and granular cells in a matrix. The peripheral portion is predominantly fibrous, whereas the internal environment is predominantly osteoblasts. The tissue is heavily supplied with blood vessels.

As ontogenetic fibers move out of the periphery, they continue to calcify and form fresh bone spicules.

A network of bone is formed from meshes containing blood vessels, and the delicate connective tissue is populated with osteoblasts.

The bony trabeculae are thickened by the additional fresh layers of bone formed by the osteoblasts on its surface, and the meshes are simultaneously encroached upon.

Layers of bony tissue are continuously added under the periosteum and around the large vascular channels that eventually become the Haversian canals, which thickens the bone.

During infancy and childhood, *longitudinal growth* occurs, where long bones lengthen entirely by growth at the epiphyseal plates.

Bones grow in thickness by appositional growth.

**Bone growth and remodeling**

The epiphyseal plates are replaced by bone in adulthood.

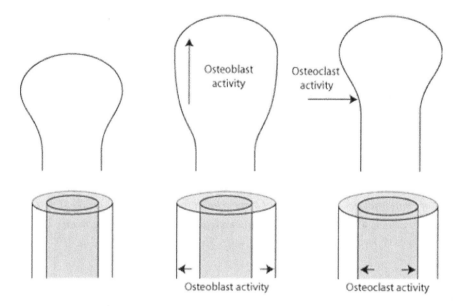

*Bone growth and remodeling: longitudinal growth (top) and appositional growth (bottom)*

The structure of the epiphyseal plate contains four zones: the *zone of resting cartilage*, which anchors the plate to the epiphysis.

The *zone of proliferating cartilage* is where the chondrocytes divide to replace those that die at the diaphyseal surface of the epiphysis.

The *zone of hypertrophic cartilage is the* site of maturing cells.

The *zone of calcified cartilage* consists of dead cells because the matrix around them is calcified.

**Dynamic bone remodeling by osteoblasts and osteoclasts**

Ossification of most bones is completed by age 25. As a child grows, cartilage cells are produced by mitosis on the epiphyseal side of the plate.

The epiphyseal plate's cartilage is destroyed and replaced by bone on the diaphyseal side of the plate.

The thickness of the plate remains almost constant, while the diaphyseal side bone increases in length.

Lengthwise bone growth occurs at the ends of long bones.

The role of osteoblasts in lengthwise bone growth is to add bone tissue at the bone ends.

Osteoblasts lengthen the knobs at the ends of the bone, while osteoclasts remodel bone tissue by degrading (chipping away) the bone ends (i.e., the knobs) until they are the right size and shape.

Along with the increase in length, bones increase in thickness (or diameter).

Appositional growth occurs in an osteogenic layer of the periosteum; osteoblasts lay down matrix (compact bone) on the outer surface. This is accompanied by osteoclasts destroying the bone matrix at the endosteal surface.

Osteoblasts' role in the diameter growth of bones is to add bone tissue to the outside of the bone.

Osteoclasts' role in the diameter growth of bones is to remove bone tissue from the inside of the bone (bones are hollow).

Without osteoclasts, diameter growth results in bones too thick and too heavy.

Even with osteoclasts, bones become thicker with age.

Age-related skeletal changes are apparent at the cellular and whole-body level.

Height begins to decrease incrementally about age 33. Bone loss gradually exceeds bone replacement.

After menopause, females lose bone more rapidly than males.

By age 70, bone loss is similar in both sexes. The likelihood of fractures increases as bones age.

Adults need more calcium in the diet than do children to promote the work of osteoblasts.

The rate of remodeling varies.

For example, the distal femur is replaced every four months, while the shift of the femur is not replaced during one's lifetime.

## Endocrine Control of the Skeletal System

### Osteoblasts and osteoclasts

The rate of bone growth is controlled by hormones, including growth hormones and sex hormones. Eventually, the epiphysis plates become ossified, the bone stops growing, and a person reaches adult height.

In adults, bone is continually being remodeled (broken down and built up again). This involves osteoblasts, osteoclasts, and the hormones calcitonin and parathyroid hormone (PTH) through the negative feedback mechanism, which affects blood calcium homeostasis.

Osteoclasts (bone-absorbing cells) break down bone, remove worn cells, and deposit Ca in the blood.

Osteoclasts secrete lysosomal enzymes that digest the organic matrix by secreting acids that decompose calcium salts into $Ca^{2+}$ and $PO_4^-$ ions, which enter the blood.

Osteoblasts (blood-forming cells) form new bone, taking calcium from the blood.

Osteoblasts become entrapped in the bone matrix and become osteocytes in the lacunae of osteons. This continual remodeling allows the bone to change in thickness gradually.

Osteoclasts determine blood calcium levels, which is vital for muscle contraction and nerve conduction.

### Nutrients for bone deposition and remodeling

Minerals needed for bone growth and remodeling include calcium, phosphorus (a component of the hydroxyapatite matrix), magnesium (normal osteoblast activity), boron (inhibiting calcium loss), and manganese (formation of a new matrix).

Several vitamins are needed for bone growth, remodeling, and repair. Vitamin D dramatically increases intestinal absorption of dietary calcium and slows its urine loss. Vitamin D deficiency causes rickets in children and osteomalacia in adults.

Vitamin C helps maintain the bone matrix and collagen synthesis; deficiency of vitamin causes scurvy.

Vitamin A is required for bone resorption and controls the activity, distribution, and coordination of osteoblasts and osteoclasts during development.

Vitamin $B_{12}$ plays a role in osteoblast activity.

Hormones needed for bone growth and remodeling include the human growth hormone (HGH), sex hormones, thyroid hormones, parathyroid hormones, and calcitonin.

The pituitary gland secretes HGH for the general growth of tissues.

HGH stimulates the reproduction of cartilage cells at the epiphyseal plate.

Sex hormones include estrogen and androgens (e.g., testosterone), which aid in osteoblast activity by promoting new bone growth. They degenerate cartilage cells in the epiphyseal plate by closing the plate.

Estrogen's effect is greater than androgen's effect.

**Bones remodeling for calcium homeostasis**

Thyroid hormones include triiodothyronine ($T_3$) and thyroxine ($T_4$).

These hormones stimulate the replacement of cartilage by bone in the epiphyseal plate.

Calcium homeostasis (blood calcium level of about 10 mg/dL) is critical for normal bodily functions.

Calcium homeostasis is controlled by PTH, vitamin D, calcitonin, and interactions of the skeletal, endocrine, digestive, and urinary systems. These body systems maintain calcium levels in the blood.

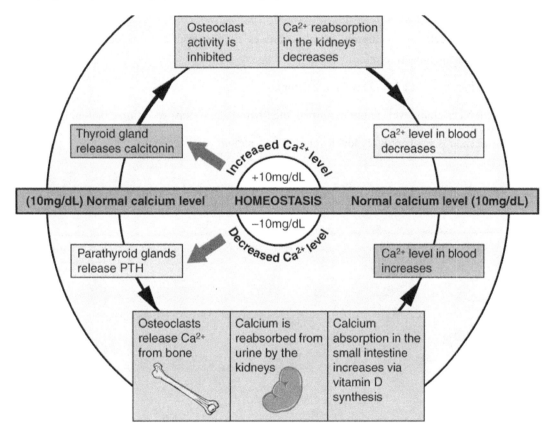

*Calcium homeostasis*

**PTH, vitamin D and calcitonin**

PTH is secreted by the parathyroid glands when blood calcium levels are low. It stimulates osteoclast proliferation, and the resorption of bone occurs. The demineralization releases calcium into the blood.

PTH causes kidney tubules to reabsorb $Ca^{2+}$ into the blood.

It causes intestinal mucosa to increase dietary absorption of $Ca^{2+}$ and causes an increase in blood calcium levels (homeostasis).

PTH stimulates vitamin D synthesis, which increases calcium absorption from food in the small intestine.

The body deposits calcium in the bones when blood levels get too high, and it releases calcium when blood levels drop too low.

This is regulated by PTH, vitamin D, and calcitonin.

When these processes return blood calcium levels to normal, there is calcium to bind the receptors on the surface of the cells of the parathyroid glands, and this cycle of events is turned off.

Calcitonin is secreted by the thyroid gland when blood calcium levels are too high (hypercalcemia).

It inhibits bone resorption and increases osteoblast activity (i.e., deposition of bone matrix).

Calcitonin causes the kidney tubules to secrete excess $Ca^{2+}$ into the urine, resulting in decreased blood calcium levels (back to normal).

 Parafollicular cells of the thyroid gland secrete calcitonin, leading to a decreased plasma calcium concentration by reducing bone resorption.

These actions lower the blood levels of calcium.

When blood calcium levels return to normal, the thyroid gland stops secreting calcitonin.

*Hypocalcemia* is an abnormally low level of blood calcium.

# CHAPTER 17

# Muscular System

- Muscle Cell

- Functions of the Muscle System

- Structural Characteristics of Muscles

- Mechanism of Muscle Contraction

- Neural Control of Muscle System

- Oxygen Debt and Muscle Fatigue

## Muscle Cell

### Muscle cell structure and function

A muscle consists of muscle cells bound by connective tissue. A single muscle fiber is a multinucleated cell formed from myoblasts during development. Muscle cells contain several parallel *myofibrils*, composed of *myofilaments* (primarily actin and myosin). Myofibrils contain the *sarcomeres*, the basic units of the contraction in the skeletal muscle. Myofibrils are packed within the multinucleated skeletal muscle cells.

The *sarcolemma* (plasma membrane) of the muscle cell contains the myofibrils and keeps them packed. The nuclei of the muscle fibers are at the edges of the diameter of the fiber, adjacent to the sarcolemma.

The *sarcoplasm* is the cytoplasm of muscle fibers and contains numerous mitochondria that produce ATP for muscle contraction. The *sarcoplasmic reticulum* is similar to the smooth endoplasmic reticulum; it extends throughout the muscle cell's sarcoplasm and stores calcium ions used in muscle contraction.

Muscle is attached to a bone by collagen bundles of tendons. After infancy, new fibers are formed from undifferentiated satellite cells and generally do not undergo mitosis to create new muscle cells after development, called *hyperplasia*.

However, muscle cells increase in size and increase the muscle's overall volume, known as *hypertrophy*. In adulthood, any compensation for lost muscles occurs mainly by an increase in the size of fibers.

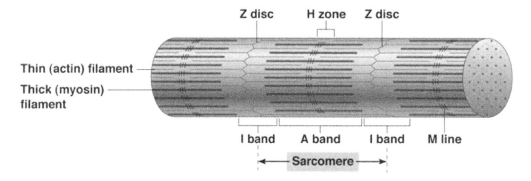

*The function unit of a muscle cell is the sarcomere*

### Transverse tubules and calcium

*Transverse tubules* (*T-tubules*) are tunnel-like extensions of the sarcolemma that pass through muscle cells from one side of the cell to another, forming a network around myofibrils. They are referred to as transverse because of the way they are oriented. The transverse tubules play a vital role in muscle contraction.

A muscle action potential (i.e., electrical charge movement) travels along the transverse tubules and stimulates the release of calcium ions from the sarcoplasmic reticulum. This allows the calcium ions to flood into the sarcoplasm and binds to troponin.

Calcium triggers the movement of various protein filaments (including *actin, myosin,* and *tropomyosin*) within the myofibrils, which results in muscle contraction. The T-tubules' general function is to conduct impulses from the cell's surface to the sarcoplasmic reticulum, where Ca is released.

**Sarcoplasmic reticulum stores calcium for contractions**

The sarcoplasm in muscle cells is equivalent to the cytoplasm of other cells. The sarcoplasmic reticulum in muscle cells is homologous to the endoplasmic reticulum.

Unlike the endoplasmic reticulum, the sarcoplasmic reticulum stores and secretes $Ca^+$, the ion essential in muscle contraction.

The sarcoplasmic reticulum forms a sleeve around myofibrils, with enlarged *lateral sacs* that store $Ca^{2+.}$ It is abundant in skeletal muscle cells and is related to myofibrils.

The sarcoplasmic reticulum membrane contains active pumps involved in moving calcium into the sarcoplasmic reticulum from the sarcoplasm. The sarcoplasmic reticulum contains specialized gates for calcium.

Action potentials lead to depolarization of the sarcoplasmic reticulum membrane, leading to depolarization of the T-tubules. This opens the $Ca^{2+}$ channels of the lateral sacs, causing the contraction to begin. To end contraction, $Ca^{2+}$ is pumped into the lateral sacs by active transport proteins, called plasma membrane $Ca^{2+}$ ATPase (PMCA).

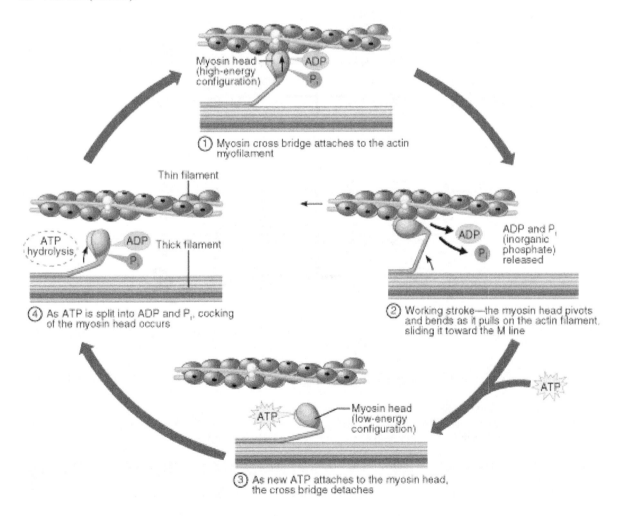

*Calcium binds to troponin to cause a conformational change in tropomyosin and expose the myosin-binding sites on the actin myofilament (step 1)*

**Sarcomere anatomy and function for muscle contractions**

Sarcomeres with I and A bands, M and Z lines, and the H zone.

Skeletal muscle cells have longitudinal bundles of myofibrils.

Myofibrils consist of thin (actin) and thick (myosin) filaments, which repeat along the myofibril in units as sarcomeres.

Organelles within the sarcomeres resemble the form and function of other types of eukaryotic cells.

In the *H zone*, the sarcomere's central region, there is no overlap between thin and thick filaments.

In the center of the H zone, the M line links the center regions of thick filaments and divides the sarcomere vertically.

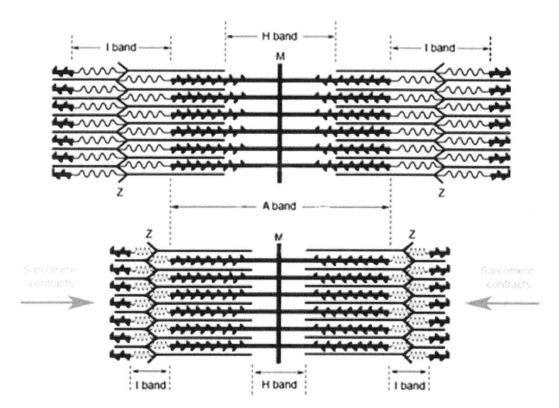

*Sarcomere with associated regions*

Each sarcomere has a band of thick filaments in the middle as the *A band*.

Sarcomeres are flanked on both sides by thin filaments.

Vertical borders between sarcomeres are *Z lines*, which anchor thin filaments.

*I bands* represent thin actin filaments, and *H bands* represent thick myosin filaments.

Titin protein fibers from the Z line are linked to the M line and the thick filaments.

Due to the banded pattern provided by thin and thick filaments, skeletal muscle is striated muscle.

## Muscle fiber types and functions

Fibers within muscle tissue are organized into fast and slow fibers.

*Fast fibers* contain myosin with high ATPase activity and have high shortening velocity.

*Slow fibers* contain myosin with low ATPase activity and have low shortening velocity. Fast fibers fatigue rapidly, while slow fibers fatigue gradually.

*Oxidative fibers* have numerous mitochondria and a high capacity for oxidative phosphorylation. ATP production is dependent on oxygen.

Oxidative fibers contain myoglobin, an oxygen-binding protein, which increases the rate of oxygen diffusion into the fiber. Myoglobin gives oxidative fibers a red color, as red muscle fibers.

*Glycolytic fibers* have few mitochondria but a high concentration of glycolytic enzymes and glycogen. Therefore, it is glycolysis, rather than oxidative phosphorylation, which fuels the contractions.

These fibers are white muscle fibers due to their pale color.

Glycolytic fibers can develop more tension than oxidative fibers because they are larger and contain more thick and thin filaments. However, they fatigue rapidly.

## Myosin ATPase activity

The types of skeletal muscle fibers, determined by their myosin ATPase activity and energy source, are:

1) slow oxidative,

2) fast oxidative / glycolytic, and

3) fast glycolytic.

Most muscles contain all three fiber types.

*Slow oxidative fibers* are one of the two main skeletal muscle fibers with abundant mitochondria and myoglobin. They generate energy predominantly through aerobic conditions.

Slow oxidative fibers twitch at a slow rate and are resistant to fatigue. The peak force exerted by these muscles is low. Slow muscle fibers have a lot of oxidative enzymes but are low in ATP activity.

*Fast oxidative / glycolytic fibers* can contract faster and produce a large peak force while being resistant to tiring even after several cycles.

These fibers have a large amount of ATP activity and are high in oxidative and glycolytic enzymes. They are used for anaerobic activities that need to be sustained for a prolonged time.

*Fast glycolytic fibers* can exert a large force and contract at a fast rate. However, this comes at the expense of the fibers tiring quickly. After a small amount of exertion, the muscle requires rest to recover.

These fibers have low oxidative capacity while ATP and glycolytic activity is high. These fibers are used during anaerobic activity for short durations of time.

## Functions of the Muscle System

**Muscles provide support and mobility**

The muscular system consists of contractile fibers held by connective tissue. Muscle contraction can result in movement, stabilization of position, movement of substances throughout the body, and generation of body heat.

Muscles provide *support* for stabilizing joints, maintaining posture while sitting or standing.

Muscles provide *mobility*. For example, skeletal muscles facilitate body movement, and smooth muscles move substances through the gut.

**Muscles assist peripheral circulation**

The heart is a muscle that pumps blood. The pumping action of cardiac muscle in the heart causes blood to flow through blood vessels. Other body muscles provide peripheral assistance outside of the heart to help keep the circulatory system flowing.

For example, contraction of the skeletal muscles of the diaphragm not only draws air into the lungs but squeezes on the abdominal veins to draw blood back to the heart.

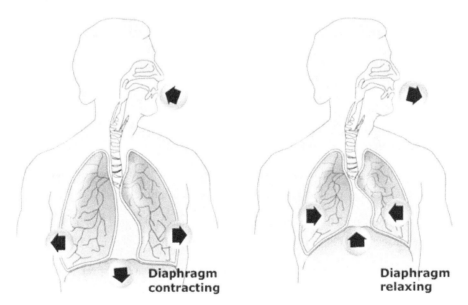

*Contraction of the diaphragm: inhaling (left) and exhaling (right).*
*During inhalation, the diaphragm contracts as the lungs expand.*
*During expiration, the diaphragm relaxes as air is expelled from the lungs.*

**Thermoregulation by the shivering reflex**

*Thermoregulation* allows an organism to keep its body temperature within a specific range. One thermoregulation method is the "*shivering reflex*," the generation of heat due to rapid skeletal muscle contractions (hydrolysis of ATP generates heat). These contractions are essential for homeostasis to maintain body temperature in cooler environments.

## Structural Characteristics of Muscles

### Skeletal, cardiac and smooth muscle comparison

All muscles are contractile fibers. There are three major types with distinctive properties: skeletal muscle, cardiac muscle, and smooth muscle.

| | Skeletal:<br>• voluntary<br>• striated<br>• multinucleated<br>• non-branched |
|---|---|
| | Cardiac:<br>• involuntary<br>• striated<br>• single nucleus<br>• branched |
| | Smooth:<br>• involuntary<br>• non-striated<br>• single nucleus<br>• tapered |

### Voluntary control of skeletal muscle

Skeletal muscle cells are multinucleated. When observed under a microscope, skeletal muscle cells appear as long, non-branched fibers with *striations* or vertical stripes. The striations occur due to the presence of sarcomeres.

The *sarcomere*, an individualized, organized structure that allows for muscle contraction, is the myofibril's basic functional unit. The myofibrils are contractile portions of fibers that lie parallel and run the length of the fiber.

Sarcomeres communicate using *transverse tubules* (T-tubules). T-tubules penetrate the cell and make contact with, but do not fuse to, the *sarcoplasmic reticulum*.

Ions are exchanged through the myofibril using this transverse system.

The ends of skeletal muscles attach to bones via tendons, allowing skeletal muscle contractions to move the skeleton.

Skeletal muscle, under voluntary control, is responsible for the everyday movements of the skeleton.

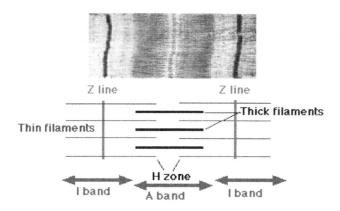

*Sarcomere with electron micrograph showing striated pattern and illustration of thin (actin) and thick (myosin) filaments with associated A and I band and H zone*

In a healthy state, the skeletal muscle never fully relaxes to its entire length. There is always *muscle tone* (some degree of tension) in the muscle, which provides essential protection to the fibers.

The muscle tone gives the muscle fibers a passive resistance to stretching. This is driven by natural viscoelastic properties of the muscle fibers and a degree of alpha motor neuron activation (lower motor neurons of the brainstem and spinal cord).

*Hypertonia* is a high muscle tone resulting in brief spasms, prolonged cramps, or constant rigidity.

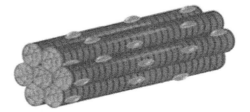

*A skeletal muscle with multinucleated myofibrils*

**Cardiac muscle comprises the heart**

*Cardiac muscle* has a striated appearance due to sarcomeres, and cardiac muscle cells contain one or two central nuclei. Unlike skeletal muscle, cardiac muscle is branched. The cardiac muscle is under involuntary control and is exclusively in the heart.

The *myocardial* (cardiac muscle) cells are separated by intercalated discs with gap junctions to allow action potentials to flow through electrical synapses. The cardiac muscle has a high mitochondria concentration and is stimulated by autonomic innervation.

Cardiac muscle and smooth muscle are myogenic and can contract without stimuli from nerve cells.

Some myocardial cells do not function in contraction; instead, they form the conducting system, which initiates the heartbeat and spreads it throughout the heart.

Blood is supplied to cardiac muscle cells by coronary arteries and drained by coronary veins.

Blood pumped through the chambers does not exchange substances with the heart muscle cells.

The vital cardiac muscle cells are innervated with a rich supply of sympathetic fibers, which release norepinephrine, and parasympathetic fibers, which release acetylcholine.

*A cardiac muscle with branching between myocardial cells*

**Involuntary control of smooth muscle**

Smooth muscle fibers are composed of spindle-shaped cells with a single nucleus. Smooth muscle fibers are *nonstriated* because they do not have the highly-organized sarcomeres that form the basic units of skeletal and cardiac muscle.

However, they have intermediate filaments involved in the sliding filament mechanism for contraction using myosin and actin.

The thick (myosin) and thin (actin) filaments run diagonal to the long axis of the cell, and they are attached to the plasma membrane or *dense bodies* as cytoplasmic structures.

Like skeletal muscle, smooth muscle requires $Ca^{2+}$ ions for contraction, which (like skeletal muscle) is released from the sarcoplasmic reticulum inside the cell.

While cardiac and muscle cells do not generally divide in adult humans, smooth muscle cells maintain the ability to divide throughout life. They are controlled by the autonomic nervous system under involuntary control.

Smooth muscle is in the lining of the bladder, the uterus, the digestive tract, and blood vessel walls.

*A smooth muscle with spindle-shaped cells and a single*

The plasma membrane of smooth muscles receives excitatory and inhibitory inputs, and the contractile state of the muscle depends on the relative intensity.

However, some smooth muscle fibers generate action potentials spontaneously. The potential change during spontaneous depolarizations is the *pacemaker potential*.

Unlike skeletal muscles, smooth muscles do not have motor endplates. The postganglionic autonomic neuron divides into branches in the smooth muscle fibers, with each branch containing a series of *varicosities* (swollen regions). The varicosities contain vesicles filled with a neurotransmitter released from an action potential. The same neurotransmitter can produce excitation in one fiber and inhibition in another.

Varicosities from a single axon may innervate several fibers, and a single fiber may receive signals from varicosities of sympathetic and parasympathetic neurons.

Smooth muscle plasma membranes bind and respond to hormones. Paracrine agents, acidity, oxygen concentration, osmolarity, and ion composition can influence smooth muscle tension, providing a response mechanism to local factors.

**Single-unit and multiunit smooth muscle**

*Single-unit smooth muscle* (or *visceral muscle*) cells are connected by gap junctions, intracellular channels allowing the passage of molecules between cells. Therefore, an action potential can influence many single-unit smooth muscle cells, causing a unified contraction.

In a single-unit smooth muscle, the fibers undergo synchronous activity due to adjacent fibers being linked by gap junctions; an action potential occurring on any of the fibers propagates to the other cells. This allows the whole muscle to respond to stimulation as a single unit. Some of the fibers may consist of pacemaker cells, which can control the contraction of the entire muscle. However, most of the smooth muscle fibers consist of non-pacemaker cells.

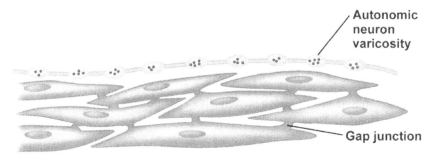

*A single unit smooth muscle with autonomic neural innervation and gap junction*

*Multiunit smooth muscle* is made of cells that contract independently from one another. This is because each multiunit smooth muscle cell is directly attached to a neuron. In addition to the neuronal response, smooth muscle cells can respond to hormones, changes in pH, $O_2$ and $CO_2$ concentration, temperature, and ion concentration.

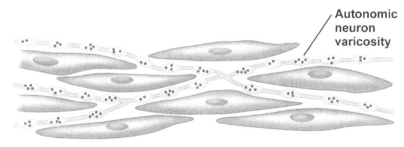

*Multiunit smooth muscle contracts independently*

## Mechanism of Muscle Contraction

### Actin and myosin filaments

A skeletal and cardiac muscle cell shows dark and light bands under a microscope. An electron microscope shows that the placement of protein filaments within sarcomeres forms the striations of myofibrils. The light and dark bands correspond to two types of proteins, actin and myosin.

*Actin filaments* (thin filaments) are long actin protein chains in a spherical conformation that include the proteins troponin and tropomyosin, which wrap around the actin protein. Thin myofilaments are comprised of two chains that coil around each other. Actin molecules have a unique combination of strength and sensitivity.

These molecules are constantly destroyed and renewed as needed to contribute to the muscle tissue's function. This is controlled by the ATP attached to each actin monomer. The state of the ATP determines the stability of the actin molecules.

*Myosin filaments* (thick filaments) consist of myosin protein molecules arranged in a bipolar structure. They are made of protruding club-like heads that lie towards the thick filaments' ends, while their shafts lie towards the middle.

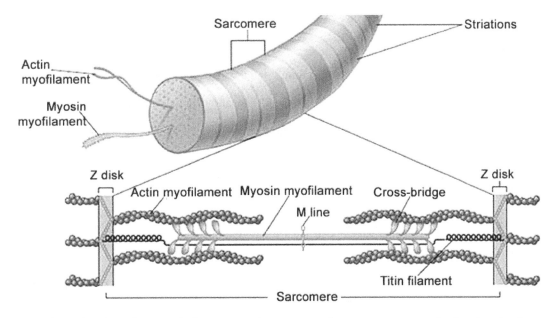

*Skeletal and cardiac muscle have striated appearance from sarcomeres as the functional unit*

Each myosin protein thick filament has a central bare zone and an array of protruding heads of opposite polarity at the ends. Myosin molecules possess a tail forming the core of the thick myofilament, while the head projects from the core filament. These myosin heads are cross bridges.

Myosin heads have ATP binding sites and actin-binding sites. The myosin head contains a hinge at the point where it leaves the core of the thick myofilament to allow the head to swivel, and this swiveling action is the cause of any muscle contraction.

The swiveling action occurs when actin combines with the myosin head, leading to the ATP associated with the head hydrolyzing ATP → ADP + energy. Actin molecules contain a binding site for myosin; myosin molecules contain a binding site for actin and ATP.

**Sliding filament theory for muscle contractions**

The sliding filament model proposes that a muscle fiber contracts, causing the sarcomeres within the myofibrils to shorten. As a sarcomere shortens, actin filaments slide past the myosin; the I band shortens, and the H zone disappears.

The swivel movement of the cross-bridges makes the overlapping thick and thin filaments slide past each other. Actin and myosin fibers do not change in length during a contraction.

The *Z line* is the boundary of a single sarcomere and is involved in anchoring thin actin filaments. Visually under an electron microscope, it is a zigzag line on the sides of the sarcomere that connects the filaments of adjacent sarcomeres.

The *M line* is a line of myosin in the middle of the sarcomere linked by accessory proteins.

The *I band* is the region containing thin filaments (actin) only.

The *H zone* is the region containing thick filaments (myosin) only.

The *A band* is made of an actin end overlapping with a myosin end.

The H zone and I band reduce during contraction, while the A band remains constant.

In the sliding filament model, cross-bridge forms, and the myosin head bends, the *power stroke*.

The power stroke causes actin to slide toward the M line, allowing the muscle fiber to contract.

Next, ATP binds to the myosin head and is converted to ADP + Pi, which remains attached to the head.

The release of myosin $Ca^{2+}$ binds to troponin and results in a conformational change in tropomyosin.

Tropomyosin exposes myosin attachment sites, and cross bridges are formed between myosin heads and actin filaments.

Subsequently, ADP + Pi are released, causing a sliding motion of actin to bring the sarcomere's Z lines together (contraction, power stroke).

A new ATP molecule attaches to the myosin head, and the cross-bridges unbind, resulting in sarcomere relaxation, as phosphorylation breaks the cross-bridge.

Though counterintuitive, ATP is not directly needed for the power stroke.

ATP binding is needed to detach the myosin head from actin and reset the power stroke by cocking the myosin head (in preparation for the next power stroke).

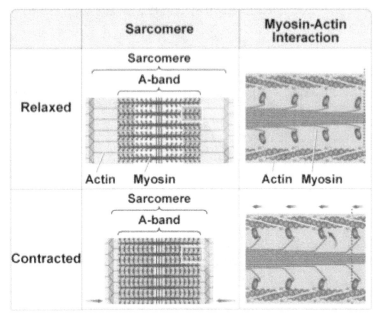

*Sliding filament model: thick (myosin) and thin (actin) filaments slide*
*past each other during muscle contraction, shortening of the sarcomere*

Nerves stimulate muscle cells during muscle contraction. An action potential runs along the muscle cell membrane and deep into the muscle cell via T-tubules.

This stimulates the *sarcoplasmic reticulum* (terminal cisternae) to release calcium ions.

Calcium causes muscles to contract via the sliding filament mechanism.

**Temporal and spatial response to force**

*Muscle spindles* monitor muscle length changes and the rates by stretch receptors present in modified muscle fibers as *intrafusal fibers*. The other fibers responsible for skeletal movement are *extrafusal fibers*. Stretching the muscle fires these muscle spindles, while muscle contraction slows the firing.

Passive tension in a relaxed fiber increases with increased stretch due to the elongation of *titin filaments*. However, the maximum tension during contraction depends primarily on the overlap between the thick and thin filaments, depending on the *resting length* of muscles.

Two main factors allow for the highest maximum tension during contraction.

*Increased resting length* increases the maximum tension because it allows the thick and thin filaments room to slide, allowing more cross-bridge cycling.

Additionally, the *decreased resting length* can increase the maximum tension. Tension can arise due to increased overlap between thick and thin filaments, allowing greater interaction during contraction.

These two factors that allow for maximum tension in a muscle are opposed: 1) increasing the resting length too much does not permit enough interaction between filaments, and 2) decreasing the resting length too much causes the thick filaments to hit the Z lines and stop the contraction.

Hence, there is an optimal resting length between the two extremes that result in the greatest possible maximum tension during contraction.

Most fibers are near this length, $l_0$, and are relaxed.

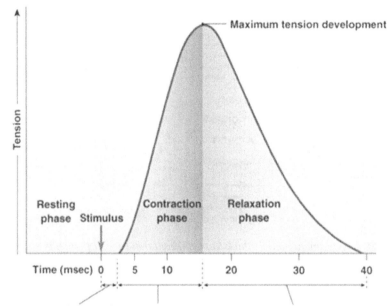

*Muscle contraction with tension vs. time. The contraction phase produces a maximum force of tension before the relaxation phase returns muscle to the resting phase for a 40 msec twitch*

Skeletal muscles are attached to the skeleton by tendons made of fibrous connective tissue.

When muscles contract or shorten, they cannot inherently lengthen on their own. Instead, skeletal muscles work in antagonistic pairs for skeletal muscles to return to their original length.

One muscle of an antagonistic pair bends the joint and brings a limb toward the body. The other straightens the joint and extends the limb. In this mechanism, the shortening of one muscle leads to the lengthening of another.

**Muscle tension responds to force applied**

Force exerted on an object by a contracting muscle is *muscle tension*, while the force exerted on the muscle by the object (weight) is *load*. These are opposing forces, and whether the exertion of force leads to a change in fiber length depends on the relative magnitudes of the tension and the load.

*Isometric contractions* are when a muscle develops tension but does not change in length. When a muscle supports a load in a constant position or attempts to move a supported load greater than the tension.

During such a contraction, the cross-bridges bound to actin do not move. In isometric contractions, the *latent period* is when the muscle receives the stimulus and develops tension in the fiber.

The following phase is the *contraction time*, the time required for the fiber to reach maximum tension. The *relaxation period* releases the fiber's tension. The fiber rests until a new stimulus is received.

Isometric contractions *do not* move a load; they develop tension in a muscle fiber without any change in fiber length. Therefore, the isometric contractions do not perform physical work, and it is appropriate that they be compared to isotonic twitches.

Isometric twitches have a *short latent period* and a *short contraction time*.

*Isotonic contractions* occur when the load remains constant while the fiber length changes. If the fibers shorten, the contraction is *concentric*. In such a contraction, the cross-bridges bound to actin move, shortening the fibers.

Before an isotonic shortening, there is a period of *isometric* contraction when the tension of the fiber increases to meet the load and move it. In isotonic contractions, the latent period is between when the stimulus is received and when shortening occurs in the fiber. The time from the beginning of shortening to the maximum shortening is the contraction time.

During the relaxation period, the fiber relaxes to a greater length. If the fibers lengthen, the isotonic contraction is an *eccentric contraction*. This occurs when the load on a muscle is greater than the tension, forcing the muscle to lengthen.

The components of isotonic twitches are compared at loads of different forces.

At a heavier load, a longer time is required in the isometric component of the twitch to build tension to meet the load. Thus, increasing the load leads to a longer latent period.

Heavier loads decrease the shortening distance that a single stimulus can provide.

Although the contraction time is slightly shorter with a heavier load, the decreased shortening distance leads to a slower velocity of contraction (or distance shortened) per unit time.

The relaxation phase depends on the load helping the fiber return to its original length; increased loads lead to a shorter relaxation phase. Isotonic twitches *do* move a load and *do* involve a change in fiber length.

Compared to isometric twitches, they have a long latent period and long contraction time. Even though eccentric isotonic contractions involve muscle lengthening over time, they involve temporary fiber shortening to give a controlled movement of the load.

For example, slowly lowering one's body from a pull-up requires eccentric muscle effort from the latissimus dorsi, whereas quickly dropping from pull-up to a dead-hang position while maintaining a grip on the bar would not involve isotonic contraction from the lats (and is painful).

Isometric twitches have a shorter contraction time but have a longer relaxation period, a *longer overall duration* than isotonic twitches.

Isotonic twitches have a shorter relaxation period due to a load, bringing the muscle to its original length.

## Neural Control of the Muscle System

**Motor and sensory neurons**

Motor neurons are *efferent neurons* that send signals to muscles and organs. Motor neurons have cell bodies in the CNS and contain large, myelinated axons that can propagate action potentials at high velocities.

*Autonomic motor neurons* control the sympathetic and parasympathetic branches of the nervous system, while *somatic motor neurons* control skeletal muscles.

Muscle fibers of a single muscle do not all contract at once.

A single motor neuron innervates multiple muscle fibers, collectively called a *motor unit*.

Motor units have varying amounts of muscle fibers. Usually, smaller motor units are activated; first, larger ones are activated as needed. This leads to smooth increases in force. Fine movement only uses smaller motor units.

The total tension a muscle develops depends on the tension in each fiber and the number of fibers contracting. The number of fibers contracting depends on these muscle fibers' recruitment (or activation).

Sensory neurons, or *afferent neurons*, are the opposite of motor neurons.

Afferent fibers from receptors can take one of four pathways. Some fibers go directly to motor neurons of the same muscle without the interposition of any interneurons, as *monosynaptic stretch reflex arcs.*

Some fibers end on interneurons that inhibit the antagonistic muscles as *reciprocal innervation.*

Some fibers activate motor neurons of synergistic muscles. Some fibers continue to the brainstem.

A *motor program* is the pattern of neural activities required to perform a movement. It is created and transmitted via neurons organized hierarchically and is continuously updated.

A skill is learned if the program is repeated frequently enough. Local control of motor neurons is important in keeping the motor program updated by gathering information from local levels through afferent nerve fibers.

**Alpha and gamma motor neurons and reflex response**

*Alpha motor neurons* are the larger motor neurons that control the extrafusal fibers responsible for skeletal movement.

*Gamma motor neurons* are the smaller motor neurons that control the intrafusal fibers. The neurons in these intrafusal fibers are excited or co-activated with the neurons in the extrafusal fibers to get continuous information about muscle length.

*Withdrawal reflex* is a stimulus that activates flexor motor neurons and inhibits extensor motor neurons to move the body away from an external stimulus. The effect is produced on the same (ipsilateral) side of the body where the stimulus arose.

An opposite effect (*crossed extensor reflex*) may be produced on the other side, the contralateral side, to compensate for any lost support due to the withdrawal.

Interneurons are synapses that integrate inputs from higher centers and peripheral receptors.

Afferent inputs to local interneurons bring information such as the tension of muscles or movement of joints, which influence movements.

*Golgi tendon organs* are receptors in tendons to monitor a muscle's tension.

Complex muscular activities (e.g., maintenance of posture and balance) require a carefully coordinated effort from several muscles. The afferent vestibular apparatus pathways of the eyes and the somatic receptors must first relay sensory information to the brain centers. The information is compared with an internal representation of the body's geometry, and corrections to skeletal muscles are made through alpha motor neurons in the efferent pathways.

Walking is a coordinated effort of multiple muscles. On one leg, extensor muscles are activated to support the body's weight.

At the same time, contralateral extensors are inhibited through reciprocal inhibition, allowing flexors to swing the non-supporting leg forward.

## Voluntary and involuntary muscles during human activity

*Voluntary muscles* are consciously controlled muscles with cylindrical fibers.

These muscles are generally attached to bones (i.e., skeletal muscles), and the brain is involved in the movement of these muscles.

An example of voluntary muscles is the biceps in the upper arm.

*Involuntary muscles* cannot be consciously controlled. They are spindle-shaped fibers associated with the autonomic nervous system.

Smooth muscles of the gut and cardiac muscles of the heart are involuntary muscles.

Contractions of voluntary muscles are usually rapid and forceful, while contractions of involuntary muscles are usually slow and rhythmic.

Motor behaviors are a continuum of these two types of contractions, having components of voluntary and involuntary muscles to differing degrees.

## Oxygen Debt and Muscle Fatigue

**ATP levels regulate muscle fatigue**

Muscle fatigue occurs when there is a decline in muscle tension from the previous contractile activity. A fatigued muscle has decreased shortening velocity and a slower rate of relaxation.

The onset and rate of fatigue depend on the type of skeletal muscle and the duration of contractile activity. If a fatigued muscle is allowed to rest, it recovers.

The recovery rate depends on the duration and intensity of the previous exercise.

Fatigue is not due to low ATP; a fatigued muscle still has a high ATP concentration but is an adaptation to prevent the rigor that results from a low ATP level.

High-frequency fatigue accompanies high-intensity; short-duration exercise is due to failure in the T-tubule's conduction of action potential.

Recovery from fatigue is rapid. Low-frequency fatigue (low-intensity, long-duration exercise) is due to lactic acid buildup, which changes the conformation of muscle proteins.

Recovery from fatigue is slow. The basic molecular mechanism behind muscle fatigue is the continuous synaptic activity causes depletion of the required neurotransmitter, leading to fatigue.

# CHAPTER 18

# Digestive System

## Introduction to the Digestive System

### Six processes of the digestive tract

Digestion provides the energy necessary for routine metabolic activities and to maintain homeostasis.

The digestive tract ingests food, breaks it down into small molecules, crosses plasma membranes, absorbs the nutrients, and eliminates indigestible remains.

The human digestive system is a coiled, muscular tube (6-9 meters long when fully extended), beginning at the mouth and ending at the anus.

Several specialized compartments occur along this length: mouth, pharynx, esophagus, stomach, small intestine, large intestine, and anus.

Accessory digestive organs are connected to the main system by a series of ducts: salivary glands, parts of the pancreas, the liver, and the gallbladder (*biliary system*).

The digestive tract performs six processes:

1. *Ingestion* – bringing food into the system

2. *Movement (peristalsis)* – moving food along the system

3. *Digestion* – breaking down food using mechanical and chemical processes

4. *Secretion* – releasing enzymes and bile into the digestive tract

5. *Absorption* – moving food molecules from the digestive tract into the blood

6. *Defecation* – eliminating solid waste from the large intestine.

### Four macromolecules in the digestive tract

Four groups of macromolecules are digested and absorbed by the digestive tract.

These include starches, proteins, triacylglycerols (fats), and nucleic acids.

Starches are broken down (i.e., catabolism) into glucose.

Proteins are broken down into amino acids.

Triacylglycerols (fats) are broken down into fatty acids and glycerol.

Nucleic acids are broken down into nucleotides.

**Gastrointestinal structures**

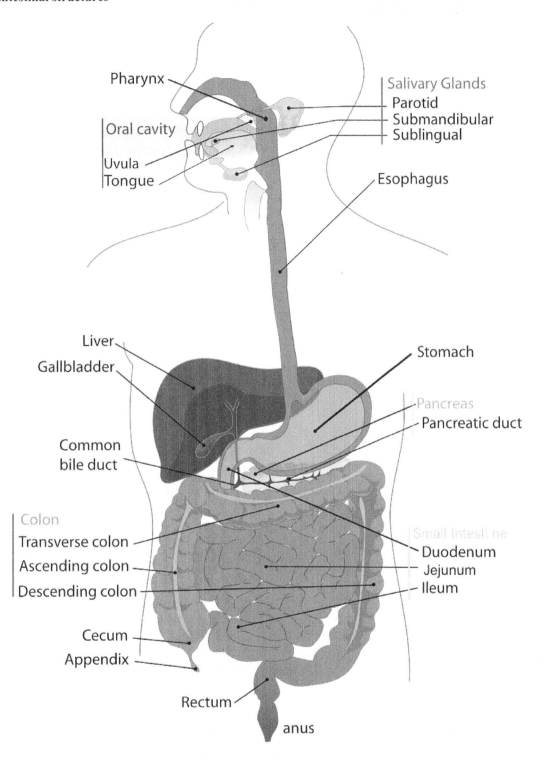

## Ingestion

**Saliva and digestive enzymes**

The gastrointestinal (GI) tract begins at the mouth, where a mechanical form of digestion begins (i.e., chewing or mastication).

Saliva, a form of chemical digestion, contains mucus and amylase (enzymes end with ~*ase*). It is secreted from 3 pairs of salivary glands around the oral cavity. Mucus moistens the food, and amylase partially digests polysaccharides (starches).

Swallowing moves food (bolus) from the mouth through the pharynx into the esophagus, past the esophageal sphincter, and into the stomach.

Human *dentition* (i.e., teeth structure) has specializations because humans are *omnivores* (i.e., a diet of plants and animals).

Food is masticated (chewed) in the mouth and mixed with saliva. Food is manipulated in the mouth by a muscular tongue containing touch and pressure receptors.

*Taste buds,* receptors stimulated by the chemical composition of food, are primarily on the tongue but the surface of the mouth.

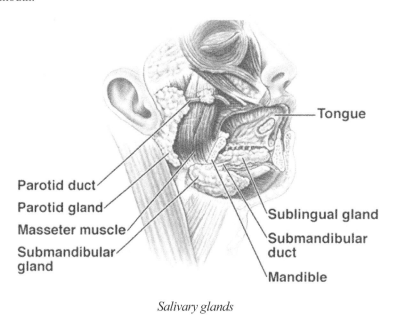

*Salivary glands*

Three pairs of *salivary glands* secrete saliva into the mouth by ducts. Saliva, a form of lubrication and a source of enzymes, dissolves food and contains mucin.

*Mucin* is a protein that lubricates the bolus. Saliva contains amylase, an enzyme that breaks down polysaccharides (starch and glycogen), as well as antibodies and lysozymes that kill pathogens.

*Salivary amylase* (enzymes end with ~*ase*) begins digesting starch (α-linked glucose polysaccharide). It breaks down the complex carbohydrates into the simple sugar maltose (a disaccharide of two glucose monomers).

Mucus (composed of mucin) moistens food and lubricates the esophagus.

Bicarbonate ions in saliva neutralize the acids in foods.

$$\text{Starch} + H_2O \xrightarrow{\textit{Salivary Amylase Mechanism}} \text{maltose}$$

## Pharynx, epiglottis and peristalsis

The *pharynx* (i.e., throat) is between the mouth and the esophagus and is where the food and air passage cross. It is a muscular tube that squeezes and routes food to the *esophagus* when swallowing.

The pharynx closes pathways to the nasal cavity and airway to prevent choking.

In the pharynx, the *bolus* (i.e., an ingested food substance) triggers an involuntary swallowing reflex that prevents food from entering the trachea (directed to the lungs) and moves the bolus into the esophagus (directed to the stomach).

The digestive and respiratory passages join in the pharynx and separate as air moves into the rigid trachea while food descends the flexible esophagus into the stomach.

During swallowing, the bolus is moved to the back of the mouth by the tongue.

If food were to enter the trachea, the pathway of air to the lungs could be blocked.

The *epiglottis* is a flap of cartilage that closes off the airway during swallowing.

It covers the opening into the trachea as muscles move bolus through the pharynx into the esophagus.

After the food and saliva are swallowed, they are pushed into the esophagus, a tube that uses muscular contractions to propel food toward the stomach.

*Peristalsis* is the involuntary muscle contractions that move food *via* the esophagus past the esophageal sphincter into the stomach, then the small intestine, large intestine, and rectum.

## Stomach

### Stomach anatomy and function

The stomach, an essential component of the digestive system, is an elastic, muscular sac that stretches to store food. The bolus (food) passes through the *gastroesophageal sphincter* (or *lower esophageal* or *cardiac sphincter*), a ring of smooth muscle fibers connecting the esophagus and stomach. The stomach secretes hydrochloric acid (HCl), which destroys bacteria and other harmful organisms, preventing most food poisonings.

When *gastric* (i.e., stomach) *juices* leak through the cardiac sphincter, irritation of the esophagus causes acid reflux or heartburn. The stomach's acidic environment (pH 1.5–3.0) provides the optimum conditions for the enzyme pepsin to function. The stomach secretes pepsin, which begins digesting proteins into smaller polypeptides and amino acids. These smaller amino acid molecules can be absorbed by the villi (small finger-like projections) that protrude from the small intestine's epithelial layer.

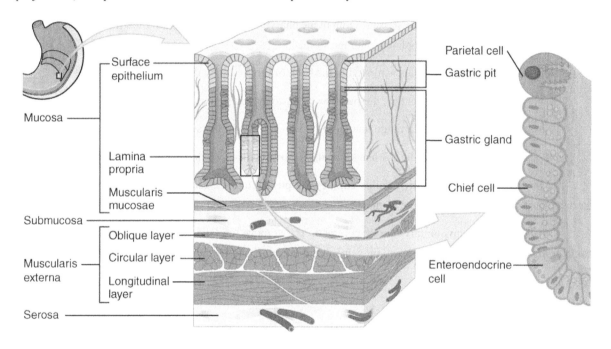

### Mechanical digestion, storage and churning of chyme

The stomach stores partially digested food (i.e., bolus in the stomach), freeing humans from continually eating for energy. During a meal, the stomach gradually fills from an empty capacity of 50-100 ml (i.e., milliliters) to a capacity of 1,000 ml (1 liter); with discomfort, the stomach distends to 2,000 ml (2 liters) or more.

The muscles in the stomach are responsible for the mechanical breakdown of food. This process is churning, where food is mechanically digested and mixed. Walls of the stomach contract vigorously, mixing food with juices secreted when the food enters. The mixing of food with water and gastric juice generates a creamy medium called *chyme*.

Food is mixed in the lower part of the stomach by peristaltic waves that propel the acid-chyme mixture against the pyloric sphincter. During 1 to 2-hours, increased contractions (i.e., peristalsis) of the stomach muscles push chyme (food) through the pyloric sphincter and into the duodenum (first of three sections) of the small intestine. High-fat diets generate satiation by significantly increasing the period for food to remain in the stomach.

**Mucus, low pH and gastric juice**

Gastric glands are *exocrine glands* (secreted by duct) within gastric pits. *Gastric pits* are indentations in the stomach that denote entrances to the gastric glands, containing secreting epithelial cells (chief cells, parietal cells, and mucous cells). These epithelial cells line the stomach's inner surface, secreting about 2 liters of gastric juice per day. Gastric juice contains several digestion components (e.g., HCl, pepsinogen, and mucus).

*Chief cells* secrete *pepsinogen,* a zymogen (i.e., precursor) to pepsin. Pepsinogen is activated to form *pepsin* by low pH in the stomach. Once active, pepsin begins protein digestion. *Parietal cells* secrete HCl and intrinsic factor, which is important in vitamin B-12 absorption.

*G cells* secrete *gastrin,* a large peptide hormone that is absorbed into the blood, stimulating parietal cells to secrete HCl. Acetylcholine increases the secretion of all the types, while gastrin and histamine increase HCl secretion.

*Mucous cells* (Goblet cells) secrete mucus that lubricates and protects the stomach's epithelial lining from the acidic environment. The mucus forms a protective barrier between the cells and the stomach acids. Additionally, pepsin is inactivated (i.e., pepsinogen) when it contacts the mucus. Bicarbonate ions reduce acidity near the cells lining the stomach by increasing the pH. For protection, tight junctions link the epithelial, stomach-lining cells, preventing stomach acids from affecting other structures.

*Goblet cells* secrete mucus to lubricate and protect from mechanical or chemical damage.

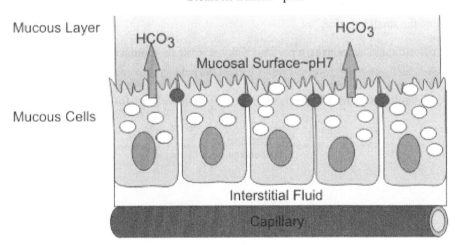

*Stomach with mucus cells and bicarbonate*

**Ulcers**

*Peptic ulcers* result from the failure of the mucosal lining to protect the stomach. Ulcers are eroded areas of the gastric surface or breaks in the mucosal barrier. Ulcers expose the underlying gastric muscle tissue to acid and pepsin's corrosive action.

---

Bleeding ulcers result when tissue damage is so severe that blood enters the stomach. Perforated ulcers are life-threatening emergencies that occur when a hole forms in the stomach wall.

About 90% of peptic ulcers are caused by *Helicobacter pylori*, a strain of bacteria that burrows into the mucous lining of the stomach, exposing the underlying epithelial cells to the acidic environment of the stomach. Other factors contributing to ulcers are stress, excess HCl, and aspirin.

**Production of digestive enzymes and site of digestion**

Carbohydrate digestion begins with salivary amylase in the mouth and continues as the bolus passes into the stomach. The bolus becomes acid chyme as it is broken down in the lower third of the stomach.

Hydrochloric acid does not directly function for digestion, but it lowers the pH of the gastric (stomach) contents to about 2.

The low pH stops salivary amylase activity and promotes pepsin activity; protein digestion begins.

Pepsin is an enzyme that controls the hydrolysis of proteins into peptides.

Chyme leaves the stomach and enters the small intestine.

$$\text{protein } + \text{ H}_2\text{O} \xrightarrow{\text{pepsin}} \text{peptides (small chains of amino acids)}$$

**Cardiac and pyloric sphincters of the stomach**

The stomach has an inner membrane of dense folds as *rugae*, allowing it to accommodate stretching.

The stomach is sealed off at the top by the *cardiac* (or *gastroesophageal*) sphincter.

At the bottom, the stomach is sealed by the *pyloric sphincter*, a circular muscle that controls the release of the acid chyme into the small intestine.

When the pyloric sphincter relaxes, a portion of chyme exits the stomach and enters the duodenum (i.e., the first section of the small intestine). A neural reflex causes the sphincter to contract, closing off the opening.

The slow, rhythmic pace with which chyme exits the stomach allows for thorough digestion.

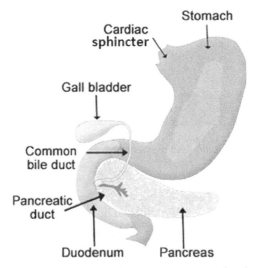

*Stomach and duodenum with accessory organs for digestion*

## Liver

### Structural relationship of the liver in the gastrointestinal system

The liver is a large glandular organ that occupies the top of the abdominal cavity, below the diaphragm. Being the largest gland in the body, it spans both sides of the abdomen (the right side occupies more space) and has ducts that drain into the duodenum and gallbladder.

The liver is responsible for the detoxification of blood (metabolizing and removing poisonous substances), synthesis of blood proteins (making plasma proteins such as albumin and fibrinogen), production of bile, destruction of old erythrocytes, storage and regulation of blood glucose, and the production of urea from amino acids and ammonia.

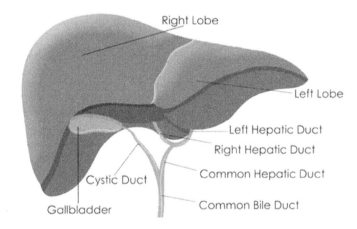

*Liver with lobes and ducts that connect the liver to accessory glands*

### Nutrient metabolism and vitamin storage

The liver stores glucose as glycogen and catabolizes (i.e., breaks down) glycogen to maintain a constant blood glucose concentration. Blood vessels from the large and small intestines lead to the liver as the *hepatic portal vein*. The liver maintains the blood glucose level at 0.1% by removing glucose from the hepatic portal vein to store as glycogen. As needed, glycogen is catabolized, and glucose monomers reenter the hepatic portal vein.

Amino acids are converted to glucose by the liver, but deamination (removal of ammonia from amino groups) must occur first. The liver produces urea from these amino groups and ammonia. By complex metabolic pathways, the liver converts amino groups to urea. Urea is the common human nitrogenous waste; the blood transports it to the kidneys (see "excretory system").

The liver provides storage for important nutrients, vitamins (A, D, E, K and $B_{12}$), and minerals (e.g., iron, copper), releasing these essential substances to the tissues as needed. These compounds are absorbed from the blood as they go through the hepatic portal system.

Glucose is stored in the liver in its polysaccharide form, glycogen. Under the influence of insulin, glucose is transported to the liver cells (hepatocytes). *Hepatocytes* absorb and store fatty acids in the form of digested triglycerides. The storage of nutrients allows the liver to maintain homeostasis of blood glucose levels.

**Blood glucose regulation and cellular detoxification**

The liver acts as a storehouse for glycogen, the storage form of glucose. Through gluconeogenesis, glycogenolysis, and glycogenesis, the liver regulates glucose levels in the blood.

When blood sugar is too low, the liver conducts gluconeogenesis (synthesizing glucose and increasing blood glucose count) and glycogen lysis (breaking down stored glycogen and increasing blood glucose count). When blood glucose is too high, the liver engages in glycogenesis, converting the extra glucose in the blood into glycogen as a form of storage.

*Insulin*, an important hormone in glucose regulation, is released to increase glucose levels. Therefore, insulin promotes glucose conversion into glycogen, whereby the excess glucose is stored in the liver for later use.

*Glucagon*, a hormone antagonist to insulin, is released in response to decreased glucose levels, promoting glycogen conversion into glucose. Low glucose is compensated for by the glucose supply by glycogen.

The liver is responsible for the detoxification of the body. It metabolizes alcohol with *alcohol dehydrogenase* (enzymes end with ~*ase*), removes blood ammonia, and inactivates drugs and toxins.

The liver excretes detoxified chemicals as part of bile (or polarized to be excreted by the kidneys).

*Kupffer cells* are macrophages in the liver that phagocytize the intestines' bacteria. Although most red blood cells are destroyed in the spleen, Kupffer cells help destroy irregular erythrocytes.

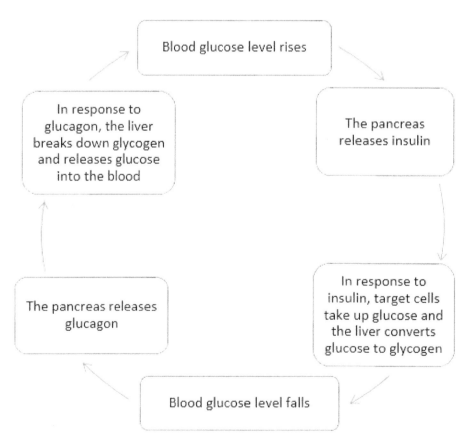

*Homeostasis of glucose by the antagonistic actions of insulin and glucagon*

## Bile

### Bile is produced in the liver and stored in the gallbladder

The liver makes bile from cholesterol and stores it in the gallbladder. To produce bile, hepatocytes in the liver destroy old red blood cells.

Bile is a green byproduct resulting from hemoglobin breakdown, converted into the two key components of bile, bilirubin, and biliverdin.

Bile subsequently enters the duodenum from the gallbladder to emulsify fats.

Bile reaches the gallbladder through hepatic ducts and is stored there for later use. When needed, the bile flows through the *cystic duct*, merging with the *pancreatic duct* to form the *common bile duct*.

The sphincter of Oddi is a muscular valve that controls the entry of digestive juices (bile and pancreatic juice) from the liver and pancreas into the duodenum of the small intestine.

When the sphincter is closed, secreted bile is shunted into the gallbladder. The presence of fat in the intestine releases CCK, relaxing the sphincter to discharge bile salts into the duodenum.

Excess, unused bile is concentrated and stored in the gallbladder. The excess bile is secreted when needed. For example, during a meal, bile is secreted from the gland by smooth muscle contraction. It reaches the duodenum as the first portion of the small intestine by the common bile duct.

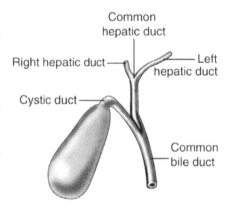

*Gallbladder and associated ducts*

### Bile emulsifies fats during digestion

Bile salts solubilize fats, while bicarbonate ions neutralize stomach acids.

*Emulsification* breaks fat globules into microscopic droplets.

Bile salts, secreted by hepatocytes (liver cells), enter the GI tract, are reabsorbed by transporters in the intestine, and are returned to the liver via the *portal vein*.

This recycling pathway is the *entero-hepatic circulation*.

$$\text{fat} \xrightarrow{\text{bile salts}} \text{fat droplets (by emulsification)}$$

This process increases fat digestion by increasing the surface area of fat globules exposed to lipase (enzymes end with ~*ase*).

Bile emulsifies fats, facilitating their breakdown into progressively smaller fat globules until they are acted upon by lipases. Bile contains cholesterol, phospholipids, bilirubin, and a mix of salts.

Fats are digested in the small intestine, unlike carbohydrates (i.e., by salivary amylase in the mouth) and proteins (predigested in the acidic stomach).

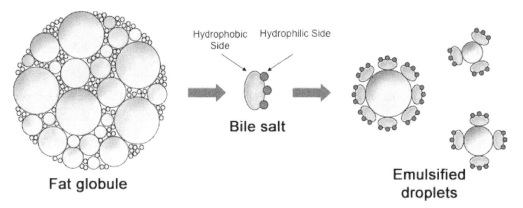

*Bile salts emulsify fat into smaller goblets for absorption in the small intestine*

Due to their hydrophobic nature, digested fats are not soluble.

To compensate for insolubility, bile salts surround fats, forming micelles that pass into the epithelial cells. Afterward, bile salts are recycled into the lumen to repeat the process.

Fat digestion is usually completed when the food reaches the ileum (lower third) of the small intestine.

Bile salts are absorbed in the ileum and are recycled by the liver and gallbladder.

Fats pass from the epithelial cells to the small lymph vessels that run through the villi.

**Gallstones and jaundice**

Excessive secretion of water-insoluble cholesterol in bile results in crystals called *gallstones*.

Gallstones can obstruct the opening of the gallbladder or the bile duct.

If a gallstone prevents bile from entering the intestine, the rate of fat digestion and absorption decreases.

If a gallstone blocks the pancreatic duct's entry, pancreatic enzymes cannot enter the intestine, preventing the digestion of other nutrients.

Blocked bile secretions result in the accumulation of bilirubin in tissues.

High levels of bilirubin produce a yellowish coloration as jaundice.

*Jaundice* is common in newborns and patients with liver disease.

## Pancreas

### Endocrine and exocrine functions

The *pancreas*, an elongated, tadpole-shaped organ, lies deep within the abdominal cavity. It is below the stomach along the posterior abdominal wall and leads to the duodenum.

The endocrine functions of the pancreas include secreting the glucose regulatory hormones (i.e., glucagon and insulin) into the bloodstream using two types of cells.

Depending on the blood glucose concentration, one of two hormones targets the liver.

From its exocrine function, the pancreas secretes digestive enzymes and a fluid rich in $HCO_3^-$ ions to neutralize the acid from the stomach.

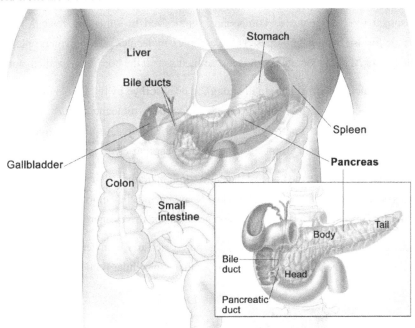

*Pancreas as an endocrine and exocrine organ aiding in digestion*

The pancreas secretes pancreatic juice, a mixture of enzymes and ions. The pancreas releases its major enzymes from pancreatic cells, *acinar cells*, into the duodenum via the pancreatic duct.

These major enzymes include *trypsin* and *chymotrypsin* (enzymes that digest proteins), lipase (i.e., digests fats), pancreatic amylase (i.e., digests starch), and deoxyribonucleases and ribonucleases (i.e., digests nucleic acids).

These enzymes exist first as zymogens / proenzymes (inactive forms). Once trypsin becomes activated by the intestinal *enterokinase*, it activates the other digestive enzymes released earlier by the pancreas. However, certain enzymes (e.g., pancreatic amylase, lipase) are secreted in active forms.

The pancreas secretes bicarbonate ions ($HCO_3^-$) to neutralize the HCl from the stomach. The pancreas enzymes function best in alkaline (pH > 7) solutions.

The digestive enzymes produced by the pancreas travel to the small intestine, where the process continues. These enzymes enter the small intestine through the *pancreatic duct* (or *duct of Wirsung*).

## Small Intestine

### Site of complete digestion and absorption of monomers

Most digestion and absorption of nutrients occurs in the small intestine. The intestinal wall secretes enzymes and receives enzymes from the pancreas. The small intestine's primary function is to complete digestion and absorb the monomers (i.e., individual building blocks comprising polymers) of food particles after chemical digestion. The small intestine contains many villi, structures increasing the surface area for absorption.

### Absorption of digested food molecules

Most animals need to digest food into small molecules to cross the plasma membranes. There are two primary reasons why the complete digestion of complex food molecules is essential for proper absorption.

First, consumed food originates as compounds synthesized by other organisms. Not all the ingested compounds are suitable for use by human tissues. These complex molecules (i.e., polymers) must be broken down into mostly individual subunits (i.e., monomers) and reassembled so that the body can use them appropriately.

Second, the food molecules must be small enough to be absorbed by the villi in the intestine by diffusion, facilitated diffusion, or active transport. Therefore, large food molecules must be broken down for absorption. Intestinal folds, villi, and microvilli increase the surface area to absorb digested compounds into circulation. Absorption involves lacteals for fats into lacteals and capillaries for amino acids (proteins) and sugars.

Active transport absorbs molecules against the concentration gradient. The intestinal lumen has less glucose than the enterocyte; secondary active transport is by the $Na^+/K^+$ pump and $Na^+/$glucose symport. Facilitated transport (passive diffusion) absorbs glucose down its concentration gradient and drives energetically unfavorable reactions.

The enterocyte (i.e., intestinal lining) now having more glucose. It transfers its glucose to the extracellular fluid using facilitated diffusion. The glucose then moves from the extracellular fluid to the blood.

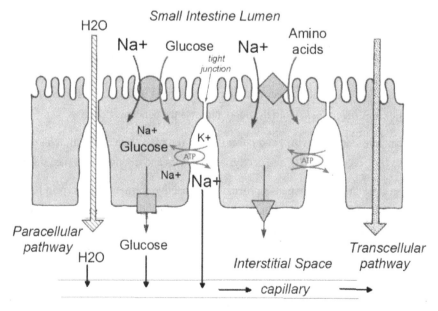

*Absorption of glucose in the small intestine*

**Function and structure of villi**

Most absorption occurs in the duodenum and jejunum (second third) of the small intestine. The intestine's inner surface has circular folds that more than triple the surface area for absorption. Finger-like projections as villi cover the mucous membrane in these ridges and furrows.

Villi increase the surface area for greater digestion and absorption. They are covered with epithelial cells that increase the surface area by another factor of 10.

The epithelial cells are lined with microvilli that increase the surface area; a 6-meter tube has a surface area of 300 square meters. The small intestine is specialized for absorption by the massive number of villi lining the intestinal wall. If the small intestine were merely a smooth tube, it would have to be 500–600 meters long to have a comparable surface area.

The structure of the villus is specific. Their numbers increase the surface area for absorption in the small intestine. The villi have projections (microvilli). Microvilli are minute projections (collectively as the brush border) on the intestinal villi's surface of cells. These microvilli have protein channels and pump in their membranes to allow the rapid absorption of food by facilitated diffusion and active transport.

The villi contain an epithelial layer (one cell layer thick) so that food can pass through easily and be absorbed quickly. The blood capillaries in the villus are associated with the epithelium so that the distance for the diffusion of the food molecules is negligible. This thin layer of cells contains mitochondria to provide the ATP needed for the active transport of specific food molecules. There is a lacteal branch at the center of the villus that carries away fats after absorption.

**Lacteals**

Sugars and amino acids enter villi cells and are absorbed into the bloodstream. Glycerol and fatty acids enter villi cells, reassemble into fat molecules, and move into lacteals. Villi have *lacteals*, a lymphatic vessel

*Intestinal villus with lacteals for fat absorption and capillaries for other nutrients*

surrounded by a capillary network in an intestinal villus that aids in fat absorption.

Absorption involves diffusion and active transport, requiring the expenditure of cellular energy.

Villi have cells that produce intestinal enzymes that complete the digestion of peptides and sugars. The villi contain large numbers of capillaries that take the amino acids and glucose produced by digestion to the hepatic portal vein and the liver.

*Absorption* occurs in the small intestine's specialized villi when food molecules pass through a layer of cells and into the body's tissues.

Absorption is followed by *assimilation*, occurring when food molecules become part of the body's tissue.

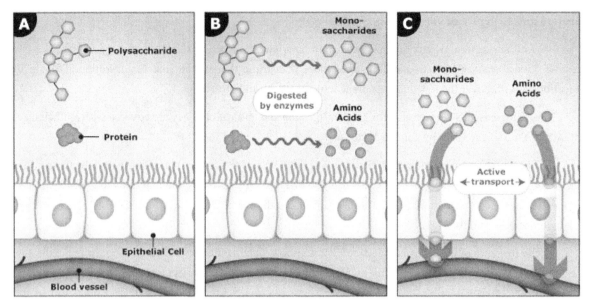

*Digestion and absorption of amino acids and monosaccharides in the small intestine*

### Enzyme production and site of digestion

As chyme enters the duodenum, proteins and carbohydrates are partially digested. No fat has been digested yet because the liver and pancreas' secretions released into the duodenum are essential for fat digestion.

Digestion of carbohydrates, proteins, and fats continues in the small intestine.

Starch and glycogen are broken down into maltose.

Proteases (enzymes secreted from the pancreas) continue the breakdown of proteins into small peptide fragments and individual amino acids.

The upper part of the small intestine, the duodenum, is the most active during digestion. The duodenum uses secretions from the liver and pancreas to break down ingested compounds.

Epithelial cells of the duodenum form *Bruner's glands* and secrete watery mucus. The mucus aids in protecting the duodenal epithelium from the acidic chyme (entered from the stomach), lubricating the intestinal walls and providing an alkaline environment for pancreatic enzymes to operate.

### Peptidase and maltase

Epithelial cells of villi produce the intestinal enzymes attached to the plasma membrane of microvilli. Intestinal secretions complete the digestion of peptides and sugars; peptidases digest peptides into amino acids:

peptides + $H_2O$ + *peptidases* → amino acids

Maltose (from the first step in starch digestion) is converted by maltase to glucose:

maltose + $H_2O$ + *maltase* → glucose + glucose

Maltose, sucrose, and lactose are the main carbohydrates in the small intestine; the microvilli absorb them. Starch is broken down into two-glucose units (maltose).

Epithelial cell enzymes convert disaccharides (i.e., two sugars) into monosaccharides (i.e., single sugar) that exit the cell and enter the capillaries.

Lactose (milk sugar) intolerance results from the genetic lack of lactase (enzymes with ~*ase*) produced by the intestinal cells. The lack of lactase results in the incomplete digestion of lactose to glucose and galactose.

While the pancreas is the primary source for the enzymes used, the small intestine does make some enzymes, including *protease*, *amylase*, *lipase,* and *nuclease*.

Cellulose, a polysaccharide similar in structure to starch, cannot be digested by humans. Humans lack cellulase needed to hydrolyze *β* glycosidic bonds of cellulose.

**Anatomical subdivisions of the small intestine**

The small intestine is divided into three segments: the duodenum, the jejunum, and the ileum.

The small intestine is a coiled tube up to 6 meters long and 2 to 3 cm wide.

Coils and folding, along with villi, give this 6–meters tube the surface area of a tube 500-600 meters long.

Food moves from the stomach to the small intestine through the *pyloric sphincter* (into the first 25 cm of the small intestine, the duodenum).

The duodenum has a pH of 6, mainly due to bicarbonate ions secreted by the pancreas.

In the duodenum, the breakdown of starches, proteins, and remaining foods (fats and nucleotides) continues.

The *ileocecal valve* separates the small intestine from the large intestine.

The duodenum is responsible for digestion, with the jejunum and ilium mainly responsible for absorption.

90% of digestion and absorption occurs within the small intestine.

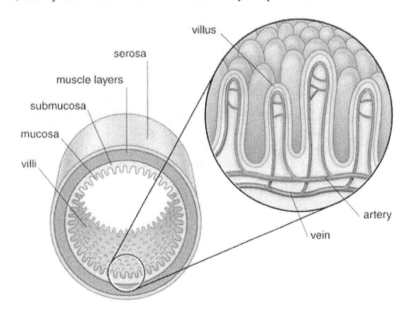

*Small intestine*

**Tissue stratification of the small intestine**

While the entire intestinal tract's length contains lymphoid tissue, only the ileum has abundant *Peyer's patches* (i.e., unencapsulated lymphoid nodules) containing large numbers of lymphocytes and immune cells.

The small intestine's luminal surface is covered by a single epithelium layer containing exocrine and endocrine cells.

The epithelia, with an underlying layer of *lamina propria* (connective tissue) and *muscularis mucosa* (muscle), are *mucosa*.

Below the mucosa is a layer of inner circular and an outer longitudinal smooth muscle of *muscularis externa*, providing the force for moving and mixing the GI contents.

*Serosa* is the outermost layer of the tube made of connective tissue.

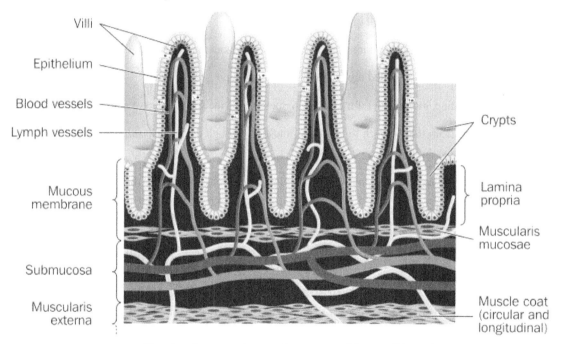

*The circulatory and muscular system of the small intestine*

## Large Intestine

**Structure of large intestine**

The large intestine is the gastrointestinal tract region following the small intestine.

The large intestine has four parts: cecum (blind pocket; the appendix), colon, rectum, and anal canal.

Chyme enters the cecum through the ileocecal sphincter, relaxing and opening by the gastroileal reflex.

The large intestine terminates at the anus, an external opening.

The large intestine has lobes (pockets) along its length due to muscle tone.

Unlike the small intestine, the large intestine has no folds or villi because its primary function is to store and concentrate fecal material for elimination.

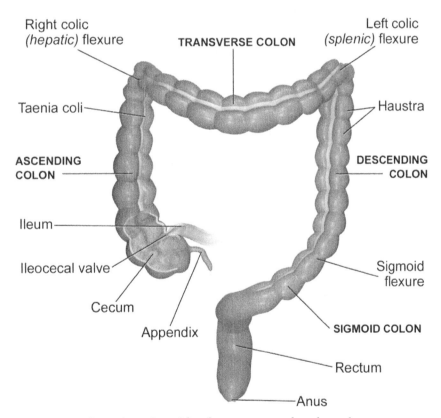

*Large intestine with colon, rectum, and anal canal*

The *appendix* is a finger-like projection extending from the cecum, a blind sac at the junction of the small and large intestines. It may play a role in fighting infections.

If an infected appendix bursts, the result is a general abdominal infection as peritonitis.

The large intestine secretes an alkaline mucus ($HCO_3^-$ ions) into the lumen, protecting epithelial tissue and neutralizing acids produced by bacterial metabolism.

**Water absorption by the large intestine**

Material entering the large intestine is mostly indigestible residue and liquid.

Undigested chyme is passed to the large intestine, temporarily stored and concentrated by reabsorption of salts and water.

About 2,500 milliliters (2.5 liters) of water enters the digestive tract daily by consumption.

The *small intestine* reabsorbs most of this liquid.

The *large intestine* (or *large bowel*) absorbs most remaining water not absorbed by the small intestine.

If the water is not reabsorbed, it causes diarrhea, which can cause severe dehydration and ion loss.

However, if too much water is reabsorbed, the result is constipation with a blocked passage.

Sodium ions ($Na^+$) are absorbed whenever water is reabsorbed.

**Rectum stores and eliminates waste**

The large intestine moves material that has not been digested from the small intestine.

Water, salts, and vitamins are absorbed in the large intestine.

The remaining contents in the lumen form feces stored in the rectum and egested through the anus.

Feces consist of about 75% water and 25% solid matter.

One-third of the solid matter is intestinal bacteria. The remainder is undigested wastes, fats, organic material, mucus, and dead cells from intestinal linings.

Following a meal, there is a wave of intense contraction (i.e., *mass movement*).

The mass movement of fecal material into the anus initiates the defecation reflex.

Contractions of the rectum expel the feces through the anus.

During defecation, the anal sphincter opens, and feces are released through the anus.

## Muscular Control

### Sphincter muscles

The *cardiac sphincter* (gastroesophageal sphincter) is between the esophagus and the stomach.

It prevents the backflow of food.

The *pyloric sphincter* is between the stomach and small intestine.

It releases food into the small intestine, a small amount at a time.

The *anal sphincter* is at the end of the rectum and ties the end of the rectum.

The *internal anal sphincter* is made of smooth muscle and closes the anus, while the *external anal sphincter* is made of skeletal muscle and is under voluntary control.

Both sphincters regulate the anal opening and closing.

The defecation reflex, mediated by mechanoreceptors, causes the two anal sphincters to open and expel the feces. If defecation is delayed, rectal contents are driven into the colon by reverse peristalsis until the next mass movement.

### Peristalsis

*Peristalsis* is regular contractions of the circular smooth muscle that produces a slow, rhythmic, bidirectional segmentation movement similar to the unidirectional material movement. The undigested material moves back and forth slowly to provide resident bacteria time to grow and multiply.

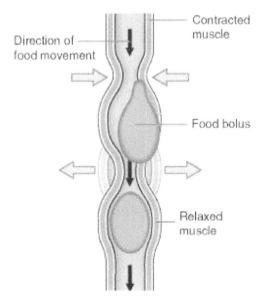

The bacteria of the large intestine (e.g., *E. coli*) are symbiotic organisms that ferment undigested nutrients, making gas as a byproduct. These bacteria produce vitamins (vitamin K) as an essential component in blood clot formation.

Undigested polysaccharides (fiber) are metabolized to short-chain fatty acids by the residing bacteria and are absorbed by diffusion. Bacterial metabolism produces *flatus*, a mixture of gases.

Peristalsis is the involuntary movement of smooth muscles that squeeze food along the digestive tract. Chyme moves through the intestines via peristalsis.

Layers of circular and longitudinal smooth muscle enable the chyme (partly digested food and water) to be pushed along the ileum by waves of muscle contractions as peristalsis.

The remaining chyme is passed to the colon.

The stomach produces peristaltic waves in response to the arrival of food.

---

The pyloric sphincter between the stomach and duodenum opens to release small amounts of chyme into the duodenum with every wave.

These waves are generated by pacemaker cells in the longitudinal smooth muscle layer and are spread by gap junctions.

Distension of the stomach with gastrin and other factors stimulates gastric motility, while distension of the duodenum inhibits it.

**Segmentation by the small intestine mixes chyme**

The typical motion of the small intestine is stationary contraction and relaxation, called segmentation.

Segmentation mixes chyme with digestive juices but results in little net movement.

The chyme is mixed and brought into contact with the intestine wall and is moved slowly toward the large intestine.

The movements are initiated by *pacemaker cells* in the smooth muscle layer.

After most materials are absorbed, segmentation is replaced by peristaltic activity as a migrating motility complex, moving undigested material to the large intestine.

The intestinal hormone *motilin* initiates migrating motility.

In the large intestine (due to involuntary contractions), movements shuffle contents back and forth, and propulsive contractions move material through the large intestine.

**Summary of the Gastrointestinal Tract**

**Anatomy and function of the gastrointestinal (GI) tract**

The human digestive tract is a complete tube-within-a-tube system. Each part of the digestive system has a specific function.

In humans, the digestion of food is an extracellular process.

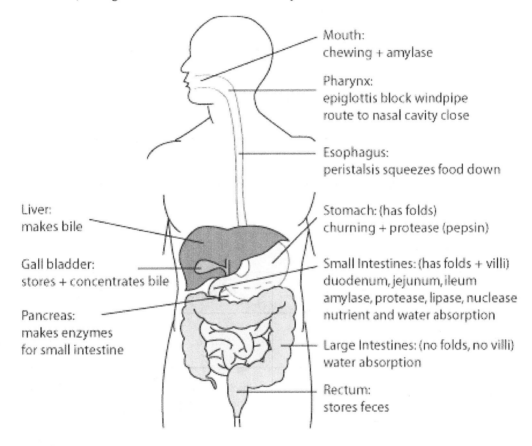

Mouth:
chewing + amylase

Pharynx:
epiglottis block windpipe
route to nasal cavity close

Esophagus:
peristalsis squeezes food down

Stomach: (has folds)
churning + protease (pepsin)

Small Intestines: (has folds + villi)
duodenum, jejunum, ileum
amylase, protease, lipase, nuclease
nutrient and water absorption

Large Intestines: (no folds, no villi)
water absorption

Rectum:
stores feces

Liver:
makes bile

Gall bladder:
stores + concentrates bile

Pancreas:
makes enzymes
for small intestine

Enzymes are secreted in the digestive tract by nearby glands.

Food is never within the accessory glands, only within the tract.

Digestion requires a cooperative effort by producing hormones and the actions of the nervous system.

**Summary of the digestive system**

- *Mouth*: grinds and moistens food by mastication (chewing for mechanical digestion); begins the chemical digestion of starch by amylase (*~ase* for enzymes) and lipase in saliva.

- *Esophagus*: moves food to the stomach.

- *Stomach*: churning chyme (i.e., mechanical digestion), acid digestion by HCl, protein digestion by pepsin (chemical digestion), and temporary food storage.

- *Small intestine*: the longest and extensively folded part of the GI tract is where most digestion and absorption of nutrients and water occurs.

  Chyme is subjected to bile (to emulsify fats) from the liver and digestive enzymes (amylase, protease, lipase, nuclease) for chemical digestion.

  The enzymes are predominantly from the pancreas.

- *Large intestine*: remaining water is reabsorbed from chyme to produce a relatively solid indigestible waste (i.e., feces).

  Bacteria in the large intestine produce vitamin K.

Enzymes are needed for digestion as biological catalysts breaking large food molecules into mostly monomers for absorption in the small intestine.

Enzymes are vital because they speed the digestive process by lowering the activation energy required for the reaction to occur at body temperature.

**Amylase, protease and lipase**

|  | **Amylase** | **Protease** | **Lipase** |
|---|---|---|---|
| **Enzyme** | Salivary amylase | Pepsin | Pancreatic lipase |
| **Source** | Salivary glands | Chief cells in the stomach lining | Pancreas |
| **Substrate** | Starch | Proteins | Triglycerides (e.g., fats and oils) |
| **Products** | Maltose | Small polypeptides | Fatty acids and glycerol |
| **Optimum pH** | pH 7 | pH 1.5 – 2 | pH 7 |

## Endocrine Control

**Digestive glands and associated hormones**

- Gastric glands produce *gastrin* in the stomach lining by sensing food reaching the stomach.

  Gastrin stimulates increases gastric motility.

  Its secretion is stimulated by meals rich in protein.

- *Secretin* is produced by cells lining the duodenum when food enters the duodenum.

- Secretin stimulates the pancreas to secrete fluids rich in $NaCO_3$ into the duodenum.

  This secretion is stimulated by acidic chyme.

- *Cholecystokinin* (CCK) is produced in the duodenal wall of the small intestine in response to fats.

  CCK stimulates the pancreas to increase pancreatic juice.

  It induces the liver to increase bile output and causes the gallbladder to release bile.

- *Gastric Inhibitory Peptide* is produced by the duodenal wall in response to fat and protein as chyme enters the duodenum.

  It causes a mild decrease in the rate of digestion in the stomach by inhibiting gastric gland secretion and stomach motility.

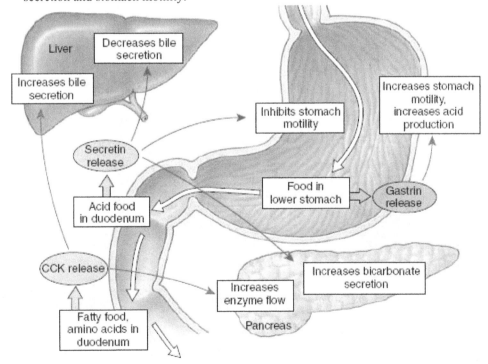

*Digestive tract with glands and associated hormones*

Endocrine cells are scattered within the GI epithelia, and the surface of these cells is exposed to the lumen.

Chemical substances in the chyme stimulate endocrine cells to release hormones into the blood.

## Islets of Langerhans, gastrin, histamine and HCl secretions

Scattered throughout the stomach lining are *enterochromaffin-like* (ECL) cells and other cells that secrete *somatostatin*, an inhibitory protein influencing the release of glucagon and insulin.

*ECL cells* are neuroendocrine digestive tract cells; gastrin stimulates them to release histamine, stimulating parietal cells to produce gastric acid.

The *pyloric antrum*, a lower portion of the stomach, secretes gastrin.

The *Islets of Langerhans* of the pancreas are irregularly shaped patches of endocrine tissue that secrete insulin and glucagon.

The islets contain specific cell types, including *alpha cells*, *beta cells*, *delta cells*, *F-cells*, and *C-cells*.

Increased protein content in a meal stimulates gastrin and histamine release, stimulating HCl secretion.

Somatostatin inhibits acid secretion by inhibiting the release of gastrin and histamine.

*Enterogastrone* in the duodenum inhibits gastric acid secretion.

The precursor pepsinogen produced by chief cells is converted to pepsin by excess acid in the stomach.

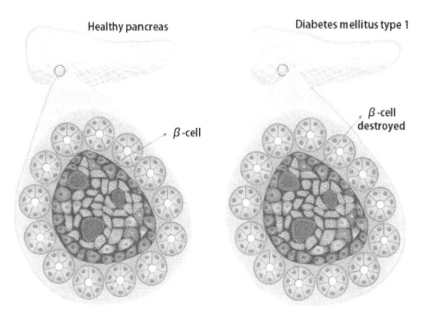

*Islets of Langerhans with β-cells producing insulin in nondiabetic patients*

**Vitamin D and calcium**

Vitamin D is a fat-soluble nutrient that promotes calcium absorption in the digestive system.

Vitamin D is involved in modulating cell growth, supporting the immune system, and reducing inflammation.

Cells in the digestive system have vitamin D receptors necessary for protein synthesis.

Vitamin D provides nerve cells with the calcium they need to send adequate signals, which is essential because nerves in the digestive tract must communicate to control the digestive process.

**Receptor regulation and gastrin**

Eighteen endocrine cell types have been identified within the gastrointestinal tract.

*Agonists* are peptide ligands that bind with a target cell receptor and stimulates the target cell to respond.

*Antagonists* are peptide ligands (i.e., a molecule that binds a receptor) that bind the receptor but do not cause a reaction within the cell.

An antagonist's (no response) ability to occupy a receptor prevents access for an agonist (elicits response). This inhibition is the mechanism for treating peptic ulcers with histamine receptor blockers.

By occupying the receptors on the parietal cells, antagonists (e.g., medication) inhibits histamines production of hydrochloric acid, a significant cause of peptic ulcers.

The discharge of granules of gastrin from the G cells occurs when a meal is consumed.

While the concentration of hydrogen ions remains low because of the buffering effect of the food, the release of gastrin continues.

As digestion occurs and the stomach starts to empty, acidity increases because of the diminishing neutralizing effect of food.

When the stomach contents contact the mucosa of the antrum, reach a certain level of acidity, the release of gastrin stops.

Failure of this process causes the inappropriate secretion of acid when the stomach is empty and may cause peptic ulcers in the duodenum.

Some endocrine cells contain microvilli on their surface that project into the lumen of the gland, stomach, or intestine's main channel. These cells can sample the luminal contents in their vicinity continuously.

When gastrin is secreted into the blood by a tumor of G cells (gastrinoma) of the pancreas, it is a continuous process because there is no mechanism at that site to inhibit secretion.

This process increases the number of parietal cells in the stomach with acid overproduction, and ulceration ensues.

## Neural Control by the Enteric Nervous System

**Neural regulation of the GI tract**

Impulses to the GI muscles and exocrine glands are supplied by the enteric nervous system, the local nervous system of the GI tract.

The neural regulation allows local; short reflexes are independent of the CNS.

Long reflexes through the CNS are possible via sympathetic and parasympathetic nerves innervating the GI tract.

Somatic nerves control chewing by skeletal muscles and the reflex activation of mechanoreceptors on the palate, gums, and tongue.

Autonomic nerves stimulate saliva secretion in response to chemoreceptors and pressure receptors in the mouth.

Swallowing is mediated by pressure receptors on the pharynx walls, sending impulses to the swallowing center in the *medulla oblongata*.

The swallowing center activates muscles in the pharynx and esophagus.

Multiple responses occur in a temporal sequence. The palate is elevated to prevent food from entering the nasal cavity, respiration is inhibited, and the epiglottis covers the glottis to prevent food from entering the trachea (windpipe).

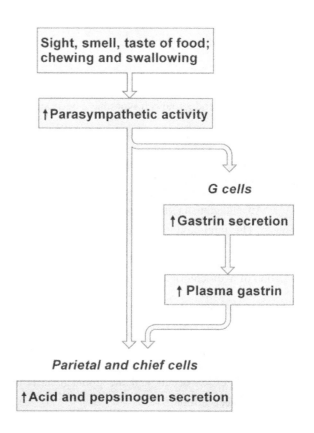

**Unidirectional movement of food**

The upper esophageal sphincter opens, and food enters the esophagus and moves toward the stomach by muscle contractions as peristaltic waves.

Food moves to the stomach when the lower esophageal sphincter opens.

A less efficient (or faulty) lower esophageal sphincter results in the reflux of gastric contents into the esophagus (gastroesophageal reflux); this reversal results in heartburn over time, contribute to ulceration of the esophagus.

---

**Vomit reflex as a survival mechanism**

The *vomit reflex* results in the forceful expulsion of toxic gastric contents and is coordinated by the vomiting center in the medulla oblongata.

Various mechano- and chemoreceptors in the stomach and elsewhere can trigger this reflex.

Increased salivation, sweating, heart rate, pallor accompanies the reflex.

Abdominal muscles contract to raise abdominal pressure, while the lower esophageal sphincter opens, and gastric contents are forced into the esophagus (retching).

If the upper esophageal sphincter opens, contents are expelled from the mouth (vomiting).

Excessive vomiting can lead to loss of water and salts, which results in dehydration and degradation of teeth enamel from the stomach's hydrochloric acid.

**Three phases of gastrointestinal control**

Each phase is named by the location of the receptor for a reflex.

These phases do not occur in a temporal sequence.

1.  The *cephalic phase* is initiated when sight, smell, taste, chewing, and emotional states stimulate receptors in the head.

    Reflexes mediated by sympathetic and parasympathetic fibers activate secretory and contractile activity.

2.  The *gastric phase* is initiated by distension, acidity, and amino acids and peptides in the stomach.

    This phase is mediated by short and long reflexes and activates gastrin secretion.

3.  The *intestinal phase* is initiated by the distension, acidity, and osmolarity of digestive products in the intestine.

    The phase is mediated by GI hormones and short and long neural reflexes.

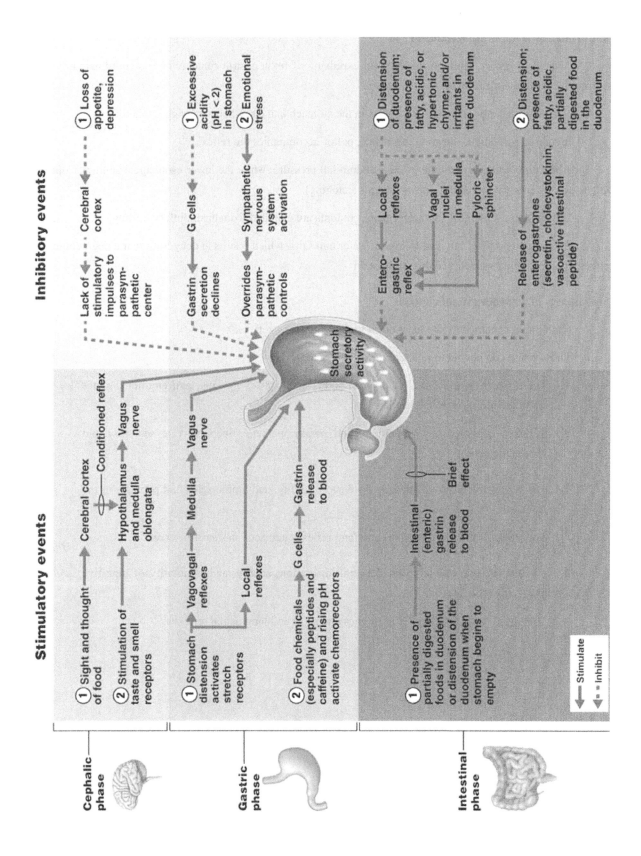

# CHAPTER 19

# Excretory System

- Introduction to Excretory System

- Kidney Structure and Function

- Nephron Structure and Function

- Roles of the Kidneys in Homeostasis

- Urine Formation

- Storage and Elimination of Urine

- Muscular Control

**Excretory system and kidneys**

The *human excretory system* is an organ system that removes excess fluids and materials to prevent damage to the body. It consists of several parts.

The human *kidneys* are two bean-shaped, reddish-brown organs about the size of a fist.

Kidneys are on each side of the vertebral column (below the diaphragm) and are partially protected by the lower rib cage.

The kidneys are urine formation sites, and each is connected to a *ureter*, which moves urine from a kidney to the *urinary bladder*.

The urinary bladder stores urine from the kidneys until it is voided through the *urethra*.

**Urinary bladder and urethra**

The male urethra runs through the penis and conducts semen. In females, the urethra opens the ventral to the vaginal opening.

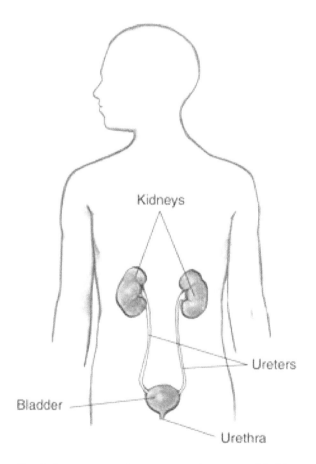

*Two kidneys connect by ureters to the urinary bladder.*

## Kidney Structure and Function

**Kidneys regulate fluid volume**

The kidneys remove and add substances to and from the plasma. The kidneys are responsible for regulating water concentration, inorganic ion concentrations, and the aqueous volume of the internal environment by controlling excretion.

The kidneys excrete metabolic wastes (e.g., urea, uric acid, creatinine, and foreign chemicals) in the urine. They synthesize glucose from amino acids and other precursors through gluconeogenesis.

The kidneys secrete hormones, erythroproteins, renin, and 1,25-dihydroxyvitamin $D_3$.

**Anatomy of the kidney**

The kidney has three regions: the renal cortex (outer part), medulla (inner part), and renal pelvis (innermost, the hollow structure of the kidney).

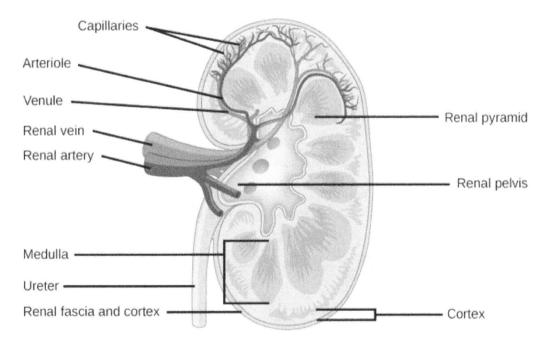

*Anatomy of the kidney with renal cortex, medulla, and renal pelvis*

The *renal cortex* is the thin, outer region (or shell) of the kidney, and it is composed of many convoluted tubules that give it a granular appearance.

The *renal medulla* is the inner part of the kidney consisting of the striped, pyramid regions that lie on the cortex's inner side and the loop of Henle.

The *renal pelvis* is a hollow, funnel-shaped structure in the kidney's innermost part that collects urine.

The renal pelvis receives the urine from collecting ducts and papillary ducts, and it releases urine into the ureter, which leads to the urinary bladder.

## Nephron Structure and Function

**Nephron as the functional unit of the kidney**

Each kidney has approximately one million subunits, called *nephrons*.

Nephrons are the functional units of the kidney because they reabsorb nutrients, salts, and water.

Nephrons are composed of the *renal corpuscle* and the *renal tubule*.

**Glomerulus as a capillary bed for the filtration of blood**

The *glomerulus* is a ball of fenestrated capillaries that acts like a sieve (or colander).

Small molecules dissolved in the fluid pass through the glomerulus (e.g., glucose, which is later reabsorbed), while large molecules such as plasma proteins and blood cells do not.

If blood cells or proteins are in the urine, this likely indicates a problem with the glomerulus.

The *juxtaglomerular apparatus* (JGA), named for its proximity to the glomerulus, consists of the macula densa cells and juxtaglomerular (JG) cells.

The *macula densa* cells are essential in blood flow regulation and can affect the glomerulus filtration rate. They are in the part of the ascending limb passing between the afferent and the efferent arterioles.

The wall of the afferent arteriole near the Bowman's capsule has *juxtaglomerular* cells, which secrete the hormone renin.

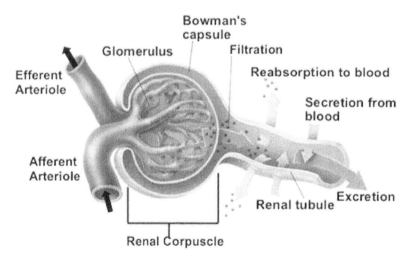

*The nephron as the functional unit of the kidney.*
*Blood enters via the afferent arteriole and exits via the efferent arteriole*

## Bowman's capsule

Bowman's capsule is a structure surrounding the glomerulus. It is responsible for performing the first step in the filtration of blood to form urine.

Bowman's capsule encloses the glomerulus involved in filtering liquids and microscope components from the blood.

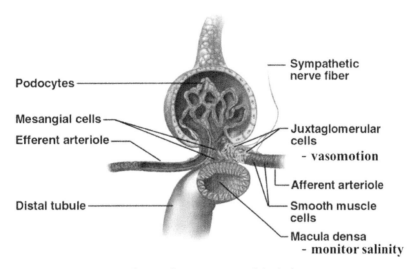

*Juxtaglomerular apparatus of the kidney*

## Proximal tubule

The *proximal tubule* is a convoluted tubule on the side of the Bowman's capsule and is the major site of active reabsorption of glucose, ions, and amino acids.

Additionally, it is responsible for the secretion of ions, except potassium.

The proximal tube divides into an initial convoluted portion and a straight (descending) portion.

Fluid in the filtrate entering the proximal convoluted tubule is reabsorbed into the peritubular capillaries. This reabsorption includes approximately two-thirds of the filtered salt as well as the water filtered out by the glomerulus.

The proximal convoluted tubule secretes chemicals, such as ammonium, formed by the deamination processes that convert glutamine to alpha-ketoglutarate. It drains into the loop of Henle.

## Loop of Henle structure

Most of the nephron is the *loop of Henle*, a U-shaped tube that extends from the proximal tubule and consists of a *descending limb* and an *ascending limb*.

The loop begins in the cortex, receiving filtrate from the proximal convoluted tubule.

The loop of Henle extends into the medulla as the descending limb and returns to the cortex as the ascending limb continues into the distal convoluted tubule.

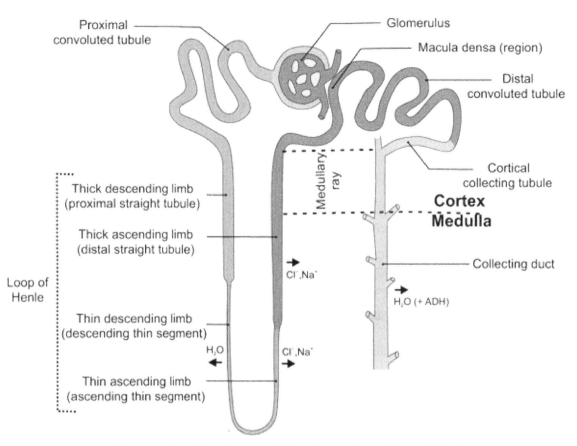

*Cross-section of a nephron including glomerulus and loop of Henle*

**Loop of Henle reabsorbs salts and water**

The primary role of the loop of Henle is to concentrate salt in the surrounding tissues (interstitium). This is accomplished using a countercurrent multiplier mechanism.

The *descending limb* of the loop of Henle is the site of water reabsorption.

The *ascending limb* of Henle is the site of salt absorption.

Their considerable differences distinguish the ascending and descending limbs of the loop of Henle.

The *thin descending limb* is permeable to $H_2O$ and noticeably less permeable to salt. This part of the loop of Henle indirectly contributes to the concentration of the interstitium.

Excess water is picked up by the *vasa recta* and returned to the blood.

As the filtrate descends deeper into the renal medulla's hypertonic interstitium, $H_2O$ flows freely out of the descending limb by osmosis until the tonicity of the filtrate and interstitium equilibrate.

Longer descending limbs allow time for $H_2O$ to flow out of the filtrate; thus, longer limbs make the filtrate more hypertonic than shorter limbs.

The thick ascending limb of the loop of Henle is impermeable to $H_2O$, a critical feature of the countercurrent exchange mechanism.

The *ascending limb* actively pumps $Na^+$ out of the filtrate, generating the hypertonic interstitium that drives countercurrent exchange. This is done through secondary active transport via Na-K-Cl cotransporters.

In passing through the ascending limb, the filtrate becomes hypotonic since it has lost much of its sodium content. This hypotonic filtrate is passed to the distal convoluted tubule in the renal cortex.

**Distal tubule regulates calcium levels**

The loop of Henle leads to the *distal convoluted tubule* on the side of the collecting ducts.

The distal convoluted tubule is hormone-controlled and fine-tunes the affects by the proximal tubule and continues the reabsorption of salts and water. It is partially responsible for the reabsorption of glucose, ions, and water.

The cells of the distal convoluted tubule contain numerous mitochondria, producing energy (ATP) for active transport. The endocrine system regulates much of the ion transport in the distal convoluted tubule.

Additionally, the distal convoluted tubule regulates the pH by secreting protons, absorbing protons, and secreting bicarbonate ions.

Calcium reabsorption occurs in the distal convoluted tubule in response to low blood calcium levels.

When blood calcium levels are low, parathyroid hormone is released.

In the presence of parathyroid hormone, the distal convoluted tubule reabsorbs $Ca^{2+}$, osteoclast activity is stimulated ($Ca^{2+}$ released from bone), and additional phosphate is secreted.

The hormone aldosterone controls sodium levels (through absorption) and potassium levels (through secretion). When aldosterone is present, more $Na^+$ is reabsorbed (along with $H_2O$), and $K^+$ is secreted.

The atrial natriuretic peptide causes the distal convoluted tubule to secrete $Na^+$.

**Collecting ducts and the antidiuretic hormone (ADH)**

Many of the distal convoluted tubules drain into *collecting ducts*, comprised of the connecting tubules, the cortical collecting ducts, and the medullary collecting ducts.

*Medullary collecting ducts* from numerous nephrons merge and drain into the renal pelvis, connected to the ureter. The tubules are connected to another set of blood vessels, the *peritubular capillaries*.

Each collecting duct is shared by nephrons and is the place where the *antidiuretic hormone* (ADH)-controlled reabsorption of water and the hormone-controlled reabsorption / secretion of sodium occurs.

Collecting ducts are normally impermeable to water.

If the hormone ADH is present, however, collecting ducts become permeable to water and water reabsorption occurs.

ADH causes blood pressure to rise and plays an important role in homeostasis by regulating glucose, sodium, and water levels in the body.

**Role of the Kidneys in Homeostasis**

**Kidneys' role in blood pressure regulation**

The kidneys function to excrete waste, control plasma pH and maintain homeostasis of fluid volume and solute composition.

Since sodium is the major extracellular solute, changes in body sodium result in changes in the volume of extracellular fluid. These changes lead to changes in plasma volume and blood pressure, which are detected by baroreceptors.

Usually, more than 99% of the sodium filtered out at the glomerulus is returned to the blood. Most are reabsorbed at the proximal tubule, 25% is extruded by the ascending limb of the loop of the nephron, and the remaining sodium is reabsorbed from the distal convoluted tubule and collecting duct.

**Juxtaglomerular cells**

Blood pressure is continuously monitored within the *juxtaglomerular apparatus*. If the blood pressure is insufficient to promote glomerular filtration, the afferent arteriole cells secrete *renin*.

Renin catalyzes the conversion of *angiotensinogen* (a protein produced by the liver) into *angiotensin I*.

Angiotensin I is converted to *angiotensin II* by *angiotensin-converting enzyme* (ACE); the rate-limiting step of this reaction is controlled by renin from juxtaglomerular (JG) cells.

JG cells act as internal baroreceptors and receive sympathetic inputs from external baroreceptors.

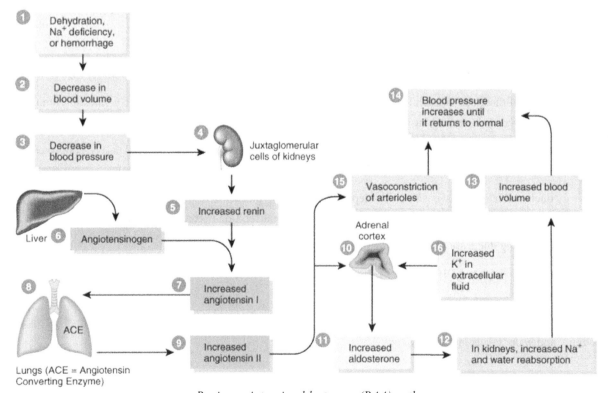

*Renin-angiotensin-aldosterone (RAA) pathway*

### Aldosterone regulates sodium ion reabsorption

Angiotensin II increases the blood pressure as a vasoconstrictor by promoting the retention of sodium ions. This hormone stimulates cells in the adrenal cortex to produce aldosterone, which stimulates sodium reabsorption by *cortical collecting ducts* (and large intestine, sweat, and salivary glands).

Aldosterone acts on the distal convoluted tubules to increase the reabsorption of $Na^+$ and the excretion of $K^+$. Increased $Na^+$ in the blood causes water to be reabsorbed, increasing blood volume and pressure.

The *renin-angiotensin-aldosterone system* triggers aldosterone production.

*Thirst* is stimulated by lower extracellular volume, higher plasma osmolarity, or angiotensin II. The brain centers for thirst are in the hypothalamus.

*Atrial natriuretic hormone* (ANH) is produced by the atria of the heart when cardiac cells stretch. When blood pressure rises, the heart produces ANH to inhibit renin's secretion and the release of ADH, which decreases blood volume and pressure.

Additionally, the heart can release atrial natriuretic peptide (ANP), which is the antagonist for aldosterone and causes the kidney to excrete more sodium ions and water, causing vasodilation.

### Kidneys' role in osmoregulation

If osmolarity differs between two regions, water moves into the region with a higher solute concentration. The excretory system regulates ions and water in body fluids. Regulation depends on the concentration of mineral ions (i.e., $Na^+$, $Cl^-$, $K^+$ and $HCO_3^-$).

Body fluids gain mineral ions when food and fluids are consumed and lose ions through excretion. Water enters the body with food or drink and by metabolism, where cellular respiration produces water. Water is lost by evaporation from the skin and lungs and through excretion (i.e., in urine or feces).

For balance, the water volume entering the body must equal the volume of water lost.

The kidneys function to eliminate wastes (urea, $H^+$) generated by the metabolic activity while reabsorbing important substances (glucose, amino acids, sodium) for reuse by the body. The generation of a solute concentration gradient from the kidney's cortex to its medulla allows a considerable amount of water to be reabsorbed.

Excretion of concentrated urine serves to limit water loss from the body and preserves blood volume.

The long loop of a nephron is comprised of a descending limb (cortex → medulla) and an ascending limb (medulla → cortex).

Salt (NaCl) passively diffuses out of the lower portion of the ascending limb, but the upper, thick portion of the limb actively transports salt out into the tissue of the renal medulla.

Less salt is available for transport from the tubule as fluid moves up the thick portion of the ascending limb. Urea leaks from the lower portion of the collecting ducts, causing the concentrations in the lower medulla to be highest.

Because of the solute concentration gradient within the renal medulla, water leaves the descending limb of the loop of Henle along its length.

The decreasing water concentration in the descending limb encounters an increasing solute concentration; this is a countercurrent mechanism.

Fluid received by a collecting duct from the distal convoluted tubule is isotonic to cells of the cortex. As this fluid passes through the renal medulla, water diffuses from the collected duct into the renal medulla. The urine delivered to the renal pelvis is usually hypertonic to the blood plasma.

**Aldosterone regulates blood osmolarity**

Blood plasma mainly contains sodium ions and chloride ions, whereas cells themselves mainly contain potassium and hydrogen ions.

Blood osmolarity is determined predominantly by the concentrations of sodium and potassium ions. If the osmolarity is too low, aldosterone is released so that reabsorption can take place.

Aldosterone controls potassium concentrations by allowing the renal system to reabsorb sodium ions and excrete potassium ions in urine. Osmolarity is regulated by secretions and reabsorptions of the kidney tubules.

**ADH increases the permeability of collecting ducts**

Antidiuretic hormone (ADH) is released from the posterior lobe of the pituitary gland. ADH acts on the collecting ducts by increasing its permeability to $H_2O$, thereby increasing $H_2O$ retention.

When ADH is released, water is reabsorbed, and there is less urine.

When ADH is not released, water is excreted, and more urine forms.

Thus, if an individual does not drink, the pituitary releases ADH; if hydrated, ADH is not released.

*Diuresis* is increased urine production, while *antidiuresis* is a decreased amount of urine.

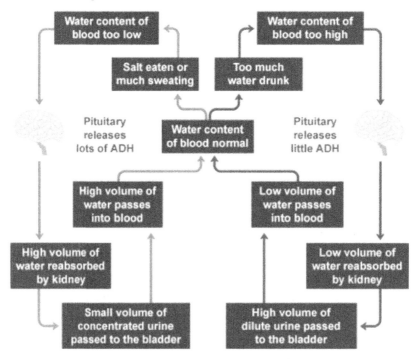

*Feedback loops used by ADH for homeostasis of blood volume*

While aldosterone and ADH ultimately do the same thing (i.e., increase water reabsorption in the kidneys), they have different mechanisms of action.

ADH directly increases water reabsorption from the nephron's collecting duct, while aldosterone indirectly increases water reabsorption by increasing sodium reabsorption from the collecting duct.

## Kidneys' role in removing soluble nitrogenous waste

The breakdown of nucleic acids and amino acids produces nitrogenous wastes.

Amino acids derived from protein are used to synthesize body proteins or nitrogen-containing molecules.

Unused amino acids are oxidized to generate energy or are stored as fats or carbohydrates.

The resulting *amino groups* ($-NH_2$) must be removed.

Depending on the organism, nitrogenous wastes are excreted as ammonia, urea, or uric acid.

*Urea* ($CO(NH_2)_2$) is a harmless form of ammonia.

Amino acids are converted into ammonia, which is converted to urea.

Urea is excreted by urination as urine, which is concentrated urea in ionized water (e.g., humans).

Mammals like humans and terrestrial amphibians usually excrete urea as their main nitrogenous waste because urea is much less toxic than ammonia.

Urea is excreted in a moderately concentrated solution, which conserves body water.

Urea is produced in the liver as a product of the energy-requiring *urea cycle*.

In the urea cycle, carrier molecules take up carbon dioxide and two ammonia molecules, resulting in urea release.

## Urine Formation

**Afferent and efferent arterioles at the glomerulus**

Urine formation follows the sequence of filtration, secretion, and reabsorption.

*Filtration* of plasma from glomerular capillaries into the Bowman's capsule is *glomerular filtration*.

The glomerular filtrate passes the glomerulus (afferent arteriole → glomerulus → efferent arterioles) to the rest of the nephron. It is referred to as a bulk flow process because water and solutes are moved together due to a pressure gradient. The glomerular filtrate contains plasma substances in the same concentrations as plasma, except plasma proteins and the molecules bound to these proteins.

The *afferent arterioles* carry blood into the glomerulus, while the efferent arterioles carry blood away from the glomerulus. Efferent arterioles exit the glomerulus and web around the nephron as *peritubular capillaries*. These peritubular capillaries surround the proximal convoluted tubule (PCT) and distal convoluted tubule (DCT). They reabsorb the nutrients and ions filtered out by the glomerulus.

**Tubular reabsorption**

The efferent arterioles continue to form the *vasa recta*, surrounding the loop of Henle (maintaining the concentration gradient) before merging with the renal branch of the renal vein.

The peritubular capillaries drain into a venule.

The venules from many nephrons drain into a small vein.

Many small veins join to form the renal vein, which enters the inferior vena cava.

During passage through tubules, substances move from tubules to peritubular capillaries as *tubular reabsorption*.

In *tubular secretion*, substances move from peritubular capillaries to tubules. Waste (e.g., urea, creatine, uric acid) and small useable ions and nutrients are filtered out.

The nutrients and usable ions are reabsorbed while the waste is excreted.

Particles too large to filter through (e.g., blood, albumin) remain in the circulatory system. This is a passive process driven by the hydrostatic pressure of blood. In the filtration process, the filtrate is pushed (hydrostatic pressure) from the glomerulus into Bowman's capsule.

The *juxtaglomerular apparatus* monitors filtrate pressure in the distal tubule via granular cells. It is responsible for the secretion of renin, which starts a signal transduction cascade involving angiotensin. The result is that the adrenal cortex is stimulated to create aldosterone, which stimulates sodium retention.

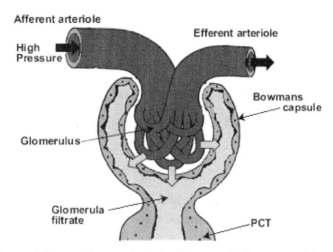

*Glomerulus and Bowman's capsule with afferent and efferent arterioles*

### Nephron regions and the passage of substances

When blood enters the glomerulus (cluster of capillaries), hydrostatic pressure (blood pressure) forces small molecules from the glomerulus across the glomerular capsule's inner membrane into the lumen of the glomerular capsule, a process of pressure filtration.

The glomerular walls are a hundred times more permeable than the walls of capillaries.

*Glomerular filtrate* are molecules leaving the blood and entering the glomerular capsules.

Plasma proteins and blood cells are too large to be part of the glomerular filtrate.

Failure to restore fluids soon causes death due to loss of water and nutrients and lower blood pressure.

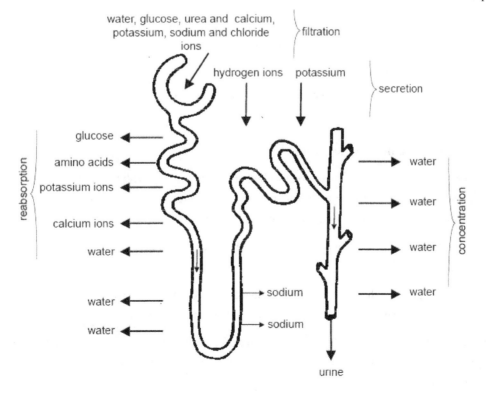

## Location and mechanism for secretion and reabsorption of solutes

During *secretion,* substances such as acids, bases, and ions (e.g., K$^+$) may be secreted by passive and active transport in *peritubular capillaries,* formed from efferent arterioles from the glomerulus.

The *proximal convoluted* tubules reabsorb the nutrients and most ions.

Soluble waste products are left in the filtrate (urea) to be excreted. NH$_4^+$, creatinine, and organic acids are excreted.

The *loop of Henle* reabsorbs water and salt using the countercurrent mechanism.

The *distal convoluted* tubules selectively reabsorb or secrete ions and compounds based on hormonal control. The collecting duct reabsorbs water to concentrate urine if ADH is present.

The *collecting duct* can secrete and reabsorb substances based on hormonal control. The regulation of blood occurs in the following manner: H$^+$ is secreted out of the blood when blood pH is too acidic, whereas HCO$_3^-$ is secreted out of the blood when blood pH is too basic.

## Tubular secretions and reabsorption

*Tubular secretion* moves substances (e.g., H$^+$ and K$^+$ ions) from peritubular capillaries into the tubular lumen by diffusion or transcellular mediated transport. Some of the movements are coupled with the reabsorption of Na$^+$ ions. Secretion back into the filtrate is primarily associated with the distal convoluted tubule. This rids the body of potentially harmful compounds that were not filtered into the glomerular capsule (e.g., uric acid, hydrogen ions, ammonia, and penicillin).

During *reabsorption,* glucose, salts, amino acids, and water are reabsorbed from the filtrate and returned to the blood.

*Tubular reabsorption* of fluids from the nephron into the blood occurs through the proximal convoluted tubule walls. Reabsorption recovers much of the glomerular filtrate.

The osmolarity of the blood and filtrate are equal, so osmosis of water does not occur. Sodium ions are actively reabsorbed, pulling along chlorine, changing the blood's osmolarity as water moves passively from the tubule to the blood.

## Proximal convoluted tubules reabsorb salts

About 60–70% of salt and water is reabsorbed at the proximal convoluted tubule. Cells of the proximal convoluted tubule have numerous microvilli, which increases the surface area available for absorption. They have numerous mitochondria, which supply the energy needed for active transport.

Only molecules with carrier proteins are reabsorbed. For example, if there is more glucose than carriers, excess glucose appears in the urine.

In diabetes mellitus, there is high plasma glucose due to a lack of insulin or insulin-resistant receptor cells. When diabetic, the liver does not correctly convert glucose to glycogen.

Waste products are excreted in the urine. Useful products are reabsorbed and are predominantly not excreted. Mediated transport is the reabsorption mechanism of many substances (e.g., glucose molecules are coupled to sodium reabsorption).

## Storage and Elimination of Urine

### The urinary bladder structure and function

The collecting ducts empty into the ureter, which drains into the bladder. The bladder stores the urine. Its special epithelium (transitional epithelium) distends to accommodate the storage of large amounts of urine.

The urine is excreted from the bladder through the urethra.

The smooth-muscle contractions of the ureter wall allow for urine to flow through. Urine is stored in the bladder and ejected during urination (micturition). The bladder is a chamber with smooth muscle walls (detrusor muscle). The contraction of detrusor muscles produces urination.

Part of the muscle at the base of the bladder, where the urethra begins, functions as the internal urethral sphincter. Below this sphincter is a ring of skeletal muscle of the external urethral sphincter, which surrounds the urethra.

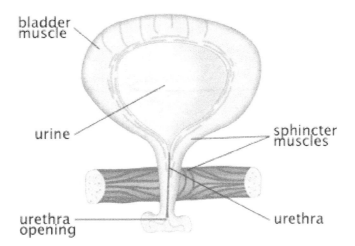

*Urinary bladder and sphincter muscles ase urine passes into the urethra*

### Renal clearance rate

*Renal clearance* measures the volume of plasma from which the kidneys remove a substance per unit time:

$$\text{Clearance of substance S} = \frac{\text{Mass of S excreted per unit time}}{\text{Plasma concentration of S}}$$

$$C_S = \frac{U_S V}{P_S}$$

where $C_S$ = clearance of S, $U_S$ = urine concentration of S, V = urine volume per unit time, $P_S$ = plasma concentration of S. $C_S$ of a substance equals glomerular filtration rate (GFR) if the substance is filtered but not reabsorbed, secreted, or metabolized.

## Muscular Control

### Neural control of the bladder

Sympathetic neurons innervate the bladder's *detrusor* (smooth) muscle from the lumbar spinal cord and parasympathetic fibers from the sacral spinal cord.

While the bladder is filling, there is little parasympathetic input to the detrusor muscle. However, there is strong sympathetic and motor input to the sphincters.

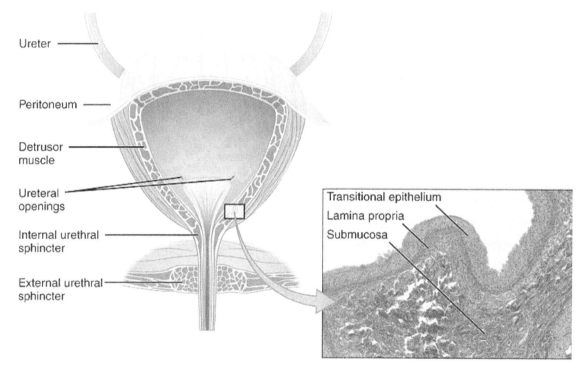

*Anatomy of the bladder with histology (inset)*

While filling, the detrusor muscle is relaxed, and the sphincters are closed.

As the bladder fills, stretch receptors stimulate the parasympathetic fibers, resulting in detrusor muscle contraction.

Consequently, sympathetic and motor input to the sphincters are inhibited, and the sphincters open to produce urination.

There is voluntary control over the external sphincter.

# CHAPTER 20

# Endocrine System

- Hormones and Their Sources
- Mechanisms of Hormone Distribution, Secretions and Modes of Action
- Hormonal Regulation and Integration of Metabolism

## Hormones and Their Sources

### Functions of the endocrine system

The *endocrine system* synthesizes and secretes hormones into the bloodstream (*endo* means "within"). The target cell of a hormone has a receptor allowing it to respond to the stimulus.

The *exocrine* system secretions travel through ducts to external environments. Several glands in the body create hormones of the endocrine system, such as the sudoriferous (sweat), sebaceous (oil), mucous, digestion, and mammary glands. A few glands, such as the pancreas, have endocrine and exocrine functions.

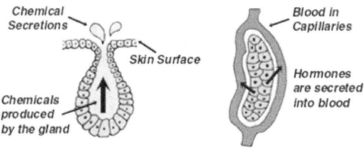

Exocrine Gland        Endocrine Gland

### Glands secrete direct and trophic hormones

*Hormones* are molecules created by glands that affect distant organs through the circulatory system. Hormones regulate the metabolism and other functions of the cells. Small amounts of the hormone may have a widespread effect.

Hormones are divided into two categories based on their target: *direct hormones* (or *non-tropic hormones*) directly stimulate target hormones, and *tropic hormones* stimulate other endocrine glands.

*Endocrine glands* are ductless glands in the endocrine system that secrete hormones into the bloodstream, which affect target cells. A single gland may produce several hormones.

Multiple glands may produce the same hormone.

The principal human endocrine glands include the hypothalamus, pineal, and pituitary glands in the brain; the thyroid and parathyroid glands (located in the neck); the ovaries (located in the abdomen); the testes (in the scrotum); and the thymus (in the thorax).

The chemical demands of an organism vary by daily function and life cycle. When a cellular demand is recognized, genes (located on DNA) are transcribed (mRNA production) and translated (making proteins). This process secretes the hormone into the bloodstream and affects the target cells (with hormone receptors).

In general, hormones instruct cells in tissues to devote their resources to protein production. For example, human adolescents require gonadotropic hormones, which target the sex organs during puberty.

Adolescent changes include the ability to produce functional gametes for reproduction and growth and develop secondary sex characteristics.

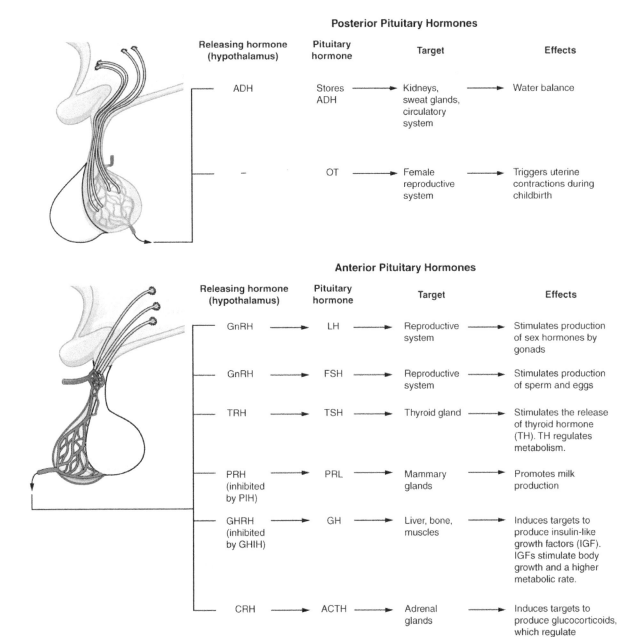

**Posterior Pituitary Hormones**

| Releasing hormone (hypothalamus) | Pituitary hormone | Target | Effects |
|---|---|---|---|
| ADH | Stores ADH | Kidneys, sweat glands, circulatory system | Water balance |
| - | OT | Female reproductive system | Triggers uterine contractions during childbirth |

**Anterior Pituitary Hormones**

| Releasing hormone (hypothalamus) | Pituitary hormone | Target | Effects |
|---|---|---|---|
| GnRH | LH | Reproductive system | Stimulates production of sex hormones by gonads |
| GnRH | FSH | Reproductive system | Stimulates production of sperm and eggs |
| TRH | TSH | Thyroid gland | Stimulates the release of thyroid hormone (TH). TH regulates metabolism. |
| PRH (inhibited by PIH) | PRL | Mammary glands | Promotes milk production |
| GHRH (inhibited by GHIH) | GH | Liver, bone, muscles | Induces targets to produce insulin-like growth factors (IGF). IGFs stimulate body growth and a higher metabolic rate. |
| CRH | ACTH | Adrenal glands | Induces targets to produce glucocorticoids, which regulate metabolism and the stress response |

*Releasing hormones from the hypothalamus and the effects on the posterior and anterior pituitary*

The releasing hormone from the hypothalamus finds its target (posterior or anterior pituitary cell). It binds to the receptor, where a chemical messenger instructs the cell to release the desired hormone. The secreted hormone targets a tissue (e.g., thyroid gland) and instructs the tissue to produce a substance.

**Structure and function of the major endocrine glands**

Humoral glands directly respond to blood levels of ions and nutrients, such as the parathyroid hormone's response to low blood calcium levels.

Neural glands release hormones when stimulated by a nerve impulse or an action potential. These glands are involved primarily with the fight or flight response.

Hormonal glands release hormones when stimulated by other hormones from another gland.

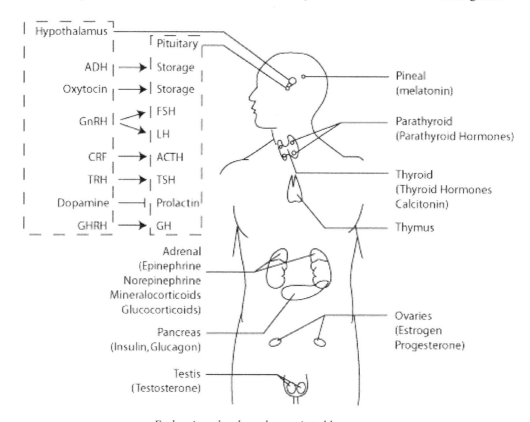

*Endocrine glands and associated hormones*

The *hypothalamus* monitors the external and internal conditions of the body. It regulates the internal environment through the autonomic nervous system, affecting heartbeat, temperature, and water balance.

The hypothalamus contains neurosecretory cells linking it to the pituitary gland, where it controls glandular secretions. The hypothalamus secretes *ADH* (vasopressin), *oxytocin,* and *GnRH* (gonadotropin-releasing hormone).

The *pituitary gland* is situated at the back of the brain and synthesizes several hormones for growth. The pituitary gland is connected to the hypothalamus by a stalk-like structure and can store hormones produced by the hypothalamus.

The pituitary gland is comprised of two parts: the posterior pituitary and the anterior pituitary.

The *posterior pituitary* does not synthesize hormones. Instead, it stores vasopressin and oxytocin produced by the hypothalamus and secretes them into the bloodstream. The posterior pituitary contains neurosecretory cells that originate in the hypothalamus and respond to neurotransmitters.

**Anterior pituitary**

The *anterior pituitary* (adenohypophysis) regulates hormone production from other glands.

The hypothalamus regulates the stimulation of the anterior pituitary. The hypothalamus controls the release of anterior pituitary hormones through a *portal system* with two capillary systems connected by a vein.

The anterior pituitary produces seven types of hormones: 1) thyroid-stimulating hormone (TSH), 2) adrenocorticotropic hormone (ACTH), 3) gonadotropic follicle-stimulating hormone (FSH), 4) gonadotropic luteinizing hormone (LH), 5) prolactin, 6) melanocyte-stimulating hormone (skin color change in fishes, reptiles and amphibians) and 7) growth hormone (GH), known as a somatotropin.

The pituitary gland regulation is via a negative feedback mechanism and by the secretion of releasing and inhibiting hormones. The hypothalamus produces hypothalamic-releasing and hypothalamic-inhibiting hormones that pass to the anterior pituitary by the portal system. *Releasing hormones* originate in the hypothalamus target cells in the anterior and posterior pituitary to stimulate the production and secretion of a hormone. Conversely, *inhibiting hormones* released from the hypothalamus target cells in the anterior pituitary inhibits a particular hormone's production and secretion. In general, each hormone from the anterior pituitary has a releasing and inhibiting hormone from the hypothalamus that controls its release.

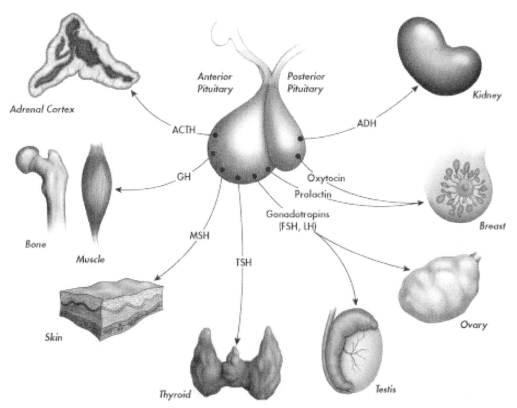

*Hormones of anterior pituitary*

Tropic effects:                          FSH, LH, TSH, ACTH, ADH
Non-tropic effects:                      Prolactin, oxytocin, MSH
Non-tropic and tropic effect:            GH

Tropic hormones have other endocrine glands as targets.

**Thyroid gland**

The *thyroid gland* is in the neck, attached to the ventral surface of the trachea below the larynx.

The thyroid is stimulated by the anterior pituitary gland, which secretes *thyroid-stimulating hormone* (TSH). Thyroid hormones increase metabolism and require iodine to function adequately.

The two hormones, thyroxine ($T_4$) and triiodothyronine ($T_3$) are produced by follicles of the thyroid gland. These hormones possess four and three iodine atoms, respectively. Iodine is necessary for growth and neurological development in children and increases basal metabolic rates in the body.

Iodine, actively transported into the thyroid, reaches concentrations 25 times greater than in the blood.

Iodine deficiency causes the enlargement of the thyroid (goiter).

Goiter is easily prevented by supplementing with fortified salt containing iodine.

The thyroid gland produces *calcitonin*, which decreases the calcium levels in the blood.

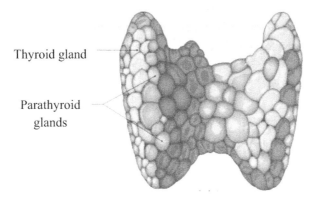

Thyroid gland

Parathyroid glands

*Posterior view of thyroid showing parathyroid glands*

**Thyroid disorders and metabolic rates**

*Hyperthyroidism* (Graves' disease) is when the thyroid gland is enlarged or overactive. The eyes protrude because of edema in the eye socket tissue as an *exophthalmic* goiter.

Additional symptoms include an increased metabolic rate and sweating. Removal or destruction of some thyroid tissue by surgery or radiation often cures it.

*Hypothyroidism* is decreased secretion of the thyroid gland and lowers the heart and respiratory rates.

Other thyroid disorders are *achondroplasia* (dwarfism) and *progeria* (premature aging).

*Cretinism* is a condition of stunted physical and mental growth in people suffering from hypothyroidism since birth. Thyroid treatment but must be begun in the first two months of life to prevent developmental delay.

Four *parathyroid glands* are embedded in the thyroid gland's posterior surface in a conformation resembling four peas.

Parathyroid glands produce *parathyroid hormone* (PTH).

Low calcium (Ca) levels stimulate the parathyroid hormone release, which increases calcium levels by stimulating osteoclasts to release calcium from the bone.

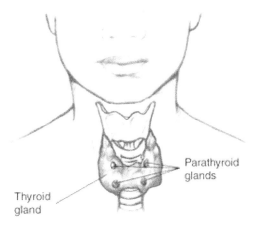

*Anterior view of the thyroid gland. Parathyroid glands are on the posterior surface*

### Adrenal glands for sex hormones and stress responses

The two *adrenal glands* are on top of each kidney. Each gland consists of two sections: an outer *adrenal cortex* and an inner *adrenal medulla*. The hormones released from the adrenal cortex provide a sustained stress response.

The adrenal cortex secretes *glucocorticoids* and *mineralocorticoids*, which are steroid hormones. It secretes a small amount of male and female sex hormones in each sex. The adrenal medulla releases *epinephrine* and *norepinephrine*, which provide an immediate response to stress (as opposed to the sustained response provided by the hormones from the adrenal cortex).

The hypothalamus exerts control over each adrenal gland. Nerve impulses travel via the brain stem through the spinal cord to sympathetic nerve fibers to the medulla.

The hypothalamus uses ACTH-releasing hormone to control the anterior pituitary's secretion of ACTH. This hormone stimulates the adrenal glands to release hormones, including *dehydroepiandrosterone* (DHEA) and *cortisol*. Adrenal hormones increase during times of physical and emotional stress.

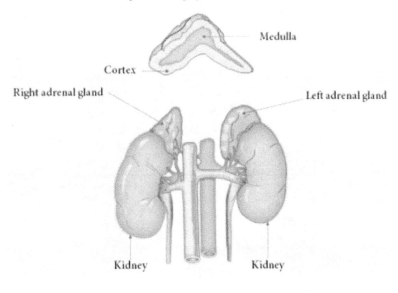

*Adrenal glands*

**Pancreas functions as an exocrine and endocrine gland**

The *pancreas* lies transversely in the abdomen between the kidneys and near the small intestine duodenum. The pancreas is composed of exocrine and endocrine tissue. Exocrine tissue produces and secretes digestive juices into the small intestine via the ducts.

*Pancreatic islets of Langerhans* are endocrine tissues that produce *insulin* and *glucagon*.

The islets of Langerhans contain two cell types, alpha cells and beta cells.

*Alpha cells* of the islet secrete glucagon.

The release of glucagon is catabolic and occurs when the energy charge is low, working to raise blood glucose levels. The term energy measures the status of biological cells related to ATP, ADP, and AMP concentrations.

*Beta cells* secrete insulin, secreted anabolically and released when the energy charge is high, where beta cells work to lower blood glucose levels. Insulin stimulates the liver and other body cells to absorb glucose.

Body cells utilize glucose; therefore, its level is subject to homeostasis and must be tightly regulated.

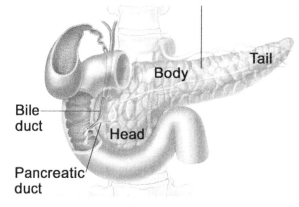

*Pancreas*

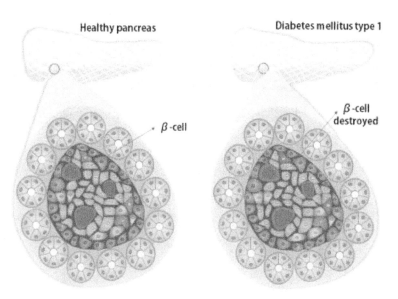

*Pancreatic Islets of Langerhans; beta cells secrete insulin in non-diabetic patients*

Male *testes* are in the scrotum and function as the human gonads, producing *androgens*, including the male sex hormone *testosterone*.

Testosterone stimulates male secondary sex characteristics, such as large vocal cords, increased muscle mass, and facial hair.

Female sex hormones include estrogens and progesterone, secreted by the *ovaries* (the female gonads).

*Estrogen* secreted at puberty stimulates the maturation of ovaries and other sexual organs.

*Progesterone* is a steroid hormone important for the menstrual cycle, pregnancy, and embryogenesis.

**Pineal and thymus glands**

The *pineal gland*, near the center of the brain, produces *melatonin*, primarily at night.

Melatonin establishes *circadian rhythms*, the basis for a 24-hour physiological cycle.

The pineal gland may be involved in human sexual development; children with a damaged pineal gland due to a brain tumor tend to experience puberty earlier.

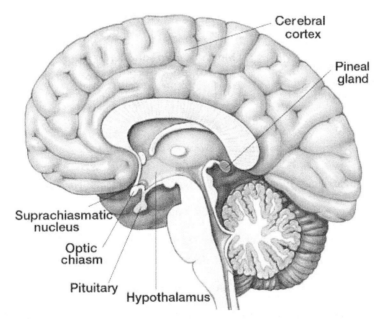

*The pituitary gland, hypothalamus, and pineal gland*

The *thymus* is a lobular gland that lies beneath the sternum in the upper thoracic cavity.

Thymus hormones (*thymo-, thymic*) stimulate the development of T cells for an immune response.

The thymus is largest and most active during childhood; it shrinks and becomes fatty with age.

Some lymphocytes originating in the bone marrow pass through the thymus and become T lymphocytes.

The thymus produces and secretes *thymosins,* which aid in the differentiation of T cells and may stimulate other immune cells.

**Major classifications of hormones and mode of action**

Three major classes of hormones: peptide, steroid, and amino acid-derived hormones.

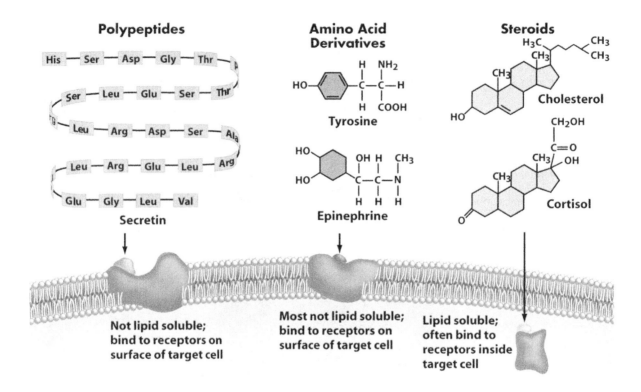

*Three classes of hormones and a schematic of their mode of action*

*Peptide hormones* are made from amino acid as peptides or proteins. Their receptors are on cell surfaces.

Their mechanism of action utilizes the secondary messenger system.

They affect their target organs rapidly; however, their effects are temporary. An example of a peptide hormone is calcitonin, which stimulates osteoblast to decrease plasma calcium levels as bone density increases.

*Steroid hormones* are made from cholesterol. Their receptors are in the cytosol (or nucleus) of a cell.

Steroids pass through the phospholipid bilayer of the cell membrane.

Once the steroid hormone binds to an intracellular receptor, the hormone-receptor migrates to the nucleus, and the complex binds to a DNA target to affect gene transcription.

Steroid hormones affect their target organs slowly, but their effects are long-lasting. An example of a steroid hormone is the growth hormone.

*Amino acid-derived hormones* are the third class of hormones derived from the amino acid tyrosine.

Amino acid-derived hormones are catecholamines (e.g., epinephrine, norepinephrine, dopamine).

Epinephrine is released from the adrenal medulla of the adrenal glands as the "fight-or-flight" response.

Amino acid-derived hormones are generally small molecules.

**Peptide, steroid and amino acid-derived hormones**

| | Peptide hormones | Steroid hormones | Amino acid derivatives | |
|---|---|---|---|---|
| | | | Catecholamines | Thyroid hormones |
| **Synthesis and storage** | Made in advance; stored in secretory vesicles | Synthesized on-demand from precursors | Made in advance; stored in secretory vesicles | Made in advance; precursor stored in secretory vesicles |
| **Release from the parent cell** | Exocytosis | Simple diffusion | Exocytosis | Simple diffusion |
| **Half-life** | Short | Long | Short | Long |
| **Transport in blood** | Dissolved in plasma | Bound to carrier proteins | Dissolved in plasma | Bound to carrier proteins |
| **Location of receptor** | Cell membrane | Cytoplasm or nucleus; some have membrane receptors | Cell membrane | Nucleus |
| **Response to receptor-ligand binding** | Activation of second messenger systems; may activate genes | Activates genes for transcription and translation; may have non-genomic actions | Activates second messenger systems | Activation of genes for transcription and translation |
| **General Target Response** | Modification of existing proteins and induction of protein synthesis | Introduction of new protein synthesis | Modification of existing proteins | Induction of new protein synthesis |
| **Examples** | Insulin, parathyroid hormone | Estrogen, androgens, cortisol | Epinephrine, norepinephrine, dopamine | Thyroxine ($T_4$) |

**Insulin regulates blood glucose levels**

Most hormones are peptide hormones. They are initially synthesized together as larger *preprohormones*, which are cleaved to inactive *prohormones* in the lumen of the rough ER. The prohormone is cleaved to form the active hormone in the Golgi apparatus. In the Golgi, they may be modified with carbohydrates.

*Insulin* is a peptide hormone secreted by the beta (β) cells of the islets of Langerhans in the pancreas. Its secretion is increased during the absorptive state and decreased during the post-absorptive state. Insulin targets are muscle, adipose, and liver tissues.

The main roles of insulin are to 1) stimulate the movement of glucose from the extracellular fluid into the cells by facilitated diffusion, 2) stimulate glycogen synthesis, and 3) inhibit glycogen catabolism. Insulin is an anabolic building hormone and inhibits protein degradation. It promotes cell division and differentiation because it is required to produce *insulin-like growth factors* (IGF-I), vital for regulating normal physiology. Insulin is controlled by an increase in plasma glucose or amino acid concentration.

*Glucose-dependent insulinotropic peptide* (GIP) is a hormone secreted in the GI tract to stimulate insulin secretion. Parasympathetic nerve fibers stimulate insulin secretion.

**Peptide hormones mode of action**

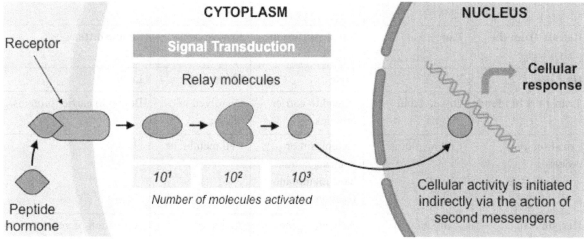

*Peptide hormones bind as a ligand to a plasma membrane receptor and initiate a second messenger cascade to amplify the cellular response. The hormone may initiate phosphorylation or dephosphorylation of molecules in the cytoplasm as the mechanism for the cellular response.*

*Hypoglycemia* refers to low plasma glucose levels that result from an excess of insulin (beta cells) or a deficiency of glucagon (alpha cells). *Glucagon* is a peptide hormone secreted by alpha (α) cells of the pancreas. Its target is the liver tissue, and its actions are antagonistic to insulin.

Glucagon increases glycogen breakdown and gluconeogenesis to increase the plasma concentration of glucose during the post-absorptive state or when plasma glucose is low (hypoglycemia). Sympathetic nerves stimulate glucagon secretion.

*Atrial natriuretic hormone* (ANH) is a peptide hormone secreted by cardiac (heart) cells when the atria of the heart are stretched due to increased blood volume. ANH inhibits the secretion of renin by the kidneys, inhibits the secretion of *aldosterone* from the adrenal cortex, and decreases sodium reabsorption when sodium is excreted along with water, the blood volume, and pressure decrease.

*Antidiuretic hormone* (ADH) is a peptide hormone produced in the hypothalamus. Antidiuretic hormone (ADH) increases the reabsorption of water by increasing the permeability of the nephron's collecting ducts, which results in water reabsorption and increased blood volume and pressure. ADH is released when there is low water content (high osmolarity) in the blood. Caffeine blocks ADH, tricking the brain that the body is over-hydrated. This causes an increased volume of fluid output, so coffee drinkers may often urinate.

*Calcitonin* is a peptide hormone produced by the thyroid gland. Calcitonin lowers calcium levels in the blood by inhibiting the release of calcium from bone. Calcitonin increases deposits in the bone by reducing the activity and number of *osteoclasts* (the type of bone cells that resorbs bone tissue). Calcium is necessary for blood clotting. If blood calcium is lowered, the release of calcitonin is inhibited.

## Hormones regulate homeostasis

The *parathyroid hormone* (PTH), a peptide hormone produced by the parathyroid gland, stimulates the absorption of $Ca^{2+}$ by activating vitamin D, retaining $Ca^{2+}$, excreting phosphates by the kidneys, and demineralizing bone by promoting the activity of osteoclasts. PTH is antagonistic to calcitonin. When the blood calcium level reaches the right level, the parathyroid glands inhibit PTH synthesis. If PTH is not produced in response to low blood $Ca^{2+}$, the body goes into tetany.

In *tetany*, the body shakes uncontrollably from involuntary, continuous muscle spasms. $Ca^{2+}$ is vital to proper nerve conduction and muscle contraction.

*Gonadotropins* are peptide hormones produced in the adenohypophysis. The two main gonadotropins, *follicle-stimulating hormone* (FSH) and *luteinizing hormone* (LH), act on the gonads (ovaries and testes) to secrete sex hormones. FSH stimulates the maturation of ovarian follicles in females, and in males, it acts on the Sertoli cells of the testes to stimulate sperm production (spermatogenesis). LH triggers ovulation and the formation of the corpus luteum in females. In males, it stimulates the interstitial cells of the testes to produce testosterone.

*Gonadotropin-releasing hormone* (GnRH) by the hypothalamus stimulates gonadotropin production.

*Oxytocin* is a peptide hormone produced in the hypothalamus which stimulates uterine muscle contraction in response to uterine wall nerve impulses markedly during childbirth. It stimulates the release of milk from mammary glands for nursing.

*Prolactin,* a peptide hormone produced in the adenohypophysis, is secreted after childbirth; it causes the mammary glands to produce milk and plays a role in carbohydrate and fat metabolism. The neurotransmitter dopamine inhibits prolactin.

*Gastrin* is a peptide hormone important during digestion in the stomach. It stimulates the secretion of HCl. *Secretin* is in the small intestine and is activated when acidic food enters the stomach. It neutralizes chyme's (i.e., partly digested food) acidity by the secretion of alkaline bicarbonate.

*Cholecystokinin* (CCK), in the small intestine, causes contractions of the gallbladder and bile release, which is involved in the digestion of fats.

*Growth hormone* (GH), or somatotropic hormone, is a peptide hormone produced in the adenohypophysis that promotes skeletal and muscular growth. GH acts to stimulate the transport of amino acids into cells and increase ribosomes' activity. GH promotes fat metabolism rather than glucose metabolism.

When there are low plasma levels of GH, *growth hormone-releasing hormone* (GHRH) is released from the hypothalamus, and GHRH stimulates GH production.

*Gigantism* is a condition from oversecretion of growth hormone during childhood and results in a person significantly taller and bigger than a typical human.

*Acromegaly* occurs when too much growth hormone is produced during adulthood and results in the disproportioned growth of some regions of the body (the parts that still respond to growth hormone).

*Adrenocorticotropic hormone* (ACTH) is a peptide hormone that stimulates the adrenal cortex to release glucocorticoids and cortisol, steroid hormones involved in regulating glucose metabolism.

**Steroid hormones mode of action**

Steroid hormones are produced by the adrenal cortex and the gonads and are specifically synthesized from cholesterol in the smooth ER. They are lipids and can freely diffuse across membranes but require protein transport molecules to dissolve in the blood. Steroid hormones have the same complex of four carbon rings but have different side chains.

Steroid hormones include the glucocorticoids (e.g., cortisol) and mineralocorticoids (e.g., aldosterone) of the adrenal cortex. They include the gonadal hormones: estrogen, progesterone, and testosterone. The placenta produces estrogen and progesterone.

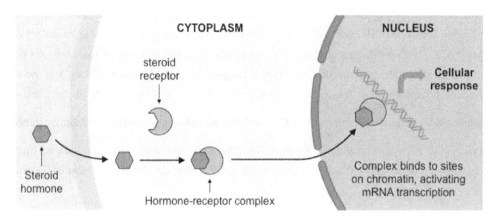

*Steroid hormones pass the plasma membrane and bind to an intracellular receptor*
*which migrates as a complex into the nucleus to affect gene transcription*

*Glucocorticoids* are stress hormones that help regulate blood glucose levels. They raise blood glucose levels by stimulating gluconeogenesis in the liver and affect fat and protein metabolism. Like glucocorticoids, *cortisol* increases energy by raising blood glucose levels. Cortisol inhibits the immune system and exerts antigrowth effects by stimulating protein catabolism. Cortisol and corticosterone affect the metabolism of glucose and other organic nutrients. Cortisol counteracts the inflammatory response and helps to medicate arthritis and bursitis. When the body is under stress, corticotropin-releasing hormone (CRH) from the hypothalamus is released, which triggers ACTH from the adenohypophysis to be released.

*Aldosterone*, a mineralocorticoid produced in the adrenal cortex, participates in mineral balance by regulating $Na^+$, $K^+$ and $H^+$ ions by the kidney. Its primary role is helping the kidneys move sodium and water from urine into the bloodstream, thus regulating the body's sodium and potassium balance. Additionally, it acts to reduce the sodium sensitivity of taste buds, and it acts on sweat glands to reduce sodium loss during perspiration. Aldosterone is stimulated by decreased blood volume and acts by increasing $Na^+$ reabsorption.

*Hyposecretion* (i.e., diminished secretion) of glucocorticoids and mineralocorticoids results in *Addison's disease*. When ACTH is in excess, it can lead to melanin buildup. The lack of cortisol results in low glucose levels. This can lead to severe fatigue, perpetuated and worsened by stress. The lack of aldosterone lowers blood sodium levels; the person has low blood pressure and dehydration. Untreated, Addison's disease can be fatal.

*Hypersecretion* (i.e., excessive secretion) of corticosteroids results in *Cushing's syndrome*. Excess cortisol leads to carbohydrate and protein metabolism changes and causes a tendency toward diabetes mellitus. As a result, muscular protein decreases, and subcutaneous fat collects, creating and an obese torso, while arms and legs usually remain proportioned. A "puffy" appearance typically characterizes sufferers of this syndrome.

*Gonadocorticoids* are another group of steroid hormones produced in the adrenal cortex. They are responsible for the onset of puberty and the onset of the female libido.

**Androgens and estrogens**

Adrenal *androgens*, responsible for developing male sex characteristics, are produced in the adrenal cortex and regulated by ACTH. The most potent androgen, testosterone, is produced primarily in the testes. The adrenal androgens are weak steroids, and some function as precursors to testosterone (e.g., DHEA, which is androstenolone). In addition to influencing male development, androgens play some role in female puberty and the adult female. The renin-angiotensin-aldosterone system controls mineralocorticoid secretion. Under low blood volume and sodium levels, the kidneys secrete renin, cleaving angiotensin I and promoting a cascade that increases blood pressure.

*Testosterone* is the major androgen secreted by the testes. Testosterone is mainly responsible for the male sex drive. Anabolic steroids are synthetic variants of testosterone used to treat some hormone issues in men. Testosterone affects the sweat glands and the expression of the baldness gene, among other characteristics and functions of the body.

*Estrogen*, a female sex hormone secreted by the ovaries, is necessary for oocyte development. It is responsible for developing female secondary sex characteristics, including forming a layer of fat under the skin and a larger pelvic girdle. Estrogen and progesterone regulate breast development and uterine cycle regulation.

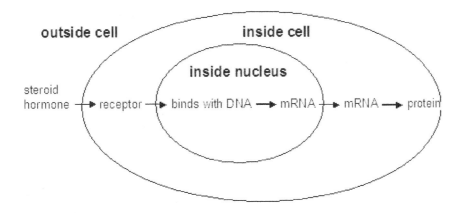

**Amino acid-derived hormones mode of action**

Amino acid-derived hormones are usually derivatives of the amino acid tyrosine. Enzymes form *tyrosine derivative*s in the cytosol or on the rough ER. The adrenal medulla secretes the amino acid-derived hormones *epinephrine* (adrenaline) and *norepinephrine* (noradrenaline), which stimulate "fight or flight" responses. They are *stress hormones* because both hormones bring about body changes corresponding to an emergency.

The fight-or-flight response initiates the glycogen to glucose conversion, vasoconstriction to the internal organs and skin, vasodilation to the skeletal muscles, and increased heartbeat. This causes the blood glucose level and the oxygen content to rise and increases metabolic rate. The bronchioles dilate, and the breathing rate increases. Blood vessels to the digestive tract and skin constrict, while blood vessels to the skeletal muscles dilate and the cardiac muscle contracts forcefully, causing the heart rate to increase.

The adrenal medulla secretes more epinephrine than norepinephrine. Both hormones are catecholamines. *Catecholamines* solubilize in water, dissolve in blood, bind to receptors on the target tissue, and mainly act via the secondary messenger system.

*Norepinephrine* is formed from the amino acid tyrosine, and *epinephrine* is formed from norepinephrine. Although the effects of these two catecholamines are generally similar, there are differences. Norepinephrine constricts almost all the body's blood vessels, while epinephrine constricts only the minute blood vessels and dilates the larger blood vessels of the liver and skeletal muscle. Epinephrine increases metabolic rate by the calorigenic effect and stimulates the catabolism of glycogen and triacylglycerols. It increases energy by raising glucose and oxygen content in the blood. It is released when the autonomic nervous system must respond to stress.

Other types of amino acid-derived hormones include the two iodine-containing hormones, *thyroxine* ($T_4$) and *triiodothyronine* ($T_3$), secreted by the follicles of the thyroid glands. $T_4$ is secreted in larger amounts but is mostly converted to $T_3$, the active form.

*Thyroid hormones* (TH) are lipid-soluble, require a protein carrier in the blood, and bind to receptors in the nucleus. TH regulates oxygen consumption, growth, and brain development.

Thyroxine is responsible for controlling the body's metabolic rate and therefore is responsible for the amount of energy consumed and the volume of proteins produced. Thyroxine is released when there is a low concentration of it in the blood.

*Hyperresponsiveness* is the hypersecretion of thyroid hormones and leads to hyperresponsiveness to epinephrine and increased heart rate.

Although tyrosine is the primary amino acid from which this class of hormones is derived, other amino acids are hormone precursors. For example, the amino acid tryptophan is the precursor to melatonin.

*Melatonin*, produced in the pineal gland, aids in maintaining balanced circadian rhythms (daily biological cycles) and sleep patterns.

*Glutamic acid* is an amino acid and the precursor to *histamine*, a hormone that is part of the body's natural allergic response. Histamine plays a vital role in the immune system.

**Neuroendocrinology intersects the nervous and endocrine systems**

Secretion of some hormones is under the control of the nervous system. This was first recognized in the brain's role (specifically the hypothalamus) in stimulating the pituitary gland to release hormones. The nervous system controls hormone release based on the body's current state.

For example, control through the hypothalamus is seen when blood glucose levels are higher from stress. The endocrine system is significantly slower than the nervous system, and hormones can modulate the nervous system. For example, low estrogen levels during menses tend to lead to mood disruptions, characteristic of premenstrual syndrome (PMS).

Neurons secrete *hypophysiotropic hormones* in response to action potentials. These hormones are named after the anterior pituitary hormone that it controls.

*Endorphins*, technically a neuro-hormone, inhibit the perception of pain.

## Mechanisms of Hormone Distribution, Secretion and Modes of Action

**Cellular mechanisms of hormone action**

*Lipid soluble hormones* cross the plasma membrane and directly activate genes.

*Water-soluble hormones* are unable to cross the plasma membrane. Instead, they bind to membrane receptors on the outside of cells. Secondary messengers (e.g., tyrosine kinase or G-coupled proteins) relaying the signal inside the cell. An example of a secondary messenger is cyclic AMP (cAMP). An amino acid hormone binds to a membrane receptor in a cAMP pathway. A G-protein is activated alongside adenylate cyclase, and cAMP is produced (discussed elsewhere).

In the *phospholipid pathway,* an amino acid hormone binds to a membrane receptor, in which a G-protein is activated. *Phospholipase C* is activated, and the membrane phospholipids split into two secondary messengers: *diacylglycerol* (DAG) and *inositol triphosphate* (IP₃). DAG triggers a protein kinase cascade, and IP₃ releases $Ca^{2+}$ from the ER.

*Hyposecretion* is when a gland is secreting too little hormone because it cannot function normally; the disorder is *primary hyposecretion.* Possible causes include a genetic lack of an enzyme, dietary deficiency of a precursor, or an infection.

*Primary hypersecretion* is when a gland secretes too much hormone.

*Secondary hypersecretion* is the excessive stimulation of a gland by its tropic hormone.

*Hyporesponsiveness* is when target cells do not respond to a hormone due to a deficiency of receptors, a defect in the signal transduction mechanism, or a deficiency of an enzyme that catalyzes the activation of the hormone. In diabetes mellitus, the target cells of the hormone insulin are hyporesponsive.

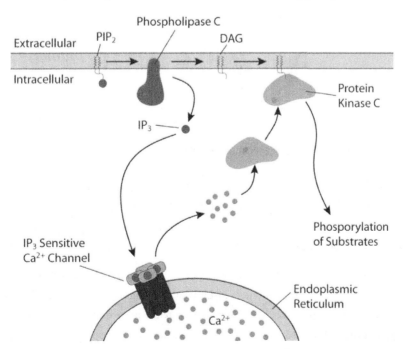

*Phospholipid pathway: Cleavage to IP₃ and DAG to release calcium for the ER*

**Hormone distribution through the blood and lymph fluid**

Hormones travel long distances via the blood and lymph. *Unbound hormones* (peptide hormones) are water-soluble hormones that dissolve in blood plasma. In contrast, *bound hormones* (steroid hormones) circulate in blood while bound to plasma proteins (e.g., serum carrier or transport proteins).

The liver and bind produce these transport proteins to hormones within the serum. Free hormones diffuse across capillary walls to encounter their target cells.

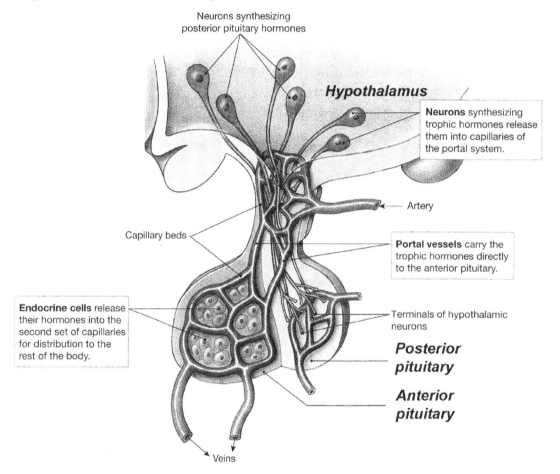

**Hypothalamic-hypophyseal and hepatic portal circulation**

*Hypothalamic-hypophyseal portal circulation* permits the transport of neurohormones by the hypothalamus' neuroendocrine cells directly to the pituitary cells. Usually, these hormones are excluded from the general circulation. In this system, capillaries from the hypothalamus go through the plexus of veins around the pituitary stalk and into the anterior pituitary gland.

*Hepatic portal circulation* allows for the transport of hormones from the Islets of Langerhans in the pancreas. The hormones of the pancreas include insulin and glucagon. Various nutrients absorbed from the intestine and transported into the liver use this pathway. This pathway occurs before general circulation occurs. In this system, capillaries originating from the gastrointestinal tract and the spleen merge to form the portal vein. The vein enters the liver and divides to form portal capillaries.

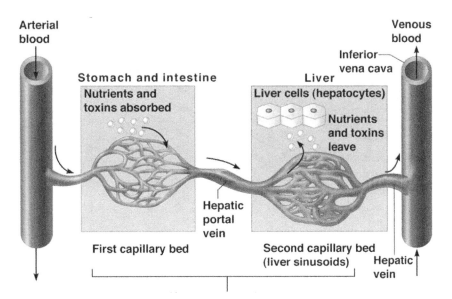

*Hepatic portal circulation*

**Target tissue specificity of hormones**

Hormones reach tissues via the blood, but cells with specific receptors act as target cells for a hormone. Specificity depends on the unique receptors on the target cells and the lack of receptors on non-target cells for the hormone. Hormones bind to cells with receptor sites for that hormone.

Peptide hormone receptors are on the cell's surface, while steroid hormones bind a receptor in the cytoplasm (or nucleus). Cells can *upregulate* (increase production) or *downregulate* (decreased production) the receptors they express. A low concentration of a hormone may be compensated for by increasing the number of receptors. In contrast, a high concentration of a hormone can decrease the number of receptors.

Receptors for peptide hormones and catecholamines are present on the plasma membrane's extracellular surface, while those for steroids are mainly in the cytoplasm. Hormones that bind to surface receptors can influence ion channels, enzyme activity, G proteins, and secondary messengers. Genes can be activated or inhibited, resulting in a change in the synthesis rate of proteins encoded by these genes.

Some hormones can reduce the number of receptors available for a second hormone, resulting in decreased second hormone effectiveness.

The hormone that blocks the second hormone is the *antagonist,* and this process is *antagonism.*

A hormone can induce an increase in the number of receptors for a second hormone, increasing the latter's effectiveness, a process of *permissiveness.*

There are cell-to-cell signaling pathways that allow hormones to bind to various target cells. In *endocrine signaling*, hormones are distributed into the blood and bind to long-distance target cells.

**Autocrine and paracrine signals**

*Autocrine* signals are local chemicals released by cells that bind to receptors on the same cell.

*Paracrine* signals act through short distances on other cells. Signals involve messengers with short lifespans since a short distance needs to be covered. Neurotransmitter secretions are a type of paracrine signaling.

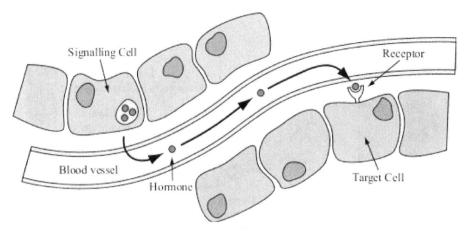

*Hormones are released from a gland, travel in the blood*
*and affect a target cell that has the receptor*

Some signals are local since they affect neighboring cells and do not travel through the bloodstream. *Prostaglandins* are potent chemical signals produced within cells from arachidonate, a fatty acid. Prostaglandins cause the uterus to contract and are involved in menstrual discomfort. The effect of aspirin on reducing fever and controlling pain is due to its effect on prostaglandins.

*Growth factors* promote cell division and mitosis.

*Pheromone*s are chemical signals that act at a distance between individual organisms. Ants produce a pheromone trail for other ant colony members to find food. Female silkworm moths release pheromones to lure male moths from miles away. Axillary secretions from the armpits of men and women are thought to affect the opposite sex. Some women may prefer men's axillary odor with a different plasma membrane protein. Women may synchronize their menstrual cycles with other women living nearby.

**Endocrine integration with the nervous system by feedback control**

The effects of hormones are controlled by negative feedback and by antagonistic hormone actions.

*Negative feedback* is where the product of a process decreases the rate of that process.

*Long-loop negative feedback* is when the last hormone in a chain of control exerts negative feedback on the hypophysis-pituitary system. If an anterior pituitary hormone exerts a negative feedback effect on the hypothalamus, it is *short-loop negative feedback*. This mechanism is seen in pituitary hormones that do not influence other endocrine glands. The pancreas produces insulin when blood glucose rises, causing the liver to store glucose. When glucose is stored, blood glucose level decreases, and the pancreas stops insulin production.

Antagonistic actions of hormones are essential factors in regulation. For example, the effect of insulin is offset by the pancreas' production of glucagon. The thyroid hormones lower blood calcium levels, while the parathyroid hormones raise blood calcium levels.

The concentration of a hormone in the plasma depends on its secretion and removal rates. The kidneys can excrete hormones or are metabolized by the target cells. Plasma concentrations of ions (or nutrients) may control the secretion of a hormone, and the hormone may control the concentration of its regulators through negative feedback.

When nerve cells in the hypothalamus determine that blood is too concentrated, ADH is released, and the kidneys respond by reabsorbing water. As the blood becomes dilute, ADH is no longer released, an example of negative feedback. Oxytocin is made in the hypothalamus and stored in the posterior pituitary; it is *positive feedback* as it increases intensity. Positive feedback does not maintain homeostasis.

During the normal control of hormones, *humoral glands* directly respond to chemical levels in the blood (e.g., parathyroid responds to low blood calcium).

*Neural glands* release hormones when stimulated by nerves (fight-or-flight response).

*Hormonal glands* release hormones when stimulated by other hormones (tropic hormones).

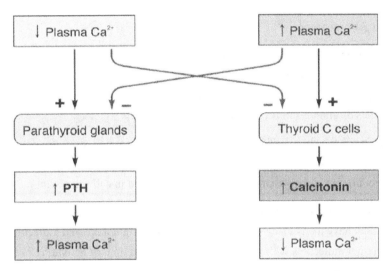

*Positive and negative feedback loops to regulate plasma Ca²⁺ levels*

## Regulation by second messengers

The secondary messenger system utilizes non-steroid hormones. In this system, the hormone binds to a membrane receptor but does not enter the cell. When the hormone binds to a membrane receptor, it initiates some reactions that activate an enzyme.

The hormone receptor binding causes the adenylate cyclase in the membrane to be activated. This activation converts ATP to cAMP, and cAMP activates protein kinases. These protein kinases activate various enzymes, stimulate cellular secretions, and open ion channels.

Peptide hormones cannot enter a cell independently, so they use vesicles to cross the membrane. Typically, they act on the surface receptors via secondary messengers. The peptide hormones bind to a receptor protein on the plasma membrane, a receptor-mediated endocytosis process.

Epinephrine is an example of a peptide hormone that binds to a receptor protein. A relay system leads to the conversion of ATP to cAMP.

Peptide hormones are the first messengers, while cAMP and calcium are the second messengers.

The second messenger may set an enzyme cascade in motion. Activated enzymes can be used repeatedly, resulting in a thousand-fold response. These hormones may serve as neurotransmitters.

## Hormonal Regulation and Integration of Metabolism

### Higher-level integration of hormone functions

*Hormones* are signaling molecules produced by glands in multicellular organisms and travel in the bloodstream to their target cell, organ, or tissue. These molecules are essential for regulating cell metabolism, as evidenced by several hormonal regulation examples in this chapter.

There are three main categories of hormones based on their chemical structure: peptide hormones, steroid hormones, and modified amino acid hormones.

### Peptide hormones target receptors

*Peptide hormones* range from three amino acids to folded proteins with subunit structures. When they have longer amino acid chain lengths, they are protein hormones. These hormones, which include insulin and parathyroid hormone, are initially produced in endocrine tissue as large products and undergo extensive processing before they are stored in vesicles or granules in preparation for release.

Peptide hormones have short half-lives in the bloodstream, so they are released at the precise moment they are needed. The response is rapid because these hormones are stored in large quantities. When released, peptide hormones target protein and glycoprotein receptors embedded in cell membranes.

The binding of the hormone to the receptor on the cell's surface can initiate a signal transduction cascade within the cell, which may have many effects. These include increasing uptake of a molecule, phosphorylation or dephosphorylation of target molecules within the cell, triggering secretion, or activating mitosis.

### Steroid hormones affect gene transcription

*Steroid hormones*, such as glucocorticoids and progestins, are synthesized from cholesterol, usually in the adrenal glands and the gonads.

The synthesis of these hormones occurs in the mitochondria and smooth endoplasmic reticulum, where a series of enzymatic reactions convert cholesterol into the specified steroid hormone.

Unlike polypeptide hormones, steroid hormones are not stored in large quantities. Most hydrophobic steroid hormones circulating in the bloodstream are bound to carrier proteins, and the unbound steroid hormones are the steroid molecules entering the target cells.

Steroid hormones easily pass through cell membranes because they are hydrophobic and fat-soluble. Inside the cell, they bind to intracellular receptors, causing a conformational change in a transcriptional complex.

This increases or decreases the transcription rate (DNA→RNA) of genes and consequently affects the rate at which specific proteins are produced.

An example is glucocorticoids that bind to the glucocorticoid receptor complex, which inhibit pro-inflammatory transcription factors, thus having an anti-inflammatory effect.

## Modified amino acids affect cell metabolism

*Modified amino acid hormones* are the third category of hormones. Examples are norepinephrine, epinephrine, and the thyroid hormones thyroxine ($T_4$) and triiodothyronine ($T_3$). The chemical modifications creating modified amino acid hormones include methylation, decarboxylation, or hydroxylation.

Modified amino acid hormones may have a long half-life like steroid hormones or a short half-life like peptide hormones.

Depending on the hormone, they may bind to receptors on the cell-surface (like peptide hormone) or to intracellular receptors (like steroid hormone).

They are a group of hormones with significant effects on cell metabolism.

## Tissue-specific metabolism

Each tissue of the body has a specialized function reflected in its anatomy, biomolecules, and metabolic activity. Skeletal muscle tissue, for instance, allows for directed motion, while adipose tissue stores and releases energy in the form of fat. The brain pumps ions across the neurons' plasma membranes to produce electrical signals. The liver processes and converts nutrients that include carbohydrates, fats and proteins, and distributes them to the appropriate locations.

The liver detoxifies foreign compounds like drugs, preservatives, and food additives. The liver is responsible for synthesizing fats. The process of lipogenesis, where acetyl-CoA is converted to fatty acids through the addition of two-carbon units, occurs in the cytoplasm.

Most of the enzymes involved in fatty acid synthesis are arranged into a multienzyme complex as fatty acid synthetase. In animals and humans, fatty acids are usually stored in adipose tissue and the liver as a triglyceride.

## Insulin regulates blood sugar levels

The hormone insulin is an indicator of blood sugar levels. The level of insulin increases as blood glucose levels increase. Insulin increases the rate of storage pathways (e.g., lipogenesis) by stimulating the pyruvate dehydrogenase complex (PDC), leading to the formation of acetyl-CoA and acetyl-CoA carboxylase (ACC), which forms malonyl-CoA from acetyl-CoA.

As insulin levels increase, the malonyl-CoA levels increase; this is important because the synthesis of malonyl-CoA is the first committed step in the fatty acid synthesis.

Insulin affects ACC in a way similar to PDC; dephosphorylation leads to the enzyme's activation.

## Glucagon for glycogenolysis

Glucagon has an agonistic effect and increases phosphorylation, inhibiting ACC and slowing fat synthesis.

Muscle tissue is involved in the mechanical movements of the body. Additionally, muscle tissue, which consumes large quantities of oxygen, is an ATP generator.

Muscular activity releases epinephrine from the adrenal medulla; epinephrine binds to a receptor on the muscle cell membrane and initiates adenyl cyclase in the membrane, triggering the cAMP cascade (described previously).

Epinephrine is involved in glycogen breakdown in the muscles and occasionally in the liver.

The protein kinase, activated by cAMP, causes phosphorylations on a series of enzymes to produce glucose-1-phosphate, later converted to glucose-6-phosphate.

Simultaneously, enzymes activate glycogen breakdown (glycogenolysis), while other enzymes such as glycogen synthetase are inactivated to inhibit glycogenesis.

The two hormones involved in the control of glycogenolysis are the peptide hormone glucagon (released from the pancreas when blood glucose levels are low) and the catecholamine epinephrine (released from the adrenal glands in response to a threat or stress).

Glucagon and epinephrine activate enzymes to initiate glycogen phosphorylase to start glycogenolysis, and they inhibit glycogen synthetase.

**Hormonal regulation of biochemical molecules**

Thyroid hormones are essential for controlling metabolism and play a permissive role in developing and maintaining the nervous system. Thyroid hormones are essential determinants of basal metabolic rate (BMR). They can increase BMR by increasing oxygen consumption, and heat-production in most body tissues termed a *calorigenic effect*.

Blood glucose concentration levels fluctuate throughout the day. Homeostasis targets plasma blood glucose levels of around 80 to 120 mg/dl. Through negative feedback, specific target organs affect the rate at which glucose is taken up from or released into the blood.

When glucose levels are too high (above the homeostasis set point), β cells in the pancreatic islets produce insulin, which stimulates muscle cells and liver cells to take up glucose from the blood and convert it into glycogen.

Glycogen is stored as granules in the cytoplasm. Some cells are stimulated to take up glucose and use it immediately for cell respiration. These processes lower the levels of glucose in the blood.

When glucose levels are too low (below the homeostasis set point), α cells in the pancreatic islets produce glucagon. Glucagon stimulates the liver cells to convert glycogen into glucose and release it into the blood, thereby raising the blood glucose level.

Cholesterol in the body comes from the diet and *hepatic synthesis* (i.e., production by the liver). The liver excretes cholesterol by adding it to bile. The homeostatic control that keeps the plasma cholesterol level constant mainly involves hepatic synthesis.

The ingestion of saturated fatty acids (animal fats) raises plasma cholesterol levels, while the ingestion of unsaturated fatty acids (vegetable fats) lowers it. Low-density lipoproteins (LDL) deliver cholesterol to cells throughout the body. High-density lipoproteins (HDL) remove excess cholesterol from blood and tissue and deliver it to the liver for excretion. The ratio of LDL to HDL is important, and the lower the ratio, the lower the deposition of extra cholesterol in the blood vessels.

**Summary table of hormone secretions, targets and effects**

| Hormone | Secreted by: | Target | Effect at the target site |
|---|---|---|---|
| Growth hormone (GH) | Anterior pituitary | Bone, muscle, fat | Growth of tissues |
| Thyroid-stimulating hormone (TSH) | Anterior pituitary | Thyroid | Stimulates the release of $T_3/T_4$ hormones from the thyroid, which increase the basal metabolic rate |
| Prolactin (PRL) | Anterior pituitary | Mammary glands | Production of milk in the breasts |
| Adrenocorticotropic hormone (ACTH) | Anterior pituitary | Adrenal cortex | Stimulates the adrenal cortex to secrete stress hormones called glucocorticoids |
| Luteinizing hormone (LH) | Anterior pituitary | In males: interstitial cells in testes; In females: mature ovarian follicle | Males: testosterone secretion Females: ovulation; estrogen secretion |
| Follicle-stimulating hormone (FSH) | Anterior pituitary | Males: seminiferous tubules of testes; Females: ovarian follicle | Males: sperm production Females: follicle growth during menstruation; ovum maturation |
| Triiodothyronine ($T_3$) & thyroxine ($T_4$) | Thyroid | All cells | Regulates metabolism |
| Aldosterone | Adrenal cortex | Kidney tubules | Increases $Na^+$ reabsorption and $K^+$ secretion at the distal convoluted tubule and the collecting duct; net increase in salts in the plasma, increasing osmotic potential and subsequently, blood pressure |
| Cortisol | Adrenal cortex | All cells | Stress hormone that increases gluconeogenesis in the liver, thus increasing blood glucose levels; stimulates fat breakdown |
| Estrogen | Ovarian follicle | Gonads (Ovaries) | Stimulates female sex organs; causes LH to surge during menstruation |
| Progesterone | Corpus luteum | Uterine endometrium | Preparation for implantation (thickens lining), growth and maintenance of the uterus |
| Testosterone | Seminiferous tubules | Gonads (Testes) | Stimulates formation of secondary sex characteristics and closing of epiphyseal plates |

**Summary table of hormone secretions, targets and effects** (*continued*)

| Hormone | Secreted by: | Target | Effect at the target site |
|---|---|---|---|
| Anti-diuretic hormone (ADH) | Posterior pituitary | Distal convoluted tubule (DCT) | Causes collecting duct of the kidney to become highly permeable to water; concentrating the urine |
| Oxytocin (OT) | Posterior pituitary | Uterine smooth muscle | Contraction during childbirth; milk secretion during nursing |
| Parathyroid hormone (PTH) | Parathyroid | Kidney tubules and osteoclasts | Reabsorption of $Ca^{2+}$ into blood, bone resorption (increases blood $Ca^{2+}$) |
| Calcitonin | Thyroid | Kidney tubules and osteoblasts | Secretion of $Ca^{2+}$ into urine, bone formation (decreases blood $Ca^{2+}$) |
| Insulin | β Islets | All cells, liver, and skeletal muscle | Pushes glucose into cells from blood, glycogen formation (decreases blood glucose) |
| Glucagon | α Islets | Liver and skeletal muscle | Stimulates gluconeogenesis, the breakdown of glycogen (increase in blood glucose) |
| Epinephrine | Adrenal medulla | Cardiac muscle, arteriole, and bronchiole smooth muscle | Raises heart rate, constricts blood vessels, dilates pupils, and suppresses the immune system |
| Norepinephrine | Adrenal medulla | Cardiac muscle, arteriole, and bronchiole smooth muscle | Raises heart rate causing glucose to be released as energy and blood to flow to the muscles |
| Melatonin | Pineal gland | Limbic system | Emotions/behavior; circadian rhythm |

## Hormonal Control of Perspiration, Vasodilation and Vasoconstriction

### Hormone modulations of skin and fluid balance

Hormones are chemical messengers that relay information throughout the body, usually maintaining homeostasis. One hormone is estrogen, which is the primary sex hormone in females but is present in males. Estrogen affects skin thickness, elasticity, and fluid balance. It increases glycosaminoglycans (GAGs) production, such as hyaluronic acid, which maintains the skin's structure and fluid balance. Additionally, estrogen increases collagen production to maintain epidermal thickness and smooth the appearance of wrinkles. Estrogen insufficiency, which occurs in menopausal women, can cause excessive perspiration.

Thyroid hormones affect body temperature and skin dryness. Excess thyroid hormone causes the skin to become warm, sweaty and flushed.

Conversely, a deficit of thyroid hormone causes the skin to become dry, coarse, and thick. An imbalance of serotonin, a hormone involved in mood, sleep, digestion, and memory, can lead to excessive perspiration.

Testosterone is present in both sexes but is the primary male sex hormone. Coarser hair, oily skin, and general skin aging are due to testosterone activity. Females can experience increased oiliness and acne when their hormones are not balanced.

### Hormones regulate blood flow during thermoregulation

Vasodilation and vasoconstriction control blood flow distribution and heat loss. They are influenced by chemical factors ($CO_2$, $H^+$ and $K^+$), sympathetic nerves, and autonomic nerves.

Hormones play an essential role in regulating this system.

Vasodilation involves the relaxation of smooth muscle around the blood vessels. Muscle relaxation depends on the intracellular concentration of calcium ions related to the myosin contractile protein's light chain phosphorylation.

Vasodilation occurs when there is a decrease in intracellular calcium levels or dephosphorylated myosin.

Hormones promote vasodilation through specific pathways by decreasing calcium content within the cells. These endogenous vasodilators include epinephrine, histamine, prostacyclin, and prostaglandins.

Vasoconstriction involves the constriction of blood vessels. This process works to increase intracellular calcium levels.

Hormones involved in vasodilation are norepinephrine, dopamine, thromboxane, and vasopressin (ADH).

Although epinephrine and norepinephrine have the same effect on the heart, these two hormones have vastly different effects on the blood vessels.

Epinephrine causes vasodilation, while norepinephrine causes vasoconstriction. This is because the heart contains beta-2 receptors, while blood vessels contain alpha and beta-2 receptors.

Epinephrine preferentially activates beta-2 receptors, so if there are sufficient beta-2 receptors, vasodilation occurs.

*Notes for active learning*

# CHAPTER 21

## Reproductive System

- Female and Male Reproductive Structures and Their Functions

- Gametogenesis by Meiosis

- Sperm and Ovum Formation

- Hormonal Control of Reproduction

- Reproduction Mechanism

## Female and Male Reproductive Structures and Functions

### Genitalia of the reproductive system

The *female reproductive system* includes the ovary, oviduct, uterus, and vagina.

The *male reproductive system* consists of the testes, epididymis, vas deferens, prostate gland, bulbourethral glands, and penis.

*Genitalia* is the external genital organs of the reproductive system.

The major difference between the male and female reproductive structures is that male structures are mostly external for the delivery of sperm. Female structures are mainly internal to nurture a growing fetus.

There is one opening for urine and sperm in males, while females have separate openings for urine and menstruation, and sexual intercourse.

### Female genitalia

The external genitalia of females is collectively the *vulva.* The urethra opens into the vulva.

The *vulva* (pudendum or external genitalia) includes the *clitoris, mons pubis, labia majora,* and *labia minora.* The labia are on each side of the vaginal and urethral openings.

The *clitoris*, a short shaft of erectile tissue capped by a pea-shaped gland at the front juncture of the labia minora. This structure is homologous to the male penis.

Additionally, the vulva contains the vaginal orifice, *greater* and *lesser vestibular glands*, *paraurethral glands,* and *vestibular bulbs* (erectile tissues).

### Female reproductive structures

The *vagina* is a tubular organ at a 45° angle with the small of the back. The vagina is connected to the uterus by the cervix, which is a cylinder-shaped neck of tissue about 1 inch across.

The *cervix* is cartilage covered by smooth, moist tissue. The vagina tilts posteriorly between the urethra and rectum. It has no glands but is moistened by transudation of serous fluid through the vaginal wall and mucus from glands in the cervical canal.

The adult vagina is lined with a stratified squamous epithelium with antigen-presenting *dendritic cells.*

The vagina's mucosal lining lies in folds, extending as necessary in childbirth. The vagina receives the penis during copulation.

*Copulation* is a sexual union that facilitates the reception of sperm by a female. During birthing, the vagina is where the fetus passes out of the body (i.e., the birth canal).

The *uterus* has an upper *fundus,* middle *corpus* (body), and a lower *cervix* (neck), where it meets the vagina. A narrow *cervical canal* connects the uterine lumen with the vaginal lumen.

*Cervical glands* in the canal secrete mucus, preventing vaginal microbes from spreading into the uterus.

The *uterus* is a hollow, thick-walled muscular organ superior to the urinary bladder. Its size and shape are comparable to that of an inverted pear; it is where the fertilized ovum develops until birth.

The uterine wall has three layers: an outer serosa *perimetrium,* thick muscular *myometrium,* and an inner mucosa *endometrium.*

The endometrium contains numerous tubular glands divided into two layers – a thick superficial *stratum functionalis* (shed during menstrual periods) and a thinner basal *stratum basalis* (retained from cycle to cycle).

The uterus is supported by a pair of lateral wing-like *broad ligaments* and cordlike *cardinal, uterosacral,* and *round ligaments.* It receives blood from a pair of *uterine arteries.*

The *Fallopian tubes* (oviducts) are two tubes that branch from the uterus and provide a passage to the uterus for the ovum released by the ovary. Fallopian tubes, uterine tubes, and salpinges (singular salpinx) are the expected site of fertilization. They are lined with ciliated epithelia. After fertilization, the embryo is slowly moved by ciliary movement toward the uterus.

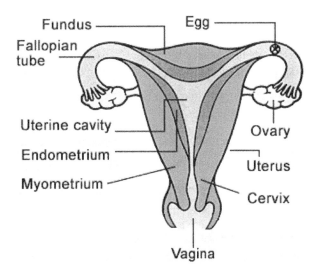

The flared distal end of the Fallopian tube, near the ovary, is the *infundibulum* and has feathery projections of *fimbriae* to receive the ovulated egg. Its long midportion is the *ampulla,* and the short, constricted zone near the uterus is the *isthmus.* A ligamentous sheet of mesosalpinx supports the tube.

*A female reproductive system with associated structures*

## Male genitalia

The external genitalia of men consists of the penis, male urethra, and scrotum.

The *penis* is a cylindrical copulatory organ that introduces semen (a fluid containing spermatozoa) and secretions into the female vagina.

The penis is divided into an internal *root* and an external *shaft* and *glans.* It is covered with loose skin that extends over the glans as the *prepuce* (foreskin).

Internally, the penile shaft consists mainly of three spongy long *erectile tissues*—a pair of dorsal *corpora cavernosa* (engorge with blood and produce most of the effect of erection), and a single ventral *corpus spongiosum* (contains the urethra).

All three tissues have *lacunae* (blood sinuses) separated by *trabeculae* composed of connective tissue and *trabecular muscle* (smooth muscle).

At the proximal end of the penis, the corpus spongiosum dilates into a *bulb* that receives the urethra and ducts of the bulbourethral glands.

The corpora cavernosa diverges into a pair of *crura,* anchoring the penis to the pubic arch and perineal membrane.

A pair of internal *pudendal arteries* supply the penis. Each branch into a *dorsal artery*, which travels dorsally under the skin of the penis.

The *deep artery* travels through the corpus cavernosum and supplies blood to the lacunae. The dorsal arteries supply most of the blood when the penis is flaccid, and the deep arteries supply blood during an erection.

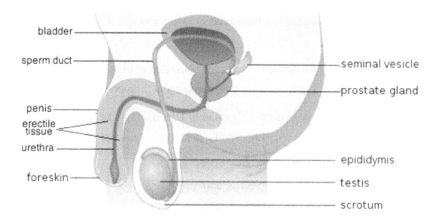

*A male reproductive system with anatomy and glands*

The *scrotum* is part of the external male genitalia behind and underneath the penis. It is a pouch of skin surrounding and protecting the testicles.

The scrotum contains the testes and the *spermatic cord*, a bundle of connective tissue, testicular blood vessels, and *ductus deferens* (sperm duct).

The spermatic cord passes up the back of the scrotum and through the external inguinal ring into the inguinal canal.

*Spermatic ducts* carry sperm from the testes to the urethra.

They include *efferent ductules* (leaving the testes); *duct of the epididymis* (highly coiled structure adhering to the posterior side of the testes); muscular *ductus deferens* (travels through the spermatic cord and inguinal canal into the pelvic cavity); and a short *ejaculatory duct* (carries sperm and seminal vesicle secretions towards the last 2 cm to the urethra).

The *urethra* completes the path of the sperm to the outside of the body.

The urethra is the duct by which urine is conveyed out of the body from the bladder and by which male vertebrates convey semen.

**Gonads for gamete production**

Gonads are primary sex organs specialized in producing gametes (haploid cells of egg and sperm).

There are two types of gonads: testes, which produce spermatozoa (sperm), and ovaries, which produce ova (singular ovum, or egg).

**Female gonad anatomy and functions**

The female gonads are the *ovaries*, which house immature eggs that mature one (or more) at a time (monthly).

The *ovary* is where the ova (or eggs) are produced (ovaries produce a secondary oocyte each month) along with female sex hormones, estrogen, and progesterone, during the ovarian cycle.

The ovaries are in the abdominal cavity. Females typically have two ovaries.

The *oviduct* (Fallopian tube or uterine tube) is a tube through which eggs move from the ovary to the uterus. Each ovary is associated with an oviduct. The ovary has a central *medulla*, a surface *cortex,* and an outer fibrous capsule of the *tunica albuginea.* Fimbriae are finger-like projections that sweep over the ovaries and waft the egg into the Fallopian tubes when it is released from the ovary. Generally, the ovaries alternate in producing one oocyte every month.

The ovary is supported by a medial *ovarian ligament*, a lateral *suspensory ligament,* and an anterior *mesovarium.* The ovary receives blood from a branch of the *uterine artery* medially and the *ovarian artery* laterally.

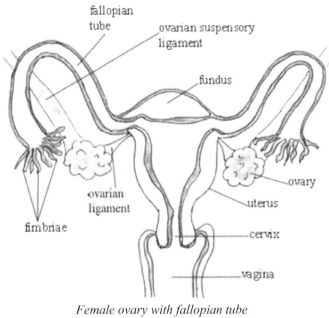

*Female ovary with fallopian tube and ovarian ligament*

**Male gonad anatomy and functions**

The male gonads are the *testes*, which produce sperm and testosterone.

Paired testes are suspended in the scrotal sacs of the scrotum. Shortly before birth, the fetal testes descend through the inguinal canal into the scrotum.

The low temperature in the scrotum is vital to normal sperm production. If the testes do not descend, surgery or hormonal therapy is required; otherwise, sterility results.

The testis consists of *seminiferous tubules* for the production of sperm and *interstitial cells* (Leydig cells) for the production of testosterone.

The epithelium of a seminiferous tubule consists of *germ cells* and *sustentacular cells.*

The germ cells develop into sperm. The sustentacular cells support and nourish the germ cells by forming a *blood-testis barrier* between them and the nearest blood supply.

Like the ovary, the testis has a fibrous capsule of the *tunica albuginea.* Fibrous septa extend from the tunica and divide the interior of the testis into 250–300 compartments of *lobules.*

Lobules contain one to three sperm-producing seminiferous tubules. Testosterone-secreting interstitial cells lie in clusters in between the tubules.

A long, slender *testicular artery* supplies each testis and drained by veins of the *pampiniform plexus,* which converge to form the *testicular vein.* The testis is supplied with *testicular nerves* and lymphatic vessels.

*Semen* (seminal fluid) is a thick, whitish fluid containing about 10% sperm, 30% glandular secretions from the prostate vesicles, and 60% secretions from the seminal vesicles and bulbourethral glands.

It contains about 50– 120 million sperm/mL and seminogelin (seminal vesicle protein), a serine protease (prostate-specific antigen), fructose, prostaglandins, and other substances.

The male has three sets of accessory glands: a pair of *seminal vesicles* posterior to the urinary bladder, a single *prostate gland* inferior to the bladder (enclosing the prostatic urethra) and a pair of small *bulbourethral glands* that secrete into the proximal end of the penile urethra.

The seminal vesicles and prostate secrete most of the semen. The bulbourethral glands produce a small amount of clear, slippery fluid that lubricates the urethra and neutralizes its pH.

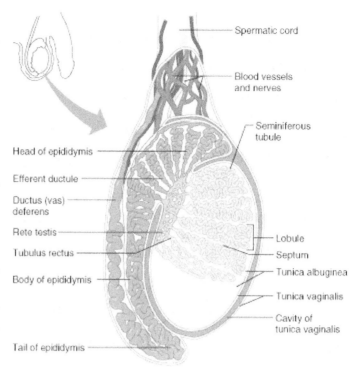

*Male reproductive system*

The seminal vesicles lie at the urinary bladder base, which contains two glands that join the *vas deferens* (pl. *vasa deferentia*) to form an ejaculatory duct that enters the urethra.

A thick fluid containing nutrients, including mucus (liquid for the sperm), fructose (for ATP), and prostaglandins, is secreted into the ejaculatory duct.

The prostate gland is below the urinary bladder and surrounds the upper portion of the urethra. It secretes a milky, slightly alkaline solution that promotes sperm motility and viability. This fluid neutralizes urine acidity that may still be in the urethra and neutralizes vaginal acidity.

The prostaglandin secretions neutralize seminal fluid, which is too acidic from the metabolic waste of sperm. The bulbourethral glands are below the prostate gland and on either side of the urethra; they release mucous secretions that provide lubrication.

The *epididymis* is a coiled tube attached to each testicle for the site of maturation and storage of sperm.

The vas deferens and epididymis store sperm until ejaculation. Sperm is non-motile at this time. During the passage through the epididymis, they are concentrated by fluid absorption. When a male is sexually aroused, the sperm enters the urethra, extending through the penis.

Sperm travels through the vas deferens into the ejaculatory duct, which leads to the urethra and penis.

The urethra transports urine from the bladder during urination.

**Pathway for sperm**

The mnemonic for the path of sperm is "Seven Up" (<u>S</u>eminiferous tubules, <u>E</u>pididymis, <u>V</u>as deferens, <u>E</u>jaculatory duct, <u>n</u>othing, <u>U</u>rethra, <u>P</u>enis).

Sperm cannot develop at the core body temperature of 37 °C. The testis is kept about 2 °C cooler than average body temperature by three structures in the scrotum: *cremaster muscle* of the spermatic cord, *dartos muscle* in the scrotal wall, and the *pampiniform plexus* of veins in the spermatic cord.

The cremaster muscle relaxes when warm and contracts when it is cool, lowering or raising the scrotum and testes. The dartos muscle contracts and tautens the scrotum when it is cool.

The pampiniform plexus acts as a countercurrent heat exchanger cooling blood on its way to the testes.

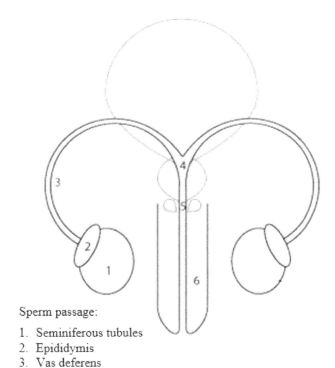

Sperm passage:
1. Seminiferous tubules
2. Epididymis
3. Vas deferens
4. Ejaculatory duct
5. Urethra
6. Penis

*Path of sperm from the seminiferous tubules and through the penis as "Seven Up"*

## Gametogenesis by Meiosis

**Formation of gametes**

*Gametogenesis* is the meiotic cell division that produces eggs (oogenesis) and sperm (spermatogenesis). *Meiosis* is a nuclear division that is broken into two broad stages (meiosis I and meiosis II), which reduces the chromosome number from diploid (2N) to haploid (N). The haploid number is half of the diploid number of chromosomes. Meiosis of one diploid cell produces four haploid cells. These daughter cells, containing half the genetic information, are *gametes.*

Before fertilization, the building blocks to create that cell must be available so that the initial fertilized cell (zygote) can develop into an embryo, fetus, and adult. Developing gametes (egg and sperm) are germ cells. The first stage in their development is the proliferation of primordial germ cells by mitosis (replication via cell division); daughter cells receive a complete set of chromosomes identical to the original cell.

In females, germ cells' mitosis activity occurs during embryonic development, while in males, it begins at puberty and continues throughout life. For years, it was believed that females contain all their egg cells at birth. However, recent findings of mitotic activity in female gonads and the idea that females do not produce new eggs during their lifetime are actively researched.

The next stage of development is meiosis; each daughter cell receives half of the chromosomes of the original cell. During meiosis, chromosomes stay in their homologous pairs.

For example, instead of 46 individual chromosomes lining up in humans, there are 23 pairs of chromosomes. Gamete production via meiosis occurs in sexually reproducing eukaryotes, including animals, plants, and fungi.

Sexual reproduction forms gametes. Human males produce small, motile sperm in the testes, and human females produce a large, immobile, nutrient-laden egg or ovum in the ovarian follicles. These gametes fuse to form a *zygote*. A zygote has the full or diploid (2N) number of chromosomes.

If gametes contained the same number of chromosomes as somatic (body) cells, the zygote would have twice the correct number of chromosomes. When the gametes fuse, the chromosomes from both parents naturally combine. Each fertilized egg (zygote) cell has a pair of homologous chromosomes, one 1N homolog from the mother (egg) and one 1N homolog from the father (sperm).

The chromosomes align within the daughter cells in many possible combinations during meiosis. $(2^{23})^2$ or about 70 trillion combinations are possible without crossing over. This allows for genetic variability in sexually reproducing organisms.

Crossing over is the process during meiosis I, where homologous chromosomes are paired with another (synapsis) and can exchange their genetic material to form genetically unique (recombinant) chromosomes.

If crossing over occurs once, $(4^{23})^2$ or 70 trillion squared genetically unique zygotes are possible for one couple. Crossing over is unique to prophase I of meiosis.

## Phases of meiosis I

Meiosis I and meiosis II have four phases: prophase, metaphase, anaphase, and telophase. Before meiosis I, DNA replication occurs in S phase of interphase, and each chromosome has a pair of sister chromatids; attached at the centromere (like mitosis for somatic cells).

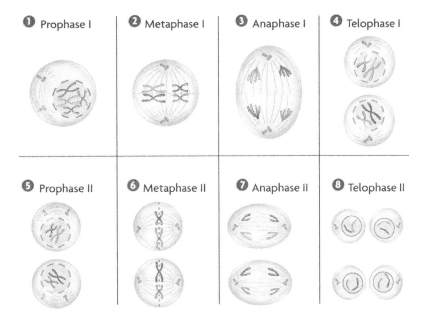

*Meiosis I is a reduction stage (2n → 1n), meiosis II separates sister chromatids at the centromere*

## Meiosis I: reduction phase of diploid to haploid (2N → 1N)

During meiosis I, homologous chromosomes line up at the synapsis. The two sets of paired chromosomes (1 from mother and 1 from father) alongside each other as bivalents (tetrads) held by a chiasma complex.

### Prophase I

1. Nuclear division occurs: nucleolus disappears, nuclear envelope fragments, centrosomes migrate away from each other, and spindle fibers assemble.

2. Homologous chromosomes undergo synapsis, forming bivalents; crossing over may occur as sister chromatids exchange genetic material by recombination.

3. Chromatin condenses, and chromosomes become microscopically visible.

### Metaphase I

1. During prometaphase I, bivalents held by chiasmata move toward the metaphase plate at the equator of the cell.

2. The fully formed spindle aligns the bivalents at the metaphase plate.

3. Kinetochores are proteins associated with centromeres; they attach to *kinetochore spindle fibers* anchored to the centrioles at each pole of the cell.

4. Homologous chromosomes independently align at the metaphase plate.

5. Maternal and paternal homologs may be oriented toward either pole.

**Anaphase I**

1.  The homologs separate and move toward opposite poles.

2.  Each chromosome is attached with a centromere and two sister chromatids (replicated previously during the S phase).

**Telophase I**

1.  In animals, this occurs at the end of meiosis I.

2.  The nuclear envelope reforms, and nucleoli reappear.

3.  This phase may or may not be accompanied by cytokinesis for portioning the two nuclei with separate plasma membranes (i.e., two daughter cells).

**Interkinesis**

1.  This period between meiosis I and meiosis II is similar to the interphase between mitotic divisions.

2.  However, no DNA replication (as in S phase of mitosis) occurs; the chromosomes are 1n (each chromosome has a sister chromatid).

**Phases of meiosis II: 1N → 1N**

Before meiosis II begins, the DNA does not replicate, and the centromere still attaches to the sister chromatids. During meiosis II, the centromeres split, and the sister chromatids separate.

Chromosomes in the four daughter cells contain one chromatid. Counting the number of centromeres verifies the number of chromosomes. Fertilization restores the diploid number (2n) in the zygote and somatic cells originating from this zygote.

1.  During metaphase II, haploid chromosomes (with sister chromatids) align at the metaphase plate.

2.  During anaphase II, sister chromatids separate at the centromeres, and the two daughter chromosomes move toward the poles.

3.  Due to crossing over in prophase I, each gamete contains chromosomes with gene combinations, unlike either parent.

4.  At the end of telophase II and cytokinesis, there are four haploid cells (1 sperm for males and 1 egg, and 3 polar bodies for females).

5.  In animals, the haploid cells mature and develop into gametes, which may eventually fuse into a zygote (2n) from a 1n sperm and 1n egg.

6.  In plants, the daughter cells become spores and divide to produce a haploid adult generation.

7.  In some fungi and algae, a zygote results from gamete fusion and immediately undergoes meiosis; therefore, the adult is haploid.

**Haploid gametes fuse during fertilization**

DNA is replicated once before mitosis and meiosis I and II; in mitosis, there is one nuclear division, while in meiosis, there are two nuclei divisions between syntheses of DNA.

In humans, meiosis occurs in reproductive organs to produce gametes, while mitosis occurs in somatic cells (not germline cells) for growth and repair.

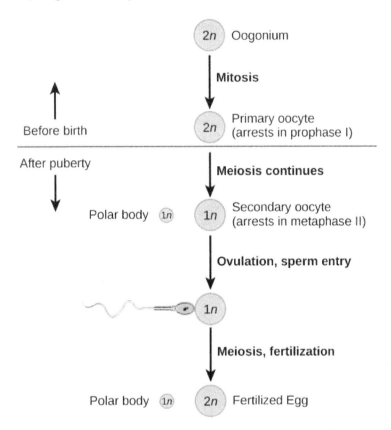

*Meiosis generates 4 unique haploid cells, while mitosis generates two identical diploid cells.*

- During prophase I of meiosis, homologous chromosomes pair for crossing over, which increases genetic variation. Crossing over does not occur during mitosis.

- During metaphase I, homologous chromosomes align at the metaphase plate; in mitosis, individual chromosomes align.

- During anaphase I, homologous chromosomes, with centromeres intact, separate and move to opposite poles. (In mitosis, sister chromatids separate and move to opposite poles.)

- Events of meiosis II are now the same stages as in mitosis; however, the nuclei contain the haploid number of chromosomes in meiosis.

- Mitosis produces two genetically identical diploid daughter cells; meiosis produces four genetically unique haploid daughter cells (4 sperm or 1 egg and 3 polar bodies).

## Sperm and Ovum Formation

**Spermatogenesis**

In human males, meiosis is part of *spermatogenesis*, the production of sperm, and occurs in the testes. In human females, meiosis is part of *oogenesis*, the production of egg cells, and occurs in the ovaries.

Spermatogenesis occurs in the seminiferous tubules in the testes and produces sperm from primary spermatocytes. *Spermatogonia* are undifferentiated germ cells that divide by mitosis and differentiate into *primary spermatocytes*. Primary spermatocytes grow and undergo the first meiotic division to form *secondary spermatocytes*. In the secondary spermatocyte stage, cells undergo a second meiotic division to form *spermatids*.

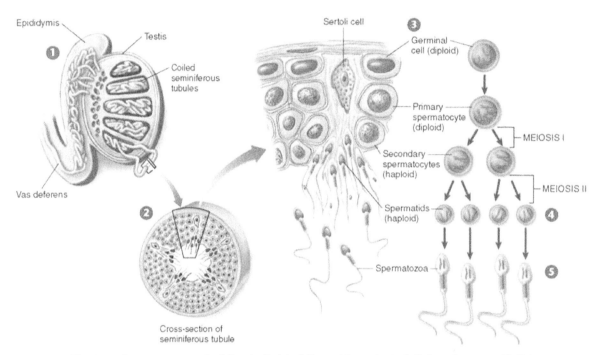

*Testis and spermatogenesis. Mitosis (2n) is followed by meiosis I (1n) and meiosis II (1n)*

The spermatogonium replicates all its chromosomes during interphase. It has 46 primary spermatocyte chromosomes, and each chromosome is made of two sister chromatids joined by a centromere. The cell undergoes prophase I, where homologous chromosomes line up on spindles at the equator. The cell undergoes anaphase I (reduction phase of meiosis), but the centromeres do not divide; the homologous chromosome pairs separate.

During telophase I, two cells are formed. Each cell is a secondary spermatocyte that contains 23 chromosomes, and each chromosome has two chromatids joined by a centromere.

These cells are haploid and undergo meiosis II: prophase II, metaphase II, anaphase II, and telophase II.

This second set of divisions DOES resemble mitosis.

Chromosomes condense (but do not pair up) during prophase II. The chromosomes align by spindle fibers during metaphase II, and the centromeres divide during anaphase II. The cells finish dividing during telophase II. At the end of meiosis II, there are four haploid cells with 23 chromosomes.

Spermatids, formed from the division of the secondary spermatocytes, develop into mature spermatozoa (sperm). *Sertoli cells* are stimulated by follicle-stimulating hormone (FSH) in the seminiferous tubules and surround and provide nourishment to spermatids during differentiation. They complete maturation (e.g., gain of motility) in the epididymis.

*Sertoli cells* secrete the peptide hormone *inhibin* (acts on the pituitary gland to inhibit FSH release) and *androgen-binding protein* (binds testosterone and acts as an intermediary between germ cells and hormones). The Sertoli cells divide the tubules into compartments with separate environments where stages of spermatogenesis continue. *Leydig cells* between the tubules produce testosterone in the presence of the luteinizing hormone (LH).

Sperm produced in the testes mature within the *epididymides*. These are tightly-coiled tubules outside of the testes. The maturation time in the epididymis is required for sperm to develop the ability to swim. Once sperm has matured, they are propelled into the *vasa deferentia* by muscular contractions. Sperm is stored in the epididymides and the vasa deferentia.

## Oogenesis and the ovarian cycle

Oogenesis produces a single ovum from a single primary oocyte. Unlike spermatogenesis, the *ovarian cycle* occurs in a monthly rhythm and usually produces one gamete (egg) per month. Each egg develops in its bubble-like *follicle*, located primarily in the cortex.

Each month, about 20 to 25 *primordial follicles* resume their development. The single layer of squamous follicular cells around the oocyte thickens into cuboidal cells. The follicle is a *primary follicle*. As the egg enlarges, the follicular cells multiply and pile up into multiple strata; the follicle is a *secondary follicle*, and the follicular cells are *granulosa cells.*

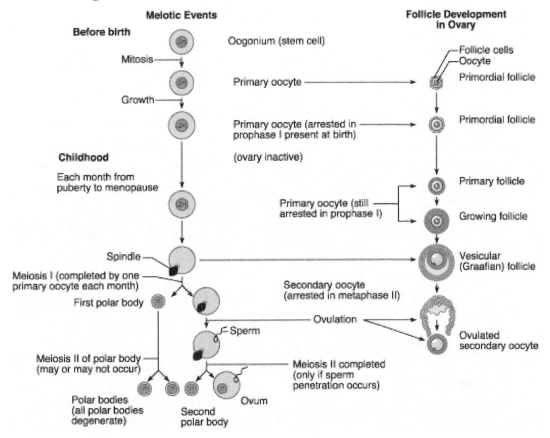

### Oogenesis, polar bodies and oocytes

*Oogonia* are primitive germ cells that undergo mitosis and develop into *primary oocytes* (with 46 chromosomes), the initial cells in oogenesis. Primary oocytes remain in meiotic arrest (i.e., begin first meiotic development but do not complete it). The germ cells in a female are believed to be at this developmental stage at birth. However, this is an area currently under investigation by researchers.

Primary oocytes are in the ovaries of the female reproductive system. Oogenesis occurs monthly, beginning at puberty and ending at menopause. At puberty, primary oocytes are destined for ovulation and complete meiosis, and each daughter cell receives 23 chromosomes.

Although some primary oocytes undergo *atresia* (immature and degraded) during childhood, there are about 300,000 to 400,000 oocytes at puberty. When the primary oocyte divides, one of the two daughter cells, the *secondary oocyte*, retains most cytoplasm. The *first polar body* is the other daughter cell, is nonfunctional, and (often) does not proceed to meiosis II. The secondary oocyte proceeds to the metaphase II of meiosis and suspends. Meiosis II resumes if fertilization occurs. Completing meiosis II allows the secondary oocyte to become a fertilized egg (2n zygote when fused with the sperm).

The meiotic division produces two *second polar bodies* that disintegrate because they receive insufficient cytoplasm. The body absorbs second polar bodies and retains most of the egg's cytoplasm. The cytoplasm serves as a source of nutrients for the developing embryo. This is different from spermatogenesis, in which four functional, mature sperm are produced from a single spermatogonium.

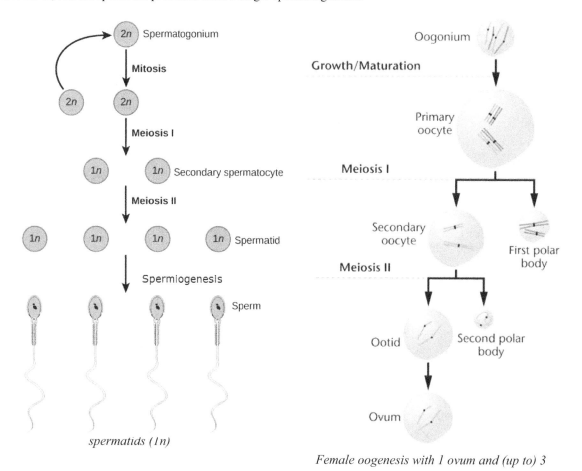

*Female oogenesis with 1 ovum and (up to) 3 polar bodies*

---

A single ovum is produced per month. Typically, one of the tertiary follicles becomes a fully mature *vesicular* (Graafian) *follicle* or the *tertiary follicle* destined to ovulate. Ovulation occurs around day 14 of a typical cycle. The follicle swells and bursts, releasing the egg and *cumulus oophorus* (a mass of follicular cells surrounding the ovum in the vesicular ovarian follicle) into the mouth of the uterine tube.

**Sperm morphology and mechanisms**

Sperm is compact cells of DNA with flagella that provide motility.

Eggs are non-motile and filled with cytoplasm.

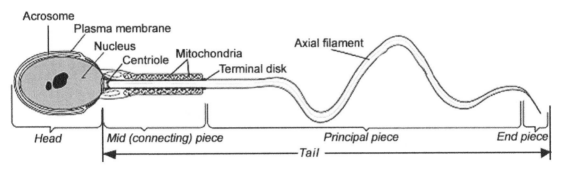

*Human spermatozoon with head, midpiece, and tail*

*Spermatozoa* (mature sperm) have three parts. The sperm *head* (haploid with 23 chromosomes) contains a nucleus and DNA covered by an acrosome. The *acrosome* is a cap-like covering over the anterior end of the nucleus that stores enzymes to help the sperm penetrate the several layers of cells and thick membrane enclosing the egg. The *middle piece* contains multiple mitochondria for energy wrapped around microtubules of the flagellum in a 9 + 2 microtubule array. The *tail* contains microtubules as components of a flagellum for its whip-like movement, propelling the sperm. The ejaculate of a human male contains several hundred million sperms. Fewer than 100 reach the vicinity of an egg, and usually, only one sperm enters an egg.

| Male | Female | Difference |
|---|---|---|
| Spermatogonium (2N) | Oogonium (2N) | Spermatogonium renews its population by mitosis throughout life. Oogonium stops renewing its population before birth |
| Primary spermatocyte (1 N) | Primary oocyte (1N) | Primary oocyte arrests at prophase I |
| Secondary spermatocyte (1N) | Secondary oocyte (1N) | Secondary oocyte arrests at metaphase II |
| Sperm (1N) | Ovum (1N) | Between the secondary spermatocyte and sperm is the spermatid |

**Male *vs.* female gamete**

The ovum (unfertilized egg cell) is the female gamete. Unlike sperm, the egg is not capable of active movement. The egg is much larger than the sperm (it is visible to the naked eye). Human sperm is about 55 micrometers (μm) in length (head is 5 μm, and the flagellum is 50 μm). A mature ovum is between 120-150 μm in diameter. Therefore, the ratio of the length of the sperm to the diameter of the egg is about 1:3. Compared with the width of a sperm cell (~3 μm) to an egg's diameter, the ratio is about 1:50.

The *granulosa cells* produce a glycoprotein gel layer as the *zona pellucida* around the egg; the connective tissue around the granulosa cells condenses into a tough fibrous *theca folliculi*. The granulosa cells secrete *follicular fluid*, which forms small pools. The follicle is a *tertiary follicle*. The fluid pools eventually coalesce to form a single cavity, the *antrum*. The egg is now held against one side of the antrum by a mound of cells of the *cumulus oophorus*; the innermost layer of these cells is the *corona radiata*.

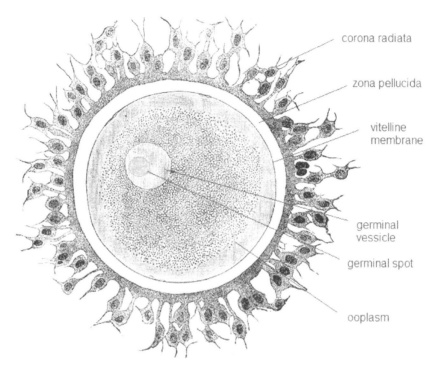

*Human ovum with the protective glycoprotein layer of zona pellucida and inner vitelline membrane enclosing the ooplasm*

**Egg and sperm contributions during fertilization**

Sexual reproduction produces offspring that combine genes from each parent. It entails the union of two gametes (ovum and sperm) to form a zygote (fertilized egg). The gametes contain half the genetic information needed to produce the 2n progeny.

Sperm contributes to the chromosomal DNA, as the egg actively destroys any mitochondria in the sperm. The egg contributes chromosomal DNA and everything else (mitochondria, organelles, and biomolecules within the ooplasm) within the large volume of cytoplasm (i.e., 1 large egg and 3 small, non-functional polar bodies). The egg contains the cytoplasm nutrients and biomolecules needed by a developing embryo.

A diploid zygote (haploid sperm and haploid egg) represents the first stage in developing a genetically unique organism. The zygote contains the essential components needed for development as the genes of chromosomes. The genes of the zygote are not activated to produce proteins until after several cleavage divisions.

During cleavage, the large zygote subdivides into cells of conventional size via mitosis. After initial cleavage, blastomeres are the initial cells of an organism's development.

## Hormonal Control of Reproduction

### Male and female sexual development

Ovaries produce the hormones *estradiol* and *progesterone*. Estradiol is the female hormone estrogen. Testes produce *testosterone*, which is the main sex hormone in males. Testosterone is an androgen, which has masculinizing effects. Androgens are not unique to males, and estrogens are not unique to females.

Many organs of the male and female reproductive systems develop from the same embryonic organs.

Organs with the same embryonic precursor are *homologous*. For example, the scrotum and labia majora are homologous because each develops from the labioscrotal folds.

*Secondary sex organs* are other anatomical structures needed to produce offspring, such as the male glands, ducts, penis, female uterine tubes, uterus, and vagina.

*Secondary sex characteristics* are features not essential to reproduction but help attract mates by indicating sexual maturity (e.g., breasts). Secondary sex characteristics comprise the external differences between males and females.

### Reproductive organs mature during puberty

*Puberty* is when reproductive organs mature, and reproduction becomes possible. Puberty is initiated by the secretion of *gonadotropin-releasing hormone* (GnRH) by the hypothalamus. GnRH stimulates the release of *follicle-stimulating hormone* (FSH) and *luteinizing hormone* (LH) by the anterior pituitary.

FSH and LH act upon the gonads to stimulate the development of sperm and ova and the secretion of sex hormones. The sex hormones exert negative feedback on the secretion of GnRH, FSH, and LH.

The visible changes at puberty are from hormones (e.g., testosterone, estrogens, growth hormone). After puberty, the individual attains fertility. Adolescence continues until the full adult height is attained.

### Secondary male characteristics

The earliest visible sign of male puberty is an enlargement of the testes and scrotum; the ejaculation of motile sperm marks the completion of puberty.

Testosterone has three prominent roles:

1) stimulating the development of prenatal genitalia,

2) stimulating the development of the male secondary sexual characteristics, such as the growth of the skeletal muscle (longer legs and broader shoulders), development of pubic hair, facial hair, and chest hair, and

3) the maintenance of sex drive during adulthood. It stimulates the secretion of oil and sweat glands (i.e., attributed to body odor and acne).

Additionally, testosterone prompts the larynx and vocal cords to enlarge, resulting in a deeper voice.

It is involved in triggering baldness if "baldness genes" are present and regulates testosterone synthesis by acting on Leydig cells to stimulate testosterone secretion.

## Secondary female characteristics

Female puberty is marked by *thelarche* (e.g., the onset of breast development), *pubarche* (e.g., the appearance of pubic and axillary hair), and *menarche* (i.e., the onset of menstruation). Regular ovulation and fertility are attained about a year after menarche.

Estrogens maintain the normal development of the related organs and the secondary sex characteristics of females. Compared to males, females have less body and facial hair and more fat beneath the skin (i.e., a rounded appearance). In females, the pelvic girdle enlarges, and the pelvic cavity is larger for wider hips. Estrogen and progesterone are required for breast development.

The female breast has a conical or *pendulous body* and a narrower *axillary tail* extending toward the armpit. The breast contains 15–24 lobules, each with a mammary duct. The *nipple* is at the apex and is surrounded by a zone of darker skin as the *areola*.

The areola has small *areolar glands* that may appear as bumps around the nipple. They produce a secretion that prevents chafing and cracking of the skin in a nursing mother.

The mammary duct begins at the nipple and divides into numerous ducts that end in alveoli (blind sacs).

Prolactin hormone is for *lactation* (milk production) to begin. The feedback inhibition suppresses the prolactin production that estrogens and progesterone have on the anterior pituitary during pregnancy. Therefore, it takes a couple of days after delivering a baby for milk production to begin.

Before this, the breasts produce a watery, yellowish-white fluid (*colostrum*) similar to milk but containing more protein and less fat, rich in IgA antibodies that provide immunity to a newborn.

Breast cancer is a common form of cancer in females; women should have regular breast exams and mammograms as recommended.

At midlife, sexes go through a period of hormonal and physical change of *climacteric.* This is marked by a decline in testosterone or estrogen secretion and a rise in FSH and LH's secretion. In females, climacteric is accompanied by *menopause*, the cessation of ovarian function, and fertility.

Menopause is the cessation of menstrual periods with age from a decrease in the number of ovarian follicles and their hypo-responsiveness to gonadotropins.

Plasma estrogen levels decrease, resulting in high gonadotropin secretion.

A decrease in bone mass of osteoporosis occurs, hot flashes or the sudden dilation of arterioles, which increases body temperature and sweating.

## Male reproductive cycle

The hypothalamus has control of the testes' sexual function through the secretion of GnRH.

GnRH stimulates the pituitary to produce the gonadotropic hormones FSH and LH in the anterior pituitary gland.

FSH promotes spermatogenesis in males by stimulating primary spermatocytes to undergo meiosis I (forming secondary spermatocytes).

FSH enhances Sertoli cells (nurse cell that helps develop sperm) by causing them to bind to androgens effectively. In males, LH is an *interstitial cell-stimulating hormone* (ICSH).

LH acts on the cells of Leydig and stimulates the production and secretion of testosterone.

The *sustentacular cells* of the seminiferous tubules release the hormone *inhibin*, which regulates the rate of sperm production and produces an androgen-binding protein, making the testes responsive to testosterone.

The hypothalamus-pituitary-testis system uses a negative feedback relationship that maintains a relatively constant production of sperm and testosterone. Although hormone and gamete production is constant in males, this is not true for females.

**Female reproductive cycle**

In a longitudinal cross-section, an ovary shows cellular follicles, each containing an oocyte (egg). A female is born with up to two million follicles. The number is reduced to 300,000–400,000 by puberty, and a small number of follicles (about 400) fully mature. As a follicle matures, it develops from a *primary follicle* to a *secondary follicle* to a vesicular follicle (Graafian).

As oogenesis occurs, a secondary follicle contains a secondary oocyte that is pushed to one side of the fluid-filled cavity. The vesicular follicle fills with fluid until the follicle wall balloons out on the surface and bursts, releasing a secondary oocyte surrounded by a *zona pellucida* and *follicular cells.*

During the *follicular phase*, FSH and LH stimulate primary follicles (containing primary oocytes) to grow and stimulate *theca cells*, express receptors for LH to produce androstenedione (androgen).

**Endometrium formation**

As a response to LH, androgens are converted into estrogen by follicle-stimulating (FSH-induced) hormone by granulosa cells. Estrogen leads to the thickening of the endometrium (uterine epithelium).

As the estrogen levels rise, it exerts feedback control over the anterior pituitary secretion of FSH, causing the follicular phase to end.

As FSH decreases, the follicles cannot be maintained, and all but one follicle degenerates.

The one dominant follicle (Graafian follicle) survives because 1) it is hyperresponsive to FSH and can maintain itself under low FSH, and 2) it becomes sensitive to LH.

Estrogen levels in the blood rise, causing the hypothalamus to secrete GnRH, causing a surge in LH secretion. LH does not drop but shoots up (LH surge) because increased estrogen exerts positive feedback on the pituitary's LH-releasing mechanism. The LH spike triggers ovulation.

*Ovulation* is the vesicular follicle's rupture with the discharge of the 2° oocyte into the pelvic cavity.

The *secondary oocyte* completes a second meiotic cell division when fertilization occurs. Meanwhile, the follicle develops into the *corpus luteum* (promoted by LH), which secretes progesterone.

Progesterone is the hormone responsible for maintaining the endometrium. If pregnancy does not occur, the corpus luteum degenerates in about 14 days, and estrogen and progesterone levels recede.

The lack of estrogen and progesterone collapses the vascular endometrium, leading to menstruation.

**The menstrual cycle**

The endometrium undergoes cyclic histological changes are the *menstrual cycle*, governed by the shifting hormonal secretions of the ovaries.

FSH, LH, estrogen, and progesterone are in a complex interaction to regulate menstruation. An average 28-day uterine cycle is divided into four phases.

The *proliferative phase* is the mitotic rebuilding of tissue lost in the previous menstrual period and is primarily regulated by estrogens.

The *secretory phase*, regulated primarily by progesterone, consists of a thickening of the endometrium by secretions (not by mitosis).

The *premenstrual phase* is ischemia and necrosis of the endometrium.

The *menstrual phase* begins when endometrial tissue and blood are first discharged from the vagina and mark day 1 of a new cycle. It is triggered by the decline in ovarian secretions of progesterone and estrogens.

The menstrual cycle begins on day 1, with *menstruation* (sloughing of the endometrium resulting in bleeding). During days 1 to 5, low levels of estrogen and progesterone cause menstruation.

*Menstruation* is the periodic shedding of tissue and blood from the endometrium; this lining disintegrates, and the blood vessels rupture.

*Menses* is the flow of blood and tissues discharged from the vagina. FSH from the anterior pituitary stimulates the growth of a follicle in the ovary (the follicular phase), which secretes estrogen as it grows.

After day 5, the rising estrogen levels stimulate the uterus to grow a new inner lining.

Between days 6 and 13, increased production of estrogens by an ovarian follicle causes the endometrium to thicken and become vascular and glandular (proliferative phase).

By day 14, the endometrial lining is thick. A surge in LH from the anterior pituitary gland releases the oocyte and some of the ovary's follicular cells (ovulation).

**Follicular and luteal phases**

Ovulation usually occurs on day 14 of the 28-day cycle.

LH causes the remaining follicular cells to become the corpus luteum.

Days 15 through 28 have increased progesterone production by the corpus luteum, causing the endometrium to double in thickness. Uterine glands mature, producing a thick mucoid secretion (secretory phase).

The endometrium is now prepared to receive an embryo.

If no pregnancy occurs, the progesterone and estrogen levels decline, and the corpus luteum degenerates.

With low levels of progesterone, the uterine lining begins to degenerate.

During menstruation, the anterior pituitary increases FSH production; a new follicle begins maturation.

The ovarian cycle controls the uterine cycle.

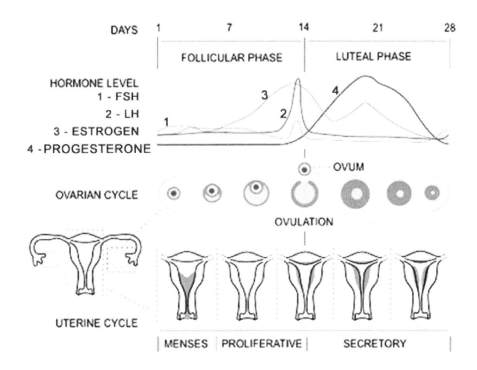

*Female ovarian and uterine cycles with associated hormone levels*

If fertilization and implantation do not occur, the corpus luteum degenerates after about 14 days.

The drop in progesterone and estrogen causes the lining to degrade and shed, initiating the next cycle.

**Hormonal response to fertilization**

The ovarian cycle is under the control of gonadotropic hormones FSH and LH in females. The gonadotropic hormones are not present constantly but are secreted at varying rates during the cycle.

The *luteal phase* in the ovary (corresponding to the uterus's secretory phase) is the second half of the ovarian cycle following ovulation.

Progesterone and estrogen from the corpus luteum inhibit the normal functioning of GnRH, which slows the production of FSH and LH.

Progesterone converts the endometrium into a secretory tissue full of glycogen and blood vessels, ready to receive a fertilized egg. As progesterone levels in the blood rise, negative feedback decreases the anterior pituitary's secretion of LH, and the corpus luteum degenerates. If fertilization does occur, the corpus luteum persists for about three months.

Emergency postcoital contraceptives (e.g., Plan B) include progesterone antagonists that prevent progesterone from binding to their receptors, leading to erosion of the endometrium.

When oral contraceptives (i.e., birth control pills) are used, a combination of synthetic progesterone and estrogen inhibits pituitary gonadotropin release, thereby preventing ovulation.

## Neural control of sexual arousal

The penis contains vascular compartments and arteries. Typically, these vessels are constricted so that there is little blood in them, causing the penis to remain flaccid.

During sexual arousal, nervous reflexes cause an increase in the arterial blood flow to the penis.

Nerves of the penis converge on a pair of *dorsal nerves*, which lead via the *internal pudendal nerves* to the sacral plexus and then the spinal cord.

The penis receives sympathetic, parasympathetic, and somatic motor nerve fibers.

Sexual excitation in higher brain centers, stimulation of mechanoreceptors in the penis, inhibition of sympathetic fibers, and the release of nitric oxide contribute to dilating these arteries. Dilation causes these compartments to engorge with blood at high pressure.

The increased blood flow fills and distends the erectile tissue, making the penis elongated and rigid, like an *erection*.

Erectile dysfunction is the inability to achieve an erection due to various physiological or psychological causes. Viagra and related products release nitrous oxide (NO) and block the breakdown of cGMP, a messenger involved in the relaxation of the arterial smooth muscle, promoting erection.

## Ejaculation and orgasm

The stimulation of sympathetic nerves contracts the smooth muscles lining the ducts and discharges semen through the urethra. The sphincter at the base of the urinary bladder is closed so that sperm cannot enter the bladder and urine is not expelled.

*Ejaculation* is the expulsion of semen and is achieved at the peak of sexual arousal.

*Emission* is the first phase of ejaculation. Nerve impulses from the spine trigger the epididymides and vasa deferentia to contract. Subsequent motility causes the sperm to enter the ejaculatory duct.

Secretions are released from the seminal vesicles, the prostate gland, and the bulbourethral glands.

A small amount of secretion from the bulbourethral glands may leak from the end of the penis to clean the urethra of acid but may contain sperm.

*Expulsion* is the second phase of ejaculation. Rhythmical contractions at the base of the penis and within the urethral wall expel the semen in spurts.

Rhythmical contractions are a release from *myotonia* (muscle tenseness), an important sexual response.

Ejaculation lasts for a limited time, and the penis returns to a flaccid state following ejaculation.

A *refractory period* follows when stimulation does not result in an erection.

An *orgasm* is the physiological and psychological sensations that occur at the climax of sexual stimulation. During an orgasm, heart rate and blood pressure increase, and skeletal muscles contract throughout.

The *clitoris* in females contains many sensory receptors as a sexually sensitive organ.

A female orgasm releases neuromuscular tension in the genital area, vagina, and uterus muscles.

## Reproduction Mechanism

### Human sexual reproduction

In sexually reproducing organisms, *fertilization* is the first step of embryogenesis. It marks the combination of sperm and egg to form a zygote. Reproduction may be sexual or asexual.

*Asexual reproduction* does not involve fertilization, as only one parent is required. Asexual reproduction is the primary form of reproduction for single-celled organisms (e.g., bacteria, many protists, fungi).

Rarely are animals exclusively asexual, but most animals that can reproduce asexually use a combination of sexual and asexual reproduction.

In *sexual reproduction*, the *ovum* (egg) of one parent is fertilized by the sperm of the other.

The ovum and sperm are *gametes* produced by sexually mature organisms in *gametogenesis*.

Sexually-reproducing animals use various strategies to ensure that their gametes find each other.

Fertilization of the ovum by the sperm may occur externally (e.g., in water) or internally (i.e., within the organism).

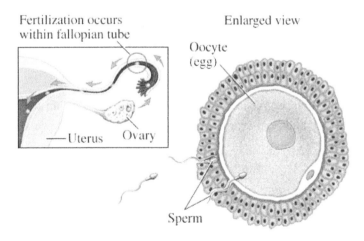

Most mammals, including humans, use internal fertilization, and their young develop within the mother's uterus until birth.

Reptiles, birds, and a class of mammals called monotremes fertilize internally but subsequently lay eggs in which their young develop.

To preserve the existence of the species and pass on their genetic material, mature adults must be capable of producing fertile offspring. Many animals are fertile during specific periods.

In human females, the ovum is available for fertilization by sperm once per cycle, during *ovulation*.

**Fertilization mechanism**

An ovary releases an ovum during ovulation, swept by ciliary cells into the *uterine tube* (the oviduct or Fallopian tube).

During intercourse, millions of sperm are ejaculated and move through the vagina, uterus, and uterine tube towards the ovum using their *flagella*, whip-like tails.

Temperature and chemical signals direct the sperm towards the ovum. They are aided in their journey by rhythmic propulsions of the vagina and uterus.

However, most sperms die before reaching the ovum due to their depleted energy supply (ATP) and the acidic vaginal environment.

A sperm secretes proteins that bind to receptors on the glycoprotein layer surrounding the plasma membrane of a same-species ovum, preventing cross-species fertilization.

This glycoprotein layer is the *vitelline layer* or *zona pellucida* in mammals.

**Polyspermy**

Upon binding, the *acrosome* in the sperm head digests a path through the zona pellucida with the release of hydrolytic enzymes. The sperm body follows into the ovum.

Most of the sperm cells that reach the ovum are viable and have the potential to fertilize it. Sperm cells attach to the ovum, but only one should succeed in penetrating the ovum.

*Polyspermy* occurs when more than one sperm penetrates the ovum.

Usually, a fertilized ovum has 2 copies of each chromosome, but an ovum affected with polyspermy has 3 or more copies, which usually leads to the formation of a non-viable zygote. Down's Syndrome is trisomy 21.

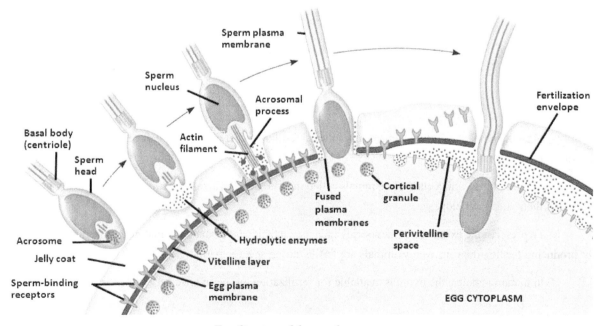

*Fertilization of the egg by sperm*

## Mechanisms to avoid polyspermy

Prevention of polyspermy depends on specific changes that occur when a sperm cell first binds and fuses to an ovum. During this time, the ovum is vulnerable to other sperm attempting to fertilize it, so immediate action must be taken to avoid this scenario by two mechanisms: fast block and slow block to polyspermy.

The *slow block* is a slower and longer-term process.

Many species other than mammals utilize *both* a fast and slow block because although the fast block is effective, it is transient, and another countermeasure to polyspermy is often needed.

The slow block is initiated upon fertilization, as the ovum secretes various hormones to prevent it from being overwhelmed by the hundreds of sperm attempting fertilization.

In most species that use this technique, the slow block is the *cortical reaction.*

The cortical reaction involves calcium release from the ovum, causing *cortical granules* in the ovum to secrete calcium, modifying the zone pellucida.

Proteases lift the vitelline layer as hyaluronic acid pushes the vitelline layer away from the ovum's surface, forming a barrier that prevents the entrance of other sperm.

Hyalin and peroxidases harden the fertilization envelope and inactivate the sperm-binding sites to prevent additional sperm cells from fusing.

## Zona reaction in humans

The vitelline layer is the *fertilization envelope.*

In mammals, the vitelline layer is the zona pellucida, so the cortical reaction is the *zona reaction.* The zona pellucida hardens, and its binding sites become inactivated.

The zona reaction of mammals is less effective than the cortical reaction in other species.

Research shows that in the zona reaction, the contents of the cortical granules inactivate ZP2 and ZP3 sperm receptors on the zona pellucida.

Mammals use only a slow block to polyspermy and not a combination of a fast and slow block as in other species (e.g., sea urchins).

Even after the sperm binds to and fuses with the ovum, fertilization is not complete until the gametes fuse their two haploid nuclei, as *pronuclei.*

The pronuclei form a single diploid nucleus containing the zygote's unique genome.

In most animals, including humans, the sperm contributes more than just its pronucleus to the zygote. The sperm centriole enters the ovum along with the pronucleus and flagellum.

Recent evidence suggests that sperm mitochondria enter but are destroyed by the ovum. The centriole replicates and is assembled into a centrosome, replicating the first mitotic spindle assembly in the zygote.

This explains why extra mitotic spindles form in polyspermy cases since several sperm cells contribute their centrioles to the ovum.

**Pregnancy**

The cells of the placenta produce human chorionic gonadotropin (HCG), which maintains the corpus luteum. This hormone is detected about 11 days after conception. Home pregnancy tests rely on the presence of HCG to confirm pregnancy.

In general, the level of HCG doubles every 48 hours during the first four weeks of pregnancy, every 72 hours by 7-8 weeks, reaches a peak at 11-12 weeks of pregnancy. The corpus luteum produces progesterone and estrogen to maintain the uterus during the first trimester of pregnancy. HCG maintains the corpus luteum until the placenta produces its progesterone and estrogen, as the corpus luteum regresses.

Progesterone and estrogen have two effects at this stage. They inhibit the anterior pituitary, so no new follicles mature. They maintain the lining of the uterus, so the corpus luteum is not needed, thus eliminating menstrual cycles during pregnancy.

Major causes of female infertility are

1) blocked oviducts,

2) failure to ovulate due to low body weight (<10-15%), and

3) *endometriosis*, the spread of uterine tissue beyond the uterus.

The common causes of male sterility and infertility are low sperm count and abnormal sperm from disease, radiation, chemical mutagens, or excessive heat near the testes.

Mammals, including humans, are *viviparous*, as the embryo remains in the female's body during development. There are many forms of viviparity, but the most developed form is *placental viviparity*, where the mother constantly supplies the nutrients needed for development (e.g., placenta).

Typical human pregnancies last for about 40 weeks from the first day of the woman's last menstrual period. When the fetal brain matures, the hypothalamus causes the pituitary to stimulate the adrenal cortex to release androgens.

**Parturition**

The placenta uses androgens as precursors for estrogens that stimulate prostaglandin and oxytocin production. The hormones estrogen, prostaglandin, and oxytocin cause the uterus to contract rhythmically and expel the fetus. *Labor* is a series of strong uterine contractions and has three stages:

1) cervix thins and dilates; amniotic sac ruptures and releases fluids;

2) rapid uterine contractions, followed by the birth of a newborn;

3) uterus contracts and expels the umbilical cord and placenta.

The cervix dilates, and the newborn moves through the vagina. Following birth:

- oxygen is now supplied by breathing with functional lungs;

- switch from fetal circulation, which bypasses the lungs and liver, to normal circulation (closing ducts and openings);

- nutrients now come from suckling rather than from the mother's blood.

# CHAPTER 22

# Development

- Reproduction Mechanism

- Mechanisms to Avoid Polyspermy

- Embryogenesis

- Primary Germ Layers

- Mechanisms of Development

- Tissue Formation

- Gene Expression

## Reproduction Mechanisms

**Human sexual reproduction**

Reproduction may be *sexual* or *asexual*. In sexual reproduction, *fertilization* is the first step of embryogenesis.

*Asexual reproduction* does not involve fertilization, as only one parent is required. Asexual reproduction is the primary form of reproduction for single-celled organisms (e.g., bacteria, many protists, fungi).

Rarely are animals exclusively asexual; animals that reproduce asexually combine sexual and asexual reproduction.

*Sexual reproduction* is when the *sperm* fertilizes the other parent's *ovum* (or *egg*).

Ovum and sperm are *gametes* produced by sexually mature organisms in *gametogenesis*.

Sperm and egg fuse to form a *zygote*. Sexually reproducing animals use various strategies to ensure that their gametes (1N *germ line cells*) fuse.

*Germ line cells* are "*sex cells*" (i.e., *eggs and sperm*) that sexually reproducing organisms use to pass on their genomes to the next generation (i.e., parents to offspring).

Egg and sperm cells are *germ cells*, in contrast to "*body cells*" (or *somatic cells*).

The ovum is available for fertilization by sperm once per cycle during ovulation in human females.

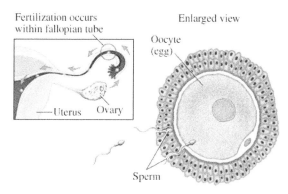

*Human reproductive structures and enlarged view of a fertilized ovum*

**Internal *vs.* external fertilization**

To preserve the species and pass genetic material, mature adults must be capable of producing fertile offspring. Many animals are fertile during specific periods. Fertilizing an ovum by a sperm may occur *externally* (e.g., in water) or *internally* (i.e., within the organism).

Animals that use external fertilization (e.g., fish and amphibians) release thousands (or millions) of gametes (egg or sperm) since the chance of fertilization is low.

The advantages of external fertilization are greater genetic variation and low disease transmission. Most externally fertilizing animals synchronize the release of their gametes using environmental signals. Tides, which fluctuate with the lunar cycle, are one such trigger.

Most mammals, including humans, use internal fertilization, and their young develop within the mother's uterus until birth. Animals that use internal fertilization, including all terrestrial vertebrates, require one (or few) ova and are selective about reproductive partners. The disadvantage of this reproductive strategy is that it reduces genetic variation and requires direct contact between males and females, promoting disease transmission.

Reptiles, birds, and monotreme mammals fertilize internally but subsequently lay eggs in which their young develop.

**Fertilization mechanisms**

*Ovary* releases an *ovum*, swept by ciliary cells into the uterine tube (*oviduct* or *Fallopian tube*) during *ovulation*.

During intercourse, millions of sperm are ejaculated and move through the vagina, uterus, and uterine tube towards the ovum using their *flagella*, whip-like tails.

*Temperature* and *chemical signals* direct sperm towards the ovum. *Rhythmic propulsions* of the vagina and uterus aid sperm in their journey.

Most sperms die before reaching the ovum due to their depleted energy supply (ATP) and acidic vaginal environment.

Sperm secretes proteins that bind to receptors on the glycoprotein layer surrounding the plasma membrane of a same-species ovum, preventing cross-species fertilization.

This glycoprotein layer is the *vitelline layer* or *zona pellucida* in mammals.

Sperm cells reaching the ovum are viable and have the potential to fertilize it. Sperm cells attach to the ovum, but only one should penetrate the ovum. *Acrosome* in the sperm head digests the *zona pellucida* with releases *hydrolytic enzymes* upon binding.

Fertilization requires gametes to fuse haploid (1N) nuclei as pronuclei. After fusion, the sperm body follows the haploid (1N) pronuclei into the ovum. Two pronuclei form a diploid nucleus containing the zygote's unique genome.

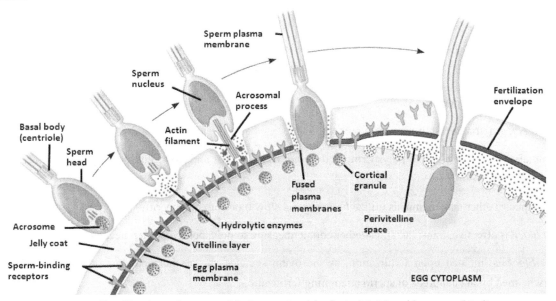

*Fertilization of an egg with time series (clockwise) initiated by sperm binding*

## Mechanism to Avoid Polyspermy

### Polyspermy

*Polyspermy* is when more than one sperm penetrates the ovum.

Usually, a fertilized ovum has 2 copies (2N or *diploid*) of each chromosome, but an ovum affected with polyspermy has 3 or more copies, forming a non-typical zygote. For example, Down's Syndrome is trisomy 21.

Prevention of polyspermy depends on specific changes when a sperm cell first binds and fuses to an ovum.

The ovum is vulnerable to sperm attempting to fertilize it, so immediate action must be taken to avoid this scenario by two mechanisms: *fast block* and *slow block* to polyspermy.

### Fast block to polyspermy

In marine invertebrates (e.g., sea urchins), fertilization triggers an influx of sodium ions into the ovum, which causes its membrane potential to depolarize rapidly.

Sperm cells cannot bind to the positively charged ovum, so *fast block* quickly prevents polyspermy.

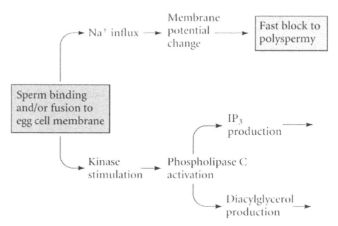

*Fast block to polyspermy involves a change to the membrane potential*
*that inhibits additional sperm from penetrating the fertilized egg*

### Slow block to polyspermy

*Slow block* is a gradual but longer-term process.

Mammals use a slow block to polyspermy and do *not combine* fast and slow blocks as some species (e.g., sea urchins).

Many species other than mammals utilize *both* fast and slow blocks to polyspermy.

*Fast block* is effective, transient, and another countermeasure to polyspermy is often needed.

*Slow block* is initiated upon fertilization, as the ovum secretes various hormones to prevent it from being overwhelmed by the hundreds of sperm attempting fertilization.

In most species using this technique, the slow block is the *cortical reaction.*

*Slow block to polyspermy uses cortical granules to create a physical barrier around the zygote*

*Cortical reaction* is calcium-dependent exocytosis when secretory granules release into the *perivitelline space* immediately after fertilization, modifying the *zone pellucida* to prevent polyspermic fertilization.

Proteases (i.e., *proteins digesting proteins*) lift the *vitelline layer* as *hyaluronic acid* pushes the vitelline layer away from the ovum's surface, forming a barrier and preventing the entrance of other sperm.

*Hyalin* and *peroxidases harden* the *fertilization envelope* and *inactivate sperm-binding sites*, preventing fusion by additional sperm.

## Zona reaction

*Vitelline layer* is the *fertilization envelope.*

In mammals, the *vitelline layer* is the *zona pellucida*, so the *cortical reaction* is the *zona reaction.*

Zona pellucida hardens, and its binding sites become inactivated.

*Zona reaction* of mammals is less effective than the cortical reaction in other species. The zona reaction and cortical granules' contents inactivate ZP2 and ZP3 sperm receptors on the zona pellucida.

Evidence suggests that sperm mitochondria enter but are destroyed by the ovum. Sperm centrioles and pronucleus (i.e., gametic nuclei) enter the ovum. Sperm contributes more than its pronucleus to the zygote.

Centrioles replicate and are assembled into a centrosome, replicating the first mitotic spindle assembly in the zygote. This supports observations of extra mitotic spindles in polyspermy since several sperm cells contribute centrioles to the ovum.

## Embryogenesis

### Zygote as a fertilized egg

Zygote is propelled by *ciliary movement* through the uterine tube (*oviduct* or *Fallopian tube*) into the uterus; it begins cell divisions as *cleavage*.

*Development* describes the changes in the life cycle of an organism.

*Embryogenesis* begins the process of growth and development of an embryo.

Once the diploid (2N) fertilized zygote begins mitotic division, it is an *embryo*.

### Cleavage

*Cleavage* is rapid cell division *without cell growth*; therefore, *blastomeres* (cells) become smaller with each division.

Cleavage is *indeterminate* or *determinate*.

When cleavage is indeterminate, blastomeres can individually complete development if separated.

Blastomeres formed by *determinate cleavage* do not develop if separated; each is a necessary part of the embryo.

*Determinate cleavage* is typical for *protostomes*, a superphylum of animals (e.g., annelids, arthropods, nematodes, platyhelminths, rotifers, mollusks). They are the counterpart to *deuterostomes*, the well-known of which are *chordates* (i.e., *vertebrates*) and *echinoderms* (e.g., *sea urchins*).

**Spiral and determinate**   **Radial and indeterminate**

*Spiral and determinate vs. radial intermediate cleavage at the eight-cell stage*

*Deuterostomes* typically display *indeterminate cleavage*, which gives rise to identical twins.

*Identical twins* are *monozygotic* twins originating from a single zygote division into two separate embryos.

*Fraternal twins* result when two separately fertilized ova implant and independently develop in the uterus.

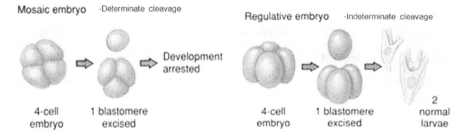

*Mosaic embryo with determinate cleavage vs. regulative embryo with indeterminate cleavage*

**Egg polarity**

Ovum has an *animal pole* (upper) and *vegetal pole* (lower hemisphere) in many species, known as *embryo polarity*.

*Vegetal pole* contains larger cells filled with *yolk*, a nutritious substance that feeds the embryo.

*Yolk* is denser than the cytoplasm, which causes it to settle at the bottom. It differentiates into extraembryonic membranes that protect and nourish the embryo in mammals.

*Animal pole* is smaller, more rapidly dividing cells and forms the *embryo proper*.

*Animal pole is on the upper portion of the egg while vegetal pole is the lower portion of the egg; pronucleus is at the boundary above marginal zone*

*Archenteron* is the center cavity formed by gastrulation, and its opening is the *blastopore*.

Deuterostomes and protostomes are defined by the fate of the blastopore.

*Protostome* ("first mouth") has the blastopore first form the *mouth*, and the *anus* develops second.

*Deuterostome* ("second mouth") has the blastopore first form the *anus*, and the *mouth* develops second.

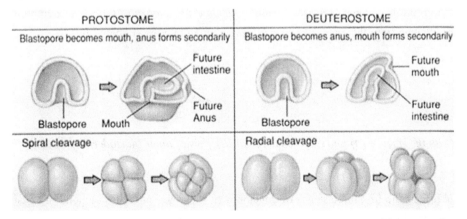

*Protostome vs. deuterostome and spiral vs. radial cleavage comparing blastopore fate*

The first cleavage is *polar* for the zygote and divides the ovum into two segments along the *vegetal-animal axis*. It is followed by cleavages *perpendicular* to the vegetal-animal axis, which is *equatorial*.

*Radial cleavage* alternates polar and equatorial cleavage and is a hallmark of deuterostome development. In contrast, protostomes typically display *spiral cleavage*.

The amount of yolk in the zygote influences the manner of cleavage.

Species laying external eggs (e.g., birds, some fish, reptiles, most insects) have much yolk, leading to *meroblastic* (i.e., *incomplete*) *cleavage*.

Mammals, worms, insects, and fish have eggs with less yolk, leading to *holoblastic* (i.e., *complete cleavage*).

**Blastula formation**

A few days after fertilization, cleavage creates a *morula*, a solid ball of cells in humans. By the fifth day, the morula is transformed into a hollow *blastula* (*blastocyst* in humans).

*Blastocyst* consists of an outer ring of cells as a *trophoblast* and an inner cell mass, the *embryoblast*. The blastocyst is formed as *blastomeres migrate to the outside* of the morula, leaving behind the *blastocoel*, a *fluid-filled cavity.*

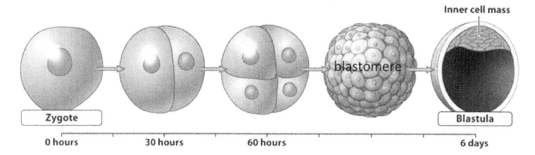

*Fertilized egg is a zygote that proceeds by cytoplasmic cleavage to form a morula, becoming a blastula*

*Trophoblast* accomplishes blastocyst implantation by embedding into *endometrium*, the nourishing epithelium of the uterus.

Upon implantation, the trophoblast releases *human chorionic gonadotropin* (HCG) to maintain estrogen and progesterone production from the *ovary's corpus luteum*, maintaining the endometrium.

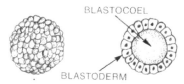

*Blastula with the surface (A) and a cross-sectional (B) view of outer blastoderms and inner blastocoel*

**Yolk**

*Amount of yolk* affects the first three stages of development (i.e., cleavage, blastulation, and gastrulation). The lancelet and frog develop quickly in water and travel into the larvae to feed themselves. The chick provides a significant amount of yolk inside a hard shell, and its development continues until the chick can exist on its own.

*Early stages of human development* resemble the chick due to our shared evolutionary history.

Frog embryo cells at the animal pole have little yolk; cells at the vegetal pole contain more yolk. Frog blastocoel is formed at the animal pole. The presence of yolk causes cells to cleave more slowly, so cells at the animal pole are smaller.

Chick cell cleavage is *incomplete*; only those cells lying on top of the yolk cleave and spread out over the yolk surface, in contrast to the ball-like morula of the lancelet.

Yolk cells do *not* participate in gastrulation and do *not* invaginate; instead, when animal pole cells evaginate from above, slit-like *blastopore* forms.

Other pole cells move down over the yolk; the blastopore becomes rounded. These yolk cells temporarily left in the region form a *yolk plug*.

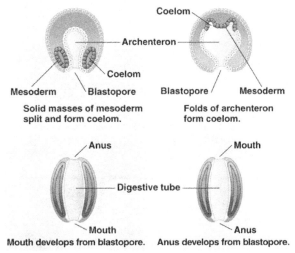

*Protostome vs. deuterostome comparing blastopore formation and mouth vs. anus sequence*

**Dorsal lip**

*Dorsal lip* cells of the blastopore migrate between the ectoderm and endoderm, forming *mesoderm*. Later, the *coelom* is created by splitting off from the mesoderm.

For example, a blastocoel is created in a chick when cells lift from the yolk and create space between cells and yolk. There is so much yolk that endoderm formation does not occur by invagination.

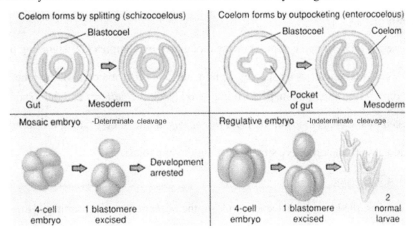

*Protostomes (left) form coelom by splitting compared to deuterostomes that use out pocketing*

The upper layer of cells differentiates into *ectoderm*, and the lower layer differentiates into the *endoderm*.

*Mesoderm* arises by an invagination of cells along the edges of the longitudinal furrow in the embryo midline, named the primitive streak. Later, the newly formed mesoderm splits to form the coelomic cavity.

**Gastrulation**

After fertilization (3 weeks in humans), *gastrulation* is when an invagination of cells into the blastocoel forms the *primary germ layers*. These are the initial cell layers from which all body tissues develop.

Vertebrates and higher animals are *triploblastic* with three primary germ layers.

Primitive animals (cnidarians and sponges) are *diploblastic*, with two germ layers.

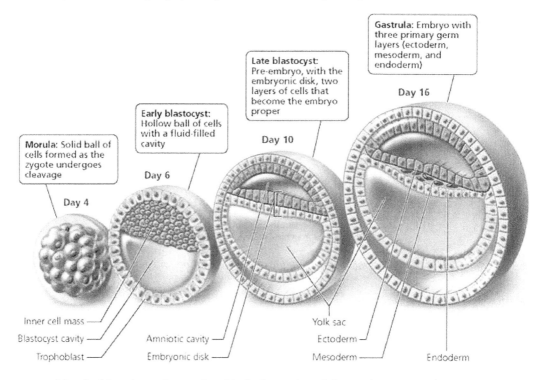

*Morula, blastula, and gastrula with the formation of three primary germ layers*

**First cell movements**

*Gastrulation* is a series of orchestrated cell movements modulated by complex cell-signaling pathways.

The exact manner of gastrulation varies by species. In humans (and other mammals), the inner cell mass flattens into the embryonic disc before gastrulation, divided into two layers: the *epiblast* and the *hypoblast*.

Gastrulation is marked by the appearance of the *primitive streak,* a line of cells along the *embryo's midline*.

*Epiblast ingresses* along with the primitive streak, pushing the hypoblast.

*Blastopore* is this first ingression.

As invagination continues, the blastopore deepens to form the *archenteron*, the primitive gut.

*Hypoblast* becomes the amnion, one of the extraembryonic membranes.

## Primary Germ Layers

### Endoderm, mesoderm and ectoderm

The first epiblast cells that migrate inwards differentiate into the *mesoderm* (middle germ layer).

*Diploblastic* animals (e.g., sponges, cnidarian) develop *mesoglea*, a non-cellular layer, instead of a mesoderm.

*Epiblastic* cells that continue to invaginate the blastocyst become the *endoderm* (*inner* germ layer), while those that remain outside are the *ectoderm* (*outer* germ layer).

After gastrulation, the germ layers develop into the entire array of structures and organs in the body.

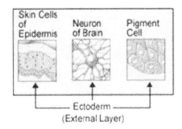

*Ectoderm is the outermost layer and gives rise to skin, nerve tissue, and epidermal skin cells*

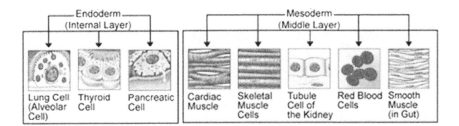

*Primary germ layers of endoderm and mesoderm and representative tissue types formed from each layer*

### Neurulation

Newly formed *mesoderm cells* of the gastrula coalesce along the central axis, forming a dorsal *notochord*.

*Notochord* is a stiff rod that supports lower chordates and is replaced in amphibians, birds, and mammals by the *vertebral column*.

The portion of the ectoderm just above the notochord develops into the nervous system in *neurulation*.

At first, the ectoderm cells on the dorsal surface of the embryo thicken, forming the *neural plate*.

*Neural groove* develops down the midline of the neural plate; on either side of the neural groove, *neural folds* move upward and fuse. This forms the *neural tube*, which becomes the central nervous system.

At this stage, the embryo is a *neurula*.

**Neural tube formation**

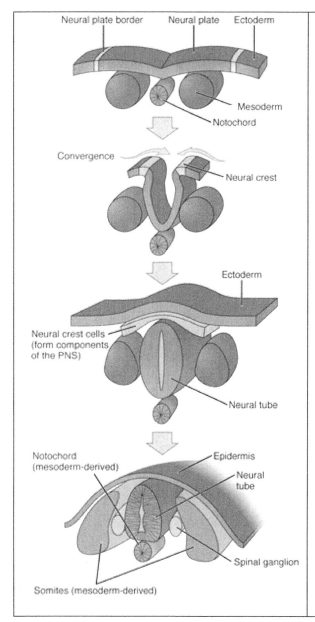

1 – Neuroectodermal tissues differentiate from ectoderm and thicken into neural plates. Neural plate borders separate the ectoderm from the neural plate.

2 – Neural plate bends dorsally, with two ends joining at the neural plate borders, which are now the neural crest.

3 – Closure of the neural tube disconnects the neural crest from the epidermis. Neural crest cells differentiate to form most of the peripheral nervous system.

4 – Notochord degenerates and persists as the nucleus pulposus of the intervertebral discs. Other mesoderm cells differentiate into the somites, the precursors of the axial skeleton and skeletal muscle.

**Neural crest**

*Neural crest* is the ectoderm at which the two neural folds close together to form the neural tube.

Neural crest cells *migrate and differentiate* into various cell types, including neurons, glial cells of the peripheral nervous system, melanocytes of the epidermis, epinephrine-producing cells of the adrenal gland, portions of the heart, and connective tissue of the head.

Although derived from ectoderm, *neural crest* is referred to as the *fourth germ layer* because of its importance.

*Neural crest is ectoderm that forms during neurulation*

## Structures arising from primary germ layers

Aside from the nervous system, ectoderm gives rise to skin epidermis, the epithelial lining of the mouth and rectum, and several glands.

*Ectoderm* gives rise to the nails, hair, skin glands, and epidermal derivatives.

During neurulation, midline mesoderm cells not contributing to the notochord formation become two longitudinal masses of tissue as *somites*, a process of *somitogenesis.*

*Mesoderm* forms the excretory and reproductive system, the heart, blood vessels and blood cells, and linings of all body cavities (coeloms). Vertebrate somites give rise to the dermis, skeletal muscle, tendons, cartilage, and axial skeleton bones. The other portions of the mesoderm develop into connective, muscular, and skeletal body portions.

*Endoderm* gives rise to the digestive tract, respiratory tract, and excretory tract epithelial linings, along with associated organs and glands of the digestive and respiratory systems.

| Primary Germ Layer Structures | | |
|---|---|---|
| Ectoderm | Mesoderm | Endoderm |
| Epidermis<br>Nervous system<br>Epithelial linings: mouth and rectum<br>Glands: adrenal medulla, pineal, and pituitary | Dermis<br>Skeletal and muscular, excretory, reproductive, circulatory, and lymphatic systems<br>Epithelial linings: coelom<br>Glands: adrenal cortex | Epithelial linings: respiratory, digestive, and excretory systems<br>Glands: pancreas, thymus, thyroid, and parathyroid<br>Liver |

## Mechanisms of Development

### Development

*Development* is the changes in the life cycle of an organism due to growth, differentiation, and morphogenesis. Most animals undergo the same embryonic stages: zygote, morula, blastula, and gastrula.

Gastrulation is succeeded by neurulation, the first organogenesis event when body organs begin to develop.

Neurulation is when the embryo transitions from the embryonic stage and becomes a *fetus.*

Organogenesis is related to *morphogenesis,* developing an organism's body plan and shape.

### Cell specialization

*Specialization* refers to the cell type; cells are specialized when they have a specific function.

For example, epidermal cells produce keratin to protect the skin against abrasion, myocytes produce actin and myosin to make muscles contract, and neurons produce neurotransmitters that transmit electrochemical impulses.

*Stem cells* are undifferentiated cells that have yet to specialize. As an embryo develops, its stem cells differentiate to give rise to specific tissues.

*Cell specialization* is achieved in two stages: *determination* and *differentiation.*

### Determination

*Cytoplasmic influences* cannot change the final form of a determined cell. Cytoplasmic influences are narrowed with successive cell divisions; complete determination usually occurs late in cell specialization.

Determination begins with specification (reversible) and ends with an irreversible commitment (differentiated) to a cell type.

*Determination* is the period when the cell commits to a particular cell type, and it can be divided into two states: a cell is *specified* and *determined.*

*Specified cells* placed into different body tissue alter their differentiation pathway to match that tissue. In this regard, specification is *reversible.*

However, once the cell is determined, it is *irreversibly committed* to its differentiation pathway and does *not* adapt to a different environment by altering its differentiation.

### Differentiation

*Cellular differentiation* is when cells become specialized in their structure and function.

*Determined* and *differentiated* are sometimes used interchangeably; *determined* is when cells have restrictive potential and commit to specific cell types, while *differentiation* is an observable morphological and biochemical process into the cell's final form and function.

*Differentiation* is an action, while *specialization* is a state of being.

Differentiation is an essential component of *morphogenesis* when the overall form of the organism and its body parts are shaped, including early cell movements and later *pattern formation,* the process by which cells assume distinct functions in specific parts of the body.

As cells differentiate, their functions change, and they interact, eventually organizing into body tissues. Cells can be traced during differentiation to build a lineage map of their development by *fate mapping*.

## Cytoplasmic segregation and induction

Each body cell contains a complete set of chromosomes and, therefore, all genetic information required to perform the functions of any cell.

Cells have the same genome but differ in which genes they express (i.e., transcription) and to what degree.

Cells do not differentiate because they receive different genes, or genes are lost as cells divide. Instead, cell specialization is accomplished via *differential gene expression.*

*Cytoplasmic segregation* and *induction* are two crucial developmental mechanisms of differential gene expression.

The foundation of cell specialization in an embryo is laid before fertilization. Ova contains mRNA and proteins as *maternal determinants* that influence development.

Blastomeres receive different concentrations of maternal determinants, which lead to *differential gene expression.*

*Cytoplasmic segregation* concentrates maternal determinants as cleavage occurs for differential gene expression.

Experimentally, the cytoplasm of a frog zygote is not uniform. After the first division of the frog zygote, only daughter cells receiving portions of the *gray crescent* develops into a complete embryo.

*Induction* is a more common mechanism of differential gene expression, in which one group of cells influences development by changing the behavior of an adjacent group of cells. Hans Spemann (1869-1941), who received the Nobel Prize in 1935 for *embryonic induction*, found that chemical signals within the *gray crescent* activate the *genes regulating development.*

## Tissue Formation

### Tissue types

Tissues of animals are four types: epithelial tissue, connective tissue, nervous tissue, and muscle tissue. Each tissue type contains specialized cells and an extracellular matrix that the cells secrete.

Connective tissue

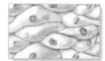
Epithelial tissue

*Epithelial tissue*s may be multilayered or one cell thick and usually function in secretion, absorption, or protection. Epithelial tissues are in the linings of glands, organs, body cavities, blood vessels, and the skin and mucous membranes.

Muscle tissue

Nervous tissue

Various epithelia are derived initially from all three germ layers.

*Connective tissue*s tether tissues and organs but can have structural and support functions. Cartilage, bone, blood, and adipose tissue (fat) are special connective tissues. These are the most versatile and widespread of the body tissues.

Proper connective tissues divide into *loose* and *dense connective tissues* divided into subtypes. These tissue types are derived initially from the *mesenchyme,* a portion of the mesoderm.

*Nervous tissue* includes the neurons and glial cells of the nervous system. Neurons (nerve cells) transmit electrical signals, while glial cells protect and support the neurons. Central and peripheral nervous tissue arises from the ectoderm during neurulation.

*Muscle tissue* is contractile tissue divided into skeletal muscle, smooth muscle, and cardiac muscle.

*Skeletal muscle* tissue is muscles under voluntary control attached to the skeletal system by tendons.

*Smooth muscle* is involuntary and in the walls of hollow organs (e.g., uterus, stomach, blood vessels).

*Cardiac muscle* is under involuntary control but is found only in the heart, where it creates powerful contractions which move blood throughout the body.

All three muscle types are originally derived from *mesoderm.*

### Embryonic and fetal development

*Human gestation* is nine months, calculated by adding 280 days to the start of the last menstrual cycle. About 5% of infants arrive on their forecasted birth date due to several complicating variables.

*Embryonic development* is during months 1 and 2 with zygote *cleavage* and initial organ development (organogenesis).

*Fetal development* occurs during months 3 through 9 when organ systems grow, mature, and increase in size and weight by a factor of nearly 600.

After fertilization, implantation of the blastocyst in the endometrium occurs at about one week.

Upon implantation, the trophoblast secretes *human chorionic gonadotropin* (HCG) to stimulate the corpus luteum to maintain the endometrial lining.

As the weeks progress, the inner cell mass detaches from the trophoblast to become the *embryonic disc*, while the yolk sac forms below.

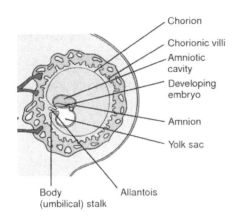

The *yolk sac* is a membranous sac attached to the embryo. It is one of several *extraembryonic membranes* which lie outside the embryo and protect and nourish it and, later, the fetus.

Evolution of extraembryonic membranes in reptiles made development on land possible. An embryo that develops in water receives oxygen from water, and wastes float away. The surrounding water prevents desiccation and provides a protective cushion. However, extraembryonic membranes perform these functions for an embryo on land. These membranes are modified depending on whether the organism undergoes internal or external development. In birds and reptiles, the *yolk sac* nourishes the developing embryo.

**Placenta**

In placental mammals, the *umbilical cord* and *placenta* nourish the embryo, so the "*yolk sac*" is empty of yolk and instead functions as an early blood supply for the embryo before becoming part of the primitive gut later in gestation.

Therefore, it is an *umbilical vesicle* to distinguish it from the yolk sacs of egg-laying animals.

As the yolk sac forms, a second extraembryonic membrane of the *amnion* encloses the embryo. The amnion surrounds the amniotic cavity, containing protective amniotic fluid that bathes the developing embryo.

Whether externally or internally, chordate animals develop in water, in bodies of water, or within *amniotic fluid*. Amniotic fluid is a buffer for mechanical and chemical disturbances and thermal regulation. Some genetic disorders can be diagnosed by sampling this amniotic fluid in a prenatal test (i.e., *amniocentesis*).

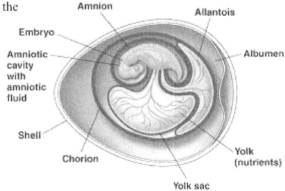

*Egg-laying animals have large yolk sacs with nutrients needed during embryogenesis*

*Chorion* is another extraembryonic membrane that, in birds and reptiles, lies next to the shell of an egg and carries on gas exchange. In placental mammals, the chorion implants into the endometrium and projects treelike extensions called *chorionic villi* into the maternal tissues. Maternal blood circulates around these villi so that an exchange of molecules between the fetal and maternal blood may occur. $CO_2$ and wastes move from the fetus, and $O_2$ and nutrients flow from the maternal side. As the embryo develops, the interface of the chorionic villi and the uterine tissue becomes an organ, the *placenta.*

Placental formation begins at about week 1 after the embryo is fully implanted in the endometrium. The placenta is the life support structure of the developing embryo, providing oxygen and nutrients while removing wastes (e.g., $CO_2$).

**Umbilical cord**

In humans, maternal blood contacts the chorion, but gas, nutrients, and wastes cross the chorion without the maternal and fetal blood mixing. Thus, the placenta facilitates gas and nutrient exchange, but not fluid exchange.

*Umbilical cord* stretches between the placenta and the fetus and contains 2 fetal arteries and 1 fetal vein. The umbilical cord allows fetal blood to reach the placenta and exchange molecules with the maternal blood.

Umbilical arteries transport $CO_2$ and waste molecules to the placenta for disposal; the umbilical vein transports $O_2$ and nutrient molecules from the placenta to the fetal circulatory system. Although the fetal umbilical artery transports deoxygenated blood, it is an artery because it carries blood away from the fetus's heart. Likewise, the fetal umbilical vein carries oxygenated blood and is a vein because it brings blood to the fetus's heart.

*Allantois* is an extraembryonic membrane that evaginates from the archenteron of the gastrula. The allantois initially stores waste products such as uric acid in birds and reptiles. It later fuses with the chorion. In mammals, the allantois initially transports waste products to the placenta but regresses in later stages of gestation. After birth, it may remain as a vestigial structure or disappear altogether. In birds and reptiles, the allantois and chorion form a double membrane next to the shell and function in gas exchange.

**Early gestation stages**

*Gastrulation* occurs during week 3 of gestation, followed by *neurulation* that initiates nervous system development.

*Neural tube* is visible as a thickening along the entire *dorsal length* of the embryo as *ectoderm* develops into *neural folds* as the *neural tube*. Towards the end of the first month, the heart starts to form, while designated cells form the basic structure of the limbs, spine, nervous and circulatory systems.

*Limb buds* appear on arms and legs. The head enlarges, the sense organs become more prominent, and the rudiments of the eyes, ears, and nose are evident.

*Heart* development begins and continues into week 4. The veins enter this largely tubular heart posteriorly, and the arteries exit anteriorly. Later the heart twists so that all major vessels are located anteriorly. The right and left heart tubes fuse, and the heart begins pumping blood, although the chambers are not fully formed.

Weeks 4 and 5, a bridge of mesoderm called *body stalk* connects the caudal (tail) end of the embryo via the *chorionic villi.* The head and tail lift, and the body stalk moves anteriorly by constriction. *Allantois*, found in the body stalk, extends into blood vessels of the umbilical cord. Organs such as the heart, lungs, and liver continue developing.

Weeks 6 through 8, the developing embryo becomes more human-like in appearance. The brain develops, and the head achieves its typical relationship with the body as the neck region develops. The nervous system exhibits reflex actions like the startle response to touch.

Week 7, the fetus, regardless of sex, initially exhibits the same external and internal genital structures. Externally, the fetus exhibits a *genital tubercle,* a pair of *urogenital folds,* and a pair of *labioscrotal folds.*

Week 8, the embryo is about 38 millimeters and weighs no more than an aspirin tablet; however, all organs are established.

By week 12 of prenatal development, the genital tubercle differentiates into the glans (head) of the penis or clitoris, the urogenital folds enclose the urethra of a male or become the labia minora of a female, and the labioscrotal folds become the scrotum of a male or labia majora of a female. The gender of the fetus can be identified anatomically.

## XY chromosomal influences

Fetus has an internal pair of *gonadal ridges*, *mesonephric* or *Wolffian ducts*, and *paramesonephric*, or *Müllerian ducts.*

In XY males, the *SRY gene* encodes for the protein *testis-determining factor*, which initiates the development of male genitalia. The gonadal ridges become a pair of testes, which secrete testosterone and *Müllerian-inhibiting factor* (anti-Müllerian hormone).

By week 8, these hormones cause the *Müllerian duct* to degenerate and induce the *Wolffian duct* to develop into the male reproductive tract. In a female fetus, where there is no Y chromosome, the gonads become ovaries. Around week 10, in the absence of anti-Müllerian hormone, the Wolffian ducts degenerate, and the Müllerian ducts develop into the female reproductive tract.

By week 10, the placenta is fully formed and produces progesterone and estrogen. Due to negative feedback control by the hypothalamus and anterior pituitary, no ovarian follicles mature. Instead, ovarian follicles maintain the uterus lining and ensure no menstruation during pregnancy. Facial characteristics of the fetus become recognizable.

By week 14, the characteristics of the fetus have mostly developed. A fetus at first can only flex its limbs; later, it moves its limbs so vigorously that the mother can feel movements beginning in the fourth month.

Fetus soon acquires hair, eyebrows, eyelashes, and nails. Fine, downy hair *lanugo* covers the limbs and trunk of the fetus but sheds shortly before or after birth. The skin grows so fast that it wrinkles.

*Vernix caseosa* is a waxy substance that protects the skin from the watery amniotic fluid.

After 16 weeks, *fetal heartbeat* is heard by a stethoscope.

At 24 weeks, a fetus born prematurely survives; however, the lungs are immature and cannot capture $O_2$ adequately. From this time onwards, the fetus grows in *size rather than complexity*.

At 38 weeks after fertilization, the fetus is mature enough for live birth.

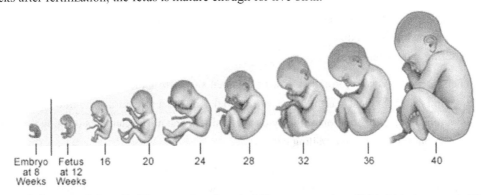

*Fetal growth from week 8 to 40. The gestational period (from conception till birth) in humans is 38 weeks; however, in obstetrics, the term is counted from the first day of the last menstruation (which is usually 2 weeks earlier), making the length of pregnancy to be 40 weeks.*

**Cell-to-cell communication**

*Development of the embryo* is mediated by communication between cells.

*Induction* is an important mechanism of differentiation using cell-to-cell signaling. The inducer is the cell sending the signal for others to change, while the responder (or target) is the cell that receives the signal and changes accordingly.

For example, *optic vesicles* are embryonic brain structures that induce ectoderm to develop into lenses of the eye.

*Induction* may result from *juxtacrine* or *paracrine* mechanisms. *Juxtacrine* signaling involves communication between two cells that touch.

*Paracrine* signaling is when an inducer cell releases a chemical signal which diffuses through space and is received by a target cell a short distance away.

In the early 20th century, amphibian embryologists Hans Spemann and Hilde Mangold experimented on the dorsal side of the embryo, where the notochord and the nervous system develop. They observed that notochord tissue induces the formation of the nervous system, even when placed in a separate tissue environment such as beneath the belly ectoderm.

Spemann and Mangold showed that the dorsal lip of the blastopore, as the *primary organizer*, is necessary for development. The primary organizer directs the formation of germ layers during gastrulation. Those cells which invaginate first are closest to the primary organizer, so they become endoderm. The next cells at an intermediate distance from the primary organizer become mesoderm. Finally, the cells furthest from the primary organizer become ectoderm.

**Cell migration**

For development, it is not enough for cells to differentiate; they must also move. This movement of cells to predetermined areas in controlled, organized *cell migration*. Migrating cells have polarity and a distinguishable front and back (posterior). Without polarity, cells would not maintain controlled movement; all sides would move at once in various directions.

Researchers hypothesize that no matter the exact model behind cell migration, cytoskeletal filaments help establish and maintain a cell's polarity. The mechanisms of cell migration are not fully understood, but the foremost models are the cytoskeletal model and the membrane flow model.

*Cytoskeletal model theory* is based on the action of cytoskeletal elements. These elements interact to support and alter a cell's plasma membrane. Experimentation has shown that rapid actin polymerization of the cytoskeleton occurs at a migrating cell's front edge.

Some researchers propose that the formation of actin filaments (microfilaments) at the cell's front edge is the driving force behind cell movement. Furthermore, microtubules may act to contract the trailing edge of the cell. Thus, this model relies on a collaboration of the cytoskeletal filaments: microfilaments pushing the front edge of the cell and microtubules retracting the trailing edge.

*Membrane flow theory* is based on changes in the plasma membrane rather than the cytoskeleton. Cells undergo membrane recycling by continually returning membrane sections brought into the cell during endocytosis back to the plasma membrane. This process is the basis for the membrane flow theory, which posits that cell migration occurs by adding plasma membrane to the cell front.

The membrane flow model states that integrin proteins attached to the plasma membrane "walk" the cell along its migratory path. Under this hypothesis, microfilaments at the cell's front edge are stabilizing agents. Integrins are continually recycled by endocytosis to the posterior as fresh integrins are brought to the front of the cell by exocytosis.

The two models are not mutually exclusive, so a hybrid theory may explain cell migration.

### Stem cells and pluripotency

In the early stages of embryogenesis, stem cells are *totipotent* and capable of differentiating into any cell.

Only the zygote and subsequent cells of the morula are *totipotent*. A single totipotent stem cell can give rise to an entire organism, provided the organism displays indeterminate cleavage.

After a few cell divisions, the embryonic stem cells become *pluripotent*, as each cannot individually divide into an entire organism but may differentiate into any embryonic cell.

As pluripotent embryonic cells continue dividing, they gradually become committed to a specific path. These cells, which have become committed to a single cell type, are *unipotent* and represent most cells in an adult human.

However, adults have stem cells, and their pluripotency is debated, and most adult stem cells are *multipotent*.

Multipotent stem cells are between pluripotent and unipotent; they have a narrow range of possible cell types but greatly benefit the organism by regenerating and repairing damaged tissue. Adult stem cells are in body tissues that must be frequently replaced (e.g., skin, bone marrow, liver).

Stem cells, both adult and embryonic, are the subject of intense research into their medical applications for tissue repair and treatment of degenerative diseases.

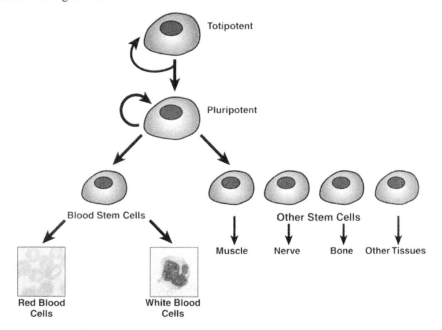

*Stem cells undergo determination before differentiation, where they exhibit the morphology*

*and biochemistry of the specialized (differentiated) cell*

## Gene Expression

### Gene regulation in development

*Gene regulation* of embryonic cells is the basis for cellular migration and differentiation during development.

Knowledge of developmental gene regulation has been primarily based on research on *Caenorhabditis elegans* (roundworm) by 2002 Nobel laureate Sydney Brenner (1927-2019), *Drosophila melanogaster* (fruit fly) by 1933 Nobel laureate Thomas Hunt Morgan (1866-1945), and other animal models.

*Maternal determinants* are usually homogeneously distributed throughout the ovum. However, *Drosophila melanogaster* exhibits cytoplasmic segregation of maternal determinants. The developing *Drosophila* ovum (oocyte) asymmetrically distributes *maternal effect genes.*

### Maternal effect genes

*Maternal effect genes* produce mRNA and proteins (maternal determinants) in the mature ovum, remaining asymmetrically distributed. Maternal determinants influence the expression of specific zygotic genes. In this way, the mother's genotype influences the phenotype of the zygote.

*Gap genes* are the first class of zygotic genes regulated by maternal effect genes. Proteins produced by *gap genes* regulate *pair-rule genes*, influencing the transcription of *segment polarity genes*.

Proteins produced by *gap genes*, *pair-rule genes,* and *segment polarity genes* interact to influence *homeotic genes*.

Together, *gap genes*, *pair-rule genes*, *segment polarity genes*, and *homeotic genes* partition the developing *Drosophila* embryo into body segments (i.e., pattern formation). Their function has been studied extensively by mutating these genes and observing the ensuing malfunctions in the body plan.

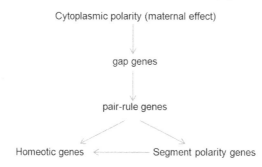

*Gene regulation in development follows a sequence of upstream gene expression and protein production*

Initial gradients of maternal determinants are not the only method of gene regulation in a developing embryo. As in the cells of adult organisms, gene regulation is a complex process due to the multitude of ways in which genes may be regulated.

During the path from DNA to protein, and even after protein synthesis, gene expression can be regulated. At the highest level is transcriptional regulation, which includes *histone modifications* that make chromatin accessible (or inaccessible) to RNA polymerase, along with modulation of transcription factors that facilitate (inhibit) the binding of RNA polymerase during transcription.

**Post-transcriptional regulation**

*Post-transcriptional regulation* occurs after transcription and before translation, targeting mRNAs transcript moving from the nucleus to cytoplasm. This may be accomplished by modulating nuclear export, RNA splicing, RNA editing, and modifications such as capping and polyadenylation, which protect the RNA from degradation in the cytoplasm.

Once mRNA is processed (splicing of exons and removal of introns, adding a 5' G cap and 3' poly–A tail) and exported from the nucleus, the cell may continue altering gene regulation at the translational level by promoting (or inhibiting) ribosome recruitment to the mRNA.

Gene regulation does not cease once a protein is translated. Post-translational gene regulation acts upon proteins that have been synthesized. For example, proteins may be sequestered to certain cell parts or assembled with proteins to form a working unit. Additionally, *zymogens* are enzymes cleaved (or modified) to become active.

Post-translational modifications to histones, such as phosphorylation and acetylation, are responsible for chromatin rearrangement and an active area of research.

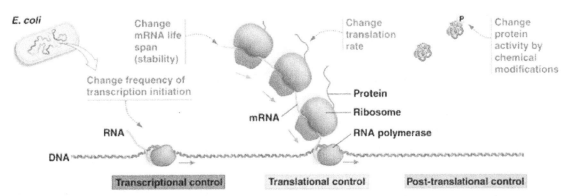

*Regulation of gene expression: transcriptional (DNA → RNA), post-transcriptional (e.g., splicing), post-translational control (e.g., glycosylation).*

**Environment–gene interaction in development**

Genetic and environmental factors contribute to the complex etiology of congenital disabilities by disrupting the highly regulated embryonic developmental processes. Intrauterine environment of the developing embryo and fetus is easily altered by maternal factors such as health and disease status, lifestyle, medications, maternal genotype, and exposure to environmental teratogens.

*Teratogens* are agents which cause congenital abnormalities. They may cause mild to severe congenital disabilities or terminate the pregnancy. Radiation, harmful chemicals, certain drugs, and pathogens may be classified as teratogens.

Congenital disabilities (1 in 33 babies in the US) continue to be the leading cause of infant death (about 5,500 per year) in the U.S., and therefore is a field of intense biomedical and clinical research. The field of teratology has focused on the causes and underlying mechanisms of congenital disabilities for decades, yet our understanding of these critical issues remains vague.

Each organ has a sensitive period when toxic substances can alter development. While the placenta is an effective mediator between the fetus and the mother, it is highly susceptible to penetration by chemicals. This is of particular concern during the embryonic period (fertilization through the 10th week of gestation or 8th week of embryonic age) when crucial structures are in the vulnerable first stages of development.

For example, between 1958 and 1961, it was typical for a pregnant woman in England and other countries to take the tranquilizer thalidomide between days 27 and 40 of pregnancy, which likely resulted in an infant born with deformed limbs. After this period, the fetus is resistant to the effects of thalidomide, and the child is born healthy.

Studies conducted over the last few decades have suggested that the relationship between genes and environmental factors plays a major role in propagating these congenital disabilities. The study of gene-environment interactions leads to a better understanding of the biological mechanisms and pathological processes contributing to the development of complex congenital disabilities.

### Programmed cell death

*Apoptosis* is programmed cell death and is a part of development. Apoptosis is a central player in gametogenesis, embryogenesis, removal of damaged cells, and aging.

During apoptosis, *caspases* (proteases) and nucleases digest the cell from within. These enzymes are inactive in a typical cell. They are activated by a complex signal transduction pathway, which may be initiated by external commands or by internal recognition of cell malfunction, infection, or DNA damage.

The basis for apoptosis in embryogenesis and fetal development has been extensively studied in animal models. Fate maps of *C. elegans* show that 131 cells must undergo apoptosis for worm development. The cell-death protein in these cells is normally inhibited, but when the cells are signaled via induction, the cell-death cascade becomes active and produces proteases and nucleases to slice proteins and DNA.

Apoptotic cells undergo characteristic changes: *protrusion of the plasma membrane* (*blebbing*), *shrinkage, nuclear fragmentation, chromatin condensation, and chromosomal DNA fragmentation*.

Apoptotic cells attract nearby cells, which consume the dying cell to avoid harmful cell contents from spilling into the extracellular fluid and affecting other cells or causing inflammation.

### Apoptosis for tissue development

During embryonic development, apoptosis removes harmful, abnormal, or unneeded cells.

Dysregulation of apoptosis during gestation can lead to severe congenital disabilities.

Apoptosis is present from the beginning of development when cells in the blastula die off to form the gastrula. Morphogenesis is accomplished through apoptosis; organs overproduce cells and "prune" excess cells to sculpt the intricate shape of organs. This is readily visible in fingers and toes, which are webbed early in gestation but lose their webbing and become recognizable digits.

Another example of apoptosis-assisted morphogenesis occurs in the center of ducts and tubes to hollow them out.

Many fetal structures must be shed via apoptosis before birth.

For example, female fetuses must degrade the Wolffian duct, while males must degrade the Mullerian duct.

Apoptosis continues after birth as a tissue remodeling and immune system maintenance in the adult organism. Cancer, autoimmune diseases, and neurodegenerative diseases result from dysregulated apoptosis. The absence of proper apoptosis allows dangerous cells to divide and invade other tissues, leading to malignant tumors.

However, excessive apoptosis leads to tissue degeneration. Both malfunctions are implicated in aging and disease.

## Regenerative capacity in various species

*Regeneration* is the reactivation of development to regrow a missing (or damaged) body structure. While regenerative abilities are limited in humans, many animals retain the capacity to regrow entire limbs after embryonic development.

For example, most echinoderms have robust regenerative powers. Some sea stars can regrow an entirely new organism from a single arm, while others can only replace lost limbs. Regrowth is not assured; it takes months or years, and sea stars are vulnerable to infection during the regrowth period. Separated limbs must survive off nutrient stores until they regenerate the rest of the sea star and feed.

Newts and salamanders (particularly the axolotl) are noted for their regeneration. Newt and salamander regeneration proceeds in two stages. First, adult cells at the site of the limb's separation de-differentiate into *progenitor cells*. Second, the progenitor cells proliferate and differentiate until they replace the missing tissue.

Humans exhibit regeneration via progenitor cells, although regrowth of entire limbs is impossible. Remarkable regeneration is observed in the liver. Through several complicated signaling cascades, the liver manages to restore any lost mass and adjust its size to that of the organism while fulfilling its duties.

Human embryos do have the ability to regenerate complete organs and limbs. However, like many vertebrates, this ability is lost during embryogenesis, leaving adult humans with a limited capacity to restore tissue damage.

## Senescence and aging

*Senescence* is the gradual deterioration of function in an organism, eventually leading to death.

Except for a few with remarkable properties of immortality, all organisms undergo senescence.

One of the puzzling questions humans currently face is *why* they age. Some have suggested that senescence avoids cancer, while others blame environmental factors such as radiation and oxidative agents, causing DNA and cellular damage. The reasons for senescence are likely a combination of factors.

Senescence refers to a cell that can no longer divide at the cellular level. Generally, cells are limited to 50 to 70 divisions, a threshold of the *Hayflick limit.*

A senescent cell is not dead; it actively continues its metabolic functions. The condition may be initiated by activating oncogenes or by the cell's recognition of its DNA damage.

*Oncogenes* signal abnormal cells to avoid senescence or undergo apoptosis to avoid tumor development.

**Factors damaging DNA**

Causes of DNA damage include radiation, oxidation (free radical damage), and telomeres shortening.

*Telomeres* are nonsensical DNA of 300 sequence repeats added to the 3' ends of DNA strands by *telomerase*.

Replication inevitably shortens DNA, leading to severe DNA damage that the cell cannot continue dividing.

Telomeres prevent losses from DNA replication to protect the encoding regions from destruction.

Telomerase allows cells to proliferate for prolonged periods because they are not affected by DNA replication loss.

Cells are subject to the *Hayflick limit*, but embryonic cells and specific adult cells contain high telomerase levels to divide continually.

The shortening of telomeres is associated with diseases involving premature aging, such as pulmonary fibrosis (scarring of the lungs). Shortened telomeres prevent the cells from dividing without losing genes, leading to cellular senescence.

The lack of sufficient telomeres may cause chromosomes to fuse, corrupt genetic blueprint, and chromosomes appear broken. Cells recognize DNA damage and thus enters apoptosis.

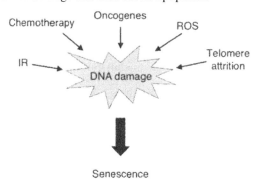

*Environmental and biochemical factors contributing to senescence*

Certain hydra, jellyfish, and flatworms are *biologically immortal*, exhibiting negligible senescence, and do not age. However, these organisms cannot truly escape death because they experience disease, injury, and predators.

There is intense research into modeling therapies based on these organisms and their "*immortal*" cells, hoping that aging and mortality can be slowed. For the present, however, senescence is inevitable with human development.

Made in the USA
Monee, IL
07 April 2025

15315692R00326